LOWER POTOMAC RIVER TIDEWATER AREA

SCALE
MILES

FISHING GROUNDS
ONLY THE MORE FAMOUS OYSTER BARS ARE SHOWN ON THIS MAP. PRACTICALLY THE ENTIRE SHORELINE ON BOTH SIDES OF THE RIVER FROM MARYLAND POINT (MD) AND METOMPKIN PT (VA) TO POINT LOOKOUT (MD) AND SMITH POINT (VA) IS GOOD OYSTER GROUND INCLUDING THE TRIBUTARIES. ST. MARY'S RIVER IS FAMOUS AS A SEED OYSTER GROWING AREA. INSHORE FROM THE OYSTER GROUNDS ARE THE MANINOSE OR SOFT SHELL CLAM AREAS. POUND (TRAP) NETS FORMERLY LINED THESE SHORES BUT NOW ARE FOUND MOSTLY FROM COLONIAL BEACH TO NOMINI BAY (VA) AND FROM POSEY'S BLUFF TO ST. GEORGE'S ISLAND (MD).

MARYLAND

VIRGINIA

CHESAPEAKE BAY

POTOMAC RIVER

THE NORTHERN NECK

MONTGOMERY COUNTY · DISTRICT OF COLUMBIA · PRINCE GEORGE'S COUNTY · FAIRFAX COUNTY · CHARLES COUNTY · PRINCE WILLIAM COUNTY · STAFFORD COUNTY · KING GEORGE COUNTY · ST. MARY'S COUNTY · WESTMORELAND COUNTY · RICHMOND COUNTY · NORTHUMBERLAND COUNTY

Cartography by CHESTER BLACKFORD

POTOMAC RIVER DORY

E.W.B. JR.

LIFE
ON THE
POTOMAC
RIVER

by Edwin W. Beitzell

HERITAGE BOOKS
2011

HERITAGE BOOKS
AN IMPRINT OF HERITAGE BOOKS, INC.

Books, CDs, and more—Worldwide

For our listing of thousands of titles see our website
at
www.HeritageBooks.com

A Facsimile Reprint
Published 2011 by
HERITAGE BOOKS, INC.
Publishing Division
100 Railroad Ave. #104
Westminster, Maryland 21157

— Publisher's Notice —

In reprints such as this, it is often not possible to remove blemishes from the original. We feel the contents of this book warrant its reissue despite these blemishes and hope you will agree and read it with pleasure.

International Standard Book Numbers
Paperbound: 978-0-7884-1935-5
Clothbound: 978-0-7884-8930-3

LIFE ON THE POTOMAC RIVER

By Edwin W. Beitzell
of St. Mary's County, Maryland

Life on the Potomac River describes the activities of some of the people who have lived along the tidewater banks of this great river from colonial times until the present.

It is dedicated to the rivermen of the Potomac and their families, and to John, Kate, Joe, and Charlie Quinnette who are learning to love the river as their Grandfather does.

C O N T E N T S

Page

THE POTOMAC

What tales you could tell mighty river,
If you would speak
Of your birth, in the misty ages
A tiny rill, seeking the seas,
Meandering across field and meadow
Blocked here, blocked there, by great rock
You patiently probe, now south, now east
Fighting your way
Growing stronger with each age
Until that day, with a mighty roar
In one of Nature's labors
You are birthed and overrun the land.

Joyously, with your new found strength,
You channel southeastward,
Giving freely of yourself,
To bring life to the parched land.
At the Great Falls, cascading gracefully
The plunge is made
To the rocky gorge below,
Leaping merrily, tunefully but sinuously
As you continue on to the sea.

You grow through the ages,
And now a great river
You join the Chesapeake
And the Ocean.
Patiently you build your soft bed
And as you continue your work
A broad bay is etched here,
A beautiful creek there.
Feeling the pull of Luna's force
You respond to your Sister
In God's Universe,
And your bosom rises and falls
As with each long breath,
You bring life's touch to your children,
The spawn of your union with Nature.

But now you notice
Along your shores
That God, who rules Nature
Has added a creature, man,
Created in His Own Image,
Red of skin, with intelligence
Which He reserved for those
Of His Own Image.

Soon the red man learns
To take of your bounty,
Gathering first the shellfish
Upon your shores.
But later he takes his needs
Of your fishes of the deep,
The sporting rock fish,
The fat shad, the great drum.
Your broad and ofttimes gentle surface
Is the travelled highway
For his log canoe.

And so, for many ages, until
The white man came, as did the red,
But in ships of sail,
Which catch the winds
To glide gracefully upon
Your blue-green waters,
Now quiet, now turbulent
But ever restless, ever moving
Between your banks,
And onward to the sea.

These white men, as the red ones
Build their homes, but of nobler kind.
Where the red men
Built their rude shelters,
They build great houses
Of the red clay from your banks,
And space them
Along your verdant ways.

The red man is pushed back
From your shores,
Shaded by the virgin forest,
And is followed
By all the wild creatures,
The sweet birds of song,
The gentle deer, the fat beaver,
The playful otter, who retreat
In dismay, as they are hunted
By this new man, who hunts,
Not for sustenance alone,
But for skins and feathers
To adorn his fair-skinned maidens.

Your shores are shorn
Of their primeval beauty.
The great pine and oak are fallen
And no longer, with supplicant arms
Reach up to their Creator.
Soon towns and cities
Dot your great length,
And at many points
The white men harness your tides,
To grind the grains
Mother Nature so abundantly supplies.

Along both of your verdant banks
Excrement fouls your ways,
Once so pristine pure.
But you, great river, struggle on
Seeking to protect your own,
The lonely loon,
The heron of great dignity,
The countless wild fowl,
Who sing myriad tunes
Of the Wind, and the Sun
And the Moon.

Yet the white man who knows
No limit to ambition,
Pursues his conquest
Of your gifts.
With courage, he braves
The mighty storms, now in ships
Great as Noah's Ark,
Harnessed by conquered
Iron and fire and water
Which turn noisy, foul smelling machines,
That defy your tides
And the four winds,
And travel your depths at will.

To those who dispute his way
He answers,
With an instrument of death,
Whose mighty roar
Rivals the thunder
Of the angry elements.
He knows no fear, nor limits
And finally,
Spans your great width
With a pathway of steel.
Now compassionate, now cruel,
He berefts you of your children,
And perversely, by laws, makes
Small endeavors to amend.

But you, oh great and goodly river,
Roll onward to the seas
Ever seeking with the ebb
And flood of your strong tide
To wash the unclean away,
To hide the evidence
Of witless policy,
That abuses your resources
Rather than conserve
And multiply them.

Your tender efforts joined
With all Nature,
Fight for your dumb and helpless ones,
The oyster and the clam.
You tug with might and main,
To tear away the traps
That impound countless numbers
Of your fleet and beautiful fishes.
You build up great sand bars,
Far from shore,
As a refuge for the stately swan,
The goose of gray feather,
The raucous gull and
All his kindred birds,
Who love every foot
Of your flowing length.

God made you great river
But man, the despoiler,
Also can help make and keep
Your cool blue-green depths
Clean and sweet.
Now, at long last
Some of those
Who love your beauty
And your worth
Join hands, to fight those
Who would destroy you.
They pool the same intelligence
That sought, sometimes with avarice,
Sometimes without thought,
To rob you
Of your greatest treasures.

Mighty Potomac, Queen of Rivers,
Gift of God to the generations,
May we humbly help Him
Keep you clear and flowing
For this sweet land.

Edwin W. Beitzell

Completed May 31, 1961, while
at anchor off the shores of
Blackistone (St. Clement's)
Island.

FOREWORD

This is an appropriate time for the publication of <u>Life On the Potomac River</u>.
On February 8, 1965, President Johnson said the Potomac River "should serve as a
model of scenic and recreation values for the entire country." This task will require the talents and efforts of many people for many years.

These environmental specialists will need the widest possible knowledge of
the Potomac and its history. In this book, Edwin W. Beitzell has contributed much
to that knowledge.

There is a bond between a man and the river of his boyhood. This is especially
true when both sides of his family have been river people for generations. The
author's forebears, of St. Mary's County, Maryland, have plied the Potomac as master
pilots, oystermen, seiners, fishermen, and boat builders. From their rich store of
experiences and his own life on the Potomac, Mr. Beitzell has produced an interesting narrative. There are also two extremely readable chapters on the river's early
history.

The author cites, for example, the silting of the Potomac before 1800. In
1791 Georgetown was perhaps the best tobacco market in America. "By the early
1800's the deep sea ships could not reach Georgetown," Mr. Beitzell reports.
Between 1792 and 1797 "erosion had shallowed the Washington Channel and the
Virginia Channel two feet and was continuing." The Potomac's problems are deep-
rooted.

In more modern times are the fish kills of 1962 and 1963 as the result of
pollution and other ecological disturbances. Mr. Beitzell compares the booming
commercial fishing of the 19th century with the skeleton industry of today. As a
fish and wildlife resource the Potomac has declined. The bald eagle is seen only
occasionally. On the brighter side, the osprey and great blue heron exist "in
goodly numbers."

We are reminded that the Potomac is the site of a landing that "ranks in
importance with Jamestown and Plymouth." On March, 1634, Governor Leonard Calvert
landed with Maryland colonists on St. Clement's (Blackistone) Island where he issued
the first proclamation of religious freedom in the New World, in accordance with
the instructions of his brother, Lord Baltimore. The State of Maryland is making
a commendable attempt to preserve the historic island from erosive forces.

"On the surface the Potomac has changed little over the years," the author
finds. The real damage is in the waters, the ecological relationships, the
unplanned and often unsightly shores, the decline of fish and wildlife.

There is a certain excitement in <u>Life On the Potomac River</u>, as those who live
here know, and Mr. Beitzell has conveyed this feeling with warmth and clarity.
His readers will share his trust that the President's plans for the Potomac Valley
must and will "undo the things that thoughtless men have done in the past."

                                        STEWART L. UDALL
                                        Secretary of the Interior
                                        Washington, D. C.

                                        December 1, 1967

INTRODUCTION

It is astonishing that we have had to wait until now for a book on the lower Potomac River. I think we have gotten one just in time. In a few decades from now, it seems very unlikely that anyone of Edwin Beitzell's qualifications will be alive. In fact, it is doubtful that anyone living today is equally qualified. His family has been an intimate part of the life of the river for generations, and much that Edwin Beitzell knows and depicts has the immediacy of direct experience. In addition, few men today possess such a generous store of knowledge concerning the tidal Potomac: its history, its folklore and anecdote, the people of its banks, past and present, and the rise and fall of its fortunes.

To extend the scope of experience through the lives of others is surely one of the enduring pleasures, and it is here liberally supplied. Their lives, whether of farmer or fisherman, are shown within a continuous context: the bustle and commerce of a busy river opening upon a bay active with the shipping of the world and teeming with the vessels and workboats of a vigorous fishery which was especially energetic in the tidal Potomac. These men, their trades and crafts, their vessels and gear, their courage and hardships, are all returned to us, perhaps for the last time.

The story of the Potomac River is of especial interest, since it is part of the very fabric of our history. In this nation, where even the immediate past has generally been altered beyond recognition; there the memories and associations of a single lifetime are often swept entirely away, it is easy enough to feel cut off at the roots. This malaise may not have a clear outline. It may take the form of an intuition or simply of an image; but it is not the less acute or widespread for that. Behind us, the bridges are down.

In the absence of history, our lives are curiously flat. It is part of the value of books like Life On the Potomac River that they add another dimension to existence: that of the past. I share Edwin Beitzell's hope that the river and the fullness of its life may flow from the past to the present, and from the present to the generations of the future.

VARLEY LANG

AUTHOR'S STATEMENT AND ACKNOWLEDGMENTS

After reading the excellent books on the lives of the Eastern Shore watermen, Follow the Water by Varley Lang, and The Lord's Oysters by Gilbert Byron, the writer was moved to tell something concerning the life of the rivermen on the Western Shore. It should be understood at the outset that this story of life on the Potomac River does not include the history of the great river front plantations along both the Maryland and Virginia shores. These stories have been ably told by Paul Wilstach, Henry Chandlee Forman, and others. Actually, except for a few families such as the Hebb, Fenwick, Lee, Slye, and a few others who owned ocean-going vessels in the early days, the river front plantation owners did not engage to any appreciable extent in the river commerce. Many of them, of course, like General George Washington, had fishing shores where herring and shad were caught in the spring, but mostly for use on the plantation. General Washington was exceptional in his thinking of the river as a great channel of commerce, but he was thinking primarily in terms of transporting farm and industrial products from the hinterlands to far away markets and bringing in supplies for the new capital city, Washington, and to Alexandria and Georgetown.

This book is concerned primarily with the tidewater Potomac, its myriad of fishes, oysters, clams, crabs, and wildfowl, the generations of men who have worked, fought, and sailed its waters for over three centuries, and the development of their boats over this same period. Frederick Gutheim has done a fine job in relating the story of the upper Potomac River, so this book relates to the area from Washington, D. C. to Point Lookout only.

The Beitzell family, although they have been on the Potomac River for six generations, going back to 1830, are comparative newcomers, for there are many river families, such as the Baileys, Cheseldines, Gibsons, Mattinglys, Morris', and Thompsons, to mention a few, whose ancestors go back to colonial days and who are still actively engaged in the water business. However, the writer has soaked up a considerable store of river lore during the past half century, not only from his own family but from related families, friends, and neighbors. Coupled with this, for many years, has been a continuing interest in all of Maryland's colorful history. So if an excuse for writing this story is needed, this is it. It is an interesting and exciting story, but one with overtones of sadness, for during the period of the past century the tremendous water resources of Maryland and Virginia have been greatly depleted. Shall we save what is left and build up from there or shall we go on to total exhaustion as has happened in many European waters where segments of the seafood industry survive only in the form of private artificial propagation? This is the question today.

Technical descriptions of the river sailing vessels have been omitted as these may be found in the fine works of M. V. Brewington, Robert H. Burgess, and others. It will be noted also that the title "Captain" is used liberally in referring to the rivermen. This is a courtesy title accorded to just about every professional waterman on the river who owns a boat.

The writer has included considerable material concerning the effect of the several wars on the Potomac because the sufferings of the river front people in these wars have been publicized very little and because it is firmly believed that the wars had a most depressing effect on the growth of shipyards and other river industries and the development of towns along the fine waterways of the lower Potomac.

This is not a fictionalized account. The data in Chapters I and II are documented material although references have been omitted. A bibliography is included for those interested. The data in the remaining chapters are factual, or as near so as human memory permits, and all of the events described as taking place on the Potomac River did actually happen there.

Many relatives and friends contributed data for the book, including my cousins, Lily (Cheseldine) DeWaard, Reginald Kenelm Cheseldine, Gladys (Cheseldine) and John Hall, Fred and Hilda Cheseldine, Richard and Joe Gibson, Bessie Gibson Ellis, William Owens, John Lawrence and Elsie Lawrence Hoover, John Garrett Beitzell, Louise Beitzell, Josephine Beitzell, and Mazie Lebarron; my brothers, Joe, Charlie, and Clem, and sister, Alice Beitzell Husemann; my uncles, Charles Beitzell and Benjamin Norris; friends, Capt. Sam and Robert Bailey, Capt. Golden Thompson, Capt. Garner Gibson, Capt. Tilton and Elton Hayden, Capt. Ben Brown, Capt. George Woodhall, Mr. and Mrs. Charles E. Fenwick, Mr. James C. Wilfong, Jr., Mr. J. Webster Jones, Mr. James Oliver, Mr. Robert E. Pogue, Mrs. William J. Corcoran, Mrs. Florence Dunn, Mr. Edward Collins, and a host of others. I am indebted and grateful to all of them for their assistance in making this book possible.

Mr. Walter R. Thomas of St. George's Island generously made available his extensive collection of data and pictures of the Island sailing vessels, and their masters, and added a great deal to the completeness of the story of the river. In addition, Capt. Joseph Henderson of the Island gave invaluable assistance not only on the Island vessels but identified and confirmed many others observed during his three-quarters of a century on the river.

The writer also wishes to express his appreciation to Robert H. Burgess, Curator of Exhibits, Mariners Museum, Newport News, Virginia, who made available the fine resources of the museum and furnished a number of pictures used in the book; and to Miss Jane F. Smith, Chief - Social and Economic Branch of the U. S. National Archives, and her staff for much research and data on the Potomac River commercial sailing vessels that also is included in the book.

The writer is indebted particularly to Varley Lang, Ph.D., one of the best informed watermen of the Chesapeake Bay, who not only has encouraged the project since its inception over seven years ago, but who has acted as a sounding board for ideas, has read the text, offering many excellent suggestions, and, in addition, has contributed a good deal of valuable data; to Frederick Tilp, an architect, a sailing enthusiast, and authority on the lower Potomac, who currently and for the past 35 years has been the Skipper of the Sea Scouts of the Corinthian Yacht Club in Washington, who not only generously made available his extensive library and collection of Potomac River data, but also has been kind enough to read the text and offer valuable suggestions. Mr. Tilp also spent many hours in research to complete, insofar as possible, the data contained in Appendix "F", "Derivation of Potomac River Place Names." Much of the data therein is the result of a unique interest in the river going back to boyhood days. He has generously permitted it to be included in this book to make the story of the lower Potomac more complete.

Many friends and relatives contributed pictures found in the book. The drawings are the work of Edwin Beitzell, Jr., Frederick Tilp, and Peter Egeli of Piney Point. Mr. Egeli is well known in art circles not only for his beautiful paintings of Potomac River scenes but also for his portrait work and paintings of historical subjects. My debt to them is large indeed.

For the publication of this book the writer is indebted to William Eskew Grant, President of the Kirby Lithographic Company of Washington, D. C., another lover of the Potomac from boyhood; and to Nancy Bartz Turner, a St. Mary's Countian, who did the final typing of the manuscript and she is thanked for an excellent job.

Finally, the writer is indebted to Secretary Stewart L. Udall, United States Interior Department, who not only took time out of his busy life to read the text and offer suggestions but also found time to write a foreword.

Truly, the destiny of our great river is in good hands and it must and shall become a model for our nation as envisioned by President Lyndon B. Johnson.

                                        EDWIN W. BEITZELL

                                        December 15, 1967

xii

LIFE ON THE POTOMAC RIVER

Chapter I

COLONIAL TIMES

".....Then on the 3 of March [we] came into Chesapeake bay, at the mouth of Patomecke. This baye is the most delightfull water I ever saw, between two sweet landes, with a channel 4:5:6:7: and 8 fathoms deepe, some 10 leagues broad, at time of yeare full of fish, yet it doth yeeld to Patomecke, wch we have made St. Gregories. This is the sweetest and greatest river I have seene, so that the Thames is but a little finger to it. There are no marshes or swampes about it, but solid firme ground, with great variety of woode, not choaked up with under-shrubs, but commonly so farre distant from each other as a coach and fower horses may travale without molestation."

Thus wrote Father Andrew White, S. J., in his "Brief Relation" of the settle-ment of Maryland in 1634. Here Father White described the maiden voyage of settlers coming from England into Lord Baltimore's newly established colony, Terra Mariae, which 142 years later was to become the state of Maryland. In 1634, the Potomac River had been explored by only a few white men and no settlement of colonists had yet been made upon its shores. Into the great river sailed two ships, the Ark and the Dove, carrying about twenty gentlemen, some three hundred laboring men, and two Jesuit priests and a lay-brother.

The Ark and the Dove continued to sail: ".....some 20 leagues up the river to Herne - Iland, so called for infinite swarmes of hernes thereon. This we called St. Clements, here we first came ashoare..... The ground is heare, as in very many places, covered with pokiberries, (a little wilde walnut hard of shell, but with a sweet kernell) with ackhornes, black walnut, cedar, saxafras, vines, sallad-herbes, and such like. It is not above 400 acres, and therefore too little to seat upon for us: therefore they have designed it for a fort to Command the river, meaneing to raise another on the maine land against it, and soe to keep the river from foraigne trade, here being the narrowest of the river. In this place on our b:[lessed] Ladies Day [March 25, 1634], in lent, we first offered, [the sacrifice of the mass], erected a cross, and with devotion tooke solemne possesstion of the Country."

In the pamphlet "A Relation of Maryland" published in London in 1635, the first landing is described in the following words:

".....They sayled up the River [Potomac] till they came to Heron Island which is about 14. leagues and there came to an Anchor under an Island neere unto it, which they called S. Clements. where they set up a Crosse and tooke possession of this Countrey for our Saviour and for our Soveraigne Lord the King of England....."

Good St. Clement was martyred by having an anchor fastened around his neck and being cast into the sea. It is fitting that the spot where the colonists first cast anchor in Maryland was named in his honor.

Today, Father White would be shocked by the fact that historic St. Clement's (Blackistone) Island has been reduced to 40 acres by erosion and is in danger of disappearing; that although a great 40 foot cross of concrete was erected on the Island in 1934, to commemorate the 300th anniversary of the founding of religious liberty in America, the Island has not, as yet, been made Maryland's first shrine; that the great virgin forests he so admired have disappeared, with little or no thought of perpetuating a few trees for future generations, and that now the "sweetest and greatest river," in its upper reaches is so polluted as to become a cesspool, and the silted channel will no longer permit our great ships to reach the ports of Alexandria, Washington, and Georgetown. He would be pleased, however, to learn that the great blue heron continues, unmolested, to make his home on the Heron Islands of St. Clement's, St. Katherine's, and St. Margaret's.

The Indians plied the Potomac River for countless generations before the coming of the white settlers, and lived along its one hundred and seventeen mile tidal reaches. Below the Falls, some ten miles above the city of Washington, the waters are brackish for approximately half its length, becoming more salty as the union with the Chesapeake is approached. The average rise and fall of the tide is about three feet. The Potomac, including the north and south forks of its tributary, the Shenandoah, has a drainage area of 5,960 square miles. Father White recorded in his "Relation" that Governor Leonard Calvert, guided by Captain Henry Fleet, of the Virginia Colony, explored the river as far as Piscataway and upon his return to St. Clement's ".....by ffleets directions, we came some 9 or 10 leagues lower in the river Patomecke, to a lesser river on the north side of it, as bigge as Thames,

THE LANDING ON ST. CLEMENT'S ISLAND

MARCH 25, 1634

HERON ISLAND BAR

Heron Island Bar is located near St. Clement's Island and it is believed that it remains about the same as when it was first viewed by the Maryland colonists in 1634. Most of it is invisible at high tide.

It is a favorite spot for herons, swan, geese, ducks, and gulls. In the past it has been a famous "dredging" bar and continues to be a good clam, oyster, and fishing ground.

ST. CLEMENT'S (BLACKISTONE) ISLAND

More than three-fourths of the Island area has washed away in storms. Work to prevent further erosion is under way.

1925

1935

1964

which we call St. Georges. This river makes 2 excellent bayes, wherein might harbour 300 saile of 1000 tunne a peece with very great safetie, the one called St. Georges bay, [afterward called St. George's Creek] the other, more inward, St. Maries. On the one side of this river lives the king of Yoacomaco, on the other our plantation is seated, about halfe a mile from the water, and our towne we call St. Maries."

Captain Fleet had a trading post at Yeoacomaco and traded with the Indians along the Potomac shores to the head of navigation at the Great Falls. But prior to this time, in 1608, Captain John Smith had explored the river thoroughly as far as his boat would take him, presumably as far as the Falls. He recorded that the fish were ".....lying so thicke with their heads above the water, as for want of nets (our barge driuing amongst them) we attempted to catch them with a frying pan: but we found it a bad instrument to catch fish with: neither better fish, more plenty, nor more variety for smal fish, had any of vs euer seene in any place so swimming in the water."

Captain Fleete also recorded in his journal on a trip in 1631 that the river ".....aboundeth in all manner of fish..... And as for deer, buffaloes, bears, turkeys, the woods do swarm with them, and the soil is exceedingly fertile."

Father White likewise recorded in his "Relation" that ".....the soyle, which is excellent so that we cannot sett downe a foot, but tread on Strawberries, raspires, fallen mulberrie vines, acchorns, walnutts, saxafras, etc.: and those in the wildest woods. The ground is commonly a blacke mould above, and a foot within ground of a readish colour. All is high woods except where the Indians have cleared for corne. It abounds with delicate springs which are our best drinke. Birds diversely feathered there are infinite, as eagles, swans, hernes, geese, bitterns, duckes, partridge, read, blew, partie coloured, and the like, by which will appeare, the place abounds not alone with profit, but also with pleasure."

Henry Spelman who accompanied Captain Smith on his exploratory journey of the Potomac in 1608 also traded on the river until he was killed by the Indians in 1623. Henry Fleet was a member of Smith's party on this expedition.

John White, an English sea captain who made several voyages to Virginia, had prepared a map about 1586 that showed the lower reaches of the James, York, Rappahannock, and the Potomac Rivers. White came to America with Sir Walter Raleigh's first expedition in 1585, but returned to England after nearly a year on Roanoke Island, and the nearby mainland of what later became North Carolina. He returned to the Island as governor in 1587 but soon sailed to England for supplies, leaving more than a hundred colonists, among them his daughter and his new granddaughter, Virginia Dare, the first English child born in the New World. Upon his return in 1590 he found that the entire colony had vanished.

White was interested greatly in the American Indian and not only wrote about them but also produced a series of water color paintings depicting many of the activities and ceremonies of the natives. Included among the paintings is one of the Virginia Indians fashioning a dugout canoe from a log by fire. He reported, ".....For whereas they want instruments of iron, they knowe howe to make them as handsomlye to sail with whear they liste in their rivers and to fishe with all as ours....."

Actually, the Spanish appear to have been the first to explore the Chesapeake Bay and its tributaries, although it is possible that Amerigo Vespucci found the Chesapeake on a search for a short cut to the Moluccas in 1497. As early as 1527 the official Spanish Padron General maps carried the Chesapeake Bay as the Bahia de Santa Maria (St. Mary's Bay), and they considered the area as part of their territory. In 1566 an unsuccessful attempt was made by the Spanish to establish a mission in what was to become the colony of Virginia. A second attempt was made in 1570, which was successful. A landing was made on the James River in the vicinity of what is now Williamsburg and a mission was established across the Neck on the York River. The mission was wiped out by an Indian massacre in 1572. The Spanish continued to be fearful that the English or other nations would attempt settlements in the Bay area and frequently sailed up the coast from their holdings in Florida to check the area. In 1609 a scouting expedition entered the Bay, and undoubtedly discovered the English settlement at Jamestown but withdrew without action. The Spanish Empire was too widespread and vulnerable to merit the military expenditure necessary to dislodge the English. As late as 1611 a Spanish Caravel, on the pretext of looking for a lost vessel came to Point Comfort to spy on the fortifications. Three leaders went ashore and were imprisoned. In retaliation the Spanish seized John Clark, a pilot, as a hostage. Molina, one of the Spaniards imprisoned, displayed considerable knowledge of the area waters. There is little doubt that the Spanish had explored thoroughly the tributaries as well as the bay.

From the settlement of Jamestown in 1607, until 1634, the Potomac remained in the hands of the Indians, who watched from the banks for the occasional explorer or trader who ascended the river in his unfamiliar boat. Indian villages and their cornfields were scattered along the forested shore on both sides of the river where the natives gathered oysters, fished, and hunted the wild fowl from their log canoes. Indeed, there was little need for the Indians to go far inland to hunt, for the deer liked the marsh grass and unending supply of fairly fresh water at the head of the creeks that dotted the area. It was an idyllic existence for the natives except for the frequent raids made upon them by the dreaded Susquehannas, and even more feared "naked" Indians, the Senecas from the far North.

In the early years of the settlement of both Maryland and Virginia there is scarcely any evidence that the colonists made any commercial use of the natural resources of the Potomac and the other tributaries of the Chesapeake. It is understandable that the shellfish, oysters, and clams could not be shipped to England, but salted and dried fish could have been and perhaps were, to a limited extent. The English were, of course, familiar with oysters and other forms of seafood found in the new land. If they did not know the art of scalding or roasting oysters, the Indians soon taught them, for this was a favorite dish of the River Indians, which is attested by the mounds of oyster shells that may still be found in the fields along the river front. One shell heap at Pope's Creek, Maryland, covered 30 acres and was 15 feet high. Many accounts are found of efforts to purchase corn from the Indians in the early years, during times of shortages, and there was much traffic back and forth across the Potomac to replenish supplies. Corn, together with game, was an important commodity in the food budget of the colonists but that this was supplemented by fish and oysters there can be no doubt. In later years, it became necessary for the Maryland Assembly to pass legislation that indentured servants and slaves would be fed food other than oysters and terrapins several days each week.

The Potomac during these pioneer years served as a highway from one settlement to another, in the absence of roads; as the port of call for hundreds of English ships to transport the tobacco crop and furs, and return laden with supplies for the colonists. Water front was essential to the settlers no matter how high up an inlet for the water was their means of transportation and it was necessary for all to become good sailors including the Jesuit Fathers, who had a string of mission stations from St. Mary's City to what is now our Federal City. Father White established missions at White's Neck Creek, Port Tobacco, Piscataway, and Anacostia where he ministered to the spiritual needs of both the Indians and the whites in the area.

It was only when the weather-protected creek shores had been occupied that the settlers took up land on the river proper, except in the case of scattered land-holders, such as Thomas Gerard, whose holdings encompassed both.

The inlets along the river, although generally known as creeks (locally called "cricks"), are in a few cases known as rivers and bays. The reason for the distinction is unknown. Some of the creeks are larger than the rivers and bays. Generally the branches or forks of the creeks are called coves, although sometimes a large cove is given another creek name. The inlets are tidal and also are fed by springs, runs, branches, and freshes so that their waters at the head are brackish. In-shore of St. Katherine's Sound, between the Island and the mainland, is the ancient Blackistone home, "River Springs", so named because fresh water springs bubble up along the shore in the waters of the Sound.

There are in tidewater Potomac 98 navigable bays or creeks, with 49 along the Maryland shore and 49 along the Virginia shore. In sequence from the mouth of the river on the Maryland shore are Calvert Bay; Smith or Trinity Creek (with Jutland Creek branching from it); St. George's Creek (with Price Cove); Piney Point Creek; Herring Creek; Blake Creek; Flood's Creek; Bretton Bay (with Combs Creek and Cherry Cove); St. Clement's Bay (with St. Patrick's Creek, Canoe Neck Creek, Deep Creek, and Tomakoken Creek); White's Neck Creek; Wicomico River (with Mill Creek, Bromley Creek, Manahowic Creek, also known as Gerard's Creek and Taveau Creek, Chaptico Bay, Dolly Boarman's Creek, Hatton Creek, and Charleston Creek); Cuckold Creek; Piccowaxen Creek; Pope's Creek; Port Tobacco Creek; Goose Creek; Nanjemoy Creek (with Burgess Creek and Hill Top Fork); Wades Bay; Blue Banks; Mallows Bay; Goose Bay; Chicomuxen Creek; Mattowoman Creek; Pomonkey Creek; Piscataway Creek; Swan Creek; Broad Creek; Oxon Creek, and the Anacostia River (Eastern Branch).

On the Virginia shore from the mouth of the river are Little Wicomico River; Hack's Creek; Cubitt's Creek; Hall's Creek; Presley Creek; Coan River (with Kingscote Creek and the Glebe branching from it); Yeoacomaco River (with South Yeoacomaco River, Mill Creek, West Yeoacomaco River, and Northwest Yeoacomaco River); Jackson Creek; Gardiner Creek; Lower Machodoc River (with Glebe Creek and Branson Cove); Buckner Creek; Nomini Bay (with Nomini Creek and Peirce Creek); Currioman Bay (with Currioman Creek, Poor Jack Creek, and Cold Harbor Creek); Pope's Creek; Bridge's Creek; Mattox Creek; Monroe Bay; Rosier Creek; Upper Machodoc Creek; Jotank Creek; Potomac Creek (with Accokeek Creek); Aquia Creek; Chopawamsic Creek; Quantico Creek; Neabsco Creek; Occoquan Bay (with Belmont Bay and Occoquan Creek fed by Bull Run); Gunston Cove (with Pohick Bay and Accotink Bay); Dogue Creek; Little Hunting Creek; Great Hunting Creek and Four Mile Run.

The fur trade on the Potomac (and undoubtedly the other bay tributaries as well) was one of great importance. In the early years of the settlement Father White was told that a merchant in a single year exported beaver skins of a value of 40,000 gold crowns and the profit was thirty fold, and for nearly a century the fur trade was important in forming the pattern of early exploration, trade, and settlement. The Potomac beaver trade was known to the French who were active in the Chesapeake Bay region. Henry Fleet's activity in the fur trade was not limited to the lower Potomac and about 1627 he was the first to tap directly the rich fur resources of the upper Potomac and the interior. The trade continued to boom and among the new traders was William Claiborne who established a post on Kent Island in the upper Chesapeake Bay and who was to cause Lord Baltimore, the Proprietor of Maryland, much difficulty in a few years. The fur trade was carried on under strict license of the Proprietor but there was a good deal of illicit trading and conflict.

Meanwhile those not engaged in the fur trade were busy growing tobacco on the great river front plantations that stretched from Point Lookout to the Great Falls. In these early days it was necessary for the Maryland Assembly to pass a law to require that a certain portion of the land be devoted to raising corn, and apparently this had the desired effect because at one time Cuthbert Fenwick was commissioned to sail all the way to New England to barter corn for other needed supplies.

Everyone, including the Proprietor, wanted to get rich quick in this new beautiful and bountiful land. The Baltimore family fortune had been sadly depleted in the unsuccessful attempt to found a colony in Newfoundland, and most of the gentry were land-hungry younger sons of the old English families, determined to rival the manor holdings of the family at home. In a few years, there were large land holdings along both shores of the Potomac and its tributaries and "rolling roads" were built to the water's edge to haul the great casks of tobacco to the designated ports of call, which were, in the main, no more than ship's landings. The search went on for gold and other precious metals and the fur trade continued to grow. The highway to all the hoped for riches was the broad Potomac.

The search for quick riches in the early days, which was detrimental to the development of the colony, was a matter of concern to many of the leading colonists, as is attested by a series of letters to Lord Baltimore in 1638. Father Thomas Copley, S. J., who was to play a prominent part in provincial affairs for twenty years, wrote as follows:

"Certainly I conceive that your Lordship will rather think it fit to nourish and support young sprigs than to depress them; and to go about to gather fruit before it be planted, and ripe, is never to have fruit. But perhaps some may be of opinion, that if your Lordship can but have the trade of Beaver and Corne to your self, the plantation is not much to be regarded. And the fewer there are the better cheer will be for them, and that among ruins they shall always find something. Yet against this I would desire your Lordship to reflect that in a flourishing plantation, your Lordship shall ever be sure of a growing profit and honor. But in these petty trades and in raking out of mens necessity, the honor will be little, and the profit very uncertain. Some that are immediate actors perhaps may get some things, but your Lordship shall be sure if you yourself have the profit to make large disbursements, and to receive large accounts and besides I am of opinion that God will not prosper such design, where if your Lordship rejecting them stick to your first designs. God in time will give them a happy success, and raise to yourself and your seed no small blessing. Here certainly nothing is wanting but people, let it be peopled, and it shall not yield to the most flourishing country for profit and pleasure, the promoting then of this must be your first aim, and this your Lordship must encourage by all means, and when the fruits are ripe, it will be time to gather them. Now only you must nourish plants, and while you expect fruits from others, by yourself seek fruits from the earth, which may be gathered in plenty, if your Lordship please to come and see, and resolve on the best, for mine own part I have so good an apprehension of the country, that I no way repent me of my journey, but live very contentedly and doubt not but if I can have patience and expect the seasons, I shall find as happy fruit here as in any other part of the world. But indeed, the old sayings are true that Rome was not built in a day, and that such as will leap over the stile, before they come at them, shall break their shin, and perhaps not get over the stile so quickly, as those, who come to them, before they go over."

Father Andrew White and Captain Thomas Cornwaleys likewise wrote similar letters to Lord Baltimore. Captain Cornwaleys, who was a tower of strength in the provincial government in the early years of the colony, went on to describe the building of his home, in these words, ".....in the meane time I am building of a house toe put my head in, of sawn Timber framed a story and half hygh with A seller and Chimnies of brick toe Encourage others toe follow my Example, for hithertoe wee live in Cottages....." This type of architecture was followed in home building by the planters along the river for many years. Later, many built all of brick but preserved the style - a story and a half with a great sloping roof in which dormer windows were spaced. Many of these old houses still survive, and excellent examples are "River View" on Canoe Neck Creek in St. Clement's Bay in Maryland and "Gunston Hall" at Gunston Cove in Virginia. The old Newtown Manor house, which overlooks both St. Clement's and Bretton Bays, also was of this type, but a half-story was added in 1815 which is clearly discernable in the brick work. Beginning in the late 1600's and early 1700's more pretentious homes were built along the Potomac shores, such as Tudor Hall, St. Inigoes Manor, West St. Mary's, Mulberry Fields, Bushwood, St. Thomas Manor, and Causine's Manor on the Maryland side, and on the Virginia side, Wilton, Bushfield, Nomini Hall, Stratford, and many others.

Some of the early landholders were able to amass sizable holdings on both sides of the Potomac River. An example may be cited in the case of Dr. Thomas Gerard whose holdings in Maryland totaled some 20,000 to 25,000 acres (St. Clement's, Basford, and Westwood Manors) and in Virginia 3,500 acres (Gerard's Reserve). Nathaniel Pope, an ancestor of the Washingtons, and others likewise had sizable holdings on both sides of the river. As a matter of fact, there is a Pope's Creek on both sides of the Potomac today. Many of the early colonists, however, did not bother to take possession of their lands but sold their land claims to newer colonists or others, so that there was a brisk real estate operation going on in the earliest years. There are some indications that a few planters claimed and received land in both Maryland and Virginia for transporting the same individuals to first one colony and then across the river to the other.

In Gerard's case, after the failure of Fendall's Rebellion in 1659, in which he seemed to be the real leader, he had to flee for his life across the Potomac to sanctuary in Virginia until the affair quieted down and he could secure a pardon from Lord Baltimore. Evidently he made many friends there at that time and in 1662 made his 3,500 acre purchase. After the death of his first wife, the former Susannah Snow, in 1667, he removed permanently to his lands on the lower Machodoc River in Virginia and married a young widow, Rose Tucker. Here together with Henry Corbin, John Lee, and Isaac Allerton, he built in 1670 a "banquetting house" near the head of Jackson's Creek (then known as Cherives Creek), where their estates cornered. Bishop Meade cited the parties here as an example of "riotous living." The old Gerard Manor house, "Wilton", two stories high, with its thick brick walls, beautifully laid about 1685, with glazed headers forming an attractive pattern, is still standing and in excellent condition.

During these early years, and indeed for a century or more afterwards, there was much intermarriage between the families residing on opposite sides of the river. Gerard's youngest son, John, and three of his seven daughters married Virginians. Two of his daughters, Anne and Frances, married Colonel John Washington, the great-grandfather of George Washington, although he had no issue by either of them.

Little is known definitely concerning the boats used in the very early years on the Potomac. Among small boats the Indian log canoe, as described by John White and others, or some variation of it was used by the colonists. It was of a pirogue type, for Father White reported that when the Indians first came out to St. Clement's Island, after the landing of the colonists, they wondered "where that tree should grow, out of which so great a canoe should be hewen, supposing it all of one peece, as their canoes use to be." It is of interest to note that a few miles inshore from St. Clement's Island there is a Canoe Neck Creek (spelled Canow in the very early records).

Father White recorded also that a barge, which was brought in pieces out of England, was assembled while they were at St. Clement's Island, but a few ships of both the pinnace and bark type were being built in Massachusetts and Virginia, prior to this time. It is unknown when boat building was begun on the Maryland side of the Potomac but it was soon after the settlement, because Lord Baltimore's colonists came much better prepared than those of Virginia and there are many references to boat ownership in the early colonial records. Governor Leonard Calvert had several pinnaces under his command during the troubles with William Claiborne over Kent Island. In the battle of the Pocomoke, when Governor Calvert's forces under Captain Thomas Cornwaleys and his Lieutenant, Cuthbert Fenwick, fought and defeated Claiborne's men, pinnaces and other boats are mentioned, and the same ships were used to reduce Kent Island to subjection. The boat of the Jesuit Fathers is described as a pinnace or galley and it was not so large but that it could be rowed by two men, "when the wind is adverse or fails." Probably a somewhat smaller boat was used by Father Copley when he crossed the Potomac to visit the Virginia Catholics, notably the Brent family, who were located on Aquia Creek.

Four vessels are named in the Indian trade during 1637-1638, and undoubtedly many more were in general use. Inventories in connection with the settlement of estates during the period 1638-1642 mentioned several canoes and other small boats, generally valued at 30-150 pounds of tobacco, and a boat was appraised in 1647 at

1200 pounds of tobacco. A review of Navigation Bonds for Maryland ships 1679-1689 disclosed that Calvert County led with 49 and St. Mary's County was next with 26. During the period 1690-1696, the Eastern Shore came into prominence with 43 as compared with 39 on the Western Shore. Talbot led with 25, Calvert - 19, Anne Arundel - 10, and St. Mary's County - 8. Apparently as more of the country was opened up the registrations shifted.

In a census of ships and ship building in Maryland during the years 1689-1697, it is mentioned that one sloop and one brig were built in St. Mary's County and two sloops and one brig were built in Prince George's. In addition, it is recorded that 5 shallops and 3 sloops were in operation in Charles County, one sloop in Prince George's, and in St. Mary's, four shallops, five sloops, and three other ships whose origins were not given. In this census for all of the Province there were included 13 classed as ships, 6 pinks, 12 brigantines, 66 sloops, 55 shallops, and 8 other craft. Some were sea-going ships as large as 450 tons; 67 were built on the Western Shore and 93 on the Eastern Shore.

This census or survey was in response to an order of Governor Francis Nicholson dated May 28, 1697, and since the reports of the sheriffs of the several counties contains much information concerning the types of vessels owned and being built, the owners, masters, etc., it is included from the Council Proceedings (Archives of Maryland XXV, pp. 595-601).

Ships built in Maryland.

Maryland, Sct.

In obedience to an Ordr of his Excy the Govr and Council bearing date the 28th day of May 1697, Commanding the severll Sheriffs of this Province to make strict enquiry of what Shipps and Vessels trading to Sea have been built within their respective Countys since his Majtys happy Reign, as also what Sloops and Shallops to the County belong, and what are now a building, together with the number of seafaring men. Pursuant whereto they make their Returns, vizt.:

The Sheriff of Ann arundll County.

The Brigantine George, built by Jno. Buck of Bytheford.
The Annapolis, built by Jno. Buck of Bytheford
The Ship Marygold, built by Jno. Davis of Bytheford
The Betty Brigantine purchased into this County by his Excy the Govr etc. Capt. Richard Hill, Capt. Wm. Holland, Capt. Richard Hill for Mr. Richard Johns, Mr. Wm. Cole, Senr, Mr. Saml Chew, Mr. Richard Harrison, Mr. Nehemia Birckhead, Mr. Mordica Moore, and Commanded by Mr. Hen Hill.
The Adventure, purchased and owned by the same owners and commanded by Mr. Thomas ffrancis.
The Susannah Brigantine, built by Richard Beard, Commanded by Edwd Balter, bound to New England and lost att Cape May three years since.
One Brigandyne in building by Mr. Jno. Buck of Bytheford
One Vessel in Building by Thomas Hardin, Jno. Baldwin, Neal Clarke, Tho. Rutland, Richd Snowden and some others who expect to be fitted to Sea by the Spring and design for Barbadoes. Comanded by Tho. Goodwin, have shippt no men yet. In all, 8 Sloops built within this County.
Abrm Childs built one Sloop, wch was lost in the Bay 3 or 4 years since.

Thomas Tench Esqr I Sloope
Mordicah Moore I Sloope
Abra Childs I Sloope

Nicho. Spurne I Sloope
Steph. ffrancis I Sloope

Mr. Jeffries built I sloope and sold her to Thomas Beale and Richd Bars last year. Major John Hamond partly built a sloop and sold her on the stocks to Capt. Deane Cock last year.

Shallops belonging to this County

Samuel Chambers	I	Joshua Merricken	I
Gabriel Parrott	I	James Collins	I
David Macklefist	2	Richd Kilbourne	I
Humph. Jervis	I	Marny Deveran	I
Jno. Baldwin	I	Majr Jno. Hamond	I

In all II

Seafaring men borne and belonging to this Coy

```
Capt. Rd Hill Jr
     Henry Hill          > Commanders
     Tho. Francis
Benj. Burgess        sons to
Charles Burgess    >  Col. Wm. Burgess
Edwd Dorsey, son of Capt. Jno. Dorsey
Joshua Dorsey        sons to
Samll Dorsey      >  Maj. Edwd. Dorsey          > Apprentices
Thomas Knighton, son of Thos. Knighton
Nathan Smith, son of Nathan Smith
```

The Sheriff of Calvert Coty

Esq. Plater, a shallop	I	Coll Henry Mitchell, a shallop	I
Wm. Pollard, a sloop	I	Coll Jno. Bigger, a shallop	I
Saml Holdswort, 2 sloops	2	Wm. Fields, a sloop	I
Mrs. Ashcom, 2 sloops		Richd Keen, a sloop	I
ditto I shallop	3	Mr. Walter Smith, a sloop	I

In all I2 Sloops and Shallops, and no Seafaring men to be found belonging to any of the sd Sloops or Shallops

The Sheriff of Prince George Coy

Mr. John Brown is now building two sloops.
Mr. Thomas Hollyday hath now on the Stocks one Brigantine
Mr. David Small hath also one sloop belonging to Capt Thomas Ennis.

Seafaring men

Mr. Tho. Hollyday Willm Boys and Robt Boys.

The Sheriff of Baltimore County

Mr. Edward Boothby, I shallop
John Ferry, I shallop
Benjn Wells, I shallop, and no vessel as yet built here

The Sheriff of Charles County

No Ships or Vessels trading to Sea built here.

Sloops and Shallops

Majr Wm. Dent's sloop about 18 or 20 Hhds.
Mr. John Stone, I shallop, about 16 or 18 Hhds.
Mr. Philip Lyne, I sloop about 36 or 40 Hhds.
Mr. John Bayne, I shallop about 14 or 16 Hhds.
Coll John Coats, I shallop about 16 or 18 Hhds.
Madam Diggs, I sloop about 45 or 50 Hhds.
Mr. James Neale, I shallop, about 18 or 20 Hhds.
Mr. Saml Luckett, I shallop about 12 or 14 Hhds.
In all, 8

```
Mr. Jno. Thomas
Jno. Harris belonging to Mr. Lyne
Joseph Leving in Wm. and Mary parrish   > Seafaring men
ffra. Sheffield in do. parrish
Wm. Pontingall in Nanjemy parrish         In all 5
```

May the 4th 1698

This is a true Extract of the Severall Sheriffs Returns
W. Bladen, Clk. Councll

The Sheriff of St. Maries County

Mr Jacob Mowland	I sloop
Col Henry Lowe	I sloop
Adam bell	I sloop and I shallop
Edwd Parsons	I shallop and I sloop building
Jno. Savadge	I shallop

Majrs John Lowe built I ship called the Planter now belonging to Liverpool, he hath 3 ships and I shallop

Robt Mason	I sloope
Edwd Hilliard	I sloope

A list of men tht goe by water when employ'd:--

Jeaffrey Jnoson	Tho: Hebb
Edwd Hilliard	Edwd Kelsy
Rd Shovebottom	Ed Parsons
Jno Savage	Chs Bonak
Richd Sherly	Richd Hortrop.

A List of such Vessells trading to sea as have been built in Somerst County since his Majties happy govt here as also what are building together wth what Sloops and Shallops to the said County belonging, taken by virtue of his Excy the Govr etc. their order bearing date the 28 day of May anno dom 1697

Vessells built.
Stephen Dorsey, two 2
Liven Denwood, one

Vessels building
I belonging to Capt. Wm. Pipes

Sloops	Shallops	To whom they belong
3	I	Liven Denwood
	I	Wm. Whittington
2		Wm. White
	I	Wm Smith
I		Mr. James and Wm. Roord
	I	John Kirk
I		Affrodosia Johnson
I		Hu. and Nath. Horsey
I		Thoms Dixon
I		Thos Everenden
I		Richd and John Waters
	I	Samll Handy
	I	Alexr Xyle
	I	Petr Elsey
	I	Thos Jones
	I	Col. Browne
I		Madam King
	I	St Col Winder
	I	Mr James Murray
	I	Daniel Hart

Seafaring men I know of none but Tho Butler and Mica Holland.

A List of Ships, Sloops, Shallops and Seafaring men belonging to Dorst County.

Col. Charles Hutchings Sloope abt 30 hhds. burthen
Major Ennalls a Brigantine goes to Seas about 50 hhds. and another a building.

Wm. Stephens a Sloope about 4 hhds. under her deck
John Anderson a Sloope about 20 hhds.
John Gladstanes a shallope about 16 hhds.

Mr. Walter Campbell a sloope 24 hhds
Mr. Rogr Woolford a shallop about 12 hhds.
John Ellitt a sloope abt. 30 hhds.
Mr Alexr Fisher a sloope abt. 30 hhds.
Presidt. Smith a Brigantine went for England.
John Thompson a Shallope abt. 16 hhds.

Caecill County

Capt. Wm. Hill	I Brigantine
Mr. Wm. Harris	I shallope
Esqr Frisby	I shallope
Capt. Thos Robinson	I shallope
The Family of the Lappadees [Labadists]	I shallope

Madam Harman one large sloop and one shallop
Thos Kelton one shallope

Kent County etc. 1697

A List of Ships and other Vessells lately built and now a building as also of wt sloopes and Shallops withn the said County.

The Torrington Loyalty built at the Towne of New Yarmouth by Jon. Olliver burthen 200 hhds or thereabout loaded att the port of Annapolis, belonging to the towne of Torrington in the county of Devon. Gone to Europe

A Brigantine belonging to Robt Smith esqr built in Choptank and brought hither to be finished, burthen 60 hhds or thereabout, Gone to Europe.

A Ship in the Stocks belonging to the sd Esqr Smith, burthen 500 hhds, or thereabouts.

A Stock of the said Esqr Smiths, burthen 30 hhds, or thereabouts.

A Deck Sloope of Capt. James Smiths, 35 hhds.

A sloop of Andrew Tonnards, 40 hhds.

A Deck Sloope of Capt. John Hawkinses, 60 hhds.

A Shallope of Mr. Michael Millers 10 hhds.

The Ship Factor of Cediford built by Mr. Geofry power, burthen 500 hhds or thereabouts, now riding in Chestr Rivr bound for Europe

The Sloop Assistance built by the sd Power now Rideing in the freshes of Chester Rivr

A Ship on the Stox a building for Mr. Jeophry Power, burthen 200 hhd or thereabouts, wth by gods assistence will be launched in 6 weeks time.

Of Seamen wthin the sd County

Sailors belonging to the Factor of Bediford: John Yeo, Master; Thos Black and Edwd Collins, mates; John Gunion, Simon Heath, John Bathead, John Glannitt, Arthur Say, Geo: Cole, John Murrow, James Betty, Thos Tucker, Saml Glear, George Owen, Tho. Stevens, carpenter, Philm Piles.

Carpenters and Sailors belonging to Mr. Powers ship in the stocks:
Danll Haynes, Wm. Miles, Christopr Reveclipp, Peter Jones, Nicho. Frand, Henry Laudmer, Jon. Wilcock, Walter Clagg.

Sailors belonging to the Loves Increase of Whitehaven:
Francis Grindal, Mastr David Davis and Henry Cragg, mates, John Osthmotherly, Wm. Askew, John Roddry, Giles browne, Joseph Woods, Jona Hodgson, Wm. Walker, Phines Boyes.

A List of Vessels etc. in Talbot County.

A pink now belonging to Capt. Sutton, built at Kingstowne by Robt Graison, about 300 hhds. burthen.

Another about the same burthen built at Great Choptank, belonging to Wm. Dickyson and Robt Graison

Another built at Island Creek by Solon Sumers for Capt. miller about 400 Tonn

AN EARLY 18TH CENTURY SLOOP

Circa 1720

AN EARLY 17TH CENTURY PINNACE

Purportedly the "Virginia," first English boat built in America.
Built in 1607 at Sagadaboc, Maine, she was a frequent visitor in
Maryland and Virginia waters. She also made regular voyages be-
tween the colonies and England and eventually was lost on the
Irish coast.

Another built in Miles Rivr by Robt Graison for himself and R. Bennet and others, abt 120 Tuns

Another built in Island Creek by S. Sumers for Capt abt 70 Ton

Another built in the Island Creek by Andw Tonnard and Wm. Sharpe for the said Sharpe about 50 Tonn

A Brigantine

Another Brigantine built at Ralph Fishbournes about 40 Ton for himselfe

A Sloope built by Andrew Tonnard at Porridge Creek, burthen about 40 Tons, sold to Col Sayers

Another built by the sd Tonnard and sold to Nicho. Lowe about 40 Tons

Another built by George Ferguson at Wm. Stephenses in the dividing Creek about 35 Tons for the sd Stephens

Another Sloop built by the sd Ferguson in Tridhaven Creek for Edwd Pollard about 40 hhds. burthen

Another built by the same man in the same Creek for Tho. Skillinton about 40 hhds

Another Sloope built by Wm. Whitaker in Tridhaven Creek for Nicho. Lowe about 40 hhds

Another Shallop of Tho. Skillingtons 25 hhds

Another Sloope built by Andw Tonnard and sold to Robt Grundy about 40 Tons

Another Sloope built in Chester Rivr for Capt. James Smith about the burthen of 40 hhds.

Another of Wm. Sharpes 25 hhds.

A Shallop sold to Nicho. Lowe of 16 hhds.

A Shallop of James Berryes of 16 hhds.

A Shallop of Mr. Berrys of abt. 20 hhds.

A Shallop of Wm. Aldernes of 12 hhds.

A Sloop of Andrew Tonnards of 40 hhds.

A Sloop built for Capt. Murphey of 4 hhds

Another for Daniel Sherwood of 70 hhds

A Sloop of Wm. Sharpes of abt 45 Tons

One of Obadiah Judkins about 60 hhds.

One of John Hankinses of abt. 60 hhds

A Ship of about 300 Tons on the stocks in Island Creek by Saml Summrs for Capt Millar

Another Ship about 300 hhds. at Ralph Fishbournes

Another at Island Creek belonging to Capt. Elisher James, abt 300 Tons.

Another Ship on the Stocks at Tho. Skillingtons in Tridhaven Creek belonging to English owners, abt 450 Tons

Another building at Wm. Sharpes for himselfe about 90 Tons

A Sloop on the Stox att Wm. Dicksons for himself abt 45 Tons.

Another of Nicho. Lowes ready to launch of 40 Ton

Another building att Sol. Sumrs for Capt. Miller abt 45 Tons

A Sloope on the Stox at Jeremiah Hookes for Jeremiah Simpson abt 40 hhds.

A Shallop at Jno. Salters abt 30 hhds. belonging to him

Another abt the same burthen belonging to Jon. Lowe.

Seafaring men, viz.:

Owen Silviant, Hugh Spondines, Henry Jackson, James Dynam, Jereh Simpson and David Mills.

True Extract of the sevrall Sheriffs Returns
                                    W. Bladen, Clk Concil.

Perhaps the estates of the planters who dwelt along the river is typified by that of Thomas Dent, lawyer, planter, and merchant. He settled in Maryland about 1658, engaged in the practice of law, was appointed a member of the County Court of St. Mary's in 1661, was elected to the assembly in 1669, engaged in trade as a merchant, and by the time of his death in 1676 owned sizable tracts of land, mostly along the Potomac, from St. Mary's City to Anacostia. He named his holdings of 850 acres in Anacostia "Giesboro" and the point at this location still carries this name. It is evident from the inventory of his estate that the home plantation was located on the west side of Nanjemoy Creek, a 900 acre holding. A sail boat is mentioned among his possessions there. His store was located on the St. Mary's River, where he had a boat landing, and the inventory mentions another boat, and a "canou" and considerable merchandise in the store. It is likely that Thomas Dent had a trade route between Nanjemoy (perhaps as far up the Potomac as Anacostia) and St. Mary's City. His presence in the city was required frequently at the court and assembly sessions and to superintend his mercantile operations. He had, perhaps, a town house in or near St. Mary's City, but the plantation at Nanjemoy was firmly established as the inventory mentions four negro slaves, three white indentured servants, much livestock, farm implements, and home furnishings.

It is evident that those members of the Council and the Assembly who lived some distance from St. Mary's City, such as Thomas Gerard and William Bretton, who lived at the mouth of St. Clement's Bay, must have been boat owners since roads were almost non-existent. Gerard was accused on a boat trip to a court session of having drunk something extraordinary (but not so much he couldn't get out of a cart's way) and of having castigated the Puritans of Anne Arundel. There were quite a number of witnesses in the group, so it is evident that sizable boats were being built by 1640. There was a great need for boats and the colonial shipyards must have been kept busy.

It sounds like a fairy tale today to speak of the troubles that the Maryland and Virginia colonists had with pirates, but this was a real problem up to the time of the American Revolution. As soon as there was a steady flow of tobacco and other products to England and the continent, pirates began to appear in the vicinity of the Virginia Capes. It soon came to a point that few of the colonial shippers would risk a single ship and the great "tobacco flotillas" came into existence. After gathering the season's crop they would rendezvous in the Chesapeake before the passage through the Capes. Sometimes the English government would even send an old warship or two to accompany the fleet like war convoys! It was particularly infuriating to the Marylanders that when certain pirates were successful in making a capture, they would sail for Philadelphia, where they were welcomed by the merchants there with open arms to buy and sell their booty at considerable profit. The pirates boldly walked the streets of the city and brawled in the waterfront dives. This matter was of concern to the Assembly of Maryland and representations were made to the Pennsylvanians with notable lack of success. This state of affairs, added onto the Baltimore-Penn boundary dispute where sanctimonious William laid the foundation to win his case with a map that many felt was fraudulent, did nothing to cement the bonds of friendship with the neighbors to the north.

Little is recorded regarding fisheries in early colonial times, although seining is mentioned at Herring Creek in the lower Potomac as early as 1639. It is certain that the river front planters owned seines and fished for supplies for their families and servants, and probably some of the freemen followed the water for a living, establishing markets in their neighborhoods. Undoubtedly there was a fish market at St. Mary's City from the earliest days and the industry grew with the establishment of towns along the Potomac. By the middle 1700's one reads about Potomac shad and other fish being hawked about the streets of Annapolis and Baltimore. The seining shores of General George Washington at Mt. Vernon were notable and he sold much of the excess of his catches that could not be used on the plantation. However, tobacco remained the key item in colonial trade, particularly with the decline of the fur trade.

Some of the large plantation owners on both sides of the Potomac River owned their own ocean-going vessels in the late 1600's and through the 1700's. Typical of the Maryland side of the river was the brig, William and Hopewell, which was built locally on the St. Mary's River around 1750. It was owned by Vernon Hebb, and sailed by his brother-in-law, Captain Edward Fenwick. Hebb's family had been ship owners before him, and these vessels were used to transport the products from their plantation and the plantations of their neighbors to the Indies, England, and points in Europe. The Lee family, located at Stratford, on the Nomini Cliffs on the Virginia side of the river likewise had their own sea-going ship or ships in the early 1700's and there were others, including Captain Robert Slye of the Wicomico River. In later years Captain Ignatius Fenwick was the owner of an ocean-going vessel and made many trips to London and other ports of the old world. His cousin, James Fenwick, of "Cherryfields" on the St. Mary's River, sailed the same routes and had in 1785 a fine new ship which could carry five hundred hogsheads of tobacco, as is disclosed in a letter of Bishop Edward Dominic Fenwick, the nephew of James, to Captain Ignatius. General Washington and other planters on both sides of the Potomac had fine schooners, built locally, that they used in the river commerce.

Most of the water front plantations were on or near water deep enough for ocean-going vessels and there was little need for ports. Ships from Boston, London, Jamaica, Cadiz, the Barbadoes, and other ports deposited their wares at the planter's wharf and reloaded, mostly with tobacco, the staple crop of the colonists. In prosperous years more than a hundred ships sailed from Maryland.

After ports of entry were established by law, warehouses were built and those landings became favorite meeting places for the men of the colony. One of these warehouses stood not far from the plantation "Porto Bello" in the St. Mary's River. Upriver towards Great Mills stood St. Mary's Warehouse and many ships touched this port. Other warehouses were located at Leonardtown, Chaptico, Cedar Point, Port Tobacco, and Piscataway.

A warehouse was erected also at Dent's Landing on Nanjemoy Creek in 1748, during the time of William Dent (1706-1757), a great-grandson of Thomas Dent, the immigrant. Throughout these generations of the Dent family at Nanjemoy Creek, ownership of shallops, canoes, and other boats is mentioned in the inventories of their estates.

In Virginia, Justices of the Peace were appointed inspectors at the tobacco warehouses in 1730, and such officials were appointed in Maryland under the law of 1748 by the church vestries of the "Established Church." While tobacco continued as the principal medium of exchange and was used to pay state taxes, church tithes, and most other obligations, "crop notes" were given to the planters for their tobacco when it passed inspection and as they were drawn to convey title, they passed freely from hand to hand. There were a dozen inspection houses along the Virginia shore and some named were Aquia, Quantico, Occoquan, Hunting Creek, and the Falls.

The town of Annapolis was incorporated in 1696 and received a charter in 1708. In the latter year Leonardtown on Bretton Bay was incorporated also. Baltimore was created in 1729 and Garrison's Landing on the Eastern Branch of the Potomac became the town of Bladensburg and was laid out in 1742 when 60 lots were placed on sale. Even prior to this time Bladensburg was already a settlement with some social and economic status. Here a Market Master's House was erected in 1757 and still stands. By 1760 the docks and warehouses had reached a capacity of 2,000 hogsheads of tobacco, and both local vessels and ships from Europe were utilizing these facilities. The Market Master's House is built of stone, not indigenous to the area, and this stone was perhaps brought in as ship's ballast. For this reason it is also known as Ship's Ballast House. In Virginia, the General Assembly authorized in 1748 the establishment of a town for Fairfax County at "Hunting Creek Warehouse" to be named Alexandria. Georgetown was laid out in 1751 on land adjacent to the inspection house called "George Gordon's Rolling House." The roads leading to these warehouses were called "rolling roads," since the hogsheads of tobacco were rolled by hand or team to these ports.

It is evident that locally built sloops and schooners were put into service on the river in these early years, and by the time of the outbreak of the American Revolution there were many engaged in the river trade. References are found which give indication of the size of the boats, such as a schooner of 1800 "bush" (bushels), a sloop of 1200 "bush", and the like; and these boats were used in hauling grain, wood, fish, oysters, and tobacco to the river settlements and towns. At the larger ports, such as Annapolis, Baltimore, Georgetown, and Alexandria, ocean-going vessels were taking on tobacco, grain, and other products destined for the Indies and Europe.

LIFE ON THE POTOMAC RIVER

Chapter II

WAR ON THE POTOMAC

For a period of almost 150 years prior to the outbreak of the Revolutionary War in 1776, there were a series of actions or revolts in Maryland designed to unseat the government of Lord Baltimore. The first action, which has been mentioned previously, was the difficulty with William Claiborne over Kent Island which occurred coincident with the settlement at St. Mary's City. In a few years the action culminated in the naval battle in the Pocomoke River and the reduction of Kent Island by Governor Leonard Calvert. In the battle of the Pocomoke, the Maryland ships were under the command of the most renowned of the early Potomac River mariners, Captain Thomas Cornwaleys and his Lieutenant, Cuthbert Fenwick.

In a few years more trouble appeared on the horizon. During the rise of the Parliamentary Party in England, Governor Calvert, in 1644, had occasion to visit his brother, Lord Baltimore, in the mother country. Richard Ingle, a mariner of England, arrived in the Potomac in January of this year in his ship, the "Reformation." While at anchor at St. Clement's (Blackistone) Island, just off Longworth's (Colton's) Point, he was visited by Thomas Gerard, William Hardwick, and Walter Broadhurst (Broadhurst and Hardwick later became sons-in-law of Gerard). The trio soon after testified that Ingle had spoken seditiously against the King. A warrant was issued to Hardwick and he arrested Ingle for treason while the ship was at anchor in St. Mary's River. Due to a mix up of instructions between the Acting Governor and members of the Council, Ingle was permitted to escape. Upon his return to England, Ingle complained to Parliament that his ship had been seized in Maryland because it was a London ship, and that Maryland was a stronghold of papists and supporters of the King against Parliament. Ingle then procured letters of marque against all ships opposed to Parliament and sailed for Maryland to avenge himself against the Government and the Catholics.

Ingle put in at St. Mary's City on February 24, 1645, with the avowed purpose of burning or destroying whatever belonged to the Catholics and to put the Protestants in possession of everything not destroyed. The pinnaces of the Maryland Navy were no match for the heavily armed "Reformation" and they fled or were captured. Ingle and his men captured the forts at St. Mary's City and St. Inigoes and then set out to rob and ravage the countryside. The Chapel-House at St. Mary's City was robbed and burned. Many fine manor houses, including that of Thomas Gerard at Longworth's Point, suffered a similar fate. Thomas Cornwaleys of St. Inigoes was robbed of all of his possessions. Catholic mission property valued at more than 2,000 pounds sterling was seized or destroyed and many of the government records disappeared. During the years 1645 and 1646, there was no government in the colony and much disorder, so that this era is known as the "plundering years." Claiborne, who never missed an opportunity to make trouble for Lord Baltimore, repossessed Kent Island during the difficulty with Ingle, but he fled early in 1647 when Governor Calvert was able to restore order and reassume the reins of government.

It is interesting to note that Andrew Monroe, mariner, an ancestor of President James Monroe, commanded a pinnace under Cuthbert Fenwick of Lord Baltimore's Navy. He "threw in" with Ingle during his invasion of Maryland and fled across the Potomac when Ingle was repelled. He settled in the vicinity of what is now Colonial Beach and nearby Monroe Creek still carries his name.

In 1654 the Puritan Uprising occurred in Maryland following Oliver Cromwell's success in England. Lord Baltimore, as a Roman Catholic in a period of religious upheaval in the mother country, was fair prey to those who were envious of his land holdings and power in Maryland and those who disliked the Roman Church. In 1649, after the Virginians had refused religious toleration to the Puritans in that colony, Lord Baltimore invited them to settle on the Severn River where they would have religious freedom. When the settlement had increased in numbers, they took advantage of the unrest caused by the difficulties in England, and with the help of other dissidents rose against Lord Baltimore's government. The Maryland Navy, some ten or twelve small ships, which seem to have been sloops and pinnaces, transported the men of Governor William Stone from St. Mary's City, at the mouth of the Potomac, up the Severn to put down the rebellion. The Puritans were aided by a heavily armed English ship, the "Golden Lion," and a barque armed with two pieces of ordnance, both under the command of Captain Roger Heamans. The barque bottled up Governor Stone's ships in a creek on the Severn, then called Herring Creek, and the heavy

14

fire from the Golden Lion forced the surrender of Stone and his militia, after the loss of some fifty of his men, four of whom were executed after surrender although they had been promised quarter.

The Puritans, again with William Claiborne in the forefront, abolished Maryland's famous "Toleration Act of 1649" and remained in power until Cromwell restored the government of Maryland to Lord Baltimore on February 26, 1658.

The smoke had hardly cleared away from the Puritan battle before the so-called "Fendall's Rebellion" occurred in 1659. Josias Fendall had been appointed Governor following the settlement of the Puritan difficulties but the prime mover behind the rebellion appears to have been Thomas Gerard, of Longworth's Point, Lord of St. Clement's Manor on the Potomac. In view of the long, trusted, and friendly relationship between Gerard and Lord Baltimore, extending over a period of more than twenty years, it is difficult to understand why Gerard threw in with Fendall when the show-down came in 1659. Certainly he had no love for the Puritans on the Severn (who sided with Fendall), after his experiences at Herring Creek in the Chesapeake Bay in 1655 when several of his close associates and friends were executed and he himself narrowly escaped the same fate. Keeping this fact in mind, it is easy to understand the statements attributed to him prior to the rebellion in the charges made before the Council when he was accused of saying that Governor Fendall was a tool of the people of Anne Arundel and was not above helping himself to the Provincial revenues, that Captain Stone, Job Chandler, and Dr. Luke Barber were secretly playing into the hands of the Puritan, Richard Bennett, Lord Baltimore's chief opponent, that the whole Council was a bunch of rogues and he would not sit with them. Perhaps the best conjecture for Gerard's action has been made by F. E. Sparks in his study, "Causes of the Maryland Revolution of 1689," wherein he states:

"The real causes of the disturbance that now arose [Fendall's Rebellion] are scarcely explained by Maryland historians. Governor Fendall is charged with being the chief cause of the Rebellion. It is true that Fendall tried to keep in favor with the party of resistance [the Anne Arundel Party] and that he was intimately connected with Gerard whose party was destined to triumph in 1689; but it was really the question of taxation that caused the so-called Fendall's Rebellion. It is sometimes said it was a Puritan move, and so it was in one sense; but Gerard who seemed to be the real leader, was a Catholic who had been and was then a member of the Council. In 1647 an act was passed by the Assembly granting the Proprietor a duty of ten shillings on every hogshead of tobacco exported from the province. This act, by the admission of the Proprietor, was the cause of complaints."

Aside from the matter of taxation, an event occurred in 1659 which may have influenced Gerard in his decision to break with Lord Baltimore. He had, in the right of his wife, laid claims to 1,000 acres of land (Snow Hill) which had been granted in 1640 to Abel Snow, his brother-in-law, who was now deceased. The land was repossessed by Lord Baltimore under the Act for Deserted Plantations and had been granted by him in 1652 to Richard Willan and James Lindsey. Apparently there had been litigation for some time. Finally Philip Calvert, Secretary of the Province, appealed the case to Lord Baltimore who ruled against Gerard and in his own favor. It should be remembered also that only a few years had elapsed since the time of the Ingle Rebellion and the Puritan Uprising and that the government of the Province was far from secure. Under such conditions there was a great temptation for any strong man to take the Government into his own hands rather than again risk the loss of all his possessions.

It seems fairly evident that Gerard faced such a dilemma, with at least some fancied justification for his action. After he had reached a decision, it is evident that Gerard maneuvered to have the Assembly and the Council meet at a location where he would have a better opportunity to dominate the meetings. The ideal location was at St. Clement's Manor, which was far removed from the usual meeting place, St. Mary's City, and where Gerard would be sure of the attendance of all his friends and adherents. The first and second meetings were held at the Gerard home at Longworth's Point on February 28, 1659. All subsequent meetings, including the final meeting, were held in the home of Robert Slye (Gerard's son-in-law) at Bushwood on St. Clement's Manor.

After a two week struggle, a majority of the Upper House or Council voted with the Lower House that the laws governing Maryland could be enacted without the assent of the Governor or the Proprietor, which meant they would be able to enact their own tax laws, and the Revolution was on. As Gerard and Fendall and their adherents controlled the militia and the navy, it was useless for Philip Calvert, the Secretary, and brother of the Proprietor, to protest. This was a bloodless revolution and life went on much the same until May, 1660, when Charles II returned to the throne of England and the Proprietor was restored to favor at the Court when the rebellion collapsed. Gerard was forced to flee for his life across the Potomac to his lands on the lower Machodoc, until affairs quieted down and he could secure a pardon and return to Maryland. It is significant that he did not invite Fendall to share the safety of his Virginia refuge.

Life appeared to go on quietly in the Province from 1660 until the Orange Rebellion in England in 1688, although there is evidence of undercover activity and unrest concerning the governing of the colony. Lord Baltimore, in order to better protect his interests, awarded most of the lucrative positions in the government to his relatives and trusted friends, many of whom were Catholics. Following the Orange Rebellion and the unseating of the Catholic, James II, certain leading Protestants and other malcontents in the Province saw their opportunity and made the most of it.

The Rebellion was led by a group of Potomac rivermen, headed by John Coode, who had married the widow of Robert Slye and thus became a son-in-law of Thomas Gerard, who had died in 1673. Coode, who at one time had been the Captain of Lord Baltimore's private yacht, was living on the Slye Plantation, "Bushwood," near the mouth of the Wicomico River. (Later when the Slye heir, Gerard Slye, became of age the plantation was divided and Coode and his wife received "Bluff Point" at the mouth of the Wicomico.) Adjoining "Bushwood" was the plantation "White's Neck" owned by Kenelm Cheseldine and adjoining "White's Neck" was the Plantation of Nehemiah Blackistone, "Longworth's Point." Both of these plantations were on the Potomac River. Cheseldine and Blackistone also were sons-in-law of Thomas Gerard.

Coode, Cheseldine, and Blackistone, with the assistance of Henry Jowles of the Patuxent River, who was in command of the Maryland militia, and others, were able to overthrow the government of Lord Baltimore in July 1689, after a sudden march on St. Mary's City. Coode and Cheseldine were sent to England to petition the new Sovereigns, William and Mary, to deprive Lord Baltimore of his authority to govern the colony and to take it under their royal jurisdiction, which they did. In the following year they sent out the first Royal Governor, Lionel Copley. The Toleration Act of 1649 again was repudiated and the Church of England became the "Established" Church of Maryland. The success of this rebellion put an end to religious freedom in Maryland for almost eighty years and it was not until the American Revolution that Maryland again became the "Free State."

Other than a good deal of sailing back and forth across the Potomac River, when Coode was trying to catch the Catholic priests and other refugees who sought and found sanctuary in Virginia, there was no naval action on the river.

From this time until the American Revolution life was quiet on the Potomac River, and the rivermen, left to their own devices, set about developing shipyards, building ships, and establishing ferries across the river to connect key points along the Maryland and Virginia shores. By the middle 1600's ferries had been established across Bretton Bay, and the Wicomico River. The Bretton Bay ferry between the east and west shores of the bay was operated by John Hammond, an innkeeper, who agreed on December 5, 1654, to provide it "for the Convenient passage of people over Newtown River." The Wicomico ferry was operated by Samuel Harris of Charles County. The order which established the ferry on June 4, 1658, reads as follows:

"It is ordered by the Gouernor & the rest of the Councel and Commissioners aboue ritten that Samuel harris shoold keepe the ferre ouer Wicokomeko River that is from Metomkin Poynt to the end of Trews march it is ordered that the sayd Samuel Harrise shal attend this ferrie from Sone Rising to Sone set in consideratione whereof it is enacted that the sayd samuel Harris shal haue payed him yearlie too thousand Pound of tob: and that to bee payed out of this Charleses Countie it is also enacted that this Countie shall furnish him with a boate for which the commissioners of this sayd Countie haue couenanted with Goodman Smote [Smoot] in the behalf of the inhabitants for 700 lb of tob: this the 4th of June Ao 1658 by the governor & rest of the councel and commissioners eiusdem curiae."

The route of this ferry is not clear since the only Metomkin Point known today is on the Virginia side of the Potomac River in the vicinity of Mathias Point. However, there is little doubt that this ferry operated between the opposite shores of the Wicomico River as a subsequent order was issued on January 12, 1664, which read as follows:

"It is ordered that Thomas Brandson shall have 2000 lb of tobacco allowed him out of the leauy of the next year hee obligeing himself twise a day to go over Wicohomeco River wheather thear bee any occasion or No And as often every day as Passengers Shall Requir."

It would be interesting to know if Mr. Brandson made the two trips required on the days when no passengers showed up for the crossing. On December 7, 1665, he was paid his fee of 2000 pounds of tobacco. On November 14, 1659, the Sheriff of Charles County was authorized to levy "13 lb of tob on each tithable person in the County to pay for the ferrie and wolves heads."

On May 20, 1695, an agreement was made by a Captain Perry to carry the mails on the route between the Potomac and Philadelphia, eight times a year. Starting from Newton's Point on the Wicomico, he went to Allen's Fresh at the head of the Wicomico, to the Potomac at Leonardtown and across the Patuxent to Annapolis. This route was one of the links to connect with the Williamsburg-Philadelphia route. In the same year a post route also was established from Port Tobacco on the Potomac through Upper Marlboro, then by ferry to London Town on South River to Annapolis and on to Philadelphia.

The area around Nanjemoy and Port Tobacco seems to have been the favorite crossing spot to reach points in Virginia and particularly to pick up the route to Williamsburg. Between 1745 and 1747 there was a total of five ferries over the Potomac and a keen rivalry was carried on in advertisements in the Maryland Gazette. Robert Dade and Richard Harrison operated ferries out of Nanjemoy and advertized they had five boats, always manned. Charles Jones' ferry operated from Lower Cedar Point and he boasted not only of good boats, but also of skillful hands, and that his route was some 20 miles nearer Williamsburg. George Dent of Port Tobacco advertised that his ferry was safer than his rival, Thompson, and that he had a marked road from the town to his landing place.

Earlier in 1720, Colonel Richard Hooes ran a ferry from his plantation on the Virginia Shore to lower Cedar Point and made a charge of two shillings per head, be it man or horse.

Fox Ferry, which ran continuously for over 100 years between Oxon Creek and Alexandria, did not cease operations until early in the 1900's.

It was during the period 1700-1750 that the rivermen along the Potomac commenced to realize some of the commercial possibilities of the river that was loaded with oysters and crabs, and teeming with an almost endless variety of fish. Commercial operations were limited largely to taking shad, herring, and rock fish during their "runs" up and down the river, but undoubtedly oysters and crabs also were sailed in locally built schooners and sloops to Alexandria, Georgetown, Annapolis, and Baltimore, along with lumber, firewood, salted fish, tobacco, and other farm crops during the appropriate seasons.

In March 1755 the people of the river plantations saw the greatest armada ascend the Potomac in its history to that time. The French had been threatening the Virginia frontier on the Ohio so the British Government sent General Edward Braddock with an army of 1,300 men to clear them out. The fleet was under the command of Commodore Keppel, and in addition to his flagship, the Norwich, there were included the Sea Horse, the Nightingale, the Garland, and many transports. The armada proceeded up the Potomac to Alexandria where the General was joined by Colonel George Washington and his colonial volunteers for the march from the Potomac to the Ohio.

Some 21 years later the river people saw another British fleet enter the Potomac but this time the English were not welcomed with dinners, balls, and concerts, for they brought with them terror and destruction instead of protection for the people on the frontiers.

Prior to the American Revolution, in August 1774, the river people on the Potomac had their "tea party" when the British brigantine, Mary and Jane, arrived in St. Mary's River, near the mouth of the Potomac. Captain George Chapman, Master, was informed that if he valued his life, his ship, and his cargo, he had best depart promptly, which he did with his load of hated tea intact. This was no idle threat, as is attested by the burning of the Peggy Stewart at Annapolis later that year. Captain Chapman, however, sailed up the Potomac and made stops at Bladensburg and Georgetown but was turned away at both points and finally returned to London with his tea.

On July 15, 1776, the people of St. Mary's County had their first actual battle of the Revolution when Lord Dunmore, the Royal Governor of Virginia, invaded Maryland with a fleet of seventy-two vessels. The armada was made up of the following:

Ships	Roebuck of 44 guns, Commodore Hammond, Comdr. Fowey of 20 guns, Commodore Montague, Comdr. William of 2 four-pounders a side, - Squires, Comdr. Anna, Dun Luce, Grace, Levant (Governor Robert Eden aboard), and the Logan
Frigates	Dunmore, mounting 8 six-pounders and the Lively
Brigantines	Fincastle, Dolphin, Maria, Fanny, Betsy, Hammond, the William and Charles, the Helena (used as a prison ship), and two unidentified brigantines
Sloops	Otter, a ten gun Sloop of War, Campbell, Lady Augusta, the Peace and Plenty, Lady Gower, a tender, John Wilkie, Comdr.; Lady Stanly, a tender, Wm. Younghusband, Comdr.; Lady Susan, a tender, Briger Goodrich,

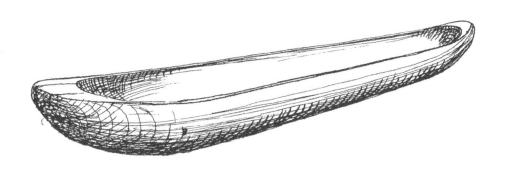

COLONIAL LOG CANOE

A SEVENTEENTH CENTURY SHALLOP

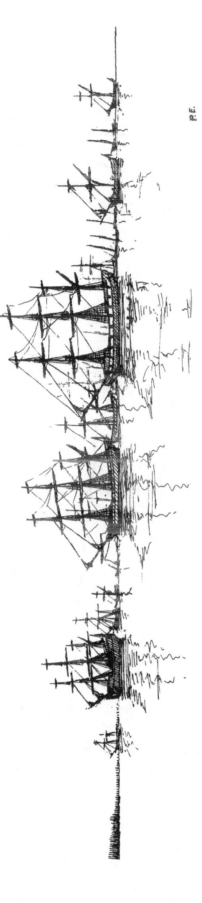

P.E.

DUNMORE'S FLEET AS IT MUST HAVE APPEARED, OFF ST. GEORGE'S ISLAND IN JULY, 1776

Sloops	Comdr.; Fincastle of 12 guns belonging to the Otter; Lady Gage, a tender to the Fowey, and eight unidentified sloops
Schooners	Thomas, Charlotte, the Gaze, a tender to the Roebuck, and two unidentified schooners
Snows	Unicorn, equipped with a blacksmith shop and a Spanish Snow, Prize Master, Super Cargo, Capt. and Crew on board
Small Craft	Twenty eight small vessels that were not fit to go to sea, i.e., to England

Dunmore occupied St. George's Island, but an attempt made to land on the mainland was repulsed by the county militia under Captain Rezin Beall, who was seriously wounded. Dunmore also was wounded in the battle.

Colonel Jeremiah Jordan's report is as follows:

St. Mary's County, July 15th 1776

"Gentlemen:

This (is) to inform you that there is now lying, off the mouth of the St. Mary's River, between seventy and eighty sail of vessels. I am now at Leonard Town on my way down with part of the 6th Battalion under my command, where I received an Express from Col. [Richard] Barnes (who is now at St. Inegoe's Neck with the lower Battalion) informing me that this morning Ten Boats full of men landed on St. George's Island and had returned for more. I expect to be opposite the Island some time this night and shall endeavor to get the best intelligence I can of their numbers and give the earliest notice. We shall want more powder and lead and also flints, if they are to be had.....

Gentlemen: Your mo;obedt Servt"

On July 17, 1776, Colonel Jordan reported:

"I arrived down here on the 15th Inst with about one hundred of the Militia, where I found Capt. Beall with part of his Company and one Company of Colo. Barne's Battalion. About daybreak yesterday we were visited by a Row Galley or Row Gondola carrying 5 Swivels on each side and a six pounder in her head, and another in her stern, they rowed along side our centinals and not a man to be seen and instantly began a very heavy firing which lasted about one hour without doing any execution, altho their shot reached the ground on every spot where the men were stationed. In the evening she returned again and engaged us again for upwards of two hours, and at the same time the troops landed from the Ships in St. George's Island to the amount of about 300 pushed down to the point opposite to us with swivels and musketry, and kept up a heavy fire, from which Capt. Beall was dangerously wounded in the shoulder by a ball (as he says from a riffle) which has rendered him incapable of duty. I shall endeavour to keep the post we are at present if possible if not shall retreat to the woods about half a mile. From a report we had given us yesterday they are constructing another vessel like the above and that they intend attacking us on the Potowmac side. I think from all appearances the Fleet will continue some time, if so, some Cannon and Swivels will be absolutely necessary to dislodge the men they have landed on the Island. With what assistance we can give in this quarter, I think 500 of the Militia of the upper Battalions will be full enough to appose the enemy. We have now at different posts about 600 men.....Col. Barnes with his Battalion is on the other side of the river, watching the motions of the enemy there....."

John Dent of Charles County, who was elected Brigadier General, in command of all the Militia of the Lower District on the Western Shore by the Maryland Convention, January 6, 1776, in a dispatch to the Council of Safety dated July 19, 1776, reported as follows:

"Gent'n

On my arrival at this place [St. Mary's River] on the 16th Inst. I found there had been an engagement with the Enemy with no loss but the misfortune of Capt. Rezin Beall being badly wounded, tho' its hoped not mortal. By four Deserters who came over to us yesterday we are informed the mate or midshipman of the Roe Buck was killed in the action. By the best information the Enemy have not more than 50 Regulars of the 14th Regiment, about 150 Tories and 100 negroes that bare arms; all of whom are landed every morning and embarked in the evening under cover of the Fleet, which continues in the mouth of St. Mary's River opposite the lower end of St. George's Island. Our strength at present is about 400 Militia exclusive of the Independent and Capt'n Forrests Company. I made bold immediately on my arrival (the strength of the Enemy being much magnified) to order to our assistance three full companies of Militia from Col. Hawkins Battalion, to be selected from the interior part of the County, which I expect will arrive about tomorrow evening, when I shall discharge an equal number of the most necessitous of those now on duty. The Fleet (which at first consisted of eighty sail) is now reduced to little more than half that number, many of the Tenders and Square Rigged vessels have gone to Virginia opposite the mouth of Potowmack where a pretty constant Cannonade has been kept up ever since I have been here. We are told by Deserters (two more of which have come over since I began to write) that the fleet intend only to wood and water on the Island, burn all, or most of their small craft and proceed to sea. Had we a few great guns at a place called Cherry Fields Point, well planted and served, we might annoy the Fleet so as to oblige them to quit their Station. Capt. Forrest's Company has relieved an equal number of the Militia who readily parted with their arms, such as they were. I shall as often as anything of consequence happens communicate it to you with the utmost dispatch, 'til when I am your most obedient Serv't.

Jno. Dent"

On July 20, 1776, General Dent reported as follows:

"Gent. From the accts given me by several deserters that the Fleet entered up Potomack River to water, and from the motions of the Roebuck, five other ships and a sloop I have the greatest reason to believe they are now on their way for that purpose. Nanjemoy, we suppose to be the place of their destination. I have by letter informed the Committee of Correspondence of the motions of the above ships and shall endeavour to watch their motions and prevent their Depredations with all my Might. There was a brisk and severe Cannonade from two or three tenders and row galley of Smith's Creek about six o'clock this morning the consequence of which I have not yet heard."

The Council of Safety advised General Dent on July 21 that Major Thomas Price had been ordered to his assistance with three field pieces and one nine pounder together with Captain John Allen Thomas' Independent Company. Major Price sent the following report to the Council on July 23rd:

"Gentlemen. I arrived at this place the 21st Inst with one of the four Pounders, the other two I left at Leonard Town, 'till further orders. After inspecting this Camp and giving the necessary orders I went over to the Lower Camp commanded by Colo. Barnes who is stationed much nearer the fleet than this Camp. I think a nine pounder could reach The Fowey from one of the points, 'tho I doubt our doing her much damage. The rest of the fleet lay outside of her, they are very quiet and give us no disturbance. The Roebuck and three or four large ships went up the river the evening before I got here, since which a number of cannon have been fired as I suppose near the mouth of Nanjemoy. I have ordered the other two peices of Cannon to the Lower Camp and shall as soon as the nine pounder arrives order that there and if intrenching tools which I have sent after can be had thro up an entrenchment as near the Fowey as possible.....we have several Deserters from the Enemy most of them in the small pox.....The shores are full of Dead Bodies chiefly negroes. I think if they stay here any time they must be ruined, for by Deaths Desertions and the Worm I think their business must be done compleatly. The officers who have been here some time immagine about fifty corps have been thrown on the shores....."

Major Price forwarded a report, dated July 26, 1776, as follows:

"Sir. The enemy comes on St. George's Island in the day time to get water and wood and in the evening retire on board their ships: they have no manner of Fortification on the Island. The Fleet lays from the North East side of St. Georges River a Bout a mile.....There is three pieces of Cannon on Cherry field point (about

a mile from the Fowey) one a nine pounder one a four the other three. I have another
on the South West side of the river, the narrowest water between the land and main,
is a four pounder. I have about four hundred men (half of which is well armed, the
other but poorly) placed on each side of St. George's River. I have good reason to
think that with the force I have I can prevent the Enemy's landing or plundering the
Inhabitants. I yesterday morning sent one hundred on the Island about half after
two o'clock. They marched silently through the Island till day appeared and there
lay hid 'till they came from the ships to water, the advanced party being rather
eager was too soon discovered and the whole Enemy ran to their boats, my people then
pursuing them with all speed and firing on them as they were getting into their boats
when our people say that they killed three or four that they saw fall and several
wounded and one taken prisoner. The Fowey then fired on them and compelled them to
retire after destroying their water casks and filling up a well, the best on the
Island....they returned to the main without loss. By the best advice I can get from
the Prisoners and many deserters the whole fleet does not intend to stay here longer
than those up Potowmack comes down which they expect everyday. Capt. Beal who was
wounded in the first engagement is recovering fast."

Captain James Nicholson of the ship, Defence, aided in the attempt made to
recapture St. George's Island and lost two small boats. Price maintained a strategic
position on the mainland, immediately opposite the island, and stationed a battery on
Cherry Fields Point from which place he made the British holding so untenable that
he drove the sloop-of-war, Fowey, out of the river, causing the British to abandon
the island, leaving several vessels and some military stores behind them.

There is evidence that there was a battle in the St. Mary's River between
Captain Nicholson and the smaller vessels of Lord Dunmore's fleet. Captain (later,
Lieutenant Colonel) Vernon Hebb, who owned the brig, William and Hopewell, was a
member of the Committee of Observation in St. Mary's County and in his report to
Timothy Bowes, Clerk of the Council of Safety, he stated that the vessels from Lord
Dunmore's fleet which had drifted ashore, (apparently after the battle) had been
examined. The vessels from Kitt's Point (lower end of St. Inigoes Manor) were one
pilot boat, one schooner of 1,400 "bush," and one sloop of 2,000 "bush." Captain
Hebb believed that the sloop could be removed if anchor and cable were provided.
Off the shore at Cherry Fields (also in St. Mary's River) there were two vessels;
a sloop and a schooner, both of which needed repair to make them usable. He proposed
that the unfit vessels should be disposed of in some way.

On July 22, 1776, Lord Dunmore in the Roebuck with part of his fleet ascended
the Potomac as far as Quantico. He did considerable raiding on his way up the river.
At Aquia Creek, on July 25th, he landed troops, burned the home of William Brent,
and as Dunmore reported in an official dispatch, "having done all the mischief in
our power," he returned and rejoined the remainder of the fleet on July 29th and
left the Potomac. For a hundred years or more the people of Southern Maryland
referred to the Revolution as "Lord Dunmore's War."

Due to the resistance of the militia of Prince William and Stafford Counties
and because a violent storm had come up, his Lordship decided not to include Alexandria in his visit. Founded in 1748, Alexandria was laid out by John West, Jr.,
Fairfax County surveyor and clerk of the city's Board of Trustees, and his 16 year
old assistant, George Washington. Two public landings were included in the plan of
the city. The first wharf, built by John Carlyle and John Dalton in 1759 was located
between King and Cameron Streets, the site of the Naval Torpedo Station during World
War II. In 1762 Thomas Kirkpatrick is said to have built the first vessel constructed
in Alexandria at Point Lumley, a wharf at the foot of Duke Street.

From that time on shipping played an important role in the life of the city and
free wharfage was given to vessels bringing tobacco to the public warehouses. Many
of the city's finest early homes on and around Lee Street, overlooking the Potomac,
were built and occupied by sea captains who made their fortunes trading from Alexandria's harbor. Point West, a wharf at the foot of Princess Street, was built by
popular subscription in 1769.

The American Revolution found Alexandria, a focal point in the construction
of ships for the defense of the Potomac, with Colonel Hugh Mercer empowered in March
1776, to "procure proper boats to be built and kept for the passage of troops at
Ocoghaun and, in conjunction with Colonel Peachy, procure proper beacons to be erected
for communicating intelligence from the mouth of the Potomack to Alexandria." Also
in that year, two galleys were built in the city and Colonel George Mason supervised
the building of ten other vessels to patrol the river. The largest ship, of 110 tons,
appeared to have been the American Congress, built by the Virginia Committee of
Safety. It mounted 14 guns of 4 and 8 pounders and carried a crew of 96 men. The
Committee also built four other war vessels. This little "Potomac Navy" was forced
to engage in "hit and run" tactics as they were outmatched by the British men-of-war.

Soon after the outbreak of the Revolution the regular British Navy appeared in the Chesapeake Bay and its tributaries. The Bay, the Potomac, and Patuxent were blockaded at various times and the water front plantations were ravaged to provide supplies for the fleet. Due to their vastly superior strength they were able to establish themselves at will on the Bay islands and also on the Potomac islands of St. George's, St. Clement's (Blackistone), and St. Katherine's. The islands provided safe harbors, fresh water, protection from the state militia, timber for masts and spars, and from these headquarters the British could send out raiding parties to the mainland whenever supplies were low.

If the British suspected that American troops were being quartered on a river front plantation, they did not hesitate to fire at the manor houses or land a force of marines and burn them. Bishop Benedict Fenwick reported in 1778 that the General Monk, a British sloop of war, fired a ball through old St. Inigoes house on St. Mary's River, which narrowly missed Reverend John Lewis, S. J. The patch in the brick wall could be seen until the manor house burned in 1872.

The General Monk and other ships were detached from the British fleet which sailed up the Chesapeake in 1778 and were instructed to harass the bay and river water fronts. The main portion of the fleet proceeded up the Elk River at the head of the bay where the British landed and took up their march to Philadelphia. In 1782, Lieutenant Joshua Barney, in command of the Hyder Ally, engaged the General Monk and after the two vessels had fought desperately for half an hour, the General Monk struck her colors. This ship was formerly the General Washington, captured by the British and put into their service under her new name. Barney restored the old name.

On February 8, 1778, two frigates were sighted at the mouth of the St. Mary's River. These proved to be English ships under the command of John Lewis Gideon, Commander of the Richmond. A proclamation was sent to Lieutenant Colonel Vernon Hebb by Commander Gideon which stated that if the duty of His Majesty's ships was not interfered with, they would not land men or destroy the houses. It was stated also that there were two Americans on the Richmond who would be sent ashore in exchange for an equal number of prisoners. Colonel Hebb reported at once to Colonel Richard Barnes at Leonardtown. In his report Hebb stated that Captain William Barton Smoot and Lieutenant Alexander Watts with men of the Lower Battalion of St. Mary's County Militia had been ordered out and the ships had retreated to St. George's Island. He felt that twenty or thirty guns were needed to pursue the British who had captured Captain Ignatius Fenwick and his ship, the Lydia. (Captain Fenwick was one of the two Americans held by the British and was a cousin of Colonel Ignatius Fenwick of Coles Farm or Wallington on the Patuxent River, who was Colonel Hebb's commanding officer.) Colonel Hebb feared that Captain Thomas Smith's brig might be the next victim of the enemy. Colonel Barnes sent on the report to Governor Thomas Johnson and stated further that no part of the state was so badly armed as Southern Maryland, and that the arms sent were "a parcel of refused things," but thirty of the best guns would be in Colonel Hebb's hands by morning. He noted also that the arms sent were not approved of by the Commanders of the Upper St. Mary's County Battalion of Militia, Colonel Jeremiah Jordan, Lieutenant Colonel John Reeder, and Major John Allen Thomas.

Captain Fenwick was either rescued or was exchanged, for in 1779 he was the master of the brigantine, Sally, a privateer. On June 10, 1780, the Captain married somewhat late in life Mary (Hill) Carroll, the widow of Charles Carroll of Carrolsburg in what is now a part of Washington, and bought the plantation "River View" on Canoe Neck Creek in St. Mary's County. It is interesting to note that Richard Fenwick, a marine, and a brother of Colonel Ignatius Fenwick, was blown up in a barge in 1777. These barges were loaded with explosives and drifted down on the anchored British fleet at night, which annoyed the British no end. The men in the barges had little chance of escape because the fuses could not be lit until the boats had made contact with the fleet. Other county men who were blown up in the barges were Joseph Sewell, William Sewell, Enoch Medley, Vachel Yates, and Richard Yates. Other known county men who served in the American Navy in the lower Potomac in 1776 were Henry Carbery, Hoshier Cole, Patrick Cole, Vachel Yates, and William Decourcey on the ship "Defence" and Joseph Bullock on the sloop "Molly" in 1777. Daniel Friend, a ship's carpenter, is mentioned as a nine months draftee in 1778.

When the war was transferred to Virginia toward the end of 1780, the British fleet again began raiding the water front plantations along the shores of the Chesapeake Bay, the Patuxent and Potomac Rivers, to destroy boats that might be used to transport troops to Virginia, to obtain supplies for their forces, and to intimidate the people. St. George's Island, due to its strategic location, was again utilized as a base. General Washington directed his Commissioners of Supplies to purchase grain, bacon, barrelled pork, and beef cattle throughout the area since it was the most exposed to the ravages of the enemy, who in their raids took away everything that could be transported and if any resistance was offered, burned the plantation house, the barns, and all out-buildings. The Jesuit farm account books of St. Inigoes, Newtown, and St. Thomas at Chapel Point of this period record large quantities of wheat, beef, bacon, pork, and tobacco sold to the American forces. Reverend John Ashton, the Jesuit procurator at Georgetown, wrote in 1785 to Reverend James Walton, the Superior of St. Inigoes Manor: "I thank you for the account you give of the stock which, considering the calamities of the war, is surprising."

General Washington also did not hesitate to "press into service" at this time both the rivermen and their ships. An example may be cited in the case of William Fenwick, of St. Mary's County and later Kentucky, who testified in open court in connection with his application for a pension (#5444) that he was in the service at the time Dunmore's Fleet occupied the mouth of the Potomac and, afterward, at the time General Lafayette mustered his troops at Baltimore he was the owner of two vessels, a sloop of 50 tons, and a pilot boat, the "Fair Maid." He, with the vessels, was pressed into service and was employed on the Chesapeake with the French Fleet until after the surrender of Cornwallis at Little York. During this time he commanded the "Fair Maid" and was engaged in transporting provisions from Baltimore to the mouth of the Little York and was subject to the command of the Admiral of the French Fleet.

The British continued their raids in the area until the end of the war and the water front plantations on both sides of the Potomac were devastated. On August 23rd and again on September 16th, 1780, the British in two separate raids destroyed most of the property of Robert Armstrong of St. Mary's County. In the meantime the people along the river were petitioning the American government for arms, ammunition, and supplies with which to defend themselves but little help was forthcoming. On January 3, 1781, Captain Joseph Ford, who headed the Commissary Department in St. Mary's County, wrote from Leonardtown to Governor Lee of Maryland that he had purchased a large supply of pork, beef, corn, and salt in the county but the "enemies barges so closely watches Patuxent and Potomac Rivers that I have thought it too dangerous to send forward my supplies." Later in 1781, a sloop of the enemy entered the St. Mary's River and destroyed the state tobacco warehouse with upwards of 200 hogsheads of tobacco. They also plundered the neighboring plantations and carried off large quantities of cattle, sheep, hogs, and other supplies.

Colonel Richard Barnes wrote Governor Lee from Leonardtown on February 16, 1781, "We have for some time past been ravaged in this County by the enemy. They on Friday last landed and plundered several families on Smith's Creek together with a quarter of mine there....." Two days later he asked for five cannon, powder, and ball. While the people near the mouth of the Potomac received the brunt of the devastation, the British did not confine themselves to this area but raided up and down and on both sides of the river, and it is certain that few of the rivermen's boats survived the three year period of destruction.

Early in the year 1781 several vessels of the British Fleet ascended the Potomac as far as Mount Vernon which was robbed but not burned as disclosed in a letter of General Washington to Lund Washington in which he wrote: "I am sorry to hear of your loss. I am a little sorry to hear of my own, but that which gives me most concern is that you should go on board the enemy's vessels and furnish them with refreshments. It would have been a less painful circumstance to me to have heard that in consequence of your non-compliance with their request, they had burnt my House and laid the Plantation in ruins."

On April 8, 1781, the Maryland Council reported: "We have just received intelligence from Colonel Joshua Beall of Prince George's County that there are six of the enemy's ships in the Patowmack supposed to be on their way to Alexandria after plundering Colonel Richard Barnes.....of all his property and burning all his houses with Priest Hunter's house in the mouth of Port Tobacco Creek."

In a letter of the same date, T. Stone of Charles County reported: "Two of the enemy's vessels came up the Potomac on Thursday last in the Evening. They dispatched two of their barges in the night to plunder; the men from these landed at Port Tobacco Warehouse.....from thence they crossed over to Mr. Walter Hanson's and robbed him of all effects to considerable value. They then went to the Priest's where they pillaged and took with them everything, not sparing the church furniture. On Friday morning they landed at Captain George Dent's before the militia could be collected in sufficient force to oppose them and burnt all his houses. On Saturday they took from Cedar Point Warehouse nearly all the tobacco, and robbed several persons in different parts. We are informed they have near 300 men and five or six barges. The militia turn out with alacrity and spirit, but we have neither arms nor ammunition sufficient to defend all the points in which we are accessible. I am desired to request your Excellency and Council to send 60 muskets and such quantity of powder and lead as you may think proper. A few pieces of cannon are also very much desired and if you can send two or three field pieces the people of this County will be extremely obliged. The enemy have small pieces under the cover of which they can land at any point without being hurt by musketry.....The enemy's vessels moved around Cedar Point yesterday afternoon and now be at Swan Point, and it is said several other vessels were seen yesterday afternoon endeavoring to come up the river, but the wind blowing fresh from N.W. they made little way....."

In another letter to Governor Lee, dated April 24, 1781, Colonel Barnes wrote: "Mr. James Adderton was taken when the Enemy landed at St. Inigoes.....four negroes of Rev'd Mr. Walton [at Newtown] have been taken by the British....."

On June 16th he wrote: "On my return to this County I found that a small ship under Flag was near Blackiston's [St. Clement's] Island (since which she has proceeded up Potomack) and a six and thirty gun Frigate, with two schooners, laying at the mouth of St. Mary's River, where they have been for several days, and have ever since continued without ever attempting to land, but on St. George's Island, which they have regularly done every day. On the 13th a Brig with two Schooners appeared off the mouth of St. Clements Bay, and landed two barges loaded with men at Mr. Herbert Blackestone's House [Colton's, formerly Longworth Point], which they burned and carried Blackstone with them, where he has continued....."

On June 18th he wrote: "All the vessels of the Enemy left the Potomack on Saturday last. They landed at Mrs. Egerton's house, below Smith's Creek, and plundered and destroyed all her household furniture. Since I last wrote to you, I have been informed the crew of the Frigate that layed at the mouth of St. Mary's River were employed the whole time they were there in getting masts for ships off St. Georges Island where there is good pine for that purpose....."

A few days later Colonel Barnes wrote: ".....In short if something is not immediately done for the protection of the County ruin must be consequence to many of the inhabitants. The enemy have plundered many since I last wrote you and are still on St. Georges Island....." But little, if any, help was forthcoming and the river and coast people were left to their own defenses, as were those on the New England frontier.

During the summer of 1781 the enemy continued their depredations and many of the Potomac River planters were forced to abandon their homes and move back from the water front. After again calling on Congress for defensive ships in vain, they equipped a ship of their own and sent it out to do battle with the enemy. On July 2nd this brigantine, the "Ranger," a privateer of 20 men and 7 guns, under Captain Thomas Simmons, sailed down the river from Alexandria. At the mouth of the St. Mary's River he was attacked by two enemy barges with crews of 30 men to each vessel under the command of two desperados, Anderson and Barnett. The battle was a desperate one, lasting for three hours, during which time the enemy lost 15 killed and 34 wounded, and were forced to abandon the fight. Captain Simmons lost only one man, but he, his second lieutenant, and a number of the crew sustained severe wounds and he was obliged to put back to Alexandria for medical assistance.

While this action was a great morale booster to the river people, the "Ranger" was no match for the many enemy ships and even pirates that continued their operations in the Potomac. In July 1782 a group of a hundred armed white and black men appeared at the mouth of the river, apparently from bases in the lower part of the Chesapeake Bay. They robbed, pillaged, and burned a number of houses in Northumberland County, Virginia, including that of Colonel Presley Thornton and attacked a brig in St. Mary's River loaded with flour bound for Boston. They were commanded by "Whaling and Penny, two notorious pirates" who threatened to import five hundred armed negroes from New York to extend their piracy. However, the British had left small pickings along the river front and they soon moved on to more profitable areas.

Many articles in the newspaper, the Maryland Journal, dated in 1781 and 1782, complained of plunder and pillage along the water front. Colonel Barnes in his letters of 1782 and 1783 continued to report the operations of the British raiders and on March 7, 1783, William Paca of the Maryland Council wrote Barnes, ".....It gives us a great concern to hear that the Enemy's barges continue their depredations.."

Excerpts from a letter of the times written January 10, 1783 by Colonel Vernon Hebb of "Porto Bello" on St. Mary's River to his sister, Mrs. Elizabeth Wilson, in England typifies the condition of the river planters during the war:

"Dear Sister:

I have been very much injured by the war, having lost my negroes and been plundered and robbed by the privateers acruising in the Potomac River, which has obliged me to remove far from the water.

Much talk we have about Peace. God grant it can soon take place, for what with our heavy taxes, and the very high prices of every article (provisions excepted) added to the losses I have had, makes the times very disagreeable.

Home we have had all our warehouses burned by the Privateers, and many gentlemen's houses on the water. This must be another loss you must expect to come to me, having tobacco in both warehouses, though our Assembly has agreed to pay the holder of new notes 6.3 per cent discount in taxes, which makes it like nothing....."

Hebb went on to state that if:

"Peace should take place and any vessel should be coming for Potomac or Balti-more, should be very glad to have sent me 2 pieces of Oznabuges with 2 pieces of the best Kindalcollens, for we have not been able to clothe our negroes or ourselves, being obliged to manufacture the most we wear, and make all our salt which had brought about much trouble and difficulty."

In a subsequent letter dated Baltimore, November 12, 1783, he stated: "One or two vessels have just arrived here from Liverpool who have sold their cargoes for 133 percent in the invoice payable in three months and one third in each month. Exchange at 70 percent which must have large profits though I must think that goods must be much lower in the Spring as the importation must be larger as the demand for goods is now very great. I have been obliged up here to get goods for my family use, leaving not a store in our County nor in but very few of the Counties.....To-bacco is now up to 35 shillings, wheat 6 a bushel, flour at 15 shillings and 12. If Mr. Hicks would ship me about 500 pounds of well bought goods early in the Spring I will engage to make his full remittance in the 12 months if not sooner. Many vessels have lately arrived here from Ireland full of passengers who pay ten guineas for passage and they take back flour, wheat, tobacco which trade must be very advan-tageous to the merchants."

The people of the lower counties of Maryland and along the Potomac in Virginia suffered a great deal during the Revolutionary War. They not only lost many of their finest young men in battle but also were robbed by the British raiders, their homes and property destroyed, and many of their slaves were abducted by or ran off to the British. The rivermen likewise suffered with the plantation owners, for their boats were confiscated or destroyed by the British to prevent action with or pursuit of the raiders. Even the small work boats were destroyed along with every boat yard. During the years 1780-1783, the sizable fleet that supported the British land forces in Virginia lived on the plunder of the water fronts of the Potomac, the Patuxent, and the Chesapeake.

So great was the devastation that beginning about 1785 over 300 families from St. Mary's, Charles, and other Southern Maryland counties emigrated to Kentucky to start anew. Many of them held land bounties for their services in the Revolution.

On the rolls of the St. Mary's County militia of 1794, there are named 37 pilots among the total of 1,372 men. This appears an excessive number for a single county and would seem to indicate that with the destruction or confiscation of many boats during the war, a considerable number of former ship owners must have turned their talents to piloting on the bay and river. The pilots listed are as follows:

John Beane	John Gough	Barton Lynch	Thomas Swann
William Bullock	Thomas Gough	John Price	Richard Taylor
Austin Cissel	James Griggs	Robert Price	Augustine Templeman
Jeremiah Cissel	Thomas Jones	George Reese	James Thompson
George Clarke	William Jones	Isaac Sanner	Charles Welch
Ignatius Clarke	James Keirk	Biscoe Smith	John Welch
Theodocius Courtney	Lewis Leigh	McKay Smoot	Tunsil White
Robert Crain	John M. Leland	Bennett Spalding	Vernon White
George Gough	William Loker	Joseph Sutton	William Zachariah
			Zachariah Zachariah

John Smith was listed as a ship's carpenter.

Aside from Henry Fleet who piloted Governor Calvert up the Potomac at the time of the settlement, the first Maryland pilot to be mentioned was one John Rablie in 1644, who had to sue for his fee - "15lb. Sterl. in goods.....a new P. of shoes & a new Saile for his shallop....." after he had piloted a ship from St. Michaels Point (Point Lookout) to James Point on the Eastern Shore. In 1676, Colonel William Burges, in command of an expedition sent from St. Mary's City to the Nanticoke Indian lands on the Eastern Shore, was instructed to take a "Pilott" in order to reach the Indian town of Chicacone. A few years later, Thomas Hebb of St. Mary's County, the birthplace of most of the early pilots, was held for trial in Virginia because he had piloted a vessel through Virginia waters without a license.

Outstanding among the late 18th century pilots of Maryland was Anthony Smith of St. Mary's. In 1776, Robert Sayer and John Bennett of London published "A new and Accurate Chart of the Bay of Chesapeake.....Drawn from several Draughts made by the most Experienced Navigators Chiefly from those of Anthony Smith, Pilot of St. Mary's....." The Patapsco and the Potomac, although they had received the attention of hydrographers before, were carefully charted, and even some of the plantations, such as General Washington's, Mr. Rozier's, Col. Fairfax, and Col. Addison's are located. An officer of the Royal Navy noted on the chart, "These & all other Remarks, Additions, or Alterations which I have made were done upon the Spot and with the Assistance of My Pilot Anthony Smith of St. Mary's." Unfortunately, the British made good use of this map during the Revolution.

With the outbreak of the Revolution, most of the Maryland and Virginia pilots gave valiant service to their country. Much of the revenues for the conduct of the war came from the sale of tobacco and wheat in the French and Dutch West Indies, and in Europe. During the war the Bay and its tributaries were largely controlled by the Royal Navy and Tory privateers. The pilots did not leave the ships at the Capes but remained on board so that there would be no delay waiting for a pilot when the vessel returned loaded with gunpowder, muskets, clothing, and other supplies. A number of the pilots were captured by the British and several died in British prisons or on-board the prison ships. A few pilots such as Joseph Whaland of Deal's Island, Andrew McCurley of St. Mary's County, and David Hunter of Calvert County, turned Tory and gave their service to Dunmore and other British raiders. Near the end of the war the pilots aided the French Fleet in the Bay both before and after Yorktown.

On November 5, 1787, Maryland passed "An Act to Establish Pilots and to Regulate Fees" and set up a Board of Pilot Examiners. In 1790 a second board of examiners was created to take care of pilotage on the Potomac River. Benjamin Stoddert, selected as a member of the first board, later became the first Secretary of the Navy.

Fees for piloting were fixed by law. The fee from the Capes to Baltimore was 8s. 9d. for each six inches of draft. However, the fee for the return trip was at the rate of 7s. 6d. If the ship went up the Potomac to Georgetown, the pilot collected one fifth more and the same for the return trip.

Vernon Hebb mentioned in a letter dated October 10, 1779, from St. Mary's that "our whole trade is now carried from Baltimore," and so effective was the blockade and destruction during the war that only a total of five letters to and from his sister in England came to hand. Father (later Archbishop) John Carroll in his correspondence with Father Charles Plowden in England stated in a letter dated April 10, 1784, "And if your other letters never came to hand you have only to blame the unsleeping avidity of your own cruisers, whom I would call pirates, were I inclined to follow your example of abusing the political measures of our adversaries."

Trade on the Potomac was cut off and diverted to Baltimore. With the destruction of ships, shipping and the water front plantations, it was not easy to restore it. In the 1790 census of St. Mary's County, only one individual, Lawrence Walter, is shown in command of a vessel, the sloop "Hope."

When a system for the collection of duties on imports and exports was provided by an Act of Congress, July 31, 1789, Georgetown was made a port of entry for all the region on the east side of the Potomac from Pomonkey Creek to the head of the navigable waters, while Alexandria was made the port on the west side.

Joseph Fenwick, one of seven sons of Colonel Ignatius Fenwick of Cherryfields in St. Mary's County, Maryland, arrived in France in 1787 and established a firm trading in tobacco and general merchandise between Georgetown, D. C., and Bordeaux. He was transported there by his cousin, Captain Ignatius Fenwick, probably in his brigantine, "Sally," which had been used as a privateer during the Revolution. Captain Fenwick had been a shipmaster in the tobacco trade between Maryland and Great Britain in his ship, the "Royal Charlotte," before the Revolution. He also lost a ship, the "Lydia," to the British during the war as previously noted.

The partners of Joseph Fenwick in his undertaking were his brother, Captain James Fenwick of Cherryfields, also a shipmaster, and Captain Ignatius Fenwick, who advanced much of the firm's capital. In 1788, John Mason, of Analostan Island in the Potomac opposite Georgetown, and a son of George Mason of "Gunston Hall," was added to the firm as a full partner. The firm was highly successful in its operations and received large consignments of tobacco from Richard Henry Lee and other Virginia and Maryland planters. On return voyages, French wines, cloth, clothing, and other manufactured goods were transported and their commercial interests gradually expanded to include New England whale oil and bone, and tar and rice from the Carolinas.

In June, 1790, Joseph Fenwick was appointed United States Consul at Bordeaux and his term of service coincided with the French Revolution. He was sympathetic to the Revolution but decried the excesses that were practiced during the reign of terror that began in 1793. He remained in office until he was succeeded by William Lee in 1801. During these years and until his death in Bordeaux he continued to participate in the activities of the firm, and at times had as many as five vessels in port, as in July, 1791, when he wrote he was dispatching one vessel to St. Petersburg, one to Providence, one to Philadelphia, one to Virginia, and one to the Cape Verde Islands.

Uriah Forrest, also of St. Mary's County, who rendered distinguished service in the Revolution, went to England after the war and established the firm of Forrest, Stoddert, and Murdock. The firm engaged exclusively in trade of the Potomac, was quite successful and did much to restore the river trade. Mr. Forrest later made his home at "Rosedale" in Georgetown.

On the heights of Georgetown the Jesuits established their college in 1789. The view of the Potomac from the tower of the Healy Building of Georgetown College is magnificent and surpasses the view from the Capitol. This is the view that caused one of Georgetown's student-poets to write many years ago:

> "Beautiful river, bold and free,
> Thy waters glide, how gracefully.
> Queen 'midst waters, 'tis to thee,
> I give the crown of sovereignty."

During the 175 year history of the college, which is coincidental with that of our great capital city, Georgetown's students have never ceased their tributes to the mighty Potomac. In the Georgetown University Anthology will be found five such tributes selected from many that have been written, including the Alma Mater song, "Sons of Georgetown." Undoubtedly since Georgetown is now a co-educational institution the girl students will make their contribution in the years to come.

Perhaps the best loved lines that have been written are those of James S. Ruby - '27, one of Georgetown's most honored sons, student, professor, writer, organizer, and secretary of the Alumni Association, who devoted his entire career to the university, except for his service in the armed forces during World War II. The lines of his poem "Vigil" follow:

> "Listen! there comes through the darkness
> The song of old Georgetown's bell
> Chanting the hour of midnight
> To the echoes that know it so well.
>
> It sings o'er the silent river,
> Each ripple with melody thrills,
> And teaches its song to the waters
> That race from Maryland's hills.
>
> It's whispered by stately pine trees
> That guard Virginia's shore
> And loses itself in the valleys
> To be sung by the echoes once more.
>
> On rush the laughing waters
> And ever the song repeat
> Till the echoes sing with the pine trees
> Where hill and lowlands meet."

Another student, Edmund R. Smith of the Class of 1848 wrote the following lines:

To The Potomac River

> I love to view thy varied scene
> Thy rugged rocks, thy islands green
> And gaze upon thy placid mien.
> Potomac!
>
> Upon the brightest page of fame
> In golden letters stands thy name,
> O mayest thou ever flow the same,
> Potomac!
>
> With rev'rence past that humble grave
> Where sleeps the bravest of the brave
> In silence glides thy limpid wave,
> Potomac!
>
> In majesty where rolls thy tide,
> His country's Father and her pride
> He rests thy verdant banks beside
> Potomac!

When every race with freedom's blow
Shall strike and prostrate ev'ry foe
Then ev'ry clime thy name shall know,
    Potomac!

Each pilgrim crossing o'er the sea
Shall treasure up sweet thoughts of thee,
As by thy shrine he bends his knee,
    Potomac!

Then let our praise in streams combine
And gently flowing on with thine
Lay down our tribute at that shrine,
    Potomac!

General Washington, ever an advocate of the Potomac, as early as 1770 pointed out in a letter to Governor Robert Eden of Maryland the advantages to Maryland and Virginia of making the Potomac "a channel of commerce" between the mother country and the immense territory that bordered on the river. Shortly after the Revolution, in his retirement at Mt. Vernon, he resumed the advocacy of his favorite project, particularly the matter of making the upper Potomac navigable, because he foresaw the general as well as the local advantages of making the Potomac the center of trade of the Ohio Valley. The General had one or more vessels in the river trade with Alexandria and Georgetown as their home ports.

On July 12, 1790, President Washington was presented by the Congress with a bill to establish Washington, the capital federal city, somewhere on the east side of the Potomac between the Eastern Branch (Anacostia River) and the Conococheague River in the upper Potomac, a stretch of some 67 miles. During the late summer and fall the President toured the area and at supper at a tavern in Hagerstown made the toast, "The River Patowmac, may the residence law be perpetuated and Patowmac view the Federal City."

The decision as to the location of the city was made known by the President to the Congress in a message on January 24, 1791 and it was recommended that the territory be limited to the ten mile square on both sides of the river as to include Georgetown and extend to the Eastern Branch. This problem being resolved, the President again turned his attention to making the Potomac navigable to the new federal city.

As early as 1793, Tobias Lear, a former secretary to General Washington, formed Lear and Company, which included Tristam Dalton and James Greenleaf, and acquired a wharf site on the Potomac in Washington at 26th Street and "F" and "G" Streets and there erected a stone warehouse where the business of the firm was conducted. James Barry, an Irishman from New York, built the Barry Wharf at the foot of New Jersey Avenue in the fall of 1795 where he engaged in the East India trade. Lewis Deblois had a wharf at the foot of South Capitol Street and later built a wharf between 11th and 12th Streets, S. E., for a Mr. Nicholson. The Commissioners of the District of Columbia had a wharf at the foot of New Jersey Avenue and another located between 21st and 22nd Streets. The Greenleaf Wharf was located at the foot of 6th Street S. W., while Notley Young had a wharf at the foot of 7th Street. All of these wharves were built around 1795. About 1800 Davidson's Wharf was erected near Maryland Avenue at the foot of "D" Street. It is evident from these activities that the new capital city was competing with Alexandria and Georgetown for the Potomac River commerce.

In 1794 fortifications were provided at Jones Point south of Alexandria. Henry Foxall built the Columbian Foundry in 1800 on the river about a mile north of Georgetown and manufactured ordnance for the Government for about fifteen years. On February 25, 1799, the Congress appropriated $1,000,000 for ships and $50,000 for dry docks to be located along the water front between 8th and 11th Streets, S. E. This installation was officially designated as the Washington Navy Yard on October 2, 1799, and continued in service for over 150 years. Much of the heavy ordnance used in the period subsequent to the War of 1812 was manufactured here.

It had commenced to look as if the dreams of our first President had come true and the future of the port of Washington and the Potomac was assured. In 1791, one of the promoters of Georgetown had described the city as "the best market for tobacco in the state, perhaps in America." But this picture was not as rosy as painted.

It was determined that during the period 1792-1797 silt from erosion had shallowed the Washington middle channel and the Virginia Channel about two feet and was continuing. By the early 1800's the deep sea ships could not reach Georgetown because the flats that made out from shore left no room to maneuver these ships. The construction of the Chesapeake and Ohio Canal to bring the products from the upper

Potomac areas moved at a snail's pace and the Napoleonic Wars in Europe were disrupting trade. A final blow was added with the outbreak of the War of 1812.

In 1800 the United States capital was moved officially from Philadelphia to Washington. Late in May of that year when the sailing vessels carrying government records and the personal belongings of federal officials from Philadelphia docked at Lear's Wharf, the new national capital bore little resemblance to a city, although L'Enfant had completed his magnificent plan in 1792.

About a half-mile below Lear's Wharf, Goose or Tiber Creek, in its meanderings flowed through the tidal flats, approximately along "B" Street, N.W. (now Constitution Avenue). Thomas Pope, one of the early land owners in this area, in 1663 named his holdings which bordered on Goose Creek, Rome. Even at this early date Goose Creek is called the Tiber in the deed but as late as the early 1800's both names are found in use. It is evident that the Tiber flowed into a bay known locally as Goose Creek, because of the great number of geese that fed there, and hence the confusion in the names. Above this marshy estuary rose the painted sandstone Executive Mansion, flanked on one side by the brick Treasury building and on the other by the partly built headquarters for the State and War Departments. At this time the Mall was a cow pasture and with the site of the Washington Monument was called "The Island," separated from the city by the Tiber.

Many of the early English visitors to the new capital were derisive in their reports, to put it mildly. The pro-British Irish poet, Thomas Moore was no exception, particularly after a fancied slight by President Thomas Jefferson when he visited the Executive Mansion in 1804, and was received by the President at his levee, in "homely costume, comprising slippers and Connemora stockings." Moore's reports on the new federal city and the President were most unfavorable but the most satiric fling at the "embryo capital" was contained in his "Odes and Epistles" which included his much quoted lines on the Tiber. Some of these verses are as follows:

"In fancy now, beneath the twilight gloom,
Come, let me lead thee o'er this Second Rome,
Where tribunes rule, where dusky Davi bow,
And what was Goose-Creek once, is Tiber now -
This embryo capital, where Fancy sees
Squares in morasses, obelisks in trees;
Which second-sighted seers, ev'n now, adorn
With shrines unbuilt and heroes yet unborn,
Though naught but woods and Jefferson they see,
Where streets should run and sages ought to be."

* * * * *

"Even here beside the grand Potomac's streams,
The medley mass of pride and misery
Of whips and charters, manacles and rights
Of slaving blacks and democratic whites."

President Jefferson who had perhaps overdone the democratic appearance a bit in his receptions was irked considerably at Moore and when handed the poet's "Irish Melodies" to read in 1814, remarked, "Why this is the little man who satirized me so." However, as he read on he remarked further, "Why he is a poet after all." Moore is best remembered, perhaps, for his beautiful composition, "The Last Rose of Summer."

Later the Tiber was connected with two canals that ran to the Eastern Branch (Anacostia River) and was opened to navigation in 1816. Much wood and produce was brought here in schooners, sloops, and longboats, and much of the adjacent ground was given to woodyards. The Tiber later degenerated into an open sewer and was covered over in the 1870's.

An early incident in 1807, which had its beginning on the Potomac River, contributed to the cause of the War of 1812. In the spring of 1807, the U.S.S. Chesapeake was being outfitted at the Navy Yard in Washington. In her crew were three seamen who claimed American citizenship but who were demanded as deserters by the British. The American government refused to surrender them. On June 22nd the Chesapeake sailed down the river on a cruise to the Mediterranean. At the capes the ship was stopped by H.M.S. Leopard and again delivery of the men was refused. The Leopard attacked and the men were seized. From this incident and similar subsequent seizures of American seamen by the British grew the second war with England.

The actions of the British during the War of 1812 followed the same pattern established in the Revolutionary War except that they were even more ruthless in their raids along the waterways. Again their ships blockaded the bay and the rivers of Maryland. Newspapers of the times report the British fleet, under the command of Sir John Bolase Warren, in the Potomac in July 1813, pillaging and burning plantations and villages which were without defenses.

On July 14, 1813, five barges from one of Warren's ships attacked a three-gun sloop, the Asp, commanded by Midshipman James B. Sigourney in Yeoacomico Bay. The Americans were outnumbered five to one but a murderous battle ensued in which eight British and ten Americans were killed, including both commanders. The Asp was fired by the British but Midshipman Henry M. McClintock who succeeded to the command, by a heroic effort, rallied his men, extinguished the flames and saved the ship. The Americans brought their dead commander ashore to the "Great House," home of the Bailey family, on the Bay where he was buried and a suitable monument, probably of Aquia Creek stone was erected.

On July 21 the British again took possession of St. George's, St. Clement's, and St. Katherine's Islands. Captain James Forrest, in command of the Leonardtown Cavalry, reported on July 27 that the situation in the lower counties was extremely critical. The British landed more than 2,000 men at Point Lookout. Here they organized several parties which committed all kinds of depredations along the shores of the Potomac and Patuxent Rivers, capturing and burning a large number of small boats. They burned also many houses and other valuable property. Anything and everything was plundered, even the women and children were robbed of their clothing, and such articles as it did not suit them to carry away were destroyed. On their return march they drove all the cattle, sheep, and hogs they could find before them. In this raid Messrs. B. Williams, R. Armstrong, M. Jones, and J. Biscoe were captured and carried off as prisoners. In this same month a landing was attempted at Mattox Creek in Virginia, but the British were driven off with severe loss by Captain Hungerford's Company of Light Infantry.

All during the summer of 1813 marauding expeditions of the enemy continued to make frequent raids on the plantation owners along the Potomac. William Marine in his history of the war wrote: "In consequence of these depredations, the inhabitants .....were compelled to perform military duty with very little intermission from early April. Their plantations, therefore, were neglected and pillaged, their slaves ran off to the enemy, and sickness prevailed to a great extent....." In response to a request by the Daily National Intelligencer during this period for an account of the difficulties being experienced, a subscriber wrote: "We are so harassed in St. Mary's [County] that very few have time or inclination to give long and detailed statements of the conduct of the enemy, or it would probably have been done by some body long ago." However, he followed this with a lengthy list of incidents with "things plundered" ranging from handkerchiefs to horses. Those named in this report who were robbed included William and Elizabeth Smoot, the Widow (Rebecca) Loker, Ann Bennett, Captain William Smith, James Kirk, Tyler Thomas, Robert Duncanson, Josiah and McKay Biscoe, Benjamin Williams, Robert Armstrong, and Mr. and Mrs. Richardson. The devastation continued throughout the year 1813, and during this year in four months alone, the British captured 129 prizes within the Chesapeake and its tributaries.

On November 22, 1813, Reverend Francis Neale wrote from St. Inigoes to Reverend John Grassi, the Superior at Georgetown College: "Last Wednesday I visited St. George's Island and viewed with affliction the great devastation made by the English. .....From the face of things they could have had no other view than to have completely destroyed the whole of the property." The letter goes on to say that every house on the island was burned, including the fences, most of the large trees had been cut and carried away for masts and spars, and the island was completely burned over which ruined most of the fine pasture land. A second burning later finished the job when the British attempted to capture some deserters.

After the British evacuated Point Lookout near the end of August, 1813, and took possession of Kent Island, the situation quieted down on the Potomac until their return in force in the summer of 1814. But it was only a lull in the storm because on their return the British systematically visited every bay and inlet on both sides of the Potomac leaving havoc in their wake. The luckless Widow Loker was again visited, together with Jenifer Taylor and John Walsh, and all lost cattle, sheep, and geese. Two sons of Mrs. Holton were captured and carried off, and everything in her home was destroyed.

On July 19, 1814, the enemy made their raid on Leonardtown in Bretton Bay. A force was landed on Newtown Neck on the west side of the Bay and on Medley's Neck on the east side to form a pincers to enter the town from the rear, while Rear Admiral George Cockburn led a contingent of his boats up the bay to land on the water front. Altogether he had a force of about 1,500 men, which so outnumbered the 36th Maryland Regiment that they retreated to avoid capture. It was reported that "every housekeeper was plundered except one - to the Court House they did great injury; not a sash or pane of glass but what they destroyed; much of the inside work cut to pieces, all the tobacco about 70 hogsheads carried off, and property belonging to individuals and the United States, to the amount of $4,000. Although Cockburn gave some of the inhabitants a guard, yet his men plundered almost within reach of the guards' muskets." Mrs. Thompson and Miss Eliza Key are given credit for saving the Court House, having informed the Admiral that it sometimes was used for divine worship. It is said that on the return march down Newtown Neck the British troops stopped to cook their dinner and used the tombstones of St. Francis Xavier Cemetery for field ovens, and this is the reason that, although the cemetery has been in use since 1640, few stones prior to 1812 remain. Captain Joseph Ford's shipyard near the Newtown Manor house was destroyed and the Jesuits lost a "battow."

The Rear Admiral in his own report stated: "A quantity of stores belonging to the 36th Regiment and a number of arms of different descriptions were found here and destroyed; a quantity of tobacco, flour provisions and other articles were brought away in the boats and in a schooner lying off the town. Not a musket being fired, nor an armed enemy seen, the town was accordingly spared."

On July 21, 1814, Admiral Cockburn went up the Nomini River to Nomini Ferry where he beat off the Virginia forces. He reported: "After taking on board all the tobacco and other stores found in the place, with a quantity of cattle, and destroying all the store-houses and buildings, re-embarked; and dropping down to another point of the Nominy observed some movements on shore upon which we again land with marines. The enemy fired a volley at us, but on the advance of the marines, fled into the woods. Everything in the neighborhood was therefore also destroyed or brought off; and after visiting the country in several other directions, covering the escape of the negroes who were anxious to join us, quitted the river and returned to the ships with 135 refuges negroes, two captured schooners, a large quantity of tobacco, dry goods and cattle and a few prisoners." One British Captain reported that they carried off between 1,500 and 2,000 slaves from the bay area during the war.

The Rear Admiral's reports continue: "July 24 - The rear-admiral gives an account of his having gone up St. Clement's creek, St. Mary's County, with the boats and marines, to examine the country. The militia showed themselves occasionally, but always retreated when pursued; and the boats returned to the ships without any casualty, having captured four schooners and destroyed one. The inhabitants having remained peaceably in their houses, the rear-admiral did not suffer any injury to be done to them excepting at one farm, from which two musket shots were fired at the admiral's gig, and where the property was therefore destroyed."

"July 31 - The rear-admiral reports, that having on the 29th proceeded to the head of the Machodick river, in Virginia, where he burnt six schooners, whilst the marines marched without opposition, over the country on the banks of that river, and there not remaining any other place on the Virginia or St. Mary's side of his last anchorage that he had not visited, he, on the 28th, caused the ships to move above Blackstone's Island, and on the 29th proceeded with the boats and marines up the Wicomoco river; he landed at Hamburgh and Chaptico, from which latter place he shipped a considerable quantity of tobacco and visited several houses in different parts of the country, the owners of which living quietly with their families, and seeming to consider themselves and their neighborhood at his disposal, he caused no farther inconvenience to them, than obliging them to furnish supplies of cattle and stock for the use of his forces."

"Aug. 4 - The rear-admiral states, that on the 2d the squadron dropped down the Potomac, near the entrance of the Yocomoco river, which he entered the following day with the boats and marines and landed with the latter. The enemy had here collected in great force and made more resistance than usual; but the ardor and determination of the rear-admiral's gallant little band carried all before them; and after forcing the enemy to give way, they followed him 10 miles up the country, captured a field piece, and burnt several houses which had been converted into depots, for militia, arms, etc. Learning afterwards that gen. Hungerford had rallied his men, at Kinsale, the rear-admiral proceeded thither; and though the enemy's position was extremely strong, he had only time to give the British an ineffectual volley, before they gained the height, when he again retired with precipitation, and did not re-appear. The stores found at Kinsale were then shipped without molestation, and having burnt the storehouses and other places, with two old schooners, and destroyed two batteries, the rear-admiral re-embarked, bringing away five prize schooners, and a large quantity of tobacco, flour, &c. a field piece and a few prisoners. The American general, Taylor, was wounded. The conduct of the officers, and men on this occasion calls for the rear-admiral's particular commendation; with 500 men they penetrated ten miles into the enemy's country, and skirmished back surrounded by woods, in the face of the whole collected militia of Virginia, under generals Hungerford and Taylor; and after this long march carried the heights of Kinsale in the most gallant manner."

"August 8 - The rear-admiral gives an account of his having, on the 12th, proceeded up St. Mary's creek and landed in various parts of the country about the extensive inlet, but without seeing a single armed person, though militia had formerly been stationed at St. Mary's factory [Great Mills or Clifton Factory] for defence; the inhabitants of the state appearing to consider it wiser to submit than to attempt opposition."

The American version of Cockburn's raid at Mundy's Point in the Yeoacomico River (from the Bulletin of the Northumberland County Historical Society, Vol. 1, No. 1) is as follows:

<u>Richmond Enquirer</u>   August 10, 1814

ENEMY IN THE POTOMAC

Dispatches were received on Sunday by Express from Gen. Hungerford, from the neighborhood of Kinsale, (Westmoreland) dated on the 3d, which inform that the British had landed their troops from about 20 barges and several tenders, at Mundy's Point--they were fired on, before they touched the beach by Capt. Henderson of the Northumberland Militia, who disputed the ground until his ammunition was expended-- he retired with his piece--they persued him to his own house which they burnt to ashes--in a subsequent attack at Kinsale, the same day, Lt. Crabb's detachment of artillery, did considerable damage to a barge's crew.

Extract of a letter from Col. T. D. Downing of Northumberland County to the Adjutant General, dated
         H. Q. Northumberland, C. H. 4th August 1814
"Sir--I have the honor to communicate to you for the information of his excellency the commander in chief, that on Wednesday morning the 3rd inst. Capt. Henderson, who was stationed at Monday's Point on Yeocomoco, with one of his four pounders and a detachment of his artillery, was attacked by a very superior force of the enemy, and after an obstinate contest, in which he expended the whole of his round shot, was compelled to retreat. Being closely pursued for the distance of five miles into the country, he suddenly diverged from the main road, and concealing his piece in the bushes, effected his retreat to Lottsburg. The enemy having missed him by this manoeuvre, proceeded about one mile farther, into nearly the centre of the country between the Potomac and Rappahannock, and destroyed Capt. Henderson's dwelling house, store-house and out-houses, with all his furniture and goods--& the houses and property of John King just opposite, across the road in Richmond County, about 9 miles from this place.

"Before a sufficient force to oppose them could advance from this place, they made a retreat to their original point of debarkation, having burnt almost all the houses near the main road, & laid waste the country thro' which they marched. They took from their families & homes, seven unarmed persons of whom several were exempt by age from military service. One of those, they compelled to shew them the concealed four pounder, which they dragged a considerable distance, until meeting with a party of cavalry from Westmoreland, they, in their turn, secreted the piece, and I have no information that it has yet been discovered.

"About 3 hours after the affair at Monday's Point, a barge was discerned entering another branch of the Yeocomoco, near Exeter-Lodge by a detachment of Capts. Henderson's & Train's companies united. This detachment had been stationed near the mouth of the river, but being in danger of capture from the very superior force which had ascended the river, had taken a position several miles higher up, and was considerably reduced by an escort which had attended Capt. Henderson's second piece to a place of safety. Of this little party, of about 40 men, Major Claughton assumed the command, & observing where the enemy intended to land, placed his men in a thicket near the shore, just opposite. Reserving his fire until the barge had grounded, he opened upon the enemy a most severe and destructive discharge from his musketry and carbines, at the distance of only forty or fifty yards. They immediately pulled off with much precipitation amidst a continued and well directed fire from the shore. Their loss was certainly very considerable; several were set down by the first fire, and were seen to fall at almost every shot. Instead of fifteen or twenty oars with which they reached the beach before they got out of the range of our musketry and carbines, they could only man five or six. In this affair an unlucky discharge of grape from their bow-piece, severely wounded Lieut. Barnes of the infantry, and a private of the artillery--the only loss we sustained.

"Much credit is due, sir, to the officers and men engaged in those little affairs. Captain Henderson with only 30 effective men contended for 15 minutes against a force of the enemy from thirty-two barges, and at last retired in good order, with only one in the least injured, who was wounded by the accidental explosion of some cartridges. He thinks that the enemy suffered severely, he is positive that he struck their barges with his round shot at least three times before they were expended, and that the fire from his carbines, which was continued some time longer, was severe and destructive in the extreme. I trust, sir, that from his conduct on this occasion and his activity and usefullness upon every alarm, that the Executive will think him worthy of another piece, should the missing one not be found.

"I have ascertained, sir, that the species of force landed by the enemy in this county was only infantry; in the van of which were placed some blacks--Among them was recognized a fellow who deserted last fall from Major Claughton of this regiment. Their knowledge of persons, roads and places, was unquestionably derived from a source of this description. Only one officer was mounted when they reached Capt. Henderson's, and he had no saddle--a proof that the horse was caught by the way.

"The force of the enemy now lying off the upper end of this county is a ship of the line, three frigates, a brig, and an unusually large proportion of tenders and barges. In the conflagration of Capt. Henderson's houses, were destroyed two boxes of 4 lb. round cartridges--a further supply of those and of every description of ammunition for artillery, musketry and riflemen is, at this crisis, deemed indispensable. Some of Capt. Jett's rifles have proved worthless, and some have been casually broken--a supply of about 20 of this effective weapon of defense would, at this time, be found highly serviceable in completely equipping Capt. Jett's very valuable corps."

FURTHER PARTICULARS

Extract of a Letter, dated
                    Camp near Kinsale, August 5.
"On the 2nd, early in the morning, information was received that the Enemy was moving down the River, with all their force, and by 12 o'clock they had reached Ragged Point.--After sunset they anchored opposite the mouth of Yeocomico. On the next day before day-break they were in motion; for, by day-break they were distinctly seen in the Yeocomico.--Their first attempt was on Monday's Point, where they were gallantly met by Capt. Henderson's 30 men (with a piece of Artillery) who were soon compell'd to retreat. Him they followed 6 miles, into the country to his own house, and burnt it together with all the houses there, and very many on the road. The direction of the road being around our right flank, and it having been reported that they were very near us, it was supposed they intended to turn us, and cut off our retreat--We were then moved about a half a mile from Kinsale.--Whilst in this situation, the troops and Cavalry of Capt. Carter and Stewart were fired on and a horse killed--& Gen. Parker and a trooper, who ventured within sight of Monday's Point, were intercepted on their return by a party of the enemy, and very narrowly escaped with the loss of their horses--The General was grazed by two balls, and followed several miles by negroes."

"On the enemy's return from Monday's Point, they approached Kinsale. Two Companies had been ordered there, one of Riflemen and the other of Infantry--and after giving the enemy a fire, were driven back by their grape-shot, rockets, &c. with the loss of a man shot through the head.

"In the meantime we had retired further into the country to our baggage-waggons--but hearing of the enemy's landing we marched back within 1/4 of a mile of Kinsale, and there formed. The enemy gave us 12 or 15 cannon shot, but did not march to give us battle; and we could not approach them (with our force) under cover of their tenders, &c. In the meantime they went on the left bank of the river, and collected there and in Northumberland, perhaps, 100 or 150 negroes, broke the windows of houses, &c.

"Yesterday, it appears, they were in Northumberland about Cherry Point and Coan, by the great smoke everywhere rising."

We learn from the Express, that the Buccanneers spared nothing at Kinsale but the hovel of a poor old negro woman--the houses (about 20 or 30) were burnt--every article was taken of which they could carry, the rest was destroyed--all the tobacco, which they found in the Ware-house was shipped, except about 20 H'bds. which they burnt, as night-fall prevented their carrying it on board.--The unfortunate soldier, of Capt. Pitts' Company from Essex, who was killed by a grapeshot, was taken from the ground, where he fell, to within 10 steps of the spot where they dined--his pockets turned inside out and rifled.--The enemy landed in Kinsale in 27 barges, which were supposed to contain near 1000 men.--Admiral Cockburn is said to have been on shore, mounted on a grey horse--sanctioning by his presence as well as by his orders, all the atrocities which were perpetrated by his band.--The enemy landed at Monday's Point 5 or 6 black platoons in red, commanded by British officers.--Weep, Briton, weep--and blush at the destitution of shame, which marks thy countrymen!

We understand that Orders have issued from the Adjutant General's Office of this State, calling Maj. General Alex. Parker to the command of the troops in the

Northern Neck.

Richmond Enquirer

August 20, 1814

"Camp, August 8, 1814.

"SIR,
     "Since my last of the 5th, I have learnt that the following prisoners are now in the squadron under your command, taken near Monday's Point on the 3d instant, viz:--Elisha Williams, aged about 66 years; Luke Dameron ages about 53 ditto; Thomas Beacham, aged about 49 ditto; Christopher Dawson, John King and Thomas Nutt. It is my duty to represent to you that the three first are over the military age prescribed by law, and that none were taken in arms, but were, as I understood, peaceably remaining at their own homes--from which, they were forcibly taken, and the houses of several burnt; under these circumstances, their detention would be manifestly contrary to the laws and usages of civilized nations, and to the declarations of British commanders in similar cases--and I request their discharge.
     "I have the honor to be your very obedient servant,

                         JOHN P. HUNGERFORD,
                         "B. G. commanding."

"P.S.--Since writing the foregoing, I have understood from the Lt. Col. to whose regiment Thomas Beacham was formerly attached, that he once held a commission in the militia as captain, but, that about 9 months since, his company was dissolved, and that he holds no command, also that Thomas Nutt is a supernumerary officer in the militia. "J.P.H."

————————

               "His Britannic Majesty's Ship Albion,
                 in the Potomac, the 11th August, 1814.

"SIR,
     "I have the honor to acknowledge the receipt of your letter, bearing date the 8th Inst. respecting six Prisoners in the Squadron under my command; and representing to me that three of them are above what you are pleased to term the military age prescribed by law, and that none of them were taken in arms; and, therefore, that their detention is manifestly contrary to the laws and usages of civilized nations, and to the declarations of British Commanders in similar cases, in consequence of which you request their discharge. As, Sir, I beg permission to judge for myself how far the people in question can be considered to have conformed to the declarations and usages you have quoted, I am sorry that it is neither in my power to agree with, or meet your ideas hereon.
     "I have the honor to be, Sir, your most ob't humble servant,

                         G. COCKBURN.

"Brig. Gen. Hungerford, &c. &c. &c."

————————

     The Rear Admiral's report of July 31 touches very lightly on the invasion of Chaptico on July 30, 1814, and if it is typical of his other reports, much is left to one's imagination. None of it is good. It is no wonder he was called the scourge of the Potomac, and some other names besides. The following are several reports of the newspapers of the times:
     "On the 30th, the same worthy body of men landed at Chaptico, in this country (except a few that the Virginia militia killed and wounded when they landed near Nominy on the 20th and 21st). In this little village they got about 30 hhds. of tobacco and no other plunder; the inhabitants having removed all their property out of their grasp. Yet here they made a most furious attack on every window, door, and pane of glass in the village; not one was left in the whole; the places was given up to the fury of their men, and if the prince regent had commanded in person, the victory and destruction could not have been more complete. They picked their stolen geese in the church-dashed the pipes of the church-organ on the pavement; opened a family vault in the church-yard, broke open the coffins, stirred the bones about with their hands in search of hidden treasure--all this in the presence of their worthy admiral. During all this havoc, not a man was in arms within fifteen miles of them, and they worked until ten o'clock at night, before they got the tobacco on board their vessels, owing to the shallowness of the creek that leads up to Chaptico warehouse, they rolled more than half the tobacco one mile. General Steuart was encamped with the militia near sixteen miles from these free-booters;

I presume he is waiting for a regular field action with the British. He had no confidence in our trees and bushes, as our militia had in the revolutionary war."

"To the Editors of the Herald. Gentlemen, I have no recollection of having seen any account of the conduct of the enemy at Chaptico published in any of the public prints; you are at liberty to publish the following extract of a letter to a friend, written shortly after that affair. It is a very imperfect account written in a hurry amidst the bustle of a camp, but contains most of the facts. My name is enclosed, which you are at liberty to make public, if any respectable person should deny the truth of the following statement

A Citizen of Maryland."

"I passed through Chaptico shortly after the enemy left it, and I am sorry to say that their conduct would have disgraced Cannibals; the house was torn to pieces, the well which afforded water for the inhabitants was filled up, and what is still worse, the church and the ashes of the dead shared an equally bad or worse fate. Will you believe me, when I tell you, that the sunken graves were converted into barbecue holes! The remaining glass of the church windows broken, the communion table used as a dinner table and then broken to pieces! Bad as the above may appear, it dwindles into insignificance, when compared with what follows: The vault was entered and the remains of the dead disturbed. Yes, my friend, the winding sheet was torn from the body of a lady of the first respectability, and the whole contents of the vault entirely deranged! The above facts were witnessed by hundreds as well as myself, and I am happy to say, that but one sentiment pervaded our army."

"I immediately shewed it to General Philip Stewart, lately commanding the American troops at that place, who read and declared it strictly true; that Cockburn was at the head of it; that they also destroyed the organ; that Judge Key's lady who had been last put into the vault was the person alluded to, that her winding sheet was torn in pieces, and her person wantonly exposed; and that his men were exasperated to desperation by his conduct. You will publish this.

Yours, &c.

Robert Wright.

October 19, 1814.

N. B. I hope every American printer will also publish it. R.W."

"The above facts, detailed by Governor Wright, were confirmed by General Philip Stewart, who lately commanded the American troops at that place; who declared the statement to be every way correct. But this, horrible as it was, was nothing to what followed. We are authorized to state, that General Stewart informed a member of the Senate of the United States, that the British Officers Stripped Young Ladies Entirely Naked, and obliged them to stand before them in that condition for an hour and an half; when they the British officers, at length permitted these distressed females again to clothe themselves!"

A newspaper of August 7, 1814 reported: "On Tuesday morning one frigate, two tenders and several barges proceeded up St. Mary's and landed on the St. Inigoes side with a plundering party of about 1000 men, headed by Admiral Cockburn." They spent several days going through the Neck gathering stock. In this same month, Cockburn with 1,200 marines and 40 sailors landed on the farm of John Kilgour near the mouth of St. Clement's Bay. They took much stock but notified the people that they would respect private buildings unless fired upon. With a force of this size there seems little likelihood that they would be fired upon and even less likelihood that much of value escaped the raiders. A detachment of the enemy about this same time landed at Benedict Heard's looking for stock. Colonel Ashton sent Captain Blackistone's rifle corps and Captain Brown's Company of infantry in pursuit and the British retreated to their barges but returned the next day and burned every house on Heard's land.

Late in August 1814 a large part of the British fleet ascended the Patuxent, landed their forces at Benedict and under the command of Admiral Cockburn and General Ross marched overland to Bladensburg where they defeated the American forces on August 22nd, captured, looted, and burned Washington, including the Capitol and White House. Thus, Cockburn made good his word to Mrs. Dolley Madison (although she had fled) that "he would make his bow" in her drawing room. During this time another part of the British fleet consisting of two frigates, four bomb ships, a sloop of war, fitted as a rocket ship, one brig, one schooner, and two barges, mounting a total of 173 guns, under the command of Captain James Alexander Gordon, was proceeding up the Potomac to join the main British forces. The larger ships were the Sea Horse, the Euryalus, the Devastation, the Aetna, the Meteor, the Erebus, the Fairy, and the Anna Maria.

It took Captain Gordon over ten days to reach Fort Washington in Prince George's County which he captured without opposition, after the commanding officer, acting on garbled instructions, blew up the works and spiked the guns. On August 27th he reached Alexandria, which was surrendered without a shot being fired. Captain Gordon, in a special report to Admiral Cochrane, explained that his delay was due to the fact that each of his ships had been aground no less than twenty times during the trip up the river. Undoubtedly the Captain arrived at Alexandria in a bad temper for the city was plundered ruthlessly and his ships were so loaded with booty that their free-boards hardly cleared the water.

Upon Gordon's return down the Potomac, a serious attempt was made by the Americans to destroy his fleet, which was notable mainly as showing that the humiliating affair of the invasion of Washington had not entirely demoralized the government. A battery, under the command of Commodore David Porter, was established about 16 miles below Washington on the historic Virginia estate of "Belvoir," sometimes called the White House, which fronted on the Potomac River and extended from Dogue Creek, formerly the southern boundary of Mount Vernon, to Gunston Cove and Accotink Creek. Porter's force consisted of a regiment of Virginia militia under General John P. Hungerford, together with a detachment of marines and sailors, the latter being a part of the crew of his old ship, the Essex.

A second battery, under Commodore Oliver H. Perry, was established at Indian Head on the Maryland side of the river. In addition, several fire ships, under the command of Commodore John Rodgers, were provided to attempt to burn the British ships.

For five successive days and nights the battery of Commodore Porter kept up their fire on the British ships but his guns were too small and no effective damage was done. Actually it was a one-sided affair for the small American force, fighting without intrenchments or other defensive works, was no match for the flotilla of eleven British ships with a total armament of 173 guns, that kept up a galling fire. The Americans suffered a loss of 11 killed and 18 wounded while the British casualties were 7 killed and 35 wounded. As the fleet passed Indian Head, Commodore Perry opened fire but again the guns were too small to be effective and Commodore Rodgers was no more successful in his attempt to burn some of the ships of the enemy. There was no want of enterprise and courage on the part of the Americans but they got there too late with too little, the result of hurried and incomplete preparation, and Captain Gordon, who had carried out the expedition with an almost utter disregard of the ordinary British prudence, escaped with a battered but complete flotilla, augmented by many prize vessels.

Colonel Fenwick reported a skirmish on September 27th, near St. Inigoes in a letter to the Secretary of War. Another report stated Cockburn destroyed all the oyster boats and wood flats in addition to the usual pillage. This action probably occurred in the St. Mary's River and creeks of Bretton and St. Clement's Bays.

The people along the river continued to complain to the government officials in Washington; and shortly before the British burned the Capitol, the inhabitants of St. Mary's again complained to President James Madison concerning their exposed situation and requested his aid and protection. The President, who had a few other problems on his mind, is said to have returned a somewhat pettish answer: "It cannot be expected that I can defend every man's turnip patch in St. Mary's County." When the people of St. Mary's learned that the enemy was in Washington burning and pillaging, they observed that "the enemy was not in the turnip patch, but in the corn field."

It was on October 30, 1814, that the British landed at St. Inigoes, robbed the manor house, and desecrated the chapel therein. Brother Joseph Mobberly, a Jesuit Coadjutor, reported that they had just been at the house of one of the tenants and taken a number of things. The wife pleaded poverty, her daughters wept and the officer finally ordered his men to restore everything, promising that they might do what they pleased at the Big House. She begged him not to make such promises, observing that there was a chapel in the house, and that the inhabitants were good people. The officer then said, "Then Madam, you are too poor, and they are too good; so at this rate, we are to get nothing; but Madam, we must live." He then ordered his men to row him to the Big House. Brother Mobberly very aptly headed his report to his Superiors:

"St. Inigoes - All Saints (Oct. 31, 1814)
Abominatio Desolationis in loco Santo."

In his lengthy narrative Brother Mobberly describes the happenings and losses in detail, which totaled over $1,000, a sizable sum in those days. Excerpts from the report read, "have come.....with the avowed purpose to burn this house down," "the prophanation is distressing, our losses are great," "never was a mechanic more perfect in his trade than these villians - the whole was completed in about 10 or 15 minutes," "I happily escaped being shot," "the times call for an immediate removal," "who can be secure on the water?"

It is interesting to note that Brother Mobberly in his report stated, "We have now been plundered and robbed twice within a few weeks and may soon expect the third." St. Ignatius Church, a brick edifice completed in 1788, located on the manor, was in a badly damaged state when the war was over and required a new roof and extensive repairs. Could the British have fired it on their previous raid? The records are silent.

A treaty of peace was signed at Ghent on December 24, 1814, and ratified by the United States on February 17, 1815, but the British remained on St. George's Island for ten days after the latter date. During this time they went ashore at the mouth of Smith's Creek and took four or five negroes from George Loker and continued to take wood and timber from the island.

A second war with the British within a period of thirty years had a disastrous effect on the rivermen along the Potomac and the Patuxent Rivers. They were overpowered and bottled up by a vastly superior fleet of ships. This powerful enemy systematically captured or destroyed every boat, large or small, and every shipyard; they impoverished the entire water front by feeding on it for ten years out of the thirty-eight year period, during which time many of the homes and barns were destroyed, the slaves confiscated and the stock and valuables stolen, to say nothing of the greatest loss, many of their fine young men.

All of this resulted in a complete paralysis of the good beginnings that had been made on the Potomac in the development of shipyards, river industries, ports, and the growth of towns. So great was the damage done that recovery had little more than begun when the worst of all tragedies came, stopping all progress on the river dead in its tracks - Civil War!

During the War of 1812 and perhaps earlier, the Lucas family of Georgetown operated a fleet of sloops and schooners out of this port to points along the Potomac, as disclosed by the records of the Collector. John Lucas, the father, lived at the foot of 21st Street and his son, William, lived on Cherry Hill in Georgetown. Another son was Ignatius Lucas who married Nancy (Ann) Cumberland, a daughter of John Cumberland, and lived south of 26th Street on a road above the canal. John Cumberland lived on the next lot and in 1843 owned the schooner, Mary Ann. He fished and hunted on the Potomac and his nets and huge ducking guns were objects of curiosity to the neighboring children.

The names of Augustus, Henry, and Richard Lucas also appear in the Collector's records and they were perhaps other sons or relatives of John Lucas. During the war years 1813-1815, John and William Lucas are shown as owners and masters of three sloops, the Polly and Sally, the Tartar, and the Infant, and three schooners, the Nancy, the Polly, and the James. No mention is made of these vessels after the war and they were, undoubtedly lost to the British. In 1816, they owned the sloop, Catherine, and the schooner, Eliza Ann. By 1822, William Lucas owned another sloop, the Miranda and John, named for his daughter and son, which he sold to a Mr. Fearson in 1825, and the sloop, Lively. By 1838 the Lucas fleet had included the following vessels - in 1827, the sloop Dove; the ocean-going ship, Eagle, cleared for Amsterdam for Augustus Lucas and a Mr. Chew; in 1828, the steamboat, Tyber, owned by William Lucas; the sloop, Dash; in 1834, the schooner, Commerce; in 1836, the schooner Mechanic, and the sloop, Delight; and in 1838, the schooner, William and Thomas. Undoubtedly, many of these vessels had been built in the shipyard of the Cumberlands. Prior to his death in 1844, William Lucas was a member of the Board of the C. and O. Canal Company.

As late as 1840, it is evident that the Potomac had not been charted thoroughly for the census records of St. Mary's County alone disclose that some 82 men were employed in navigating the river, while 5 were engaged in ocean navigation. It is small wonder that the British went aground so often in their invasion of Washington via the Potomac in 1814, particularly in view of the fact that such markers as were in use had been removed. It was a foolhardy risk on the part of Captain Gordon but as usual the British "muddled through."

On February 28, 1844, the Potomac was the scene of a great tragedy. The U. S. Frigate, Princeton, a new steam warship and one of the first propeller type built for the Navy, was being shown to a large party of government officials, including President John Tyler and his Cabinet when an accident occurred. Mounted on the Princeton's deck was a 225-pounder, a Paixhans gun, of special design known as the Peacemaker. It was a very large gun for those times. When cruising past Mount Vernon a salute to George Washington was fired from the Peacemaker. Later, on the return trip when opposite the mouth of Broad Creek, Commodore Stockton consented to fire the great gun a second time. As the gun was fired the breech was blown off and among those killed were Secretary of State, Abel P. Upshur, Secretary of the Navy, Thomas W. Gilmer, Commander Kennan of the Navy, Representative Virgil Maxey of Maryland, Representative Sykes of New Jersey and a New York Legislator, David Gardiner, the father-in-law of President Tyler. At President Tyler's direction the dead were brought to the White House from whence they were taken for burial on

36

March 2nd.

During the War Between the States the armies of both the North and the South crossed and recrossed the upper Potomac many times. In 1862 the Confederate Army of Northern Virginia crossed at White's Ford to open battle at Sharpsburg and Antietam, where on September 17, the bloodiest single day of the war occurred. After the battle, General Lee and his men recrossed the Potomac at Boteler's Ford. In July 1863, he once again invaded the North and was followed by the Army of the Potomac under General George Meade who crossed the Potomac at Edwards Ferry near Leesburg. The main body of the invading Confederate Army under General James Longstreet waded across the river at Williamsport. After the bloody days at Gettysburg, the Confederate Army returned to Virginia. At Williamsport the river was high due to heavy rains and it was necessary to build pontoon bridges to effect the crossing.

It had been the hope of the South that even though Maryland had been kept in the Union, through the machinations of its Governor, Thomas Hicks, and the suspension of the writ of habeas corpus by President Abraham Lincoln, that with the invasion of the North, the Marylanders north of the Potomac would flock to the Confederate standard. But this hope was not realized, for once the "die had been cast" these Marylanders elected to stay with the North or remain uneasy neutrals.

The story was quite different among the people of the Southern Maryland Counties. Here the younger men had crossed the river to serve with the Confederates and the sentiments of their families were overwhelmingly with the South. Indeed in St. Mary's County no one seems to remember any white resident who fought for the North, although the writer, after a diligent search, found two and since that time several others have been brought to his attention. The people in St. Mary's County were in an uproar and undoubtedly the same situation prevailed in the other southern counties. As early as February, 1861, the citizens of the Patuxent district organized an infantry company called the "Smallwood Vigilantes" under Captain James M. Heard. Other companies included the "Clifton Guards," headed by J. Edwin Coad; the "St. Inigoes Dragoons," Captain Randolph Jones; the "St. Mary's Guards," Captain Robert Neale; the "Riley Rifles," Captain James F. Raley; the "Charlotte Company," Captain Thomas, and a company from Great Mills under Captain Reeves. The "Riley Rifles" were presented with a handsome new flag made by the ladies of Leonardtown on April 23rd. It was their own handiwork and made after the style of that adopted by the Confederate states. On the same day in 1861, a public meeting was held in Leonardtown which was attended by practically everyone in the county. Under the leadership of Benedict I. Heard, C. Combs, Chapman Billingsley, John H. Sothoron, L. W. B. Hutchins, John F. King, B. G. Harris, J. F. Dent, Thomas Martin, William Coad, Dr. J. W. Forrest, Joseph Forrest, Oscar Mills, J. Edwin Coad, Dr. R. Neale, James F. Blakistone, Theopholus Harrison, R. F. Neale, Dr. James Waring, R. H. Reeder, F. J. Stone, Thomas Loker, Thomas O. Spencer, E. S. Abell, Dr. Walter Briscoe, and H. Thomas....."The sum of $10,000 [was voted] for the purpose of purchasing arms and ammunition for our people, in order that they may be capable to defend their rights and the honor and interests of our state....." When Maryland failed to secede, the companies dissolved and the men joined regular Confederate units in Virginia.

Throughout the war both the Federal Army and Navy were active along the Potomac, south of Washington, fearing for the safety of the Capital. On the Virginia side of the river in the Northern Neck, the Federals made a few raids and there were a few skirmishes, but no major battles, although a considerable amount of property was destroyed; on the Maryland side there was much marching and counter-marching, patrolling and blockading by the Federal forces. Garrisons were maintained at strategic points along the river all during the war and this was hotly resented by the people of Southern Maryland.

But the point most germane to our story of the Potomac was the blockade which again brought industry on the river to a standstill. The writer's grandfather, a native of Washington at that time, after running the blockade a few times found the venture too risky to continue and was reduced to accepting a government contract to haul supplies from Washington to Quantico to avoid the loss of his vessels through bankruptcy.

On April 26 and 27, 1861, the Confederates destroyed the lightships on Kettle Bottom Shoals in the Potomac and moved or removed most of the buoys from Aquia Creek to the mouth of the river, in order to make navigation difficult for the Federals. By May 15, 1861, they had set up batteries at Aquia Creek and Mathias Point to close the Potomac and prevent supplies from reaching Washington. The guns for the battery at Mathias Point were transported up the river by the Confederate steamboat, the Virginia. The Federal Potomac River Flotilla was commanded by Captain James Harman Ward and he was determined to destroy these batteries. On May 29, 1861, Ward, taking the lead in the steamer, Thomas Freeborn, and supported by two smaller steamers, the Anacostia and the Resolute and later by the Pawnee, made repeated attacks over a period of several weeks at both points which ended with his death on June 27, 1861, at the hands of a Confederate sharpshooter, Andrew Pitts of Caroline County, Virginia.

A few days before this a landing was made on the Virginia shore and the home of Dr. Hooe was burned. More than a year later the Confederates still maintained a fairly effective blockade of Washington and such vessels as got through had to endure the gunfire of the batteries on the Virginia shore.

Colonel Ephraim Elmer Ellsworth in command of a regiment of Zouaves, and supported by ships of the Potomac Flotilla, occupied Alexandria on May 24, 1861. Ellsworth was shot dead by the enraged proprietor of the Marshall House, James W. Jackson, while he was descending the stairs with a Confederate flag which he had pulled from the front of the building. Jackson in turn was shot down by Ellsworth's men.

Typical of communications concerning the Confederate blockade of the Potomac during December, 1861, are the following:

"Dec 20, 1861

Last night a schooner was becalmed for nearly two hours off The Shipping Point Confederate Batteries and the damage she sustained amounted to two holes through her mainsail.

Willards Hotel"

"To the Assistant Sec. of Navy
WILLARD hotel
Dec 25, 1861
Dear Sir: I am the owner of steamers Volunteer and Reindeer, running daily from the foot of Eleventh st to Rum Point on Mattawomen Creek, but am in dread constantly of a rebel battery now or about to be erected at Hollowell [Hallowing] Point, 6 or 8 miles below Mt. Vernon, they having possession there as rebel cavalry and soldiers are seen there daily. It is the most dangerous point on the river, and would be a complete blockade of the river, as vesels drawing 6 feet are obliged to pass within a quarter of a mile of the shore. If the Government desires to land 1,000 men there to protect it, I will transport them from here or General Hookers division for nothing, immediately, if they require it.

CALEB S. WRIGHT

Cockpit Point had a heavy rebel battery and most of the commercial traffic or small naval boats passed Cockpit point at night, anchoring in Mattawoman until moon down."

Letter from the Secretary of the Navy to Lieut. Wyman, U.S.N. commanding Potomac Flotilla, regarding reported infringement of blockade.

"NAVY DEPT., Dec 16, 1861
Sir: Captain Shore of the Steamer CHAMBERLIN, called at the Dept to-day and made the following verbal statement, viz:
I was coming up the river on Wednesday last; a flag was raised on Piney Point light house, and I went in. Mrs. Marshall, the keeper of the light, wished me to report that five or six loads of rebels crossed the river every night into Virginia with provisions etc.; that there was $10,000 worth of goods, ammunition, clothing, etc., in the woods just above the lighthouse to be carried over. Men came to her every day and asked her if any of the U. S. cutters were about, and told her she had better keep away as they intended to destroy the light-house. The rebels have a small steamer in the creek just above Ragged Point which they brought from Fredericksburg.
Captain Shore also states that a small boat with provisions crossed over at Ragged Point at 12 o'clock n.
Two of our vessels were lying at Blakistone Island and could have seen this boat.
I am respectfully, etc.

GIDEON WELLES"

Point Lookout at the mouth of the Potomac was a well known watering place before the war. There was a large hotel, about 100 cottages, the lighthouse, and a steamboat landing. After the outbreak of the war, activities declined and the Federal Government established a veterans hospital there.

While stationed at Aquia Creek in June, 1861, Lieutenant Hunter H. Lewis, of the Confederate Navy, a graduate of the U. S. Naval Academy, noticed that the steamboat St. Nicholas, which ran from Baltimore to Washington and made many stops along the Maryland side of the river to pick up or unload freight and passengers, was permitted to approach the Federal gunboat Pawnee without challenge and deliver supplies. He immediately conceived a simple plan for the capture of both ships. He and others, in disguise, would board the St. Nicholas at various points from Baltimore southward, overpower the crew at Point Lookout, and then capture the Pawnee.

Lewis received little encouragement from his superiors in Richmond but he was joined by Captain George N. Hollins and Richard Thomas of Maryland, who were enthusiastic about the plan, and ultimately it was approved. Captain Hollins was an experienced naval officer who had served under Stephen Decatur and was placed in command. Richard Thomas of Mattapany-Sewall, second in command, was of a distinguished family in St. Mary's County. Although only twenty-eight years of age, he had been a surveyor on the western frontier, had campaigned against the Chinese pirates in the Far East, and, drifting to Europe, had fought under Garibaldi in Italy, where he adopted the name of Zarvona. He had lived in Paris for some time and his French was fluent, so he disguised himself as Madame la Force, a modiste, with several large trunks which contained the arms of the Confederates. At Point Lookout, the last contingent of Confederates boarded the St. Nicholas, including Captain Hollins.

Soon after leaving the Point, Zarvona clad himself in the uniform of a Confederate Zouave and he and Captain Hollins and their men took over the ship without difficulty and headed for the Coan River in Virginia. There they were to meet Lieutenant Lewis who would have part of the crew of the Confederate ship Patrick Henry and other volunteers to augment the force on the St. Nicholas. The passengers were allowed to go ashore at Coan River and while waiting for Lewis to arrive Captain Hollins learned through a Baltimore newspaper found on board that the Pawnee and most of the Potomac flotilla were anchored at Washington so that the men could attend the funeral of Captain James Harman Ward who had been killed in the attack on Mathias Point. He then decided to take the St. Nicholas up the Rappahannock and as they rounded Smith's Point, three ships were spied within a short period and all were captured. They were the brig, Monticello, with a cargo of 3,500 bags of coffee; the schooner, Mary Pierce, loaded with 200 tons of ice; and the vessel, Margaret, loaded with 270 tons of coal.

The St. Nicholas was renamed the Rappahannock and became a unit in the Confederate Navy. Richard Thomas Zarvona attempted to duplicate the feat with the steamer, Mary Washington, out of Baltimore, but was captured and remained a prisoner of war until released in broken health in April, 1863. Hollins and Lewis continued their service in the Confederate Navy.

The fear of capture of other steamboats similar to the St. Nicholas incident is disclosed in the following memorandum dated July 8, 1861, sent by Gideon Welles, Secretary of the Federal Navy, to William H. Seward, Secretary of State:

"A man of notoriously bad character named James C. Hurry of St. Mary's County has formed a plan for the capture during the present week, of one of the Steamboats plying between Baltimore and the Patuxent River, either by putting his men on board at Baltimore, or at Millstone Landing on that River. This Millstone Landing is a position whence more smuggling of men and provisions is carried on than any other place in the Chesapeake waters. Small vessels are constantly plying between that position and the Rappahannock and Coan [Va.] rivers, chiefly to the latter, where a Tennessee regiment is posted."

Throughout the war there were constant complaints to the U. S. Navy Department that the people of Southern Maryland along all of the lower Potomac water front were aiding and assisting the Confederates with every means at their command. As a consequence the Navy endeavored to keep ships stationed near most of the important landings on both sides of the river. These landings included Aquia Creek, Budd's Ferry, the White House, Mathias Point, Cedar Point, Piscataway, Nanjemoy, the mouth of the Wicomico, St. Clement's and Bretton Bays, the St. Mary's River and Smith's Point. However, the blockade was far from being effective and shortly after the outbreak of the war well defined routes were laid out by the Southern Marylanders to convey Confederate volunteers, spies, mail, equipment, medical supplies, food, and other materials across the Potomac from secret landing places that stretched from St. Mary's River to Piscataway. Generally, the Marylanders used fairly small boats that could be rowed or sailed across the river on moonless nights and had little difficulty in avoiding ships of the Federal Potomac Flotilla.

Secretary Welles stopped the steamboat and schooner traffic between Baltimore and Southern Maryland, at least for awhile, stating that after the ships reached St. Mary's River, they awaited a favorable opportunity to cross the Potomac and land contraband in the Coan River. On July 21, 1861, a petition was presented, by representatives of St. Inigoes and Point Lookout, to Commander Thomas T. Craven, in charge of the Potomac Flotilla, requesting resumption of steamboat service from Baltimore to points along the Potomac. The following names appeared on the petition:

A. J. Foxwell	John W. Bennett	W. Murphey
Randolph Jones	Thomas J. Bennett	B. F. McKay
C. M. Jones	R. B. Crane	J. B. Courtney
James F. Ellicott	W. L. Biscoe	H. M. Langley
J. W. Forrest	Robert Crane	J. H. Hopkins
J. Piett Forrest	James B. Loker	John G. Lilburn
Wm. R. Smith	O. N. Evans	James K. Jones
John A. Crane	Thomas J. Byrd	Walter Langley
Wm. C. Bayne	Joseph Milburn	N. B. Langley
Joseph T. Artis	J. E. Bruffey	T. T. Drury
		James H. Miles

Although the Naval Records are silent concerning the disposition of this petition, it is evident that Commander Craven acceded to the request, at least to a limited extent, perhaps because his flotilla was spending more time in the lower reaches of the river and he was in a better position to observe the shipping activities near the mouth of the Potomac.

The names of many Southern Maryland sympathizers and blockade runners appear in the U. S. Naval Records of this period. Mention is made during the summer of the capture of the sloop, Teaser, owned by Charles Huselman of Charles County and the schooner, Robert K. Scott, owned and sailed by John Johnson. In addition, the vessels of Henry Neitzey, a schooner, the Bachelor, and a shallop or sloop, the H. Day, were seized. Dr. Morgan of Yates Creek in Bretton Bay was under suspicion of ferrying troops to Virginia and it was stated that he was making two trips weekly. Captain John M. Goldsmith of Bedlam Neck was reported to have two cannon hidden at his home, Enfield, on St. Patrick's Creek in St. Clement's Bay and looking for transportation to Virginia. The guns and other arms had been bought in Baltimore, and apparently he got both the guns and himself safely across the Potomac, as later in the war, he caused much havoc to the river and bay lighthouses in his sailboat, the Swan.

Perhaps these cannon were those referred to by Commander Craven of the U.S.S. Yankee in a communication dated July 26, 1861, off Piney Point, Maryland.

"To Honorable Gideon Welles, Secretary of the Navy

Sir: I have received information that there are now secreted at Leonardtown, Maryland, two pieces of cannon and about forty stand of arms. The cannon have arrived but recently and are en route for the rebels. The small arms are supposed to belong to the State and should have been turned in, in obedience to a proclamation issued some time since by the Governor. Could I be assisted by the Marshall or one of the Deputies with the necessary search warrants, I have no doubt that these arms can be found and seized."

Off Aquia [Va.] August 1, 1861 [Craven to Welles]

"Sir: Acting under your authority, I yesterday proceeded to Leonardtown with the steamers Freeborn, Reliance and Yankee and landed a party from each of these vessels under the Command of Lt. Commanding Wyman, who had my instructions to visit the town and state to the chief magistrate that he was there for the purpose of searching for ordnance, small arms, etc., which I had been informed were secreted in the place. After a careful search without finding any of the articles in question, and being informed by some of the most prominent gentlemen of the town that there were nothing of the kind there, Lt. Commanding Wyman returned on board. I can not help feeling a distrust in the statement of these people, and have stationed the tenders Dana and Cobb off the mouth of Bretons Bay, with orders to cruise night and day, for the purpose of intercepting any vessels or boats which may have contraband articles on board."

Commander Craven while lying off Piney Point on August 11, 1861, reported to Secretary Gideon Welles that he had learned from a negro runaway that: ".....at Herring Creek, [in the Potomac] one Maddox, has been quite active in procuring supplies of men, munitions of war, clothing, etc., for the rebels, and that he had sent many boat loads of them to Virginia; that on Tuesday last he sent eight wagons and sixteen horses to Maryland Point [one wagon was loaded with uniforms], and on the same day eight men, who came from Baltimore, were sent across the river, cooperating with Maddox is one Dr. Coombs who has appropriated an old outhouse as a barrack for the reception of volunteers for the rebel army. Yesterday week there were ten men lodged in this barrack.....Maddox and Dr. Coombs employ their negroes, horses, and wagons in transporting recruits to the various landings, at night, watching their opportunity when our cruisers are out of sight. One Ben Hughes furnishes the recruit with shoes. His brother ran the Pocahontas with freight to and from Baltimore and has brought provisions for the rebels.....Two boats are now in Herring Creek.....from Virginia.....I started a party of eight men, under charge of Acting Master's Mate Street.....to seize the boats [they captured three]. I shall use my utmost efforts to obtain legal evidence against these people.....From all I can see and learn of the people of Maryland I am convinced that along the shores of the Potomac there is not one in twenty who is true to the Union, and I sometimes think there are many hundreds of them thoroughly organized into companies, perhaps regiments, and prepared to act against the Government at any moment."

In a communication dated August 18, 1861, Colonel William Coad of St. Mary's River is quoted as saying "You cannot find a Union man from Bretons Bay to Point Lookout, except Doctor Randolph Jones and some inhabitants of St. Georges Island."

These reports are typical of many throughout the war. Occasionally some of the men were captured and imprisoned in the old Capitol building in Washington (and later at Point Lookout) but usually they were turned loose after a short period due to lack of evidence, as the blockade runners were skillful at escape and avoided being caught with incriminating evidence.

William Fallon, master of the Buena Vista, was perhaps not so fortunate as disclosed in a letter from Secretary Welles to the Collector of Customs, Baltimore, dated July 29, 1861:

"The Navy Department deems it proper to communicate the following facts to you. The schooner Buena Vista, William Fallon, master, cleared from Baltimore about the 11th ultimo for St. Mary's River with an assorted cargo, was seized as a suspicious vessel by the Potomac Flotilla and brought to Washington. Her cargo was sold and it has just come to light that 5 barrels purporting to contain whiskey were filled with pistols. It appears that the manifest of the Buena Vista that the cargo was shipped by G. R. H. Leffler of Baltimore. I am respectfully, etc."

On September 13, 1861, Captain John Lawrence of St. Mary's County, complained to the Navy Department, that on a trip down the Potomac, with his mate, John F. Russell, his sloop, the Jane Wright, was sunk off Smith Island in the Chesapeake although his papers were in order. In his reply to an inquiry of the Navy Department, Commander Craven replied that on the morning of the sinking:

"I received a special dispatch from the Department, with an enclosure of a memorandum from the Assistant Secretary of War, relative to the intended invasion of Maryland by the rebels. In that dispatch I was authorized under certain contingencies to destroy every vessel or boat within my reach. Under that order the sloops, T. W. Riley and Jane Wright were scuttled and sunk."

Several orders of this type during the war, whenever there was a rumor of a Confederate invasion of Maryland, effectively wiped out the work boats of the Potomac River. The first such order was issued by Commander S. C. Rowan of the U.S.S. Pawnee in June, 1861, who ordered all rowboats on the Virginia shore that could be found, destroyed. The boats not captured or destroyed before the failure of the Confederate plan to free their men imprisoned at Point Lookout in July, 1864, were systematically destroyed by Commander Foxall A. Parker, then commanding the U. S. Potomac Flotilla, under an order dated September 1, 1864.

Parker's orders required the destruction of all privately owned boats on both sides of the Potomac and he reported that he destroyed a total of 39 boats during the month of September. Any boats that escaped this order undoubtedly perished after the assassination of President Abraham Lincoln by John Wilkes Booth for on April 22, 1865, Secretary Gideon Welles sent the following dispatch to the Potomac Flotilla:

"Booth was near Bryantown last Saturday, where Dr. [Samuel] Mudd set his ankle, which was broken by a fall from his horse. The utmost vigilance is necessary in the Potomac and Patuxent to prevent his escape. All boats should be searched for and destroyed and a daily and nightly patrol established along both shores. Inform the people that more than $100,000 are offered for him. Allow none of your vessels to leave except for search elsewhere."

The effect of these orders left the rivermen without boats and the means to procure new ones and resulted in an almost complete paralysis of commerce in the Potomac River for many years. In those years much of the river trade was diverted to Baltimore and the ship building industry became centered in the Chesapeake Bay.

Commander Rowan continued to complain during the summer of 1861 that many more supplies were being brought into St. Mary's County than could be possibly used and obviously they were being transported to Virginia. He stated that Benjamin Gwinn Harris of Ellenborough and Mr. Key of Tudor Hall in Leonardtown were two of the most prominent rebel sympathizers in the Bretton Bay area, and that they together with a Mr. Blackwell of Virginia had threatened the Blackistone (St. Clement's) Island Lighthouse keeper, Jerome McWilliams with violence, unless he put the light out.

He captured the schooner, Somerset, in Bretton Bay and burned her as he was sure she was being employed in carrying provisions and men to Virginia. In addition, he reported that Mr. Edwin Coad, his father, Colonel William Coad, and Captain Samuel Trader were shipping supplies to the Confederates out of St. Mary's River. Other Southern sympathizers mentioned in the reports included Randolph Walton of Leonardtown and Thomas and Joseph Maddox of St. Inigoes, all described as couriers for the Confederates.

The schooner, Remittance, of Port Tobacco was captured off Aquia Creek on August 30, 1861, and impounded at the Washington Navy Yard on suspicion of transporting contraband from Baltimore. Her owner, James H. M. Burroughs, his brother, Thomas F. Burroughs, who was mate, and his passengers, Alexander Johnson, Edward Sanders, Charles A. Yates, and a Mr. Lancaster, all of Port Tobacco were detained. They claimed they were owners of the cargo of tobacco found on board and were going to Baltimore to sell it. They probably won acquittal as no contraband was found after a diligent search. There is no doubt, however, that the government informant had been accurate, in his report, because it was well known that the Burroughs brothers were blockade runners.

An interesting report dated September 4, 1861, stated John Dent of Pope's Creek in Maryland had brought a large sailboat, the Lizzie Dodge, into the Wicomico River and hauled her four miles overland to Pope's Creek and conveyed passengers and goods to Mathias Point, thus breaching the blockade. George Dent who resided on the high bluff opposite Mathias Point was accused of signaling all the movements of the Potomac Flotilla to the Confederates and had three of his boats seized. Other residents of the Port Tobacco area mentioned as dedicated to the Southern cause were George Brent, J. H. Neil, John Ware, and Francis Delehay, who had been conveying men and provisions to Virginia. Walter and Heb Mitchell had crossed the Potomac and joined the Confederates. John Johnson, William and Alexander Campbell, Frank Clements, and Alfred Naley burned the light-boat at Cedar Point. Apparently none of these men were arrested due to lack of evidence to prove their guilt.

A negro informant reported on December 11, 1861, the names of a group of Leonardtown men who were transporting men and supplies from Bretton Bay and Piney Point to the Machodoc River. Those mentioned were Mr. T. W. Gough, Mr. Mattingly, John Blackiston, Jr., N. Ford, Mr. Fenwick, Mr. Dills, George Simms and his brother, and Mr. Moore. A report dated August 13, 1862, stated that Mr. C. C. Spalding of Chaptico was the principal furnisher of supplies to the Confederates in that area. The report went on to state that while the traffic extended generally from St. Mary's River to Swan Point, the principal depots appeared to be Leonardtown and the Wicomico River. The principal Virginia landings were Nomini Bay, Pope's Creek, Mattox, Rosier's and the Upper Machodoc. Among those mentioned as being engaged in this illicit traffic were a Mr. Raley, a Mr. Lucas, and Mr. F. J. Allston of St. Mary's County. Mr. Allston was captured with a canoe load of goods while trying to cross the Potomac on October 20, 1862. However, this traffic was not engaged in solely by white people as there are several mentions of the capture of negroes, presumably free, who were engaged in the contraband trade, and on December 1, 1862, several were captured, together with their goods, at the mouth of White's Neck Creek. It is possible that some of these negroes could have been loyal slaves, acting for their masters, attempting to get supplies across the river.

On September 6, 1862, it was reported that Mr. Richard Colton (whose son was in Virginia) was planning to make a trip to Baltimore for the purchase of arms to send to Virginia. Mr. Colton had lately been appointed as an enrolling officer in St. Mary's County by the Federals but had declined to serve.

About the middle of September, 1862, the fortifications at Mathias Point were abandoned by the Confederates and the Federals were engaged for several weeks in destroying the fortifications of this and the smaller batteries along the river. On October 8th the job was reported as completed and from then on until the end of the war the Potomac Flotilla was able to give its full attention to the blockade of the Potomac. They succeeded in bottling up the river tightly, and with the capture or destruction of most of the larger boats the traffic across the river dwindled to a trickle, carried mainly in rowboats or small bay canoes that could be hidden easily. On October 5, 1862, the Federals rented Bushwood Wharf at the mouth of the Wicomico from E. P. Plowden for $140 per month for a midpoint landing and supply depot.

In the latter years of the war, and particularly after the camp for Confederate prisoners was established at Point Lookout in July, 1863, the Potomac River Flotilla was based in the St. Mary's River, extolled by Father Andrew White at the time of the settlement of Maryland, as an excellent harbor. The landing at Cornwaley's Cross Manor was utilized as a coaling depot. Many years prior to this, in 1820, serious consideration had been given to establishing a naval base here but St. Mary's lost out to Norfolk when the final decision was made.

One of the tragedies of the war occurred here on Friday, November 11, 1864, when the U.S.S. Tulip, a converted lighthouse tender was lost. This ship was one of the flotilla based in the St. Mary's. One of her boilers had been condemned as unsafe and unfit for use and she was ordered to Washington for a new one. Her Captain, Acting Master William H. Smith, because he felt that her slow speed with only one boiler would make the Tulip easy prey to the Confederates, decided, against orders, to use the defective boiler. After the ship had passed out of the St. Mary's, some time after 3:00 P.M., she crossed the Potomac to Ragged Point and was headed up the river. About 6:00 P.M., the Captain ordered steam up in the defective boiler. All of the officers were apprehensive and the paymaster was so unstrung that he left the messroom and went to the extreme after end of the deck. When the Tulip's boilers blew up shortly after, he was blown into the water and was one of only eight survivors in the crew of sixty-nine. At this time Captain Smith, James Jackson, the pilot, Master's Mate Hammond, and the Quarter-Master were on the bridge over the boilers, and must have been blown to bits. The only trace of Captain Smith was his hat. Among the sixty-nine officers and men, other than those previously mentioned, were Ensign Wagstaff; Acting Master's Mates Davis, Reynolds, Roffenburg, and Simons; Engineers Parks, Gordon, and Teel.

The explosion ripped off the upper deck of the vessel, scalding the officers and crew and threw them in all directions. Several of those who escaped serious injury ran immediately to lower the gig, but before they could get it down the Tulip sank, carrying down with her most of those on board. Some of the survivors seized whatever they could lay their hands on and succeeded in keeping afloat for more than an hour, until they were rescued by the tug boat, Hudson. Captain James Allen and Engineer R. Granger picked up ten men which included Ensign Wagstaff, the Executive Officer and Master's Mate Davis (the only two who escaped uninjured); Master's Mate Reynolds, with a broken leg; Engineer Teel, very badly wounded; and six of the crew. Two of these men died the next day.

Eight men whose remains were among those recovered but could not be identified were buried in a locust grove on the bank of Cross Manor, where a commemorative marker was placed in 1940.

After the terrible battle of Gettysburg in July, 1863, the Federal Government converted the Hammond General Hospital which had been established at Point Lookout in August, 1862, to a prisoner of war depot. By December, 1863, there were over 9,000 Confederate prisoners at the Point and this number eventually grew to over 20,000 men, exclusive of the guards and troops stationed there. These men were crowded into tents on twenty-three acres of a sandy spit that was about two feet above sea level, where they froze to death in winter, sweltered during the summer months, and starved the year round. Drainage from the camp which seeped into the surface wells in use caused much sickness.

Typical of the conditions at the camp is the report of one of several inspections made during the two year period of its use. This inspection was made in November, 1863, by W. F. Swalm who sent his report to Dr. J. H. Douglas of the Sanitary Commission. He reported that the prisoners' hospital consisted of eighteen hospital tents and contained about one hundred of the less ill prisoners; these men were furnished with mattresses and at least one blanket a piece; (prisoners deliberately maimed themselves to get hospital accommodations); men detailed to look after the prisoners were negligent and the sick were in a filthy condition; (among the sick were two shot and wounded while trying to escape and two others had been killed); there were no stoves and the sick complained greatly of the cold; chronic diarrhea was the most prevalent disease and the seriously ill who were moved to the Hammond Hospital averaged between twenty and thirty daily; the number of patients in the hospital was 1,277, of which 493 were Union and 784 Rebels; the smallpox hospital was located about one quarter mile north of the camp in the pine bushes; nine Sisters of Charity were in charge of the "half-diet" kitchen and the store rooms; the prisoners' dispensary was extremely poor, but their hospital rations were good; he felt that the Federal doctor in charge was very slack.

He reported that the camp grounds and quarters were in filthy condition; the prisoners in general were ragged, dirty, and thinly clad, destitute of nearly everything; they had good tents and most had a fireplace and chimney built of brick, made by them from the soil and sun baked, but generally the tents were filled with smoke; the prisoners secured their own firewood but it was never enough; they were poorly supplied with blankets, generally one blanket to three men, and must have suffered severely from the cold; the prisoners complained that they didn't get enough to eat and not more than half of their meat ration; the kitchen and dining halls were six wooden buildings 160' by 30' located in the "bull pen"; the most prevalent diseases were scurvy, diarrhea, and itch; the camp was surrounded by a board fence twelve feet high with a platform on the outside for sentinels; Swalm blamed the camp authorities for the bad conditions and recommended that medicine and clothing be provided and conditions generally be improved.

Colonel W. Hoffman, Commissary General of Prisoners, wrote Brigadier General Gilman Marston, in command at Point Lookout on November 27, 1863, regarding the Swalm report, who replied on December 4th with a sweeping denial of the conditions cited in the report and ended his letter as follows: "That they (the prisoners) are a dirty, lousy set is true enough, but having afforded them every facility for cleanliness the duty of Government in this regard as respects the well men is accomplished." An unsuccessful attempt was made to suppress the report, but word got out and another inspection on December 17th showed some slight improvements, but generally conditions continued to be very bad.

The people of the Southern Maryland counties offered to aid the prisoners with food and clothing but were not permitted to do so. Hoffman's instructions to Marston were to not permit anyone to send food; members of a prisoner's immediate family were permitted to send clothing, but no luxuries and "no gifts whatsoever were to be permitted to be given by Southern sympathizers for the general benefit of the prisoners."

During the two year period that the prisoners camp was operated at Point Lookout the official government report recorded the deaths of 3,384 Confederates. Many St. Mary's Countians believe the figure was considerably higher. There is no need to fictionalize the story of the Point Lookout prison camp as has been done in the case of Andersonville, for the full record may be seen at the United States National Archives in Washington.

The monuments erected to the memory of the Confederate dead at Scotland, near the Point, provide a lasting reminder of the inhumanity of war, for many of these prisoners died from lack of sufficient food, clothing, shelter, and medical attention the Federal Government could have provided. Some writers have stated that this was in retaliation for the lack of food and medical attention to Federals imprisoned by the South, which was too destitute to provide them. The writer has found little to substantiate such a statement. It does not appear that the result was planned, nor was it a policy of the United States Government. It was rather a matter of negligence, lack of enforcement of Government orders and regulations, lack of interest or compassion by the higher officials in charge, profiteering and much brutality on the part of the colored guard, including several murders, all of which actions were condoned, if not approved, by their white officers.

During the war the Federal forces made a number of raids across the Potomac in the Northern Neck of Virginia. The Bulletin of the Northumberland Historical Society (Vol. II, No. 1) states that early in the war protection of the Northern Neck was the responsibility of the 37th Militia Regiment, but with the transfer to other units of practically every able-bodied man between the ages of 18 and 45 years after the spring of 1862, the Regiment was disbanded and the area for awhile was without defenders. This, of course, served but to entice the enemy to prey upon the countryside at will, and this it did. (Probably, the Federals were kept informed of the situation by slaves who escaped across the river.) A raid was made on Heathsville, in Northumberland County on February 13-14, 1863, and is reported by the Federal officer in charge of the expedition as follows: "Steamed down the Potomac River to Coan River, where we arrived at 10 A.M. on the 13th, disembarked and marched rapidly to Heathsville, arresting and detaining as prisoners all citizens living on the line of march, to prevent information of our approach reaching the place. The town was completely surprised. From all the information I could gain, I am convinced there is no depot of supplies in that neighborhood; none were found. I seized all mail-matter found in the place, which is herewith transmitted. I seized 43 horses and mules, 28 of which I sent under charge of officer and 27 men, by land, instructing him to seize any stock he could on the way. He will probably reach our lines today. Fifteen horses and mules I shipped on board the steamer. I seized 10,000 pounds of bacon, 1 box of shoes, 1 bale of cotton, 1 cable chain, 1 wagon, 2 sets harness. Having no transportation for any more property, I embarked my command and steamed to Nomini Bay. The property I will turn over to the quartermaster. Forage can be had in large quantities in the neighborhood of Heathsville, if gathered in from the plantations round about."

The Bulletin goes on to state that after General Judson Kilpatrick's raid through the Northern Neck in May and June 1863, Northumberland County began the organization of a Home Guard composed of boys too young for active service in the regular army, veterans discharged from the services by reason of wounds or disease, and men too old for active service. In addition soldiers home on furlough or sick leave quickly joined the ranks when an emergency occurred.

In the year 1864, at least four separate expeditions were organized at Point Lookout, which aided by units of the Potomac Flotilla, invaded the Northern Neck. The first of these expeditions was led by Brigadier General Gillman Marston, Commander of the St. Mary's District, Maryland, which included the prison camp at Point Lookout, who landed at Kinsale on January 12, 1864 with about 200 men. They wandered through the Neck for a couple of days but did very little damage. General E. W. Hinks then in command at Point Lookout reported on April 15, 1864, that he had led an expedition of 300 men of the 36th U. S. Colored Infantry under Colonel A. G. Draper, and 50 cavalrymen under Lieutenant Mix, across the Potomac to Lower

Machodoc River in search of contraband goods and to break up blockading establishments. They crossed over on the steamer, Long Branch, with three naval gun boats. In the vicinity of Nomini, they seized $40,000 worth of fine tobacco owned by Joseph H. Maddox, whom they arrested and brought back with them. ".....a couple of buildings from which our troops were fired upon by the enemy were burned." They also brought back fifty "contrabands" (negro slaves).

Between May 11 and 14, 1864, Colonel Draper led an expedition to the Rappahannock River to attempt to destroy torpedoes that the Confederates were manufacturing. He reported that with the 36th Colored Infantry he landed on the 12th at Mill Creek, where he exploded three torpedoes and raised two others; they marched across the peninsula between the Rappahannock and the Piankatank Rivers and discovered four more torpedoes in the woods; the mill of Henry Barrack was burned, as he was an accomplice of the men who were manufacturing the torpedoes; they ran into a small Confederate detachment and had a brief skirmish, ".....this little affair was conducted wholly by the black men as no officers arrived until the fight was over. The colored soldiers would have killed all the prisoners had they not been restrained by Sergeant Price, who is also colored....."; five Confederates were killed and five captured, and the Federals lost one man who was killed and two were seriously wounded and one slightly; captured thirty-three head of cattle, twenty-two horses and mules, and quite a number of vehicles, which were brought back "for use of our contraband farm on the Patuxent."

Between June 11 and 21, 1864, Draper led an expedition of about 600 men, including 475 of the 36th Colored Infantry and a detachment of the 2nd and 5th Cavalry, to Pope's Creek, Virginia, for the purpose of procuring horses for the Quartermaster Department and farming implements, wagons, etc., for use at the "contraband settlement" on the Patuxent River. After landing he divided the party into two detachments of 300, one group moving on Warsaw and the other on Montross and down to Currioman Bay. Near Union Wharf in the Rappahannock, Draper ran into some Confederates and led a cavalry charge. When they neared the Confederates, his men turned tail and ran so that he narrowly escaped capture. Later there were several skirmishes; they burned the grist mill of Robert M. T. Hunter near Laytons and brought back 375 cattle, 160 horses and mules, about 600 "contrabands," including between 60 and 70 recruits for the army, harness, carts, carriages, etc.; two transport loads in all.

The boys, old men and convalescents of the Confederate Home Guard, under the command of Colonel John M. Brockenbrough, retired from regular service, gave a good account of themselves in the defense of the Northern Neck. A final expedition in October, 1864, under the command of a Colonel Davenport, with a sizeable Federal force, landed on the west side of Coan River and advanced through Lottsburg with the intention apparently of raiding Heathsville. Colonel Brockenbrough had Home Guard Companies from Northumberland, Lancaster, and Richmond Counties entrenched at the end of the road that then went across Fallin's Mill Dam between Lottsburg and Heathsville. With the death of Colonel Davenport at the hands of the elderly lead scout, James K. Hurst, after Davenport had pursued Hurst and emptied his revolver at him, and evidence that the Home Guard was in force to meet them, the Federals retreated to their boats on the Coan. They burned "Piedmont," the home of Colonel Richard A. Claybrook, the home of Captain Dobbins, the home of Thomas Hall, and attempted to burn "Plain View," the home of William R. Claughton, but the fire was extinguished by loyal slaves.

There seems to have been little naval action on the Potomac between the Confederate and Federal forces, since the Confederates had no comparable force to cope with the Potomac Flotilla. Mostly the action took the form of the Home Guard firing upon Federal ships that came into range and retalitory shots with heavier guns on the part of the Federals. Carroll W. Adams, writing in the Bulletin of the Northumberland County Historical Society (Vol. IV, No. 1) records the following incidents:

From the log of the U.S.S. Coeur de Lion:

"June 10 [1863] - at 7:30 p.m. got under way and proceeded to Coan River in search of sloop supposed to have run the Blockade. At 9:30 came to anchor in mouth of Coan River."

"June 11 [1863] - at 4:30 a.m. sent two boats armed and manned up the river in search of the vessel supposed to be in it. At 8:15 cutter returned. At 10 gig returned after firing on two schooners named Sarah Margaret and Odd Fellow, both of the Yeocomico River."

"December 16 [1864] - Cruising up Coan and Yeocomico Rivers. At 6:30 a.m. proceeding up Yeocomico River. At 7:15 anchored in Lodge Creek and sent an armed boat ashore. From 8 a.m. to 12 received on board one suit of schooner sails from William Dawson's house, a notorious blockade runner. At 1:30 p.m. anchored in Coan River. Received reliable information that Col. Claybrook and 800 reserves of Westmoreland County lay along the river banks. At 1:45 opened fire upon them and expended 10 shells from 30 pounder Parrot, 6 shells from 12 pounder rifled howitzer, and 6 shrapnel from 12 pounder light howitzer. Carried breeching of 30 pounder rifle during the skermish. At 4:35 anchored off St. Inigoes."

From the log of the U.S.S. Currituck:

"February 24 [1864] - 9:15 a.m. steamed up the Wicomico [Va.] River, followed by the Jacob Bell. At 11:00 a.m. anchored near head of the Wicomico. At 11:30 sent the gig in charge of Acting Master Hall and Acting Ensign Walker, of the Jacob Bell, further up the river to destroy some schooners; set two on fire, the Gratitude and Charles Henry. At 12:30 ;.m. sent second cutter in charge of Ensign Felix, on shore for wood; saw some Rebel cavalry. At 1:30 the boat returned; fired two shots at some cavalry seen on a hill."
"September 17 [1864] - Cruising off Coan River, at 2:30 a.m. heard a volley of musketry in the direction of the Coan River and soon discovered the signals agreed upon of danger for the cutter. Proceeded to the mouth of the river and entered; fired the 20 pounder rifle. Soon after saw the first cutter coming out with a canoe in tow. She came alongside, and Acting Ensign Thomas Nelson came on board and reported 1 man killed, 1 wounded and 2 prisoners captured in the act of running the blocade in the canoe above mentioned. At 3:20 shelled the woods; at 4 ceased firing."

From the log of the U.S.S. Dragon:

"November 18 [1864] At 1:00 p.m. passed into Dividing Creek. At 1:30 opened fire on some Cavalry. Expended nine 10 second shells, three 15 second shells, and two percussion shells from 30 pounder Parrot. From 4 to 8 p.m. still shelling the woods at Dividing Creek."
"On July 24, 1864, the Northumberland Home Guard fired and destroyed the Federal 200 ton sidewheel steamer, Kensington, which had run aground off the Dameron Marshes. The Federal sailors escaped in lifeboats. On October 8 another naval vessel, Picket Boat #2 was burned when she grounded in the Wicomico [Va.] and was left high and dry at low tide. Her captured crew and all ordinance were sent to Richmond."
"The final naval action in Northumberland County took place in February, 1865. The steamer Knickerbocker, ran aground earlier that month on Gobb's Bar and the U.S.S. Mercury had been ordered to stand by and protect her. Several times the Confederates had tried to board her and set her on fire but were driven off by the guns of the Mercury. Finally on February 15 they succeeded in boarding the Knickerbocker under the cover of a heavy fog and setting her afire so thoroughly that when discovered by the Federals it was too late to save her. The Mercury retaliated by sending several shells into the area ashore." Undoubtedly, there were many other similar actions in the myriad of waterways along the Virginia shores of the Potomac.
It is interesting to note that in the raid of May 11-14, 1864, led by Colonel Alonzo G. Draper, the chief purpose of the expedition was to destroy torpedoes that were being manufactured by the Confederates of the Northern Neck. Information concerning the location of these torpedo plants undoubtedly was given by escaped slaves.
The use of torpedoes by the Confederates was first detected by the Federals near Aquia Creek on July 7, 1861. They were designed to drift down on a ship at anchor, become entangled in the anchor rope and eventually explode through a slow burning fuse. As the war went on many improvements were made in the device.
Stephen R. Mallory, Secretary of the Confederate Navy Department, realized from the outbreak of the war, that he could never match the Navy of the North, that they must do very much with very little and that innovations and new approaches must be developed if the Southern Navy was to be effective. The development of the torpedo was one of the great "firsts." In the beginning the torpedo was attached to the enemy ship while at anchor by swimmers but toward the end of the war the South had developed and successfully used the first submarine in naval warfare. The torpedo also was developed for land use or, in more modern terms, the land mine was developed, although there were many scruples among the Confederate leaders in regard to its use. General James Longstreet "did not recognize it as a proper or effective method of war." In addition to the torpedo and the submarine, the third in the trio of great firsts was the creation of the first ironclad vessel of war, the Merrimac (Virginia) and her sister ships, which revolutionized naval science. George F. Moore of St. Mary's County, a pilot, was killed in 1864, when the steamboat he was piloting on the James River was blown up by a torpedo.
After the battle of the Merrimac and the Monitor, members of President Lincoln's Cabinet were in a panic for two months until the Confederates destroyed the Merrimac, because the Federal Government feared that the Confederates would bring the Merrimac up the Potomac to attack Washington, and gave serious consideration to blocking the channel at the Kettle Bottom Shoals. Secretary of War, Edwin Stanton, went so far

as to order the Navy to sink ships at the Shoals to block the channel but Secretary Welles of the Navy countermanded the order. On May 11, 1862, the Confederates sunk the "iron diadem of the South" in the Elizabeth River to prevent capture by the Union forces in Norfolk. The Federals later lost the Monitor when she foundered off Cape Hatteras while being towed south.

After the establishment of the prison camp at Point Lookout, the people of St. Mary's County gave all aid within their power to get the Confederates who escaped this "burning-freezing sandy hell spot" across the Potomac to safety on the Virginia mainland. A number of rendezvous spots were established and one of them was "River View" on St. Clement's Bay. The men were hidden in the once roof-high boxwood until a crossing could be arranged.

On May 19, 1864, the Confederates raided Blackistone (St. Clement's) Island with the intent of destroying the lighthouse. There was some variance in the stories of Captain John M. Goldsmith who led the raid and Commander Foxall A. Parker of the U.S.S. King Philip. Commander Parker, of course, minimized the damage done and perhaps Captain Goldsmith maximized a bit. In any event, Goldsmith, who was a St. Mary's Countian, and who had once owned the island, and whose home, Enfield, was located nearby on St. Patrick's Creek, had crossed the Potomac and joined the Confederate service, as mentioned previously. On the fateful night, in a thirty foot sailboat, The Swan, Goldsmith slipped past a Federal gunboat anchored near and landed on the island, destroyed the lens and the lamp and made off with the oil and light tender. It had been his intention to dynamite the lighthouse, but the keeper's wife, Mrs. Jerome McWilliams, was expecting a baby and her time was near. Jerome, who knew Goldsmith well, having been a neighbor for many years, pleaded his wife's condition and that her life would be endangered if moved, so Goldsmith gallantly abandoned that part of his plan.

A story is told that Goldsmith proposed to take McWilliams away as a prisoner of war but was frustrated by Mrs. McWilliams, who insisted that he take her, too. The story goes on to relate that after the Confederates had left the island, Mrs. McWilliams heroically signaled the Federal forces at Point Lookout and repaired the light before the Union force arrived or the Confederates had reached the Virginia shore. One can be more than somewhat skeptical about the whole story for a number of reasons. Where was Jerome during all these heroics? Why didn't she signal the Federal gunboat anchored near the island? What was she doing flying around and climbing the steep stairs of the tower in her delicate condition? And finally, although there were a few white Union sympathizers in St. Mary's County, during the war, it is doubtful if one of them was a McWilliams, male, female, or in-law.

Near the end of the war, when the South was in desperate straits and there were almost as many Confederates imprisoned at Point Lookout as there were effective men in General Lee's army, the General conceived a plan to free the prisoners. At first he planned to send General Bradley T. Johnson, a Marylander from Frederick, and his Maryland volunteers across the Potomac in boats to attempt the delivery but was prevented by the movements of Generals Kilpatrick and Sheridan.

As soon as there appeared any possibility of accomplishing this undertaking, he reactivated the plan with some changes, and on July 3, 1864, he sent a confidential dispatch to President Jefferson Davis stating: "....An effort will be made to release [the prisoners] about the 12 Inst....." General Jubal A. Early received his orders by special courier on July 6th, directing him to march on Washington. Early slashed his way through the Shenandoah, crossed the Potomac at Shepherdstown and moved on toward the Capital. On July 8th he ordered General Bradley Johnson to move around to the north of Baltimore, burn the bridges leading North and cut all communications; then circle around to cut communication between Baltimore and Washington; then move on to Point Lookout and attack at daylight on July 12th, when an attack would be made from the water side by Captain John Taylor Wood, who would run up from Wilmington with a naval force and arms for the prisoners. When the prisoners, some 15,000, were released, Johnson was to assume command and march them to Bladensburg, where Early would wait for them, when Washington would be carried, communication established across the Potomac, and General Grant would be forced to release Richmond and return to recover Washington. It was General Lee's hope that Early's movements around Washington would call the Potomac Flotilla to Washington, thus giving Captain Wood's small naval force a chance.

Many things went wrong with the plan. Early moved slowly and cautiously on Washington and engaged in a skirmish at Fort Stevens trying to feel out the strength of the defenders. Had he known that at the time of his arrival, the Fort was defended by only a small force of hospital convalescents, clerks from the War Department, and teamsters and laborers from the quartermaster corp, he could have taken the city easily. In the meantime reinforcements were pouring into the city. General Johnson completed his circuit successfully, after three days and three nights in the saddle, ran into a thousand Federal cavalry and drove them into Bladensburg where he cut the railroad. He then started for Point Lookout, a distance of eighty miles, with seventeen hours in which to make it. When his column had gotten about fifteen miles south, a courier from Early arrived and informed him that the expedition would have to be abandoned because the Federals had learned of the plan, Washington was strongly reinforced and the naval force had not been able to start from Wilmington because of a delay in securing arms for the prisoners. Johnson turned back, rejoined Early and on July 13 they recrossed the Potomac at White's Ford into Loudoun County.

One of the last Confederate naval actions involving the Potomac River Flotilla is contained in the following dispatch to Commander Foxall A. Parker:

"U.S.S. Galena
Delaware Breakwater, April 4, 1865

"Sir: I arrived here yesterday afternoon, and this morning the inspector of customs, Lewistown (Lewes), Del., informed me that the schooner, St. Mary's, of St. Mary's Md., was captured in Chesapeake Bay near Patuxent River, on the 31st ultimo, by a yawl containing twenty armed rebels, commanded by Lieutenants Braine and Murdock. The captured schooner, the St. Mary's, got to sea that night or next morning and captured another schooner, the J. B. Spafford, bound to New York, and last from Wicomico. The crew and two passengers of the St. Mary's were put on board of the J. B. Spafford (having been released). She arrived here yesterday afternoon. At the time of her capture she was off Hog Island. The St. Mary's was last seen by the released crew heading to the south, with the wind from the northward, on the night of the 1st instant, and they report that there was a light in a south-easterly direction, which they supposed was a vessel the rebels had captured and set fire to. The St. Mary's is a Baltimore-built schooner of 115 tons, and had an assorted cargo valued at $20,000. Braine, the rebel commander of the piratical yawl, informed the master of the schooner Spafford that he was going to St. Marks, Fla. The crews of the St. Mary's and Spafford were generally robbed of their personal effects. The rebel party took the St. Mary's by surprise, reporting that they were in a sinking condition, when they came alongside. I shall proceed to sea today.

Respectfully, your obedient servant,

C. H. Wells
Lieutenant-Commander"

President Abraham Lincoln traveled the length of the Potomac three times during the war. His last trip was made in the spring of 1865 when he left Washington on the steamboat, River Queen, to join General U. S. Grant on the James below Richmond just before it was captured. As the President passed Pope's Creek on the Maryland shore he also passed a boat hidden near its mouth that would carry his assassinator, John Wilkes Booth, across the Potomac to his rendezvous with death in Virginia. Accompanied by David E. Herold, a youth of Port Tobacco, who was to guide him to the hidden boat, Booth was forced to stop at the home of Dr. Samuel A. Mudd, near Bryantown to have him set his broken leg. Herold led him to the woods on the Cox farm near the head of Pope's Creek, Maryland, where Thomas A. Jones hid them for six days and nights, despite the knowledge that by turning them in he, a poor farmer who had held steadfast to the South, would receive a fortune. On a moonless night Jones led Booth and Herold to his hidden rowboat in Pope's Creek and directed them to Upper Machodoc Creek across the river. Herold was unable to stem the heavy tidal current and the boat was swept back to the east shore of Nanjemoy Creek, Maryland, where they were forced to hide until the following night when they made a successful crossing. Virginia sympathizers took them to Dr. Richard Stuart at Cedar Grove but as his reception was not cordial Booth pressed on south across the Rappahannock to the home of Richard H. Garrett in whose barn he was shot to death by a Federal soldier. Herold, Mrs. Mary Surratt, and others convicted as conspirators by a Military Court, were hung on July 7, 1865, at the old penitentiary on the grounds of the Washington Barracks, which was located on Greenleaf Point on the southern extremity of Washington between the Anacostia River and the harbor.

With the war's end, the rivermen of the Potomac could again pick up their way of life, but time had definitely passed them by. The river front planters on both sides of the river were ruined by the war -- their slaves gone, fields growing up in underbrush, their investments in Confederate bonds worthless, and their plantations mortgaged, they were in no condition to supply large cargoes to be hauled to markets in the river schooners. And the rivermen themselves were in a bad way with their ships and boatyards destroyed, their income cut off during the war years and no funds to build new ships and start anew. It took years to attempt to rebuild the river industry. In the meantime steam driven boats were replacing sail as cargo carriers,

48

and the railroads were taking much of the freight and passenger traffic.
     But the river schooner was to have one final fling on the Potomac before fading
from the scene forever -- the fish and oyster bonanza which lasted for a half-century
following recovery after the end of the war.

SCHOONER, "MATTIE F. DEAN"

Photo: A. Aubrey Bodine
WORK BOAT RACES, PINEY POINT, MARYLAND - 1930
(Courtesy of The Mariners Museum)

LIFE ON THE POTOMAC RIVER

Chapter III

A RIVER FAMILY

It all started when Great-Grandfather John Beitzell left the family farm on the Little Conewago, a few miles outside of York, Pennsylvania, at the age of 21 in 1833. He was the seventh of eight children and was only two years of age at the time his father, Jonathan, died in 1814. This was only two months after the death of his grandfather, also named Jonathan. Within a week after his father's death his uncle, John, died with the result that he and his brothers and sisters inherited two farms located on a high plateau which totaled over 400 acres of good land and in addition, other land and property. The farms were complete with substantial houses, log barns, and even a still. But, without a father to manage the family affairs both farms were liquidated and all had been expended to support the large family by the time John became of age.

Three prior generations of the family had lived on the Little Conewago. John Beitzell, the immigrant, married in 1736 and emigrated from Berleburg in the Rhenish Palatinate, Germany, in the same year. The armies of Louis XIV of France, in the War of the Spanish Succession, had desolated the area and the young couple decided to try their fortunes in America. They arrived at Philadelphia on October 8, 1737, on the English ship, "Charming Nancy," from Rotterdam via Plymouth. Their first son, Jonathan, was born on the high seas on September 16, 1737. If one believed in signs and omens, this should have been the beginning of the seafaring way of life for the family, but if so, it was delayed for three generations, because the immigrant settled in York County and by 1766 had acquired 700 acres of land and a family of sixteen children. All three of the sons including Jonathan, the first born, served in the American Revolution. This was somewhat ironical, since the first John had left Germany in the hope of avoiding the wars that had been the scourge of Europe for centuries.

With the passing of the family holdings in Pennsylvania, John with his wife, Sarah, decided to try living in the new federal city of Washington, where their son Josiah was born on August 5, 1834. In a few years the ex-farmer decided to "follow the water" for a livelihood and engaged in "gill netting" and "seining" on the Potomac River along the Washington and Alexandria water fronts. Fish were plentiful in those days and the growing city of Washington provided a ready market. In order to be nearer to the river front, the family moved from 8th and "G" Streets, N. W., to 13½ Street and Maryland Avenue, S. W. Here John made many friends among his new neighbors, including Charles Husemann, Richard Bundick, Ned Weser, and George Cumberland. All engaged in gill netting, seining, boat building, duck shooting, and other river activities.

Mr. Cumberland became a boat builder of renown and later had his boat-yard at Georgetown. Ned Weser opened his famous oyster house at 12th and "E" Streets, N. W., now the site of the Harrington Hotel. Here he introduced and served steamed oysters to the famous people of his day. The Evening Star of February 21, 1907, contained a long article reporting his death and said in part: "For many years Mr. Weser had been engaged in the fish and oyster business in the District and was intimately associated with the old river Captains and Potomac fishermen. He was manifestly a self-made man, and began his career hereabouts by working on the fishing shores as· a seine hauler. He was much interested in his later years in oyster propagation. He feared the natural supply of bivalves might become exhausted in time.....he was the only oyster dealer in the District to own some private oyster beds, being the proprietor of a farm in St. Mary's County, Maryland, which had a water front of one and one quarter miles."

Mr. Husemann was a man of many accomplishments. He was a locksmith, gunsmith, and blacksmith. In addition he was a carpenter, building many gilling and gunning skiffs, and also a sail maker. He was a talented musician, had his own band, and played many seasons at Colonial Beach on the Potomac, a famed resort in those days. Mr. Husemann also was a duck hunter of renown and one of his standing contracts was to deliver several pairs of canvasback ducks to President James Buchanan at the White House every Saturday morning during the duck season.

This group of early South Washingtonians broke up after the Civil War and all except Mr. Cumberland left Washington. The war changed many things and by this time those who wished to "follow the water" for a livelihood found it necessary to go lower on the Potomac. Captain Beitzell and Mr. Bundick located at Coan River, Virginia. A landing on the Coan still carries Mr. Bundick's name. Mr. Husemann settled on St. Patrick's Creek, in St. Mary's County, Maryland, and bought land adjoining Ned Weser (who owned the old Goldsmith farm, Enfield).

Young Josiah Beitzell grew up on the Potomac, assisting his father from boy-hood in the gill netting and seine hauling operations. By the time of the outbreak of the Civil War, he had acquired two pungy boats and a schooner which were used in hauling oysters, fish, wheat, corn, lumber, cordwood, and other freight between the Chesapeake Bay and the Potomac and Patuxent Rivers to Norfolk, Baltimore, Philadel-phia, and Washington. The war cut off most of this business except when he was able to get an occasional boat through the blockade, but this was risky business. He was able to secure a contract with the military to haul food, arms, and ammunition from Washington to Quantico where there was a military encampment, and this kept him afloat during the war.

Captain Josiah told many tales about his war experiences and his favorite con-cerned the "white mule" bread. Besides the army food-stuff, he also hauled supplies for the Sutlers (Storekeepers) at the camp. No liquor was permitted to be sold in the camp and the soldiers developed a powerful thirst. Among the Sutler supplies there was much bread. The Captain soon noticed that the Sutlers were selling these loaves of bread for 50¢ when bread could be bought for 3¢ in Washington. Still it seemed that about every man in camp had a terrible yearning for bread and more bread, so he performed an autopsy on several of the loaves and found a half pint bottle of whiskey encased in each loaf. It was a simple matter to arrange for supplies and to establish his own agent in camp. By the time the authorities had discovered the source of all the camp hilarity a year later, this operation had netted him a great deal more than the army contracts.

A few years after the move to Coan River, the family moved to the bayside of Virginia and ultimately located at Fleet's Bay near Kilmarnock. Captain Josiah gave several reasons for the move from Washington -- he had been for a time a member of the original Metropolitan Police, at that time called the Auxiliary Guard, of the District and some of the "goings on" he had seen during the war (and it was no better after the war) had convinced him there was too much wickedness in the city to bring up a family decently and his wife, Mary (the sister of Ned Weser), was in hearty agreement. Coupled with this was the fact that they had the heartbreaking experi-ence of losing their first two children in a diptheria epidemic in 1865, which made them anxious to settle in the country. In addition, by settling on the Chesapeake Bay or lower Potomac, he would be near the source of his cargoes and could run as easily to any one of several ports -- Washington, Baltimore, Philadelphia, or Nor-folk. Also with his fleet of boats and $7,500 won in the Louisiana State Lottery, he was in a position to make a move without difficulty.

The family, at the time of the move from Washington, was comprised of the parents, John and Sarah; Josiah and Mary, and their infant son John; and Josiah's sister, Bathsheba Rau, and her little daughter, Mamie. A word might be said con-cerning the names of Josiah and Bathsheba. John and Sarah had wanted children so badly that they had made a solemn vow that if they were so blessed they would be named for biblical characters, and they really hung a couple of dillies on the children.

Bathsheba was not a widow as one might suspect. She had married a "character." Lewis Rau was a charmer, loved by every child and dog in town, and all the girls swooned (or whatever they did in the 1860's) whenever he passed by. Even Captain Josiah was impressed by his new brother-in-law and after a while made him Captain of one of his pungy boats. Shortly thereafter, in 1862, Lewis sailed a cargo to Baltimore, got into a card game and gambled away the cargo. This gone, in an effort to recoup the loss, he forged a certificate of ownership of the boat and gambled it away also. With nothing else tangible to lose he decided to try the fortunes of war. Here he found he had a real talent. In the meantime Captain Josiah was having the devil's own time recovering his boat. The cargo was hopelessly lost. Since Captain Josiah was a man who did not believe in half measures, he made Bathsheba wait for seven years, when Lewis was declared legally dead, and then had her get a divorce after which she was free to marry again.

Lewis was far from being dead. When next heard from, he had survived the war but no one seemed to know which side he had fought on; some were so unkind as to say he had probably fought on both sides. After the war, word drifted back that he was a freebooter down in South America and had been mixed up in half a dozen revolutions. At any rate he made quite a reputation as a mercenary, and his ser-vices to the revolutionary forces of Brazil when they overthrew the rule of the Emperor in 1889 made him a wealthy man. After this he returned to the U.S.A. for a brief period but soon bought a ranch of 3,500 acres in Mexico along the Gulf where he lived until his death.

Although the old South Washington neighbors were now widely separated, the friendships were kept alive by visits back and forth. There was considerable inter-marriage over the years among the Beitzell, Weser, Bundick, Husemann, and Cumberland families.

Captain Josiah, from 1865 to 1884, sailed his vessels from the lower Potomac to Washington, Norfolk, Baltimore, Annapolis, and Philadelphia. His cargoes were largely oysters during the fall and winter months and grain, tobacco, lumber, and cordwood in the summers, but oysters were the real payload. As pointed out by Varley Lang, in his book Follow the Water, these were the days when the oyster was "King" in the Chesapeake and its tributaries and the harvest was averaging around twelve million bushels a year in the 80's.

The Captain loved company and the home was always filled with visiting relatives and friends. During the summer months, particularly, on each trip home his schooner carried not only barrels and boxes of provisions but usually a contingent of friends and relatives from Washington or the lower Potomac. With his wife and parents, seven children, several orphans who were taken in, assorted relatives and friends, and the "hands," the home at Fleet's Bay was always crowded, but there were no dull moments. It was a happy family.

Mary, his wife, was a Roman Catholic and since there was no Catholic church in the vicinity, her home became a "Mass station" which was visited by priests from the Diocese of Richmond. During the years 1872-1875 when the Diocese was under Bishop (later Cardinal) Gibbons, the Bishop made several visits to the Beitzell home and a warm friendship sprang up between him and Captain Josiah, who later became a communicant of the Catholic Church. The friendship continued over the years and there were few trips to Baltimore that the Captain didn't find time to call on the Cardinal. One of his prized possessions was an autographed copy of the Cardinal's famous book, The Faith of Our Fathers.

As the oysters were thinned out in the bay, the "buy boats" began to move further up the tributaries. In 1882, Captain Josiah moved up to the Potomac River, in the St. Clement's (Blackistone) Island area, and bought a part of "Collingwood" (then in possession of Andrew Jackson Cheseldine) on Canoe Neck Creek in St. Clement's Bay. Shortly after the move to Maryland, on a voyage to Baltimore, his schooner, the "Harvester," was hit by an ocean liner off Sharp's Island. The bowsprit was carried away and the stem badly damaged. The collision caused the cargo of railroad ties to shift aft, bringing the bow out of the water, which saved the boat from sinking. The Captain of the liner sent a tug to tow Captain Josiah into port and he received a good settlement for the damages. It was necessary to rebuild the "Harvester" and the work was done at a shipyard in Salisbury. A new stem and bowsprit were installed and the boat lengthened, which necessitated a new stern. When the job was completed, the schooner was re-registered with a new name of the "Rosa Beitzell."

Before the removal from Virginia, Josiah's parents, John and Sarah, had died. In John's old age he relived his life on the upper Potomac in the gill netting days. The bane of his existence in those early days was the fear of being run down during the night by the many ships sailing to and from Washington. Generally the gill netters worked at night in order to get their catch to the market in the morning. Sometimes the nets were staked out in a permanent position, and other times the fisherman resorted to drifting with the tide with the net stretched out between a gill boat on one end and buoys on the other. When the tide and wind swept them out into the channel, they often were in for real trouble. After several close calls when the net was carried away and the boat swamped, the fear of being run down became an obsession with Captain John. On more than one occasion, after a few nips to keep off the cold, John would see a schooner or steamboat that wasn't there and Josiah would hear him holler out in the night, "Look out Joe, the G-d d--n bastard is bearing right down on us." On one particularly cold night, when one may suspect that Captain John had had a few more nips than usual, Josiah heard him bellow out in a voice that could be heard on both sides of the Potomac, "Joe, Joe, look alive there boy -- there's a big square rigger bearing down on us and she's going to carry us straight to hell for sure." Josiah called back, "I don't see any square rigger, Pa." John hollered, "Hell and damnation boy, there she comes. I can even see her mizzens. Pull hard for shore, pull hard....." No one could ever convince Captain John that he didn't really see that square rigger and later on he would always explain it by calling it his "vision." In his declining years, when he would doze in the summer sun on the porch at the home on Fleet's Bay, he would suddenly call out, "Bear off, boy, bear off -- she's headed right for us....." and the children would say, "Grandpa's seeing his vision again."

The rivermen generally used right salty language but they meant no offense to the deity. Most of them were totally unconscious of the use of the forbidden words and looked on them, if they thought about them at all, as figures of speech.

Captain Josiah, like his brother-in-law Ned Weser, also was concerned about the dwindling supply of oysters and as soon as he was established on Canoe Neck Creek started planting oysters along his shores, which were about two miles in length. In those spots not choked with seaweed there are still many oysters to be found today. While the creek oysters are not as salty or as well shaped as those of the

Chesapeake and the Potomac, they grow very fat in the fall of the year and are of an excellent grade.

Captain Josiah died in 1884, two years after the move to Maryland. He had been in failing health at the time of the move but despite this handicap endeavored to carry on to get his family permanently settled. Upon the doctor's advice he tried to get as much rest as possible. As the cabin of his schooner was not very comfortable, he made arrangements to spend as much time ashore as possible along his oyster buying route. One such point was the home of Mrs. Lizzie Lyons at Mill Point near the mouth of the Wicomico. As the oyster boats did not sell their catch until late afternoon, Captain Josiah would come ashore around noon for lunch and Mrs. Lyons made him comfortable in one of her bedrooms for an afternoon nap, after which he would return to the "Rosa Beitzell" to buy and load the day's catch of the oystermen. After obtaining a load he would set sail for Baltimore or Washington. As all oyster buying was a cash transaction the river captains, of necessity, carried large sums of money with them at all times and "Miss Lizzie" was forever cautioning Captain Beitzell to "be careful" lest the sight of so much cash be too great a temptation to her servants.

After the death of their father, the older Beitzell boys displayed a deep sense of responsibility to their widowed mother and the younger children of the family, and even in their teens made their contribution to the support of the family, and continued to turn over their earnings until they reached their majority. Nor did any of them marry until the financial security of the family was assured.

John, the eldest son, at 19 became the head of the family. He had sailed the trade routes with his father from boyhood and due to his experience and excellent seamanship, Captain Josiah permitted him, at the age of 16, to captain one of the family pungies. Upon the death of his father, he took over the operation of the schooner, the "Rosa Beitzell," and continued to sail her until the death of his mother in 1890. At the time of Captain Josiah's death, he owned, in addition to the schooner and pungies, a dory and three nancies. One of the pungies was under the command of his brother-in-law, Captain Sam Brown, of Fleet's Bay, Virginia. The smaller boats were built after the move to Maryland and at first were hired out but later the younger boys of the family worked them. Young Joe worked the dory named the "Scutulus"; Ernest, the nancy called the "Seagull"; Charlie, the "West"; and George, the "Boston Boy."

In 1891, John married Laura Lankford of Kilmarnock, Virginia, and lived at the home place on Canoe Neck Creek for a few years. At this time the family estate was settled under John's administration and he was so scrupulously honest and conscientious in carrying out his duties, he wound up without a boat and little or nothing for his own share. None of the boys having sufficient capital to purchase the schooner or one of the pungies, they were sold. Captain John Palmer of St. Patrick's Creek bought one of the pungies, named the "Dolphin," and rented the "Rosa Beitzell" for a season or two. The schooner later was sold to Thomas C. Eaton, Jr., of Cambridge, Maryland, on July 14, 1893. Subsequently, she was owned by James S. Pope of Baltimore. Joe was able to buy the "Scutulus." The other boys received the nancies they had been working.

While John was at the home place, he built a steamboat wharf at the mouth of the creek, opened a store there and sailed the oyster route to Washington. The ventures were not very successful. After the steamboat dropped the wharf from its route, John moved back to Kilmarnock and later to Washington. In Virginia he engaged in just about every kind of sailing activity on the bay and its tributaries from pungy boat hauling as a "carry-way" for the menhaden fishermen to bay piloting. Captain Willard Lankford of Kilmarnock, brother-in-law of Captain John, recently told the writer that he sailed for some years with John as a young man. He said, "My first trip with Brother Johnnie was on the Bugeye, George B. Faunce, and we were running fish that spring, [1896] from Coan River to Washington. We would be met by a tug boat every day, because we couldn't lose too much time in getting the fish to market or they would spoil. I was with him a lot in running oysters up the Potomac in the fall. We would sometimes go down the bay as far as Smith's Point or the York River. He sailed a lot of boats -- the Fairview, Lady Evans, the Zephyr, the Lizzie Bert -- and we ran grain to Baltimore from St. Mary's County in the Edward Dean. He also was on one of Taylor's tug boats with Ollie Crowther towing ice boats from Cape Henry to Washington."

Captain John qualified as a Bay Pilot and held his Master's license in both sail and steam. He was aided in securing his license by volunteering to pilot the steamboat "Jamestown," a sidewheeler, through the Thimble Shoals in Hampton Roads to a safe harbor during a hurricane in 1907. He was credited with saving the ship and the lives of all aboard. The "Jamestown" was running sightseers from Washington to the Jamestown Exhibition. Her first captain was Bailey Reed. Some years later, John delivered the "Jamestown" to a new owner on the Rio De La Plata Estuary on the South American coast.

In later years and until his death in 1917, Captain John was Master of a number of steamboats on the Bay and the Potomac. As a small boy, the writer remembers greeting him when he would dock the "Dreamland," an excursion steamer from Baltimore, at the great pier at Chesapeake Beach in Calvert County, Maryland, during the period 1913-1916. Uncle John, a kindly man with small boys, was a dazzling figure in his gold braid. Surprisingly enough he could do excellent house-work, including sewing and cooking, and once pieced and quilted a prize-winning quilt. He was also an accomplished dancer and always did some fancy didoes in the square dances, the Virginia Reel and other dances of the times. Captain Lankford said that prior to the "Dreamland," John captained the "St. John's," the "Queen Anne," and the "Jamestown." The Captain tried it ashore once and opened an "oyster house" restaurant in Washington, but he was unhappy ashore and the restaurant was a failure anyway. He just wasn't cut out to be a businessman and his brother, Ernest, once said: "John was a damn good waterman, but a mighty poor businessman. Why if 'Uncle Sam' was to say, 'John, go down to the U. S. Treasury and help your-self,' he'd come out with very little because he'd be picking up dollar bills in-stead of thousand dollar bills."

His brother, Charlie, said one time: "We all agreed that Captain John was the best sailor in the family, but dammit he was too careful and he never did carry enough sail to suit me."

Joe, the next eldest son, and the writer's father, did not get into the trans-portation end of the river business on the Potomac but preferred to operate in the home waters, particularly after his marriage to Mary Elizabeth Norris in 1888. His father thought that pound (trap) nets offered good possibilities as a business for some of the younger boys, and while he knew how to rig the nets, he was away from home so much of the time that he hired a rigger from Washington to come down and teach them the art. Both Joe and Charlie started trap netting while still in their teens, using their father's nets. The nets were lost in the settlement of the estate, but Joe got back in the business later. For many years these nets lined the channel all the way from the lower Potomac to Washington.

In addition to trap netting, Joe worked the dory, "Scutulus," oystering with both dredge and tongs, and turned over his earnings to the family until he was twenty-one. After his marriage he settled on 100 acres of the home place near the mouth of Canoe Neck Creek and continued fishing and oystering, which provided a good livelihood that permitted his large family to live in comfort. He developed a deep love of the river over a period of 92 years, and even in his very old age found some reason to get out on the river almost every day.

Ernest, as was characteristic with him, soon tired of the nancy, "Seagull," and while still in his teens started sailing to Colonial Beach, Virginia, with Ben Owens, who owned a 26 foot dory, the "Volunteer." The beach was a famous watering place at that time, and here during the summer months, they took out sailing parties at fif-teen cents a head. Their venture at the beach was so successful that one suspects that since Virginia was "bone dry" there may have been other attractions aboard the "Volunteer" than sailing the briny deep. Be that as it may, a warm friendship sprang up between Ernest and Ben that continued throughout their lives. Sailing was a popu-lar sport on the river in those days and they soon had plenty of competition at the beach, including 15 year old Charlie Beitzell in his nancy, the "West." One day, upon arrival at Colonial Beach they found much excitement -- one of the hotel guests had disappeared while in a swimming party. Ernest, upon learning where the man had disappeared, dove in and after several attempts located the body and brought it to the surface and with Ben's help got it ashore. But it was too late. The poor man had been submerged for over a half-hour.

Ben Owens, who was born at Mathias Point, Virginia, had shipped out when scarce-ly more than a boy and had been a deep sea sailor prior to his marriage to Lucy Norris, the sister of Elizabeth Beitzell. Uncle Ben followed the water for a living until he was forty years of age (in 1900), when he quit and went to "carpentering" at which he was quite successful. He said at the time, the river was done for, and while a little premature, he accurately predicted the final outcome of the oyster industry. Even so, he couldn't leave the river completely and would occasionally return for the oy-ster season. As a small boy the writer recalls an incident of his last fling on the river -- Uncle Ben was working with his nephew, Clem Beitzell, and the Captain of a certain "buy boat" was so glad to see Cap'n Ben back on the river that he plied him with one drink after another in celebration. Uncle Ben, who was a model of sobriety, just couldn't handle all that liquor and while his head was fairly clear, his legs became rubbery, and he had to be lifted bodily from the boat and carried ashore. By this time it was dark and Clem, who knew he would catch it from Mother for letting Uncle Ben get in this condition, on the "Q-T" enlisted his younger brothers to help him get Uncle Ben home about a mile away. After a whispered conference, Uncle Ben was hoisted into the family buggy and since use of the old horse would be too noisy and it would be time-consuming to hitch him up, the boys acted as old "Dandy." All the way up the road, Uncle Ben said over and·over, "Miss Lucy ain't going to like this -- no sir, she's going to be awful mad, boys." The boys never did find out how mad, because they deposited Uncle Ben on his doorstep and, despite his protests, high-tailed it for home. Although Uncle Ben and Aunt Lucy had a married life of 47 happy years, blessed with 12 children, their formal mode of address to each other was always used -- she was "Miss Lucy" and he was "Mr. Owens."

Soon after the venture at Colonial Beach, Ernest went into another venture with his brother-in-law, Billie Lawrence, who had married his sister, Rosa. They became co-owners of an old pungy, the "Jesse J. Parks," and following the usual Potomac River pattern, bought oysters in season and hauled grain, tobacco, lumber, cordwood, and marl when they couldn't find other freight. The marl, which is a calcareous earth mingled with clay and sand, was dug out of the Nomini Cliffs on the Virginia side of the Potomac, loaded on scows and transported to the pungy where it was taken to Baltimore or Washington to be used as a base for fertilizer. It was mean stuff to handle. Marl was used also as a building material in the early days. The present Grace Episcopal Church at Yorktown, built in 1697, was made of marl slabs taken from the York River shores and the Williamsburg garden walkways are of marl granules.

In a year or two the "Jesse J. Parks" foundered in Canoe Neck Creek, and Ernest then sailed the "Rosa Beitzell" for a season. He did well enough in these ventures to acquire his own "two topmast" schooner, the "Daisy," and while his usual ports were Norfolk, Washington, Baltimore, and Philadelphia, he went as far as Cuba and the West Indies. Billie Lawrence, with his brother, Joe, bought another pungy, the "Edward Dean," which he sailed in the river trade for some years. When the "Parks" foundered on the creek shore, Charlie Beitzell decided to salvage the masts, which were sound. He sawed a section out of the hull and deck and at the risk of life and limb knocked out the chocks at the bottom of the masts which fell cleanly into the creek without damage. His brother and brother-in-law were so pleased at his brashness that they allowed him to keep the money when they were sold to Noble Tibbs. Charlie said recently of his brother: "Ern was a doer and he had plenty of courage. While he wasn't as good a sailor as Captain John, he always got there all right. He would load his schooner to the gunwales, caulk the hatches, get on every piece of sail possible, and with water in his scuppers, take off for port."

Ernest, soon after his marriage in 1898 to Margaret Cumberland, quit the schooner trade, and with a schoolmate, West Russell, of St. Mary's County, started in the fish business in Washington as Commission Merchants. Later he made a fortune in the wholesale liquor business and running the "Crab House" concession at Chesapeake Beach. He also had a heavy investment in the Crandall Theatre chain in Washington. Unfortunately he lost most of his fortune in the early 1920's in an effort to establish a menhaden fishing industry near his old home in Virginia. His company did well for a few years and soon owned a good factory and two fine ships, the "Gloucester" and the "Louise." However, the menhaden disappeared from the Bay and coast for several successive seasons which forced practically all engaged in the industry into bankruptcy. The writer was out on the "Louise" on her maiden voyage in 1920. It was a wonderful trip, with five meals each day, which a boy of fifteen could really appreciate. The "Louise" was a World War I ship that had been remodeled and rebuilt for purse net fishing and was equipped with a modern refrigeration plant, which was a fairly new idea on the Bay at that time. But the maiden voyage of the "Louise" marked the beginning of the end, for in the ten day cruise less than a hundred thousand menhaden were caught, which didn't pay the fuel bill, and the fishing steadily worsened.

After this blow Ernest didn't give up but went back into the seafood business with his old partner, West Russell, and was making a recovery when his death occurred in 1942. As his life-long and devoted friend, Captain Ben Owens said, "When Ern had the sail bent on and a fresh breeze behind him, even Captain Jiggs of the Horse Marines had better give him room to come through, but he knew how to tack when he had to." So he lived and so he died.

Charlie, with the permission of his mother, started shipping out on bay vessels in the summers when only thirteen years of age and in subsequent years got away as far as Bermuda and the coast of Norway, always under sail. At fifteen he started to sail with his brother, John, on the "Rosa Beitzell" but there was friction between the two and the association was short-lived. Charlie admired his elder brother but John was a difficult taskmaster and Charlie resented being treated as a boy. At the first port Charlie "jumped ship" and started to wander. Located after some effort, he was persuaded to return home where he oystered and fished until he was seventeen, when he enlisted in the U. S. Coast Guard. He was stationed at Oregon Inlet and Cape Hatteras, North Carolina, during his four year enlistment and gained a lot of sailing experience during his service. However, all this experience went to naught when he returned home and got involved in a love affair. The affair turned out most unhappily when the young lady jilted him, practically at the altar. Charlie threw the wedding ring out into Canoe Neck Creek, started West, and St. Mary's County saw no more of him for twenty years. The wedding ring lies out there in the Creek in the general vicinity of Grandmother Beitzell's cooking fork and therein lies a story.

Grandfather Josiah, although he was a kindly and generous man and deeply devoted to his family, was also strict and meticulous and on occasion could be a martinet. The writer's mother told him that one time before her marriage, on a visit to the family, a cooking fork was, inadvertently, placed beside Grandfather's plate. Josiah held forth at some length concerning this and gave all present to understand in no uncertain terms that it was not to happen again. Unfortunately, planned or otherwise (Grandma was spirited, too) the cooking fork appeared at his plate at the next meal. Josiah said nothing but with ominous calmness and deliberation he marched, fork in hand, out of the house to the edge of the front yard and threw it with all his might far out in Canoe Neck Creek. Needless to say the proper fork was left at his place thereafter.

Charlie wandered through the West for some years and struck out for the Klondike in 1898. His experiences there could be a book in itself. After the "Gold Rush" days he bought a farm and settled down in the Imperial Valley of California about 1908. He returned East briefly in 1911 to marry a childhood friend, Lelia Cheseldine. Upon her death in 1914 he decided to again locate in St. Mary's County, bought St. Katherine's Island from Freeman Cheseldine, and in 1916 married his sister-in-law, Ida Cheseldine. While primarily a farmer since that time, he has oystered every season to his 87th year, and after enjoying a well-earned retirement for a few years, died on January 7, 1967. His son, George, carries on with both the farm and river activities, clamming and oystering in season.

George, the youngest of the boys, following in his older brothers' footsteps, went into the fishing and oystering business. After disposing of the nancy, "Boston Boy," he owned and sailed a flattie about 40 feet long for awhile, buying and running oysters to Washington. After his marriage in 1899 to Susan Ellis he worked with his brother John in the Oyster House in Washington (which Ernest had financed) for a couple of years. George, who was small and wiry, was the redhead of the family, taking after his Grandmother Sarah. The hair was more golden than red and was inherited by his three daughters. He had the usual temperament to go with his hair and his brothers liked to see George get fired up, which he could do in a moment. He was also a good deal like his father and when Aunt Susie dared to flour his fish before frying them one time, Uncle George was insulted, refused to eat his dinner, put on his hat, and left the house. Before leaving he delivered the following discourse: "Madam, you know I love fish and once or twice in my life I have been full of fish, but never in my life have I had enough fish. Now Madam, as much as I love fish, I will not eat them ruined by that damned goo and I want no more of it in my house." Fortunately, Aunt Susie was able to cook up another batch of fish without the flour and peace was soon restored.

In 1901, George returned to Canoe Neck Creek where he became a combination oysterman and tobacco farmer until his death in 1949.

Both of the girls of the family married rivermen. As previously noted Rosa married Billie Lawrence (in 1886) and they lived on a one-third portion of the home farm. For many summers Billie managed the Crab House for Ernest Beitzell at Chesapeake Beach. George Beitzell also worked at the Crab House during the same period. With the decline in the river business after World War I, the Lawrence family moved to Washington.

Mary, the youngest daughter, married Edwin Gibson in 1896, the son of Captain Jerry Gibson, and of a river family for many prior generations. Mary inherited the old home place with one-third of the farm land. Edwin followed the family tradition and was rated as one of the best sailing masters on the Potomac. With the decline of the oyster industry he got out of the "buy boat" business and fished trap nets, and, of course, oystered in season. As the commercial fishing played out, he turned more and more to farming and became quite successful as a tobacco farmer.

By the time of the fourth generation fishing and oystering on the Potomac was a dying, almost dead, industry, and many of the rivermen recognized it. Only two of the writer's five brothers "followed the water" and one (Captain Walter) quit about 1935 when trap net fishing was no longer profitable unless one wished to risk a sizable amount of capital in a rather uncertain venture in fishing nets in much deeper water. The other, Captain Clem, is a diehard and is still at it. He stopped fishing trap nets about 1940 but continues to oyster every season. In the year 1963, with two men in the boat, the catch was some 8-10 bushels per working day which sold for $5.25 per bushel. Several of the Gibson boys started on the river but all have given it up except Captain Henry, another diehard, who continues to use his dory as his work boat. Two nephews of the writer, Harry and Ross Husemann, of the fifth generation, and a grandnephew, James Downs, of the sixth generation continue to earn most of their livelihood from the Potomac and the Patuxent at the present time. A few, but very few of the kinfolk on the writer's mother's side of the family, mainly the Cheseldines, are still working in the river, so the river now is providing part of the livelihood of five or six members of the family whereas two generations ago most of the 50 male descendents of the immediate family would likely still be "following the water."

POTOMAC RIVER DORY BOATS

Frozen in the Ice in Canoe Neck Creek
Circa 1918

LIFE ON THE POTOMAC RIVER

Chapter IV

BOATS AND NEIGHBORS

    With the coming of the "golden age" of oysters in the Chesapeake and its tribu-
taries during the period 1870-1920, and the use of the dredge for catching them, the
Potomac rivermen realized the need for a boat of better sailing qualities than could
be had from the "nancies" and the "gill boats" which had been in use from colonial days.
The nancy was a flat bottom boat, painted black, ranging in length from 18 to 24 feet
and the width was a little more than one-third of the length. The sides, usually of
single pine boards, were about 2 1/2 feet high, topped by narrow washboards. The stern
was square and undercut at an obtuse angle. The larger boats were ribbed, the keel was
2 X 6 inches and the planking ran lengthwise. They had center-boards and could be
sailed against the wind (see drawing - p. 105). In reality it was an oversized skiff,
which lacked ribs and had crosswise planking. However, it was a poor sailer, would
ship water in a heavy breeze, and was very clumsy to work. The gill boat had been
developed, as the name implies, for the use of the gill netters, and while satisfactory
for that purpose, it was a treacherous sailer and easily upset. Generally, gill boats
were 18 to 20 feet in length with a keel and modeled like a life boat.
    Since larger boats of superior sailing qualities were an immediate need, the local
boat builders around St. Patrick's and White's Neck Creeks designed the Potomac River
dory about 1880 or perhaps a few years earlier. Grandfather Josiah's dory, the "Scutulus," a 27 footer, was rated as being one of the first of this type boat built on the
Potomac. Grandfather moved from Virginia to Maryland in 1882 and the "Scutulus" was
built shortly after the move. She was built by Captain Charlie Husemann and his son,
Zach, of St. Patrick's Creek. Some say that they were the designers of this new model
sail boat, but others say that this honor belongs to Captain Kelly (Kenelm) Cheseldine
of White's Neck. Still others say that "Rome" Thompson and his son, Willie, built the
first dory boat. However, most believe that Captain Kelly was the designer of the dory
and the writer believes this to be correct. In any event, they were a tremendous improvement over the nancy.
    It is understood that Mr. Howard Chappelle, Curator at the Smithsonian Institution,
has obtained detailed measurements and made drawings of the dory, the "Doris C.," owned
by Henry Gibson of Canoe Neck Creek in order to build a model for the Smithsonian collection. This dory is considered one of the finest specimens in the ultimate development of this type of Potomac River boat. She was built by the late John Long, and was
one of three sister dories built about the same time, around 1920. He built the "Seagull" for Captain Edwin Gibson, father of Henry, and the "Resolute" for Alfred, also a
son of Captain Edwin. All of these dories were equipped with sails and were used as
dredge boats in the Potomac. The dory was "dead rise" and something of a small edition
of the Chesapeake Bay bugeye which was developed after the Civil War to dredge oysters.
The sides of the dory were steamed, twisted and curved to form a rounded surface forward with a moderate sloping bottom resembling a wide "V". The stern was undercut,
sloping upward and rounded, somewhat resembling a shield. The boat was reinforced with
ribs from bow to stern, the planking ran lengthwise and was warped both fore and aft.
    The earlier models ranged from 25 to 30 feet in length, though in later years they
were built up to 42 feet long. Generally the width was about one-third of the length.
The boat was equipped with a "center well" and two slightly raked masts, and she was an
excellent sailer, very fast and easy to maneuver. As with the nancy, and the bugeye,
and contrary to the schooner rig, the foresail was larger than the mainsail. Likewise,
of course, the foremast was longer and heavier than the mainmast. In contrast to the
mournful black of the nancies, the dory was painted white, with gay stripes of green,
red, and yellow below her gunwales from bow to stern.
    The oyster bonanza after the Civil War also created a need for "buy boats" in the
Potomac River. These were usually bugeyes, schooners, and pungies and during the
period 1870-1900 shipyards seemed to spring up in every deep water creek from the mouth
of the river to Georgetown. From the incomplete records (see list of Potomac River
Sailing Vessels, Appendix "A") that are extant, Washington, including Georgetown,
appears to have turned out the most vessels, some 50 sloops, schooners, and pungies.
Undoubtedly, a good many of these vessels came from the yards of George Cumberland in
Georgetown. Most of these vessels ranged from 40 to 80 feet in length. Some of the
smaller were used as dredge boats in the Chesapeake Bay.
    During this period, Alexandria produced some 28 vessels. Generally, they were
larger than the Georgetown-Washington boats and with the exception of three sloops,
all were schooners. Two of these schooners were more than 150 feet in length. The
"James Boyce, Jr.," built in 1882 was 156.3 feet in length and the "Wilson and
Hunting" built in 1883 was 152 feet in length. Included on the list are 15 vessels
built at Occoquan and 10 at Hunting Creek, Virginia. The Hunting Creek boats were

POTOMAC RIVER DORY BOATS

The "Scutulus"
Built circa 1882

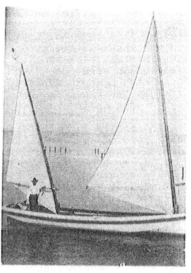

Circa 1890   Capt. Ben Owens - circa 1910

Circa 1918   Circa 1920
The "Doris C" and the "Resolute"   Capt. Ned Russell in his dory,
frozen in the ice on Canoe Neck   "Theresa," in White's Neck Creek.
Creek.

POTOMAC RIVER DORY BOATS
Dory, "Ethel M."
Built for Capt. Theodore Bailey by Capt. Kelly Cheseldine, circa 1900
Aground at Bushwood Wharf

(Courtesy of Robert E. Pogue)

Under Sail   Converted to Power Boat

Duck-tail Dory   Round Stern Dory

Built by John Cheseldine

Capt. Jerry Gibson on aft-deck
and Mr. Lewis K. Mattingly

sloops and small schooners ranging from 35 to 50 feet in length. The boats built at Occoquan, with the exception of two sloops, were schooners ranging from 63 to 82 feet in length. Included with the Occoquan vessels is a 78.8 foot schooner, the "Three Brothers" built on Pohick Creek in 1872. As late as World War I, several three-masted schooners were built at Quantico, Virginia.

Stafford County, Virginia, seems to have produced a single 98 foot schooner, the "Anna M. Estell" in 1883. Westmoreland County, largely in the 1880's produced 10 vessels ranging from 32 to 67 feet in length, including two bugeyes, the "Lola Taylor" of 56 feet built in 1886, and the "Ella Covington," 55 feet, built in 1891 in Currioman Bay. A total of 11 vessels ranging from 30-71 feet in length are credited to Northumberland County including two small bugeyes. They were the "Maguire," 49 feet in length, built in 1892 and the "Mary Priscilla," a 30 foot bugeye built in 1876.

Prince George's County, Maryland, produced two schooners, the "Ada," 50.9 feet in length in 1883, and the "Celeste" of 61.5 feet in 1892. The St. Mary's County boat-yards at St. George's Island, Piney Point, Bretton Bay, St. Patrick's Creek, and White's Neck Creek produced some 26 vessels, all sloops or small schooners ranging from 33 to 50 feet in length. One 74 foot schooner, the "Lewis C. Worrell" was built in Bretton Bay in 1910, probably by Captain Harrison Ewell or Captain Henry Wehrheim. Another schooner, the "Lizzie D. Egerton," 65.5 feet in length was built in 1870, perhaps at St. George's Island.

All of the smaller yards along the lower Potomac were, of course, turning out many dories and other smaller boats and were kept busy with repair work and sail making. While the Potomac River oyster buyers used a good many schooners and pungies in the oyster trade, the Chesapeake Bay bugeye was a great favorite.

Brewington, in his fine work "Chesapeake Bay Bugeyes," states that there were a number of small shipyards at Solomons Island near the mouth of the Patuxent River beginning with the one established by Isaac Solomon in 1859. Builders included James T. Marsh and his son, J. H. Marsh, M. M. (Cell) Davis, J. J. Saunders, R. T. Allinson, and T. Elliott. Schooners and sloops mainly were built until 1879, when Mr. Marsh built what is thought to be the first regularly framed and planked bugeye, the "Carrie." Mr. Marsh is credited with other firsts, namely the "duck-tail" stern on the Alexine in 1880 and the use of wire rigging on the "Hallie K." in 1891. In his list of over 400 bugeyes, Brewington shows that some 49 or over 13% were built at Solomons, mainly by Mr. Marsh and Marcellus M. Davis.

There were a number of railways on the Potomac that were capable of handling the larger sailing vessels but the yards at Solomons Island got a great deal of the building and repair business. Among those on the Potomac was one near the mouth of Bretton Bay, owned by Captain Joseph Ford during the War of 1812. It continues to be operated today through a succession of owners and is the largest on the lower part of the river. Sometime in the 80's Captain Henry Wehrheim became the owner of the yard and operated it until his death in 1936. In the hurricane of 1933, Captain Wehrheim suffered a severe loss when his 65 foot schooner, the "Emma V. Wills," grounded so far inland that it was impossible to refloat her and she had to be dismantled. The yard is now operated by his daughter, Mrs. J. R. Delahay and her two sons, Kenneth and Ronald.

Captain Harrison Ewell had a railway nearby on Coombs Creek when the writer was a small boy and went there with his father. Captain Ewell employed a negro black-smith named Cook who had been in the British Navy. Cook told many fascinating stories to fire a boy's imagination. He was very talented, not only in working iron, but in all phases of boat repairs and it is said that he carved many of the name boards and other wood decorations on the Potomac sailing vessels. An oil painting by Cook, of a schooner under full sail, adorns a living room wall of the writer's sister, Mrs. Alice Beitzell Husemann. This railway passed to the ownership of William Quigley who sold the equipment used in handling the larger boats. A small railway is operated there now by Philip Hurry.

The best known builders of the smaller work boats, and in particular, the dories, in the early days on White's Neck Creek were Kenelm (Kelly) Cheseldine and his sons, John and George. They also built some of the bay type log canoes and a few flatties, sloops, and small schooners. In later years Captain Kelly and his sons built a considerable number of yachts of 40 to 65 feet in length for many prominent Washingtonians, including Judge Wright, Dr. Warren, Charles F. Carr, the jeweler, and Dr. Judd, and a few barges, including the "Mildred D." for Raymond Oliver. Many of the Virginia rivermen bought their boats from the Cheseldines. The Cheseldines owned and sailed two pungies in the river trade, the "Dove" and the "Annie L." Somewhat later, Walter Cheseldine, who learned the trade under his cousin, John Cheseldine, became a boat builder of repute on White's Neck. A son-in-law of Captain Kelly, John Hall, also is well known as a boat builder.

William Thomas (Buddy) Gibson and his brother, Garner Gibson, also learned the trade under John Cheseldine and they started building dories at White's Neck about

1920, some over 40 feet in length. After the death of Buddy, Garner continued in the business and in 1928 he originated the so-called box stern boat which has largely replaced the dory in the last three decades. His brothers, John and Perry, also build boats and they are fine boats. Garner, in describing the design of the box stern boat, said he squared off the bottom about six feet back from the transom and made a square stern. This caused the boat to "plane" and attain high speed, which effect could not be obtained in the dory, even though fins or wings were projected from the stern. The smaller box stern boats are powered with outboard motors and the larger with marine inboards or converted automobile engines. In his 43 years of boat building, and he is still at it, Garner has built some 285 boats, for both commercial and pleasure use. His boats may now be seen in Baltimore, Deale, Crisfield, Washington, Alexandria, and at practically all points along the Maryland and Virginia sides of the Potomac. Garner's largest box stern was a 47 footer, built for Captain Sam Bailey, and George Kennedy recorded in the Sunday Star of Washington on June 24, 1956, that he clocked a 36-footer built by Garner at 42 miles per hour when it passed the camera. James Oliver provides a good outboard motor repair shop and a small boat haul-out service at the mouth of the creek.

Bruce Quade also was a builder on White's Neck Creek, but he built mostly small skipjacks and flatties. Captain Bruce often recalled the days when four-masted schooners hauling ice to Washington would be met by tugs at the Kettle Bottom Shoals in the Potomac and towed to the city, and then towed back to the Shoals. Here the schooners would anchor and wait for a wind from the North or West. He stated that sometimes as many as twenty of these vessels would get under way at approximately the same time. What a picture that must have been!

John Long built many dories and smaller work boats on Canoe Neck Creek over a period of about fifteen years, until he quit boat building about 1927. As many of these builders did, John worked alone and it was amazing to see these artisans bend the side boards on, always making a perfect fit. All of these builders worked without formal plans or half models and were self-taught or learned under another builder. Many of the Long, Cheseldine, and Gibson dories are still in use as powered work boats.

On St. Patrick's Creek, the builders were Captain Charlie Husemann and his sons, Willie and Zach, and Captain "Rome" Thompson and his son, Willie. Captain Willie Thompson built several types of boats and one of his specialties was a round stern dory. The writer recalls three of them around 1912, the "Tory B.," owned by Captain Edwin Gibson, the "William E. Thompson," owned by Captain Tommie Morris and one owned by Mr. Lewis K. Mattingly, who kept store near the head of Canoe Neck Creek. In the present day the builders are Wilmer Palmer and his son, Creighton, and David Lawrence. Wilmer Palmer from boyhood has seemed to have only one interest -- boats -- although his father was a successful farmer on the creek, boats and the sea were in his blood, for his grandfather had been a "deep sea" sailor and other members of the family had been in the river trade. Wilmer, undoubtedly, learned much from Captain Willie Thompson whose yard was across the creek, and much of Wilmer's time was spent there. Captain Willie also supervised the construction of several large wooden ships at the yards in Alexandria and Quantico during World War I.

David Lawrence is completely self-taught and probably hadn't built so much as a chicken coop until his return from the service after World War II. David started in building skiffs, progressed to 20 foot dead rise box sterns, and now is one of the finest boat builders on the river. While some of the boats from the Palmer and Lawrence yards are for commercial use, most are pleasure craft. Mr. Lawrence also built a fine marina at his boat-yard near the mouth of St. Patrick's Creek.

The Kopel brothers, Carl and Robert, have established a marina on St. Patrick's Creek in recent years and it is one of the finest on the river. They also engage in boat building, repair work, and build bulkheads and wharves.

In recent years many marinas and boat-yards have been established along the Potomac. Excellent facilities will be found along the Washington and Alexandria water fronts, and in practically every bay and creek along the Maryland and Virginia shores to the mouth of the river.

St. George's Island has been the scene of a good deal of boat building for well over a century after the Jesuits sold the island in 1851. Many fishermen and oystermen from Tangier Island and others from Virginia settled there.

Among those famous in Potomac River annals for generations will be found the family names of Thompson, Trice, Twilley, Thomas, Chesser, Henderson, Graham, Trader, Crowder, Simpkins, Adams, Poe, Clark, Ball, Rice, and others. Among the boat builders were Richard Ball, Richard L. Thompson, and Thomas Crowder. Pungies, sloops, schooners, log bugeyes, and log canoes were among the types of boats built. In the present day the Deagle boat-yard is producing a combination work or pleasure boat that is gaining favor all along the lower Potomac. An 18 footer powered by a 75 H.P. outboard can do up to 40 miles per hour.

Captain Clarence Biscoe of St. Mary's River is a well known sailing master. Among the vessels he owned and skippered was the pungy, "Julia and Annie." During the period 1921-1926 he owned the "Francis J. Ruth," the second largest pungy on the

POTOMAC RIVER DORY BOATS

Motorized Dories

Oyster Boats

"Rosie B, I"

In Canoe Neck Creek

Box-stern Dories

The "Sylph" and
the "Doris C"

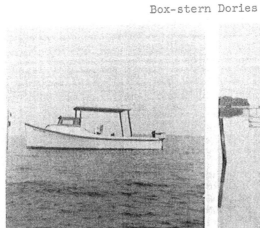

"Jody B"

"Rosie B, II"

POTOMAC RIVER BOAT YARDS AND MARINAS

Combs Creek, Bretton Bay

Ewell Railway, circa 1915

(Courtesy of The Mariners Museum)

Delahay Railway

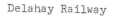

Established Prior to War
of 1812

St. Patrick's Creek

Kopel Brothers Marina

Tim's Marina

Gibson Railway, White's Neck Creek

Hall Railway, Canoe Neck Creek

Chesapeake and a beautiful vessel. In these years of sailing he was accompanied by Mrs. Biscoe. The "Francis J. Ruth" was built in 1871 in Dorchester County and during the early years was used on the Baltimore-West Indies route, hauling sugar, rum, molasses, and pineapples. In later years the "Ruth" was used largely in general freighting on the Chesapeake and Delaware Bays. While loading cargo at Millstone Landing in the Patuxent in 1933, she was anchored too close to shore and was pounded to pieces during an easterly storm. At this time she was owned by shipping interests in Baltimore.

The Foxwell family of Bretton Bay have been famous on the Potomac for generations. In the 1860 census five of the family are listed. Benjamin and Stephen, captains of freight vessels; Van Buren and Benjamin, captains of Bay vessels; and Solomon is listed as a sailing master. Solomon, at one time was owner and master of the famous schooner, "Mattie F. Dean." In the next generation, H. Webster Foxwell was notable not only on the Chesapeake and the Potomac but also was a "deep water" sailing master. His commands included such well known vessels as the "Hester A. Waters," a 92 foot schooner and the "Lizzie J. Cox," one of the great bugeyes. The St. Mary's Beacon recorded in September, 1913, that Captain Webster Foxwell had left for Baltimore and would sail from there to Savannah in his four-masted schooner, the "Salisbury." In the present generation Captain Stephen Foxwell is well known on the river and has only recently retired as a wharf builder.

All of the older heads say that the loss of Zach Husemann, at the age of 21, in January, 1886, was a great blow to the boat building business in the area, because he was a fine artisan with many original ideas. His death was caused by what was described in those days as "cramp colic" from eating oysters that had frozen, thawed, and refrozen. The passing of this very popular young man was made the more melancholy by the fact that his wedding to Miss Nora Morris was imminent at that time.

Even though the dory was found to be a superior boat, people were slow to change and nancies continued to be built for some time. Also, with the use of the gasoline engine for boats, beginning in this area about 1905, the dories were continued in use, although they were poorly adapted to motor operation because of lack of speed, despite the amount of horsepower. They were built to sail and good sailers they were-- perhaps if Zach Husemann had lived he would have come up with a better model for gasoline engines at an earlier date.

The motors in the early days were quite unreliable and slow. Most in use in the dories were 5 or 7½ horsepower and in any kind of breeze a sail boat could run circles around them. This caused a good deal of banter back and forth similar to the exchanges between the early motorists and the horse and buggy men. On a memorable occasion the writer's brother, Charlie, our cousin, John Lawrence, and Uncle Billie Lawrence had a game of tag in a dory under sail and a motorboat all the way from the lower Potomac River to Chesapeake Beach in the Bay. Uncle Ern Beitzell who operated the "Crab House" at Chesapeake Beach bought a motorboat from Wade Blackistone of River Springs and a dory, the "Ella B.," still under sail, from my father, for use at the beach. He engaged Charlie, John, and Uncle Billie to bring the boats up the Bay to the "Crab House." They started out at daybreak, John in the dory and Charlie and Uncle Billie in the motorboat. The breeze was light and John was soon left far behind but then the motor "conked out" and John had to give them a tow -- about the time they got the motor started again, the breeze died and they had to tow John. Then the breeze came on again but the motor failed again. In all the motor failed eight times and John said he almost wore out the hawser, "making fast" and untying again. But Uncle Billie and Charlie had the last word for at Plum Point the breeze died completely and it became "slate" calm, so John had to be towed the rest of the way to the beach. They made the trip in eighteen hours and perhaps proved that the motorboat was here to stay.

With the advent of the dories, the owners were very keen about racing their boats. There was a great deal of rivalry between the White's Neck Creek boats and the Canoe Neck Creekers. The championship shifted quite frequently between Captain Edwin Gibson's dory, the "Louise," and George Cheseldine's boat, the "Mabel," which was built by his father, Captain Kelly. He later sold the "Mabel" to his cousin, Garrett Cheseldine. Willie Thompson built a dory for Lee Norris that was called the "Otis." The "Otis" occasionally beat the Gibson and Cheseldine boats. Papa's dories, the "Scutulus" and the "Defender," frequently tangled with the dories of Captain Tommie Morris, our neighbor across the creek, but none were very fast sailers. The old "Defender" was very broad of beam and was not built for speed but to carry large loads of fish and oysters. My elder brothers claimed that Papa never won but one race in his life, and that was on a July day off Colton's Point when the racers were caught in a terrific wind during a thunderstorm. Everyone else had to "reef down" or drop their foresail, but Papa was able to carry full sail on the "Defender." However, it isn't quite correct to say he won only one race because the St. Mary's Beacon recorded that on July 24, 1886, ".....the boat race [at Blackistone Island]..... was quite exciting. Husemann and Beitzell raked in the change, beating the "Ella May" and others." Captain Joe owned a couple of other dories during these times, the "Ella B.," previously mentioned, bought of Captain Theodore Bostwick of Canoe Neck

Creek, and the "Alice B.," built by Uncle Willie Thompson. The latter dory was hired out to Willie Owens and Frank Norris, his nephews. She was powered by a particularly balky 7½ horsepower Mianus engine and the boys renamed the "Alice B.," the "Buck Maude," after a favorite comic strip character of the time, a balky mule, named Maude, and the name stuck. The "Buck Maude" was sold later down at Solomon's Island.

The 4th of July was, and still is, a great day for boat racing on the lower Potomac. In this area, in the old days, no one "shot off" fireworks on the 4th -- that was done on Christmas Day, beginning at daybreak. Instead there was boat racing, foot races, climb the greasy pole, catch the greasy pig, the consumption of a good deal of liquid refreshment, and generally, a few fist-fights -- all together a highly satisfactory day.

Papa told of an exciting foot race at River Springs one 4th about 1910. Wade Blackistone was our local champion and a natty dresser. Several city boys were prancing around in shorts and running shoes passing uncomplimentary remarks about the country yokels. This nettled Wade, who had not intended to run, so he removed his coat, carefully folded it, handed it to a bystander to hold, and then in a tight vest, patent leather shoes and a high-standing collar, he left the city slickers so far behind they looked silly -- and the country yokels "raked in the change."

During the period from 1880 to well past the turn of the century, many of the rivermen became "buy boat" operators, buying and hauling oysters in season and hauling grain, tobacco, cordwood, lumber, etc., the rest of the year. Their boats ranged from "flatties," 35 to 40 feet in length, sloop rigged, one mast with a sharp mainsail and jib, to sloops, pungies, bugeyes, and large schooners.

Prior to 1880 most of the Potomac rivermen were sailing schooners and pungies, but with the advent of the bugeye many acquired the new type boat, not to dredge as they were commonly used in the bay, but to run oysters, mainly to Baltimore and Washington. They were fast boats and speed was an important consideration in getting oysters to market and in the number of trips that might be made during the comparatively short season.

Among the Canoe Neck Creekers, Captain Edwin Gibson and his father, Captain Jerry, were rated the best sailers on the river. Captain Jerry at one time owned and sailed the "Winnie H. Windsor," a 27 ton, 63 foot, sharp stern, standard rig bugeye, built at Solomons Island in 1884. But some years later, needing a larger boat, he sold her and acquired the "Amanda F. Lewis," a 48 ton pungy. She was painted in the traditional pungy colors -- "pungy pink" from the waterline to the chains, or halfway up the freeboard; from the chains to the gunnels, she was painted watermelon green.

Captain Edwin first sailed the sloop, "Minnie Blanche," but sold her to Captain Ned Hayden and acquired the bugeye, the "Lottie L. Thomas," a fast and beautiful vessel. There was a good deal of friendly rivalry between Captain Edwin and his father. In one of their many races, this time from Washington, in a heavy breeze, Captain Jerry had to clew his topsails, but Captain Edwin, literally throwing caution to the winds, broke out his stasail and raising his flying jib, beat the "old man" home. As soon as Captain Jerry reached the creek, he made a "bee line" for Captain Edwin at anchor and gave him h--l for abusing a good boat.

Captain Edwin liked to travel fast and the "Lottie" was a fine sailer. On one occasion he lost his topmast in a heavy breeze and immediately put into Solomons where he had a heavier topmast installed with a larger sail. He made a remarkable run from St. Clement's Bay to Baltimore, unloaded a cargo of wheat and tobacco and returned home between suns, having a favorable breeze each way. According to Brewington, a second effort to widen the after-deck of bugeyes was made in the design of the "Lottie L. Thomas" by Joseph Brooks who built her at Madison in 1883 for William R. Thomas and Josiah Linthicum, both of Dorchester County. She was named for the daughter of Mr. Thomas. While she was gaff rigged, she was in all other respects a bugeye. She was an easy vessel to handle and Captain Edwin, who was not given to boasting, always said he could lay the "Lottie" alongside a wharf "without cracking an egg," and he could do just that.

The "Lottie" had a life of 61 years and many owners. Captain Edwin Gibson owned her from 1896 to 1907 when he sold her to Captain Matthew R. Bailey. Captain Matt sailed her in the river trade until 1924 when he sold her and the rig was changed to a gasoline screw and the gross tonnage increased to 27 tons by additional inclosures on the deck. She was then placed in service on Fall River, Massachusetts, where she was beached and badly damaged during the 1939 hurricane. By 1944 she was beyond repair and was abandoned on Fall River on March 7th of that year.

Captain Jerry and Captain Edwin not only sailed to Washington, but also the Baltimore, Annapolis, Philadelphia, and Norfolk routes. Due to his years of experience, not only on his own but also sailing with his father, Captain Edwin undoubtedly knew the Potomac River better than anyone of his time. As a young man he got into the habit of laying out compass courses and of timing with his pocket watch distances

POTOMAC RIVER "BUY" BOATS

Bugeye, "Eleanora Russell"

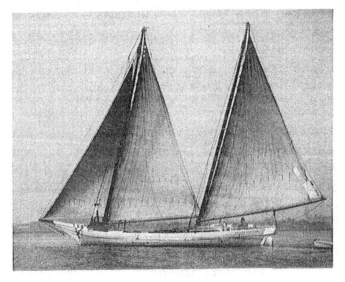

Photo: Percy E. Budlong

Pungy, "Amanda F. Lewis"

Photo: Frank A. Moorshead, Jr.

(Courtesy of The Mariners Museum)

POTOMAC RIVER "BUY" BOATS

Schooner, "Mattie F. Dean"

Photo: A. Aubrey Bodine

WORK BOAT RACES, PINEY POINT, MARYLAND - 1930

between markers and landfalls, taking into consideration the state of the tides and winds, so that sailing at night and in fogs his accuracy seemed almost uncanny. A number of rivermen have told the writer that in later years when many of the oyster boats were working the Upper Cedar Point bar, on foggy mornings, the boats would fall in line behind Captain Edwin and stay there until they would hear his call, "You can drop your anchors, boys" and they would be "smack dab" on the bar. One night when the men around Canoe Neck Creek were relating experiences around the old pot-bellied stove at Lewis Mattingly's general store, Captain Ned Hayden, who also had an extensive knowledge of the river, was bragging a little bit to the effect that he knew every bar and shoal in the river and Captain Edwin cut in good-naturedly to add, "I'm sure you do Captain, because you have run ashore on every one of them in your time" -- to which Captain Ned replied, "By golly, I guess you're right, Captain, but never the same one twice."

Captain Jerry followed the water all his life until retirement in his late 70's. His brother, Captain John Joe Gibson, also sailed the Potomac for a lifetime. His first vessel was named the "Sunny South." She has been described as a square sail bugeye but her record has not been identified. His second command was the sloop, "Fanny Shepherd." During the period May 19, 1887, to April 2, 1889, Captain John Joe owned and sailed the bugeye, "Col. R. Johnson Colton." His fourth command was called the "Wm. H. H. Bixler," a small schooner. His last vessel was the schooner, "J. R. Dixon," of 15 tons, 45 feet in length and built in Somerset County in 1879. She foundered in the Wicomico in 1936. The brothers were very devoted to one another and upon retirement spent a good deal of time together on the river, handline or bottom fishing. Quite frequently, on the way to or from the fishing grounds, they would get into an interesting conversation and because it was difficult to hear with the noisy Victor engine running, they would cut it off and drift for a while. Sometimes this would be repeated several times during a trip. Strangers were forever trying to give them a tow.

The brothers lived near each other on Canoe Neck Creek, and often carried on their conversations by hallooing across the cove that separated them. One winter when their vessels were frozen in the creek, they decided to break a track through the thin ice, using their skiffs. It was hard work and as the sun rose higher Captain Jerry first removed his coat and then his shirt. During a lull in the operation, Captain Jerry hollered out, "It's hot here today, John Joe." Captain John Joe called back, "Yes, sir, it is indeed -- first time I ever saw ice like this on the creek on the 4th of July." Captain Jerry loved to eat oysters and it is no exaggeration to state that winter or summer, day in and day out, he had a "mess" of oysters at least once every day without fail, and sometimes three times.

After Captain Jerry's retirement, the "Amanda F. Lewis" was sold to Captain Gus (G. T.) Rice of Coan River, Virginia. She was, undoubtedly, one of the best known of the many pungies to sail the Chesapeake and its tributaries. According to Robert H. Burgess of the Mariners Museum in Newport News, the "Amanda F. Lewis" was built in 1884 by Joseph W. Brooks at Madison near Cambridge for Captain M. O. Lewis, who named her for his wife. Mr. Burgess describes the pungy as a keel vessel, the only class of Chesapeake Bay commercial sailing craft not carrying a centerboard. They were schooner rigged, two-sail, raking masts, with a main topmast and a minimum of standing rigging. A raking stern and sternpost, deep draft aft, full flaring bows, and a log rail, except aft of the main rigging where an open quarter would be found, were all characteristics of the pungy. It is believed that the pungies were the direct descendents of the famous Baltimore Clippers and the absence of the foretopmast and squaretopsails on the pungy was about the only difference in the rigs of the two.

Captain Gus sailed the "Amanda F. Lewis" for 30 years between Baltimore and the Coan, hauling lumber and grain up the bay and returning with the holds filled with fertilizer for the farmers or empty cans for the Virginia packing houses. In 1939, Captain Gus sold the "Lewis" to Captain William J. Stanford, who had her converted at the Krentz shipyard in the Yeoacomico at Harryhogan, Virginia, for operation in the Bay menhaden fisheries. Her masts and bowsprit were removed and her graceful longhead with its decorative trailboards was cut off. Adorning her transom was a carved decoration displaying the likeness of her namesake, "Amanda F. Lewis," which probably was carved by Hammond Skinner. This was removed, likewise, and presented to the Smithsonian Institution for preservation. Not long after her conversion, the "Lewis" was sold for use in Florida as a shrimp boat out of Miami. On August 10, 1948, the vessel was sold to an alien and placed under Haitian registry and flag.

Captain Fred Tilp, who has skippered the Sea Scouts of the Corinthin Yacht Club for the past 35 years relates the following anecdote: "Old Capt'n Gus Rice was sailing his pungy Amanda F. Lewis up the Bay from Coan, Va. to Baltimore with a cargo of wheat. George, his faithful colored cook, was the only crew member during the more pleasant summer months. The black night was beautiful with a star-lit sky; a following fair wind kept the sails drawing full; so with a steady barometer there was no change expected in the wind or weather. 'George,' directed the aged Capt'n, 'I'm going below for a bit of sleep. You take the wheel and steer straight up the Bay, heading for that bright star up there,' pointing toward the North Star, 'and by morning we should be just off Baltimore Light.' The cook took over the wheel, feeling quite proud of the confidence that the Capt'n had placed in him. After several hours of peaceful sailing the sleeping Capt'n was suddenly awakened by George's shouting down the hatch, 'Cap'n Gus, oh Cap'n Gus, come up here quick and give me another star to steer for -- I done passed that one!'"

Mention has been made of Captains Josiah, Ernest, and George Beitzell, and Billie Lawrence and their vessels of Canoe Neck, and there were several more. Captain Billie Cullison sailed a 68 ton schooner, the "A. H. Quinby," whose name was changed later to the "Mildred" when she was rebuilt. Captain Billie did not engage in the oyster trade but hauled mostly cordwood and railroad ties up through the First World War. His brother-in-law, Captain Frank Russell, sailed a pungy, the "Pianka-tank," and later a two-topmast schooner, the "E. P. Evans," built in 1881 at Pungo-teague, Virginia. Later his sons, Sol, Stuart, and Douglas, sailed the "Evans" and other schooners on the Baltimore, Washington, and Norfolk routes. Captain Douglas, at one time sailed the schooner, the "Ostrich." On a trip to Washington loaded with wheat, the "Ostrich" was hit by a tug and sank. Captain Sol sailed the schooner, "Annie Crosswell," for many years as also the pungy, "Sea Bell." Stuart later had built and sailed the "Elenora Russell," named for his wife, the former Nora Morris. After the death of Stuart, in his thirties, Nora moved to Washington, remarried and moved to Philadelphia. Her old home, at the mouth of Canoe Neck Creek is still called "Nora's Point." The "Elenora Russell," a bugeye, was built at Solomons in 1889 and probably was a Marsh or Davis built boat. Her capacity was 15 tons, and she was 60 feet in length. Stuart sold the "Elenora Russell" in 1893 and acquired the schooner, "Joseph T. Brenan," which he sailed until his death in 1894.

Much has been said, over the years, concerning "Yankee horse traders" but they had nothing on the rivermen. It is amazing, when one looks at the records, how often the tidewater sailing vessels changed hands. The "Elenora Russell" will serve as an example. Captain Richard W. Chesser of St. George's Island bought her from Stuart Russell and sailed her until 1906. She then passed into the hands of Thomas E. and John W. Shannon of Doncaster, Maryland, until 1924 when she was bought by Captain William J. Stanford of St. Patrick's Creek. Captain Stanford sold her in 1928 to Howard Cambrill and Smith Hand of New Jersey where she had several additional owners until she was "abandoned" at Philadelphia on July 30, 1934. Although a gas screw was installed in the "Elenora Russell" in 1928, she did not suffer the ignominious fate of having her masts chopped out and bowsprit sawed off, that befell so many of these beautiful vessels that were converted to barges, but was allowed to die in all her glory. Grandfather Josiah Beitzell's schooner, the "Rosa Beitzell," (formerly the "Harvester") was not so fortunate for on July 9, 1897, she was dismantled and converted into a river barge in Baltimore. During her 37 year career as a sailing vessel she had 17 different owners and a total of 31 masters. It was not unusual in these boat sales and trades to give "boot" and cases have been found where this "boot" ranged from a horse to a house. In the fall of 1967, the writer saw the "Louise Travers," a 70 foot bugeye, built by J. Marsh at Solomons Island in 1896, at Huggins Bar, near the mouth of Bretton Bay buying oysters. She was converted to a barge rig probably 30 or more years ago but is still a handsome and well kept vessel. In her sailing days she was mastered by Captain Henry Ward, a favorite oyster buyer of the Potomac rivermen.

One of the most beautiful and best known schooners on the Potomac, the "Mattie F. Dean," during her 71 years had 17 owners and probably 50 masters. When she sank on May 10, 1955, Robert Burgess salvaged one of her trailboards, restored it, and it now hangs on his office wall at the Mariners Museum, Newport News, Virginia. The wooden figure, depicting her namesake, is on display at the "Cy Ellis" restaurant at 11th and "E" Streets, N. W., in Washington. Mr. Burgess also has the quarterboard of the "Ella F. Cripps" in his collection. Like the "Mattie F. Dean," she was a beautiful schooner and a very fast boat. An excellent account of one of her oyster buying trips to the Potomac, under the command of Captain James Sommers, was reprinted in the "Chronicles of St. Mary's" (Vol. 15, No. 11) from the Rudder magazine of August, 1911. The "Dean" and the "Cripps" raced together many times, particularly in the Work Boat Races, and died side by side in Back Creek, Annapolis, Maryland. Another favorite participant in the Work Boat Races was the handsome bugeye, "Florence Northam," owned and sailed at various dates by Captain Charles O. Chesser, and William and Shill Simpkins, all of St. George's Island. She survived until March 21, 1958, when she was dismantled as a derelict in the harbor of Nassau, Bahamas.

Captain Con Faunce sailed the "Rebecca," a round stern schooner. My eldest brother told me that about 1895 Captain Con lived near the mouth of Canoe Neck Creek in an old boat that the neighbors called "The Ark." At that time he was fishing trap (pound) nets and kept his nets stored in a shanty on the shore when he wasn't fishing them. On the "Ark" he had the first phonograph in the community, complete

POTOMAC RIVER "BUY" BOATS

Pungy, "Francis J. Ruth"

Second largest pungy on the Chesapeake
Lying in St. Mary's River

Square-rigged bugeye,
"Thomas H. Kirby"

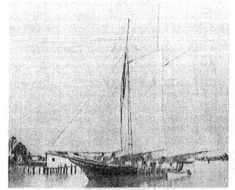

Second Round-stern Bugeye
Lying in White's Neck Creek

Unidentified schooners, waiting to load

Probably "Mattie F. Dean" in Foreground
Lying in St. Katherine's Sound

POTOMAC RIVER "BUY" BOATS

Schooner, "Joseph T. Brenan"

Bugeye "Avalon"

Under Sail

An ignominious fate --
converted to a barge.

with the so-called "Morning Glory" horn, and it was a sight to behold. Joe said, "Papa and I used to row across the creek to hear it quite often, leaving Mama alone with the small children, which she did not like very much. Occasionally Captain Con would bring the phonograph over to our house and play it for the whole community. Many came by horse and buggy from miles around to hear it." Webster Jones, who had a similar boyhood experience on the Patuxent, said, "Our family acquired one of these early machines and it was the wonder of the age. The recordings included songs, stories, and recitations and my favorite was 'The Hunter and the Bear' and we shrieked with laughter each time we heard it. It did not take much imagination to see the hunter up the tree, praying, 'Oh, Lord, if you can't help me, don't help that bear!'"

Captain John Owens and Captain Tommie Morris also sailed out of Canoe Neck. Captain John sailed a small round stern schooner named the "Becky." Captain Tommie sailed the "Hiawatha," a 37 foot bugeye built at Pocomoke City in 1884, but quit around 1901 to go into the trap net fishing business. The Morris family were good friends and good neighbors, but they were somewhat excitable and emotional in times of stress, and were great cussers, the usual failing of the rivermen. Due, I am sure, to Mama's influence, I never heard Papa swear in his life, though on several occasions when I was a boy, when something particularly aggravated him, I was sent to the house without reason and I'm sure it was to get me out of hearing distance.

Shortly after the Beitzells moved to Maryland, tragedy struck the Morris home. Because of the difficulties of coping with a large and unruly family, Mrs. Morris had, what we would call today, a nervous breakdown and had been sent to Washington to stay with relatives for a complete rest. She was due back on a particular Saturday night and that day Mr. Morris, in cleaning his gun, accidentally shot his daughter, Annie, and wounded her seriously. Mr. Morris sent his son, Tommy (then 16 years old and the same age as Papa) over to ask Grandfather to lend him his horse and carriage to meet the steamboat at Bushwood Wharf that night to bring Mrs. Morris home. Grandfather readily gave his consent but stipulated that Papa must go with young Tommy to see that no harm came to the horse and rig.

Before the boys left to meet the steamboat at midnight, Mr. Morris coached Tommy carefully as to how to break the news to his mother. The conversation went something like this: "Now, Tommy, you know that your Mama has been very sick and we had to send her away to get a good rest -- it's going to be an awful shock to her when you tell her about Annie -- you've got to break the news gently -- you hear me, now, you've got to break the news gently." "By God, Papa, don't you worry about it -- I understand, yessir, I understand -- break the news gently, yessir -- don't you worry."

Papa said the steamboat arrived on schedule but Tommy had been getting more and more wrought up by the waiting, and even before the crew had gotten out the gangplank, Tommy spied his mother on deck -- forgot all of his instructions and carefully rehearsed speech, and hollered out to her, "God Almighty, Mama, Papa's done shot Annie!" Papa said that Tommy never got any farther in breaking the news for poor Mrs. Morris swooned and there was pandemonium at Bushwood for over an hour.

Annie never fully recovered from the wound and died about three years later in 1886. She was buried in old St. Francis Xavier Cemetery on Newtown Neck, which has been in continuous use since 1640, and the river people attended the funeral, coming by boat. Until the time that automobiles became commonplace, the rivermen and their families on both St. Clement's and Bretton Bays went to services at St. Francis Xavier Church by boat. Many of them are buried there including Dr. Joseph L. McWilliams of St. Clement's Island, who died on April 16, 1885.

Captain Ned Hayden also sailed out of Canoe Neck Creek. His father, a Virginian, was captured and imprisoned at Point Lookout during the Civil War and died soon after, as his sufferings in the prison camp had greatly weakened his constitution. As an orphan boy in his teens, Ned came to live with Grandfather down at Fleet's Bay. He sailed with Grandfather until he was grown, and together with John Bryant and Portious Moore, a colored man, moved up to Maryland with the family. He sailed some of the family boats at first but soon had his own small sloop of 150 bushels named "Prohibition." During his long life on the river, Captain Ned, who was a very competent sailor, mastered many boats, some of which he owned and others that he sailed for Captain Dick Miller and Captain Allie Read of Virginia. His command included the schooners, "Edward Dean," and the "Majestic," the bugeye, "Maquire" and the pungy, "Dove." He owned and sailed the "Ethel," a sloop of 350 bushels which he traded to Tommie Simpkins on the Eastern Shore giving, to boot, of all things, a horse. He bought the sloop, "Minnie Blanche," from Captain Edwin Gibson and later acquired the sloop, "Enola," of 19 tons and 51 feet in length. She was built in 1869 at Westhaven, Connecticut, and foundered near the mouth of Canoe Neck Creek about 1917. He then acquired the "J. W. Knowles," a fine big schooner with staterooms. The "Knowles" was a 57 ton ship and 83 feet in length. When Captain Ned retired about 1926, his son, Howard, sailed the "Knowles" for several years, before she was sold. Captain Ned had no desire to retire, though well along in years, but he severely injured his hand and

wrist when they were caught in a winch while he was raising the mainsail of the
"Knowles."

After the "Enola" foundered, Richard Gibson, son of Captain Edwin, then a boy,
made a ship model of the "Mattie F. Dean" out of the "Enola's" bowsprit. The model
was fully rigged and complete with yawl boat. The late Adam T. Wible, the local
blacksmith, made the anchors and other hardware. This model is now in a museum in
Boston. Dick made many other models, including one of the "Enola," now in the possession of Ernest Morris of St. Patrick's Creek, and one of the bugeye, "Nora Phil-
ips," built at Solomons in 1901, by J. T. Marsh.

Captain Ned was a most likable character and he loved the river. After retirement he bought an old Chesapeake Bay log canoe, which he named "Polly," after one of
his granddaughters, and spent every day in summer bottom fishing around Heron Island
Bar, and anyone who liked to fish was always welcome in Captain Ned's boat.

A story is told about Captain Ned for which I cannot vouch, but it may be true.
Like most of the old timers on the river, he couldn't swim a stroke, and while he
knew every marker in the river, he was used to sailing in the channels and his extensive knowledge did not include all the depths around Heron Island Bar. One summer, when business was dull and cargoes hard to find, Captain Ned bought a seine
and with his sons and a few neighboring boys for crew, started in the seine hauling
business. They went out to Heron Island one moonless night to make their first haul
toward the end of flood tide. Somewhere in the vicinity of the bar, Captain Ned
gave the command, "overboard boys" -- the boys demurred -- they didn't believe they
were close enough to the bar. Captain Ned, with supreme confidence in his many
years on the river, said, "By golly (his favorite expression), boys, I'll show you."
He grabbed the lead line, leaped into the inky blackness with a loud splash into ten
feet of water. By the time the boys got him back into the seine boat, Captain Ned
was pretty waterlogged and they had to roll him on the water barrel of the "Enola"
to get the water out of him. As one of the boys said, "It looked more like flood
tide than ebb tide by the time we got the Cap'n bailed out."

Captain Ned Hayden was a talented musician and his performances on the concer-
tina-accordian are still remembered on the river. Although, like other river musicians, he had no formal training, he composed the words and music to several songs
and the best remembered song was entitled the "Poor Eastern Shoreman." He and his
friend, Captain John Harden, were very good ballad singers and their favorites were
"Believe Me If All Those Endearing Young Charms" and "On the Banks of the Wabash."
His years of sailing with Captain Josiah Beitzell, who was highly rated as a singer
of river ditties and of ballads, undoubtedly increased his musical repertory. The
river musicians were always in great demand for neighboring house parties. Perhaps
the best known group were Captain Ned, Captain Joe Lawrence, first violin; Captain
Sandy Ellis, second violin; and Captain Willie Husemann, the foremost performer on
the five string banjo in St. Mary's County. As a small boy, the writer recalls
attending a house party in the home of Willie Owens where Captain Joe Lawrence's
rendition of "When You Wore a Tulip and I Wore a Big Red Rose" brought forth many
encores. There were also several bands of colored rivermen and perhaps the most
famous was "Carter's Band," composed of John Carter, fiddle; William Henry Carter,
bass fiddle; and Miley Carter, banjo. They furnished music for both white and
colored affairs in St. Mary's County for many years, when the old time square dances
and waltzing were in vogue. Their talent was inherited and the music they played,
which included several Strauss waltzes, had been handed down in the family for generations, going back to slave days. The neighboring house parties were great fun where
"We danced all night, 'til broad daylight and went home with the girls in the morning."

Another of Captain Ned's sons, Tilton, sailed with his father from boyhood. In
1917 he owned a bateau or flattie, the "A. J. Lewis," of 300 bushels, which he used
as a dredge boat in the Potomac. He also owned and operated a log canoe, bought down
on the Rappahannock, in the oyster business. In later years he mastered the "Emma
V. Wills," owned by Mr. Wehrheim, and the "Mattie F. Dean," owned by Captain Matt
Bailey.

On St. Patrick's Creek, Captain Joe Lawrence sailed a sharp rig bugeye, the
"M. J. Stevenson" but she does not appear in Brewington's list of bugeyes. At any
rate she was sold to Captain Harrison Ewell. He also sailed the "Edward Dean," a
46 foot pungy, built in Alexandria in 1883. The "Edward Dean" originally was owned
by the brothers, Thomas L. N. Lawrence and William (Billie) J. E. Lawrence from 1883
to 1887, with Billie as master. During the years 1887-1889, Billie was sole owner
but in the latter year sold an interest in the vessel to his brother, Joe. On December 18, 1896, the "Edward Dean" was sold to Augustus Dean of Alexandria and she was
destroyed by fire in Monroe's Creek, Virginia on September 5, 1897. Captain Joe was
a fiddler of no small repute and in his later years grew the finest watermelons in
St. Mary's County. He had a more extensive river vocabulary than most, but he prayed
loud and fervently at church on Sunday, so probably the one offset the other. The
late Reverend Lawrence Kelly, S. J., related an amusing anecdote concerning Captain

Capt. Andrew Jackson (Jack) Cheseldine

Capt. Kenelm (Kelly) Cheseldine

Capt. Clarence Biscoe

Capt. Josiah Beitzell, Sr.

Capt. Jerry Gibson

Capt. Edwin Gibson
and sons, Alfred and Henry

Capt. John W. Henderson

Capt. Charles Chesser and Wife

Capt. J. M. (Boss) Bailey
and grandson, J. M. Downs

Capt. Ned Hayden
and son, Howard

Capt. Matt Bailey

Joe. It seemed that one fine day Father Kelly went down to Foster's Point near the mouth of White's Neck Creek and went fishing with his good friend, Captain Andrew Jackson Cheseldine. On this particular day, Captain Joe, in his dory, was sailing a boatload of watermelons up the river when Captain Jack, in his log canoe, with Father Kelly were sailing down the river to the fishing grounds. The sails obscured the vision of both skippers and they had a collision. Captain Joe, always in good voice, sounded off, making free use of his river vocabulary, that startled several Virginians on the other side of the Potomac, and when he got going good the air was "blue." By the time he had run down, the sails had been dropped and he spied Father Kelly. With complete aplomb, he touched his cap and said, "I certainly am glad you didn't overhear what I said, Father." Father Kelly reported, when asked about the ending of the story, that he never tasted finer watermelon.

Willie and Smitty Husemann sailed an old pungy, the "Splendid," for a while. They had two colored boys as crew who slept behind the cook stove in the main (and only) cabin. Both of the Husemanns loved a good joke and never lost an opportunity when an opening was presented. One night while they were laying at anchor, Captain Willie was loading gun shells and one of the boys asked, "Cap'n Willie, what would happen if you was to throw one of them gunshells in the stove?" Captain Willie winked at Smitty (who got the message) and said, "Why, John Henry, that would blow us up for sure." Smitty chimed in, "Now, Willie, don't go scaring the boys, you know one old gun shell won't blow us up." Willie said, "Yes, it will too -- you know how a shell goes off in a gun -- it's ten times worse in a stove." The boys could be observed edging out from behind the stove. Smitty said "I don't believe it and I'll prove it -- I'm going to throw one in." Willie said, "My Lord, Smitty, don't do that" and at that time the pair pretended to struggle over a shell Willie had just loaded -- but the boys hadn't waited -- they were both jammed in the companionway, fighting to gain the deck. It took some time to un-wedge them and get things quieted down again.

On the return trip home from Washington with the oysters sold, the old pungy was riding high in the water. Her sides were in bad shape and Captain Willie worried about the ice in the river. He called John Henry and Charlie Joe together and told them one would have to be on lookout on each side of the boat throughout the trip home and if a side got cut through the boys should run down in the cabin, grab a blanket from a bunk; one was to lay over the side and chunk the blanket in the hole, the other was to hold onto the feet of the first. The boys got their instructions clearly, but unfortunately Captain Willie hadn't said whose blanket was to be used. Off Swan Point the expected happened -- John Henry rushed to the cabin, grabbed the blanket from Charlie Joe's bunk, dashed back on deck -- Charlie Joe took one look at the blanket and said, "Don't you go taking my blanket, cullud boy," and made a grab for it -- in a moment there was melee on deck -- after a few fruitless moments trying to separate the warriors, with water pouring into the hold, Captain Willie grabbed the blanket that had been dropped in the struggle, and went over the side with Smitty holding onto his feet. John Henry quit at the end of the trip. He said afterward, "Ah liked Cap'n Willie, and Cap'n Smitty too -- yessir, I liked them both -- but they was too much going on all the time on that old boat -- tween the two of them a man didn't have no peace atall."

A younger brother of Captain Willie and Captain John Smith Husemann is Frank Husemann, who as a youth had the reputation of being one of the finest shots on the river. He soon attracted the attention of the leading gun manufacturing firms and over a 32 year period represented both the Remington and Winchester firms in national and international shooting meets. The high point of his career was a meet in Canada when he performed before King Edward of England.

Captain John Palmer of St. Patrick's Creek was a deep sea sailor. His ship was the "Edwin J. Palmer," built in Baltimore in 1864. It was 197 tons in capacity and 102 feet in length. With his wife, Elizabeth Creighton Palmer, he sailed the West Indies route out of Baltimore and the lower Potomac. They had five children who sailed with them though none of them were born at sea, as has been said, according to Mrs. Lillia Palmer Cryer. Shortly after the Civil War, Captain Palmer bought the farm, "Friendly Hall," near the mouth of St. Patrick's Creek, from Colonel William Blackistone and settled there. After a bad storm at sea when they were nearly lost, he retired and the census of St. Mary's County for 1870 shows him as a farmer. The "Edwin J. Palmer" was wrecked in a storm on Williams Shoal, Chincoteague, Virginia, on August 7, 1886.

In the settlement of the Beitzell estate in 1890, Captain Palmer bought the pungy, "Dolphin," and it was sailed by his son, William. Captain Will also is reported to have sailed a schooner called the "Ostrich." Windsor Palmer of St. Patrick's, a grandson, has a painting of the "Edwin J. Palmer." The tradition of the sea is kept alive by another of Captain John's grandsons, Wilmer, and his great-grandson, Creighton.

Captain Jacob R. (Jake) Faunce also sailed out of St. Patrick's Creek. He and his brothers, John B. and David Mc. Faunce of Washington had the bugeye, "George B.

Faunce," built by J. T. Marsh, at Mill Creek, Solomons Island in 1887. She was a sharp stern and sharp rig ship of 25 tons, 60.7 feet in length. Captain Jake was quite a fabulous character on the Potomac and truly representative of the old-timers on the river. On June 5, 1896, the "George B. Faunce" was sold to Captain Andrew Freeman Cheseldine of White's Neck Creek when Captain Jake decided to devote full time to trap net and seine fishing. Captain Jake later owned the small schooners, "Jacob D. Faunce," built in Washington in 1876 and the "Emma R. Faunce" built on St. Patrick's Creek in 1902 which were used in his seining operations.

Captain John Bryant was another to sail in the river trade out of St. Patrick's. Among his vessels was the "Edith Marcy," a sharp sail 60 ton bugeye he bought of Captain Dick Chesser of St. George's Island. He also sailed the "Winnie H. Windsor" which he bought from Captain Jerry Gibson and sold or traded to Captain Dick Chesser.

Captain Jimmie Dingee sailed the "Water Lily," a sloop, and Bernard Ellis had at least two boats out of St. Patrick's, the "Fanny Kemp" and the "Horn Point," a sloop.

In addition to the white masters in the oyster and general hauling trade on the river, there were several negroes out of St. Patrick's Creek who captained their own boats. Beverly Collins had a sharp sail bugeye, the "Mark Stevens," built by R. E. Tyler of St. Peters in 1888. She was 54.5 feet in length. Captain Collins displayed a great deal of courage when a January snow and sleet storm in the Bay carried away both of his masts during a trip to Baltimore. Though offered tows, Collins refused because he knew the salvage would eat up his ship. After two days and a night in terrible weather, Collins made it to port under a jury rig. A story is told that at one time Captain Collins had a boy, Fred Jones, as cook. Like most youngsters, Fred was always hungry. On this particular occasion Fred had cooked dinner and called to the Captain that everything was ready. The Captain was busy and several calls went unheeded. Fred couldn't stand the tantalizing odors of the hot cooked food and pitched in and ate his dinner. When Captain Collins came below, Fred was just finishing. It was said by the crew that the Captain's wrath was something to behold, although a good deal of it was simulated, it seems. After the Captain threatened to "keel-haul" him, to hang him from the bowsprit, tow him by a rope from the stern, give him 30 lashes and the like, Fred promised on bended knee never again to even think about eating until the Captain had been served and then only after permission had been obtained.

Other outstanding colored men on St. Patrick's Creek included Henry Stewart who captained the bugeye, "Eva Clarence," built by L. Shores in Somerset County in 1887, a 50 footer. The "Willie Clarence," a bugeye, also was built in Somerset County at Oriole in 1892, probably by the same builder. This vessel was captained by James Dickerson and was 51.5 feet in length. Both were sharp sail craft. Captain Luke Clark bought the "Hiawatha" from Captain Tommie Morris and sailed her for many years. His brother, Joe Clark, also owned his own vessel. Richard Jones of Canoe Neck Creek had a reputation as an excellent riverman and while he did not own a vessel he sailed both bugeyes and schooners on a sharing basis.

Other negroes who were well known on the Potomac were Taylor Green and Henry Branson. All of these men made good reputations on the river. Captain Collins and Captain Clark owned fine farms on the river front which are still in possession of their descendents.

In connection with the activities of Taylor Green, an interesting side light was furnished the writer by Mr. R. Johnson Colton, II, of St. Mary's County in reply to an inquiry regarding the bugeye, "Colonel R. Johnson Colton." Mr. Colton replied as follows:

"In reference to the bugeye, "Col. R. Johnson Colton," my father had the boat built for Taylor Green, a colored man. Green was a handy man around Colton's Point and bought produce up and down the river for the hotel, then run by my father and Uncle Bruce. My father esteemed Taylor so much for his honesty and faithfulness that he had the bugeye built and gave it to Taylor, who named it the "Col. R. Johnson Colton." He ran oysters each winter to Washington, D. C."

Prior to sailing the "Col. R. Johnson Colton," Taylor Green owned and sailed the sloop, "John Williams," (1880-1885), built by Captain Kenelm Cheseldine. Green was renown as the champion whistler of the area and the old-timers say that he not only whistled beautifully but also he could be heard at considerable distances. The writer's brother, Charlie, recently stated that one calm morning, when he and cousin Frank Lawrence were rowing a skiff up Canoe Neck Creek on their way to the old Oakley public school, Frank suddenly stopped rowing and said, "Listen to that fellow whistling -- that's Taylor Green, clear over on Newtown shore" (a distance of about 2 miles across St. Clement's Bay). Charlie said he listened but couldn't hear him but he didn't doubt that Frank did because Taylor "was a powerful whistler." Green lived for many years in a log cabin on "Bluff Woods" at the mouth of Canoe Neck Creek. This was the last surviving log cabin in the area and was pulled down about 1915.

The "Col. R. Johnson Colton" was built at Solomons in 1886, probably by M. M. Davis, with a so-called patent stern. After passing through many hands, she was

HOMES OF POTOMAC RIVERMEN

Canoe Neck Creek

Capt. Jerry Gibson

Capt. Josiah Beitzell, Sr.
and
Capt. Edwin Gibson

White's Neck Creek   Canoe Neck Creek

Capt. Kelly Cheseldine   Capt. Boss Bailey   Capt. Josiah Beitzell

GERARD-BLACKISTONE HOUSE

COLTON (LONGWORTH) POINT, MARYLAND
(Prior to 1933)

68

abandoned around 1928 in Little Creek, Virginia, and then resurrected and rebuilt there in 1929. She was converted for use as a yacht in 1936, to the extent of the addition of a full length "house" on her deck, and an engine was installed. For some years she was kept in the waters of the upper Bay until purchased in 1948 by N. T. Kenney, a newspaperman who planned to use her in his journalistic assignments at regattas on the Bay in summers, and to dock her at Washington in the winter time for use as his home. At the time of purchase in 1948, the "Colton" had been subjected to inexcusable neglect. She had sunk at her moorings; rainwater, seeping through frayed canvas and open deck seams, had caused rot in places. Her foremast was badly decayed at the partners; her running rigging was about gone, and her standing rigging none too good. Mr. Kenney, after a somewhat hazardous trip down and across the Bay, took her to Dick Hartge's shipyard at Galesville for the major repairs, and then on to Washington. She changed hands again in 1956, but is still afloat in the harbor of Annapolis and her present owner, George Allen Pierce, Jr., plans some extensive repairs and to get her back into good sailing condition. She continues as one of the few survivors of a fabulous age in the life of the Potomac. It would be a wonderful contribution to the children of Maryland if the "Colton" could be preserved as a typical vessel of the tidewater area of the state.

No story of the colored men on the river would be complete without a mention of Portious Moore. Portious was a West Indian negro who sailed with Grandfather, Josiah Beitzell, from the age of 12 until he was grown, and he sailed boats on his own when a man. He worked some years for Captain Con Faunce, and in his old age Portious lived in Washington. As a young man he loved children and was quite a "ladykiller" in the colored circle. The writer's brother, Harry, was somewhat sickly as a child and Portious relieved Mama many days by taking Harry with him in his boat, crabbing and fishing for the day, and of course Harry loved it and was quite content to stay with Portious as often as Mama would permit. Harry never lost contact with Portious over the years and was sent for when Portious was on his deathbed.

Prior to owning the "Mattie F. Dean" (1919-1944), Captain Matt Bailey of White's Neck Creek owned the "George B. Faunce" (1902-1907). He acquired the "Faunce" from Freeman Cheseldine, giving in trade a store on White's Neck Creek, and other considerations. In 1907, he sold the "Faunce" and bought the "Lottie L. Thomas" from Captain Edwin Gibson and for five years following World War I had two vessels, the "Thomas" and the "Dean," in the river trade. The "Faunce" wound up on the North Carolina coast and was abandoned at Beaufort in 1920.

Upon retirement from the river in 1944, Captain Matt again opened a store near his home at the mouth of White's Neck Creek, but was soon elected a County Commissioner and became quite prominent in county affairs until his death on September 24, 1959.

Captain Lum (George Columbus) Bailey who lived on Bullock's Island, near the mouth of White's Neck Creek, sailed a vessel called the "Annie Lee" and later sailed the schooner, "Ruth and Ella," named for his daughters, until his death in 1899. After this she was sailed by his son, Boss (James Mitchell), for some years and then sold to Captain Nick Norris of Charles County. This schooner was built by Captain Kelly Cheseldine for his brother, Jack, who sold her to Captain Lum.

Captain Ned Russell, also of White's Neck, owned and operated several small flatties in the oyster trade. Prior to this time he had owned the pungy, "Dove," which he sold to Captain Ned Hayden. The "Dove" foundered in Canoe Neck Creek, when the writer was a small boy, a half-century ago.

After the "Ruth and Ella" was sold, Captain Boss Bailey owned a small bugeye, the "Quick Time," and later bought the "Thomas H. Kirby" from Jim Bailey and sailed this vessel for about ten years, when she was sold, dismantled and turned into a barge. At this time he had John Cheseldine build a barge for use in the oyster trade which he named for his daughter, Helen Bailey. Due to the inroads made in river transportation by the trucking industry, Captain Boss sold this boat in 1935 and retired.

Captain Jim Bailey first owned a big sloop, the "Emmett Arthur," then the "Lizzie Lane," another sloop, and then acquired the bugeye, "Thomas H. Kirby," which was built at St. Michael's in 1882, by T. H. Kirby. She was 61.1 feet in length and was the second round stern bugeye to be built. The "Kirby" was schooner rigged. Upon leaving the river about 1922 to run a store at River Springs, Captain Jim sold her to Captain Boss Bailey, as previously noted. A colored print mounted on canvass of the "Kirby" at anchor in White's Neck Creek, with her sails up, hangs on the wall of the writer's study, given to him by Mrs. Helen Bailey Downs.

Captain Sam Bailey, a nephew of Captain Matt, has owned many boats from schooners to barges and his current assortment includes log canoes, a small pungy, some Hooper Island boats, dories, box sterns, and most anything one can name. In earlier years Captain Sam was part owner, with his brother Robert, of the "Joseph T. Brenan," and also sailed a double ender in the oyster trade, bought of Jackson Wise of Compton, named the "Five Sisters." Although he has engaged in many business enterprises, including a large truck line -- the Bailey Express, he has never divorced himself from the seafood business. With the opening of the Potomac tributaries in the summer of 1961, Captain Sam and his sons, Sam Jr., Eddie, and Bernard, as might be expected, were the first to put a fleet of clam dredgers in the river and establish a shucking industry on White's Neck. They also operate several establishments specializing in fish, oysters, and crabs and folks come from miles away on Friday nights for their steamed crabs.

Captain Robert Bailey sailed the 27 ton schooner, "Joseph T. Brenan," built at Madison on the Eastern Shore in 1883. He engaged in both the bay and river trade but gave up the business with the decline that followed the First World War in 1921. The "Brenan" was destroyed by fire on January 5, 1929, at Matts Landing, Maurice River, New Jersey.

Captain George Gibson, the father of the boat builders Buddy, Garner, John, and Perry also sailed the Potomac in the "Edward Dean." All of the rivermen saw storms in their day and Captain George was no exception. He was caught in one of hurricane proportions and went aground at Persimmon Point Light so hard it took a big tugboat from Washington to pull him off.

Captain Jack (Andrew Jackson) Cheseldine of White's Neck followed the water all of his life and for many years sailed the 39 ton pungy, "L. B. Platt," built in Dorchester County in 1873. His last boat was the pungy "Capitol." After his retirement, his son, Robert, sailed the boat for some years until October 5, 1896. On that day Robert, in company with his cousins, John and George Cheseldine, who were sailing the pungy, "Dove," were caught in a bad storm and both pungies swamped off Sandy Point. Robert and his crew of two colored men, William B. Jones and Joseph Price, were drowned. The "Capitol" was wrecked on the Point and became a total loss. Robert might have saved himself as he was a good swimmer and they were not far from shore, but he became entangled in the rigging and by the time his cousins discovered his predicament he was beyond help. John and George were more fortunate as their pungy dragged anchor and they were so near shore they were able to make it safely to the river bank by clinging to the mainmast boom.

While no sensible riverman will ever take any unnecessary chances, since life for the riverman is always risky, tragedies did happen, infrequently, but they happened none the less. Six months later Great-uncle Jack Cheseldine lost his son-in-law, James Morgan, by drowning near Stone's Wharf at the head of St. Clement's Bay. Cousin James was knocked overboard by the jibbing of the mainsail boom of his dory during a heavy breeze and drowned before anyone could reach him. In the summer of 1916 the writer's cousin, Eldridge Norris, age 16, was lost on a trip to Washington while sailing with Captain John Joe Gibson on the schooner, "J. R. Dixon." During the night a heavy thunderstorm rolled up and Captain John Joe called down to Eldridge who was asleep in the cabin to come on deck to help reef the sails. As he stepped on deck, the jibbing boom swept him overboard and although the Captain made every effort to locate him in the water, he could not be found. His body was not located until three weeks later. It is supposed that when Eldridge came on deck he was still half asleep and not alert to the jibbing boom. It fractured his skull, so when he hit the water he was unconscious. Otherwise, he would have survived for a while, even in the heavy sea since he was an excellent swimmer.

Both Captain Willie Husemann and Captain Jack Cheseldine kept "sailing canoes." They were bay log canoes and Captain Willie's was quite large, measuring about 35 feet in length. She had a foresail and a jib but no mainsail, and was a fast sailer. He kept her neat as a new pin and always freshly painted, as he did with all of his boats, including the big dory, "Sylph," which he built about 1915. The canoe was named the "Lillian Palmer" for the beautiful sister of Larry Palmer, who kept a large general store at the mouth of St. Patrick's Creek for the rivermen, where he did a thriving business.

Captain Jack's canoe was small, only about 20 feet in length, with only a mainsail. One day he decided that the canoe was too narrow for the best sailing and there wasn't enough room inboard so he sawed through the keel from stem to stern, bolted in a new keel about 12 inches in width and solved his problem very neatly. After his retirement and when he was in his late 80's, Captain Jack continued to sail out in the Narrows (St. Katherine's Sound) to fish almost every summer day. As both his hearing and eyesight were getting very poor, he couldn't hear or see the thunderstorms as they would come up. On one particular summer's day, a real bad one began to make up in the Southwest and there were great rolls of thunder in the distance but the Captain fished serenely on. His daughter, Ida, who lived on St. Katherine's Island, became more and more worried and finally prevailed on her husband, Charlie, to go out in his motorboat and give her father a tow to White's Neck. By the time Charlie reached him the storm was even more threatening and promised to break loose any moment. Charlie came alongside and hollered a warning about the storm and grabbed the anchor rope. Captain Jack allowed as how he could take care of himself and for Charlie to go on back home if he was worried about the storm. With the storm becoming

POTOMAC RIVER "BUY" BOATS

"Mattie F. Dean" leads the "Ella F. Cripps"
Piney Point in the Background

WORK BOAT RACES, PINEY POINT, MARYLAND - 1930   Photo: A. Aubrey Bodine
(Courtesy of The Mariners Museum)

POTOMAC RIVER "BUY" BOATS

Schooners, "Mattie F. Dean," "Ella F. Cripps," and Bugeye, "R. B. Haynie"

WORK BOAT RACES, PINEY POINT, MARYLAND - 1930   Photo: A. Aubrey Bodine
(Courtesy of The Mariners Museum)

more and more threatening by the minute, Charlie stopped arguing, pulled up the anchor, dropped it in his boat, started his engine and began towing the Captain in. Captain Jack grabbed his bait knife, cut the painter, got his sail up and with the deck awash but his dignity complete, he beat the storm home by a hairbreadth and informed all his womenfolk who were clucking around that by all that was good and holy he had sailed that river, man and boy for over 70 years and he wasn't through yet, and that if any of them sent Charlie Beitzell or any other upstart to tow him anywhere, they were going to wish they hadn't -- or words to that effect. Captain Jack died peacefully ashore some years later.

His brother, Captain Kelly, built and sailed several vessels in the early days and in 1882 had two schooners in the river trade. However, with the growing demands of his shipyard, he left the sailing to his sons, John and George, but by the turn of the century they also were busy with boat building. A younger son, Robert, has been employed by the Corinthian Yacht Club in Washington since 1930. In 1900, Captain Kelly temporarily gave up boat building and signed a contract with the Western Union Telegraph Company to construct a telegraph line from Cape Hatteras to Newport News. With a crew of seventeen men on a large schooner, the "Cunningham," the job was completed in less than three years. The men lived aboard the schooner and trips home were made rarely. Telegraph poles were obtained by utilizing the woods along the coast. They endured many hardships in the Hatteras area and lived through many dangerous storms, particularly in winter.

Captain Jack's other sons, Freeman and Garrett, both followed the water for some years. Garrett sailed with his father but Freeman mastered several vessels. The first was the "Annie L.," followed by the "Bessie Reed," a schooner of 28 tons. He later acquired the "George B. Faunce" which he sailed from 1896 to 1902.

Captain James H. Cheseldine sailed the sloop, "Fanny Shepherd," built by his distant cousin, Captain Kelly Cheseldine, in 1879. The sloop was sailed by Captain Kelly for three years and then passed through the hands of Captain John Joe Gibson, John H. Long, Z. Taylor Haydin, and John Bryant, before she was acquired by Captain Jimmie, who in turn sold her to his brother, Captain Charles E. Cheseldine on May 10, 1893.

Captain George Ellis of River Springs, near White's Neck, first sailed the sloop, the "Fanny Shepherd" which he bought from Captain Charlie Cheseldine in 1898. He then acquired the "Hallie K.," a 10 ton bugeye. His sons, Cyrus and Paul, sailed with him for some years. Later, Captain George bought the square rigged, round stern, bugeye, "R. B. Haynie," built at Solomons Island by M. M. Davis in 1896. The "Haynie" was a handsome boat of 31 tons, 64.6 feet in length. Captain George sold the "Hallie K." to his son, Paul, and sailed the "Haynie" until retirement in 1935. He sold the "R. B. Haynie" to George W. Clark of Belhaven, North Carolina, and she went to pieces on Gull Shoals when she grounded during a storm on January 18, 1937.

Cyrus sailed both of these bugeyes at times but later became a seafood commission merchant on the Washington water front and established the well-known "Cy Ellis" restaurant on "E" Street. The restaurant business is being carried on by his widow, Bessie Gibson Ellis, daughter of the late Captain Edwin Gibson, and her two sons, George Cyrus and James Edwin.

Captain Paul Ellis sailed the "Hallie K." in the river trade from 1923 until May 24, 1926, when he went into the seafood business with his brother, Cyrus. He sold the "Hallie K." to Captain Havie Bannigan of River Springs, who in turn sold her in 1931 for service in Florida. The "Hallie K." was built by James T. Marsh at Solomons in 1891 and Captain Havie had her rebuilt at Solomons in 1928. She foundered December 13, 1935, about 30 miles northeast of Jupiter Light, Florida, with four persons aboard, but no lives were lost. Captain Havie purchased and sailed the "J. R. Dixon" after the retirement of Captain John Joe Gibson and also ran an oyster barge, the "Thelma M." for some years.

The masters of the river and bay sailing vessels were keen on racing, and after unloading their cargoes at Washington, Baltimore, and Norfolk there were many individual races back to the oyster grounds. Often several vessels leaving port at the same time participated in these impromptu races. For many years there were annual work boat races in the Chesapeake under rather strict rules laid down by the Regatta Committee. The race of June 21, 1930, was perhaps typical and the entries will be found in Appendix "B".

In a few years after the turn of the century, with the depletion of the oyster and fishing industries, the use of gasoline engines, the steamboat and the automobile, the schooner trade on the river rapidly deteriorated. By 1930 there were only a handful of schooners, pungies, and bugeyes left as indicated by the work boat race entries. In 1880 the Alexandria custom house registered 182 sailing vessels as their home port and, undoubtedly, as many or more were registered in the ports of Washington and Georgetown. With the exception of the Chesapeake Bay dredging fleet the last commercial sailing vessel carrying oyster shells to the local fertilizer factory in Alexandria arrived in 1944.

When the oyster and fish bonanza came to an end in the Potomac, the promising ship building industry on the river also died with it because these two items of seafood had been its main support. To those who loved these beautiful sailing vessels the rotting hulks of schooners, pungies, bugeyes, sloops, and dories that lined the shores of every creek along the Potomac was heart-rending and the price of progress seemed high.

Captain Matt Bailey and his beautiful schooner, the "Mattie F. Dean," were the best known among men and boats of the Potomac River. Captain Matt spent most of his lifetime on the Maryland waters and he was the last of the long line of Potomac sailing masters. He was one of the ablest masters on the river, and he did not give up the schooner trade until 1944. When the "Mattie F. Dean" foundered in 1955 in the Annapolis harbor, it was a sad day for the rivermen because it marked finally and irrevocably the passing of the most glorious era in the history of the Potomac River. There couldn't have been a better or more representative man than Matt Bailey to bring down the final curtain, nor a fairer or more representative schooner to take a final bow. She had many owners besides Captain Matt who sailed her for a quarter of a century. They included William H. Dean, Levin T. and John A. Dunnock of Taylor's Island, Maryland; Stephen T. Norris of Baltimore; Solomon Foxwell of Leonardtown, St. Mary's County; Jesse Fagan of Mt. Holly, Virginia; John W. Vane of Cambridge; H. T. Belfield of Kinsale and J. L. Healy of Nomini, Virginia; Edgie Shores of Chance, Maryland; the Somerset Seafood Company of Deal and Harry J. Bureau of Eastport, Maryland. When old and "hogged," after 60 years of cargo carrying on the Bay and its tributaries, she spent another decade as a "dredge boat" in the dwindling Bay fleet, the proud dowager of a dying race. How many young watermen were trained on her decks? How many storms did she weather? What a saga of the Chesapeake and the Potomac she could tell of her 70 years on these waters! It is a pity she could not have been preserved for posterity.

A list of 382 sailing vessels (excluding dories) either built in Potomac River yards or used in the river trade is contained in Appendix "A". This list is far from being complete. It may be worthy to note that this list includes nineteen bugeyes not found in Brewington's list.

LIFE ON THE POTOMAC RIVER

Chapter V

OYSTERS, "DRUDGERS," AND POACHERS

Oysters have been prized as a delicacy from the time of the first recorded history of man. Accounts are extant concerning oyster feasts in the banquet halls of the Romans, and they were divided in their opinions as to which were the best oysters, those which were carried back from Britain by the conquering Roman legions or those from the Baian Lake, i.e., Lacus Lucrinus, the famous Roman oyster preserve. It is recorded also that as far back as the Middle Ages, the oyster was highly valued as a food. In America, the coastal Indians consumed huge quantities of this delicacy. Even today mounds of oyster shells left by the Indians may be found in the river front fields along the Potomac.

The early Maryland and Virginia colonists utilized the abundance of oysters along their shores and soon after the settlements, this food became an important item in their diet.

Early accounts sent home to England in 1635 and 1656 speak in glowing terms of the abundance of fish, oysters, and crabs that might be taken with small effort from the waters of Maryland. Even oyster pearls come in for a mention in the 1635 account ".....The [Indian] women affect to weare chaines and bracelets of beades, some of the better sort of them, weare ropes of Pearle about their necks, and some hanging in their eares, which are of a large sort, but spoyled with burning the Oysters in the fire, and the rude boaring of them....." However, the professional oyster industry in Chesapeake Bay and its tributaries did not start to develop until around 1760.

Early in the 19th century the New England watermen started coming into the bay because they had exhausted their beds through the use of the "dredge," an implement that caught every oyster in its path. By 1808 many New England vessels were buying oysters in the bay from the small "tonging" boats. The "tong" or "rake," is a pair of wooden shafts, joined like a pair of scissors, with a heavy wire head about a yard wide, equipped with teeth on the bottom of the head, which enables the tonger to pull up from the water about a half bushel of mud, shells, and oysters at each "lick." Since hand tonging ordinarily is carried on in 15 to 25 feet of water, the "licks" are blind and consequently spots on the bottom are missed and some oysters are left for propagation. However, at times, usually in the beginning of the season, some "sight" tonging is done in shallow water.

The New Englanders soon found that the tongers couldn't supply their needs fast enough so they started dredging. The Maryland and Virginia oystermen quickly followed suit and the oyster beds were being depleted so rapidly that both Maryland and Virginia enacted legislation in 1820 prohibiting the use of the dredge. However, the oyster market grew steadily in Baltimore, Washington, and Norfolk and the packing industry was organized in 1836, and oysters were shipped as far as Pittsburgh by wagon. The opening of the Chesapeake and Delaware Canal expanded the Philadelphia market and the rapidly growing Baltimore and Ohio Railroad greatly increased the packing trade.

During the Civil War the oyster industry was seriously disrupted and in some areas of the Bay and its tributaries activity was practically discontinued. As a result the oysters had a chance to recover and multiply rapidly. After the War dredging again was permitted and by 1880 the industry was at its height in Maryland and Virginia waters.

Brewington, in his fine work, Chesapeake Bay Bugeyes, has traced the development of this greatest of all oyster boats used in the Bay. However, as indicated previously, the bugeye was also a great favorite of the Potomac rivermen who used them largely as "buy boats" and the Potomac dory was developed for the local dredgers and tongers. As the oyster beds in the Bay were depleted, more and more of the Bay dredgers started coming into the Potomac to work Heron Island bar, Sheepshead, Kettle Bottom shoals, Cobb bar, Swan Point, and other beds and this led to the "Oyster Wars" that have plagued the river for the past century. But before getting into this story it may be well to outline the life of this bivalve and to tell something of its worth.

When the water reaches a temperature of 68 to 70 degrees, oysters begin to spawn. In the Potomac this is usually during the months of June, July, and August. After spawning, the larvae are so small that a container about the size of a man's little finger would hold about 1,000,000 of these young oysters and would produce, if they all matured, about 4,000 bushels of marketable oysters. At this stage the larvae are free swimming, moves with the tides and currents, and many are carried

SEAFOOD PLATTER - An even dozen tiny oysters dot the top and bottom shell of this 7½-inch hard crab which was caught in Eastern Bay off Lowe's Point by P. T. Hambleton, Jr., Bozman. Ernest Reitch, who was working with Hambleton, spotted the oyster-covered crab in the crab pot. This was the second hard crab reported caught during the season with a load of tiny oysters attached to its shell.

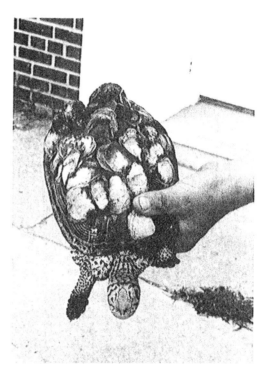

DIAMONDBACK WITH OYSTERS - The 7-inch Diamondback Terrapin caught in Harris Creek by Carroll (Pigwich) Harrison, Bozman, is covered on the top shell by 50 young oysters and 3 barnacles. At some point in the Terrapin's life it came into contact with something that severed its right rear leg. All that remains is a short stump of the leg.

HORSESHOE CRAB with three large oysters.

Photos: Mary Swaine
(Courtesy of The Star-Democrat Newspaper, Easton, Maryland)

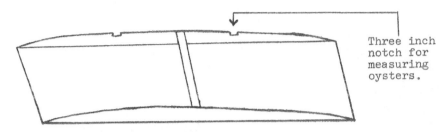

Three inch
notch for
measuring
oysters.

Oyster Culling Board
(Length is the width of the boat and width is 1/4 of the length)

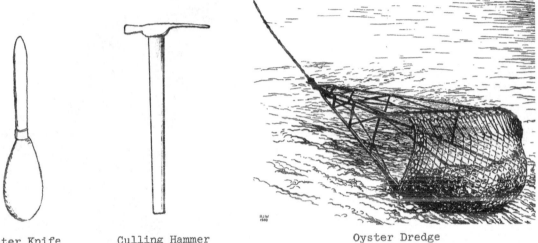

Oyster Knife   Culling Hammer   Oyster Dredge

Nippering Oysters   Oyster Tongers at Work

Courtesy of Virginia Fisheries Laboratory

far from their place of birth. The free-swimming stage is of short duration, varying with water conditions, and never exceeds a few weeks, after which the instinct to settle down and build a home prevails. So, when conditions as to temperature and saltiness of the water are favorable, it settles to the bottom to attach itself to an object. However, of the myriads of young oysters that settle to the bottom, only a few are fortunate enough to fall on a firm object. These fortunate ones then cement themselves to it almost instantly. Usually the object is inanimate and generally is an old oyster shell but sometimes it is a living thing such as another oyster, a crab, or even a terrapin. The rest perish. In a most unusual occurrence during the summer of 1965, the young oysters, called spat, were so plentiful in portions of the Chesapeake Bay that the Star-Democrat newspaper of Easton, Maryland, reported the catch in Eastern Bay, off Lowe's Point, of several live hard crabs covered with small oysters. One 7½ inch hard crab was pictured in the paper on which an even dozen tiny oysters could be counted. Subsequently a 7 inch diamondback terrapin was caught in Harris Creek, Bozman, covered with 50 young oysters.

In their first stage the oysters are invisible to the human eye for a month or more. After the attachment, the oyster remains on the object, unless during the growth of the oyster the object disintegrates. In 2 to 4 years (usually 3) they grow into tender, juicy, and succulent marketable oysters from 3 to 6 inches in length.

The age of the oyster can be determined from the successive layers making up its shell. Usually, each pronounced layer represents a year's growth, much as the rings around the circumference of a tree indicates a similar passage of time. Large quantities of water are strained by the oyster for its food which consists of plants, microscopic in size, so small that as many as 10,000,000 of them will be found in a quart of Potomac River water, which is especially rich in them. When the temperature of the water is about 75 degrees an oyster will strain about 100 quarts of water through its gills during a 24 hour period.

When foods were eaten primarily because of their taste appeal, oysters occupied a foremost rank. Later, when the medical profession showed the way to health by the proper selection of foods for a balanced diet, the oyster not only continued to occupy a foremost rank, but in certain nutritional respects led the procession. This is especially true because of the mineral content of the oyster, that no doubt imparts to it that particularly tasty flavor. Biochemical studies have shown that oysters contain appreciable quantities of all the minerals needed for the functioning of a healthy body.

A pint of oysters will supply about one-half of the phosphorous, one-third of the calcium, and all the iron and iodine required in the food of an average person daily. The human diet is commonly found to be deficient in the latter three minerals, the last of which is needed in organic combination in food for the normal functioning of the thyroid gland. The high iron, copper, and manganese content of oysters makes them valuable for promoting a good blood condition. The calcium and phosphorous in oysters make them important food to develop straight and sturdy bones. This same pint of oysters also will furnish about one-fourth of the protein required by a man daily. In addition, oysters contain vitamins A, B, C, D, and G in appreciable quantities. Glycogen, a substance resembling starch, is another important constituent of oysters, and is necessary in the diet of healthy individuals. As contained in the oyster, it is practically predigested and ready to meet the nutritional requirements of the body even when uncooked. The oyster is more nearly balanced nutritionally than possibly any other single food, resembling milk in this respect.

Because of its wonderful flavor and many nutritive constituents, the oyster is an ideal food for those in practically any walk of life, whether a homemaker, office worker, laborer, invalid, or a growing child. It is a food that can be served raw on the half shell and as a cocktail, steamed or roasted in the shell, as the base for soups, sandwiches, and salads and as a stuffing for fowl, or as the main course of a meal, stewed, fried, or baked. And it can be eaten during any month of the year and for any meal of the day. Further, the oyster is an economical food. It is entirely edible, there being no wastage from trimmings or bones. In fact, a quart of oysters is a quart of food.

Some years ago, before conservation steps were taken, a friend remarked to the writer that oysters were growing so scarce and were so expensive that they must be classed as a luxury and soon only the rich could afford them. This thought is very disturbing when one considers how delicious they are and what a fine food they are. It points up the necessity for not only continuing the efforts to conserve this valuable resource but also there should be a doubling or stepping up of the effort on all fronts to increase production. Such a program should include educating the oysterman and the general public as to its value; more adequate policing; a 100% return of shells to the oyster beds from the shucking houses and greatly increased planting of "seed" oysters on depleted grounds.

In the Potomac the oyster season generally opens in September and continues

Circa 1904
Probably the schooner, "E. P. Evans"

(Courtesy of The Mariners Museum)

POTOMAC RIVER OYSTER TONGING BOATS

Circa 1904
Huggins Bar

Circa 1912
Anchored for night in
St. Katherine's Sound

Circa 1904
Putting Out the Catch

(Courtesy of The Mariners Museum)

through March. Actually the season is much shorter because the tonger is lucky if
he averages three or four days a week, due to high winds and ice. Usually, by the
first of the year, the beds have been fairly well cleaned and the catch is small.
Dredging is prohibited in the Potomac. Such oysters as are in water too deep to
tong remain there. It would seem that no harm would be done if dredging were permitted in deep water for limited periods. The problem is that once a boat is equipped
for dredging and the oysters become scarce on the dredging grounds, it is a great
temptation to encroach upon the tonging grounds, particularly at night. Perhaps it
is time to again attempt to work out a solution.

The tonger generally carries along a pair of "nippers" for use on calm days.
"Nippers" are similar to tongs, about 10 to 15 feet in length but they are equipped
with "paws," about 4 inches in width, with three teeth or fingers on one paw and
four on the other. They are used in shallow water where individual oysters can be
sighted and picked up, one by one. The writer well remembers the fall of 1920, when,
at the age of 15, he decided that he had had enough schooling and it was now time to
become a full-fledged riverman. Over the somewhat agonized protests of his mother,
he joined his father at the beginning of the oyster season. One fine day in late
September they nippered 40 bushels of "selects" on the flats of Posey's Bluff for
which they received 60¢ per bushel, a fine price in those days. Alas, as winter drew
on, it wasn't so pleasant on the oyster grounds. In those days heavy rubber gloves
were unknown to oystermen and the only protection for the hands was a pair of woolen
mittens that instantly became soaked from handling the tongs, though they did serve
to protect the hands from the wind. When ice began to form on the shafts, oystering
got to be downright mean work, hands took on a leathery quality and feet seemed to
be perpetually numb. After the Christmas holidays, Captain "Eddie-Buck" was happy
to return to school. He is sure now that his father had told his mother privately
that this was the way it would turn out, otherwise she would not have surrendered
so early in the battle. Anyway, Mother was a farmer's daughter and she never liked
the water and always feared it. She could not understand why her menfolk were so
fascinated by "that old river." Wasn't that where those "terrible" Eastern Shore
dredgers were? Hadn't the Potomac claimed the lives of her cousins, Robert and
James, and her own nephew, Eldridge, just four years before? Weren't most of the
rivermen a rough and rowdy lot? Besides, "a living" on the river was so uncertain
and becoming more so. It was useless to argue that branches of the family had been
rivermen for generations, back to the time of her ancestor, Thomas Gerard; that the
river had seen good times and bad times; that her relatives who were rivermen were
not rowdies; that farmers' sons met with accidents, too -- she would concede only
that the river "was nice to look at." But it did not keep her from owning a small
dory, the "Katy B." which she rented and which provided a substantial part of the
cost of sending her son away to high school.

Ordinarily, the oysterman works with tongs that range from 14 to 22 feet in
length. Fifty years ago a few of the big men like Palmer Bannigan and Kep Maddox
(colored) of St. Patrick's Creek worked 24's and 26's, but they were exceptional.
Today, the young men must be stronger or have learned to better utilize their tongs,
for many of them are working 26's, 28's, and even 30's in order to reach the oysters
in deeper water.

The writer asked his friend, Varley Lang, an "Eastern Shore" waterman, who
works out of Easton, about long tongs, and he wrote as follows:

"About the long rakes. From twelve to fifteen years ago, almost no one around
here used anything longer than twenty-fours. There were two reasons for that: in
the first place, there were plenty of oysters in comparatively shoal water; in the
second place, the deep water oysters had all died due to a lack of oxygen near the
bottom, brought on in the summertime by layering and low misture of oxygenated water
near the surface with that below it. [This generally was true also in the Potomac.]
But now the long rakes are very much in favor again. For one thing, oysters are more
scarce. Speaking for myself alone, I think I could not make a living without twenty-
fours, and many men use thirties. In addition, the deep water oysters have made a
good comeback. Sometimes, if you don't work with long rakes on the bar edges, you
just don't catch oysters. Here is another thing. Anything from twenty-fours to
twenty-eights are easier to handle than eighteens or twenties; and fourteens and
sixteens will kill you, they jar and jamb you so badly. The balance on a pair of
Georgia pine edge grain twenty-fours or twenty-sixes is absolutely perfect, whereas
anything under that tends to pull down at the head and over balance. While this
drag is not important for one lick, it becomes increasingly difficult during a day's
work; and sixteens are even worse. I worked only once with a pair of Georgia pine
fourteens, and that was enough. I was a liniment case. Important thing about thirties and thirty-twos is this: it takes one hell of a long time to get them up and
dump the load: therefore, there absolutely must be something under the rake heads
to make the job worthwhile, otherwise you are wasting your time and energy. Whereas
with twenties you can come up with only four oysters and still make a day, because

the whole process is quicker. A competent tonger can really whip a pair of twenties but no one can handle thirties like switches. It can't be done. On the other hand, crawling around on your knees with a pair of twenties in order to reach the bottom is very punishing work; it will cripple your back. Besides, rakes are not meant to be worked at the ends of the shafts. You want wood level with your eyes for the most efficient leverage. Clem will tell you that. I expect he knows more about all this than I do."

Dr. Lang is being quite modest, for he is one of the most skillful practitioners of the art, all self taught. He not only knows the proper implements to use and how to use them most effectively, but his study of oyster breeding and breeding grounds makes him one of the best informed men in these matters on the Bay. His dedication to conservation and law enforcement in the oyster industry makes him one whose advice should be sought in any plan to revitalize it.

The life of the waterman is not an easy one. His hours are long and laborious in fair weather and foul, and at times his life is laid on the line. When a season is good he is apt to be a free spender and many wind up their days with little to show in worldly goods. Varley Lang, in the lines that follow, has caught the plaint of the old men, but most of them, if given another chance, would not give up their hard won independence for anything that a land boss might offer.

Nothing to Show

"I set fykes," old Morris said,
"And hauled seines and trapped for eels;
I tonged oysters, crabbed, and shed
Out crabs. I was always on the water."

"Why, all the water I ever worked
Has gone to the sky again in all
This time. I never slacked or skirked,
And nothing to show, nothing to show."

While the grey seas come and go,
The water goes back to the sky;
It returns with the rain and the snow,
And nothing to show, nothing to show.

In a letter dated October 23, 1965, Varley wrote: "I had to give up crabbing in the middle of September, although I held on that long because of the unseasonable heat. A man can kill himself with a pair of tongs in that kind of weather. It was even right warm and still today, this late in the year. I went up to a hill in the upper Miles, just for Saturday morning, and Jack Kemp came alongside, 'just to keep me company.' First, he complained about his rakes, which were 'contrary as a parson with a bad collection plate.' Then the weather was too hot. Then he said his will power was failing. Then he told me it looked bad off there, a storm was hell-brewing sure. I kept psh-pishing and pshaw-pshawing, and he said, 'Hell, man, you won't let me quit and go home, noway.' I made a slow start with tonging. Takes me a little longer every season to get the silk back, but I believe I have it now,.....and I think I have the swing back. And what a pleasure it is to use yourself so hard and enjoy the fine season along with it. Somehow, every season seems to me more interesting and more beautiful than the last. I saw my first flight of wild swan today against a vivid patch of blue sky surrounded by smoky black clouds. Wonderful. So white they were."

Tongs, in one form or another, have been used in America since the middle of the 17th century and eventually were developed into a delicately balanced implement that required a good deal of skill in their manufacture. Members of the craft were never numerous. In the St. Clement's Island area, Willie Husemann, and the local blacksmith, Adam T. Wible, were outstanding practitioners of the art for a half century. They have been followed by Bill Dickson of St. Patrick's and Sidney Lucas of Bretton Bay, both of whom also do some boat building. Probably the most famous tong maker of the early days was Charles L. Marsh of Solomon's Island, a blacksmith, who invented the so-called "patent" tongs in 1887. He was a brother of the ship-builder, James T. Marsh.

The "patent" tongs were designed for use in deep water and had a spring release that would cause the tongs to "grab" upon reaching bottom and would catch a bushel or two of shells and oysters at each lick. Originally, these tongs had long wooden shafts, but Mr. Marsh soon replaced them with short iron shafts. These tongs were raised from the bottom with a winch. They were used quite extensively in deep water tonging for many years until the scarcity of oysters made them uneconomical. They are still used to a limited extent in the Patuxent River, but they were perhaps used for the last time in the Potomac about 1919 when George and Clem Beitzell decided to

"PATENT" OYSTER TONGS

Charles L. Marsh
Inventor of the Patent Tongs in 1887

PATUXENT RIVER CIRCA 1941

Capt. Charles Husemann and sons,
Ross and Harry. Capt. Joseph Davis
of Tidewater Fisheries checking for
legal size which is minimum of 3
inches.

Patent tongers raise
catch from bar.

POTOMAC RIVER OYSTER TONGING BOATS

1964

St. Katherine's Sound

Sheepshead Bar

76

try the deep water off lower Heron Island bar. The pair worked for a day using a hand winch and they raised about a thousand bushels of shells, from which two bushels of beautiful big oysters were culled. Mr. Marsh made very little from his patent, since his tongs could be duplicated quite easily by any iron worker. In recent years most of the deep water oystering in the Patuxent has been carried on by the use of a hydraulic rig.

In the days when oysters were plentiful in the Potomac, two men in a boat would tong 50 to 75 bushels per day at the beginning of the season in September. Later in the season, the catch would drop to around 30 bushels. In 1962 the catch ranged from 6 to 12 bushels. The tongs or rakes are dumped on a "culling" board which is approximately three feet wide and in length equals the width of the boat, so that placed crosswise on the boat the debris can be raked overboard after culling. The board has a railing on each side to prevent spillage before the culling operation is started. After the board is loaded, one of the tongers stops tonging to "cull off" the board. The oysters, three inches in size or larger, are picked from the debris, any dead shell or other objects knocked off with the "culling hammer," a small specially designed implement, and the oysters then are dropped into the boat. The remaining debris, usually shells, small oysters, mud and stones, is raked overboard. This operation is continued from sunrise, when the boats generally get on the bar, until 3:30 to 4:30 P.M., when they leave to sell their catch.

Generally, the owner of the boat takes out 1/5 share for the use of his boat and the remainder is shared with his mate. In exceptional cases, when a tonger is outstanding in his craft, he receives a somewhat larger share. It is worthy of note to record that this arrangement prevails regardless of color -- the man shares strictly on his ability to produce, so that the negro waterman gets a fair break on the Potomac. Most of the oystermen work two to a boat, sometimes three, but in recent years, more small one-man boats are appearing, due to the scarcity of the oysters. When oysters are scarce and a tonger finds a patch there are always one or two on the bar who will try to push in, and unless the finder knows his way around, he is in for a very aggravating time which may culminate in some unpleasantness, such as ramming, hammer throwing, or even shooting.

In January, 1962, Varley Lang had such an encounter and in a letter to the writer, he described the incident as follows:

"Until last week, tonging had dwindled to a day or two a week with luck, but I got some solid work in for a change, though one day was spent in a sleet storm with hail the size and color of small mothballs. Very unpleasant, as I am sure your brother, Clem, would agree. I was bothered the other day by two young tongers who followed me about. I had put out six bushels the day before, and I guess the news got around, since that is a good catch these days. I would move, but I couldn't seem to shake them. They evidently thought I had a patch somewhere. However, I have played this game before. Age has its compensations. I moved to a rise on the edge of Gibson's Flats, a very steep, narrow rise, room for just one boat on the good ground. They came right behind me. By shearing the boat, I was able to drive them either on top of the barren sand or off into the mud, whichever way they jumped. They wasted two hours while I tonged five bushels right under their noses. They gave up and left me alone. I never have crowded another tonger, and I will not allow another tonger to crowd me. Everyone here knows that, including those youngsters. But they had to try me. It was what the old tongers used to call 'a very pretty piece of digging.' You don't see much of it anymore, because there is little crowding of that kind, the deliberate sort, that is; and the old men who taught me the tricks are mostly gone."

In the dredging days, the dories usually were operated by only two men on a sharing basis with two dredges, one on each side of the boat. The dredges were hauled in alternately by hand windlasses, the catch culled immediately, and the dredge returned to the water to fill while the other dredge was being hauled in and cleared. A few flatties or bateaus and skipjacks also were used in the Potomac by the local rivermen and they would be crewed by four to six men. Typical of the latter was the flattie, "A. J. Lewis," owned by Tilton Hayden of Canoe Neck Creek. In 1918, his crew consisted of Frank Morris, Frank Norris, Raymond Owens, Howard Hayden, and Ernest Lyon. In the earlier part of the season their catch averaged from 100 to 150 bushels a day while working the deep waters from Sheepshead to Cobb bar.

Occasionally there were seasons when oysters were so plentiful that tongers with several men in the boat were putting out two loads per day, from 200 to 300 bushels. The dredgers also made correspondingly larger catches in these years. These days can return if the proper conservation steps are taken and the oyster economy is managed efficiently.

Many of the oyster "buy boats" and their masters of the lower Potomac during the period 1870 to 1920 have been mentioned in Chapters III and IV. Most of them lived in the vicinity of St. Clement's and St. Katherine's Islands. Captains Benjamin and H. Webster Foxwell sailed out of Bretton Bay. St. George's Island was well represented by Captains Samuel Trader, Thomas and Oliver Crowder, George Ball, George Duncan, George Gabriel Thomas, and George H. Cullison; Captains Dick, Charles, Tyler, Ephraim, Watt, and Bill Chesser and Captains Charles, John, and Joe Henderson. Captain Bill Chesser lost his life in his bugeye, "Nettie May," as she was standing off St. George's Island, after a record run from Washington on Christmas Eve, 1895. Captain Bill had a green crew on this trip and was knocked overboard by a boom as he stood amidships drinking coffee after a long watch at the helm. The accident was caused by an inexperienced hand at the wheel.

A great riverman of the old school is Captain Joe Henderson who was born on St. George's Island, June 18, 1885, a son of many seafaring generations. He has lived on the Island all of his life and while now retired from his labors on the great river, he continues to produce the finest "nippers" that can be found on the Potomac. There is scarcely a boat or master who has plied the river in the past seventy years that he does not remember and his help has been invaluable in identifying both boats and masters during this period.

Captain Joe has been a riverman since 1902 and shipped with his father, John Henderson, in 1905 aboard his 60 ton bugeye, the "Avalon." Later he mastered his own bugeye, the "Edith Muir." On his forty-fifth birthday he went to work for the Maryland Tidewater Fisheries as an inspector and served under six governors before retirement. He rates the following vessels as the fastest sailers and their skippers as the more competent and best known on the Potomac: The "Avalon," a sharp sail bugeye, Captain John W. Henderson; the "Lottie L. Thomas," a square sail bugeye, Captain Edwin Gibson; the "George B. Faunce," a sharp rigged bugeye and the "Mattie F. Dean," a beautiful schooner, Captain Matt Bailey; the "Amanda F. Lewis," a fast pungy, Captain Jerry Gibson; the "Ethel Vail," a sharp rigged bugeye, Captain George W. (Watt) Chesser; the "Martin Wagner," a schooner, Captain Charles E. Henderson; and the "Eleanora Russell," a sharp sail bugeye, Captain Richard Chesser.

In addition to the Potomac River "buy boats," there were many buyers from the Bay. Among them were Captain Henry Ward in the "Louise Travers," a bugeye; Captain George Adams in the "William M. Powell, a schooner; Captain John Tyler in the "Richard Cromwell," a 4,000 bushel, two-topmast schooner; Captain Harvey Conway in the schooner, "Ruth Conway,' and also the "Lorena Clayton"; Captain Gus Forbush, Willard Lankford, John Guy, and his son-in-law, Arthur Marshall, who now operates a fish and oyster packing plant on Canoe Neck Creek; and Captain Ed Tyler in the "Carrie L." Josh Morris of Canoe Neck Creek lost his dory when she was heavily loaded and swamped as he was putting out his oysters on the "Carrie L." near the mouth of St. Clement's Bay.

When the "golden era" of the oyster industry in the Chesapeake Bay and its tributaries began in the 1870's, it was perhaps the most colorful period in its long history. It is true that the great square rigged ships of the "Tobacco Fleet," the British war armadas, and the famed Baltimore Clippers have contributed greatly to the nautical lore of the Chesapeake and the Potomac and were recorded in their history; they were subjects of verse and song, legend and magnificent paintings, but the end of the 19th century saw an activity in the history of sailing vessels on the Bay and its great tributaries that will never be equaled or duplicated and was worthy to bring down the curtain to mark the passing of sail work boats and of water transportation by sail. The pungies, schooners, bugeyes, sloops, skipjacks, and dories went out in a grand blaze of glory and with them almost went that silent succulent treasure of the gourmet, the oyster.

The Bay "drudgers" found in the 70's that the pungies and schooners were not well suited for dredging and the Bay log canoes, which had grown into brogans, were still too small for their operations, so the Chesapeake Bay bugeye was developed. While some of the pungies and schooners were kept in service as dredge boats, many became "buy boats." The Potomac rivermen adapted the bugeye because of its speed, for the "buy boat" use on the river and developed the dory to fill their local requirements for a small dredge boat.

It may be of interest to review the activities on the Potomac River a century ago as disclosed in the U. S. census records of 1860, 1870, and 1880. While the different classifications used by the census takers in the several counties are somewhat confusing the following tabulation gives a fair picture of river activities at that time. The 1860 figures excludes a considerable number of slaves, either working with their masters or working their master's boats for them. After the war almost 40% of the rivermen were ex-slaves working small skiffs. Many of the white rivermen either died during the war or lost their boats and no longer were engaged in river activities, but by 1880, many of them or their sons had improved their financial situation, were again boat owners, and were taking advantage of the oyster and fish bonanza that had opened up on the river.

POTOMAC RIVER OYSTER TONGING BOATS

1966

Sheepshead Bar

Heron Island Bar

Clamming Boat

Chesapeake Bay Log Canoe

St. Clement's Bay

St. George's Island

"Mattie F. Dean"

"Double-Ender"

Used both as Dredge and "Buy" Boat

Owned by Capt. Sam Bailey

78

	Fishermen 1860-70-80			Oystermen 1860-70-80			Sailors 1860-70-80			Watermen 1860-70-80			Boatmen 1860-70-80			Total 1860-70-80		
St. Mary's County	22	2	17	74	81	142	75	55	45	-	-	-	-	-	-	171	138	204
Charles County	3	21	14	14	2	62	35	34	43	-	-	-	-	-	-	52	57	119
Prince George's County	1	-	3	-	-	-	2	-	2	-	-	-	-	-	-	3	-	5
Northumberland County	1	-	83	12	45	44	64	44	90	-	-	-	-	-	-	77	89	217
Westmoreland County	-	3	2	-	-	60	-	18	20	19	-	-	-	-	-	19	21	82
King George County	2	1	7	-	-	-	8	8	-	4	-	-	-	-	-	14	9	7
Stafford County	3	2	3	-	-	-	-	4	-	2	-	-	10	2	-	15	8	3
TOTAL	32	29	129	100	128	308	184	163	200	25	-	-	10	2	-	351	322	637

NOTE: (1) Undoubtedly these figures do not include farmers along the water front who engaged in fishing or oystering during the seasons but whose main occupation was farming.

(2) Judging by the amount of personal property shown and the titles used in these censuses, it is evident that certain of the men listed were owners or masters or both of merchant sailing vessels engaged in the Potomac River trade. A list of their names will be found in Appendix "C".

During the late 70's and early 80's when the yield of oysters in Maryland waters was averaging around 15,000,000 bushels a year, there was little difficulty with the oyster fleet. But as the dredging grounds in the Bay were depleted, the dredgers started moving in on privately owned grounds and on the grounds of the tongers. They also started coming into the Potomac to dredge and they came by the hundreds so that the river was white with sails.

Near the mouth of the Potomac some fifty to seventy-five boats would work each bar. Some of the more famous oyster bottoms on the Maryland shore are James Creek Bar, between Point Lookout and Calvert Bay; St. George's Island Bar, between the Island and the mainland; Back of the Island Bar, in the Potomac off St. George's Island; Herring Run Bar, above Piney Point off Herring Creek; Huggins Bar off Bretton Bay; Heron Island Bar, below St. Clement's (Blackistone) Island; Dukeharts or the Swash, between the Island and Colton's Point, Sheepshead Bar, above the Island; St. Katherine's Sound, between the Island and the mainland; Cobb Island Bar, at the mouth of the Wicomico River; and Swan Point Bar opposite Colonial Beach, Virginia. On the Virginia shore there are Hog Island Bar, off Coan River; Lynch Point Bar off Yeocomico River; Red Bar below Ragged Point; Ragged Point Bar; Peach Orchard Bar above Ragged Point; Old Farm Bar, the largest bar in the area, between Pope's Creek and the Kettle Bottom Channel; and the Kettle Bottom Shoals.

Following the Bay dredgers, many Bay tongers also came into the Potomac. Some forty or fifty fast sailing log canoes from the Tangier Island area generally worked the "lumps" off the Lower Machodoc and the smaller Nanticoke lapstreak boats, painted a distinctive green and white, scattered far and wide up the Potomac.

Beginning about 1875, the so-called Oyster Wars began and have continued down to this day. The early difficulties in the Bay culminated in 1888 in a pitched battle in the Chester River between the police boat, "McLane," under the command of Captain Thomas Contee Bowie Howard, and about a dozen dredge boats which had been lashed together to form a massive barricade in the "McLane's" path. After several hours of rifle fire, at a range of seventy-five yards, Oliver Crowder, the mate, of St. George's Island, suggested to the Captain that they ram the dredgers. Permission granted, he circled the clustered dredgers out of range, took a compass bearing and withdrew on a set course. Since the pilot house was armored only halfway up, below the windows, Crowder removed the compass from the binnacle to the deck, turned 180 degrees on his course and ordered full steam ahead. With the men crouched on the deck, a compass course was steered straight into the blazing guns. The dredge boat, "J. C. Mahoney," sank from the force of the collision and another dredger was badly damaged. The "McLane" also was damaged but Captain Howard dodged in and out through the now disrupted fleet with guns blasting away as fast as they could be reloaded and eventually captured several of them. However, this did not mark the end of troubles in the Bay. As late as 1928 Governor Harry Byrd of Virginia dispatched three companies of militia to Mobjack Bay, where oystermen were helping themselves from a packer's preserve and shooting at patrol boats.

When the Bay dredge boats started "invading" the Potomac in the 1880's, the "Oyster War" soon spread to the river. Like the sons of all river families, the writer, during his boyhood, was nurtured on tales of the terrible "Eastern Shoreners," a term which included all foreign dredgers, whether they were from Virginia, the Eastern Shore of Maryland, or from Baltimore. By and large they were a tough bunch of characters as is attested by a reading of county papers covering the past eighty years. During the dredging season, in practically every year of this period, there have been reports of armed clashes between our rivermen and the tidewater police on the one side and the "Eastern Shoreners" on the other, with fatalities reported frequently.

It was permissible for these foreign "drudgers" to work in the Potomac. The men from Baltimore and the Eastern Shore of Maryland were entitled to this right as Marylanders, and those from Virginia, under the Compact of 1785, agreed to by Maryland and Virginia. This compact provided that in return for free entry of Maryland ships through the Virginia Capes, Maryland gave Virginia full and equal fishery rights in the Potomac.

The local rivermen did not like this invasion of their home waters by the larger bay dredge boats that "hogged" the better parts of the bars and crowded the entire area and there was trouble from the beginning. With increased depletion of the dredging grounds over the years the situation worsened.

There are many accounts of clashes in the local newspapers and as early as January 13, 1870, the St. Mary's Beacon reported trouble between the dredgers and tongers. On December 18, 1879, the Beacon reported that the oystermen of Beggars (Newtown) Neck and Bedlam Neck (St. Clement's Manor) had subjected the foreign dredgers to a withering crossfire when they were caught in St. Clement's Bay. Still another account, dated February 23, 1888, described the continuation of the oyster war and reported the death of a dredger from gunfire. One could be sure that year after year as the oyster season arrived there would be further trouble between the "Eastern Shoreners," the police and the Potomac rivermen. On January 3, 1918, the Beacon reported: "A naval battle between a fleet of eight oyster-dredging boats and the Major Murrey and Accomac, of the Maryland and Virginia oyster navies, took place today on the Potomac River off the mouth of Port Tobacco Creek, resulting in the capture of the eight oyster boats. The captains of the dredgers were taken off the boats and the whole fleet escorted by the police proceeded down the river to Bushwood."

Again the tonging grounds were being invaded, first by the "foreigners" and then by the Potomac dory dredgers themselves, who could not bear the sight of "them damned Eastern Shoreners" stealing their oysters; if any stealing was going to be done, they would do it themselves. Somehow, through some unfathomable process, the Virginians always wound up getting most of the blame and the unfavorable publicity. Generally the "Oyster Wars" have been exaggerated somewhat by writers and in news reports but a number of fatalities resulting from armed clashes are a matter of record, and probably fifty or more men have lost their lives since 1880.

In the winter of 1895, Reverend Charles K. Jenkins, S.J., was forced to call upon the State Attorney to protect the church property at Newtown Manor on St. Clement's Bay from the Eastern Shore and Virginia dredgers. When the state didn't move fast enough the people took matters in their own hands. This was a very hard winter and quite a few dredge boats were caught and frozen in the ice covering St. Clement's and Bretton Bays for a considerable period of time, with the result that the dredgers, some 140 of them, were short of provisions and firewood. Even in pleasant weather the dredgers were not averse to slipping in to shore under cover of darkness to replenish supplies from the water front farms. Thus a number of pigs, chickens, sheep, and the like never reached market, but were cooked on the dredge boats, often over a blaze made of the luckless farmer's fence rails. This did not further endear the dredgers to the county people and after Father Jenkins' complaint the neighboring men took over with the result that the dredgers were subjected to a considerable amount of gunfire which wasn't quite "cricket" since the dredge boats were frozen in the ice and couldn't make a run for it. Eventually the relatives of the dredgers heard of their plight and brought them supplies and the situation cooled off a bit.

Undoubtedly there were good men among the dredgers and the priests at old Newtown Church have recorded that some of them came to services at the church on Sundays during the winter months, although they were not Catholics. However, the general

A NAVAL ENGAGEMENT IN CHESTER RIVER. For several years the State authorities of Maryland have had much trouble with oyster dredgers working either out of season or within prohibited limits. The swift sailing schooners generally succeeded in eluding the officials when detected in unlawful dredging. At length the patience of the officers gave out, and a police boat was built expressly to prevent the dredgers from trespassing on grounds forbidden to them under the law, one of the provisions of which is that there shall be no dredging beyond the headlands of the risers and estuaries of the bay; and another provision of which is that the dredgers must cull their oysters on the natural or legal grounds whereupon they were taken.

In the thick fog of Friday, March 18th, a fleet of oyster dredging schooners passed inside of the headlands of Chester River, went up the river and there commenced taking oysters on the forbidden grounds. No trouble was experienced until late in the afternoon, when several of the fleet ran down and capsized the tongers who were at work along the stream. The tongers who are irreconcilable enemies of the dredgers, saw a chance for revenge and so sent a delegation of their men across Gray's Inn Neck to the captain of the police boat "Nannie Merryman," who at once headed for the mouth of the river to lay in wait for the dredgers. The first vessel to arrive was the schooner "Eugene," Captain John Wilson, owned by Patrick Pendergast of Baltimore. The captain of the "Nannie" ordered the "Eugene" to drop her jib and lie-to. No answer was returned, and the schooner kept on her course, when the sloop ran alongside of her and repeated the order. Still it was not heeded, and the fight commenced. The "Nannie" fired from a swivel-gun, and the "Eugene" replied from several large shotguns in the hands of the captain and crew. For a while the exchange of shots was lively. Captain Wilson stood to his helm until a tin cup on the top of the binnacle was shot away, and then he lashed his helm and dropped under the sail for safety. His vessel was the faster sailer in a light wind, and he soon got out of the way, suffering no greater loss than the cutting away of his sounding-pole by shot from the sloop, and the riddling of his bulwarks. At one time he was so close to the "Nannie" that in jibing his mainsail his boom struck the shrouds of the police sloop and knocked off the starboard light. The "Nannie" did not endeavor to pursue the "Eugene" any further, but turned back to look after the rest of the fleet of illegal dredgers. Shots were exchanged with the schooners "Merrick," "Cambridge," "Kite" and "Petrel," as they tried to run the gantlet, but all succeeded in escaping except the "Kite" and the "Merrick," which were captured, and, with their captains and crews were taken under escort of the sloop to Chestertown. Notwithstanding the briskness of the firing, it is not known that anybody was hurt beyond a man in the "Petrel," who was slightly wounded in the forearm. The "Eugene" arrived in Baltimore and discharged her cargo. The "Merrick" and the "Kite" belonged to J. Fred Bucheimer, who went to Chestertown and paid the fine of $100 and costs for each of his vessels.

Maryland Naval Engagement with Oyster Poachers
Dredging in the Chester River - 1881

Leslie's Illustrated News, April 19, 1881

OYSTER WARS

POACHED OYSTERS. The annual war between the State of Maryland and its refractory oystermen has broken out with signal force and fury. When the oystermen can reap their bivalvular harvest with as little trouble in the waters that are free as in the waters that are forbidden, it appears they do so. When the wild crop, so to speak, falls short, they invade the preserves against the peace and dignity of the people of Maryland, and the statute in such case made and provided, and this is a bad season. Love laughs at locksmiths. It is difficult to believe that a man who gets his living catching oysters with tongs can laugh at anything. But in point of fact he does laugh at the laws of Maryland; and indeed the bard who sang "Carry me back to old Virginny" has chronicled his delight in his occupation and told melodiously how he

> "spent the live-long day
> A-raking among the oyster beds;
> To me it was but play,"

or words to that effect. This year Maryland has risen in her might, not this time to spurn the Northern scum, but to avenge the ravishment of the preserved oysters which had been reposing in secluded creeks "under the protection of the law and in the gladsome light of jurisprudence," with a touching confidence in the legislature which higher organisms can never attain. The piratical navy consists of some twenty-five or thirty oyster boats, of about ten tons each, and as like each other as so many peas. In order to make detection still more difficult, the crews are reported to smear the sails with mud, so the new cloths shall not betray them, and to array themselves in weird and wonderful garments. Apparently they are only liable to arrest when found actually engaged in dredging. If they are simply sailing the forbidden waters, they are yachtsmen taking their pleasure and carrying oyster tongs for bric-a-brac. When they are taken in the act of pulling up the wards of the State, they run into shallow water, if the pursuer be a steamboat, and subsequently emerge with an innocent air, and disguised with wonderful garments which baffle identification. When they are pursued by sloops, they make for the Virginia waters, into which the writs of Maryland do not run. As their boats are always fast, by the same wonderful provision of nature by which a smuggler always outsails a revenue-cutter, a slaver a man-of-war, and a pickpocket runs away from a fat policeman, they commonly gain their refuge, and grin defiance upon their baffled pursuer.

This year the Navy of Maryland has been put upon a war footing by the borrowing of two 6-pounders from the Naval Academy for two of the oyster boats of war, and a determined pursuit of the poachers has been undertaken. Emboldened by immunity, the poachers laid in shot guns and revolvers. It need hardly be added, considering that they were organized to resist the laws of an American State, that they have also relied upon their political "influence" to make sure that the commander of the State Navy should look where they were not, and not where they were, as if they had been the business books of an eminent financier. In this reliance they have heretofore been justified. But this year the navy has been put under the command of a "theorist" who acknowledged no obligations to "the boys" who chose to break the laws which he absurdly assumed that it was his business to enforce. And, besides, the boys really presumed on their privileges by not only dredging with graceful candor under the guns of the navy, but also by assaulting the crew of a Man-of-War which attempted to interrupt their proceedings. So that even if the theorist had been a machinist, he would have been compelled to defend his flag, and to show the poachers of Maryland, as has lately been shown to the liquor dealers of New York in the person of Mr. McGlory, that there are lengths to which even a "boy" cannot go with impunity.

A general engagement took place on Sunday, February 10. The government squadron, in making its way to the forbidden water, encountered a line of sloops loaded to the gunwale with oysters presumably poached, and were fortunate enough to find two sloops busily at work engaged in a simultaneous breakage of the eighth and fourth commandments, and the statutes of the State of Maryland passed to enforce the same. The sloops were confiscated and the crews locked up to be dealt with according to law. The sad event has cast a deep gloom over the whole business of oyster-poaching.

Maryland Oyster Pirates Dredging at Night - 1884
(Harper's Weekly, March 4, 1884)

opinion of them was not flattering and this is well illustrated by the following anecdote which has come down from these times. Several oystermen, sitting around the pot-bellied stove at Lewis Mattingly's store on Canoe Neck Creek, were discussing Hell. All had had their say except one of the group. When called upon for his opinion he replied, "Oh, I ain't worried none about Hell." "Well, how is that, Cap'n Billy -- you're a God fearing man?" "Yes, sir, I am," he replied, "but there's been too many drudgers died and gone there -- they done tore that place down long ago."

A goodly number of men were "shanghaied" from Baltimore and Washington to work the dredge boats when there were shortages in the crews. The St. Mary's County Beacon, around 1900, carried a story of a young man of good family who was "shanghaied" out of Baltimore and it took his mother several months and considerable expenditure of money to locate him. After locating him, she found it necessary to resort to court action to secure his release from servitude on the dredge boat. It is true that some of these poor devils were paid off near the end of the season with "the boom," which means they were, sans pay, knocked senseless and thrown overboard on a dark night and a report given out that they had been swept overboard by a jibbing boom during the night or in a storm. More often members of the crew, particularly immigrants, were set ashore at some lonely spot at the end of the season, with little or no pay for their season's work.

In the History of the German Society of Maryland, published in Baltimore in 1909, the story of Otto Mayher, a 20 year old German immigrant, who was murdered by a Captain Williams of the pungy, "Eva," in 1884, is told. The trial was held in Somerset County in the spring of 1885 and Captain Williams was convicted of murder and sentenced to 18 years in the penitentiary. Through the efforts of the Society following this murder, the Maryland legislature passed a law to be effective January 1, 1890, to protect the dredging crews. However, the administration of the law was not effective and after several additional murders and many cases of brutal and inhuman treatment, the Society succeeded in 1906 in having Federal legislation passed that was more effective. One of the cases successfully prosecuted by the Society in 1892 was tried in Leonardtown, Maryland, after the Captain of the schooner, "Partnership," was arrested by Captain Turner, of the police boat, the "Governor McLane," near Ragged Point at the mouth of the Potomac.

During the early spring (April) of 1908, the writer's father, who, in addition to oystering also fished "pound" nets found the body of a dredger in his net on Carnishes, between St. Clement's and Bretton Bays. The body was clad in typical dredging costume -- oil skins, gum boots, sou'wester hat, polka dot handkerchief, etc., and at the coroner's inquest, a "barlow" knife and a 5¢ coin were the only possessions found in the clothing. The body could not be identified and had been in the water too long to determine if there had been foul play. It was the consensus that he was a victim of the boom, since a man had not been reported missing in the area. A pine box coffin was made and the unknown was buried on the shore of "Bluff Woods" in St. Clement's Bay, near the mouth of Canoe Neck Creek. At the time of the burial there was some discussion as to whether or not the "barlow knife" should be buried with the body. The problem was solved when one of the rivermen spoke up, this time not too unkindly, "leave it on the poor devil, he may need it to cut his way through hell." John Kobler, in a feature article in the Saturday Evening Post, November 1, 1958, stated that "In a Potomac River tributary not long ago, anglers hauled up three skeletons, the necks chained together and the skulls crushed."

In the summer of 1958, the writer interviewed the late Captain Douglas Russell, then in his 80's, who was one of the old time law enforcement officers on the Potomac. The writer had known the Captain since boyhood and had always admired him as a man who could not be bribed or intimidated. Captain Douglas began his career in January, 1901, as Mate to Captain George W. Maddox on the "Bessie Jones," a sailing vessel used to patrol the Potomac and its tributaries. At that time, the Captain's pay was $60 per month, the Mate's pay was $40 and the crew members were paid at the rate of $35 per month. The wages did not include food. Captain Douglas served from 1901 to early 1906, when he resigned due to a disagreement with authorities concerning law enforcement. However, he returned to the service in the fall of 1906, under Captain Edmund Plowden and it was during this season that one of the many shooting affrays in which he was engaged produced a fatality. The "Bessie Jones" was chasing two dredgers engaged in illegal operations near the mouth of the Wicomico River. Several of the dredgers, including Captain John Guy and Alex Harris, had the same day engaged in an argument with the police officers in the store at old Bushwood Wharf. The argument had ended with the declaration that the law couldn't keep them off Cobb bar and they were leaving to prove it. They were followed by the police boat and Captain Douglas, who was forward in the boat, started shooting at the halyards of the dredgers, in an attempt to drop their sails for a capture. The distance between the boats was only about 75 yards and one of the dredgers returned the fire and one of the shots cut a leg off the binnacle on the "Bessie Jones." Captain Douglas ran aft and returned the fire from the cabin hatchway and Alex Harris of

Oxford (on the Eastern Shore), was a dead man. It wasn't a pretty sight because Captain Douglas was shooting a 45-70 rifle which used a lead bullet about the size of a thumb that mushroomed when it hit. He was fully exonerated by a coroner's jury. Due to pressure from certain oyster interests, he was not reappointed for duty on the Potomac, but was offered duty protecting the Potomac tributaries. This he declined.

In 1916 Captain Douglas returned to the service as Oyster Inspector at $45 per month for himself and $30 per month for the use of his boat. Again, this was a very rough time, for the dredgers, particularly the owners of dredge fleets, such as Tom Webster of Deal Island were attempting to break the "Bailey Survey" (which for many years had defined the dredging areas in the Potomac). The dredge boats started to invade the "Inside," such as the tonging grounds at "Horseshoe," the "in"-side of Heron Island bar, the "Swash," "Old Wrack," etc. Captain Douglas was out at all hours of the day and night and in all kinds of weather. Once he was able to make arrests by running up on the dredge boats during a snow storm. On another day he was nearing a group of dredgers when his engine "froze up" due to the bitter cold, but he was able to transfer to the boat of William Thompson, a local boat builder and oysterman, with the result that he caught three of the dredge boats whose owners drew $100 fines and six months suspended sentences. Another time he was able to surprise and arrest a number of boats off Colonial Beach under the disguise of a "gill netter."

A story is told about a particular local dredger who bragged that he was breaking the law continually and that he was too smart to be caught by Captain Douglas. Word soon reached the Captain who said nothing but late that night hid himself aboard the dredger's boat under the stern seat. As the dredge went overboard the next morning on illegal oyster ground, the Captain crawled forth from his cramped hiding place and another law breaker learned that it didn't pay to trifle with the Captain.

He continued in the service until 1921. The "Eastern Shoreners" were infuriated at the Captain's success in keeping them out of the "Inside" and retaliated by trying to drive the local dredgers, who usually had only "dory boats" (which were quite small in comparison to the bugeyes, pungies, and sloops used by the foreign dredgers) off the dredging grounds "Outside."

The writer's brother, Clem Beitzell, who was dredging on "Sheepshead," just west of St. Clement's Island, had the foremast of his 32 foot dory knocked out by a big bugeye in 1920. The larger bugeye bore down on the small dory to the windward and came close enough to smother the wind in the dory's sails. The dredge then acted as a drag so that the dory was "sucked" in to the side of the bugeye which slackened a boom to knock out the mast (and bash out a few brains, if the men weren't quick). This was a favorite sport of the big boats and quite effective, with the result that the "Eastern Shoreners" hogged the best oyster grounds. Captain Clem came home, with such speed as he could muster, to get his gun but Mother put her foot down firmly, and that was the end of that.

Ordinarily, however, the watermen, including the "Eastern Shoreners," had a code to which they adhered rather strictly. For example, the writer's father, Josiah E. Beitzell, fished "pound" nets off the outside of Heron Island bar, which was in one of the best dredging areas. No dredger would run through the nets, although they were a nuisance and avoiding them slowed operations considerably. Nor would they steal from the nets. In a period of forty years of fishing on the river, he only caught one poacher in his nets and he believed this man was truthful when he said he only wanted a "mess" for supper, which was given him.

Captain Douglas Russell was one of the last of the great rivermen. He started his career as Captain of his own schooner at 15, through the help of his father, a sailing master before him. During the summers from 1910 to 1914 he was master of the yacht, "Iona," a 60 foot sailing boat owned by Paul Portner who was at that time the proprietor of the beautiful "Portner Apartments" at 15th and "U" Streets in Washington, D. C. In 1914, Mr. Portner purchased the ocean going yacht, the "Latona," in New York harbor. Captain Douglas sailed the boat down to Washington and continued as her skipper until 1918. This beautiful boat was 100 feet in length and had a lead keel over 36 feet long. One of the fastest sailing runs made by Captain Douglas in the "Latona" occurred when he left Baltimore at 7:15 A.M. one day and reached the Cedar Point beacon in the Potomac at dark. Much of the wind was fair that day and the breeze was moderate to heavy throughout the trip.

It seems only yesterday that the writer, then a small boy, would look out from his home on Canoe Neck Creek and see the beautiful vessel at anchor in St. Clement's Bay near Bluff Woods. In boyish dreams he sailed the Seven Seas in the "Latona" and had many wonderful adventures.

After World War I, and after the dredge rocks had been thoroughly cleaned, the Maryland legislature finally outlawed dredging in the Potomac, and the rivermen saw the last of the Bay dredgers and the last of dredging by sail in the river. Comparatively, only a handful of dredge boats continued in the Chesapeake for oyster production dropped from over 10,000,000 bushels in the 90's to about 3,000,000 bushels

Schooner, "Columbia F. C.," Leaving Coan Wharf
March 1939, Pulled by Yawl Boat Under the Jib-Boom

Schooner, "Federal Hill," Sailing Up Chesapeake Bay
with a Cargo of Lumber, 1929

POTOMAC RIVER SAILING VESSELS

Photo: Robert H. Burgess

Schooner, "Henry Disston," Loaded with Lumber
Headed Down the Patapsco River, August 11, 1935

Photo: Robert H. Burgess

Schooner, "Thomas B. Schall," Headed Down
Chesapeake Bay, May 30, 1935

annually. No longer were the waters white with sail. There were only a few dis-
masted derelicts chugging about, powered with noisy, ill-smelling and poorly adapted
engines, in place of the many slick, beautiful ships that had been built to sail and
to sail beautifully.

A low water mark was reached in the Potomac River oyster·industry prior to
World War II, but after the war, the river was discovered to be "alive" with oysters.
Tongers were catching 100 to 150 bushels daily and getting $2.00 to $2.25 per bushel
for them. This was too much for the Virginians and they moved in on the oyster bars
with dredge equipped power boats and they did not confine themselves to the deep
waters. They were joined by more than enough Marylanders, who said in effect: These
are Maryland oysters and if anyone is going to catch them its going to be us Marylanders. The tongers stood helplessly by, the tidewater police were not geared to
handle lawbreaking on a wholesale scale and by the time the police could cope with
the situation, the oyster grounds were stripped and have not yet recovered.

Alfred Toombs, in a feature article in the St. Mary's _Enterprise_ in 1955, described the happenings of this period in the following words:

"Maryland and Virginia are the only two of the United States which are still
trying to regulate their relationship on the basis of a treaty which was drafted
before the Constitution was ratified. And, from what I've seen and heard in the
30-odd years I've been around St. Mary's County, it's just as well none of the other
states are trying it."

"Things have been fairly quiet along the Potomac this winter. Only one armed
clash between The Virginia-men and the forces of Maryland law and order has been
brought to my notice, although it is possible that a few skirmishes have taken place
in the dark of night which have not been reported in the record book."

"But it has not always been this peaceful in the river and may not continue
thus for very long. I would suspect that the fact that most of the oysters have by
now been pilfered has more to do with the situation than has any onset of civic
rectitude."

"This river which flows past my front steps -- and, during hurricane season sometimes flows over them - has a dark and bloody past. In my boyhood, the blame for
most of this was fixed in my mind upon some lumbering, brawling, murderous characters
known only as Virginia-men."

"The old timers around our creek used to speak with awe of the depredations of
these Virginia-men, who would scatter the Maryland oyster fleet like leaves before
the wind. It was Virginia-men who, with blazing guns, would chase Marylanders off
the oyster bars. They would also kidnap Marylanders to work their boats and then
pay them off with the boom -- sweeping them into the icy waters. The tales the old
captains told us were enough to make your blood run cold and, what was more, it did."

"But it was not until I grew older that the Virginia-men began to emerge as
something more than boogey-men, fashioned out of the memories of the old captains
around the creek."

"During the war -- when I was away from the county on a trifling European trip --
the Virginia-men came back strong. Then it was that prices for everything were high,
including oysters. After the war, the prices got higher and the Virginia-men became
more in evidence."

"The river was fairly loaded with oysters, which were being taken up by tongs
in the legal fashion. The Virginia-men, an impatient lot, began to appear on the
river with dredges and fast boats. For a good night's work, they could make a few
hundred dollars."

"The wonderful part of it was that, in spite of the fact that this was entirely
illegal, there was no actual danger of anyone being caught and sent to jail. This
was because of the wonderful Compact of 1785 between the sovereign states of Maryland
and Virginia."

"The Compact was drafted to settle the disputes between the two states over
rights to the Potomac River and the Chesapeake Bay. It seemed that Virginia had
been collecting tolls from all Maryland boats passing through the Capes and there
were various other matters at issue. So delegates from the two states met, at the
suggestion of General Washington, at Mount Vernon to draft a treaty."

"The treaty acknowledged the fact that Maryland owned the river, right up to
low-water mark on the Virginia shore, and had the right to police the fisheries
therein. But the compact also provided that when a Virginia citizen was arrested
for illegal fishing in the river, he must be returned to Virginia for trial."

"Although treaties, as such, between the states were abrogated by the Constitution, the Compact between Maryland and Virginia, as far as it related to the river
and bay, was allowed to remain in force. So that, down through the years, whenever
a Virginia-man was arrested for poaching oysters or fish on the river, he was returned to be tried by a jury of his friends and neighbors, who were likely engaged
in the same business."

"As far as anyone knew, nobody ever got convicted under this system. And so it was that after the war, in 1945, our river was cluttered up with high powered boats out of Virginia, dredging oysters."

"Captain Chester Cullison, the doughty skipper of the Tiny Lou -- the flagship of the Tidewater Fisheries fleet in the River -- was very unhappy about this situation. He would run his boat up to Cedar Point and chase a fleet of dredgers off the oyster bars. Then he would start down the river to Swann Point to get after another crowd. While he was at Swann Point, the dredgers would reassemble at Cedar Point and Captain Chester would start up the river again. It was a frustrating existence for an honest man, trying to do his duty."

"But one day, Captain Chester took judicial note of the fact that the Tidewater Fisheries had put a machine gun on his boat and furthermore, had given him a small supply of ammunition. No one had ever told him not to use it, so next time he approached the Virginia Dredging fleet off Cedar Point, he let fly with a few bursts. The boats scattered for home. So Captain Chester went down to Swann Point and repeated the experiment with the same results."

"The howls that went up from the Virginia-men were loud and long. Captain Chester was called to Annapolis to answer to Edwin Warfield, then chairman of the conservation commission. Now the good captain is normally a reticent man, but when Mr. Warfield wanted to know what the shooting was all about, Cullison took a deep breath and unburdened himself. He talked about the days when he had first shipped out on the patrol boat which his father had skippered on the river for better than 40 years. He spoke with deep emotion of Maryland oysters -- extolling their virtues over the unappetizing varieties which grew in Virginia. He pointed out that the few remaining oysters in the river were being stolen from honest Maryland oystermen by those scoundrels from Virginia."

"Then Captain Chester described every weary, frustrating mile he had travelled between Cedar Point and Swann Point in vain pursuit of the dredgers. His peroration came when he described the beautiful path made by tracer bullets and the even more spectacular trajectory created by Virginia-men in retreat."

"When he had finished, Captain Chester stood there as Warfield eyed him sternly. Finally, Warfield spoke: 'Captain Cullison,' he said, and his voice was husky, 'Do you need any more bullets?'"

"Well, things got a little noisy out in the river after that. Somehow, the bullets never hit anyone. But there was a lot of close combat -- with dredgers trying to ram the police boats, trying to drive them on to the rock shoals and even to set them afire."

"One feature of the Compact of 1785, which provided the ground rules for all of this, was a provision that no changes in the treaty could be made unless confirmed by both the Maryland and Virginia legislatures. This was interpreted to mean that Maryland could not pass a law which said that Virginia dredgers could be tried in our local courts -- unless the other legislature agreed."

"The Maryland authorities finally decided to ignore this and to bring Virginia-men to trial in Maryland, anyway. The Governor of Virginia got pretty mad and dispatched a strong protest through diplomatic channels."

"One of the first of the Virginia-men to be arrested and tried in Maryland -- about five years ago, [1950] -- was a dredger named Nubby. He presented a unique problem to law enforcement authorities who wanted to fingerprint him. For Nubby had been born without hands. When they took off his boots, they found he was also without feet. Hardly the picture of the fierce, swashbuckling Virginia-men I had heard about in my boyhood -- but I guess they don't hardly make them anymore. Oddest thing about the handless, footless Nubby was that he had been arrested in Virginia for burglary, which goes to show how a man can overcome the worst handicaps."

"Well, its been a good deal quieter along the river recently. They took the machine guns off the boats, for one thing. And, for another thing, there are hardly enough oysters in the river to bother with. About all that's left is the Maryland-Virginia treaty."

Two extremely unfortunate killings in the Potomac in recent years resulted in a further decline in the poor relations between Maryland and Virginia that have marked the 175 year history of the Compact of 1785. In 1949, Earl Nelson, a Marylander, and a sixty year old widower with seven children, was killed by a Virginia Fisheries deputy. A few years later, Berkeley Muse, a popular young man of Colonial Beach, Virginia, and the father of several small children, was killed by the Maryland Tidewater police, while a passenger in a boat suspected of illegal dredging. These and similar shooting affrays, which did not result in casualties, resulted in complete deterioration of relations between the two states in administering the laws governing operations in the river.

In 1957, Governor Theodore McKeldin signed a bill, passed by the Maryland Assembly, abrogating the Treaty of 1785. Virginia immediately appealed to the U. S. Supreme Court on the grounds that Maryland could not, under the compact, move unilaterally to cancel it. The Supreme Court referred the case to Stanley F. Reed, a retired Justice, seeking an out-of-court settlement. A commission composed of representatives from each state worked out an arrangement whereby the river would be regulated by a bi-state agency. The proposed arrangement was bitterly opposed by the Potomac River watermen of Maryland but it was approved by the Assembly. However, under the leadership of State Senator Walter Dorsey of St. Mary's County, the matter was made the subject of state-wide referendum. Due to the lack of knowledge on the part of many Marylanders of the history and problems of the river, the action of the Assembly was confirmed. The new pact was ratified by the U. S. House of Representatives and the Senate and approved by the President in 1962. It created a Potomac River Fisheries Commission with three members from each state, and with powers to regulate the taking of all seafood from the Potomac between the District of Columbia and the Chesapeake Bay. Commission action will require the concurrence of at least two of the members from each state. In addition to regulating the watermen's activities, the Commission has authority to do research work, to impose an oyster inspection fee and to issue licenses. Each state has agreed to appropriate at least $50,000 a year for use by the Commission for purposes other than law enforcement.

Governor J. Millard Tawes of Maryland and Governor Albertis S. Harrison of Virginia observed the inauguration of the new Potomac River Compact at a luncheon in Washington which featured oysters, on December 5, 1962, the date the new compact went into effect. Both Chief Executives expressed the hope that the Compact will end oyster hostilities which have brought death to at least five persons in the past fifteen years. It is to be hoped that both states will cooperate fully to conserve, improve, and protect all of the resources of the river.

The rivermen on both sides of the Potomac have now formed "Watermen's" associations. The Maryland Association headed by Captain David Sayre of St. George's Island is quite active. There are no local representatives from the lower Potomac River counties on the Commission. This had caused a great deal of resentment because the rivermen feel, and justly so, that they should have a voice in the decisions reached by the Commission in actions that directly affect their livelihood. Further, the knowledge and recommendations of these men should be valuable to the Commission. It is hoped that the Commission will establish at least an advisory committee composed of rivermen from the counties concerned so that they may have a voice in their own affairs. It is certain that if such action is taken, committee decisions will become more palatable to the rivermen and there will be better enforcement of regulations.

Dr. R. V. Truitt, founder of the Chesapeake Biological Laboratory and former member of the Maryland Board of Natural Resources, has estimated that $1,000,000 could be added to the industry of St. Mary's County alone through proper planning and management of its tributaries. He has urged that not only the rivermen but the leaders of the County ".....organize, work out plans for restoration, by and with the advice and assistance of scientists and practical people, and work closely with the State's Tidewater Fisheries Commission.....Also, they can develop their own areas, through leased barren bottoms of which there are 14,000 acres now unproductive. But again, through planning and dynamic leadership, the watermen must themselves, become more elastic in their thinking in order that certain, but few, of the present marginal tonging bars may be set aside for shelling and seed production -- seed to be used in the County. No matter which approach is made looking to increased oyster production, that is, whether done by the State, as a public fishery or by the local people, seed production is basic. St. Mary's County can become a world leading oyster producing center and in a relatively short period, to the advantage of the watermen, the economy of the area and to the State generally."

The writer is in agreement with Dr. Truitt that the lower Potomac ".....can become a world leading oyster producing center and in a relatively short period....." However, there is no necessity for large public leases. That was tried in the 1890's with disastrous results when the creeks along the river were opened to public leasing. It brought nothing but contention and trouble and finally public opinion ran so high against it a bill was rammed through the Maryland Assembly outlawing the practice. As a result those owning the leases lost their complete investment overnight -- an investment that had been carefully built up over a period of years. It was the biggest political "headache" of those times and some of the feuds engendered are still remembered in the present generation.

If any leases are granted at all they should be restricted to local people, limited to a small area, on barren grounds in the creeks and only after a thorough investigation. It would be a much better plan to re-seed such barren grounds rather than lease them as they are excellent oyster producing areas. A case in point was the re-seeding of the area, St. Clement Shores in St. Clement's Bay in 1962. In 1964 this shore was loaded with oysters and if it is policed properly will produce for years.

In any event, no public leases should be granted in the Potomac River and its bays, and none should be granted to the packing houses of Baltimore and the Eastern Shore. The individual oystermen do not have the capital required for large public lease operation so that public leasing would be no more than an open invitation for the big packers, who have the resources, to move in, which would not benefit either the oystermen or the local economy. The use of leased ground would permit the packers to buy cheaply from the local men, plant on their private grounds and later harvest the oysters when the market was high. Further, the packers would use dredges to take up their oysters. Once a boat is equipped with a dredge it is extremely difficult for the police to control its use.

In the matter of seed production, there is plenty of barren ground that could be used by the state, but there is no necessity to take over producing grounds for this purpose. In those areas too deep for tonging, where there are oysters going to waste, limited dredging under direct police supervision might be permitted, under special license. At the end of the period, the dredges would be impounded by the police and not released until the start of the next season.

There is no real necessity for public leases. The state re-seeding program, and better police protection is beginning to pay off, and will increase rapidly in the coming years, if the dredge and clam boats are kept off the oyster bars. Continuation and expansion of the seeding program to include more barren grounds, and adequate policing is all that is necessary.

During each war oysters have made a phenominal recovery. Prior to the war, oysters were very scarce; with the outbreak of the war the young men sought jobs in shipyards or other war industries and of course, many went into the military service. This gave the oyster beds a chance to re-establish themselves. We know beyond any doubt that this has been the pattern following the Civil War and World Wars I and II, and each time the recovery took place in a period of four years or less. It is obvious that with a sound conservation program and strict enforcement of the oyster laws, the situation can be fairly well controlled. By giving nature some assistance, as suggested by Dr. Truitt, the desired results can be attained more quickly.

The account books of Newtown Manor show that the Jesuit Fathers were paying 6¢ per bushel for oysters in 1815 following the close of the War of 1812, which indicates that oysters were plentiful following this war. Likewise, a decade following the Civil War saw the beginning of the golden era of the oyster industry. Following World War I, with the return of the young men from the service and the shipyards of Washington, Alexandria, and Quantico, there was a revival of the oyster industry in the Potomac that approached for a few years, the golden days of the 80's. Two men in a boat were tonging 50 to 75 bushels a day and oysters were bringing from 60¢ to 75¢ a bushel. Engines were removed from the dories and replaced by sails and the dredgers were doing better than the tongers. There were so many sails on the Potomac River bars that, literally, one on the Maryland shore could not see the Virginia shore when there was a breeze on the river.

A few years prior to this time, in October 1911, a lawyer, Louis Sayer, who had a particular liking for sailing vessels took a cruise on a "buy boat," the "Ella F. Cripps," out of Baltimore, as mentioned in Chapter IV, and recorded the following:

".....It is some thirteen miles down the Patapsco River, and, with a nearly full moon giving light, we ate up the distance gloriously, arriving at the river mouth about ten o'clock, and finding a bad sea running up the bay, ran back under Bodkin Point and anchored for the night. Up at daylight, we found the wind due South and began a beat that lasted all that day and until dawn the next, when we worked around Point Lookout and stood up the Potomac with a light wind."

"It was a magnificent spectacle; there were in sight countless boats dredging, and the beautiful shores of the river made a suitable background for the ruffled water."

"We were bound for Bretton Bay, thirty miles up the river, and we were all day fanning along in the light air. As we turned into the bay at nine o'clock that night, I thought we were approaching the lights of a city, but when we got deep into the bight, I found we were anchored among a fleet of five hundred vessels whose anchor lights I had taken for those of a settlement."

"As night drew on the wind died out absolutely and the full moon rose over the hills to reflect the quivering spars in a sea of jet, and the only sounds were the flapping of a sail or the creaking sheave of a block. We were tired after a 48-hour thrash, followed by twelve hours of light air, than which nothing is more fatiguing, but sat spellbound 'til late, as it is such scenes as these that arouse that very passion for living that is in everybody's heart."

"Sunday morning the weather still held, and as the law prohibits dredging, the fleet was perforce idle, and I took our yawl and went about. There were schooners, bugeyes, bateaus, Long Island sloops, and boats of no known type, hundreds of them, and it seemed an opportunity to study their differences, and guage their adaptability to their business. My experience on the water had been confined to the North, so I

POTOMAC RIVER "BUY" BOATS

Schooner, "Ella F. Cripps"

Photo: A. Aubrey Bodine
WORK BOAT RACES, PINEY POINT, MARYLAND - 1930

Bugeye, "Florence Northam"

Photo: A. Aubrey Bodine
WORK BOAT RACES, PINEY POINT, MARYLAND - 1930
(Courtesy of The Mariners Museum)

POTOMAC RIVER "BUY" BOATS

Unidentified Schooner (maybe the "Annie Croswell")
Passing Ragged Point Lighthouse, near the mouth of
the Potomac River (Courtesy of The Mariners Museum)

Schooner, "J. W. Knowles,"
in Baltimore Harbor

"Amanda F. Lewis" at anchor
in Canoe Neck Creek

especially enjoyed this chance to broaden my view. Some things surprised me. I had supposed the bugeye was a narrow boat; also, that they were always rigged with raking spars and jibheaded sails. So they were, most of them, but I found them schooner-rigged, some with raking spars, but a gaff on the head of the foresail and regular mainsail. Then again that might be reversed. One boat that was much thought of in the community was the bateau, a model growing in favor for dredging. They are sharpie-rigged but sloops, built with square bilges, about 45 feet long and 14 feet breadth, but they are peculiar. They do not get their beam for two-thirds of their length aft, the mast rakes back sharply, as in so many bay boats, to get a spread for the shrouds and get the center of sail effort back where it should be. They are fast, handy, able and cheap to build, and suggest the inverted wedge model, in the handling of their lines, that design supposed to be new, yet those models are as old as the civilization on the bay, and have had an eclipse but are again coming back into their own."

"Most of the vessels that are large enough, carry a stout launch on their stern davits, with a single-cylinder, two-stroke gasolene engine of about 5 h.p., and use them for towing, or rather for showing their vessels in a calm, as they drop the stern from one davit, leaving the bow suspended just above the water, to give the wheel [propellor] better water to work in. One of these boats will push a 70-foot schooner three miles per hour."

"I boarded several vessels where there were groups gathered together and listened to their talk and unaccustomed expressions. I found these were boatmen, indeed, used to the rigors of Winter sailing as well as the pleasures of Summer, and wise in their business. Like all people, they thought the vessels they owned the very best for their work."

"One criticism made of the bugeye was that the sharp stern made for poor cabin and wheel room, and this is so; but these sterns are great for a seaway and their rig is fine for heavy weather, and some claim they are faster than the schooners in a blow, but I did not see this borne out, as, on our return, in an all-day run into Baltimore, in a stiff breeze, we ran a large bugeye out of sight."

".....In the afternoon it began to cloud up and blow harder, and I shall never forget the picture the dredge boats made as they came luffing up under our stern, jibs slapping and banging as they were hauled down, and bows plunging, throwing the spray off in sheets. Among the many boats that came alongside, from 16-foot canoes to 60-foot schooners, the handling was so exquisite that no falling short or over-standing occurred. The wind was Northwest, fair for us out of the river, and about four o'clock we tucked in one reef in the mainsail and flew down the river, loaded to the sheer plank. I went out on the end of the bowsprit, and she was piling up the foam even with her rail forward, which trailed off her sides like snow from a plow. Her topsides forward flared so that she had her full beam at the shrouds, for she was built on the codfish-head, mackeral-tail style, but once she broke the water she was all run. The breeze kept rising, and as it would be ahead up the bay, we ran into the mouth of St. Marys River and anchored just at dark. We went to bed early and by twelve o'clock the wind had gone down to a moderate breeze, so we got away again and got around Point Lookout and into the bay just at dawn. There were four other schooners and two big bugeyes in company with us, all bound for Baltimore, and a race was on in a minute. We had a close haul, everything on, including flying-jib, deck staysail, and maintopsail, and as the breeze kept rising and fairing, had a glorious run.....Along towards night we had to take in our kites, and at seven o'clock we rushed into harbor....."

Mr. Sayer recorded that the dredge boats were catching forty to sixty bushels of oysters daily and receiving thirty cents a bushel for them. He also mentioned that there were many small boats, "locally called canoes" operated by the tongers but failed to mention the Potomac River dory used both for tonging and dredging, unless they were included in the term "canoe."

A few years after World War I the dredge rocks were cleaned and there had been a lot of encroachment on the tonging grounds. By the time of the outbreak of World War II, oysters were so scarce that many of the rivermen had sold their boats and obtained employment elsewhere. After the war, it was discovered that the bars were alive with oysters and in 1944 the average boat was putting out from 80 to 100 bushels per day at $2.00 to $2.25 per bushel. Henry Gibson and Tilton (Tillie) Hayden tonged a phenominal 287 bushels of oysters in a single day on Key's Bar, near Indiantown, in the Wicomico in this same year. Everyone was getting rich, richer even than in the lush days following the first World War. But this time the prosperity was even more short-lived for faster boats and better motors had been developed. Small boats with big outboard motors that could pull a small dredge, and high powered larger boats using motorized winches to haul in big dredges, cleaned up all the bars, working day and night and outrunning the police at all times. The coordination and co-operation between the Maryland and Virginia police was not notable. One Maryland wag made the observation, perhaps a bit unfair, that the dredgers went out at 4:00 A.M.

and returned by 8:30 A.M. -- then at 9:00 A.M. the Virginia police went out and watched the tongers. One Virginia dredger reportedly made $27,000 in a single season. In any event by the time the police had gotten geared up to cope with the situation the poachers had made a clean sweep.

Prior to 1960 when the state began the shell and seed oyster replanting program two men in a boat were lucky to catch 10 to 12 bushels per day. In the year of 1962-1963, oysters were selling for $5.00 to $5.50 per bushel. Oyster landings in Maryland totaled 1,243,000 bushels in this same year, the lowest in history. In the year 1963-1964 the landings were up some 143,600 bushels for a total of 1,383,617 bushels. It was evident that the state planting of seed oysters on the barren bars had already begun to take effect.

In the Potomac the oystermen had a still better year in the 1965-1966 season as was true in the Chesapeake Bay and all of the tributaries. During the 1966-1967 season 3,014,670 bushels of oysters were landed in Maryland, more than double the figure reached in 1963-1964. Altogether 82,700,000 pounds of seafood was taken from the bay and its tributaries and was greater than in any year since 1908, when watermen harvested 113,800,000 pounds of seafood. Oysters led the seafood production in 1966-1967 with 56% of the total value. The 1967-1968 season promises to be even better. An important contribution to the success of the replanting program has been improved law enforcement.

Although the writer was certain that a replanting program, coupled with more adequate law enforcement would effect considerable improvement in a short period of time, the last three years in the Potomac River have been almost unbelievable. In 1962 only a handful of boats would be observed working the tonging bars, usually not more than 8-10 boats on a bar. In the last three years over 500 boats have been observed working just three bars in the St. Clement's Island area. A total of over 6,500 boats are now working in the Maryland waters, manned by some 9,000 men. The demand for oysters is growing. Although production has tripled in three years, first quality oysters are still selling for $5.00 to $5.50 per bushel. The price for less desirable oysters ranges from $3.00 to $4.00 per bushel.

The state plans to continue the replanting program and the police are better equipped and are able to do a more effective job. All of this gives great hope for the future. Unfortunately, there are still poachers among the oystermen. Some seed oysters are still being stolen and there is far too much "tonging in," i.e., in certain boats where the oysters lie thick on the bar the men will tong in without culling the oysters and then cover them with culled oysters. There are not enough police to cull every boat, every day, or even approach such a goal. These poachers do not sell such catches to the regular buyers where police are on hand to check. Instead, they dump them on private ground for later sale or sell to illicit buyers. This practice must be stopped by severe punishment and more police are needed to do a more effective job. But this is not the complete answer. The answer lies largely with the oystermen themselves. Will they let a handful of law breakers in their ranks deprive them of their livelihood and future or will they see that the law breakers and the buyers of their illicit oysters get their just desserts by making "citizen's arrests?" Will they plan and work to replenish the barren grounds and advise and assist the state in the conservation program that is now under way? It seems reasonable to assume that business and civic leaders will be glad to give a hand in any enterprise that furthers prosperity and the elected representatives in the Maryland Assembly have already demonstrated their interest. Today, the outlook on the river is encouraging and tomorrow can be even better. It would appear that for the oystermen the old days are in sight again and the rivermen can get all the sail on, batten down the hatches and start running before a fair wind.

LIFE ON THE POTOMAC RIVER

Chapter VI

FISHING AND CRABBING

Captain John Smith of Virginia was the first to record the fabulous quantities of fish of many sorts to be found in the Potomac, in his exploratory journey
in June, 1607, to the Great Falls above the present city of Washington. His report
was confirmed subsequently by Henry Spelman, Captain Samuel Argall, Henry Fleet,
and Father Andrew White, S. J., the first chronicler of the Maryland colony. Fleet,
during his several years of captivity with the Potomac Indians, and after the death
of Spelman at their hands, reported, "This place [the site of Washington] without
question is the most pleasant and healthful in all this country, and most convenient
for habitation, the air temperate in summer, and not violent in winter. It abound-
eth in all manner of fish. The Indians in one night will commonly catch thirty
sturgeons in a place where the river is not above twelve fathom broad." All of these
hardy pioneers in the exploration of this great river sent home exciting but truthful accounts of the Potomac, its natural beauties, its deep waters and snug harbors,
its quantities of fish and game, its fertile tidewater soil, its wonderful forests,
"with the goodliest Trees for Masts that may be found else-where in the world," and
its abundance of wild life and vegetation.
        "A Relation of Maryland," dated 1635, probably prepared by Father Andrew White
or from his original "Relatio Itineris in Marylandiam," with additional material
added, was circulated by Lord Baltimore in England to attract new colonists. It
contained the following information concerning fish and fishing: "The Sea, the
Bayes of Chesopeack, and Delaware, and generally all the Rivers, doe abound with
Fish of several sorts; for many of them we have no English names: There are Whales,
Trouts, Soules, Place, Mackerell, Perch, Crabs, Oysters and Mussles; But above all
these, the fish that have no English names, are the best except the Sturgeons: There
is also a fish like the Thorneback in England, which hath a taile a yard long, wherein are sharpe prickles, with which if it strike a man, it will put him to much paine
and torment, but it is very good meate; also the Todefish, which will swell till it
be ready to burst, if it be taken out of the water."
        Concerning the provisions the colonist should bring for fishing and hunting,
he is instructed in the pamphlet as follows: "Imprimis, necessaries for a boate of
3. or 4. Tunne; as Spikes, Nayles, Pitch, Tarre, Ocome, Canvis for a sayle, Ropes,
Anchor, Iron for the Ruther: Fishing-lines for Cod or Macrills, etc., Cod-hookes,
and Macrill-hookes, a Seane or Brasse-net, Herring netts, Leade, Fowling-pieces of
sixe foote; Powder and Shott, and Flint Stones; a good Water Spaniell, etc."
        John Hammond, in his account entitled "Leah and Rachel, or The Two Fruitful
Sisters, Virginia and Maryland," dated 1656, stated ".....for the rivers afford
innumerable sortes of choyce fish (if they will take the paines to make wyers or
hier the Natives, who for a small matter will undertake it) winter and summer and
that in many places sufficient to serve the use of man, and to fatten hogs.....huge
Oysters and store [plenty of them] in all parts where the salt-water comes.....these
with the help of Orchards and Gardens, Oysters, Fish, Fowle and Venison, certainly
cannot be but sufficient for a good diet....."
        In 1963, Army engineers in removing some old bridge piers on the Washington
water front discovered an ancient Indian weir in excellent condition below the
surface. Care was exercised in the removal of the piers to leave the weir intact.
        George Alsop, in his account, "A Character of the Province of Maryland," dated
1666, stated, "As for fish, which dwell in the watery tenements of the deep.....here
in Mary-Land is a large sufficiency, and plenty of almost all sorts of Fishes, which
live and inhabit within her several Rivers and Creeks.....which with very much ease
is catched....."
        However abundant the fish were in colonial days there were bad years from time
to time as reflected in laws considered or enacted by the Maryland Assembly. The
first such proposed law prohibited the use of seines in Herring Creek in St. Mary's
County, but failed of enactment during a session of the Assembly, February 25 to
March 19, 1638-39. The proposed legislation reads in part, "Fishing at the Creek
in St. Georges hundred commonly called the Herring Creek with a Sceyne or other
unlawfull net and the offender Shall forfeit his nett or Sceyne to the partie com-
plaining thereof....."
        On November 15, 1712, a law was passed entitled, "An Act against Striking sun-
dry sorts of Fish within the Precincts of this Province," which reads in part,
"Whereas the frequent Striking of Fish within the Precincts of this Province has
been represented to this present General Assembly, as a great Evil to the Inhabitants

thereof, in the Destruction of their Fishery; Be it therefore Enacted.....That no Person whatsoever shall hereafter strike or shoot any fish within the Precincts aforesaid with Gigs, Arrows, or any other striking instrument, nor shall presume to go out upon the Water in Canoes, Boats or other Vessels fit for that Purpose, in the Night time....." The act provided heavy penalties, a fine of 200 pounds of tobacco for the offense and 100 pounds for each fish taken, half of which was to be paid to the informer. Slaves were to be whipped, not exceeding 39 stripes for any violation. Subsequent legislation, not quite so severe, was passed from time to time, after the customary hue and cry following a bad season or two.

It appears to be uncertain when commercial fishing became an industry on the Potomac, but undoubtedly salted fish was a commodity of trade considerably before fresh Potomac shad were being hawked about the streets of Annapolis prior to 1750. The conservation act of 1712 would argue that there was enough of an industry at that time to attempt to protect it.

George Washington made frequent entries in his diary relative to his fishing shore at Mount Vernon, his seines, records of fishing conditions, his schooner built on the place in 1765, tabulations of catches he made, and his fishing trips. One entry reads: "The white fish ran plentifully at my Sein landing having catch'd abt 300 in one Hawl." Another entry recorded, "the Herrings run in great abundance." At that time shad brought "twelve shillings per hundred" and herring "five shillings per thousand." During the herring run in the spring they were salted down in barrels for use on the place or for sale in winter at a good price. Sometimes, in heavy runs, the herring were used for fertilizer on the plantation. Most of the shad were barrelled, iced, and shipped by sail boat up the Potomac to the city of Georgetown and from there they were hauled overland to widely separated settlements. Some were shipped down the Potomac, up the Bay and into the new port of Baltimore.

General Washington owned several fishing stations on the Potomac and made one available, complete with a seine, for the use of the poor in the area. On a trip to Williamsburg in the spring of 1768, he recorded in his diary:

May 10   "Rid to the Buck House & returned to Dinner; after which went a dragging for sturgeon."

13   "Went after sturgeon & a gunning."

14   "Went to my Plantation in King William by water and draged for Sturgeon & catched one."

16   "Fishing for Sturgeon from Breakfast to Dinner but catched none."

30   "Went fishing & dined under Mr. L. Washington's store."

In this same year he recorded that he "hauled the sein for sheep heads" at Currioman Bay which is quite a distance down-river from Mount Vernon. It appears likely that salted fish was a part of the export cargo carried in the ships of the Lee family at Nomini Cliffs.

Throughout his lifetime, General Washington continued to maintain his interest in the great river that flowed past his door. Elswyth Thane in a recent book, Potomac Squire, which depicts admirably the plantation and family life of the General, quotes from the account of a London merchant, Mr. Hunter, in 1785 as follows: ".....At three, dinner was on the table, and we were shown by the General into another room, where everything was set off with a peculiar taste and at the same time very neat and plain. The General sent the bottle about pretty freely after dinner and gave success to the navigation of the Potomac for his toast, which he has very much at heart, and when finished will, I suppose, be the first river in the world...."

Perhaps the most repeated entry in the General's diary is "Rid to the Fish landing." In April, 1787, he recorded, "Much fish caught and no demand for them; Salting them up....." On April 4, 1788, he recorded that he had caught about 50,000 herrings at a single draught in the afternoon. In a letter to Arthur Young in November, 1793, General Washington wrote: "No estate in United America is more pleasantly situated than this. It lyes in a high, dry and healthy Country 300 miles by water from the Sea, and, as you will see by the plan, on one of the finest Rivers in the world. Its margin is washed by more than ten miles of tide water; from the bed of which, and the enumerable coves, inlets, and small marshes with which it abounds, an inexhaustible fund of rich mud may be drawn as a manure, either to be used separatedly or in a compost, according to the judgment of the farmer."

The vast amount of fish caught in the Potomac River during the early days of the District of Columbia is almost unbelievable, and yet there is proof that at times the catch of fish was really stupendous. The industry extended beyond Georgetown as well as up the Eastern Branch as far as Bladensburg, where in 1816 the curing and packing of herring was a sizable industry.

The Metropolitan, a Georgetown newspaper, in its issue of April 25, 1836 stated: "We were not fully aware of the immense importance of the Potomac fisheries and their value to Georgetown, in particular, until this spring. Besides the larger supplies shipped daily by the canal, every night the long length of Bridge street and High street, besides many other places, is crowded with heavy four and six horse wagons from the most remote parts of Pennsylvania, Maryland and Virginia, even to the confines of Ohio, which exchange the produce they bring down, for the delicious fish which this noble stream affords in an exhaustless abundance, and return with a year's supply of these cheap and grateful delicacies to the far-off homestead of the inland farmer. Activity and enterprise are only wanting to make the fish trade a source of immense and permanent wealth to the town."

Again on May 2, 1836, the Metropolitan has this news item: "Great Haul of Fish - The fisheries on the Potomac have been unusually prosperous for several days past. Our markets have been glutted with the finest fish we have ever seen. One thousand rock or bass fish, weighing from 50 to 60 pounds each, were caught at a single haul on Friday evening last. It is said that several hundred escaped on the seine's coming in shallow water. We understand they were caught at the landing called Hollow Marsh, owned by Mr. W. King, 61 miles below Georgetown. Many of them were sold in our markets at $1."

It was not uncommon in those days to take at a single haul 4,000 shad or more, and 300,000 herring. In 1832, a record catch of 950,000 accurately counted fish (shad and herring) was taken in one haul off Alexandria. The low price that these brought was, for the herring, 25¢ a thousand, and for the shad, $1.50 a hundred. Generally, however, the former brought $1.50 a thousand and the latter from $3.00 to $4.00 a hundred. Rock fish (or striped bass) also were plentiful in the area during this year. On one occasion, about three miles below Washington, 450 rock fish averaging 60 pounds each, were taken at one haul.

During this period members of the Beitzell, Bundick, Cumberland, Faunce, Husemann, and Weser families and many others were engaged in the fishing business on the Washington water front, using both seines and gill nets, and perhaps to a lesser extent fyke and pound nets. Usually the seines were used for the great run of shad, herring, and sometimes "schooling" rock fish, in the spring, while the gill nets were used in the fall or winter for rock and perch.

In 1837, Belvoir or White House Fishery, was one of the chief fisheries on the Potomac. Others were the Sandy Bar fishing shore, Raingerfield's fishing shore, Bryan's fishing shore on Bryan's Point, and fisheries at Freestone, Oxon Run, Moxleys Point, High Point, Stony Point, Fair Landing, Longwood, Bridges Creek, Fowkes Landing, White's Shore (now Colonial Beach), Maryland Point, Windmill Point, Stump Neck, Stump Landing, Ackendale, Fallers Landing, Goose Bay, Budds Ferry, Chapmans Point, Hallowing Point, Monkey Point, Dipple, Sandy Point, Eagles Nest, Mount Moriah and Tent Landing.

One may get the idea of the competition and the magnitude of the Potomac herring and shad industry at its peak prior to the Civil War when there were then 150 fisheries on the river, employing 6,500 laborers; the number of vessels was 450, with 1,350 men used to navigate them. Although the season lasted but about eight weeks, during this time as many as 22,500,000 shad were taken and 750,000,000 herring. In curing the fish for later consumption, 995,000 barrels of salt were used and a greater number of barrels were used in a year.

At this time there was also a good deal of commercial fishing near the mouth of the Potomac where seines, gill nets, and pound (trap) nets were in use. Here too, in the good years, the catch was heavy. Many of the herring were sold locally, especially to the farmers whose "hands" consumed large quantities of "fat back" (salt pork) and salt herring. Herring and shad also were sold to local packers, generally on the Virginia side of the Potomac. The better grades of fish such as rock, trout, and perch were shipped to Baltimore, Annapolis, and Washington, first by fast sailing vessels and later by steamboat. In the 1860 census of St. Mary's, Charles, and Prince George's Counties, Maryland, and Northumberland, Westmoreland, King George, and Stafford Counties, Virginia, there were 34 men classed as fishermen and probably there were many more who engaged in the fishing business on a part time basis. Despite the casualties of war, the number was 29 in 1870 and by 1880 the number had increased to 129. The fierce competition and the consequently smaller catches were instrumental in the removal of the Beitzell, Bundick, and Husemann families, and members of the Faunce family, to new locations near the mouth of the Potomac. The Faunces remaining in Washington became Fish Brokers, and the Cumberlands gave more of their time to boat building; the Wesers opened a seafood restaurant that became famous in its day.

After the move from Virginia to Maryland in 1882, Grandfather Beitzell started his sons fishing small pound (trap) nets in the Potomac and its tributaries. After his death in 1884, the writer's father, Josiah, and his brother, Charlie, continued to fish the family nets until 1890 when Grandmother died and the nets were sold in the settlement of the estate. This made it necessary for my father to buy small fyke trap nets for fishing near his home in Canoe Neck Creek as there were no good "stands" available nearby in the Potomac and the better ones were more than he could finance. Captain Joe did well with the fyke nets in the Creek, catching small rock fish, perch, spot, butter fish, mud shad, eels, and crabs and within three years, together with the money made from oystering, he was able to buy the larger trap nets for fishing in the Potomac.

Fyke nets vary in size and rig. The type used by Captain Joe consisted of a net bag 12 feet long, distended by 5 hoops, with two funnels extending from the first and third hoops. The first hoop was about five feet in diameter and tapered down to about two feet. The wings were about 50-60 feet in length. The fyke net was set in shallow water along the creek shore with the hedging starting near the shore edge. Fish swimming along the shore would hit the hedging, follow it out to the wings and enter the trap. A few light wooden poles were used to stake the net into position and weights were used to hold it on the bottom.

The pound or trap net generally used in the Potomac is a much more elaborate and costly piece of fishing gear. In outline it appears as follows:

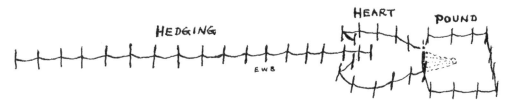

In some of the deeper water nets, the fishermen used a double set of hearts and a second smaller pound, called a pocket in front of the main pound connected by a second funnel.

Ordinarily, the fishermen in the Potomac set their trap nets in water anywhere from 12 to 34 feet deep but most are in the range of 20 to 30 feet. The number of wooden stakes or poles required to stake the nets average about 120 but there is considerable variation, depending largely on the length of the hedging. The depth of water controlled the size and length of the stakes and their costs. In 1921 Captain Joe Beitzell bought for his son, Walter, two "sets" of nets, at the end of the fishing season, from Captain Bunny Orem of Virginia, off Posey's Bluff on the Maryland shore for $1,000 cash. The nets were being fished in 32 and 33 feet of water. Both knew that the nets were rotten and the poles were in bad shape, so that, in effect, the $1,000 was the price of the "sets." It is an unwritten law of the river that anyone can stake a net on any vacant ground and the "set" or "stand" is his until sold or abandoned, and no one would think of invading another's stand. It was not unusual to see a sizable amount of money change hands for a "set" on the river, with nothing more than a stake driven in the mud to mark the spot. Captain Walter was very lucky in the buy from Captain Orem. He decided to leave the nets out for a few more days in the hope of catching enough fish to pay the expense of getting the nets and stakes up to prepare as best he could for the next season. There came a great run of large rock fish and in ten days he caught $1,700 worth of fish that brought, on an average, less than 10¢ per pound. The rock ranged in size from 10 to 60 pounds and because the net was rotten, he lost more fish than were landed. But he was able to pay off his debt to his father and have something left with which to prepare for the next season. Thus it went, as the fishermen say "feast or famine" with the disadvantage that usually during the feast periods, everyone was catching a lot of fish resulting in a glut in the market, so that prices were low, but it was an exciting and venturesome game.

The 33 foot nets required stakes about 46 feet in length which were bought on the stump at a cost of $1.00 per tree in 1925. Cutting, hauling, and skinning brought the cost to $2.50. The cost has tripled over the years. Straight, loblolly pine trees were used. Captain Willard Lankford, who fished trap nets in 62 feet of water on the Chesapeake, out of Fleets Bay, Virginia, into the middle 1940's, paid $12.50 each for his stakes, which were 75 feet in length and 14 inches across the butt. In the '40's, a 24 foot net would cost around $1,000, exclusive of stakes, weights, rope, and labor of tarring, rigging, and getting the net placed in the river. Since most fishermen had two or three nets and a crew of three to six men, they had a sizable investment and a risky venture.

Generally the stakes for nets up to 28 feet were "stuck" by hand through the use of a "Tom." The "Tom" was an iron ring to which a weight was attached, varying from 50 to 80 pounds, depending on the size of the stakes. The ring and weight with a rope attached were slipped over the stake and the weight served to bring the stake into an upright position, whereupon three men would throw their weight on the stake to push it into the muddy bottom about 6 feet. After the pole was stuck there remained only the task of pulling the "Tom" to the surface and lifting it some six feet in the air to clear the ring from the pole. Larger rigs required the use of pile driving equipment, particularly if the net was set on "hard" bottom, i.e., a sand bar or oyster lump. One of the hard bottom areas is the shallows of Heron Island Bar. The writer recalls helping his father and brothers put out stakes there and it was good for the appetite but hard on arms and back. About 10 licks with a 20 pound mall would get the stake down a couple of inches and driving about 100 stakes was a real day's work. Sometimes so much would be beaten off the top of the stake or it would break, and it became too short to go into the bottom far enough to hold so it would have to be pulled and another stake used. One warm September day we forgot the jug of drinking water but fortunately had a big watermelon aboard the "Defender." By the time the stakes were stuck there wasn't even any rind left of that watermelon. Generally the stakes are roped together in rafts and towed to the set.

The sticking of a set of stakes is a precision job that is made more difficult by the tides and winds. The fishermen endeavor to pick a fairly calm day but since the pay of the crew goes on despite the weather, they often work in fairly rough weather, short of a storm. Again, too many days cannot be lost because of the relatively short season which lasts only three months in the spring and fall. All too frequently when the fisherman starts his operation, the U. S. Navy at Dahlgren decides to do some gun testing by shooting down the Potomac. The river is cleared and the rivermen are left to fret and fume away a day that always seems ideal for the work at hand. The pound and heart stakes must be so driven that the net will fit just right and the tolerances are fairly small. "Ring" or "stay" poles are placed at the four corners of the pound in order that the net may be drawn square in the shape of a box by ropes. The ring pole has a pulley mounted at the base, together with a loop that goes around the corner pole to hold it into position. It is lashed at the top to the corner pole. A rope extending from the corner of the pound is passed through the pulley in the ring pole and after the net is pulled taut the rope is fastened to the top of the ring pole and corner pole. Similarly, the funnel from the heart into the pound is hauled taut by means of a warp and a bridle and the ropes lashed to a stake in back of the pound. The net for the hedging and heart is weighted every few feet, usually with chain which is lashed to the bottom line to hold the net on the bottom, and the top line is lashed to the stakes at high water level.

Before the nets are set in the river, in order to preserve them from rotting, it is necessary to "tar" them. This is accomplished by dumping a barrel of tar in a huge pot over an open fire. The net is immersed in the hot tar and then spread out in a field to dry. It is a nasty, hot, sticky job at best, but when the tarring has to be done in July for the early fall set, it is really no picnic. Occasionally the boiling tar catches fire and there is "hell to pay." It is small wonder that most of the rivermen develop a picturesque vocabulary. After newly tarred net dries sufficiently, the rope and weights are lashed on, the funnel and pound are rigged, and the net is ready to be set.

When the nets are fished, a corner of the pound is carefully lowered just enough to permit entry of the fishing boat and upon entry the corner is again tied up. The funnel and ring lines are loosened so that the net may be gathered up to corner the fish in a small space. The men work from the funnel side of the pound toward the front side until the fish are crowded sufficiently for the bailing operation. This is done by hand with a short-handled, large bow dip-net, in small nets, or by a power driven rig in the larger nets. After the fish are boated, a corner of the net is again dropped to permit the boat to leave. Then the lines are hauled to pull the funnel and pound back to a taut position. The fishermen time their operation to begin toward the last of a tide and endeavor to complete it during "slack water," i.e., between tides, otherwise hauling a net taut against the tide takes a prodigious amount of work and sometimes has to be abandoned until the next "slack water." Often when caught in the tide as the fisherman attempts to "haul out," the ring lines will break in the effort to "buck" the tide.

At the end of the season, the net is removed from the stakes, brought into shallow water and washed to remove the mud and any fouling or marine growth. This is accomplished by the men standing in hip deep water, swishing the net in the water vigorously. During this process the weights are removed and the net is examined for damage or rotten spots so that new supplies may be ordered for the next season. After the net is washed it is spread out in the fields to dry, after which it is stored until the next season. Generally the Marylanders have pulled their stakes (excepting one to mark the set) at the end of each season and stored them in racks on shore to dry. At the beginning of the next season the barnacles are scraped off and damaged or defective stakes replaced. Under this method most of the stakes will last for four or five seasons. The Virginia fishermen generally leave their stakes in the river and use them for two or three seasons, after which they are abandoned and another set made nearby. There is considerable objection on the part of the sportsmen on the river to the practice, since the stakes, particularly those broken off under or near the surface, are a hazard to the small fast speedboats of today. So far no legislation to require the removal of this hazard has been enacted.

In the Federal Census of 1880, a total of 129 persons are shown as engaged in the fishing business on the lower Potomac, exclusive of the employees working in the fish factories in the lower Northern Neck of Virginia. Those classed as "Sailors" evidently were the ship owners and crews engaged in hauling fish and oysters to market during these seasons, and tobacco, grain, lumber, cordwood, etc., at other times. The names of some of these rivermen will be found in Appendix "D".

FEDERAL CENSUS OF 1880

	Fishermen			Oystermen			Sailors			Total		
	W.*	C.*	Total	W.*	C.*	Total	W.*	C.*	Total	W.*	C.*	Total
St. Mary's Co., Maryland	12	5	17	76	66	142	37	8	45	125	79	204
Charles Co., Maryland	11	3	14	41	21	62	29	14	43	81	38	119
Prince George's Co., Maryland	2	1	3	-	-	-	1	1	2	3	2	5
Northumberland Co., Virginia	73	10	83	27	17	44	55	35	90	155	62	217
Westmoreland Co., Virginia	2	-	2	34	26	60	6	14	20	42	40	82
King George Co., Virginia	6	1	7	-	-	-	-	-	-	6	1	7
Stafford Co., Virginia	2	1	3	-	-	-	-	-	-	2	1	3
TOTAL	108	21	129	178	130	308	128	72	200	414	223	637

* W. indicates "White" and C. indicates "Colored"

Captain Joe Beitzell started trap net fishing on his own in the Potomac River about 1892, fishing in the spring for shad, herring, and rock fish and in the fall for rock, perch, and trout. He didn't do so well the first year or two as good "sets" were not available, but in 1894 he took over the sets of Captain Con Faunce who had moved away. He fished spring nets on "Carnishes" between St. Clement's and Bretton Bays and on the lower east side of Heron Island Bar. The fall sets were made on the south side of Heron Island, the east end of Blackistone (St. Clement's) Island, and at Carnish Point, Jones' Point, Elm Hollow, Bluff Woods and Shipping Point in St. Clement's Bay. The latter were rather small nets, 12 to 20 feet, but the spring sets averaged from 24 to 28 feet. In 1896 he went into partnership with Captain Theodore Bailey of St. Margaret's Island and they did so well in that season that Captain Theodore sold out to Captain Joe and retired. In the deal Captain Joe acquired his second dory boat, the original "Defender," a 32 footer, and a large dory for those days. The "Defender" was no beauty as she was very wide and built to carry fish and oysters, but she could carry plenty of sail and weathered many a storm that had other boats scudding for home. On calm days, she was a devil to row with six men at the oars, particularly when she was loaded to the gunwales with 20,000 herring.

When large catches were made during the herring and shad runs in the spring, the fishermen often called on the oyster buyers in their schooners, pungies, sloops,

POUND OR TRAP NETS

Off Posey's Bluff, Maryland

Capt. Clem Beitzell   Capt. Josiah Beitzell

POUND OR TRAP NETS

Off Nomini Cliffs, Virginia

"Pulling" Stakes

Capt. Walter Beitzell - 1921

and bugeyes to carry their fish to the city markets. Captain Joe Henderson of
St. George's Island, who shipped on his father's 22 ton bugeye, the "Avalon,"
engaged in hauling fish at the close of the oyster season. Sometimes they hauled
for the fishermen and other times they would buy fish for the seafood dealers. One
of the Washington dealers was the Cogswell Brothers and Captain Henderson with a
crew of three, would contract his boat and crew at $4 a day to buy fish out of the
Yeoacomico River for them. The tugs that met the "Avalon" and other buy-boats engaged in this work carried a crew of nine and were hired for $20 per day. Captain
Henderson recalls a day, the 17th of March, 1903, when the "Avalon" sailed into
Washington with 2,300 fine shad, the first of the season, and some 30,000 herring,
iced below decks. However, the buck shad brought only about 3¢ each and the roe
shad about double this price. Herring averaged about $2.50 per thousand after the
Commission Merchant had deducted his one-seventh of the sale price. The men who
cleaned herring for the buyers could cut thirty a minute and were paid 10¢-15¢ a
thousand.

Captain Joe Beitzell established a local market, mostly for herring, at the
steamboat wharves in St. Clement's Bay and in the Wicomico River. Some of these
wharves were Howard's, Abell's, Greenwell's, Stone's, Cobrum, Colton's, Morris',
and Bushwood. Herring sold for $3 to $6 per thousand generally, and shad at 60¢ to
$1 per pair, i.e., 1 roe and 1 buck. Very early in the season when the fish were
scarce, they would be sold by the "string" -- 10 to 15 herring on a wooden "splint"
for 25¢. The wooden splints were made during bad weather in the winter months when
the men were not otherwise engaged. In the late fall a number of white oak saplings
about 2 1/2 inches in diameter were selected, cut in lengths of approximately 2 1/2
feet, and left in water to prevent drying. When ready for working, the bark was
peeled off and the trunk was split into four sections with a hatchet. The four sections were then split into smaller sections and splints were peeled off with a sharp
knife and sharpened on each end. Each splint was 2 1/2 feet in length, about 1/8
inch in thickness and 1/4 inch in width. They were strong, pliable, and could be
tied in a flat knot after the fish were strung. Thousands of these splints were
made each winter, tied by short splints in bundles of 25, and stored in a cool place
for later use. The white oak saplings were used also to make the needles used in
mending the nets. In this case the saplings were cut into approximately one foot
lengths and flat layers about 1/4 inch in thickness were split off, from which the
needles were carved. The completed job looked like this:

The needles were about 10 inches in length and 3/4 inch in width. They were loaded
with tarred twine and in mending net the needle was passed back and forth between
the meshes like a shuttle in the process of repairing the torn or rotten place in
the net.

Some great catches of shad and herring were made in the 1890's and later. Captain Joe's biggest catch in a single net on Carnishes was 70,000 herring. This catch
loaded the "Enola," Captain Ned Hayden's sloop, and was taken to market in Washington. Generally 300-500 shad would be found among the herring in a catch of this size,
but more often the catch would range from 10,000-15,000 herring and 100-150 shad.
Large catches of shad and rock fish would be shipped to Washington and Baltimore by
sail or steamboat. Among the fishermen of these days in the vicinity of St. Clement's
Island, in addition to Captain Joe, were Captain Jake and Captain Con Faunce, Edwin
Gibson, Tommie Morris, Fred McWilliams, Theodore Bailey, and the Virginians, Bernard
Orem, William Balderson, and William A. Hinson.

Whenever the fish were running heavy, the market would become glutted and the
fishermen were hard put to dispose of their catches. Thousands of herring were sold
at $1-$2 per thousand to the "cutting houses" for salting. These cutting houses were
located on the Coan River, Nomini Bay, and Monroe Bay at Colonial Beach. Many of the
river schooners also were utilized for hauling the fish to Washington, Baltimore,
Annapolis, and Norfolk. Generally these sailing craft were met by tugs to expedite
delivery of the fish to market as promptly as possible. The steamboats were utilized
on "steamboat days," usually twice a week.

Perhaps the highest price paid for herring occurred in World War I when Captain
Joe received $22 per thousand for them. Roe shad were bringing $1.25 at the same
time. The writer, then a small lad, was permitted to accompany his father on Saturdays to fish the nets at Carnishes. The catch from two nets usually was around
10,000 to 20,000 herring and 100 to 200 shad. The old "Defender," now equipped with
five horsepower Mianus engine, would make the seven mile run to the head of St. Clement's Bay in about an hour and a half. The farmers with their wagons would be waiting

there at Stone's Wharf, the home of Mr. Phil Greenwell, to buy their year's supply of the herring to be salted. If there wasn't enough fish to satisfy everyone's need that day, orders would be taken for the next fish day. Depending on the run of fish, the nets might be fished anywhere from twice a week to daily. The crew at this time consisted of the writer's older brothers, Clem and Walter, Uncle Lee Norris, and a colored man, Joe Woodland. (Joe's people had been free men in Maryland from Revolutionary War days.)

Among the many men who worked with Captain Joe over the big fishing years and who still live in the memory of the writer were Norman Yates and Stoney Dent. The writer visited Mr. Yates about a year before his death, during the summer of 1962, on his farm in Newtown Neck. Mr. Yates, who was in his late 80's, left the river many years ago to become a very successful farmer but maintained his friendship with Captain Joe over the years. He had not seen the writer for many years and there were tears in his eyes as he made "Captain Joe's boy" at home. He was eager to talk about the "good old days" on the river. He told of the great flood of fishes caught a half-century before and told many tales of the river, some of which I had heard before from my father, and others that had not registered in the mind of a small boy when they happened. Perhaps their worst experience on the river was being lost in a blinding snow storm under sail and almost freezing before making shore. He told of another time when the master of a big four-masted "bald-headed" schooner stopped them in the river and wanted Father to pilot him up Bretton Bay where he was to take on a load of logs. Father wasn't anxious to do it for it was a torturous channel near the head of the bay for a big vessel under sail but they made it without mishap and the Captain paid handsomely.

Mr. Yates said there was much fine timber still left along the river in those days, second growth trees, two to two and a half centuries old, and much of it was hauled away by large sailing vessels. He said that one crew came in by vessel to Leonardtown when he was a boy, set up a mill and cut Chestnut of which they made a great wooden tepee, perhaps forty feet high, in which to live. They soon abandoned the operation, however, because of the difficulties in trying to transport the great logs from the woods to the water by oxen.

In this connection, my father once related that in 1882, when the family moved from Virginia to Maryland the Jesuits of Newtown Neck sold their second growth oak trees on the Neck to a firm in Germany which made veneered furniture. These great logs were hauled by double teams of oxen to the water's edge where they were floated out to an ocean-going sailing vessel for transportation to Germany. He said that many of these logs were 6 feet in diameter across the butt.

Both Mr. Yates and Stoney Dent lived in with the family. Stoney, as the writer remembers him, was middle-aged, of ruddy complexion, with a clipped walrus mustache, neatly dressed, with twinkling eyes and an easy smile. He was not overly fond of work, unless he happened to like you and when in very good humor, brought on by a generous amount of hard liquor, he would say much to our small boy delight, though we didn't understand it -- "Bull Madden butt the bull off the bridge, but Stoney Dent caught the goat." Stoney worked for Papa several seasons, putting down and fishing pound nets and oystering on the off days. He became fond of our family and we, likewise, were fond of him. For many years after he up and quit work permanently, and lived with his sister, he would come to visit us a couple of week-ends each year.

He walked some 10-12 miles from where he lived, getting well oiled at each store on the way. On one particular Saturday, about noon, Stoney arrived with a real jag on. Mama, seeing his condition, suggested to Stoney that he needed a rest after his long walk and he should lie down on the couch in the living room for awhile. Stoney, with all the drunken gravity and composure he could muster, assured Mama he was never finer in his life, sat down with more dignity than equilibrium on one of the kitchen chairs, and started an animated conversation with Mama as she went about preparing the midday meal (which we called dinner). Soon the conversation dwindled to mono-syllabic responses on the part of Stoney, coming to a dead stop, when with a terrific crash, Stoney took a header out of the chair and turned a complete somersault out on the kitchen floor. For a few seconds there was a startled silence, as Stoney brushed his hip pocket (to assure the wholeness of the pint concealed under his coat-tail), and Mama and I succeeded in getting him on his feet. The silence was broken by Stoney allowing as how maybe he was a little more tired than he thought and perhaps he should lie down on the couch for a little nap before dinner.

Like all of the "small fry" of the family the writer was permitted to earn his pocket money by stringing bunches of perch, small rock fish, and flounders for sale to the farmers at 20¢ to 25¢ per bunch. His sales completed, he would make a "bee-line" for the store near the foot of the wharf to buy a supply of a certain raisin cookie that was a favorite then and which he still likes to this day. His older brothers, Joe, Charlie, and Harry always told him that he was born at a luckier day because in their time there were no gasoline engines and when it was calm, the "Defender," loaded with fish, had to be rowed up St. Clement's Bay and sometimes back

96

down, when the calm held.

Captain Jake and Captain Con Faunce were rated highly among the more capable fishermen. Captain Jake fished all through the year from St. Patrick's Creek and he ranged all the way from Point Lookout to the spawning grounds in the Upper Potomac. He fished both fall and spring trap nets, gill nets in the winter, a big seine in the summer and became a legend in his own time. Undoubtedly he was one of the best known men on the river for a period of fifty years or more. A story is told that when seining, he would cup his hand, take first a sniff and then a swig of the water, to be sure that fish were there before making a decision to lay out the seine. The writer is somewhat skeptical of this approach but it was good showmanship -- and he did catch fish, more often than not. There are some who say that a large school of fish will cause the water to become oily where they are feeding so maybe Captain Jake wasn't acting. Another story is told that, being on the river so much and at all hours of day and night, he became so used to keeping his hat on that he could not be persuaded to remove it at his infrequent meals at home and it was with some difficulty that he was persuaded to take his hat off when going to bed. His knowledge of the Potomac was tremendous and he was highly regarded and respected by all the rivermen. Captain Seneca Cheseldine also of St. Patrick's Creek was a highly rated commercial fisherman of these days.

After World War I a new generation of fishermen started trap-netting in the Potomac. Clem and Walter Beitzell, Henry and Alfred Gibson, Charlie Husemann, Frank and Joe Faunce, and the Morris boys, Stuart, Foster, Con, and Frank, to name some. Several of them also gill netted in winter and seined in summer. Captain Clem fished off Knott's Cove at the mouth of Bretton Bay and also off White Point. He used nets ranging from 12 to 28 feet. The same nets were used by him for both spring and fall fishing. Captain Walter Beitzell fished nets of 32 and 33 feet off Posey's Bluff. In line with him were the nets of Captain Edwin Gibson, and his sons, Henry and Alfred. It was permissible to stake these nets right out to the channel and only a 90 foot clearance for boats was required. A light (kerosene lantern) was required on each net.

Captain Clem's biggest single catch of herring was 22,000 and 470 shad. He took over much of the market at the boat landings established by his father, Captain Joe whose stands at Carnishes were no longer very productive with many more and deeper nets being used nearer the mouth of the river. When the herring and shad run began in the spring there was again the problem of transporting the catch to the market but the day of the gasoline motor had arrived and the powered dories and barges replaced the sloops and schooners, although the steamboats were still utilized. John Harding, Sr., had a dory that would carry some 40,00 herring; Frank Faunce had a bigger dory of 60,000 capacity; Walter Beitzell loaded his dory, the "Sylph," about 7 ton, from one net and the dories of the Gibson family, Edwin, Henry, and Alfred, were used to run the catch to Washington. However, as the years went on, the catch of herring not only dwindled but also the demand for herring slackened -- apparently the farm hands no longer were content with a diet of salt herring and fat-back and people generally were able to get fresh fish and no longer used salted fish in quantity. Practically all of the fishermen on the Maryland side of the river had stopped trap net fishing by 1940.

Captain Clem, a diehard, fished on until 1943 when he too quit. In this year he went to work at the Patuxent Naval Base and Rosie, his wife, who had endeavored for years to get him out of the fishing business, took advantage of what to her was God-given opportunity to get him "out of the river" and sold his nets. It happened this way -- Rosie waited until one morning when Clem was behind schedule and it looked as though he was going to be late for work. As he went to get into his car, she called from the kitchen door, "Clem, Frank Faunce has been after you to sell him your old nets -- I forgot to tell you, but he's coming up here again today -- is it all right for me to sell them?" Clem stopped -- Rosie cut in -- "Now Clem, you're going to be late -- go on, get in your car -- you know those nets are just taking up good storage space -- shall I sell them?" Clem gave a harassed and reluctant "yes," slammed the car door and took off. Rosie rushed to the phone, called Faunce and told him he could have the nets if he would come and get them that very day, which he did.

When Clem returned home from work at the Base that day, Rosie had an extra good supper for him. As he went to sit down at the table Clem said, "Frank must have been in a big hurry for those nets, wasn't he -- I see the whole business is gone -- chain, ropes, net, everything -- don't know as I wanted him to have the chain -- might want to set again -- and where is my brand new net I paid $850 for? My God, Rosie, you didn't let him have that too, did you?" Rosie said, with all the courage she could muster, "Now, Clem, you know you've quit the fish business, so I sold the whole lot -- that's what I thought you wanted me to do -- it's what you wanted, isn't it?" "Well now, Rosie, I don't know -- but if you've done it, it's done -- How much did you get?" Rosie took a deep breath and said, "$100 cash." Clem opened his mouth but nothing came out -- after a moment he managed a groan, sat down at the dinner table, shook his head and after another short silence said, "$1800 worth of nets for $100 - one brand new net and three nets in good shape -- chain, rope -- Rosie, you sure got me out of the trap net business and there's no mistake about that." Rosie said, "Come on, Captain Clemmie, don't think about it -- eat your supper now -- I fixed all the things you like -- do you know that Jack is making eyes at that little Rosie Brown, she's a cute child....."

Perhaps Rosie didn't make such a bad deal after all for trap net fishing in the Potomac at this period was very uncertain and a couple of poor seasons could have resulted in a larger loss than $1700. Frank Faunce and his son continued to fish small nets on the Maryland side of the river for a few years as did Captain Joe Beitzell until 1946. But their catch was small. Captain Joe could never quite bring himself to believe, after catching so many fish for so many years, that shoal water trap-netting was done for and when he died, in 1959, his net shed was still full of nets awaiting the return of the fish.

Before the taking of sturgeon was prohibited, he would frequently catch some very large ones, ranging from six to twelve feet in length. It took a lot of skill and "know how" to get these fish out of the net without damage to the net and loss of the fish. Actually the fish was lassoed by slipping a noose over its head -- at a given signal, the whole crew would heave on the rope and the fish would be pulled into the boat in a continuing motion, so quickly it didn't get a chance to get in a lick with its dangerous tail which could break a man's legs or knock the bulkhead out at the main thwart. On one occasion, when the steamboat wasn't due for a couple of days, Captain Joe tied a large sturgeon to the stake in the creek where his wife's dory, the "Katy B." was moored. This was accomplished by running a strong rope through the mouth and out of the gills of the sturgeon. Later that day the "Katy B." was observed to be moving at good speed out of the mouth of the creek without a rag on her masts or a hand on her rudder. The sturgeon, in one of his lunges, had snapped the half-rotten stake and was heading for friendlier waters, "Katy B." and all.

The largest rock fish caught, in the writer's memory, weighed a little over 70 pounds and he remembers his father putting the fish singly in a sugar barrel, filling the remaining space with ice and covering the barrel opening with sacking which projected about 18 inches above the opening to cover the protruding tail of the fish. Most of the fishermen had sizable ice houses which were filled from the fresh water ponds in winter.

In his fall fishing in later years, Captain Joe would "pound" the larger and better fish in the creek for December shipping when prices generally were better. This operation was accomplished by towing a skiff, covered with netting, out to the nets. The skiff was "sunk" at the net and the fish bailed into the skiff -- the netting was made fast and the skiff was towed to the pound in the creek where the fish were released in the pound. Since the fish were kept "pounded" for a period of two months, more and more feed had to be provided as more fish were added to the pound, and this feeding process got to be quite a chore. It was accomplished by cutting up bushels of menhaden caught with the rock and perch at the time the nets were fished. It was cold, mean work when the weather got bad in December, but the "pounding" paid good dividends.

Captain Joe also seined the fresh water ponds around the Jewish holidays when carp were in great demand in the Washington and Baltimore fish markets. Several ponds on St. Clement's and Bretton Bays were utilized. Usually they were spring fed but sometimes had an inlet to the bay that would permit entry of a small skiff, or the skiff would be dragged over the beach to the pond. A small seine was employed in catching the fish, usually a mixture of fine carp, "mud shad," and perch. The carp were shipped by steamboat and brought good prices on the Jewish feast days.

Flounders were caught in moderate quantities both spring and fall but rock and perch were the main catch in the fall, although there were good runs of trout in September. In the spring fishing there was greater variety -- shad, herring, croakers or hardheads, flounder, catfish, rock, perch, some speckled trout (early in the spring), and always quantities of the lowly menhaden. It was an exciting business when the fish were running.

The menhaden were a favorite food of the gulls. We generally culled the menhaden from the good fish, throwing them overboard, as we proceeded up St. Clement's Bay. As a consequence we were followed by a flock of screaming, wheeling gulls all the way up the Bay and they would all but fly into the boat in their eagerness to obtain a fish. It was amazing, but the gull could swallow a fish that seemed almost as large as he was.

Stoney Dent told me a story about a gull that caught an eel, but he was probably "pulling my leg" though he kept a straight face and assured me it was the "gospel." He said this was a stubborn old gull because every time he swallowed the eel, though he couldn't hold him because the eel was so slippery, he kept right on trying. After the 17th try, the gull walked up and sat down on a flat rock on Heron Island Bar and

on the 18th try he was successful. Stoney even pointed out the rock to me. If he
had said it was a fish hawk (osprey), the story would have been a little more be-
lievable. These great birds often dive and catch large eels which are very strong
and hard to hold. Often the fish hawk will lose the eel a couple of times in his
flight, but will wheel, dive and catch the eel again before it hits water and carry
him successfully to his nest on an old duck blind or high in a tall pine on the
shore. The osprey, like the heron continues in goodly numbers on the river, but
the great bald eagle is seen only infrequently, though they still range from the
Great Falls to the mouth of the Potomac. The eagle has been seen on the river to
make a dive at an osprey in flight to try to cause him to drop the fish he was carrying. When this didn't work, the eagle wheeled and dove the second time -- the osprey
fell with a broken neck and the eagle caught the fish in mid air and continued on his
way.

One day in early March, 1958, the writer saw an eagle alight in the top of a
walnut tree at the head of a cove on Canoe Neck Creek near his home. At that moment
there was a flock of blackhead ducks feeding in the shallow water at the head of the
cove and they immediately noticed the eagle. Near panic was evident throughout the
flock -- the water was too shallow to dive and to fly would be to invite disaster --
they did not panic but swam as fast as possible, without commotion, out of the cove,
but with fear in their every movement. It was amazingly easy to read their alarm
and fear but not a single duck panicked and flew. The eagle either did not notice
them or had already feasted and made no movement. After a half-hour rest he continued his flight north.

Although practically all of the trap net fishermen on the Maryland side of the
river quit fishing around 1945, a number of Virginians continued operations in the
deep water, usually fishing 34 foot nets. Only four or five of the deep nets were
fished on the Maryland side of the river, off Posey's Bluff, but the nets of the
Virginians dotted the south shores from the mouth of the Potomac to Colonial Beach.
**Among these fishermen were Captain Nevil Ball, Sam Hall and his two sons, Melvin
Faunce and Ridgely Jones, who fished together, Bryant Jetts, Richard Sisson, Harry
and Everett Muse, Raymond Chatham, the Jenkins brothers and the Maguires.**

Captain Otis L. Hinson and his brother, Raymond L. Hinson, sons of Captain
William A. Hinson, didn't return to fishing until the late 1940's. They had fished
with their father as young men but were attracted to the big city (Washington) after
World War I. After World War II, they decided to return to life on the Potomac and
their enterprise and new approaches to an old game have placed them among the most
successful fishermen on the river. They have, in addition, provided badly needed
leadership in trying to protect the fishing industry. Until the 1962-1963 season
they had fished trap nets from the upper Stratford Cliffs to Colonial Beach and
caught huge quantities of shad, herring, rock, and perch. However, in recent years,
shad have been scarce and there has been little demand for herring, and consequently
they had to be sold to the cutting houses in Nomini and Monroe Bay at very low prices.

They are now fishing only smaller nets on the Rappahannock. For some years Captain Otis and his brother alternated the spring and fall seasons between the Potomac
and the Rappahannock, which was no small feat because it meant the transportation of
a forty foot boat and much gear across the Northern Neck each season. Captain Otis
solved the boat transportation problem by hooking two large farm wagons in tandem,
backing them into the river deep enough to float his boat upon them, and using a
heavy tractor for the haul. This has been a time and money-saving operation compared
with the cost of running his boat and gear from the Potomac to the Rappahannock.

The Hinson brothers have had even more spectacular success in their seining
operations and have caught hundreds of tons of rock fish and croakers (hardheads)
in the last fifteen years. Their catch of 75 tons of rock fish on February 21, 1948,
made feature news stories in all the Washington, Maryland, and Virginia newspapers.
It took several days to land these fish and since the Virginia limit on rock is 25
pounds, tons of the larger fish were released. Despite this and other large catches
in 1948, the Hinsons had a highly successful season again in 1949. One of their
largest single catches of croakers amounted to 414 boxes, weighing 100 pounds each.

Captain Otis tells a story of a frustrating problem in seining that eventually
was solved in a unique way, so unique that some of his friends thought he had lost
his mind. He located large schools of fish off the Virginia Cliffs and made repeated
attempts to catch them without success. He had no difficulty laying the seine around
the fish but there was so much seaweed on the flats where it was necessary to land
the net that when the net hit the seaweed it would roll up and the fish would escape.
Time and again the Captain would locate the fish, make his haul and spend hours un-
rolling his net with not a fish to reward his effort. Finally a possible solution
occurred to him and the Captain swung into action. He jumped into his car, drove
into Montross and stopped at the farm supplies store and said to the proprietor:
"Mr. Mothershead, I want to buy the biggest and best hay mower you have." Mr. Mothershead said, "Sure, Captain Otis, but tell me, have you quit fishing and gone farm-

ing?" Captain Otis said, "No, sir, I'm still fishing, but I'm in kind of a hurry for that mower." Mr. Mothershead said, "Well, all right, the price is $142, but what are you going to do with the mower?" Captain Otis said, "I'm going to take it down and throw it in the Potomac River -- now, here is your money, hook the mower to the back of the car so I can get on down the road." Captain Otis left Mr. Mothershead shaking his head and muttering, "Otis must have lost his mind."

Captain Hinson placed the mower in position in nine feet of water on the flats and proceeded to tow it up and down the shore with his boat and mowed the seaweed on the flats, much as a farmer would cut a field of alfalfa. The seaweed, having been cut, floated to the top of the water and was carried off by the tide. The Captain caught $700 worth of fish the first night after the mowing and many more thereafter. It was necessary for him to mow his "field" four or five times each season. His idea soon caught on among the seiners and it wasn't long before Raymond Chatham of Lower Machodoc and Frank Brown of St. Patrick's Creek were busy mowing the seaweed on their seining grounds on opposite sides of the Potomac.

The seiners, like any other type of fishermen, have had their good years and bad but on the whole over the past 30 years, they have caught a prodigious amount of fish ever since the advent of 300 fathom seines and power hauling. In addition to the Hinsons and Raymond Chatham, the Jenkins brothers and Everett and Harry Muse are seiners on the Virginia side of the river. On the Maryland side, in addition to Frank Brown and his son, there are Clem Beitzell, Stuart (Buster) Morris, Arthur and David Lawrence, John Gibson, Evans and Frank Faunce, Bill Dickson, Ernest (Tootsie) Morris, "Monk" Gass, and the sons of Captain Golden Thompson, Roy, Gussie, Golden, Jr, and Paul.

One of the most ridiculous situations that grew out of the now defunct Compact of 1785 between Maryland and Virginia was the enactment of different laws governing the size of rock fish that might be taken from the Potomac. For many years the limit on the Maryland side has been 15 pounds and on the Virginia side 25 pounds. This law finally got Captain Clem Beitzell completely out of the fishing business. In 1958 when he was seining with Roy Thompson, they made a set off St. Katherine's Island similar to the one made by Captain Otis Hinson in 1948, and brought ashore tons of rock fish. Practically all of the fish ran over the Maryland 15 pound limit and had to be turned loose so that they were able to boat less than a thousand pounds of fish. It was a catch that every fisherman dreams of and perhaps realizes once in a lifetime. To have to turn loose all of those beautiful fish was too much for Captain Clem -- so after four generations and 125 years none of the family is engaged in commercial fishing on the Potomac.

Prior to the great catch of perch by Captains Jim and West Covington of Nanticoke about fifty years ago, there was no statute to prohibit trawling in the Potomac. The Covingtons pulled their net over Kettle Bottom Shoals one March day and loaded their boat. They proceeded to Washington to sell their catch where the story leaked out and made newspaper headlines. The Maryland Legislature, upon complaints of the pound and gill net fishermen, promptly closed the Potomac to trawlers, and thus it has been ever since.

During the years of phenominal catches there continued to be poor seasons from time to time and when they occurred, the evil was laid at the door of the commercial fisherman, with everyone forgetting the good years when the fish returned by the millions. Thus, in the St. Mary's Beacon of June 10, 1858, an article appeared concerning the poor fish season and demanded the enactment of conservation laws. Again, on February 10, 1870, the Beacon carried an article stating that seines were to be restricted to 80 fathoms in length to conserve the supply of fish in the Potomac.

Back in the 1920's and earlier, the croaker (hardhead) almost was a rarity in the Potomac but they finally came into the river in important quantities. During this same period the menhaden disappeared for several years and most of the Bay and coast purse net fishermen went bankrupt. There have been few bluefish, croakers, and trout (weakfish) in the Potomac for several years past. Undoubtedly, the trawlers along the coast, the deep water pound nets in the Bay and the large seines have had their effect but this is not the complete answer to our fisheries problems according to Dr. R. V. Truitt, former head of the Chesapeake Biological Laboratory. Some of the fishes found in local waters originate in the sea and visit the Potomac and other Bay tributaries during the period of their growth. This is true of the croaker and the trout. Others, like the shad and herring, are present and abundant during the spawning run from the ocean to fresh water. The rock and (white) perch are native and usually stay in Maryland waters. The former schools up during the pre-nuptial runs and in the winter which they generally spend in the deep areas of the Bay, especially off the shores of St. Mary's and Calvert Counties, although some schools may stay in the deeper waters of the Potomac and the Patuxent.

Dr. Truitt, in a special article written for the St. Mary's County Enterprise in 1955, stated:

"Fin fish are more talked about, perhaps, in the County than any other forms of

100

economic importance due not only to local interest but to the fact that literally thousands of outsiders visit the shores to go fishing during the summer season. Receipts from the fish catchers, which are higher than those derived from crabbing, are much lower every year than the income from oystering. At this time (1955) the fish catches are lower than they have been since 1947. In 1953, some 616,000 pounds of fish, valued at $86,000 were taken by 49 licensed operators."

"There are no statistics covering the sportfishery of the County but the income from it is nearly equal to that of the commercial men, many of whom are dually engaged. The high point in the commercial fishery in recent years was reached in 1950 when 1,216,000 pounds were netted. This catch compares quite favorably with the hauls made in the early days of fishing, thus it may be said that except for trout and croakers, the fin fishes are in fair supply with reasonable assurance for the continuance of same."

"It is ironical that the sports fishermen and the county's party boat operators are in a disturbed state in regard to fish conservation, based largely on the assumption that the rock, or striped bass, has been greatly depleted and is constantly growing more so. Catch records painstakingly gathered over many years do not support the assumption. To the contrary, they indicate that this fish is holding its own quite well. In this review of the water resources, it perhaps is well to expand a bit on this matter. The rock is not the fish in very low abundance. Rather, the trout and the croaker are relatively low in supply. Now these fish are oceanic forms and spend only a limited period in local waters. During nine months of the year they are pursued strenuously at sea in trawler fisheries with consequent declines in catches, a fact reflected locally in both the net catches and those made by sportsmen. It is this situation at base that irks the angler and unfortunately he doesn't have the facts before him to reason it out accurately."

"The rock is the ultimate in local sport fishing. Since the time of George Washington, sportsmen have sought at length and more recently at high price to catch this fish. They just plain like its cunning and the way it strikes and tugs at the other end of the line. It used to be that when they failed, the situation was almost completely mitigated by the fact that there was an abundance of trout and/or croakers to take back home to wives and neighbors. Nowadays when no rock are taken, anglers go home with creel empty, 'skunked,' and expensively so, to face wives and neighbors, an awkward situation. Very naturally they conclude that 'rock are gone,' or something of the kind and begin to press for a reform of some kind. In this case, the commercial fisherman is most likely to be condemned as the culprit even though, as indicated, his rock catches have been stabilized quite largely for several years considering peak to peak of production. There is obvious need of understanding on the part of the sportsmen as well as clear and continued legitimate practices by the commercial operator together with sound leadership from Annapolis to assure fish in substantial supply for both interests since the waters are potentially able to provide adequately to meet the foreseeable needs."

"In concluding this essay on the waters of St. Mary's County, several things should be indicated.....All native Maryland fishes are maintaining a fair level of abundance, including the rock. The trout and croaker, oceanic fish that come to St. Mary's shores, are in short supply due, it is held, to heavy pressure on them by trawlers, over which there is now no control. This situation has conjured the thinking of some fishermen who hold that the rock is threatened by extermination due to commercial netting. Fish are sufficiently abundant for both commercial and sports purposes at this time and any change in this status will be detected and publicized by the scientists."

There has been a good deal of agitation in recent years on the part of our sports fishermen to curtail further the operations of the commercial fishermen, particularly in the catching of rock fish. This is a matter that requires careful consideration and deliberation, after study by experts in the field, since it involves the livelihood of the commercial fishermen. In 1960 the commercial fish catch in the Maryland and Virginia counties along the Potomac amounted to approximately $600,000.

Although there have been fish "kills" in the Potomac over the years, they were comparatively minor when measured against those of the summers of 1962 and 1963. In the 1962 kill, the bulletin, "Pollution-Caused Fish Kills," published by the Public Health Service recorded that approximately 3,180,000 alewives or branch herring were killed in September, in the Anacostia River near Washington, and this number totaled more than half of all the pollution killed fish reported by 36 states. This report points out that the totals reported probably represent only a fraction of the fish actually killed by man-made pollution and do not include fish kills where it was not definitely established that pollution was the cause of the kill.

In addition to the herring, during the summer of 1962 rock fish and perch died in the lower Potomac by the thousands. Many of the rock fish weighed from five to fifteen pounds. This kill was not included in the Public Health Service bulletin because it could not be determined that it was caused by pollution. In 1963 the kill was almost entirely perch, and they died by the millions. The shores of the river were lined with dead perch, in places a foot deep, and the stench drove many people from their homes. This kill extended to the Chesapeake Bay and was so serious that the Governor of Virginia appointed an investigating committee, which action later was followed by the Governor of Maryland. The kill continued during July and August. While nothing conclusive was determined by the committee, the consensus seemed to be that the perch were killed by the combination of high temperatures, the dissolved oxygen in the water being at a low point; over fertilization of the water (which would seem to point to pollution), with a high percentage of phosphorous and nitrogen that makes algae grow, and the great concentration of perch in the river. Only one fact seems to be certain -- the commercial fishermen cannot be blamed this time.

Dr. Varley Lang of Easton commented on the kill on August 3, 1963, as follows: "The latest guess on the perch kill in the Potomac comes from a Federal investigator who claims to have isolated a harmful bacterium. He is probably right. The only thing is that all of these enemies, harmful bacteria and viruses, anoxia and algae, fungus and food failure, are always present. Apparently any one or all of them remain fairly quiescent until conditions favor an epidemic attack, in which case one or more become killers. But what triggers the attack is environment (the entire complex), not the presence or absence of potential enemies, which are always in the environment. This is the ecological point of view, a comparatively recent discipline which has had a difficult way to make because it introduced multiple instead of single causation, complexity in place of simplicity. I'm persuaded that the ecological view, while complex and difficult, is nevertheless fruitful and essentially sound."

If this situation is repeated during the summers to follow, the fishing industry in the river will be in a bad way, to say nothing about the loss in sport fishing. It is a problem that will require the utmost in effort to solve. If it is not solved, the fracas between sports and commercial fishermen can be forgotten -- there will be no fish to fight over.

Some thirty or more years ago the season for gill netting in the Potomac was curtailed and the opening of the season delayed until March 1 of each year, although this restriction was not made effective in the Chesapeake Bay. It was a cause of considerable bitterness among the Potomac fishermen who had been making sizable winter catches in the "deep holes" in the river. Captain Joe Henderson recalls netting $2,000 worth of rock on one expedition in 1927 and Captain Edwin Gibson was making similar big catches in the deep water in the vicinity of the Potomac River Bridge about this same time. The curtailed season caused many fishermen to abandon gill netting and the river as a livelihood as it left them idle for two months when there was little else left for them to do.

In great-grandfather's day, in the spring, people would stand on the banks of Rock Creek in Washington with dip nets and in a few hours catch enough herring to last them until the next season, and they still do this along Piscattaway and other streams but times and tastes have changed. The 1960 Potomac River herring catch totaled only 13 million fish weighing about 6 million pounds, valued at $87,122. Compared with 1959, this was a decline of 21% in the number, pounds, and also in the value of the fish caught. The catch of shad in the Potomac during 1960 amounted to 71,683 fish, weighing 189,400 pounds and valued at $28,248. Although the number of fish caught was 18% greater than 1959, the poundage increased only 1% while the value declined 10%. The number of fishermen engaged in the shad and herring industry declined from 625 in 1959 to 538 in 1960. This is a far cry from the thousands of men employed in the industry a century ago when the catch was around 22 million shad and 750 million herring. Shad in those days weighed 6 to 8 pounds and some as much as 13 pounds. The average of the 1960 catch was 2.67 pounds.

In the early days of gasoline engines when the rivermen were first required to carry life preservers, a bucket of sand, a bell and a "fog" horn in their work boats, such safety precautions were looked upon as bordering on the ridiculous and compliance was half-hearted, haphazard, and in most cases, non-existent. Two happenings on the Potomac will illustrate their viewpoint. Captain Joe Beitzell was stopped one day and it turned out that his fog horn couldn't be blown. There was a good reason for this -- Captain Joe had found out that by breaking off the metal reed and using a couple of thicknesses of screen wire, the fog horn made a fairly good gasoline strainer. When he was taken to task by the Inspector, he said, "Cap'n, that thing ain't any good in a fog." "Why not?" asked the Inspector. Captain Joe replied, "Well, when you blow that thing with the engine running, nobody can hear it and I'm not going to cut my engine off in a fog and be a sitting duck for anybody -- best thing to do is to put a lookout forward and keep moving so's to be able to get out of the way. Besides, you can hear that old engine a lot before you can hear that horn." After some further words, the Inspector who was understanding but unsympathetic gave the Captain a ticket which the Captain threw overboard on his way home.

102

After that, a series of letters arrived, each a little more ominous in tone, telling the Captain to report in Baltimore to attend to the violation. Finally the Captain sat down and wrote the following letter:

Dear Sir:

"I bought a fog horn as the law said. It wasn't any good because the engine made more racket than it did. I explained all this to the Captain of the Police boat. I wanted to get my money out of it so I made a funnel out of it. I may be able to get to Baltimore some time next summer when the oyster and fish season slacks off and if I do, I will stop by and explain it to you again. If you can't wait I guess you will have to come down here to see me."

Yours truly,

J. E. Beitzell

The "law" surrendered at that point and Captain Joe bought a number of fog horns after that, over the years, all of which he used to strain his gasoline.
Captain Edwin Gibson was caught one day down off White Point where he had gone to fish his trap nets, towing a skiff used in the operation. He was short one life preserver because he had brought along his ten year old son with his crew. The Inspector told him he would have to arrest him. Captain Edwin said, "Now, look here, Cap'n, I knowed I was short a life preserver before I left home but with that skiff, I don't need any life preservers. If anything happened to my boat I would use the skiff." The Inspector insisted the law was the law. Captain Edwin said, "Cap'n, I'm on the side of the law but the law don't expect a man to do something foolish -- you know I wouldn't put one of them life preservers on my boy and put him overboard in this icy water -- he wouldn't live a half hour -- no sir, I'd put him in that skiff and the crew, too." The Inspector asked, "Well, what if the skiff foundered?" Captain Edwin replied, "We'd hang on to that skiff and I wouldn't want that damn life preserver in my way while I was doing it." The Inspector who knew how really clumsy the early life preservers were -- an arrangement of foot long oblong corks that kept one afloat but hampered every movement -- had to agree and let the Captain off with a warning.
Captain Edwin was an able riverman, and it was no accident. He worked hard to do a good job and he would stand for no nonsense from his seven sons when it came to doing a job correctly. His older boys well remember one occasion when they were "sticking" a set of trap net stakes. It happened to be Saturday and Saturday afternoons usually were free. By the time the wind had died down so they could work it was fairly obvious that the job would run well into the afternoon. The boys didn't like this and from the start of the job they began to hurry and soon it was obvious that the poles were going down out of line. Captain Edwin made them pull up a couple of poles and restick them after considerable argument. When the argument grew long and loud on the third pole the Captain gave in and had no more to say as the work grew progressively worse. The boys sensed that his silence was heavy with disapproval and kept waiting for further protest. None came, and the set was completed in record time -- 120 poles were in position, many out of line. On Monday at 4:00 o'clock in the morning, the boys got the order "roll out, boys." There were sleepy groans and protests, and finally Dick had the temerity to ask, "why are you getting us up so early, Papa -- what have we gotta do?" Captain Edwin roared, "I'll tell you what we gotta do -- we are going down that river and we are going to pull every damn one of them stakes up -- the crooked ones and the straight ones, and then we are going to stick them the way they should've been stuck in the first place." Which is exactly what they did.
Although the crab industry did not have its beginning in Maryland's great Bay and its tributaries until 1873, the Chesapeake Bay blue crab (callinectes sapidus) is mentioned as a valuable food item in "A Relation of Maryland," dated 1635, a year after the settlement of the colony. There is no doubt that crabs, both hard and soft, were used extensively as a food delicacy from the earliest years by the people along the salty waterways of both Maryland and Virginia, but the market was limited to the nearby settlements due to the difficulties of preservation and transportation. Richard Parkinson, a British traveler, reporting on the habits of Americans during his visit at the close of the 18th century, dwelt on the popularity of both hard and soft crabs, but added that they were consumed only in the immediate areas of capture.
The first distant shipment of soft crabs is credited to Captain John H. Landon of Crisfield, Maryland, to the firm of John Martin of Philadelphia in 1873. As late as 1880, with the Bay and its tributaries swarming with uncaught millions of crabs, only three crab-meat processing firms were officially listed. However, in this year, 1,167,000 pounds of hard crabs were taken in Maryland waters and 2,139,000 pounds of

hard crabs were caught in the Virginia waters. From the beginning made in 1873, the crab industry, both hard and soft, in Maryland and Virginia, including the bay fisheries grew to a catch of 9,500,000 pounds, valued at $315,000 in 1890. By 1915 the catch amounted to 50,400,000 pounds, valued at approximately $1,000,000. Due to lack of conservation measures the catch dropped to 22,700,000 pounds in 1920 but was worth $1,300,000. In 1960 the catch totaled 70,716,000 pounds, valued at $4,596,416. The crab industry owes its growth and success, in no small measure, to the pioneer studies of W. P. Hay in 1904 and E. P. Churchill, Jr., prior to 1917. Mr. Churchill continued his studies and his findings were included in a bulletin of the U. S. Bureau of Fisheries in 1917-18, entitled, "Life History of the Blue Crab." Subsequently, in 1925, the Bureau of Fisheries in cooperation with the Maryland Conservation Department and the Virginia Fisheries Commission, conducted an extensive survey of the crab fisheries of the Chesapeake Bay that confirmed most of Churchill's findings and led to the introduction of limited conservation measures that have enabled the industry to grow rather than retrogress, as has happened in the fish and oyster industry.

The Potomac River crab fisheries which depend completely on the breeding grounds of Virginia, in 1960 had a catch of 7,725, 100 pounds valued at $462,797 (see Table). These figures include the bay side of Northumberland County which probably accounts for about one-half of the total catch in this County so that the Potomac catch totaled in excess of 5,000,000 pounds in 1960.

Blue crabs have an interesting and complex life history which has been studied carefully in the Chesapeake Bay area. They have an extensive range along the Atlantic Coast from Cape Cod to Texas. They like the shallow bays, sounds and river channels and are seldom found far out at sea. In summer the crabs live close inshore, but in winter they move off into deeper water to escape the cold. They do not appear to migrate extensively up and down the coast and probably each section has its own local population. More than 40% of the blue crabs caught are taken from the Chesapeake Bay and its tributaries. The principal shipping center in Maryland continues to be Crisfield and in Virginia, it is Hampton.

POTOMAC RIVER CRAB FISHERIES 1960

	HARD CRABS		SOFT CRABS & PEELERS		TOTAL	
	Pounds	Value	Pounds	Value	Pounds	Value
MARYLAND						
St. Mary's County	960,900	$ 53,812	79,600	$ 15,916	1,040,500	$ 69,728
Charles County	455,100	25,486	2,800	560	457,900	26,046
Prince George's County	1,200	67	-	-	1,200	67
TOTAL	1,417,200	$ 79,365	82,400	$ 16,476	1,499,600	$ 95,841
VIRGINIA						
*Northumberland County	4,194,200	$190,870	333,400	$ 84,485	4,527,600	$275,355
Westmoreland County	1,288,800	58,586	38,400	9,815	1,327,200	68,401
King George County	190,200	10,000	12,200	3,100	202,400	13,100
Stafford County	156,000	7,000	12,300	3,100	168,300	10,100
TOTAL	5,829,200	$266,456	396,300	$100,500	6,225,500	$366,956
TOTAL MARYLAND AND VIRGINIA	7,246,400	$345,821	478,700	$116,976	7,725,100	$462,797

*Includes the Bay side of the County

NOTE: These figures do not include crabs caught for home consumption or those sold locally to neighbors, etc., which would add substantially to the totals.

The seasonal migrations are especially important, having a direct bearing on the problem of conservation. Every year between the first of June and the end of August a new generation of crabs is produced in the Virginia area of the Chesapeake Bay and its tributaries. The female extrudes the eggs, each about one one-hundredth of an inch in diameter, from a large yellowish mass upon the apron (referred to as the "sponge"). After spawning occurs the eggs hatch in about 15 days. When first hatched the crab resembles a tiny question mark but as it grows it sheds its shell repeatedly, and in about a month it assumes a crab-like form. Thereafter the crab molts or sheds about 15 times before reaching maturity, at first every six days, then, after gradually lengthening periods, until about 25 days elapse between the final molts. Ordinarily the crab gains about one-third in size with each molt. Crabs reach their full growth and maturity and cease to molt during their second summer, when 12 to 14 months old.

Usually the first spawning takes place when the female is about two years old. Some females are believed to live over another winter and to deposit more eggs when three years old; probably few or none live longer than this. Presumably the life span of the male is about the same length.

Most of the young crabs hatched in the lower Chesapeake Bay soon begin a northward migration though some remain to mature in Virginia waters. Cold weather often interrupts this journey and they settle to the bottom for the winter and cease to feed or grow until conditions are more favorable. Late in spring their migration is resumed, growth proceeds and finally they reach Maryland waters. The mating of the majority of the crabs takes place in Maryland. After mating, the females return to the lower Bay, but most of the males remain behind, spending the winter in deep holes or burying in the creeks and rivers. Only about one-fifth of the crabs taken in the lower part of the Bay during the winter are males. Nearly all of the sponge bearing crabs are found in Virginia waters. In the Potomac River the crabs begin to appear in the shallow waters near the end of May and range from grown to very small crabs, with a preponderance of the latter during the early part of the season.

As indicated previously, the blue crab grows by a process of molting (the rivermen call it shedding). He grows inside his shell to the point that the shell will no longer contain him. In this process he begins as a "hard shell" crab and goes through three major stages -- (1) the "peeler" stage, when he forms a new soft shell within the old, including every organ, (2) the "buster" stage, when the old hard top shell breaks loose on the back of the crab and the "shedding" process begins, and (3) the "soft shell" stage, after he pulls himself out of the old hard shell, i.e., completes the shedding process.

It will be seen from the foregoing that the so-called "soft crab" is not a distinct species. The term is applied to any crab that has shed its old shell and whose new shell has not yet hardened. As it nears the new hard stage, the crab is called a "paper shell" or "buckram." At this stage the crab is largely water and is valueless as either a soft or hard crab.

About the smallest "shedders" seen in the shallow waters of the Potomac and its tributaries are approximately an inch in length, measured from the tips of the top shell, although smaller ones may be observed swimming at the top of the water out on the river where the water is deep. In the fall and winter, all sizes of both male and unmated female crabs are caught by the oysterman occasionally in their oyster tongs and dredges.

As the soft-shelled crab is considered especially choice they are sought throughout the late spring and summer months while they are still molting. Crabs that show definite signs of approaching the shedding stage ("peelers") are kept in floats. If caught too early, however, the crab will die without shedding and state laws prohibit the impoundment of crabs that have not reached the "peeler" stage. A "peeler" crab can be detected by a pink "sign" on the last pair of legs (back fins), indicating that the new shell is fully formed underneath the old one.

After "shedding" the crab, in his soft state, is very weak and almost helpless for an hour or two. In this state, he is that great delicacy, the Chesapeake Bay soft shell crab. During the period when he becomes a "ripe" peeler until shedding he is the fishing bait par excellence for rock, trout, blues, perch, and most other Bay fish. During this period his new "skin" is tough enough to stay on the hook, the shell peels off easily and the sporting type fish love the meat just as much as the human fancier of soft crab fare. A few hours after the crab has shed (unless he is removed from the water), his shell starts to harden again, he goes into the "paper" shell stage and he is not such good fish bait as the meat doesn't stay on the hook very well. Nor is he quite the delicacy for human consumption as when he first sheds. From the paper shell stage he again progresses to the hard stage and starts to feed again, not having done so during the ripe peeler stage. It is believed that the shedding process takes from 24 to 36 hours from the ripe peeler stage back to the hard state. When a comparison of the size is made of the newly shed crab with his "shed," it doesn't seem possible that the crab could have been contained in the so much smaller "shed."

Both male and female crabs grow through the shedding process. The sex may
be distinguished by the "apron," a flap on the bottom of the crab which is hinged
to the back of the top shell and which covers the organs of reproduction. In the
female crab, before mating, the apron is shaped like a triangle and covers two tiny
openings on either side of the lower body from which the eggs issue, a considerable
time after mating to form the "sponge" that spreads over the apron.

In the male crab the apron is much narrower, having somewhat the appearance of
the letter "T" and no changes occur before or after mating, other than growth. The
apron in the male covers and protects two reproductive organs resembling a hair about
an inch in length. When grown, the male crab is generally larger than the female,
particularly before the female mates. On the last shedding before mating the female
attains full growth and while generally still not as long as the male, she becomes
considerably broader than in her previous state. There are all sizes of the adult
crab, both male and female and some grown crabs can be described as dwarfs, but most
of them are normal and of a uniform size.

The younger crabs do not have so much in the way of contrasting colors, being
a fairly uniform greenish brown until they approach the adult state. This is particularly true of the female crab which seems to blossom out in color at mating time.
Her colors are quite different from the male and at this period she can be distinguished from the male by color alone. It is not unusual to see as many as three
male adult crabs fighting over a single female. The male, after beating off his
adversaries, triumphantly grabs his bride who always seems quite willing, tucks her
under his body, holding her with his six pointed legs (three on each side of the
body) and takes her wherever he goes, sharing his food with her during the mating
period, until the time she becomes a ripe peeler as she becomes totally inactive,
although normal in every way. Sometimes the male doesn't have any competitors around
and simply chases the female until he captures her. After being captured, the female
again seems to submit quite willingly. At this stage both are "hard shell" crabs.
The mating pair are called "doublers" or "a channeler and his wife."

The male crab continues to carry his bride during the complete period required
for her to progress from hard to peeler to buster to soft, i.e., during a complete
cycle of the shedding process, estimated to be at least a week to ten days. He,
himself, does not shed during this period. When the female reaches the buster stage,
the male will bring her into shallow water for her to shed. He always hides her as
best he can, in a thin patch of seaweed or behind a log or rock. He then buries himself nearby and waits for the final shedding process, which takes approximately an
hour. This is a very great ordeal for a crab, male or female, as it is completely
defenseless during this time and if disturbed may have to drop a claw or fin because
it seems to have only strength enough to shed normally under the most ideal circumstances, i.e., without distraction or disturbance. In the case of the mating couple,
of course, the male crab is nearby to give his protection and he will tackle anything,
no matter how large, that threatens his mate.

Immediately after the female has shed and is in the completely soft state, the
male seizes her, turns her upside down under his body, holds her with the same fins
and the actual mating process begins. In the last shedding process, the female has
taken on her full adult colors and her apron has changed from the shape of a triangle
to that of a perfect shield and has broadened out considerably in the process. Sometimes the male, immediately after the bride has shed, will make for deep water with
her, come to the surface and swim on the surface with her against the tide. Many
such couples can be observed on the surface of the river during the month of August.
They also often swim on the surface while the female is still in the peeler stage.
The actual mating process continues for about 24 hours, i.e., until the female progresses from the soft state to the paper shell stage. At this point, the male reverses the female to her original position when he first captured her and continues
to carry her until her shell is quite hard again and she is fully capable of defend-
ing herself. At this point she is released to fend for herself and proceeds in due
course to the hatching grounds in the lower part of the Chesapeake.

Many are found and taken by dredges during the winter months in the Chesapeake
Bay and millions of eggs are destroyed with the destruction of the mother crabs.
However, control is exercised by Virginia who has jurisdiction of this area and
these grounds are opened or closed to crabbing following the advice of qualified
experts. Limited use of the dredge permits fresh crab meat to be on the market
during winter months and this is an important part of the industry. Other conservation measures are minimum size limits on crabs possessed or sold, specified seasons
for some types of gear and the complete prohibition of certain others. Maryland and
Virginia crabbing laws do not coincide in all respects, even though the same crabs
are common to the waters of both. Generally speaking, Virginia controls the areas
of spawning and hibernation of female crabs. The two states are interdependent as
regards the blue crab, but the effective protection of the crab demands different

POTOMAC RIVER NANCY
(Forerunner of the Dory)

Drawing by
Frederick Tilp

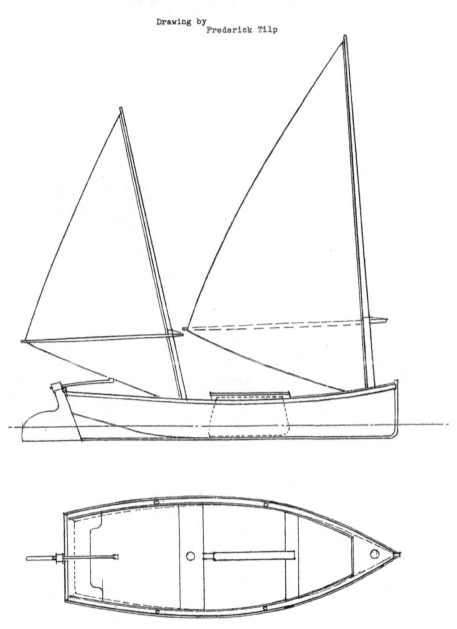

USED FOR CRABBING, FISHING, AND OYSTERING

Chesapeake Bay "Blue" Crab

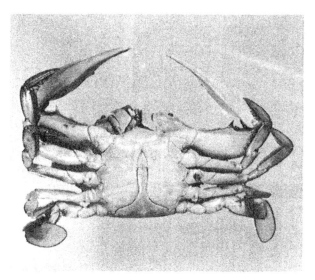

Male Crab

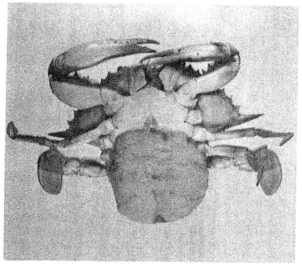

Female "Sponge" Crab Bearing Eggs

Female Crab, Before Mating

Female Crab, Ready To Mate

PHOTOS—Robert S. Bailey, Virginia Institute of Marine Science

Chesapeake Bay "Blue" Crab

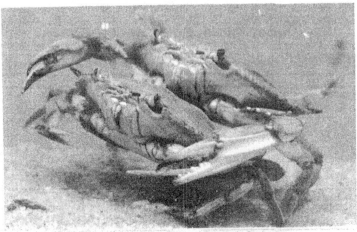

"Doublers", Male Hard Crab and Female in Peeler Stage

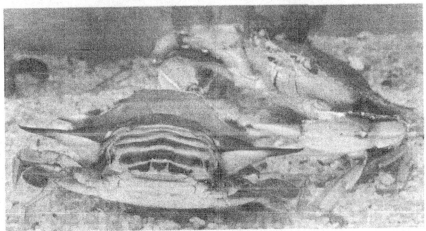

Male Crab Waiting for Female to Shed

Female Emerging from "Shed"

Hard Male Crab and Soft Female Mating
(Female "Shed" in Foreground

PHOTOS---Robert S. Bailey, Virginia Institute of Marine Science

Chesapeake Bay "Blue" Crab

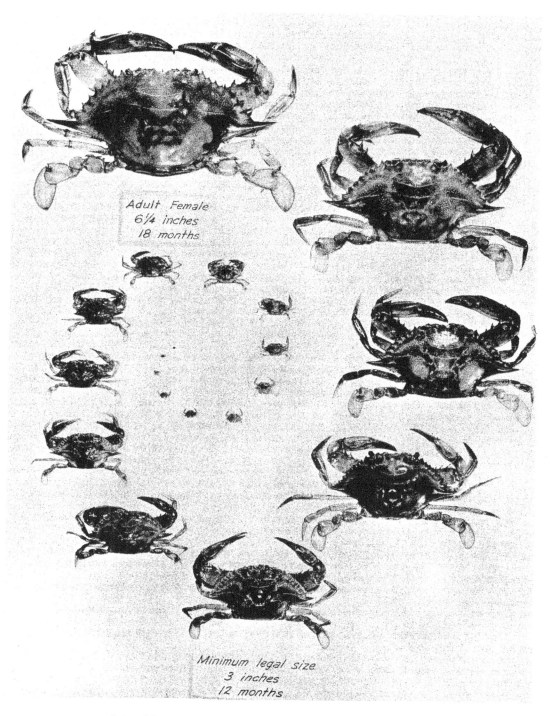

Adult Female
6¼ inches
18 months

Minimum legal size
3 inches
12 months

Series of Sheddings Showing Growth of Crab from Early Stage to Mature Adult

PHOTOS—Robert S. Bailey, Virginia Institute of Marine Science

measures in the two states.

It was of interest to the writer while he was at Fort Monroe for two weeks in June 1957, to see many of the local people who wanted a "mess" of crabs fishing traps, from the Army pier at Hampton Roads, catching many female crabs, almost all mated females, with the shield shaped apron, loaded with eggs of a bright orange color with the apron hanging loose. The few previously seen with eggs in the Potomac were quite different; the eggs were of a greenish brown color and each egg covered by a sort of tough skin and all attached firmly to the apron, forming a rather hard mass. While a few unmated females (with the triangle shaped apron) were being caught, not a single male crab was seen during this period.

Mated females are not seen in the Potomac in May when the crabs first come into shallow water to shed, and sheds of the mated female are not found since they stop shedding after mating. While it is believed that the male crab also stops shedding at maturity it is difficult to determine, as some shedders are very large.

About 20 years ago Captain Golden Thompson of St. Patrick's Creek on the Potomac River, a seafood dealer for 60 years, found a female crab with the shield shaped apron which was in the peeler stage and this crab shed in the normal course of events. It is the only case heard of, of this curiosity, and rivermen all around the area came to see it. Perhaps this crab had never actually mated, although her apron had changed from the triangle shape to the shield shape. Many "doublers" are caught before the actual mating process has begun. The female peeler is put into a float with other peelers to shed. Sometimes she becomes, through some inadvertence, a buckram before it is noticed that she has shed. Since she is then worthless she is turned loose, and thus every season a few of these unmated mature females are returned to the waters. Although she has not mated, since she must be in a soft state for this to be possible and she was separated from her mate in the peeler state, her apron changes from the shape of a triangle to the shape of a shield and she takes on all the other characteristics of the mated female. Was the case observed by Captain Thompson a freak or do such females shed again? It would be interesting to know the answer to this and many other questions.

During the summer of 1962, (and again in 1963), the writer noted an unusual phenomenon in the Potomac that caused considerable talk among the rivermen. Ordinarily the mating of crabs doesn't begin on the river until the hot days of July but in this year mating couples were observed almost at the opening of the crab season, early in June. Crabs were scarce during the early season and many of the mating crabs appeared to be unduly small or immature. It was unusually hot and dry during the late spring. The writer communicated these facts to Varley Lang of Easton, and in a letter dated July 21, 1962, he wrote: "I should tell you that a friend of mine also caught a sponge crab, the first in a couple of decades around here. She was swimming on top of the water, and he dipped her up out of curiosity. Her whole apron was covered with eggs. That was in the middle of July. I have never heard of such a thing this early. Another man (duly witnessed and published in the paper) caught a big crab on a trot line in the Wye. The entire carapace of this crab was colored a light blue, while the claws were brown. What do you make of that?.....Crabbing has fallen off here as well. In fact, it has fallen off all over the Bay, even in places like Crisfield and the Black Water. When that happens, then you just have to wait until late August and September before you can expect much of a run of crabs....."

The writer also caught a hard crab about this time whose claws and a couple of fins were brown but the carapace was normal. He was a strange sight.

On September 27, 1962, Dr. Lang wrote: ".....For a couple of weeks in September the crabbers struck it rich: ten and twelve bushels a day. I stood on the bridge over Leeds Creek and looked over the flats. The water was exceptionally clear. Every three feet, just as though spaced out by measurement and as far as I could see, there was a hard crab....." The crabs also came into the Potomac during this time, perhaps a week or so earlier.

Male crabs survive a second season and perhaps a third because in May of each year, one can catch fully grown males and some look much older than others. It is doubtful that mated females return to the Potomac after their migration to the lower part of the Bay.

The Chesapeake Bay blue crab is the fightingest, eatingest, and meanest thing in the water for his size. When he sees you he will run for safety if possible, but not from cowardice -- he's just being sensible. Who wouldn't run if he saw a dragon 180 feet long armed with a telephone pole, with a net on the end 12 feet in diameter, grabbing at him. That's what a man on the bow of a skiff, with a crab net, looks like to a crab. However, if he is cornered in shallow water he will fight to the last ditch. When dumped in a boat or on land he will literally jump in the air trying to bite his captor. If at any time he grabs hold he will hang on until beaten to a pulp. Cases are known where a crab has bitten a finger of a riverman to the bone on both sides and a riverman's hands are as tough as leather due to exposure. Cases are known, also, where children have lost fingers, the crab having severed the bone. When captured, the hard crab goes berserk, he will bite at anything, including other crabs and himself (and the hard shell female is no exception). When carrying his mate, he will run if possible, even dropping his mate if she is still in the peeler state and able to fend for herself. In the process the water is muddied, deliberately and he will always return to find her. When captured in a crab net he will sometimes bite his mate, but the writer is inclined to believe this is accidental, due to his frenzy, rather than his trying to kill her to prevent her from falling into other hands. One time the writer found a mature male crab eating what seemed to be his freshly shed mate. This was so unusual that he has wondered if this crab might have killed another male in battle and then proceeded to eat his mate.

A crab will eat almost anything, dead or alive. He is a cannibal and one often sees a small hard shell crab that has caught a large soft shell crab and is eating it. More than that, the writer once threw overboard a hard shell crab in shallow water, along with his claw which had been broken off; the crab grabbed the claw and went on his way eating it. As a boy, the writer raised ducks on the river and most of the casualties among the ducklings occurred when crabs would grab their feet, pull them under the water and drown them and then have a juicy meal. They will go into fish traps and likewise catch and eat live fish. They are scavengers also and will eat anything from old crab sheds to a dead horse. However, they won't eat a sick crab. Occasionally one will see a sick crab around the shore -- they turn a sickly yellow, move very sluggishly and eventually die. The dead crab will lie there until he disintegrates -- nothing will touch him.

Crabs have natural enemies, turtles of all kinds, bitterns, herons (cranes), fish, other crabs, and humans. They are completely vulnerable during the last of the shedding stage and are fair game for anything that comes along. If a heron "crabs" a shore ahead of you, the pickings will be mighty slim. The crab's two back fins are his swimmers, his six pointed legs help him move about on the bottom (and carry his mate) and his two great claws are his battle axes and have amazing strength. He moves sideways, rather than forward or backward and is very swift in the hard shell state. If he loses a fin or a claw, or several in battle, he is not unduly worried for he can grow replacements, if the break is at the joint which it usually is. When soft, the crab will deliberately drop a member to escape (seemingly at will). This is how a soft shell crab often escapes from a hard shell crab -- he will drop a claw when grabbed and while the hard shell crab is eating it, he will remove himself from danger. When hard, the crab doesn't seem able to drop a member but many are severed at the joint in battle. Immediately a new fin or claw, which is soft and covered for protection by a skin bag, begins to grow to replace the lost member. If the fin or claw is lost when the crab is small, the new one will be almost as large as the original when he sheds but if the crab is fairly large, the new fin or claw will be considerably smaller than the original. After shedding, the soft fin or claw hardens with the rest of the crab.

Soft shell crabs are caught in the Potomac mainly in two ways. They shed mostly on an ebb or falling tide. The crabber may push a skiff around the shore with a "dip" net, standing in the bow and sighting the shedding crab in shallow water. The other method is to wade in shallow water with a "push" net, about a yard wide and square across the front, rather than round or oval, pushing the net through patches of seaweed. In some of the bay areas small seines are used.

Hard crabs are caught in several ways. For example, by dredging them in deep water. This method is not used in the Potomac. Some are caught by the methods described for soft crabs and some are caught on individual hand lines, baited with chicken heads and such. The common commercial methods used are the crab line and crab pots.

There are three other types of crabs in the river that should be mentioned. One is the "Fiddler" crab, which when grown is about the size of your fingernail. He lives in an old oyster shell in fairly shallow water. If he ventures out of his house he is likely to become food for some fish or hard crab. This is a hermit type crab. It lives alone but mates and produces eggs each year and remains in the same locale. Another type is the oyster crab (commensal) which lives within a living oyster. Although not truly parasitic he shares the same fare as the oyster. He enters the oyster apparently as an egg or when very small and grows also to the size of a fingernail. His size causes him to be imprisoned in the oyster shell since the oyster cannot open his mouth wide enough for the crab to escape, even if he wanted to. These oyster crabs are considered great delicacies by gourmets. They are found quite frequently (perhaps one in every ten oysters) in the oysters on Heron Island bar in the Potomac, at the mouth of St. Clement's Bay. A third type of crab is the king or horseshoe crab but he is seen only infrequently in the Potomac.

When a boy, the writer's biggest source of spending money during the summer was from soft crabbing and the catch would average from three to six dozen daily which brought from 30¢ to 50¢ per dozen. Since the crabbing season began late in May and school did not close until the middle of June, he was often in difficulty with his mother and his teacher about tardiness. Up at daylight, it was hard to leave the crabbing grounds when the crabs were thick and the tide was right. Half-size crabs counted as full-size soft crabs but the smaller ones went two for one and sometimes three for one. There were no size limitations fifty years ago. The writer favored the dip net from the bow of a skiff in the creeks where the bottom was soft from mud but the push net was used in the seaweed on the flats of St. Clement's Bay and the Potomac. It was not unusual, however, with several persons to a boat to catch as many as 100 dozen soft crabs a day during the height of the season at such places as Knott's Hollow at the mouth of Bretton Bay and on the flats downriver between Huggin's Point and Posey's Bluff.

Soft crabs were sold to local buyers, such as Captain Golden Thompson of St. Patrick's Creek or some of the Morris boys of Canoe Neck Creek or to Eastern Shore buyers, mainly from Crisfield, such as John Sterling, George Nelson, John Guy, Arthur Marshall, William Wallace Evans, and John Tawes Taylor. The last two always bought in partnership. In the early days, the Eastern Shoreners came by sail but with the advent of gasoline engines, they used bateaus. Each buyer carried a sizable cloth bag of change, perhaps a couple of hundred dollars in silver, and to a small boy this seemed like a tremendous amount of money, particularly when he was allowed to "heft" the bag.

In the early years and prior to 1938, when the crab pot was invented and patented by B. F. Lewis of Harryhogan, Virginia, practically all commercial "hard crabbing" in the Potomac was done by trot lines. The trot line might be anywhere from a 1/4 mile to 1 mile in length, weighted at each end, with bait of salted eel or tripe knotted in the line every three or four feet. The line, when not in use is kept in a tub of brine to prevent spoilage of the bait. The line is re-baited after use each day. In the earlier days the method of crabbing differed somewhat from present day procedures. Slim poles that could be "chunked" down in the mud were used to mark each end of the line and the crabber sat in the bow of his skiff and pulled up the line, hand over hand, to net the crabs. He used a homemade crab net that somewhat resembled a snow shoe.

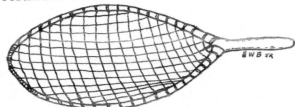

The frame of the crab net was made of a forked piece of white oak, about an inch in diameter at the butt with two branches about the size of a finger, that were shaped to an elongated oval and plaited at the top to form the bow. A shallow net bag was attached to the bow to complete the job. With care, these crab nets would last for years, as compared with the present day metal bows that scarcely last a season.

In later years, the poles used to mark the end of the line were replaced by buoys of various types, a roller is mounted aft of the crab boat over which the line passes. The boat is motorized and the crabber in a standing position dips the crabs with a "store boughten" long handle dip net.

Captain Al Norris was perhaps one of the best known old-time trot line crabbers in the Blackistone Island area of the Potomac. For reasons best known to himself, Captain Al never aspired to be a capitalist but always crabbed in partnership with his brother-in-law, Captain Joe Beitzell. Captain Joe supplied the skiff, the crab line, bait, salt, and barrels while Captain Al supplied the crab net and the labor. They shared the profits and it was a mutually satisfactory arrangement for many years. Uncle Al simply could not be persuaded to go into business for himself -- when the subject was broached, he would smile and shake his head. If pressed, he would say, "I like it the way it is," and walk away.

His success as a crabber appears to have been mainly due to his knowledge of the tides and the feeding habits of the crabs. While he had certain favorite "sets," they were varied from time to time and he could be counted on to bring in three barrels of crabs when other boats would bring in two -- all select crabs and never a "she" crab in the lot -- to him it was downright sinful to catch breeder crabs that would insure future supplies. A close observer might notice him at the edge of dark, rowing out of the creek with muffled oarlocks to stake his set for the next day. The summer night would be spent sleeping on the dry bottom of his immaculate skiff, that was scrubbed thoroughly at the end of each day's work. If rough weather or a thunderstorm came up during the night, he would slip in to shore, throw a tarpaulin over some bushes and make himself comfortable until dawn. If the wind was high he would shift his set to another favorite spot on a leeward shore.

Since the hard crabs in those days were shipped to Baltimore and Washington by steamboat and there were only two or three "boat" days a week, the crabs were pounded in "crab boxes" in the creek until shipment. These boxes were slatted affairs about twelve feet square and five feet high, fastened by ropes to the cross pieces of poles driven in the mud at each of the four corners. These boxes had to be watched night and day and raised or lowered with the tide to prevent escape of the crabs at "high water," or to prevent them from smothering if the box was too high out of water at "low water."

Crabs were plentiful in those days, and an advertisement in the St. Mary's Beacon of August 14, 1902, offered hard crabs cooked and delivered at 10¢ per dozen. Currently the price is $2.50 for steamed crabs, except on Friday nights at Captain Sam Bailey's Emporium on White's Neck Creek, where one may have all he can eat for $1.50, which is about a dozen, if you really liked steamed crabs.

A generation ago when there were many more men engaged in hard crabbing in the Potomac using trot lines, bad weather in the winter months was employed by many of them in making eel pots, usually from empty nail kegs, although some bought pots from Cambridge or Easton made of gum or white oak splints. A funnel was placed in one end of the pot and a plug was fitted into the other end so that the trapped eels might be removed. Later the pots were made of small mesh wire rolled over 3 wire hoops, 9 inches in diameter. The length of the pot was 3 feet. The pots were baited with menhaden or crushed hard crabs. The pots generally were set on the mud bottom of the creeks or between the sand and mud on the river flats in the spring and early fall. The pots were weighted and a buoy attached on a line 15 to 20 feet long.

While some of the larger eels were shipped to market in Washington and Baltimore, most were salted down for use as crab-line bait, either by the individual himself or he might sell the eels to neighboring crabbers or ship them in barrels to wholesale commission merchants in the city. A good many eels were caught also in the trap nets. The writer recalls as a boy investing in three of the new wire eel pots in 1919 at a cost of $1 a piece. He caught a "gum" barrel of eels in Canoe Neck Creek which he salted and when shipped to market they brought almost $60. He has not had so good a return on an investment since. On one occasion he had great difficulty in raising one of the pots and getting it over the side of the skiff, and found the pot packed so tightly with eels that all were dead -- they had smothered.

One of the favorite sports among the youngsters on the creek was to fish with hand-lines for eels alongside of the crab boxes, which contained about 8-10 barrels of crabs awaiting shipment on steamboat day. The eels would feed on the fins of the crabs protruding through the slats of the crab box and some whoppers were caught, as big around as one's wrist and 30 inches long. Our mothers would fry 4 inch sections of them crisp, in deep fat, and this was mighty tasty eating. But after a couple of hours of eel fishing our clothing and persons were a sight to behold from the eel slime, and the mortality rate among Papa's fish hooks ran high. It was fun though, and ounce for ounce of weight, the eel is about the pullingest fish there is.

Uncle Al Norris and his brother, Lee, were self-trained naturalists, though they probably never realized it; they were representative of a breed of men no longer with us. They knew where to find possums and raccoons and all types of game, and they were good shots. They knew how to trap the diamondback terrapin and the location of all the good fishing places. Their "educated toes" knew how to feel for the snapping turtles buried in fresh water ponds at hip depth, in the early spring and they knew unerringly which end of the turtle to reach for -- a mistake would have been extremely painful; it was natural to them to catch a jarful of bees on the flowers in the yard, release them one at a time and be guided by their flight to a wild honey tree at the edge of the woods, perhaps a mile or two away; they knew where to find chestnuts, hickory nuts, the finest huckleberry bushes, wild asparagus and the best wild berries and fruit for jellies and wine; their rabbit snares and traps furnished much game for the table; they knew how to make weirs to trap fish and each had "huddles" (green pine brush, anchored with stones) at various secret spots in the creek and bay. These were baited to attract the fish which liked to frequent these spots, huddling around or swimming through these underwater gardens -- of course, the fish didn't realize until too late that they were going to end up taking the bait dangling from Uncle's "angle" rod and provide a good meal for supper. They made their own "angle" rods for bottom fishing of cedar, 16 feet in length, worked down to 1 1/2 inches at the butt and tapered to 1/4 inch at the top -- the cork was carved from heavy pine bark. The term "angle" is obscure but probably was derived from angle worms which were used for bait when there was nothing better at hand, such as peeler crabs, a favorite bait. These men made their own wooden needles, used for making or mending nets, wooden "splints" for stringing fish, wooden bows for crab nets, and their carved whistles, toy boats and tops would delight the heart of any little boy. A sharp bladed pocket knife was the most essential thing carried on their persons,

110

and it is certain neither of them would have traded their knives for a present day social security card. Their home gardens were a joy to behold -- they loved the land and the water that gave life.

In modern times the river police have done a much more complete job of enforcing the statutes governing the river throughout the year much to the discomfiture of the old-timers, who could never understand that a riverman was not entitled to take a mess of fish, oysters, or crabs from the river whenever he felt the need, in season or out. To the riverman it is an inalienable right -- a part of being a riverman. Captain Joe Beitzell didn't have too much trouble about fish or oysters -- there was no closed season on fish and he could always slip up a cove and come home with a bucket of oysters, but catching hard crabs was another matter. It just wasn't worthwhile to bait a trot line for an occasional mess of crabs -- a few crab pots were much handier. He would set some crab pots, baited with fish, around Canoe Neck Creek and the police would promptly confiscate them, as their use in the Potomac tributaries was forbidden. He would patiently make a few more only to have those confiscated also. The police knew him and were sympathetic but if he were permitted to fish them, the commercial crabbers would soon be at it. This was explained to the Captain but his answer always was "but I just want a mess for supper." Finally it was suggested that he set his pots by boat stakes or an old duck blind, tie the cord under water and no one would be the wiser. Captain Joe was indignant -- he would never do such a thing -- it smacked of deceit and he would have no part of it -- so the game was played out to the end, when the Captain left his beloved river forever, at the age of 91.

****

SPECIES OF FISH FOUND IN THE POTOMAC RIVER

Alewife
Angler fish, Toadfish, or
    Miller's Thumb
Bluefish
Butterfish
Carp
Catfish
Cobia
Crappie or Tobacco Box
Croaker or Hardhead
Drum, Red
Eel, Common
Eel, Conger
Flounder, Winter or Blackback
Fluke
Garfish
Gizzard Shad or Mud Shad
Goldfish
Harvestfish or "Starfish"
Herring, Sea
Hickory Shad
Hogchoker
King Mackerel

Lamprey
Mackerel, Atlantic
Menhaden
Mullet
Pike or Pickerel
Scup or Porgy
Sea Bass
Sea Robin
Sea Trout or Weakfish, Gray
Sea Trout or Weakfish, Spotted
Shad
Shark
Sheepshead
Sand Perch, "King William," or
    White Perch
Skate
Spot
Striped Bass or Rockfish
Sturgeon
Swellfish, Toadfish, or Blow-
    fish
Tautog
White Perch or Gray Perch
Yellow Perch or Yellow Ned

LIFE ON THE POTOMAC RIVER

Chapter VII

STEAMBOATING ON THE RIVER

For some unfathomable reason, the beginning of any new idea, method, or activity seems always to be shrouded in mystery, leading to disputes and arguments as to the author or originator. The introduction of steamboating on the Potomac River is no exception and there are several claimants to the honor. Perhaps Americans have been too busy during the last three centuries making history to take time to record their history carefully.

If the "ingenious steam device" of James Rumsey of Berkeley County, Virginia, which he operated successfully on the Potomac in 1787 can be classed as a steamboat, then he undoubtedly deserves first honors on the river.

However, it appears to be firmly established that John Fitch of Philadelphia was the original inventor of the "steam" boat. Fitch, who was born in Connecticut, built his first model in 1785 and successfully operated a skiff powered by a 3 inch cylinder, driven by steam in July, 1786, on the Delaware River at Philadelphia. A second and improved steamboat was operated by Fitch on the Delaware on August 22, 1787. Rumsey, who previously had invented a boat propelled through a system of mechanical cranks, operated by wheels and hand power, found the device unsatisfactory and turned to steam, but did not get his boat in operation on the Potomac until December, 1787. His efforts were followed with interest by General Washington and other prominent citizens. Rumsey and Fitch engaged in a controversy and Rumsey appealed to the Virginia legislature to cancel the exclusive rights previously given to Fitch, to operate steam vessels in Virginia waters but his appeal was denied. A third steamboat built by Fitch made a 20 mile trip from Philadelphia to Burlington in July, 1788. The vessel was 45 feet in length and 12 feet wide and had room for passengers.

The research of the late John Clagett Proctor, who for many years was a featured writer for the Evening Star of Washington, discloses that the "Columbian," a clumsy, flat-bottomed steamboat, whose builder or owner is now unknown, was operating on the Potomac as early as 1813, hauling grain and wood. This was some two years earlier than the introduction of Robert Fulton's steamboat, the "Washington," on the Potomac. There seems to be some doubt concerning the statement that Fulton tried out his steamboat, or a model of it, on Rock Creek, in the Kalorama section of Washington, prior to his memorable voyage in the "Clermont" from New York City to Albany in August, 1807, but it is possible. Fulton went abroad in 1787 and did not return until late in 1806. Early in 1807, his friend, Joel Barlow, purchased Kalorama from William Augustine Washington. According to the statement of Jacob Colclazer, a blacksmith, at a meeting of the Association of Oldest Inhabitants, in Washington, in 1871, he, Colclazer helped make parts for the boat, and Fulton made his experiments on Rock Creek while a guest of Barlow at Kalorama, although Colclazer cited the date of 1805. It is possible that Mr. Colclazer may have been mistaken concerning the date, but it is also possible that he might have confused Fulton's submarine torpedo demonstrations and other activities in 1807 with the steamboat experiments.

James Clephane, a pioneer Washingtonian, stated on December 3, 1873, that the "Dandy" purchased by Joe Johnson in Baltimore was the first steamboat on the Potomac and the first to ply between Washington and Alexandria. Mr. Johnson operated a ferry from Buzzard Point. However, Mr. Clephane did not arrive in Washington until 1817, two years after Fulton's steamboat, the "Washington," was in use on the river. The arrival of the "Dandy" was most likely about 1819.

The record concerning the "Washington" appears to be quite clear. A newspaper report dated December 14, 1812, stated:

"A meeting of the subscribers to the stock for establishing a steamboat, to run between the City of Washington and Potomac Creek near Fredericksburg will be held at Triplet's Tavern in Alexandria, at 12 o'clock on Saturday, the 2nd day of January, 1813, at which the subscribers are requested to attend either in person or by proxy. The subscription proposed to be made for the establishment of a steamboat, to run between Georgetown, the City of Washington and Alexandria, under the patent of Messrs. Livingston and Fulton is suspended for the present.

B. Henry Latrobe,
Agent for Messrs. Livingston and Fulton."

The next report concerned the launching of the boat, and appeared in a New York paper under the date of June 12, 1813: "Yesterday was launched from the shipyard of Mr. Charles Browne, the steamboat Washington, and this morning the steamboat Richmond, built under the direction of Mr. Fulton, for companies in Virginia; the first to run on the Potomac from Washington to Marlborough, a distance of about 40 miles; the second to navigate the James River, from Norfolk to Richmond. They are in strength of timbers and plank equal to ships of 200 tons. The cabins which are finished are superior to anything which have yet been done for this elegant mode of conveyance."

Two years later the "Washington" arrived at Norfolk, Virginia, on its way to the District of Columbia, and a report dated at Norfolk, May 24, 1815 states: "The Potomac Steamboat Novelty. We were last evening, for the first time, gratified with the sight of a steamboat, entering our harbor! This distinguished stranger is called the Washington, commanded by Capt. O'Neale, and owned by a company of gentlemen of Washington. We were in hopes that she was intended to ply between this place and Richmond, but understand she is destined for the Potomac. In her leaving New York many were doubtful that she would be able to perform the voyage, no vessel of that description having ever tried the sea before; but she has made the trip in perfect safety, without the smallest injury, and in a period of 50 hours. Her cabin is superbly fitted up, and every convenience for the comfort and accommodation of passengers, and she is, on the whole an object that cannot fail to delight the eye and interest the understanding."

The National Intelligencer of Washington, dated June 8, 1815 carried the following item: "The steamboat Washington has arrived in the River Potomac, and has made two trips to Aquia Creek and back. She certainly is a very fine boat and fitted up at a very considerable expense, in an elegant style for the accommodation of passengers; but from the necessary absence of Capt. Mix of the Navy our present commander (a gentleman highly respected for his professional skill and polite manners) her regular operation will be suspended until Thursday, the 7th instant, when she will take passengers from Georgetown, Washington, and Alexandria, leaving Washington every morning at 4 o'clock for Aquia Creek, where she will arrive at 12, and leave the creek at 1 o'clock with passengers from the South for the before-mentioned places, where she will arrive early in the evening. The fare of each passenger will be $5, including one meal -- anything extra will be a separate charge. No passenger can be admitted on board and land again at a sum short of one dollar."

The steamboat "Camden" is recorded as operating out of Washington in 1817. Captain Gird was its owner and Captain Moffat its commander. The "Cygnet," "Phoenix," "Chesapeake," "Fredericksburg," "Sydney," "Salem," "Paul Jones," and other boats followed.

Captain John Shrieve seems to have been the first to use actual horsepower to operate water craft on the Potomac. His boat made regular trips between Washington, Alexandria, and Georgetown, stopping at Long Bridge and also at Van Ness' Wharf, as did other boats of this type in the early days. This wharf once occupied the site of the Pan American Building at 17th Street and Constitution Avenue, close to which was also the Van Ness Mansion and David Burnes' cottage. For many years excursion boats took on passengers at about 12th Street and Constitution Avenue.

John Sessford wrote the "Sessford Annals" for the National Intelligencer for many years, which were reprinted in the "Records of the Columbia Historical Society." In them he described the growth and development of the city. He noted in 1823 that an extensive wharf had been erected for the accommodation of the Southern Steamboat Line, in the Fifth Ward, which at that time included the water front. In 1829 he gave the following steamboat schedules:

Two boats daily from Washington to Alexandria at 9:00 A.M. and 5:00 P.M.
Two boats daily from Georgetown to Alexandria
A boat daily at noon from Washington to Alexandria and Fredericksburg
A boat every Tuesday from Washington to Baltimore, Maryland
A boat every Wednesday from Washington to Norfolk, Virginia

A new wharf was erected at the U. S. Navy Yard in 1841 and the channel would accommodate vessels up to 24 feet draught. Nine steamboats were plying from the city to various ports. In 1851 dredging operations were begun in the channel between 15th and 17th Streets so that vessels bringing coal through the Chesapeake and Delaware canal could pass up as far as the bridges would permit. It would also permit vessels of 7 foot draught, hauling lumber, to pass up and unload on the line of wharves instead of having to transfer their loads to scows at the mouth of the Tiber. The wharf at 7th and "M" Streets was enlarged by Mr. Page, who also built and launched three steamboats from it with great success. Mr. Lambell's inclined plane building and repair yards were meeting with much encouragement. The arrival and departure of steamboats to Alexandria, Acquia Creek, Baltimore, Norfolk, Richmond, and other points were regular, and other vessels plying the river were numerous.

In 1852 Sessford noted that steamboats were running hourly between Alexandria and Washington. There was a daily boat to Acquia Creek and a weekly boat to Baltimore and Norfolk. Occasional trips (excursions?) were made to Mount Vernon. A new steam ferry boat was plying from the south end of 7th Street to Alexandria. Beginning January 2, 1860, a regular line of steamboats began to run from New York City to Alexandria and Washington. The steamboats, "Great Eastern," "Keyport," and "Lady of the Lake" were mentioned but their runs were not given.

At the beginning of the Civil War, which gave a great impetus to the further development of steamboats, a number of vessels were berthed along the Washington water front, some of which were seized by the Government, armed at the Navy Yard and used both as fighting ships and for transporting troops and supplies. Four of these, the "Powhatan," "Mount Vernon," "Philadelphia," and "Baltimore," were turned over to Companies "A" and "E" of the Washington Light Infantry, under the command of Captains Towers and Powell. At the same time the steamboat "St. Nicholas" (later captured by the Confederates in a daring exploit) was seized at her wharf at the foot of 10th Street, and Company "A" of the National Guard, Captain Lloyd, put aboard. It was on the first four vessels mentioned and the "Pawnee" that the Ellsworth Zouaves made their trip to Alexandria, and it was on the "James Guy" that Colonel Ellsworth's body was brought back to the Navy Yard after his encounter with James Jackson on May 24, 1861.

While the Potomac River channel has been mapped and buoyed since late colonial days, and there was a light ship at upper Cedar Point as early as 1820, the first lighthouse was not built until 1851, on Blackistone (St. Clement's) Island. A fog bell was added at the edge of the channel in 1881. Lighthouses were erected at other points in the following years: Fort Washington - 1857; Smith Point - 1868; Mathias Point - 1876; Cobb Island - 1889; Maryland Point - 1892; Jones Point - 1900 (tower added 1926); Persimmon Point - 1909; Ragged Point - 1910; Occoquan - 1913; Glymont - 1915; and Hallowing Point - 1928. Many of these well known land or water marks have been de-commissioned and no longer are in use. The Blackistone Island light was discontinued in 1939 and on July 18, 1956, the old lighthouse was destroyed by fire after being hit by lightning. The Ragged Point Lighthouse which was mounted on steel stilts out over the water was removed in 1962. A year or so before the removal, the keepers got the scare of their lives when a couple of young lieutenants from the Patuxent Naval Air Station fired a few rounds from their plane, presuming the lighthouse to be vacant and abandoned. They found out otherwise, to their sorrow. Their aim was very good and the house was riddled, but fortunately the keepers escaped without injury.

A terrible tragedy occurred during a hurricane on October 23, 1878, when the steamer, "Express," of the Potomac Transportation Company was lost in the Chesapeake Bay. She started on her regular run from Baltimore to Washington, Alexandria, and Georgetown on Tuesday, October 22, 1878, at 4:00 P.M. Beginning around midnight the wind began blowing in gale proportions and between 4:00 and 5:00 A.M. Wednesday morning, in the vicinity of Point Lookout, the wind having increased to a frightful velocity, the steamer could not make headway, became unmanageable and rolled in the trough of the sea. At this point the Captain decided to let go the anchors to bring her head into the wind and attempt to ride out the storm. The effort was futile as the cables parted and the steamer went adrift. A huge wave broke over her on the port bow, staved in her upper works and a flood of water rushed through the saloon, carrying away all the furniture and the life-boats. Again and again the fierce waves swept over the ill-fated steamer until the passengers and crew were swept overboard together with the upper deck housing. With the coming of the gray dawn, the survivors clinging to pieces of the wrecked steamer, sighted the hulk of the "Express" about a half-mile away floating bottom up.

All of the passengers, excepting Captain John I. Walmsley, of Frederickstown, Cecil County, were lost, including Mrs. Randolph Jones of Cross Manor at St. Inigoes; Mrs. Mary A. Bacon of Bacon's Wharf, St. Mary's River; Dr. Dennis C. Burch, Postmaster at Milestown, St. Clement's Bay; Mrs. Mary A. Tarleton, wife of J. P. Tarleton, and her six year old son, William; all were natives of St. Mary's County, Maryland. In addition, passengers Henry Ulman and a Mr. Levetine of Baltimore, and Chloe Dyson and a Mrs. Thomas, both colored, lost their lives.

The crew consisted of the following: Captain James T. Barker; F. J. Stone, purser; L. J. Howard, of Piney Point, Maryland, first officer; Joseph Haney, second officer; Charles W. Bailey, chief engineer; Edward Prior, assistant engineer; James E. Douglas and John Douglas, quartermasters, Fillmore Rice, colored lookout-man; Robert Hawkins, fireman; David Wyatt, colored, steward; Thomas Carrington, colored, steward; Nathaniel Carrington, colored, waiter; William Grant, colored, cook; George Green, colored, baggage-master; Matilda Isaacs, a colored chambermaid; William Barker, aged 17 years, son of the Captain, and five deck hands, including H. Lewis, William Holt, and Charles Cassell.

The survivors included Captain Barker, James Douglas, and an unknown colored man who were picked up by a small pungy, the "Samuel R. Waite" under the command of Captain Parks, after they had drifted about 20 miles. F. J. Stone, John Douglas (who was badly injured), William Barker, Charles W. Bailey, Captain Walmsley, William Grant, George Green, David Wyatt, Robert Hawkins, William Holt, Charles Cassell, and Hiram Lewis were rescued by a boat from the steamer, "Shirley," grounded near Barren Island, off the mouth of the Patuxent River. Mr. Stone, the purser, of St. Clement's Bay, had the unusual experience of locating a piece of wreckage of the housing that contained a port hole and he had an easier time than most of his companions because he was able to put his head and arms through the porthole which provided excellent support. By the time the rescues had been effected the wrecked "Express" had drifted to the vicinity of Hooper Island, across the Bay.

It is obvious that Captain Barker in his anxiety to save his ship, passengers, crew, and cargo was faced with many terrible decisions as he steamed down the Bay. Undoubtedly, he saw the several grounded steamers at the mouth of the Patuxent and decided that an attempt to negotiate the narrow entrance at this point was too risky. Should he attempt the long and perilous return trip to Annapolis or Baltimore or cross the raging waters of the Bay to seek safety in the Choptank River; or since he was so near Point Lookout, should he attempt to battle on and round the Point to gain the comparatively safer waters of the Potomac? It is apparent that he decided on the latter course, knowing full well the risk entailed in negotiating the rough waters he would encounter in rounding the Point. We know now that his decision was tragic, but who can say that any other decision would have been less tragic? We know from the reports that he took all safety precautions possible under the circumstances and that he was successful in equipping his passengers with life preservers. It must be marked down as another tragedy of the sea.

The "Express" was built in 1841 and during the Civil War was in the Government service, running between Fortress Monroe and Newport News, Virginia, as a dispatch boat for General Benjamin F. Butler. A small cannon was mounted in her bow and she was one of the swiftest dispatch boats in the service. After the war she was placed on the Potomac River run and in 1873 was rebuilt at a cost of $20,000 and 40 feet added to her length. She was 200 feet in length, had a 25 foot beam and her capacity was 602 tons. During the winter of 1877 she was completely overhauled and was in good condition when caught in the hurricane. The value of the "Express" and her cargo totaled $35,000.

The newspapers of Maryland, Virginia, and Washington featured articles concerning the tragedies that grew out of the hurricane for several days. A highly descriptive feature article by an unknown writer in the Washington Post of October 25, 1878, in which he describes the last moments aboard the "Express," under the caption "Gone to the Bottom," was not overdrawn when he wrote: "The scene was weird and thrilling in the extreme. The rushing roar of the hurricane, sounding with appalling violence upon the ears of the doomed Mariners, the pitiless swash of the driving rain, the steady and terrible dash of the waves over the ill-fated craft, sweeping remorselessly from stem to stern; the black, sweltering mass of waters on either side running mountain high, the fitful glare of the deck lanterns illuminating the scene just enough to heighten its terrors and make darkness visible; all these accessories made up a picture startlingly frightful to the mere looker-on, had there been such, but inexpressibly horrible and appalling to those whose destines were mixed up in its tragic features, and who heard the knell of their own dirges ringing in the roar of the rending wind and sounding in the ominous dash of the angry waves. On the other hand, an interminable waste of engulfing waters black as the night that enveloped them, the very foam caps of the breaking billows invisible in the pitchy darkness, the ceaseless rush of the driving rain that poured in sullen torrents from the inky clouds above, lending its monotonous voice to the frightful and awe-inspiring tumult of wind and wave; with the dread certainty that for the ill-fated crew and passengers no morrow's sun would ever again lighten up the ineffable blackness of the night into which, as into a yawning grave, the pitiless forces of nature had forever driven them; it was an hour whose supreme but hopeless agony may not be written, and can but feebly be imagined. Of the horror of that dread moment and the weathering gloom that enveloped the twenty souls who were buried by wind and wave in one whelming wreck, no tongue may ever speak."

"At the point where the Express went down, the Potomac is more like an estuary than a river. Fully nine miles across from shore to shore, where the storm-wind blows in its fury, the waves hold high carnival, and dash in angry roar like the billows of the sea. The river here is properly an arm of the bay, and is famous for the ocean-like character of its gales. In calm weather it glides on with the smooth current of a land-locked lake, between low sloping banks, sometimes wooded to the very line of the waters, and sometimes trending to the tide in grassy marshy plains. It is the 'blue Potomac' in hours of calm, its waves silvered by the breezes and ruffled only by the wing of the white swan or the glancing rays of the sunshine. In storms it is the foaming, dashing, wrathful waste of waters, magnificent in the ocean-

like grandeur of its tempests and terrible in the whelming might of its angry fury."
This storm created much havoc in and about the Chesapeake Bay and its tributaries. Apparently the ship masters were caught without warning. A tugboat towing 19 barges in the Bay lost 11 of them, the remainder having grounded. In addition to the "Shirley," the steamboats, "Massachusetts," of the Maryland Steamboat Company, the "J. S. Ide" of the Wilmington Line and the "Louise" of the York River Line, grounded while attempting to anchor during the storm at the mouth of the Patuxent River. The steamer, "Florida," returned to Baltimore after its bow was stove in by the sea off Point Lookout. Two steamers of the Weems Transportation Line, the "Matilda" and the "Theodore Weems" were feared lost for several days. The "Matilda" rode out the storm grounded in the Rappahannock River while the "Theodore Weems" was towed into Crisfield by the steamer, "Tangier," after her captain had been unable to beach the steamer in Tangier Sound, when the rudder was torn away in the attempt. Dozens of schooners were blown ashore and grounded far from water by the receding tide.

As indicated in the wreck of the "Express" a hurricane is a fearsome thing on the water and pity the poor sailor caught in one. Periodically over the 300 years of recorded history of the Chesapeake Bay and its tributaries these storms have occurred. The storm of 1878 is perhaps the worse on record. In these days most heavy No'theasters are called hurricanes and for some unknown reason are given girl's names but storms such as that of 1878 seem to come only about once a decade with some fairly bad ones in between. The writer read a description of one written about 1650 by a Virginia chronicler that could duplicate the one that occurred in 1933 on the Potomac. Both storms started about midnight and by 4:00 A.M. the wind from the Northeast had reached gale proportions. This heavy wind continued throughout the day but gradually swung around the compass to the Northwest, and the weather cleared about sundown, with a tide almost 10 feet above normal. Wharves were carried away, small boats were found in neighboring cornfields, and many larger boats dragged anchor and were grounded and damaged or lost. Hurricane Hazel which occurred in 1954 was another humdinger in this area.

In October, 1878, Captain L. L. Blake, formerly master of the "Mary Washington," brought the "W. W. Corcoran" to Washington from New York where she had been built. This steamboat became one of the most famous on the Potomac. In 1879 the "Lady of the Lake" was making runs to Norfolk, Fortress Monroe, and other points South. The steamer "John W. Thompson" also was in commission. In 1883 the river front was occupied with the wharves of the Inland and Seaboard Coasting Company, the Mount Vernon Line, with the "W. W. Corcoran," and the Potomac Steamboat Company which operated the "George Leary" and the "Excelsior." The steamers "Mystic" and the "T. V. Arrowsmith" were doing the river landings along the Potomac and the Upper Potomac Steamboat Company was running the "Mary Washington" with Captain P. Hilman in command. The Potomac Transportation Line was stopping at the river landings with the steamers "Sue" and the "Mattano." Beginning about 1885, and in later years, may be mentioned such well known vessels as the "Armenia," "Charles Macalester," "Jane Mosely," "Wakefield," "St. Johns," and "Pilot Boy," the "River Queen," "Samuel J. Pentz," and others. The well-known Norfolk and Washington Steamboat Company, although chartered in 1890, actually dated back to 1876, when it succeeded the Potomac Steamboat Company.

It is interesting to note that the old "River Queen," built in 1864, did notable service during the Civil War and was the vessel that carried President Lincoln on his memorable trips to City Point, Virginia, to confer with his commanders and to meet the Confederate Peace Commissioners.

The "Mary Washington" was a steamboat of an unusual design. She was a large flat-bottomed vessel, with a hull like a box with pointed ends, the only vessel of her kind, it is recorded, that ever plied the Potomac. She was built in 1874 at Occoquan Creek, Virginia, by a syndicate of farmers that included Colonel Edward Carriel of Gunston and P. H. Troth of Accotink, Virginia. The idea of the builders was to construct a light-draft boat with which they could navigate the small streams and thus enable the farmers to get their produce to market at a reduced cost. She was fitted out and equipped at Alexandria, and when tried out it was found that she was a failure for the purpose intended. The owners lost no time in disposing of their interest, and the boat found her way into the excursion field. She had a carrying capacity of 1,500 people and in her day she is said to have carried more passengers than any other vessel on the Potomac.

John Clagett Proctor who loved to reminisce about the old river steamboats has written about the "Mary Washington" as follows: "The writer's first recollection of going on an excursion on this boat was on July 4, 1876,.....and one will recognize from the date that the vessel was then quite new. The trip to Mount Vernon Springs, long since off the map as an excursion resort, but which was then just south of the wharf of Mount Vernon and only separated from that estate by a cove which makes up at this point. As an excursion place it soon gave way to other and more popular resorts, but the old pavilion, with its weather-worn timbers, could for years be seen

116

from the passing boats, until it finally toppled over from its own weight. Since
the entire saloon deck was one large pavilion, dancing on the Mary Washington was
the principal attraction, and such square dances as the quadrille and the lancers
were enjoyed by the excursionists. The polka, the schottische and the waltz were
also among the dances of this period, the waltz being the only one in vogue today,
and it is generally danced in modified form. Another place, quite popular, especially as a Sunday school resort, was Occoquan Falls. The Mary Washington was peculiarly
adapted to shallow water, and it was invariably of great interest to see the long
trail of mud left in the wake of the steamer as she churned up the creek bed, the
water of which seemed not over three feet in depth."

The "Mary Washington" was bought at an early date by Captain Ephraim S. Randall,
and he may have owned the "Tygert." The "Mary Washington" ran for many years between
Washington and River View on Swan Point, Maryland. After this she was used for colored excursion parties to Notley Hall and other points on the river. Later the vessel
was sold to Robert Holtzman who converted it into a clubhouse and anchored it at
Analostan Island, near Georgetown. In her last days the old steamboat was anchored
near Four-Mile Run, and there she caught fire on November 22, 1902, and that was the
end of the "Mary Washington."

Other favorite excursion points were Glymont, Fort Washington, Fort Foote,
Marshall Hall, Lower Cedar Point, Chapel Point, River View, and Colonial Beach. Going down or coming up the river, the old Arsenal where the Army War College is now
located, always had an especial attraction for the youthful excursionists. During
its existence as an arsenal, two very serious explosions occurred here. One of these
took place August 25, 1814, when the British were wreaking vengeance on Washington.
Dr. James Ewell, who gave medical attention to the wounded, left the following account
of the disaster: "About 2 o'clock on the 25th. a British captain with a company of
soldiers marched down on Greenleafs Point to destroy the powder magazine. On reaching the spot, they found the magazine empty, the powder the day before having been
taken out and thrown into a dry well. The British, being strangers to this fact,
threw a lighted match into the well. A most tremendous explosion ensued, whereby the
officers and about 30 of the men were killed and the rest most shockingly mangled.
Some of these unfortunate victims of gunpowder were seen flying in the air to great
distances and others were totally buried alive under tons of earth thrown upon them.
The survivors were carefully brought upon Capitol Hill and those in the most distressed situation were lodged in Carroll's buildings, adjoining my house. I never
saw more endearing marks of sympathy than were here exhibited on the countenance of
Gen. Ross. He observed, looking at me with an eye of searching anxiety, 'I am much
distressed at leaving these poor fellows behind me. I do not know who is to mitigate
their sufferings.' I understood his meaning and instantly assured him that he need
not make himself uneasy on account of his wounded soldiers. 'The Americans, Gen.
Ross,' said I, 'we are of the same origin as yourself. We have, I trust, given you
many splendid instances of our humanity in the course of this unfortunate war, and
you may rely on it, sir, no attentions in my power shall be withheld upon them.'"

The second terrible explosion at the arsenal occurred during the Civil War, on
July 17, 1864, when the city was just recovering from the threat of invasion by General Jubal A. Early and his troops only a week before. Many Federals were killed or
injured and among them was Judge Hosea B. Moulton, a neighbor of the writer in Washington, some 35 years ago. Judge Moulton was wounded during the Battle of Gettysburg, and was on inactive duty, although again injured in the explosion, he survived
to live to a ripe and useful old age. At the time the arsenal was destroyed, the
rope walks of Ringgold, Heat & Co., and those of John Chalmers in the immediate vicinity also were destroyed.

Among the many river steamboat captains of bygone days were Captain "Traverse"
Moncure, Captain William C. Geoghegan, of the "Calvert," the "Westmoreland," the
"Three Rivers" and others, Captain Isaac R. Bowen and Captain William E. Luckett,
who once piloted the Presidents' yacht on the river; Captain Tom Ross and John Henry
Turner, who piloted the "Macalester"; S. E. Hows, Captain of the "Mattano"; Captain
Joseph White of the "George Leary," Captain Bohannon of the "Dorchester," and Captain
Joe Smith of the "Northumberland"; Captain Charlie Entwisle of the "Arrowsmith,"
Captain Bailey Reed and Captain Joseph T. Barker of the "Jane Mosely"; Captain John
Beitzell of the "St. John's" and others, Captain Chap Slye (father of Commander Wal-
ter C. Slye, Captain and pilot for three Presidents and Captain Harry E. Slye, in
command in 1963 of the Wilson's Line 221 foot diesel-powered "George Washington") of
the "Charles Macalester," "Queen Anne," "Anne Arundel" and others; Captain Chapman
Posey of the "Norfolk" boat, the "District of Columbia," and Captain Ephraim S. Randall, who owned the Randall Line, which included the "Pilot Boy," the "John W. Thompson," which he changed to the "Harry Randall" (and which was later changed to the
"Capital City"), and the "Lovie Randall." Mr. James E. Nicholson of Baltimore in a
letter to the writer in 1962 gave the following information on the steamboat fleet:

"The Baltimore Boats -- Weems Line, later Maryland, Delaware, and Virginia
Line --

Anne Arundel	*The Talbot and the Dorchester were later than the
Calvert	others. These were side wheelers, as was the Three
Northumberland	Rivers; the others were screw steamers. The Anne
Three Rivers	Arundel was the last one in service when the Western
Talbot*	Shore Steamboat Company attempted to revive interest
Dorchester*	but failed."

"The Norfolk and Washington Line (Queens of the river in their day)

Norfolk	Later	Northland
Washington		Southland
Newport News		District of Columbia"

"The Randall Line -- Potomac River Landings all the way to Piney Point at times.

Harry Randall	Kent	All were side wheelers ex-
Wakefield	Samuel J. Pentz	cept the Estelle Randall
T. V. Arrowsmith	Estelle Randall	which was a small single
		screw steamer."

"The Randall Line was owned by Washingtonians.....I remember the senior Captain Randall [Ephraim S.] very well. He was President and principal owner of the line. He had a son, Harry Randall, also a Captain, for whom the steamer was named, as was the Estelle Randall named for one of the family. The old Samuel J. Pentz was the River View boat, but she needed help many times in handling the crowds and was assisted by one or two of the other boats on heavy days. The Wakefield and others made lower Potomac landings as well as Colonial Beach, Virginia."

"All old time Washingtonians remember the Charles McAllister of Marshall Hall and Mt. Vernon fame. Then there was the St. Johns that ran to Colonial Beach every summer, one of the biggest sidewheelers on the River, if not the biggest. There was another steamer that made the lower Potomac landings too -- I don't remember her line, but her name was the Majestic."

"The old Jane Moseley was used for colored excursions and docked at the foot of 10th Street and if you want to go back a little farther the name Columbia comes to mind. She was a double end Ferry boat used between Washington and Alexandria and burned at her pier in Washington in the early 1900's."

"It is hard to realize that all of these steamers were, at one time, berthed along old Water Street between the Washington Barracks and 10th Street, S. W. There was room for them all in those days but, alas, I doubt if there is even one left, and southwest Washington is no more."

Over the years the river counties on both sides of the Potomac, particularly St. Mary's County, have furnished many pilots for the river. Captain Harry Slye, now known as the dean of the river captains, who came up to Washington from St. Mary's County with his father over 40 years ago, said in an interview in 1963 with Carol LaVarn, who did a special feature in the Potomac magazine of the Washington Post:

"It was a good life. When I was with the Maryland, Delaware and Virginia Company's Marine Division, we had 36 steamboats up and down the Chesapeake Bay and its tributaries. We made 24 landings in the 98 miles of the Potomac from Washington to Point Lookout. Two boats made three trips a week from Baltimore to Washington. We'd leave here Wednesday at 4 p.m. and arrive in Baltimore on Friday at 7 p.m. We'd have Friday night in port and go out again. There were crews of 35 or 40, even 50 on some boats. We had every facility on board a hotel could offer. There were a lot of new people to talk to all the time. The food was out of this world, and when you were off watch you could read or talk to some of the girls who were aboard. We used to play the Victrola to entertain the girls with our new records. That all lasted from 1918 until 1930 or so."

It has been estimated that since the days of Fulton's "Washington" there have been at least 150 different steamboats in service on the Potomac River. In the earlier years the "George Leary" was representative of the elegance to be found on board during the steamboating era. The "Leary" had pile carpets, grapevine chandeliers and on the tables were found "elegant flowers, both natural and of the finest French wax work." Her salon was "painted with pure lily white, while upon the panel work, the painter's pencil has drawn some very beautiful and chaste devices, pleasing to the eye and appreciative to the refined mind for the ideals of the beautiful and pure."

Mr. Henry Burroughs, who also came to Washington from St. Mary's County, was

STEAMBOATS, MASTERS, AND RIVER LANDINGS

Circa 1910
Stone's Wharf or Bayside
St. Clement's Bay

Capt. Chapman Posey

Capt. John Beitzell

Bushwood Wharf
Mouth of Wicomico River

"Dorchester"

"Anne Arundel"

Steamboat "Northumberland" Docking at Bushwood
Wharf at the mouth of the Wicomico River with
Police Schooner, "Bessie Jones," in background.
(Courtesy of Robert E. Pogue)

one of the former owners of the "Potomac," a steamboat of recent years. Mr. Burroughs has stated that the "Potomac" "went from Washington to Colonial Beach in day service until three years after the war (World War II). She had carpet on the second deck, wood paneling and oil paintings. In the heyday of the name bands, they all played aboard the Potomac -- Paul Whiteman, Harry James, Benny Goodman. It wasn't unusual to carry several thousand people."

It is sad to record that the "George Leary" became a lumber barge and foundered at sea in 1901. Sadder still, the "Potomac" was reduced to a hull and used as a barge in the pulp wood trade on the York River. In 1963 she was tied up at Norfolk.

In the writer's generation, beginning in 1905, and for some years earlier, among the sidewheelers coming into the Potomac from Baltimore were the "Sue," the "Three Rivers" and the "Dorchester," which was later renamed the "Robert E. Lee." The "Sue" is mentioned in the St. Mary's County Beacon of 1886 as having transported a group of "capitalists" from Baltimore to Leonardtown, whose visit concerned the building of the railroad from Washington to St. Mary's City. Among the propeller type were the "Northumberland," the "Potomac" and the "Endeavor." The latter had twin propellers. Everyone said the "Endeavor" could turn on a dime, and it was true that she could maneuver in a small space because one of her landings was Morris Point at the mouth of Canoe Neck Creek. She ran regularly from Baltimore to Nomini, Virginia. In the late 1920's, Stuart Morris persuaded the owners to put in at his oyster shucking house at the mouth of the creek. At that time the steamboats had stopped coming into St. Clement's Bay and it was necessary for the rivermen to meet the "Endeavor" off Blackistone (St. Clement's) Island and get their catch aboard out in the channel. This could be a ticklish business when the weather was bad, as is attested by the writer's brothers, Clem and Walter, and cousin, Henry Gibson. Other Baltimore boats included the "Westmoreland" and the "Talbot."

The St. Mary's Beacon reported in May, 1902, as follows: "The new steamer Calvert, of the Weems Line made her first trip to Leonardtown and the Potomac River Landings Wednesday. At every point she was enthusiastically received, the people turning out in force to meet her. Captain William C. Geoghegan who is in command, was showered with flowers and compliments. The Calvert is a sister ship of the Northumberland, but her saloon is more roomy and more artistically furnished. She is a very pretty boat and is complete in all her appointments."

In 1910 the Beacon noted that the Christmas traffic was so heavy on the river that an extra steamboat was put into service in an effort to accommodate the patrons.

In those winters when the Potomac River would freeze over it would disrupt the steamboat service and cause a great deal of inconvenience.

The writer well remembers the winter of 1914 when the Potomac was frozen solid as far as the eye could see and people were skating out around St. Clement's Island. The storekeepers were getting desperate for supplies when the "Northumberland" finally broke through to reach the head of St. Clement's Bay. We watched her progress up the bay and it seemed she would never make it. She would back off a hundred yards or so and smash ahead a couple of boat lengths and then do it again and again. It was very exciting. Con Morris, who was the champion skater on Canoe Neck Creek, made a running jump on his skates from the ice into the gangplank entrance aboard ship with room to spare. He was quite a hero. About this same time there were reports of suffering at Leonardtown and when the steamboat finally made it through the ice, it was noticed that many barrels but few boxes were unloaded. Some wag remarked that it was apparent that the people were suffering a great deal more from thirst than hunger.

The St. Mary's Beacon of February 27, 1914, reported that "the steamer Tivoli had no trouble cutting her way through the ice on her last trip from Baltimore to Leonardtown," so it was apparent that the ice was becoming "rotten" and the great freeze began to break up about that time.

As a boy, it was a delight to see the schools of porpoises that followed the steamboats into the landings. Now these sporting fish are rarely seen in the Potomac. Shipping days, particularly Saturdays, were always looked forward to by the younger members of the family for this meant a trip to the steamboat wharf at Cobrum, near the head of St. Clement's Bay, or at Colton's Point, at the mouth of the bay. At first these trips were under sail but later by motorboat, powered by a 5 H.P. Mianus or Victor engine that made a powerful amount of noise, and sometimes attained a speed of 5 miles per hour. It was always exciting at the landings, the Captain of the steamboat, standing on deck resplendent in his uniform, the mate shouting instructions to the sweating stevedores, doing a fast "cake walk" with their hand trucks, loading barrels of crabs, fish, apples, and peaches, grain, tobacco, crates of chickens and ducks, and live pigs and calves, which contributed in the general clamor. Every once in a while a pig or calf would break loose, jump overboard and have to be caught by using one of the smaller boats at the wharf. In these cases, the wrath of the mate was something to hear and behold; mothers put their fingers in the children's ears and said, "It's disgraceful, that's what it is, Joe Brown," and the husbands would make the stock reply, "Now Nellie, he don't mean any harm -- that's just river talk."

Oh, those were lovely, exciting, carefree days.

One of the tragedies of the earlier days when local hospitals were non-existent was sudden illness such as a case of acute appendicitis. If the victim was fortunate enough to be taken ill on a steamboat day there was some chance of making it to a Washington or Baltimore hospital for an operation, but some were not so fortunate. Helen Dent, a daughter of Dr. Walter B. Dent, of Deep Creek in St. Clement's Bay was one of these unfortunates. She became very ill and a considerable and time consuming effort was necessary to secure a U. S. Revenue cutter, which took her to Washington. Unfortunately the effort was in vain, due to the delay, and she lost in the race with death.

Although Papa still preferred to sail to Baltimore for his annual trip with Captain Matt Bailey or one of our other neighbors, it was the great thrill of my boyhood to make the annual steamboat trip with Mama each summer to visit our relatives and friends in Washington, when she would do the family shopping for the coming year. We would take the boat at Cobrum Wharf, near the head of St. Clement's Bay or at Bushwood at the mouth of the Wicomico about 3-4 o'clock in the afternoon. The long summer evening was a continuing delight as stops were made along the river to take on more passengers and freight. There would be a couple of blasts on the steamboat whistle to warn the last-comers to hurry, and to call the wharf tender to his duties. As the steamer drew up to the wharf there was much jangling of bells as she was warped in, with the mate shouting instructions "lively with that spring line, ready with the gangplank" punctuated by some picturesque language when the men didn't move fast enough.

Despite a boy's natural, healthy appetite, justice often was not done at the Captain's sumptuous table due to the excitement. Mama would not permit me to bother the Captain or his mate in the Pilot House because she was always somewhat concerned when on the river and probably felt they needed no distraction by a small boy and should give their full attention to their duties, but sometimes there was an opportunity to slip below to see the great engine at work for a few moments. There was a great reluctance to settle down for the night, but the time would finally come when Mama "put her foot down firmly" and after the exciting afternoon, sleep came quickly to be blasted by the ship's whistle as the boat drew in to the next landing. This continued most of the night, but after the first blast or two, it seemed to be a welcome sound, faint in the world of half-sleep, and reassuring that all was well. Early morning found us safe at the landing on the Washington water front, with Uncle Ern there to greet us. It seems strange now, but it is no longer possible for me to identify in my mind the engine noises of the "Three Rivers" and the "Northumberland," which were quite different, since one was a sidewheeler and the other was a propeller. But the memory of those trips is still vivid after a half-century or more. While the return trip was pleasurable, it was not quite as much fun, as we would leave Washington about the same time in the afternoon and arrive at Bushwood Wharf at midnight, where we had to land without having "bedded down." Then there was the long drive by horse and carriage to reach home at an ungodly hour for country folks. Perhaps the realization that school opening was near and there wouldn't be another trip for a whole year had something to do with the sort of let-down feeling. But all in all it was great fun and a wonderful experience for a youngster.

The late Oliver Martin wrote extensively about the Chesapeake and Potomac country back in the 1920's. In September, 1926, he made the steamboat trip from Baltimore to Washington and his account of the journey is quite interesting. Excerpts from the account follow:

"The distance from Baltimore to Washington, if you follow the route of a crow in flight, is about 40 miles, and you can cover that distance in an express train in something like 50 minutes.....But it will take you a day and two nights to make the trip and you'll wander through a large section of colonial America in doing it. You leave Baltimore on Monday afternoon, for instance, and spend part of what is left of the daylight hours on the Patapsco River, which is another name for Baltimore Harbor, and Monday night on the broad waters of the Chesapeake Bay; during Tuesday and Tuesday night you are stopping at and starting away from various landings on the Potomac River, both in Maryland and Virginia, and you wake up on Wednesday morning at or near the wharf in Washington -- 40 miles from where you started."

"The first-timers begin their saunterings around the boat even before it leaves the wharf, and eventually reach that part of the ship which is occupied by the cargo-- and in the case of the Northumberland, it is as miscellaneous a cargo as was ever trundled aboard a sturdy ship by singing stevedores. These husky, dusky, lithe-limbed lads come swinging down the gangway, each propelling a handtruck with speed, grace, and skill, the truck containing anything from a pile of automobile tires to a side of beef. Or perhaps the burden consists of a box of groceries, a barrel of paint, a bag of cement, a crate of live chickens, or a sack of sugar."
****
"If you have ever been in Baltimore's inner harbor, you will recall the congestion there, with fussy little steamers coming in from or starting out for various

120

points on the Chesapeake and its rivers and creeks. As the Northumberland leaves the pier, three other steamers get the same notion and before the outer harbor is reached, the passengers begin guessing which boat will start down the bay first. The Talbot has made a good getaway and the others string along behind. The Eastern Shore is second, but the Northumberland soon passes her. Puffing along in the rear is the Potomac. But she gains foot by foot and eventually is abreast of us, within speaking distance. For a few minutes, it is a bow-and-bow race, the Negro crews calling taunts to each other across the intervening stretch of water. Slowly the Potomac pulls ahead and from her crew comes bursts of triumphant laughter and yells of delight, mixed with expressions of amused contempt. Finally, one of the dusky group produces a rope and shakes it in the direction of our crew. This is the crowning reproach. For every sailor knows that to 'shake a rope at 'em' is the last word in insult -- meaning, of course, that the ship at which a rope is shaken is in sore need of being taken in tow."

"Down the harbor plows the good ship, passing on the way the famous old Fort McHenry, the flag over which inspired Francis Scott Key to write the Star Spangled Banner and Fort Carroll, built on an artificial island, and constructed under the supervision of Robert E. Lee, then a young army engineer and later the famous and well-beloved leader of the Lost Cause of the Confederacy. Fourteen miles from the city the river loses itself in the bay. And about here the eager watchers of tramp steamers, schooners, bugeyes and other craft realize that evening has stolen on them unawares.....inside the boat there is plenty of light and activity, and downstairs in the dining room a hot chicken supper awaits appetites sharpened by salt sea breezes."

"Once more on deck for a look at the night. What a change! Darkness everywhere, except for the faint light shed by the moon and the stars, and the blinkings of distance lighthouses.....A chill breeze.....Midnight comes.....one must go to bed sometime. A pleasant stateroom. Sleep. At least sleep until the first landing is reached, which is at Solomon's Island, at the mouth of the Patuxent. Then across the Patuxent to Millstone, where is unloaded a calf that protests in a loud and mournful voice.....More sleep. And while the passengers are lost in slumber the boat makes a big sweep around Point Lookout.....leaving the bay and entering the wide mouth of the Potomac river."

"Along about dawn, a few early birds among the passengers.....watch the stevedores trundle off the merchandise for Wynne, formerly Miller's, on Smith's Creek, called Trinity Creek by Calvert in 1634 but later renamed by others in honor of Captain John Smith. Wynne is only a little settlement.....but it stands on historic ground. Just back of the village is 'Calvert's Rest,' marked by a fine old colonial dwelling.....where lived William Calvert, son of the first governor. Smith's Creek is separated from St. Mary's River by a neck of fertile land [St. Inigoes Neck].....

****

"The ship has now started on an in-and-out journey among the rivers, bays, creeks, coves, inlets, islands, necks, points and other geographical features that nature has sprinkled here rather carelessly -- a journey that will take until late afternoon, although no point among those visited in this group is much more than ten miles from any of the others. Perhaps you have seen a milkman making his morning delivery, crossing and re-crossing the street, diving into alleys and passage-ways. Well, that's the way the boat performs among these bays and inlets."

"From Wynne the boat proceeds to St. Mary's City, or rather to the wharf known as Brome's, near the site of Maryland's ancient capital where Leonard Calvert and his little group.....established their town and proclaimed religious liberty throughout the colony. But St. Mary's City is no more. A church, a monument, a school, a wharf, a little group of houses and a beautiful view of the river -- these are the things that may now be seen."

****

"As the boat slides up to the next wharf, we read 'Porto Bello' on the weatherbeaten sign nailed to the weather-beaten wharf house. Porto Bello recalls to mind the adventure of three Potomac River lads who sailed with Admiral Vernon of the British Navy as midshipmen in his campaign against the Spaniards in the West Indies, where they took part in naval engagements at Porto Bello and Carthagena. When the young men returned to the Potomac and built themselves homes they incorporated into the names of reminder of their experiences. Lawrence Washington named his estate Mount Vernon, William Hebb called his place Carthagena and Edwin Coad* borrowed the

*Actually both Carthagena and Porto Bello were owned by
the Hebbs at this time and named by them according to
Charles E. Fenwick, President of the St. Mary's Historical
Society. The Coad home place was Cherryfields.

name of Porto Bello for his home. All of these homes are still standing.* The most famous of course, is Mount Vernon, on account of George Washington, who inherited the place from his brother Lawrence."

"The boat chugs along to Grason's Wharf on St. Inigoes Creek [where is located] Cross Manor House.....[said to have been] built in 1644.....we are now approaching the mouth of the St. Mary's and shall soon again be in the Potomac. We pass Fort Point, on which in early colonial days was Fort St. Inigoes.....Out of St. Mary's River we now take our way and steer directly across the Potomac to the Virginia shore and enter the mouth of the Coan River, where are more wharves to be served.....The Coan, like the St. Mary's is a succession of beautiful vistas and delightful surprises .....the navigation of the Coan requires a master hand. The river is narrow and full of shoals, and that is why the boat navigates it like a drunken man staggering up a street. At the head of navigation we come to twin wharves -- Coan and Bundicks -- directly opposite, one on each side of the river. The distance between them is hardly more than the steamer's length, but, until a ferry was established there a few years ago, there was no other way to get from one hamlet to the other without going around the head of the stream.....Coan Landing is situated at the foot of a hill on which the village is located. Life here is tranquil, indeed.....Now the boat twists and turns and eventually finds itself alongside the wharf at Bundicks, facing downstream. A few packages are put ashore at Bundicks and the boat pushes off for Lake. A stop here and then across the Coan to Walnut Point."

"The peninsula on which the Point is located shoots out into the river so far that it seems that it will block the passage of the boat, and it is so narrow that a fine view can be had of the Potomac beyond. The oyster shells at the landing indicate that there is an oyster packing plant nearby, which serves in turn to remind the traveller that the lower Potomac is rich in oysters, both natural and cultivated. Crabs, too, are plentiful here, and trot-line crabbers may be seen in their small boats at the mouth of the river. On another point of land, directly opposite Walnut Point, is Cowart's Landing, and a little nearer to the mouth of the Coan lies Lewisetta, a fishing village. From the upper deck of the boat, while she is lying at the wharf at Lewisetta, may be obtained a fine view of the mouth of the Potomac. The steamer is barely out of the Coan and into the Potomac again when she turns into a stream called the Yeocomico."

****

"The ship plows up the peaceful stream to Lodge Landing.....[which].....according to the captain, received its name from the fact that here was established the original lodge of Masonry in Virginia. Mundy's Point is the next stop, after which the boat heads up a winding stream, the Kinsale River, to Kinsale, a larger village than most of the others visited, boasting a hotel and more than one street. Incidentally, it is as old as Philadelphia."

"Back to the Maryland side goes our good ship Northumberland, to do some more wandering among bays, islands and little rivers. It is now the middle of the afternoon. We have been in the Potomac since dawn. Yet, on account of our meanderings on both sides of the river, we are still near enough to the mouth to see plainly the trees on Point Lookout, where the Potomac and Chesapeake join. It must be remembered that the Yeocomico, the Kinsale, the St. Mary's and the other rivers mentioned are not really rivers at all, in the true sense of the word. They do not rise in mountains and flow to the sea, but are arms or estuaries of the Potomac, and resemble a chain of lakes more than anything else."

"At the mouth of the St. Mary's, where we were early in the morning, is St. George's Island, once noted as a summer resort. On crossing the Potomac in the afternoon.....we pass to the north of the island and touch at Piney Point, where there are several summer cottages. If the voyager is seeking sheer beauty, he finds it here. The island is so close to the mainland that the shore seems continuous, as it curves around into a semi circle of white, glistening sand, above which rise clumps of pine trees. Standing on the top deck of the boat and looking down on this scene, with a hot sun shining overhead, it does not take much imagination to conjure up thoughts of the South Seas."

****

"No more landings now for two hours. Just a straight run up the river, with plenty of time to sit back on the deck and talk or to roam about the boat on discovery bent. Down on the freight deck one.....finds a bantam rooster that has achieved

*When the replica of the State House at St. Mary's City was erected in 1934, Carthagena, which was in ruinous condition, was taken down and the bricks used to erect the wall in front of the State House. It is said that Esperanza, on the Patuxent, also was named by another unknown Maryland midshipman who sailed with Admiral Vernon in company with Washington, Hebb and Coad.

122

something that many grown-up human beings have not. He has succeeded in getting his picture in the paper, with a write-up of about a column. This bird, Billy, adopted the ship. Walked aboard one morning at a landing and refused to leave. And that's not all. It is said that on one of his visits to shore he made the acquaintance of a dimunitive hen, which fowl followed him on board just before the boat pulled out. At any rate, there is also a bantam hen on the boat. The story, as we have set it down here, and as it appeared in the newspaper, was given us by the purser of the boat, who may be a truthful man."

"Two hours of conversation and watching the scenery, and the captain remarks we are approaching Leonardtown. But where? For no sign of a town can be seen. And then we learn that Leonardtown is not on the Potomac, but is hidden away at the edge of the hills that come down to the waters of Bretton Bay, and that the steamer must do a lot of winding in narrow channels before the town is reached. And because groups of trees grow on every little neck of land, the wharf does not come in sight until the boat is almost upon it. Getting into Leonardtown is an adventure all by itself. Next to St. Mary's, Leonardtown is probably the most historic place in Southern Maryland, and is probably more interesting to the present-day tourist than St. Mary's City for it has continued as a going town ever since it was laid out in 1708..... Leonardtown today [1926] is a quaint mixture of old and new. One may see colonial houses with massive brick chimneys and also little bungalows, and on the same street may be enjoyed the experience of passing ox-carts and Ford automobiles. As an indication of the peculiar geographical layout of this part of Maryland, it may be mentioned that a couple of years ago we rode in an automobile across the peninsula from Leonardtown to Millstone, on the Patuxent, in about an hour. The time consumed between the two points on this trip by boat is nearly 18 hours."

****

"Steaming out of Bretton Bay in the late afternoon and skirting around Newtown Neck, the steamer enters St. Clement's Bay, where it makes two stops, one at Bayside and one at Cobrums. At the entrance to St. Clement's Bay, and seeming to prevent access to it, is Blackistone Island, originally called St. Clement's Island. Here Calvert and his little band first landed on March 25, 1634, when they sailed up the Potomac, and here they celebrated the first Mass in English -- speaking America..... As the boat is leaving the bay the shades of evening are fast falling and the passengers.....watch the turning of the ship as she follows the channel.....More sailing through the night, and the mouth of the Wicomico is reached, passing St. Katherine's Island and St. Margaret's Island. The influence of the Catholic colonists on the geographical names in Southern Maryland may be seen in the fact that even today a list of the towns, rivers, islands and bays sounds like a Litany of the Saints."

"By the time the boat enters the Wicomico the evening is growing late, but there are still a few of the more inquisitive ones on deck as the landings at Bushwood and Rock Point are reached, and the obliging captain turns his searchlight on the latter settlement, picking out of the night the little rustic church and other points of interest. The Wicomico is one of the larger streams of Maryland and on it was once located the chief town of the Wicomico tribe of Indians."

"Some of the passengers are in bed when the steamer passes Wakefield, on the distant Virginia shore.....Wakefield, situated between two creeks that flow into the Potomac, was the original Washington home in Virginia, and here, in 1732, George Washington was born. Only a few miles away were born two other Presidents of the United States, James Madison and James Monroe, as well as Lighthorse Harry Lee of Revolutionary fame, and his illustrious son, Robert E. Lee.....at the next stop.....[is] Colonial Beach, a popular summer resort for Washingtonians. The main building at the resort was once the home of Lighthorse Harry Lee.....There are no more stops until morning.....By the time Alexandria is reached most of the passengers are up and dressed and out on deck, watching the river activities. Only a little farther now and the end of the journey will be reached. Soon the boat enters Washington harbor and slides up to the dock. The passengers file ashore, having had the remarkable and delightful experience of making a journey of 40 miles in 40 hours in an age in which speed has been set up as something to which one should bow down and worship."

It is evident from Mr. Martin's closing words that he realized that the days of the steamboats were near their end, another victim of "progress." By 1930 most of the freighting by steamboat was ended though a few excursion boats continued in service until World War II.

Mr. O. A. Reardon of Alexandria, Virginia, whose father was once the Alexandria agent for all the steamboat companies feels that the development of roads, following the coming of automobiles, killed the river traffic. "Fresh seafood (caught by the rivermen) could go by road so much faster. Freight was what kept the boats going -- the passenger business was really only in summer." In this Mr. Henry Burroughs agrees. In three months of the year it was impossible to make a fair return on the capital investment in these steamboats. Captain Harry Slye who has seen the river hauling trade die, adds: "The farmers stopped shipping their produce to agents. As the roads came in, the tractor trailers could drive.....right there."

And so the automobile put the steamboat out of business, and with the schooner, the "goose" gun and the five string banjo, they have disappeared in the fog of the river to return no more. To those who knew these things, their passing is reviewed with sadness. It is true that we now have planes buzzing over the river, a sleek yacht pulling a huge swell as she highballs down the Potomac, a darn fool in a 16 footer with ninety horsepower doing figure eights in the creek, juke boxes that destroy the calm of a summer's evening with hillbilly and rock and roll noises, and swan that make a nuisance of themselves but can't be shot, but this is not quite the same -- or so it seems to the writer. And one wonders sometimes how much longer the real rivermen will be around. Their numbers seem to grow smaller and smaller.

But there are some encouraging signs -- we see more pleasure sailing craft on the Bay and its tributaries each year, the state is gaining in the renewal of the oyster beds, some of the old Bay log canoes have been saved and there is talk now of trying to preserve a few of the Potomac River dories. Perhaps even the bugeye, "Col. R. Johnson Colton," may be rescued for posterity.

Joseph Goldstein of the Wilson Lines is still operating a couple of steamboats in an excursion service from Washington to Mount Vernon and Marshall Hall. In 1965, a new company appeared on the scene briefly. The Chesapeake Bay Line offered a three-day cruise from Washington to Yorktown, Jamestown, Williamsburg, Norfolk, and Virginia Beach, Virginia, at attractive rates that included fine food, dancing to the ship's orchestra, and other entertainment. The company had bought the old steamboat, "District of Columbia" for this service. Unfortunately, they could not get the boat through the Coast Guard inspection without costly repairs which very quickly sank the whole project. There is interest in such an undertaking though and perhaps another try will be made in the future.

The newest ship on the Potomac is the Hydrofoil. The following news item appeared in the Washington Daily News on April 13, 1964:

"A speedy water bus for commuters and sightseers will be in service in the Potomac at the end of the month."

"The $100,000, 24-passenger Hydrofoil will cost about $5 a ride, and its owners hope to take passengers from Indian Head, Md., to Georgetown and pick up riverfront apartment dwellers. The foil will also have access to such spots as D. C. Stadium and Arena Stage."

"Its owners, Joseph Goldstein of Wilson Lines and Frank Luchs, District realtor, say it is the first of a fleet of 10 and part of a transportation system that will include helicopters."

Mr. Goldstein placed the Hydrofoil in commuter service from Washington in the spring of 1965.

Is this the new medium of water transportation that will renew travel and industry on the river? Modes of transportation are ever changing -- we have seen sails replaced by motors, the locomotive kill the canals, the automobile finish the steamboat, and now the airplane and the trailer-truck take much of the traffic of the railroads -- all of this has happened in a lifetime. But what would the Hydrofoil threaten on our rivers? With more leisure time almost everyone wants a place on a waterway. And we need a fast passenger and light freight vehicle on our waterways for trips of a hundred miles or less. Will the Hydrofoil come and stay? It is an interesting question. The writer is inclined to believe it will, even though the first trial might be unsuccessful. First trys often are unsuccessful. In April 1966, the writer enjoyed a 60 mile run on Lake Maracaibo in Venezuela in a Hydrofoil. Although the waters of the lake were quite rough, the ride was smooth at 40 m.p.h. While this was strictly a passenger boat it could easily have been adapted for light freight as well as passengers.

Views of Potomac River landings as seen from the channel by the steamboat captains and sailing vessel masters during the past century will be found in Appendix "E". These sketches were made by Coast and Geodetic Survey artists about a century ago.

POTOMAC RIVER DISTANCES

	Washington D. C.		Point Lookout		Colonial Beach	
	N.M.	S.M.	N.M.	S.M.	N.M.	S.M.
Hains Point, D. C.........................0		.0	89.4	102.8	57.0	65.5
Alexandria, Va. (Jones Pt. Light).......3.8		4.4	85.6	98.4	52.9	60.8
Notley Hall (Rosier Bluff)..............5.0		5.8	84.4	97.1	52.0	59.8
Ft. Washington Light....................8.6		9.9	80.8	92.9	49.1	56.5
Mt. Vernon, Va. (Entrance to).........11.2		12.9	78.2	89.9	45.8	52.7
Marshall Hall, Md. (Wharf)...........12.0		13.8	77.4	89.0	45.9	52.8
Gunston Cove, Va. (South Entrance).....14.7		16.9	74.7	85.9	43.2	49.7
Indian Head, Md. (North Wharf).........18.8		21.6	70.6	81.2	39.1	45.0
Occoquan, Va. (Town of)...............25.3		29.1	75.1	86.4	43.6	50.1
Mattawoman Creek, Md. (Mouth of).......23.0		26.5	66.4	76.4	34.9	40.1
Chicamuxen Creek, Md. (Mouth of).......25.2		29.0	64.2	73.8	32.7	37.6
Quantico, Va. (Wharf).................26.7		30.7	62.7	72.1	31.2	35.9
Sandy Point Light......................28.5		32.8	60.8	70.0	29.0	33.4
Smith Point Light......................32.4		37.3	57.0	65.5	25.1	26.1
Maryland Point Light...................38.0		43.7	51.4	59.1	19.5	22.4
Nanjemoy Creek (Mouth of)..............42.2		48.5	47.2	54.3	15.3	17.6
Upper Cedar Point Light................44.2		50.8	45.2	52.0	13.3	15.3
Mathias Point Light....................46.0		52.0	43.4	49.9	11.1	12.8
Potomac River Bridge...................49.9		57.4	39.5	45.4	7.4	8.5
Lower Cedar Point Light................51.2		58.9	38.2	43.9	6.0	6.9
Morgantown, Md........................52.1		59.9	37.3	42.9	6.2	7.1
Upper Machodock (Ent. Light)...........52.2		60.0	37.2	42.8	3.9	4.5
Dahlgren, Va..........................55.3		63.6	34.1	39.2	5.6	6.4
Colonial Beach, Va....................57.0		65.5	32.4	37.3	.0	.0
Wicomico River, Va. (Mouth of).........63.0		72.8	26.4	30.4	6.0	6.9
Rock Point, Md. (Town of).............64.7		74.4	29.0	33.4	7.7	8.8
Blakistone Island, Md. (Nun "N-4A).....66.7		76.7	22.7	26.1	11.0	12.7
Nomini Creek, Va. (Outer Light)........70.1		80.6	19.3	22.2	13.3	15.3
Leonardtown, Md........................75.6		86.9	27.3	31.4	20.0	23.0
Lower Machodoc River, Va. (Entrance)...72.8		83.7	16.6	19.1	16.2	18.6
Ragged Point Light....................74.0		85.1	15.4	17.7	18.2	20.9
Piney Point Light, Md..................77.2		88.8	12.2	14.0	21.7	25.0
St. Mary's River (Mouth of)............83.0		95.5	6.4	7.4	27.2	31.3
Yeocomico River (Mouth of).............82.7		95.1	8.4	9.7	26.7	30.7
Smith Creek, Md. (Mouth of)............85.0		97.8	4.4	5.1	29.3	32.9
Kinsale, Va. (Town of)................85.6		98.4	12.0	13.8	31.1	35.8
Lewisetta, Va. (Town of)..............89.9		103.4	7.2	8.3	31.7	36.5
Pt. Lookout, Md. (Buoy, south of).....89.4		102.8	.0	.0	34.1	39.2

NOTE: Many of these points were the entrances to the Potomac River steamboat landings.

LIFE ON THE POTOMAC RIVER

Chapter VIII

BOYHOOD REMINISCENCES

Great fun was had on the river when there was a freeze. The Potomac does not freeze every winter but frequently the creeks and small bays do, so there is a good deal of sport, skating and ice boating.

Perhaps the first mention of a great freeze in the Potomac River is contained in a report of the Jesuits to the Superiors in England in 1642. A portion of this report reads as follows: "Father Andrew [White] suffered no little inconvenience, from a hard-hearted and troublesome sea-captain of New England, whom he had engaged for the purpose of taking him and his effects, from whom he was in fear a little while after, not without cause, that he would either be cast into the sea, or be carried with his property to New England, to the Puritan Calvinists - that is, the very dregs of all Calvinist heresy. Silently committing the thing to God, at length in safety he reached Potomac, which in the vernacular is called Patomake, in which harbor, when they had cast anchor, the ship stuck so fast, bound by a great quantity of ice, as if on land, the Father departed for the town; and when the ice was broken up, the ship, driven and jammed by the force and violence of the ice, sunk, the cargo however being in a great measure recovered."

When there is a prolonged freeze of the river the oystermen are in for a bad time and in the old days the dredgers and oyster buyers sometimes were caught and frozen in for weeks at a time. When firewood and supplies were exhausted it was a very nasty predicament. In the great freeze of 1914 many of the local oyster buyers were caught at the mouth of Canoe Neck Creek with their vessels loaded with oysters. Among the vessels were the "Lottie L. Thomas," the "R. B. Haynie," the "Thomas H. Kirby," and the "Hallie K." The captains were forced to seek assistance from Mitchell Davis of Washington who sent a tugboat under Captain Toby Taylor to break them out and tow them to Washington. The first of this freeze was a strange phenomena. Ordinarily one thinks of ice as a surface smooth as glass and generally the freezes on the river are, but in this instance the wind was blowing of gale proportions and the ice froze in irregular ridges -- it was a strange sight. After the first thaw that lasted for a few days, the ridges melted down and the river re-froze smoothly. As the writer recalls, this freeze lasted throughout January and February.

During the 1914 freeze a small yacht which was tied up at Captain Edwin Gibson's wharf at the mouth of Canoe Neck Creek was frozen in, much to the concern of the owner and his friend, both men with German names, now forgotten. They said they were traveling the river, showing "moving pictures" at the towns and they did indeed show their movies at the old Abell public schoolhouse twice a week during the extended period that they were frozen in. These were the first movies seen in this area and caused quite a sensation, and they played to a full house throughout their stay. The men became quite popular but it was thought a little strange that though they were entertained throughout the neighborhood, no one was ever invited aboard their yacht, and some of the prying youngsters were ordered away from the vessel rather sharply, and when they persisted, told harshly to go away and stay away. A week after the ice broke up in the river, the pair were picked up by a Naval patrol boat near Washington and it was discovered that they were mapping the Potomac. The "movie operators" turned out to be two German agents who had done a thorough job of mapping the Bay and its tributaries. We prying youngsters, though not very capable as junior Sherlock Holmes', were the envy of our friends and the arrest was the talk of the area for weeks afterward.

The winter of 1814, following the invasion of Washington by the British, was so severe that loaded wagons crossed the frozen Potomac in perfect safety. During the winter of 1856-1857 it was reported that the ice was thick enough on the Bay and its tributaries to walk from Washington to Norfolk. Undoubtedly it was true enough if one did not hit what was called locally, "an air hole." Strangely enough, even on the river, there were open spots, sometimes to the extent of several acres in which the ducks, geese, and swan would gather, which provided great targets for the river gunners.

In January, 1887, the St. Mary's Beacon reported that the river was frozen on the average about 9 inches in thickness and that the children on Bretton Bay were crossing the ice to attend school. The previous year also was a bad one and the Chesapeake was frozen over as late as March. If one reviews the newspapers of the counties along the Potomac during the past century it will be found that these heavy freezes can be expected periodically. The Washington Post reported on February 6, 1934, that the "Firefighter," the District of Columbia fireboat, spent the morning breaking up the heavy ice just below Key Bridge in the Georgetown Channel. The ice had stopped all traffic of small craft but it was the first time since 1918 that the ice had caused serious congestion on the river. During 1918, the heavy floes blocked the channel and wrecked boat houses all along the Georgetown shore. The freezes in recent years seem to have occurred largely in the bays and creeks that are tributary to the Potomac, when ice from five to eight inches in thickness have immobilized the oyster fleet for weeks at a time.

For over a hundred years until the big guns (the so-called punt or goose guns) were outlawed in the 1920's, the commercial river gunners made some of their biggest kills during periods when the river was frozen. In the night they would push their gunning skiffs on the ice into the wind to approach the air holes in the ice where ducks, geese, and whistling swan were massed in the only available water. Captain Willie Husemann of St. Patrick's Creek made his biggest kill on one such occasion when he killed twenty-two geese at a single shot. It was not uncommon for Captain Kelly Cheseldine to bring home fifty geese after an evening hunt. This was a hazardous sport and an extremely dangerous way to make a living, but the river gunners loved it and it was a sad day for them when the big guns were outlawed. Captain Willie's gun, which was typical of those in use, was inherited from his father, who did some commercial gunning together with the Cumberlands and others along the Washington water front prior to the Civil War. It was a muzzle loader, the barrel of which John Husemann, the grandfather of Willie, ordered made in England about 1840 at the cost of $100 in gold. The stock and locks were made by the Husemanns and the gun is slightly over 10 feet in length, including the stock, and weighs about 80 pounds. The charge consists of a quarter pound of powder and a pound and a quarter of shot, which is loaded in the barrel with proper wadding. The barrel is 3 inches in diameter at the locks and tapers to 2 inches.

The gun is mounted in a sling on the punt or gunning skiff and the recoil upon firing is taken up by the skiff being hurled backward in the water (or on the ice). A gunning skiff is a tricky boat and required a man of great skill, patience, endurance, and courage to engage in this type of hunting. The skiffs varied from 14 to 16 feet in length, were about 2 feet in width and were only about 15 inches out of the water. It was propelled by a double bladed paddle. In "creeping up" on the birds a pair of short paddles were utilized to reduce noise to a minimum. The gun was laid in a groove in the bow of the skiff so that it was the skiff that was aimed at the wild fowl rather than the gun. The best ducking season was in the cold winter months, particularly when there was much ice and snow and the "big gunner" always did his hunting at night.

Captain Willie had one serious accident and he said afterward that he wasn't sure whether he might have forgotten to remove the cork from the end of the barrel (to keep out water when caught in bad weather) or he might have rammed in a second charge when he thought the gun was empty. In any event the barrel burst about midway and blew out the side of the skiff and the charge untwisted the "Damascus" steel barrels of his 12 gauge shotgun, used for killing crippled ducks. Captain Willie was stunned by the explosion and the skiff immediately filled with water. Fortunately, Captain Kelly Cheseldine was hunting with him that night and came quickly to his assistance. He got Captain Willie ashore, made a fire and soon brought him around. The big gun was saved, the undamaged sections of the barrel were rejoined and the gun had much subsequent use. Both the gun and the skiff are in the possession of his grandson and namesake, William Husemann.

Captain Willie made some extraordinary shots -- once he killed 50 canvasbacks and 14 blackheads at a single shot. He also killed many whistling swan and every variety of Potomac River ducks. Primarily, he hunted for the better variety of ducks, mallard, redheads, canvasbacks, and geese and swan, as a good portion of his income came from marketing these ducks in Washington and Baltimore. On one occasion when the family larder was rather bare, his wife, Miss Jennie, said, "Willie we are going to have to use some of your ducks." Willie said, "But Jennie we don't have any trash ducks, they are all canvasbacks for market." Their small daughter, Ethel, who always had a healthy appetite spoke up quickly, "Mama don't we like canvasbacks?" The family dined on canvasbacks that day because no one enjoyed a good laugh more than Captain Willie.

Captain Willie, like all of the old-timers on the river, felt that it was his right as a riverman to have a mess of ducks when he felt like it and he didn't take kindly to the outlawing of the big guns, and continued on occasion to slip out on the river, make a quick shot and come home with enough ducks to last the family quite a while. But as time went on and the law was more strictly enforced it got rather risky, so he solved the problem by getting himself elected game warden for the area. It is said that he had one of the best seasons that year, that he had had in many years.

While Captain Willie built an occasional dory, his skill in making oyster tongs was known not only on the Potomac, but on the Wicomico, the Patuxent, and the Chesapeake Bay. It takes craftsmanship of the highest order to make tongs that are properly balanced, with teeth on just the right slant to insure that they will catch proper-

PUNTS OR GUNNING SKIFFS

Capt. Fred Cheseldine in the Punt of his father, Capt. Walter Cheseldine

Tide Mill - Virginia Shore

Poquoson River (Va.) Log Canoe

River View
(Late 17th Century)

Early River House on Canoe Neck Creek

Colton (Longworth) Point

Prior to the Hurricane of 1933

1964

ly -- in a word, they must "work right," and Captain Willie was a perfectionist. He had a wonderful personality and his friends were legion. He was always interested in people, had a prodigious memory and knew more about the history of the people of the river and the bay than any man in St. Mary's County. He had a gift of telling interesting stories and his wit and good humor made him a favorite of old and young. Like his father, he was very talented on the five-string banjo, and it will always be a matter of regret that his repertoire of old folk songs and ballads could not have been recorded and preserved.

A story is told that when Captain Willie was living on the old Waterloo farm which fronted on the Potomac, things got pretty slow on the river and times were so bad that the Captain was reduced to trying his hand at farming. One of his immediate problems was the fact that no matter how hard he tried he just couldn't plow a straight furrow. One day, as the story goes, he was seen to stop plowing and make his way to a big tree near the edge of the field where he sat down in the shade, loaded his pipe with care, and gave the matter some serious thought. Pretty soon he tapped out his pipe and moved with resolute steps down to his wharf where he boarded his boat and soon returned to the field with a compass in his hand. When last seen by the observer, the compass had been lashed in place between the handles of the plow and the Captain was plowing a direct course south to north, and hollering to his horse, "move to starboard, you blasted hunk of crowbait."

He would have delighted in having shared the view with the writer, in February, 1964, of a flock of whistling swan on Heron Island Bar, estimated to have been more than a thousand of these magnificent birds, the largest flock seen in a half-century of observation on the river.

The late Walter Cheseldine of White's Neck was the last "big gun" hunter on the Potomac. His punt and gun are now mementos kept by his son, Fred Cheseldine, of St. Patrick's Creek. His gun was a 10 foot steel tube obtained in Philadelphia, with a bore of 1 1/2 inches. The walls of the barrel are 1 inch in thickness. Walter reamed the barrel 18 times by hand, using an expansion reamer and then polished the inside with emory cloth. The stock was made by hand from a black walnut, blown down in a hurricane, on Charlie Cheseldine's place nearby. A lock and hammer from an old Springfield rifle was utilized to complete the gun. The finished barrel was 7 feet 6 inches in length and the bore 1 9/16 inches. The measuring charge was a steer's horn of powder and 1 1/2 pounds of single FG shot. Single strands of wad rope wound up, was used for wadding, one before the shot and one after. The gun rest on the punt was made from the same piece of walnut as the stock, and covered with elkskin. Captain Walter's biggest shot occurred one New Year's night when he killed 72 canvasbacks at one shot and a total of 108 ducks in two shots.

The tide mills, used for grinding grain, on the Potomac all seem to have disappeared, along with the steamboat wharves and lighthouses. One of these mills dating back to colonial times was located near Bushwood Wharf at the mouth of the Wicomico River. A more modern mill was operating there when the writer was a small boy. The great wheel of another mill may be seen on the shore of the Nomini Cliffs where a small stream from the river flows into a pond on the flood and reverses on the ebb. The old Lee Mill at Stratford nearby has been restored but this doesn't seem to be a true tide mill because drainage from the land fills the mill race to operate the mill, which then flows on to the river. My father, in the days of sail boats, bought much of the flour and corn meal used by the family from mills in this vicinity of Virginia. On one of his trips to the mill, and it probably was the Lee Mill in the days when Stratford was owned by Dr. Stuart, the dam gave way as he reached the landing and a wall of water hit the old "Defender" bows on, but other than filling the dory no great damage was done. The story might have been very different if the boat had been hit broadside. Papa said it was one of the most frightening experiences of his life on the river.

There were many things on the river to intrigue a boy and fire his imagination. The writer cannot remember when he couldn't swim -- not very expertly, but it seemed to come as natural as walking and we could dive from the rigging of the bugeyes and schooners anchored at the mouth of Canoe Neck Creek. When about 12 years of age, with his cousins, Dick, Joe, and Jack (Bernard) Gibson, and Albert Beitzell, they would be permitted, during the summer, to go off on camping trips on St. Clement's Bay. A rowboat, loaded with an old sail from the "Defender," to serve as a tent, a few cans of beans, some Irish potatoes for roasting, a crab net, fishing lines and a .22 rifle brought in a variety of fish and game that filled all our needs. None of us owned a bathing suit - our underpants sufficed, and we did a lot of swimming.

Each summer too we would row about seven miles up the Potomac to St. Katherine's Island to spend a few weeks with Uncle Charlie Beitzell. We caught perch by the hundreds in St. Katherine's Sound, had a swim about every hour, rode Uncle's horses bareback over the Island in the afternoons, raided his watermelon patch at will and around sundown sat at the edge of the alfalfa patch and with our .22's came home with enough young and luckless rabbits for Uncle to make one of his famous "Mulligan" stews. One summer Uncle, tired of his widower status, and remarried. It was necessary for us to sleep in the barn on the hay, while his house was being rebuilt for his new bride. This was the best summer of all. Uncle never laid down but one rule -- no smoking in the barn -- and we never did, but we always wondered how he knew we were beginning to sneak smokes when no one was around.

There were unending arguments among the boys on Canoe Neck Creek, Tommie Morris, Willard Lawrence, Gilbert and Delmas ("Bee") Ellis, the Gibson boys, Ralph and Elmer Norris, Larry Owens, Arthur and Francis Lawrence and the Woodhall boys, Joe and George, about what boat was fastest, the prettiest, the best sailer, had the biggest engine, which engine had the nicest sound and the like. You were put down as a traitor of some sort if you didn't maintain to the end that the boats in your family had most of all the merits. The debates didn't stop at the family boats -- the merits of every steamboat, schooner, pungy, and bugeye known on the river were argued without end.

School days could be endured except in September and June. There were still good fishing days in September and having to wear shoes every day added to our unhappiness. It was true we had to wear shoes to church on Sundays but we could take them off as soon as the service was over, tie the laces together, swing them around our necks and be as free as the wind again. Our feet seemed to spread in the summer but they probably only grew -- in any event the shoes always seemed tight and uncomfortable. Soft crabs appeared late in May and from that time until June 15th when school closed it was almost more than a body could bear to be cooped up in school.

The schoolhouse, about a mile from the writer's home, was a one room affair set at the edge of the woods. Its location was very handy for playing "hounds and hares" during our lunch hour, when lunch carried in a small tin pail was "bolted" to have more playtime. Several boys were designated as the hares and the others formed the pack of hounds. The hares were given about a hundred yard start, when at a signal from the leader, the pack took off after them through the woods. We would run for miles in the woods in a wide circle so that we would not get out of range of the school bell that marked the end of the lunch period. If the hares made it back to the school at the bell signal without being caught they were the winners. If a hare was caught he automatically became a hound and had to join the pack. It was exciting and great fun and we never seemed to tire of the game.

In good weather the morning and afternoon recess periods were usually occupied in shooting marbles. A ring about four feet in diameter was drawn on a bare smooth piece of ground and each boy playing would place an agreed number of marbles, usually about five, in the center of the ring. The first to shoot was determined by dropping our "toy" or shooter from waist height at a straight line drawn on the ground. The boy whose "toy" was nearest to the line on either side got to shoot first and the remainder in precedence to their nearness to the mark. The first shot was a matter of considerable importance among first class marble shooters. As long as a marble was knocked out of the ring on a shot but the "toy" remained in the ring the shooter could keep shooting. Dewey Blackistone was the champion in the St. Clement's Bay area and many times he would clean out the ring without missing a single shot. He could put "English" on his "toy" to maneuver it into position for the next shot just like an expert shooting pool. Unfortunately for Dewey he so far outclassed all the other boys that only the very best shooters would play with him. We had a great time whenever an unsuspecting stranger could be inveigled into a game with Dewey. The outcome always reminds me of a skit of the actor, W. C. Fields, where he enticed a "pool shark" into a high stakes game. After the balls had been racked, Fields had the opening shot. He shot with apparent carelessness and without looking at the table, walked over and racked his cue, adjusted his tie with care and put on his coat. By this time all of the balls had rolled into the pockets and he pocketed his winnings with a flourish. But Dewey's show was the real thing and he made it last by picking off most of the marbles one at a time. Occasionally he would spin out two marbles at once just to show it could be done. We sometimes played "knucks down," which meant at the end of the game the loser had to rest his knuckles on the opposite edge of the ring and let the winner shoot (as hard as he could) at them. Since the most popular "toys" were hollowed steel balls about the size of a thumbnail the loser got a stinging crack on his knuckles. Most of the good marble shooters were earmarked by a dirty right knee from kneeling to shoot, and dirty knuckles, and the mortality to stockings in the winter months when shoes were worn was high.

The old Abell Public School housed seven grades so the children ranged in age from six to fourteen years. During most of the writer's seven years in this school the teacher was his sister, Alice, who played no favorites when a switching was in order. She was a good sport though and never reported my transgressions when we got home as this would have called for more punishment. I am sure she felt she had done a thorough job and I would have been the first to agree with her. When one of the boys was summoned to go cut a black gum switch we knew we were in trouble.

One memorable occasion occurred when the County Superintendent, "Professor" George W. Joy, paid his annual visit to our school. The Professor made it a point to arrive fairly early in the morning (it was a long drive by horse and buggy from Leonardtown), listen to us recite for awhile, spend the recess with the teacher and after more recitations, leave at lunch time and give us the afternoon off. On this particular occasion he didn't arrive until lunch time and we could see our holiday go "a glimmering" as the afternoon wore on. At the afternoon recess the boys held a council of war and the decision was reached that since we were being cheated out of our holiday we would give him a "spit-balling," the likes of which mortal eye had never before seen.

A short length of hollowed out elder branch was used as a blow-gun to shoot the "spitball," which was a bit of masticated paper. (If it were wet enough and blown full force one could make it stick to the ceiling of the schoolroom.) We really let the Professor have it. He always sat up on the platform with the teacher and there must have been a hundred spitballs on the floor around his chair. Every shot must have been a hit but the Professor never batted an eyelash which infuriated us no end and although Sister Alice looked like she would likely explode any minute and gazed longingly at times at the window stick nearby, we kept up the barrage. The Professor left shortly before closing time, with a pretty fair idea, I'm sure, how Alice would utilize the remainder of the time. He was hardly out of the schoolyard before some six or seven of us were told to go and cut our own switches and not to come back with any flimsy ones. We knew she meant business and each cut a black gum about little finger size and took our switching in turn and Alice laid it on with a will. She must have had a sore arm that night. The following afternoon we were given a holiday and I have wondered ever since whether this was an understanding order on the part of the Professor or Alice's idea after she had cooled off. I had some welts on my legs and thighs to brag about for almost a week.

The boys and girls played a form of baseball together, choosing sides from both sexes so that the teams would be fairly well balanced. The ball was homemade with a walnut for the center and then many layers of tightly sewn rags covering it. It was slightly smaller than a regular baseball. The bat was a flat piece of board about two and one-half inches wide and three-quarters inch in thickness, with a carved handle. The overall length was about thirty-two inches. We had no baseman except the catcher. All of the players except the pitcher and catcher were fielders. The pitch was made underhand and whoever caught the batted ball threw it at the batter or another runner unless it was a long hit when it was relayed in for throwing. If any runner was hit while off base it was an out. The in-fielders moved in to try to cover each throw and considerable skill was developed so that there were frequent double and sometimes triple plays. Three outs for each side completed an inning. The number of innings varied depending upon the amount of available time. There might be anywhere from five to ten on each side. The game was a lot of fun for 10-14 year old youngsters.

Another game played by the boys and girls was called "nicky-nicky-nee." Here again the rag ball was used and sides were chosen from both sexes. Each team got into position on opposite sides of the schoolhouse. At the call of "nicky-nicky-nee" the ball was thrown over the schoolhouse. The side catching the ball dashed around the schoolhouse and threw the ball at an opponent. As soon as the other team saw who had the ball and knew in which direction to run they made a dash around the school to escape being hit. A complete circuit of the school had to be made to be safe. Any one hit had to become a member of the opposing team. Although the schoolhouse rested on short locust posts and one could see the feet and legs of the opposing team by looking under the school it couldn't be determined who caught the ball and "false" runners were started around each end of the school to confuse the opponents. It wasn't considered fair to "spy" around the corner of the school and anyone caught was put out of the game. Eventually all became one team and that was the end of the game.

At thirteen, the writer matriculated to the Oakley Public School, a two-room building with two teachers and 10 grades, about three miles from home by land and two by water if one wanted to row a skiff for a mile and walk alone for the remainder of the way. He usually preferred the former, joining schoolmates all along the route. There was much opportunity for "skylarking" along the way and we did all the things that country children had done for generations such as trying to ride the farmer's yearlings, catching harmless snakes, turtles, frogs, and crayfish; climbing trees; walking rail fences, occasionally we ran down a small rabbit, and the glass insulators on the telephone poles presented excellent targets for our "bean" shooters (in which we used stones) and slingshots. Occasionally a rabbit or frog found its way into the teacher's desk but we never tried a snake or crayfish -- that would really be asking for trouble. As we grew older whippings were rare and punishment for misdeeds took the form of having to stay in during recess or after school and copy a hundred or two hundred lines from our history books or commit poetry to memory. One time I had to commit the whole of Thomas Gray's "Elegy Written in a Country Church-Yard" and it seemed like there were a thousand verses. Actually there were 32 four-line verses. I still remember a few lines. This was occasioned, as I recall, by the fact that I found a crazy old horse who liked to chew tobacco and over a period of time, with my approving schoolmates looking on, I fed him quite a few "sticks" of tobacco from the luckless farmer's barn, which was on our route to school. I never did know whether the old horse was hungry or really liked tobacco -- anyway he never refused and took all I tendered him.

One youthful prank backfired to haunt me for several weeks. One drizzly winter evening about dusk when I was later than usual getting home from school I saw a housewife's wash hanging on a rickety wire fence. The family was somewhat on the lackadaisical side and were not noted for clotheslines and such like conveniences. Under the cover of the enveloping darkness I did a masterful job of knotting stockings, shirt sleeves, pants legs and the like in the wire. I got carried away with the task and did a thorough and painstaking job. It was not done out of meanness -- I was just overcome by temptation. It was an opportunity that could not be passed up lightly. I expected the lady would be some aggravated in the morning but failed to take in account the state of the weather. There had been a thawing period for several days but that night it turned cold, very cold, and the "cold snap" lasted for three solid weeks and that poor old lady's wash stayed there on the fence, the knots frozen solid. I had to pass it morning and evening during this period with a growing sense of guilt and remorse. Even a snowstorm could not hide my guilt from me. The fact that I saw the old lady gazing wistfully out of her kitchen window at her frozen wash on several occasions did nothing to relieve my guilty conscience. But perhaps something was gained -- I did some growing up and was pretty well cured of playing pranks.

When I was ten years old, Papa had a twelve foot skiff built for my personal use. Prior to this time I had been using the family "rowboats" for crabbing and fishing, but the new skiff was somewhat unusual because it was primarily a "pleasure" boat rather than the usual work boat. Papa was even persuaded to have it equipped with "wash-boards," which made it the envy of all the boys on the creek. He said from the beginning the skiff was too small for practical use and he was right because when one stood on the bow to look for soft crabs in the shallow water the stern "cocked up" and the bow went deep so that one could not get in close to shore where most of the crabs like to go when shedding. However, I "tacked" a narrow board along the keel, my brother Clem made me a mast from a young loblolly pine, and also a rudder, and with Mama's help a "leg-of-mutton" sail was made of light canvas and I had a real sailboat. She sailed so well I named her the "Greased Lightning" and she gave me and my friends many pleasurable hours and a few wettings when we tried to carry too much sail in a heavy breeze.

The next year I had my own crabbing skiff built, fourteen feet, three inches in length. Clem and I went across the Potomac in the old "Defender" to Nomini Bay and bought all the lumber necessary for $8 from a sawmill located there. John Long built the skiff for $5 so that my total investment was $13, not including the oars and oarlocks. This skiff was in use for over forty years. A similar skiff built in 1952 cost $125.

When I was a little older I was permitted to sail Mama's small dory, the "Katy B.", during the summer months when she was brought home after being hired out during the oyster season. One of Papa's hired men was a young man who had been raised in a city orphanage and he also enjoyed sailing the "Katy B." but never seemed to comprehend the necessity for "coming about in the wind" when attempting to dock the dory. Despite repeated instructions he would simply grab the tie stake or wharf as he passed by, usually going adrift or aground in the process and knocking off some paint to boot. This annoyed Papa considerably. One day in October when the water in the creek had become quite chilly, with a stiff breeze blowing, Bert did his usual of grabbing the tie stake as he went by. The "Katy B." was moving so fast that Bert found himself hanging on the stake as the dory proceeded up the creek to be grounded at the head of the cove. Bert hollered to me to come to his rescue in the skiff but Papa, who was standing by said, "No sir, let the durn fool swim ashore -- maybe next time he will know enough to come about." So Bert had to swim ashore in the icy water, but he never did learn to sail a boat properly.

Papa was a firm believer that work was a therapy that kept all young people out of mischief. It was unthought of for youngsters to get into serious trouble in those days other than smoking corn silk or grapevine, and that was a punishment in itself. All were assigned specific chores and the youngest started out picking up chips and other small pieces of wood from the "woodpile" for kindling to start the fire in the kitchen range at daylight in the morning. The fire in the range was lit every morning of every day in the year and the stove remained hot for a couple of hours after supper

131

when the family had finished the evening chores and retired to the living room. It burned a prodigious amount of "cordwood," which was cut from the family woods of loblolly pine (we called it "long leaf" pine) during late summer and the windy days of the fall when it was too rough to work in the river. Mama always kept both the coffee pot and the teapot simmering on the back of the range, which was enjoyed as much then as now.

As we grew a little older bringing in the firewood was added to the list of chores and when you grew big enough to chop and split cordwood, usually around the age of 10-12 years, one found the chores around the home were endless. Bailing the boats (and there was usually a half-dozen or so of assorted kinds and sizes) wasn't so bad -- that only happened after a rain or snowstorm in winter. Scraping the dead barnacles off the hundreds of trap net poles with a piece of iron, similar to an old automobile tire iron, was something else again -- it took days of tedious work, pole after pole having to be shifted, scraped and returned to the pile. The fact that the pole usually was slightly warped and tended to return to its original position when one tried to scrape the underside, did not add to the pleasure. Picking the dried seaweed from the meshes of the net before it could be tarred for the new season was no better job, particularly in the summer months when there were a thousand interesting things to do on the river.

However, Papa allowed us time for fishing and swimming and you could generally count on being allowed to go swimming with the gang around 4:00 P.M. in the afternoon. He, himself, liked sport fishing and there were plenty of fish to catch in those days. Although trout in those times seemed to bite well with every change of tide, we liked to be on our favorite fishing grounds, the Tompkins, off the mouth of Bretton Bay, about daylight when the tide was right. One memorable morning with my brother, Clem, we caught 145 trout, ranging from 1 to 3 pounds, in a little over an hour. Those that weren't eaten for supper that day were salted down for winter. Great runs of "Norfolk" spot could be expected during the summer and these were caught and also salted down for the winter. Thousands of herrings were salted down in the spring for winter use also but, of course, our favorite salted fish were trout, spot, and shad. Mama knew how to prepare them to a "T", as the saying went. She would soak them overnight, boil them in clear water, butter generously and season well and serve with freshly baked biscuits and syrup. It was a breakfast fit for a king. Unfortunately, we always seemed to run out of good salted fish about Lent and had to fall back on salted herring. And Mama was a stickler for Lent. She never, never missed a fish day. Frequently, in good weather, Papa would take me fishing off Heron Island Bar in the late afternoon. We would have an early supper and be in the shallows of the bar about 5:00 P.M. We would sit very quietly and soon the fish would start to bite. By dark we would have a bushel basket of good-sized rock, trout, blues, spot, and perch. Usually there would also be a few flounders and several big eels. The eels generally put an end to our outing as the darkness gathered over the river.

The meanest chore of all to any river boy was the cornfield. How we hated those cornfields. Most river families kept a couple of horses, several cows, and a lot of chickens. Corn and fodder (dried corn leaves) were their staple diets. Planting corn wasn't so bad. You walked along and dropped two or three grains in each hill, but the easy part stopped right there. About the time the soft crabs started to come and fish were biting in the creeks that damned corn had to be thinned. This was in the days before the modern hybrid corn and only one stalk was left per hill. It was a backbreaking job to pull out the extras and care had to be exercised in pulling up the surplus not to pull up all in the hill. One day the writer had a rather unusual experience "thinning" corn. His next older brother, Walter, unknown to him had killed a snake which he arranged with care around a hill of corn on the next row I was due to thin. In due course I arrived at this particular hill and bending low to get at the extra corn sprouts I found myself looking eye to eye with a sizable and very live appearing snake. What happened then is left to the imagination of the reader. It is sufficient to say that it was almost as memorable a day as the Christmas day Walter dared me to shoot at him with a Roman candle. The dare was accepted and the aim was deadly, with the result that Mama whipped me for being so bad as to shoot my brother's new Christmas suit full of holes on Christmas day, and she then whipped Walter for being so foolish as to dare me to shoot at him.

However, the corn thinning was only the beginning. Those pesky plants had to be worked with a cultivator to keep the grass down. Twice each row with the cultivator behind a reluctant and plodding horse, and always at the time the fishing and crabbing were best on the river. One particularly hot day when I wanted the worse way to go swimming with the boys I was told "no swimming" until the corn was cultivated. Hoping to get in at least on the tail end of the swimming, I took a wrench and "spread" the cultivator and went down each row only once when I was supposed to go twice. Since I was the youngest in the family and Papa had learned all of his son's tricks, he, of course, caught me before I had completed one-third of the field. The net result was that the cultivator was restored to its normal width, I had to start from the begin-

132

ning, and was lucky not to have gotten a thrashing to boot.

In those days nothing was lost in the cornfield. About the middle of August, usually when it was hotter than Hades, and if there was a breeze the tall corn cut it off, it was time to "strip fodder." This operation consisted of pulling off the lower leaves, from the ground up to the ear of corn, tying them into bundles and after they had dried, storing them in the barn. The sharp edges of the corn leaves cut minute gashes in the hands during the stripping and the fuzz from them seemed to prickle every inch of skin as it permeated every stitch of clothing. Next the "tops," above the ear of corn, were cut off with a heavy knife or a machete and carried an armful at a time to make "shocks" in the field, like small tents, for drying. After drying the shocks were brought in near the barn where a framework of fence rails was made resembling an Indian hogan, and the dried tops were used to cover the frame, making a fodder house that would gradually disappear during the winter as the "tops" were removed to feed the cattle. Inside the fodder house the shucks from the corn were stored and also used for feed. Now the remaining chore was to pull off the corn from the remainder of the stalk, throw it in piles, for later removal to the barnyard by horse and wagon, which was utilized also to bring in the bundles of fodder and the "tops." The young people then had great fun at the "shucking bees" when the boys would bring their girl friends, who got "bussed" everytime a red ear was shucked. Good apple cider added to the merriment. The fun part of corn growing was lost to the writer because when he was sixteen he went away to high school and mercifully was released from the cornfield. Prior to his sixteenth year he would rather have wrestled an eel than hug a girl, although he later had a change of heart. Thus the whole corn operation was a complete loss to him from beginning to end. He is fond of the lines concerning corn in the beautiful music of "Oklahoma," but to this day, his interest in growing corn stops right there.

"Hog killing time" always was an exciting occasion for the boys on the river. This time arrived after the weather had definitely turned cold, the latter part of November or early in December. I seem to recall that some phase in the moon got into the selection of the time. I know it did with the spring planting and the first soft crabs could be expected on the full moon in May when the locust bursts into bloom. In any event on the day the hogs were to be slaughtered we were up hours before daylight. The previous day a big "gum" barrel had been set in the ground on a slant so that the mouth was somewhat above ground and it would hold about one-half its full capacity of liquid. This permitted the hogs to be immersed, first one end and then the other with a minimum of effort since they weighed between 200 and 300 pounds each. A great pile of wood and chain (used to sink the fishing nets) also was placed near the barrel; the barrel was filled with water to its restricted capacity and oyster culling boards were placed on "sawhorses" nearby so that all was in readiness for the big day. A roaring fire was kindled before daylight that looked beautiful in the dark and felt wonderful on the frosty morning. Then the chain was placed in the fire to heat. When it became "red hot" it was removed by a pair of oyster "nippers" and immersed in the water to heat it. This operation was continued until the water was boiling. After a hog was immersed, placed on a culling board, and the hair removed, the water was re-heated for use on the next hog. Two or three colored men were hired to be the butchers and to dress and hang the hogs to cool but Papa always cut up his own meat and he was quite skillful in doing the job.

The fresh hog meat, including the tenderloin and spareribs, tasted wonderful after a year of salted hog meat. Mama had extra colored women in to help during the hog killing time and they were busy for a week cooking up the fat to make the coming year's supply of lard. The fat was boiled down in great kettles on the kitchen range; the clear liquid was drained off and stored in the lard cans, and the residue known as "cracklins" was saved to season greens, such as cabbage and kale. Great quantities of sausage meat was ground. Some was made into cakes and stored in large earthen jars and sealed by pouring liquid lard over the top and then stored in the dairy. The remainder of the sausage meat was made into links. The small intestines of the hogs were utilized for the casings after being scraped and washed many times. The larger intestines were made into "chitlins" which our family never seemed to relish very much so that most of them were given to the colored helpers, though some were kept for the regular colored help who fancied them. There was much "head cheese" or "souse," scrapple, pickled pigs feet and the like to be made and nothing was wasted. Scrapple was made from the cooked hearts, livers, and lean meat from the heads of the hogs. The stuff one buys as scrapple today is a rather weak imitation of the real thing. The brains also were preserved and when combined with scrambled eggs made a very tasty dish. A considerable amount of the fresh pork also was cooked and canned for future use. Even the hog's hair was utilized on occasion when some plastering was necessary around the house.

After the hams and shoulders had been down in brine for the proper length of time it was then time to hang them in the meat house, along with the link sausage and sides of bacon, for smoking. This was generally started early on a Saturday morning, with the writer in the role of "fire tender." I never could understánd how green hickory would burn for it was unlike pine, which when green has much gummy sap. But burn it did, making the dense but savory hickory smoke so essential to fine ham. The fire tender was kept at his duties all day, periodically entering the smoke house to re-plenish the fire. The smoke house was so filled with the pungent smoke that little could be seen even with open eyes if one had been so foolish as to attempt to open them wide. The trick was to slit the eyes momentarily to locate the fire, dump on more hickory and exit as expeditiously as possible. Even so by the end of the day the fire tender was as red-eyed as the Mad Hatter and fairly well smoked himself. But it was great fun and thoroughly enjoyed. The fire was continued through the night but here the grown-ups took over.

"Hog killing" was about the final step in getting ready for winter. It was a wonderful feeling to know that the home was well supplied come the winter ice and snowstorms. Mama's shelves were lined with canned pork, vegetables, peaches and pears, preserves and jellies, relishes and pickles, and dried fruits. Cider and wine had been made and stored along with barrels of Winesap apples and Bartlett pears. The boys in the family had harvested a large quantity of walnuts, chestnuts, and hick-ory nuts. Cabbage, turnips, beets, and parsnips filled a large dirt kiln in the gar-den and many bushels of "Irish" and sweet potatoes were safely stored. Firewood and coal was laid in near the kitchen. An adequate supply of fish had been salted for winter use and now the meat supply was assured. Even the cattle were remembered and a large pile of pine chaff (pine needles from loblolly trees) filled a good portion of the barnyard for their winter bedding. When snow came dancing in on the beginnings of a heavy Nor'wester one had the good feeling that all was in readiness and the fam-ily would be snug and warm and well fed, come what may. It was a great feeling. Little work was done from Christmas to March except to fill the ice-house, check on fishing gear, make splints and needles, huddled in the warmth of the kitchen range. We sort of followed Nature's lead when she rested her things of the earth. It was a good life, even with the cornfield thrown in.

Raising ducks was a good source of pocket money for boyhood pleasures. I first started in this business when nine years of age and continued until I was sixteen. It was a most successful and foolproof piece of business for me. Originally Captain Willie Husemann secured for me a "setting" of wild mallard eggs and thereafter I had a flock of approximately fifty ducks ready for market by early fall. A few of the ducklings were lost to crabs, but the ducks fed themselves from the creek all summer and it was only necessary to pen them for a week before shipping and fatten them on Papa's corn. This was only fair in return for my labors in the cornfield. A few ducks were held out to assure a crop for the next year and the remainder shipped to the wholesale market in Washington at 100% profit and very little labor. The mallards were beautiful ducks and it was easy to become attached to them. They could and did fly like their wild kindred and wandered far from home during the day but would always come flying home at eventide. Alas, they fell victims to commercialism and during my last couple of years in this venture white Pekings were substituted for the mallards because they were larger and heavier and brought a better price in the market place. These were shipped off to market without a twinge of conscience.

My venture into trapping muskrats on the creek was not so successful. The mar-ket during my time was somewhat uncertain and the work was most distasteful. Musk-rats really are a nuisance in the creeks as they tunnel under the banks causing ero-sion and a colony of them will soon strip the edge of a cornfield along the shores. During the second season the venture was abandoned and it is doubtful that the reve-nue obtained covered the cost of the traps. The traps had to be emptied before high tide or the muskrat would knaw off his foot and escape before the rising tide would drown him. This often meant rising at 3:00 or 4:00 A.M. on a freezing winter morning to tend the traps, sometimes in snow or sleet. It was a long pull in the rowboat to tend the trap line and a heavy breeze made the task more onerous. If there was ice on the creek it meant a long walk over marshy ground in heavy clothing and "gum" knee boots, and lugging the dead "rats" on the return trip. As time passed the venture grew increasing distasteful and culminated one cold winter morning around 5:00 A.M. when I stepped into a muskrat "lead" and sank in the slimy ooze over both boot-tops, about a mile from home. It was very easy to convince myself on the return trip home, which was made in record-breaking time, that I just didn't have the makings of a good trapper. As a consequence the muskrats on the creek are still making a nuisance of themselves, including their continuing effort to undermine the sea-wall along the front of my home on "Gerard's Cove." But the challenge is now accepted with reason-ably good grace. Somehow I feel that I owe them something and they are interesting little animals to observe. One cannot help but admire their cockiness, and bravery in the face of death, and their skill and speed in the water, although I would appre-ciate it if they would quit using my wharf for a diving board, where they invariably leave evidence of their presence.

The writer graduated from a .22 rifle to a double-barrelled 12 gauge shotgun the

Christmas he was 14 years of age -- undoubtedly this was the most thrilling Christmas present of his life. There was a good deal of shooting around the place for awhile that resulted in some "borrowing" of Papa's gunshells until he started keeping a check of his shells. He had been having some difficulty about his supply of gunshells for some time prior to this time and remarked several times for the benefit of all present, usually looking hard at sons, Clem and Walter, that he couldn't understand why he always seemed to be low on shells. The writer could have explained it, if he had been asked a direct question -- fortunately he wasn't. The truth of the matter was that Valentine Woodhall, the father of Joe and George, had an old Civil War musket that the boys would sneak out of the house. The writer would rendezvous with them at an appointed spot in the woods with a supply of shells that would be unloaded and used to charge the musket. The peace of mind of every red squirrel for miles around was upset but there never was a casualty, and that old musket kicked like a horse, at least to a 12 year old.

Arthur Lawrence, Tommie Morris, Gilbert Ellis, and George Woodhall are the only ones in this crowd of boys who have stuck with the river as their main source of livelihood. In talking with George sometime back, he related an experience on Ragged Point, at the mouth of the Potomac a few years ago. George said, "We laid out our big seine that night on the Point fairly far out on the bar, and got around some fish. We had noticed the makings of a thunderstorm in the West but decided that it wouldn't amount to much, which was probably the poorest decision of a lifetime. We had the seine half in when it hit. In no time, the breakers over the bar turned knee deep water into water up to our armpits and there was so much pressure on the seine it seemed like all was going to be swept away. It was a good ways to shore and we couldn't buck the breakers. There was nothing to do but to hold on, dig in our heels and fight that seine to keep from being carried off the bar. I had thought I wasn't much of a praying man but I learned to pray that night and it come very easy. I've been a better churchman ever since. That was about the closest call in 40 years on the river and all of us were lucky to get out of it alive, I can tell you."

Richard (Dick) Gibson, while he did not follow the water for a livelihood, is well known as a Charter Boat Captain by weekenders seeking the great sporting fish of the Potomac, the striped bass or rock fish. The fish are pursued from June through February, weather conditions in the winter months permitting. Captain Dick and his beautiful boat, the "Enterprise," is a familiar sight on the Potomac, where over the past 40 years he has caught literally tons of these fish. When he doesn't have a charter he is still to be seen on the river and one suspects, that from his viewpoint, these are the very best days.

While a heavy summer thunderstorm can be awesome when caught on the river, it is generally the heavy No'theasters that do most of the damage as they are lengthy affairs compared with thunderstorms. The writer and his daughter, Jean, were caught on the Potomac in a sudden thunderstorm in a 20 foot boat in the summer of 1958. At full speed of 25 m.p.h. a run was made for the comparative safety of St. Clement's Bay. In less than 10 minutes that it took to reach the bay the wind had risen to a velocity of 55 miles per hour and the waves were so high that the motor had to be throttled to prevent wrecking it when the propeller was out of the water due to the pitching of the boat, which literally "stood on end" as it took the waves. Fortunately, enough power could be applied to keep the boat "bow on" so that it did not turn over in the trough of the waves. The rain came down in "sheets" and we could not see off the side of the boat for more than a dozen feet. The storm was over in 20 minutes but it was undoubtedly the longest 20 minutes of our lives and we were thankful to have reached the bay before we were hit by the full force of the storm. Perhaps one of the heaviest thunderstorms recorded occurred during invasion of Washington by the British in August, 1814. Most of the British armada ascending the Potomac were grounded and their anchored ships in the Patuxent River, awaiting the return of the invasion force, were driven ashore. One troopship, at anchor, with bare spars was capsized.

Ducking was perhaps the favorite sport of most of the boys along the river 40 years ago when there was a longer season. Blinds were not the fancy affairs of today -- just enough pine brush on a frame of poles stuck in the mud to hide a skiff. A couple of dozen homemade decoys, a gun and shells was all that was necessary. The writer with his cousin, Andrew Cheseldine, of White's Neck got 34 ducks, mostly blackheads, one memorable afternoon in St. Katherine's Sound and finally had to quit because practically all of the decoys had become ice-logged and turned over. It was blowing so hard the decoys were dipping their bills in the waves and it was so cold great icicles formed on their bills to turn them over. We had to fight our way to shore through falling snow and a skim of ice that was forming but it was all great fun and this was fine ducking weather.

Periodic visits to relatives and friends on the Heron Islands always were a pleasure, during boyhood days. Captain Theodore Bailey, Papa's old fishing partner, lived on St. Margaret's Island and a weekend there was great fun. There was not only much river talk to listen to in the evening but during the day there was a chance to explore the island with cousin, Fred Cheseldine, a grandson of Captain Theodore.

The great blue heron is a tremendously interesting bird. Father Andrew White named these islands St. Clement's, St. Katherine's, and St. Margaret's, but called the group "The Heron Islands," because they seemed to be favorite nesting spots for these birds. Lord Baltimore, evidently under the impression that these were fine game birds, had a clause inserted in the early land deeds to protect herons and their nesting areas, along with certain other wild fowl. However, the heron's diet is largely fish and since it affects the taste of his flesh, he has always been a privileged bird and he is permitted to go his way in peace. The writer has been interested in the heron all of his life but it was not until the summer of 1963 that he was lucky enough to stumble on a herony and it was a thrilling sight. Over a hundred nests were seen high in the tall pines and oaks on about two acres of a densely wooded area, and though great care was exercised the parent birds soon discovered the intruder. Soon there was a screaming pandemonium of both old and young birds. Some of the baby birds were seized in the beak of a parent and flown out of the danger area. Some of the larger of the young encouraged by their parents succeeded in hopping or making short flights to higher and safer locations. One clumsy young fellow fell to the ground without injury, breaking his fall on projecting limbs on his descent.

Ordinarily when a heron is seen in flight he seems to be a slow, lumbering bird, incapable of speed. Here in alarm, the parent birds zoomed in like jet airplanes, displaying great speed and skill in avoiding the treetops and projecting limbs. Some sixty-two parent birds were counted at the herony and they seemed to fill the air over the area. Since the birds continued in a state of alarm though the observer remained motionless for a few moments, he withdrew hastily to put an end to the birds' anguish. Several shells of the birds' eggs were picked up in the hasty retreat and they were light blue in color and about the size of hen's eggs. It would seem that the heron, like his beloved river, is destined to go on until the end of time.

Another interesting bird often seen along the shores of the Potomac is the bittern. One of the most beautiful sights a boy can see in the spring is a mother bittern with her chicks. The chicks appear as bits of black fluff and are miniatures of the ordinary offspring of chickens. They pad about with their mother on the muddy shores and are as cunning as the bobwhite and her brood.

Today, the boys and girls on the river front continue to swim, crab, fish, and skate on the Potomac and its tributaries. Outboard motors have been substituted for sail on the small boats and a new sport, water skiing, has been added. The steamboat and the beautiful schooners, pungies, and bugeyes have disappeared, along with most of the big fishing nets. But there are countless wild fowl still on the river and an occasional school of porpoises is to be seen. The hated cornfields are scarce on the river front, and these few are harvested by machines. Hog killing is almost a thing of the past, milk is bought at the grocery store, the horse has been replaced by the automobile, and oil has been substituted for cordwood to provide heat. There is a good deal of racing with high-powered speedboats and duck shooting continues to be a popular sport. Marinas dot the inlets of the river, housing an amazing variety of pleasure boats, including a few sailboats. Perhaps the new things compensate for the old, and there is still much to observe and to learn on the river. More and more of the city people are taking up bits of land on the Potomac, for weekend retreats, to escape the hurly-burly of the crowded cities. So the Potomac will see more of youth on her shores and this is good for they will learn to love the river and help undo the damage done in the past.

LIFE ON THE POTOMAC RIVER

Chapter IX

THE FUTURE

It now appears at long last that a serious effort is being made to eliminate the pollution of the Potomac at Washington at Alexandria and in the upper reaches. Attention also is being given to deepening the channel to encourage more water borne commerce. One of the big problems has been the reluctance of the water shipping industry to haul freight to Washington and Alexandria and have to return with empty holds due to the lack of industries to provide freight for the return trip. This problem has been aggravated by the difficulty of navigating the shallow channel.

In recent years, through the efforts of the Metropolitan Washington Board of Trade, a few steamship lines have started running ocean-going pleasure cruises from Washington and a number of large tank ships have been bringing oil to both Washington and Alexandria. The Board also has made a great effort to attract light industry into the metropolitan area.

With the opening of Dulles International Airport a tremendous impetuous has been given to all of these activities. Presently the National Capital area accounts for 1 1/10% of the nation's population but it supplies almost 5% of the air traffic in the United States. This figure will increase considerably with the full utilization of the Dulles facilities. Directly northeast of Dulles more than 7,000 acres of land have been zoned for light industry and more of such zoning is under way.

Plans are under consideration to install a pipeline on the Virginia side of the Potomac to receive jet fuel shipments, via sea-going tankers, for Dulles, which is the largest jet installation in the United States. If this pipeline becomes a reality, it will justify deepening the channel to 36 feet to accommodate the tankers. As a result, other water borne commerce will follow.

The Dulles interceptor sewer should help to alleviate pollution along the Washington water front, particularly in the Georgetown area. This will lead to a growth in water sports and should attract many pleasure boats from the Bay and its other tributaries, that are now giving this area a wide berth because of the filth.

With this increased traffic it is not difficult to foresee the need for many more marinas and shipyards all along the Potomac. In addition, now that Maryland and Virginia have gotten together in the matter of commercial fisheries, with added emphasis on conservation, we may see a revitalization of the oyster, crab, and fish industries.

Also under consideration are plans for a free port at Dulles. If this project wins approval, many plants will be established to assemble components from abroad for distribution in this country and trans-shipment to other nations in this hemisphere.

With the five-day work week and increased vacation intervals being given by both government and business establishments there is more and more demand by city-dwellers for weekend homes, motels, parks, and amusement places along all of the waterways of the Chesapeake Bay. In some of the inlets of the Potomac practically all of the water front has been taken up and land prices have sky-rocketed in a few years. The increased sales of pleasure boats is almost unbelievable and the demand for more marinas and boatyards continues.

All of this will give impetus to the restoration of historic river cities, such as St. Mary's City, and other famous river landings on both sides of the Potomac. Undoubtedly, one of the most historic bits of land on the river is St. Clement's (Blackistone) Island, where Governor Leonard Calvert, acting under the instructions of his brother, Cecilius, Lord Baltimore, first proclaimed the doctrine of religious freedom in the New World at the landing of the Maryland colonists on March 25, 1634. This landing ranks in importance with Jamestown and Plymouth, and when the blessings that flow from religious toleration are counted, it can with justice be said that it was the most important.

After more than ten years of effort the St. Mary's County Historical Society is succeeding in its efforts to save the island from disappearing through erosion. In 1964, the state of Maryland spent $100,000 on erosion control on the south end of the island in the vicinity of the commemorative cross erected in 1934. This area now is under the jurisdiction of the Society and the Maryland Parks Commission. It is hoped that the remainder of the island soon will be placed under the supervision of the Parks Commission and declared a state park. In 1966 an additional $100,000 was spent by the state to provide erosion control on the east shore. Future plans include completion of erosion control on the west shore; establishment of ferry service with the mainland; erection of another wharf on the south end of the island; erection of an exhibits building; erection of a replica of the old lighthouse, where a perpetual

light will be maintained as a torch signifying the establishment of religious liberty; and other improvements.

The Potomac has a new presidential champion. On September 17, 1964, President
Lyndon B. Johnson told an election audience at Portland, Oregon, "A national program
of scenic parkways and scenic riverways is on the horizon. I hope, for instance, to
make the Potomac a conservation model for our metropolitan areas." Wolf Von Eckardt,
a Washington Post staff writer, in an article dated January 2, 1965, stated, "The
President's intense interest in the Potomac presents a bright hope for the continued
beauty and future livability of this capital and its burgeoning suburbs. Like no
other in the country, the future of Metropolitan Washington is linked with the future
of its great river. Its rapid growth is along both sides of the Potomac, upstream
and downstream."

There can be no mistake concerning the President's interest and championship of
the Potomac River, for in his "State of the Union Message" to the Congress on January
4, 1965, the President reiterated, "We hope to make the Potomac a model of beauty and
recreation for the entire country -- and preserve unspoiled stretches of some of our
waterways with a Wild Rivers bill." On February 8, 1965, the President in a special
message to the Congress, placed the Potomac River program under the jurisdiction of
Secretary of the Interior, Stewart L. Udall.

Here now is high hope for the future of our great river. There is no doubt that
President Johnson's action is one that would have the hearty approval of President
Washington, who truly loved its magnificent sweep and all of its life sustaining qual-
ities. After 200 years the Potomac is again in good hands.

Actually on the surface the Potomac has changed little over the years. Man-made
things along her shores come and go and the activities of men on her surface wax and
wane. She suffers pollution in her upper reaches, her channel has been shallowed and
her fishes and wild fowl have been reduced, but now a great leader who realizes her
worth has come to the fore and sets about to undo the things that thoughtless men
have done in the past. Through it all the Potomac's ebb and flood goes on and on,
sustaining life, changing a shore line here and there, at times calm, at others turbulent, but ever interesting, challenging, beautiful.

So, flow on great river, for our children and for our children's children. May
the new generations love you even more than those of the past.

POTOMAC RIVER SAILING CRAFT

(Late 1800's and early 1900's)

Crabbing Skiffs

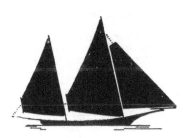

Log Canoe   Pilot Boat   Skipjack

(Off the Virginia Capes)

Sloop   Bugeye   Schooner

Ram   Pungy   3-Masted Schooner

Drawings: Frederick Tilp   Photographed by H. W. Piper

POTOMAC RIVER SAILING VESSEL

Photo: Robert H. Burgess

Three-Masted Schooner, "Josephine Wimsatt," Anchored
in Canton Hollow, Baltimore, June 24, 1936

APPENDIX "A"

Name of Vessel	Ship #	Ton-nage	Type	Length	Year Built	Where Built
Ada	106187	16	Schooner	50.9	1883	Prince George's Co., Md.
Ada Ballenger	107410	14	Schooner	49.2	1898	Alexandria, Va.
Ada Wood	71	10	Sloop	34	1856	-
Addie	106603	11	Sloop	37	1888	Westmoreland Co., Va.
Addie	106516	8	Bugeye	46	1884	Fairmount, Md.
Admiral Dewey	107389	8	Sloop	41.2	1898	Crisfield, Md.
A. H. Quinby	105669	68	Schooner	78	1887	Wilmington, Del.
A. J. Lawson	106217	24	Bugeye	57	1883	Pocomoke City, Md.
A. J. Lewis	202518	-	Flattie	41.5	1905	Hopkins, Va.
Alabama	201431	6	Schooner	39	1904	Hunting Creek, Va.
Alice	209262	8	Schooner	38	1906	Hunting Creek, Va.
Altrurian	107127	10	Sloop-yacht	39.5	1894	Washington, D. C.
Amanda F. Lewis	106304	48	Pungy	67	1884	Madison, Md.
Anna M. Estell	106157	134	Schooner	98	1883	Stafford Co., Va.
Annette	107213	9	Schooner	46.2	1895	Washington, D. C.
Annie	1993	6	Bugeye	39.8	1871	Somerset Co., Md.
Annie Crosswell	-	-	Schooner	-	-	-
Annie Gibson	1429	16	Schooner	47.6	1868	Washington, D. C.
Annie L	-	-	Schooner	-	c.1890	White's Neck Creek, Md.
Annie Lee	-	-	-	-	-	-
Annie E. Proctor	106815	7	*Sloop	26.2	1891	Washington, D. C.
Annie N. Mason	1554	33	Schooner	78.5	1868	Washington, D. C.
Asp	-	-	Sloop	-	c.1812	-
Avalon	106861	22	Bugeye	59	1891	Pocomoke City, Md.
B. H. Lambert, Jr.	2773	15	Sloop	41.5	1871	Alexandria, Va.
Bachelor	-	-	Schooner	-	-	-
Becky	-	-	Schooner	-	-	-
Belle	3408	17	*Sloop	58.6	1880	Washington, D. C.
Belmont	3860	34	Schooner	70	1900	Occoquan, Va.
Bertha May	3586	9	*Schooner	35.4	1893	Occoquan, Va.
Bessie Ford	3304	26	Bugeye	59	1884	Somerset Co., Md.
Bessie Jones	-	-	Schooner	-	-	-
Bessie Reed	3352	28	Schooner	59.6	1886	St. Michaels, Md.
Betty Smith	-	-	Flattie	-	-	-
Billy Buck	3509	6	*Sloop	32.2	1891	Occoquan, Va.
Blue Wing	3596	-	Bugeye	62	1893	Solomons Island, Md.
Buckshot	3444	20	Sloop	66	1886	Occoquan, Va.

RIVER SAILING VESSELS

Master**	Home Port or Sailed From	Remarks
-	Richmond, Va.	Abandoned at Richmond 4-8-1922.
-	Alexandria, Va.	
Bernard Thompson	St. George's Island, Md.	
-	Tappahannock, Va.	
Tom Bland	St. George's Island, Md.	Built by S. Parks.
Joe Ed Trice	St. George's Island, Md.	
Frank Twilley	St. George's Island, Md.	
Grude Clark	St. George's Island, Md.	
William Cullison	Canoe Neck Creek, Md.	Rebuilt by Wm. Thompson at Ewell's Boat Yard in Bretton Bay and name changed to "Mildred" about 1912.
Randolph Thomas	St. George's Island, Md.	Square sail.
Tilton Hayden	Canoe Neck Creek, Md.	Sharp sail bateau (sloop rig).
-	Crisfield, Md.	
-	Crisfield, Md.	
-	Baltimore, Md.	
Jerry Gibson	Canoe Neck Creek, Md.	Operating with shrimp fleet in Florida in 1948. August 10, 1948, Hatian registry and flag. Converted to a barge.
Gus Rice	Coan River, Va.	
-	Baltimore, Md.	
-	Washington, D. C.	
Wes. Chesser, Jr.	St. George's Island, Md.	
Sol Russell	Chaptico, Md.	
John Robey	Alexandria, Va.	
Freeman Cheseldine	White's Neck Creek, Md.	Built by John Cheseldine.
George Columbus (Lum) Bailey	White's Neck Creek, Md.	
-	Washington, D. C.	
-	Alexandria, Va.	
J. B. Sigourney	Washington, D. C.	Three gun sloop of war -- owned by U. S. Government. Converted to a barge.
John W. Henderson	St. George's Island, Md.	
Ned Henderson	St. George's Island, Md.	
Charles Henderson	St. George's Island, Md.	
-	Alexandria, Va.	
Henry Neitzey	Washington, D. C.	
John Owens	Canoe Neck Creek, Md.	Round stern.
-	Washington, D. C.	
-	Alexandria, Va.	
-	Alexandria, Va.	
Burton Graham	St. George's Island, Md.	Built by E. S. Wiley.
Benjamin Foxwell	-	Potomac River Police Boat.
Freeman Cheseldine	White's Neck Creek, Md.	Changed to gasoline screw in 1924 -- abandoned 4-23-1941.
Andrew J. Cheseldine		
Golden Thompson	St. Patrick's Creek, Md.	Sharp sail bateau.
-	Alexandria, Va.	
-	-	Built by M. M. Davis. Abandoned in Canoe Neck Creek c. 1954.
-	Alexandria, Va.	

APPENDIX "A"

Name of Vessel	Ship #	Ton-nage	Type	Length	Year Built	Where Built
Buena Vista	-	-	Schooner	-	-	-
Capitol	4404	27	Pungy	50	1854	Somerset Co., Md.
Carl Castillo	127460	8	Sloop	42	1897	St. Patrick's Creek, Md.
Carrie	125856	-	Bugeye	52	1879	Solomons Island, Md.
Catherine	-	35	Sloop	-	c.1816	
Cavalier	126464	8	Sloop	38	1887	Northumberland Co., Va.
Cecilia	126175	6	Sloop	31	1883	Washington, D. C.
Celeste	26881	38	Schooner	61.5	1892	Prince George's Co., Md.
Centennial	125692	9	Bugeye	51.5	1878	Crisfield, Md.
Charles Lewis	125058	22	Schooner	47.2	1872	Accotink, Va.
Chas. H. Daiger	125399	7	Schooner	48	1875	Dorchester Co., Md.
Col. R. Johnson	126410	10	Bugeye	56	1886	Solomons Island, Md.
Colton						
Columbia F. C.	125285	49	Schooner	79	1874	Mundy Point, Va.
Clara May	125778	7	Sloop	29.7	1879	West Creek, N. J.
Columbia	126986	6	Sloop	31.4	1888	Coan River, Va.
Columbia	127572	6	Sloop	39.3	1901	Hunting Creek, Va.
Comet	126894	12	*Sloop	38.6	1892	Washington, D. C.
Commerce			Schooner	-	c.1834	-
Copia	125820	11	Schooner	35.6	1880	Somerset, Mass.
Cora L. McKenney	125535	21	Schooner	50.8	1875	Alexandria, Va.
C. R. Lewis	126450	10	Bugeye	55	1887	Somerset Co., Md.
Daisie	95291	17	Schooner	63.5	1874	Rocky Hill, Conn.
Daisy	157250	13	Sloop	50	1887	Alexandria, Va.
Daisy	157332	5	Sloop	31	1891	Alexandria, Va.
Daniel	157608	60	*Schooner	64	1901	Alexandria, Va.
Daniel J. Ballard	6504	16	Pungy	46	1867	St. George's Island, Md.
Dash	-	-	Sloop	-	c.1828	-
Dashaway	157218	16	Schooner	51.6	1883	Washington, D. C.
Defence	-	-		-	c.1770	-
Defy	-	-	Pungy	-	-	-
Delight	-	-	Sloop	-	c.1836	-
Dirigo	6809	12	Schooner	43.5	1873	Northumberland Co., Va.
Dolphin	-	-	Pungy	-	-	-
Dove	-	-	Sloop	-	c.1827	-

Master**	Home Port or Sailed From	Remarks
William Fallon	-	
Robert Cheseldine	White's Neck Creek, Md.	Wrecked at Sandy Point, Md. 10-5-1896.
John Gandy	Crisfield, Md.	Probably built by "Rome" or Wm. Thompson. Abandoned at Crisfield 11-23-1909.
-	-	Built by J. T. Marsh.
William Lucas	Georgetown, D. C.	
-	Tappahannock, Va.	
-	Annapolis, Md.	
-	Norfolk, Va.	Changed to auxiliary gasoline screw in 1906.
Henry Dickens	St. George's Island, Md.	Square sail -- owned by Adams Bros., St. George's Island.
-	Alexandria, Va.	
Joe Ed Trice	St. George's Island, Md.	
Taylor Green	St. Patrick's Creek, Md.	Still afloat -- docked at Annapolis, Md. 1965.
John H. Long	-	
John Joe Gibson	Canoe Neck Creek, Md.	
George Duncan	Mundy Point, Va.	—(Named for Columbia Fishing Club.
Frank Twilley, Sr.	St. George's Island, Md.	(Sold in Cuba in 1948.
-	Alexandria, Va.	
-	Crisfield, Md.	
-	Washington, D. C.	
- Lucas	Georgetown, D. C.	
Henry Stevens	St. George's Island, Md.	
-	Alexandria, Va.	
Joe Ed Trice	St. George's Island, Md.	Built by W. Lawrence.
George Dickens	St. George's Island, Md.	
H. Chesser	St. George's Island, Md.	
A. E. Beitzell	Canoe Neck Creek, Md.	Originally named "Henry B. Anthony" and 52.5' in length. Rebuilt at Wilmington, Del. in 1883 and lengthened to 63.5' and capacity increased to 34 tons. Abandoned at Norfolk, Va., on 10-6-1914.
-	Alexandria, Va.	
-	Alexandria, Va.	
-	Alexandria, Va.	
Charles Chesser	St. George's Island, Md.	Owned by George Duncan, Yeocomico River, Va.
- Lucas	Georgetown, D. C.	
-	Washington, D. C.	
Capt. Nicholson	St. Mary's River, Md.	Fought in Revolutionary War.
Samuel Trader	St. George's Island, Md.	
- Lucas	Georgetown, D. C.	
-	Norfolk, Va.	
Josiah Beitzell	Canoe Neck Creek, Md.	
John Palmer	St. Patrick's Creek, Md.	
John William Palmer	St. Patrick's Creek, Md.	
- Lucas	Georgetown, D. C.	

142

APPENDIX "A"

Name of Vessel	Ship #	Ton-nage	Type	Length	Year Built	Where Built
Dove	6387	17	Pungy	44.6	1856	Hunting Creek, Va.
Duck	157313	9	*Sloop	37.7	1889	Washington, D. C.
E. P. Evans	135539	37	Schooner	62.5	1881	Pungoteague, Va.
Eagle	-	-	Ship	-	c.1827	-
Earl Biscoe	135982	41	Schooner	79.5	1888	Washington, D. C.
Edith M.	135959	10	Bugeye	55.10	1875	St. Peter's, Md.
Edith Marcy	136497	27	Bugeye	69	1895	Solomons Island, Md.
Edith Muir	136403	13	Bugeye	54	1893	St. Peter's, Md.
Edna & Nellie	136085	10	Bugeye	51	1889	Pocomoke City, Md.
Edward Dean	135711	19	Schooner	46.2	1883	Alexandria, Va.
Edna J. Cox	136644	6	Skipjack	37.4	1897	Fairmount, Md.
Edwin H. Stuart	135052	22	Schooner	51.5	1874	Northumberland Co., Va.
Edwin J. Palmer	7030	197	Schooner	102	1864	Baltimore, Md.
Elenora Russell	136042	16	Bugeye	60	1889	Solomons Island, Md.
Elexena	8378	21	Schooner	48.3	1846	Northumberland Co., Va.
Eliza Ann	-	30	Schooner	-	c.1816	-
Elizabeth Clarke	209891	38	Schooner	69.3	1912	Washington, D. C.
Ella Covington	136184	16	Bugeye	55	1891	Currioman, Va.
Ella F. Cripps	136851	47	Schooner	69.2	1900	St. Michaels, Md.
Ella G. Pride	-	29	Bugeye	67.5	1892	Pocomoke City, Md.
Ella Hill	136326	11	Schooner	47.4	1892	Occoquan, Va.
Elsie May	207848	6	Skipjack	35.8	1910	St. George's Island, Md.
Emma	135525	8	Sloop	33.4	1880	Washington, D. C.
Emma Berry	135330	9	Pungy	34.9	1876	St. George's Island, Md.
Emma Grant	136080	16	*Sloop	50.4	1886	Washington, D. C.

Master**	Home Port or Sailed From	Remarks
Alec Marmaduke	St. George's Island, Md.	
William Finn	St. George's Island, Md.	
Kenelm Cheseldine	White's Neck Creek, Md.	
John Cheseldine	White's Neck Creek, Md.	
Ned Russell	White's Neck Creek, Md.	
Ned Hayden	Canoe Neck·Creek, Md.	
-	Washington, D. C.	
Frank Russell	Canoe Neck Creek, Md.	Dismantled and converted
Wes Chesser	St. George's Island, Md.	to a barge in Philadelphia
Richard Chesser		in the 90's.
Augustus Lucas	Georgetown, D. C.	Cleared for Amsterdam 8-16-1827.
-	Washington, D. C.	
George M. Thomas	St. George's Island, Md.	
Richard Chesser	St. George's Island, Md.	Built by M. M. Davis. Rig
John Bryant	St. Patrick's Creek, Md.	changed to oil screw. Still afloat 11-24-1964.
George W. Thomas	St. George's Island, Md.	Changed to gas screw 1-12-1924.
George E. Thomas	St. George's Island, Md.	Abandoned at Crisfield, Md.
Joseph Henderson	St. George's Island, Md.	7-27-1936.
J. Foster Thomas	St. George's Island, Md.	
Frank Twilley, Sr.	St. George's Island, Md.	
TLN & Wm. J. E. Lawrence	Canoe Neck Creek, Md.	
John Beitzell	Canoe Neck Creek, Md.	Destroyed by fire in Monroe's
George Gibson	White's Neck Creek, Md.	Creek, Va. 9-5-1897.
Joseph A. Lawrence	St. Patrick's Creek, Md.	
Ned Hayden	Canoe Neck Creek, Md.	
Augustus Dean	Alexandria, Va.	
Willie Twilley	St. George's Island, Md.	Abandoned in St. George's Creek.
G. Edward Thomas	St. George's Island, Md.	
-	Norfolk, Va.	
John Palmer	St. Patrick's Creek, Md.	Sailed the West Indies route. Wrecked-Chincoteague, 8-7-1886.
Jeb Stuart Russell	Canoe Neck Creek, Md.	Changed to gasoline screw
Richard (Dick) Chesser	St. George's Island, Md.	10-26-1928. Abandoned at
William J. Stanford	St. Patrick's Creek, Md.	Philadelphia 7-30-1934.
-	Tappahannock, Va.	
William Lucas	Georgetown, D. C.	
-	Washington, D. C.	
-	Crisfield, Md.	Abandoned at Baltimore 10-14-1955.
James Sommers	Baltimore, Md.	Abandoned in Back Creek, Annapolis, Md., in 1955.
Burton Graham	St. George's Island, Md.	
-	Alexandria, Va.	
Clint Henderson	St. George's Island, Md.	Built by Richard L. Thompson.
Bernard Thompson	St. George's Island, Md.	
-	Washington, D. C.	
Thomas L. Crowder	St. George's Island, Md.	Built by Capt. Tom Crowder.
E. Chesser	St. George's Island, Md.	Wrecked 4-15-1904 in the
William O. Chesser	St. George's Island, Md.	Tappahannock River, Va.
-	Washington, D. C.	

144

APPENDIX "A"

Name of Vessel	Ship #	Ton-nage	Type	Length	Year Built	Where Built
Emma R. Faunce	136996	13	Schooner	42.7	1902	St. Patrick's Creek, Md.
Emma V. Wills	135741	46	Schooner	64.9	1883	St. Michaels, Md.
Emmett Arthur	135282	22	Sloop	50	1877	Bayport, N. Y.
Enola	8508	27	Sloop	42	1869	West Haven, Conn.
Enquire	136090	14	Sloop	44	1889	Washington, D. C.
Ethel	135822	7	Sloop	40.8	1884	Accomack Co, Va.
Ethel Vail	201810	18	Bugeye	54	1905	Solomons Island, Md. Md.
Etta	135144	31	Schooner	62.5	1825	St. Michaels, Md.
Eula K	137006	13	Schooner	50	1902	Elizabeth City, N. C.
Eunice S	136635	5	Skipjack	35.7	1897	Hopewell, Md.
Eva Clarence	135952	10	Bugeye	50	1887	Somerset Co., Md.
Eva Lee	136187	6	Sloop	31.2	1889	Georgetown, D. C.
Fair Maid	-	-	Pilot Boat	-	c.1770	-
Fairplay	9243	9	Sloop	34.7	1863	Washington, D. C.
Fairview	140385	8	Schooner	-	1879	Somerset Co., Md.
Fannie	211514	23	Schooner	58.2	1900	Georgetown, D. C.
Fanny Kemp	-	-	-	-	-	-
Fanny Shepherd	120382	13	Sloop	36.6	1879	St. Mary's Co., Md.
Federal Hill	9679	72	Schooner	84.1	1856	Baltimore, Md.
Father & Sons	9942	24	Schooner	45.9	1870	Newtown, Md.
Five Brothers	120283	12	Schooner	45.4	1877	Georgetown, D. C.
Five Sisters	120119	34	Schooner	81.8	1872	Occoquan, Va.
Five Sisters	-	-	Flattie	-	-	White's Neck Creek, Md.
Five Sisters	-	-	Double Ender	-	-	-
Five Sons	212732	20	Sloop	46.5	1914	Hunting Creek, Va.
Flora	120599	14	Pungy	40	1884	Alexandria, Va.
Florence Northam	120803	26	Bugeye	65	1890	Solomons Island, Md.
Four Sisters	120832	14	*Sloop	38.8	1891	Washington, D. C.
Fox	9215	-	Pungy	-	c.1845	-

Master**	Home Port or Sailed From	Remarks
Jacob Faunce	St. Patrick's Creek, Md.	Probably built by Willie Thompson. Abandoned at Annapolis, Md. 9-20-1926.
Wes Chesser, Jr.	St. George's Island, Md.	Owned by Richard Chesser.
Tilton Hayden	Bretton Bay, Md.	Owned by Henry Wehrheim.
James Bailey	River Springs, Md.	Foundered in Bretton Bay in 1933 hurricane.
Ned Hayden	Canoe Neck Creek, Md.	Foundered in Canoe Neck Creek about 1917.
-	Washington, D. C.	
Ned Hayden	Canoe Neck Creek, Md.	
George W. Chesser	St. George's Island, Md.	Built by M. M. (Cell) Davis.
Richard Chesser	St. George's Island, Md.	Still afloat 2-11-1964.
George W. Thomas	St. George's Island, Md.	
Richard Chesser	St. George's Island, Md.	
Billy Sinclair	St. George's Island, Md.	
Millard Twilley	St. George's Island, Md.	
Henry Stewart	St. Patrick's Creek, Md.	Built by L. Shores.
-	Washington, D. C.	
William Fenwick	St. Mary's River, Md.	Used in Revolutionary War -- 1783.
-	Washington, D. C.	
John Beitzell	Canoe Neck Creek, Md.	Owner unknown.
-	Alexandria, Virginia	
Bernard Ellis	St. Patrick's Creek, Md.	
Kenelm Cheseldine	White's Neck Creek, Md.	Built by Kenelm Cheseldine.
John Joe Gibson	Canoe Neck Creek, Md.	Abandoned at Crisfield, Md.
John H. Long	St. Mary's Co., Md.	6-17-1914.
Z. Taylor Hayden	Alexandria, Va.	
John Bryant	Alexandria, Va.	
James H. Cheseldine	River Springs, Md.	
Charles E. Cheseldine	River Springs, Md.	
George W. Ellis	Colton's Point, Md.	
William J. Stanford	Colonial Beach, Va.	Abandoned Monroe Cr., Va. 1941.
Thomas H. Milburn	Bretton Bay, Md.	Built in Bretton Bay. Burned
A. C. Tennesson &		and abandoned at Alexandria,
R. K. Forrest	Bretton Bay, Md.	Va. on 6-30-1915.
Benjamin Foxwell	Bretton Bay, Md.	
Massena Kendrich	Nanjemoy, Charles Co., Md.	
Richard A. Wright	Pisgah, Charles Co., Md.	
Thomas P. Simms	Ironsides, Charles Co., Md.	
-	Washington, D. C.	
-	Alexandria, Va.	
John Harden	St. Patrick's Creek, Md.	Built by Douglas Goode.
Samuel M. Bailey	White's Neck Creek, Md.	
-	Baltimore, Md.	
Will Taylor	St. George's Island, Md.	Owned by Dick Courtney, St. George's Island, Md.
Charles O. Chesser	St. George's Island, Md.	Built by M. M. Davis. Dismantled 3-21-1958. Was a
William Simpkins	St. George's Island, Md.	nuisance in the harbor at
Shill Simpkins	St. George's Island, Md.	Nassau, Bahamas.
-	Washington, D. C.	
Joe Ed Trice	St. George's Island, Md.	

APPENDIX "A"

Name of Vessel	Ship #	Tonnage	Type		Year Built	Where Built
Frances Miller	120643	59	Schooner	79	1886	Washington, D. C.
Francis J. Ruth	120011	60	Pungy	73	1871	Dorchester Co., Md.
French Smoot	120905	11	Schooner	44	1892	Alexandria, Va.
G. A. Kirwan	85735	45	Pungy	62	1882	Madison, Md.
General Hancock	10849	11	Sloop	42.3	1867	-
George	215645	14	*Schooner	50.9	1917	Alexandria, Va.
George B. Faunce	85983	27	Bugeye	60.7	1887	Solomons Island, Md.
George H. Bunker	85813	22	Bugeye	56.5	1883	Pocomoke City, Md.
George T. Ash	10990	51	Schooner	72.2	1868	Baltimore, Md.
Gilman Dove	86123	53	Schooner	71.4	1890	Occoquan, Va.
Gracie Lee	86226	6	Sloop	35.7	1892	Onacock, Va.
Grape Shot	86067	19	Sloop	66.4	1886	Washington, D. C.
Gussie C	200387	21	Pungy	55	1903	Fairmount, Md.
Gypsy	86139	16	*Sloop	48.6	1891	Washington, D. C.
Hallie K	96131	10	Bugeye	53	1891	Solomons Island, Md.
H. Day	-	-	Sloop	-	-	-
Harp	96390	39	Schooner	67.5	1895	Kinsale, Va.
Harry & Charlie	95905	34	Schooner	71.3	1887	Washington, D. C.
Harvester	11920	41	Schooner	67	1860	Talbot Co., Md.
Hazeline	95892	9	Bugeye	51.4	1886	Somerset Co., Md.
Hector	96034	13	Sloop	42.4	1885	Washington, D. C.
Henry and Rebecca	-	54	Schooner	56.1	1816	St. Mary's Co., Md. (Maiden Bower Creek)
Henry Disston	95644	41	Schooner	73	1881	Portsmouth, Va.
Hester A. Waters	95835	97	Schooner	91.6	1884	Pocomoke, Md.
Hiawatha	95824	8	Bugeye	37	1884	Pocomoke, Md.
Hope	-	-	Sloop	-	c.1785	-
Horn Point	95618	12	Sloop	38.3	1880	Annapolis, Md.

Master**	Home Port or Sailed From	Remarks
- Shill Simpkins Clarence Biscoe	Washington, D. C. St. George's Island, Md. St. Mary's River, Md.	Second largest pungy on the Bay. Foundered at Millstone Landing, Patuxent River, in 1933.
- Charles Chesser	Norfolk, Va. St. George's Island, Md.	Owned by - Webster of Baltimore, Md.
Walter Chesser - Jacob R. Faunce John Beitzell Freeman Cheseldine Matt Bailey	St. George's Island, Md. Alexandria, Va. St. Patrick's Creek, Md. Canoe Neck Creek, Md. White's Neck Creek, Md. White's Neck Creek, Md.	Converted yacht. Built by J. T. Marsh. Changed to gasoline screw 3-16-1911. Abandoned at Beaufort, N. C. on 7-6-1920.
Joe Ed Trice John J. Allston James S. Saunders - Burton Graham -	St. George's Island, Md. St. Mary's River, Md. St. Mary's River, Md. Alexandria, Va. St. George's Island, Md. Washington, D. C.	Wrecked and abandoned at Washington, D. C. on 6-13-1899. Abandoned Lower Machodoc Creek, Va. in 1932.
Burton Graham George W. Ellis Paul Ellis Cyrus Ellis Havie Bannigan	St. George's Island, Md. Georgetown, D. C. River Springs, Md. River Springs, Md. River Springs, Md. River Springs, Md.	Center board. Built by J. T. Marsh. Foundered 30 miles N. E. Jupiter Light, Florida on 12-13-1935.
Henry Neitzey George H. Sheldon	Washington, D. C. Alexandria, Va.	Abandoned at Alexandria, Va. 4-15-1901, because of decayed condition (probably worms in bottom).
- Andrew Jackson Cheseldine George Cheseldine Josiah Beitzell Samuel P. Brown Josiah Beitzell	Washington, D. C. White's Neck Creek, Md. White's Neck Creek, Md. Fleet's Bay, Va. Fleet's Bay, Va. Canoe Neck Creek, Md.	Rebuilt in 1882 and renamed the "Rosa Beitzell."
George Dickens - - Ed Cox H. Webster Foxwell	St. George's Island, Md. Georgetown, D. C. Wicomico River, Md. Colonial Beach, Va. Bretton Bay, Md.	Square sail. Owned by Adams Bros., St. George's Island. Built for Philip Turner, Henry M. Clements, and George Morgan. Abandoned in 1945. Owners - Francis E. and Hester A. Waters. Last record at Miami, Florida, on 8-13-1945. Probably sold down in the West Indies.
Thomas Morris Luke Clark	Canoe Neck Creek, Md. St. Patrick's Creek, Md.	Built by E. J. Tull.
Lawrence Walter Bernard Ellis Billy Ellis Kenelm Cheseldine	St. Mary's Co., Md. White's Neck Creek, Md. White's Neck Creek, Md. White's Neck Creek, Md.	In service in 1790.

APPENDIX "A"

Name of Vessel	Ship #	Ton- nage	Type	Length	Year Built	Where Built
Humming Bird	11921	12	Pungy	41	c.1867	St. George's Island, Md.
Infant	-	18	Sloop	50.7	1888	Washington, D. C.
Isaac Solomon	100077	27	Pungy	57	1872	Solomons Island, Md.
Island Belle	100436	10	*Sloop	50.7	1888	Washington, D. C.
Iva	206813	5	Sloop	35.8	1902	Hunting Creek, Va.
I. Z. Graves	100437	20	Schooner	50	1888	Mundy's Point, Va.
J. J. Hogan	-	-	Flattie	-	-	St. Patrick's Creek, Md.
J. M. (Jim) Jones	76543	8	Bugeye	43	1884	Somerset Co., Md.
J. P. Robinson	76291	53	Schooner	71	1882	Alexandria, Va.
J. R. Dixon	76098	15	Schooner	45.2	1879	Somerset Co., Md.
J. S. Smith	75415	30	Pungy	55	1872	Somerset Co., Md.
J. W. Knowles	77514	57	Schooner	83	1901	Sharpstown, Md.
J. W. Padgett	76670	8	Skipjack	49	1883	St. George's Island, Md.
Jack Bowling	77047	10	*Sloop	33.2	1892	Washington, D. C.
Jacob D. Faunce	75879	17	Schooner	42.4	1876	Washington, D. C.
James	-	20	Schooner	-	c.1814	-
James A. Whiting	75326	35	Pungy	61	1871	Somerset Co., Md.
James Boyce, Jr.	76375	730	Schooner	156.3	1882	Alexandria, Va.
James H. Beach	77306	23	Schooner	53	1898	Alexandria, Va.
Jane Wright	-		Sloop	-	c.1860	-
Jannett	77366	8	Sloop	38	1898	Leonardtown, Md.
Jeannette	77033	18	*Sloop	46.3	1886	Washington, D. C.
Jesse J. Parks	13919	30	Pungy	55.3	1866	Somerset Co., Md.
John Bush	211517	26	Schooner	67.5	1890	Alexandria, Va.
John Fisher	211516	30	*Schooner	75	1891	Alexandria, Va.
John Henry	77276	7	Pungy	41.6	1897	Fishing Creek, Md.
John Neely	75945	10	Schooner	37.8	1877	Hunting Creek, Va.
John Taylor	208888	57	*Schooner	75	1911	Alexandria, Va.
John S. Harvey	77330	5	Skipjack	34.5	1898	Guilford, Va.
Julia & Annie	75164	42	Pungy	64.5	1869	Talbot Co., Md.
John Tolbert	77046	8	*Sloop	29.8	1891	Washington, D. C.
John Williams	75892	9	Sloop	34.7	1876	St. Mary's Co., Md.
Josephine Wimsatt	92364	149	Schooner	95	1891	Milford, Del.

APPENDIX "A"

Master**	Home Port or Sailed From	Remarks
George Pearson	St. George's Island, Md.	Built by Richard Ball.
-	Washington, D. C.	
Grude Clark	St. George's Island, Md.	
-	Washington, D. C.	
-	Crisfield, Md.	
Tyler Chesser	St. George's Island, Md.	Owned by Tyler Chesser.
Wes Chesser, Jr.	St. George's Island, Md.	
Charles A. (Sandy) Ellis	St. Patrick's Creek, Md.	Built by Wm. Thompson.
Richard Chesser	St. George's Island, Md.	Built by J. M. Jones.
-	Alexandria, Va.	
John Joe Gibson	Canoe Neck Creek, Md.	Rig changed to gasoline screw
Havie Banagan	River Springs, Md.	on 5-8-1924 and on 11-30-1925 rig changed back to sail. Foundered at the mouth of Wicomico River on 7-30-1936.
Howard J. Chesser	St. George's Island, Md.	
Ned Hayden	Canoe Neck Creek, Md.	Owned by Ned Hayden. Abandoned at Humphrey's Shipyard, Weems, Md. in 1935.
Howard Hayden	Canoe Neck Creek, Md.	
R. T. Ball	St. Mary's Co., Md.	Built by Richard Ball-2 masts.
S. D. Lankford	Northampton Co., Va.	Abandoned at Cape Charles, Va. 3-15-1913.
-	Washington, D. C.	
Jacob Faunce	St. Patrick's Creek, Md.	
William Lucas	Georgetown, D. C.	
John W. Henderson	St. George's Island, Md.	Owned by Andrew Lewis, Coan
Charles Chesser	St. George's Island, Md.	River, Va.
-	Perth Amboy, N. J.	
-	Crisfield, Md.	
John Lawrence	St. Patrick's Creek, Md.	Burned and scuttled by U. S. Navy off Smith's Island in 1861.
D. B. Robertson	Palmer's, Va.	Converted to pleasure yacht 5-3-1919.
George Cumberland	Washington, D. C.	
William Lawrence	Canoe Neck Creek, Md.	Foundered in Canoe Neck Creek
Ernest Beitzell	Canoe Neck Creek, Md.	in 1894.
-	Crisfield, Md.	
-	Crisfield, Md.	
Lum Downey	St. George's Island, Md.	
-	Onacock, Va.	
-	Alexandria, Va.	Rebuilt in 1911.
Henson Blackwell	St. George's Island, Md.	
Clarence Biscoe	St. Mary's River, Md.	
-	Annapolis, Md.	
-	Washington, D. C.	
Kenelm Cheseldine	White's Neck Creek, Md.	Built by Kenelm Cheseldine.
Taylor Green	St. Patrick's Creek, Md.	Abandoned at Norfolk, Va. on
Edward Lucas	St. Patrick's Creek, Md.	6-30-1917.
George F. Owens	River Springs, Md.	
Joseph Hayden	-	
L. R. Cole	-	
-	Alexandria, Va.	Original name "May and Anna Beswick" - 3-masts. Sold to British and renamed "Ruby W." Wrecked off Texas coast 8-26-45.

150

APPENDIX "A"

Name of Vessel	Ship #	Ton-nage	Type	Length	Year Built	Where Built
Joseph T. Brenan	76422	27	Schooner	54	1883	Madison, Md.
Kate	14001	19	Schooner	51.5	1853	Occoquan, Va.
Katy Hines	-	-	Schooner	-	-	-
Klondike	211515	18	*Schooner	60.6	1901	Alexandria, Va.
L. B. Platt	15944	39	Schooner	61.6	1873	Dorchester Co., Md.
L. E. Coulbourn	40571	20	Bugeye	59	1882	Crisfield, Md.
Lady Evans	140385	7	Bugeye	45.3	1897	Somerset Co., Md.
Laura	141193	15	*Schooner	44.4	1892	Washington, D. C.
Laura G. Walker	-	-	Flattie	-	-	-
LeDroit	140941	12	Sloop	50.5	1885	Washington, D. C.
Lena	40797	8	Bugeye	49.3	1885	Somerset Co., Md.
Lewis C. Worrell	207552	55	Schooner	74	1910	Compton, Md.
Lillie F. Evans	200777	8	Sloop	47	1904	Alexandria, Va.
Lilly	141168	39	*Schooner	69.4	1891	Alexandria, Va.
Lily of the Valley	140947	12	Sloop	50.4	1888	Greenback, Va.
Little Dorritt	15540	10	Schooner	40.7	1868	Hampton, N. H.
Lively	-	10	Sloop	-	c.1820	
Lizzie Burt	15859	28	Schooner	55	1872	Dividing Creek, N. J.
Lizzie D. Egerton	15685	34	Schooner	65.5	1870	St. Mary's Co., Md.
Lizzie Dodge	-	-	Sloop	-	c.1860	-
Lizzie J. Cox	202376	23	Bugeye	67.6	1905	Fishing Island, Md.
Lizzie Lane	15745	10	Sloop	36.5	1874	Sayville, N. Y.
Lola Taylor	140844	10	Bugeye	56	1886	Westmoreland Co., Va.
Loon	14516	83	Schooner	90	1873	Norwalk, Conn.
Lottie L. Thomas	140621	24	Bugeye	65.6	1883	Madison, Md.
Lottie M	141810	6	Sloop	30.6	1902	River Springs, Md.
Louise Travers	141457	32	Bugeye	70	1896	Solomons Island, Md.
Lucy J. Stewart	15467	27	Pungy	51.6	1869	Somerset Co., Md.

APPENDIX "A"

Master**	Home Port or Sailed From	Remarks
Jeb Stuart Russell	Canoe Neck Creek, Md.	Changed to gasoline screw 3-3-1927. Destroyed by fire 1-19-1929 at Matts Landing, Maurice River, N. J.
Robert P. Bailey &	White's Neck Creek, Md.	
Samuel N. Bailey	White's Neck Creek, Md.	
-	Alexandria, Va.	
Thomas Howard	-	Potomac River Police Boat, Ollie Crowder - Mate.
-	Alexandria, Va.	
Andrew Jackson	White's Neck Creek, Md.	Abandoned at Baltimore, Md. on 4-17-1930.
Cheseldine		
Charles Chesser	St. George's Island, Md.	
George W. Thomas	St. George's Island, Md.	
John Beitzell	Fleet's Bay, Va.	Owned by Calvin Disharvon, Chance, Md. Abandoned at Crisfield, Md. on 2-10-1913.
-	Washington, D. C.	
Kenelm Cheseldine	White's Neck Creek, Md.	Rebuilt by Kenelm Cheseldine.
-	Washington, D. C.	
Watt Chesser	St. George's Island, Md.	Rebuilt.
James O. Carter	Washington, D. C.	Built by Ewell or Wehrheim in Bretton Bay. Abandoned at Washington, D. C. May, 1944.
-	Tappahannock, Va.	
-	Tappahannock, Va.	
-	Chincoteague, Va.	
Tom Bland	St. George's Island, Md.	
William Lucas	Georgetown, D. C.	
Charles Chesser	St. George's Island, Md.	Owned by Tyler D. Chesser.
Tyler D. Chesser	St. George's Island, Md.	Rig changed to gasoline screw on 5-8-1924. Sunk at wharf at Bowers, Del. 1-21-1936.
Tyler D. Chesser	St. George's Island, Md.	Abandoned at Crisfield, Md. 12-4-1901. Owned by Tyler Chesser.
John Beitzell	Fleet's Bay, Va.	
John Dent	Charles Co., Md.	
H. Webster Foxwell	Bretton Bay, Md.	Built by John Branford. Wrecked in storm 9-21-1938 in Bristol Harbor, R. I.
James Bailey	River Springs, Md.	Purchased from James Covington.
Randolph Thomas	St. George's Island, Md.	Square sail. Abandoned at Cross Roads, Va. on 9-29-1939.
Arthur Johnson	St. George's Island, Md.	Rebuilt. Owned by Tom Moore.
Edwin Gibson	Canoe Neck Creek, Md.	Built by J. W. Brooks. Abandoned at Fall River, Mass. 3-7-1944.
Matt Bailey	White's Neck Creek, Md.	
Joe Martin	White's Neck Creek, Md.	Built by Kenelm Cheseldine. Changed to pleasure yacht 6-30-1913.
Henry Ward	Crisfield, Md.	Built by J. Marsh. Converted to a barge -- still afloat in the fall of 1967.
Charles Chesser	St. George's Island, Md.	Abandoned at St. George's Island.

152

APPENDIX "A"

Name of Vessel	Ship #	Ton-nage	Type	Length	Year Built	Where Built
Lottie E. Carter	140802	25	Schooner	56.7	1885	Alexandria, Va.
Lucylena	141024	21	*Sloop	53	1889	Washington, D. C.
Lula Scott	140653	7	Sloop	36.5	1883	St. George's Island, Md.
Lydia	-	-	Ship	-	c.1770	-
Lydia	140282	12	Schooner	45	1878	St. Mary's Co., Md.
M. J. Daugherty	93268	17	Pungy	49	1902	Crisfield, Md.
M. J. Stevenson	91367	16	Bugeye	55	1881	Crisfield, Md.
Maggie E. Smith	92333	10	Bugeye	51	1891	St. Peter's, Md.
Maggie E. Turner	91412	19	Schooner	46	1882	Alexandria, Va.
Maggie L.	16072	-	Schooner	-	1867	Dorchester Co., Md.
Maggie May	92418	41	*Schooner	67.7	1891	Washington, D. C.
Maguire	92481	10	Bugeye	49	1892	Northumberland Co., Va.
Majestic	93182	26	Bugeye	67.3	1901	Fairmount, Md.
Major Todd	91808	10	Bugeye	50.3	1885	Somerset Co., Md.
March Gale	208057	6	Sloop	38	1906	Hunting Creek, Va.
Margaret Ella	90317	16	Schooner	43.7	1870	Alexandria, Va.
Mark Stevens	92050	10	Bugeye	54.5	1888	St. Peter's, Md.
Martha Ann	92506	11	*Sloop	38.7	1893	Washington, D. C.
Martha Avery	17877	32	Pungy	57.5	1864	Baltimore, Md.
Martin Wagner	91482	33	Schooner	60.1	1882	Pocomoke City, Md.
Mary Ann	-	-	Schooner	-	c.1841	-
Mary E.	93185	6	Skipjack	39	1901	Hopkins, Va.
Mary Ellen	-	-	Pungy	-	-	St. George's Island
Mary Elvis	92833	9	Sloop	40.8	1897	Wayside, Md.
Mary Hunt	92032	7	Sloop	59.2	1887	Washington, D. C.
Mary Parker	16389	34	Schooner	60	1847	Northumberland Co., Va.
Mary Priscilla	90935	7	Bugeye	30	1876	Northumberland Co., Va.
Mary Thomas	92276	7	*Sloop	30.1	1891	Washington, D. C.
Mary & Rebecca	16540	18	Schooner	44.7	1860	Washington, D. C.
Mary J. Bond	90662	35	Pungy	61.6	1874	Crisfield, Md.
Mary Ann Shea	90550	51	Schooner	78.7	1873	Occoquan, Va.
Mascotte	92347	7	Sloop	28.7	1885	Alexandria, Va.
Mattie A. Walston	92820	7	Skipjack	39.6	1897	Crisfield, Md.
Mattie F. Dean	91695	48	Schooner	68	1884	Madison, Md.

Master**	Home Port or Sailed From	Remarks
-	Washington, D. C.	
-	Washington, D. C.	
James T. Waters & James Scott	Chincoteague, Va.	Changed to gasoline screw in 1914 and abandoned at Cape Charles 7-6-1953.
Ignatius Fenwick	St. Mary's River, Md.	Ocean-going vessel used in Revolutionary War.
A. C. Tennesson	St. Mary's Co., Md.	Abandoned at Baltimore, Md. 9-1-1896.
Howard Chesser	St. George's Island, Md.	
Joseph A. Lawrence	St. Patrick's Creek, Md.	Abandoned 9-27-1911.
John Twilley, Sr.	St. George's Island, Md.	Built by I. S. Somers.
-	Baltimore, Md.	
George Thomas	St. George's Island, Md.	
-	Washington, D. C.	
Ned Hayden	Canoe Neck Creek, Md.	Owned by W. E. Hopkins of Virginia. Rig changed to gasoline screw on 9-25-1915. Abandoned at Newport News, Va. on 12-29-1938.
Richard C. Miller	Colonial Beach, Va.	Rig changed to oil screw on
Ned Hayden	Canoe Neck Creek, Md.	10-13-1938. Sunk near Key
William J. Stanford	Colonial Beach, Va.	West, Florida on 1-7-1943. Built by J. Branford.
Randolph Thomas	St. George's Island, Md.	Owned by James Hall.
-	Crisfield, Md.	
-	Norfolk, Va.	
Beverly Collins	St. Patrick's Creek, Md.	Built by R. E. Tyler.
-	Washington, D. C.	
Charles Chesser	St. George's Island, Md.	
Howard Chesser	St. George's Island, Md.	
Charles Edward Henderson	St. George's Island, Md.	Foundered at Crisfield, Md. 6-3-1934.
John Cumberland	Washington, D. C.	
Foster Thomas & Ned Henderson	St. George's Island, Md.	
Thomas Crowder	St. George's Island, Md.	Built by Thomas Crowder.
Walter L. Jackson	Charles Co., Md.	Abandoned at Washington, D. C.
James N. Morris	Charles Co., Md.	12-5-1913.
S. Spearman Lancaster	Charles Co., Md.	
John W. Furbush	Charles Co., Md.	
-	Washington, D. C.	
-	Baltimore, Md.	
-	Tappahannock, Va.	
-	Washington, D. C.	
-	Washington, D. C.	
Charles Chesser	St. George's Island, Md.	Owned by - Webster, Baltimore, Md.
-	Alexandria, Va.	
-	New York	
Shill Simpkins	St. George's Island, Md.	
Solomon Foxwell	Bretton Bay, Md.	Abandoned and sunk at Annapolis,
Matt Bailey	White's Neck Creek, Md.	Md. 5-10-1955.
Tilton Hayden	Canoe Neck Creek, Md.	Owned by Matt Bailey.
Havie Bannigan	St. Patrick's Creek, Md.	Owned by Matt Bailey.

APPENDIX "A"

Name of Vessel	Ship #	Tonnage	Type	Length	Year Built	Where Built
May	92218	8	Bugeye	44.8	1890	Jones Creek, Md.
May	91203	6	Sloop	32.4	1879	Alexandria, Va.
May Flower	92179	47	Schooner	73	1890	Alexandria, Va.
Mechanic	-	-	Schooner	-	c.1836	-
Melia & Bee	91509	6	Sloop	35.6	1882	Dorchester Co., Md.
Mildred	208729	81	Schooner	82	1911	Solomons Island, Md.
Minnie Blanche	91956	8	Sloop	32	1887	Pocomoke City, Md.
Minnie Kershaw	91167	10	Schooner	49.4	1879	Washington, D. C.
Minnie Titlin	92349	21	Schooner	63	1891	Occoquan, Va.
Minnie E. Gaskins	91414	18	Schooner	47.5	1882	Northumberland Co., Va.
Miranda & John	-	50	Sloop	-	c.1822	-
Model	16018	27	Pungy	50.4		Somerset Co., Md.
Mollie	90220	13	Sloop	35.5	1870	Washington, D. C.
Mount Vernon	50524	42	Schooner	75.3	1869	Occoquan, Va.
Nancy	-	32	Schooner	-	c.1814	-
Nancy Ann	-	-	Ship	-	c.1812	-
Nautilus	130080	9	Sloop	38.2	1876	Absecon, N. J.
Nellie	130514	21	*Sloop	65.1	1883	Washington, D. C.
Nellie Bly	130503	36	Bugeye	48.5	1884	St. Peter's, Md.
Nellie Richards	130592	9	*Sloop	38.3	1882	Washington, D. C.
Nellie Somers	209267	8	Sloop	42	1911	Hunting Creek, Va.
Nellie White	136635	6	Skipjack	39	1901	St. Peter's, Md.
Nettie May	130989	10	Bugeye	52	1902	Whitestone, Va.
Nettie A. Foxwell	130320	-	Bugeye	50	1884	Dorchester Co., Md.
Nettie B. Greenwell	130754	-	Bugeye	72	1897	Madison, Md.
Nora Phillips	130945	-	Bugeye	75.5	1901	Solomons Island, Md.
Norah	18776	8	Schooner	42.5	1873	Northumberland Co., Va.
Northumberland	130610	9	Sloop	40.7	1892	Alexandria, Va.
Ocean Queen	19235	22	Pungy	48	1855	Somerset Co., Md.
Onward	155000	14	Schooner	36.8	1878	St. Mary's Co., Md.
Oriental	19257	19	Pungy	45.6	1852	Crisfield, Md.
Osceola	155231	40	Schooner	78.3	1892	Occoquan, Va.
Oscar	205242	54	Schooner	79	1908	Washington, D. C.
Ostrich	19255	47	Schooner	60	1864	Somerset Co., Md.
Oyster Boy	55135	7	Sloop	37	1881	Calvert Co., Md.
Peri	150224	58	Schooner	80.9	1881	Alexandria, Va.
Piankatank	-	-	Pungy	-	-	-
Pocahantas	-	-	Pungy	-	-	-
Polly	-	32	Schooner	-	c.1814	-
Polly Lawrence	150139	19	*Sloop	43.4	1878	Washington, D. C.
Polly & Sally	-	34	Sloop	-	c.1813	-
Prohibition	150431	6	Sloop	30.5	1887	Sinnickson, Va.
Puritan	150675	6	Sloop	31	1894	Alexandria, Va.

Master**	Home Port or Sailed From	Remarks
George Garner	St. George's Island, Md.	Owned by Adams Bros., St. George's Island.
-	Annapolis, Md.	
-	Alexandria, Va.	
- Lucas	Georgetown, D. C.	
Frank Crowder	St. George's Island, Md.	Abandoned at St. George's Island.
Wes Chesser	St. George's Island, Md.	Owned by - Clark, Alexandria, Va. Changed to gasoline screw.
Edwin Gibson	Canoe Neck Creek, Md.	
Ned Hayden	Canoe Neck Creek, Md.	
-	Annapolis, Md.	
-	Alexandria, Va.	
-	Baltimore, Md.	
William Lucas	Georgetown, D. C.	
William Simpkins	St. George's Island, Md.	
-	Crisfield, Md.	
-	Alexandria, Va.	
William Lucas	Georgetown, D. C.	
Jacky Bright	St. Mary's Co., Md.	Ocean-going ship captured by the British during War of 1812.
John Twilley, Sr.	St. George's Island, Md.	Changed to gasoline screw.
Henry Dickens	St. George's Island, Md.	Sharp sail.
-	Washington, D. C.	
Tyler Chesser	St. George's Island, Md.	Log bugeye. Foundered off
Walter Crowder	St. George's Island, Md.	Black Walnut Cove, Md. in November, 1917.
-	Washington, D. C.	
-	Cape Charles, Va.	
Grude Clarke	St. George's Island, Md.	
William Chesser	St. George's Island, Md.	
-	-	
-	-	
-	-	
-	Crisfield, Md.	
-	Alexandria, Va.	
Tyler Chesser	St. George's Island, Md.	
R. T. Ball	St. Mary's Co., Md.	Abandoned at Annapolis, Md.
A. C. & W. C. Combs	St. Mary's Co., Md.	on 6-30-1893.
J. Thomas Swann &	St. Mary's Co., Md.	
John T. Adams	St. Mary's Co., Md.	
Wes. Chesser, Sr.	St. George's Island, Md.	
-	Alexandria, Va.	
-	Washington, D. C.	
John Wm. Palmer	St. Patrick's Creek, Md.	Hit and sunk by tugboat near
Douglas Russell	Canoe Neck Creek, Md.	Washington, D. C.
Arthur Johnson	St. George's Island, Md.	
-	Alexandria, Va.	
Frank Russell	Canoe Neck Creek, Md.	
George Duncan	St. George's Island, Md.	
John Lucas	Georgetown, D. C.	
Matthew M. Taylor	Washington, D. C.	
William Lucas	Georgetown, D. C.	
Ned Hayden	Canoe Neck Creek, Md.	
-	Alexandria, Va.	

156

APPENDIX "A"

Name of Vessel	Ship #	Ton-nage	Type	Length	Year Built	Where Built
Quick Time	20608	10	Bugeye	52	1893	St. Peter's, Md.
R. A. Golden	110410	12	Schooner	39.5	1873	Washington, D. C.
R. B. Haynie	111134	31	Bugeye	64.6	1896	Solomons Island, Md.
R. H. Stuart	111158	17	Schooner	56.3	1897	Stratford, Va.
R. M. Blundon	110617	43	Schooner	71	1883	Northumberland Co., Va.
Raymond Oliver	111066	11	Schooner	41.2	1894	White's Neck Creek, Md.
Rebecca (Becky)	-	-	Schooner	-	-	-
Rebecca Smith	110998	9	Schooner	40	1892	Alexandria, Va.
Remittance	-	-	Schooner	-	-	-
Republican	-	-	Schooner	64	1805	St. Mary's Co., Md.
Robert E. Lee	111047	9	Sloop	42	1893	Currioman Bay, Va.
Robert K. Scott	-	-	Schooner	-	-	-
Rosa Beitzell	110542	50	Schooner	73.3	1860	Pocomoke City, Md.
Ruth	201261	38	Schooner	50	1904	Mt. Holly, Va.
Ruth & Ella	111139	10	Schooner	38.5	1897	White's Neck Creek, Md.
S. Wimsatt	116136	8	Schooner	34.4	1886	Washington, D. C.
S. A. Guyther	116705	8	Schooner	41.5	1895	Piney Point, Md.
S. C. Kemble	115447	25	Schooner	49.5	1875	Newport, N. J.
St. Mary's	-	-	Schooner	-	c.1860	-
Salisbury	-	-	Schooner	-	-	-
Samuel J. Tilden	115741	7	Bugeye	49	1876	Crisfield, Md.
Samuel S. Smith	116297	10	Bugeye	53	1889	Monie, Md.
Samuel T. White	115976	20	Bugeye	50.5	1883	Pocomoke City, Md.
Samuel W. Thomas	23629	8	-	49.10	1857	Somerset Co., Md.
Sans Souci	116439	29	Schooner	48.4	1891	Washington, D. C.
Sarah Jane	115659	9	Sloop	37.5	1877	Alexandria, Va.
Sea Bell	-	-	Pungy	-	-	-
Seabird	116654	9	Skipjack	38	1894	Whitehaven, Md.
Sea Gull	115418	9	Sloop	38	1875	Dorchester Co., Md.
Sea Witch	116019	8	Bugeye	44	1874	Somerset Co., Md.
Seeker	23641	8	Sloop	36	c.1866	Crisfield, Md.

Master**	Home Port or Sailed From	Remarks
"Boss" (J. M.) Bailey	White's Neck Creek, Md.	Rig changed to gasoline screw on 8-9-1918. Abandoned at Weems, Va. on 9-16-1946.
-	Cape Charles, Va.	
George W. Ellis	River Springs, Md.	Built by M. M. Davis, wrecked on Gull Shoals, N. C. 1-18-1937.
T. W. Bryant	Alexandria, Va.	Changed to gasoline screw in
R. H. Stuart	Alexandria, Va.	1911 and converted to a house-boat in 1917.
-	Tappahannock, Va.	
E. T. Oliver	White's Neck Creek, Md.	Built by Kenelm Cheseldine.
Raymond Oliver	White's Neck Creek, Md.	Abandoned at Reedsville, Va.
George M. Owens	White's Neck Creek, Md.	on 6-30-1921.
Con. Faunce	Canoe Neck Creek, Md.	
-	Alexandria, Va.	
James H. M. Burroughs	-	
Matthias Clarke	Calvert's Creek, Nanjemoy, Md.	Pilot boat built by John Hopkins.
T. W. Bryant	Westmoreland Co., Va.	Abandoned at Alexandria, Va.
Wm. J. & John J. Foxwell	Westmoreland Co., Va.	on 9-27-1906.
John Johnson	-	
Josiah Beitzell	Canoe Neck Creek, Md.	Formerly the "Harvester." Re-
Mary Beitzell	Canoe Neck Creek, Md.	built in 1882. Dismantled and
John Beitzell	Canoe Neck Creek, Md.	converted to a barge at Balti-
Ernest Beitzell	Canoe Neck Creek, Md.	more, Md. in 1897.
-	Alexandria, Va.	
Geo. Columbus (Lum) Bailey	White's Neck Creek, Md.	Built by Kenelm Cheseldine. Dismantled and converted to
"Boss" (J. M.) Bailey	White's Neck Creek, Md.	a barge.
Nick Norris	Charles Co., Md.	
-	Newport News, Va.	
Charles H. Guyther	Piney Point, Md.	Changed to sloop rig 1-30-1909.
Philip Greenwell	St. Clement's Bay, Md.	Abandoned May 20, 1910.
Charles Chesser	St. George's Island, Md.	Owned by Tub Hall, St. George's Island.
-	St. Mary's Co., Md.	Captured by the Confederates in 1865.
H. Webster Foxwell	Bretton Bay, Md.	Four-masted schooner.
Jim Moore	St. George's Island, Md.	Owned by Adams Bros., St. George's Island.
George Pearson	St. George's Island, Md.	Square sail.
John Crowder	St. George's Island, Md.	Square sail.
Bun Rice	St. George's Island, Md.	Square sail. Abandoned at St. George's Island.
-	Washington, D. C.	
-	Crisfield, Md.	
S. W. (Sol) Russell	Chaptico Bay, Md.	
Charlie Poe	St. George's Island, Md.	Two masts.
Jim Brown	St. George's Island, Md.	
Ned Robrecht	St. George's Island, Md.	
George (Axe) Poe	St. George's Island, Md.	

APPENDIX "A"

Name of Vessel	Ship #	Ton-nage	Type	Length	Year Built	Where Built
Shamrock	117071	5	Sloop	37.5	1901	Hunting Creek, Va.
Shining Light	22410	20	Pungy	53	1856	-
Silver Spray	116116	10	Bugeye	45.8	1886	Somerset Co., Md.
Silver Star	115361	20	Schooner	67	1874	Occoquan, Va.
Skysjack	115971	7	Schooner	30.4	1883	Washington, D. C.
Sodonia Curley	116018	79	Schooner	91	1892	Alexandria, Va.
Somerset	-	-	Schooner	-	-	-
Southern	-	-	Skipjack	30	-	-
Splendid	23614	15	Pungy	44.6	1867	-
Star	23604	8	Sloop	28	1849	Worcester Co., Md.
St. Mary's	-	-	Schooner	-	-	Baltimore, Md.
Sunny South	115290	-	Bugeye	48.6	1873	Somerset Co., Md.
Susan E. Parker	115802	23	Schooner	66	1881	Northumberland Co., Va.
Swan	-	-	Sloop	-	-	-
T. W. Riley	-	-	Sloop	-	-	-
Tartar	-	-	Sloop	-	c.1815	-
Teaser	-	-	Sloop	-	-	-
Tennessee	145528	15	*Sloop	47	1885	Washington, D. C.
Thomas Franklin	24962	13	Schooner	41	1873	St. Mary's Co., Md.
Thomas Warren	145531	8	Sloop	32.4	1889	Westmoreland Co., Va.
Thomas H. Kirby	145316	28	Bugeye	61	1882	St. Michaels, Md.
Three Brothers	145387	7	Sloop	33.4	1884	White's Neck Creek, Md.
Three Brothers	24977	24	Schooner	78.8	1872	Pohick, Va.
Three Sisters	59435	36	*Schooner	61	1887	-
Tom Young	-	-	Schooner	-	-	-
Tropic	24535	18	Pungy	47.8	1866	Somerset Co., Md.
Thomas B. Schall	145302	55	Schooner	75.3	1882	Baltimore, Md.
Tryall	145534	7	Sloop	33	1890	Alexandria, Va.
Twilight	145414	9	Bugeye	45.8	1885	Somerset Co., Md.
Venus	-	-	Schooner	-	-	-
Village Belle	25507	21	Bugeye	50.2	1851	Somerset Co., Md.
Virginia	25940	10	Schooner	36.6	1877	Washington, D. C.
Wallace W. Hawkins	80622	20	Schooner	50.4	1877	Hunting Creek, Va.
Wanda	81575	9	Skipjack	43.8	1897	Wittman, Md.

APPENDIX "A"

Master**	Home Port or Sailed From	Remarks
-	Crisfield, Md.	
George Gabriel Thomas	St. George's Island, Md.	
Charlie Poe	St. George's Island, Md.	
Ben Moore	St. George's Island, Md.	
-	Washington, D. C.	
-	Alexandria, Va.	
-	Alexandria, Va.	
-	-	
Joseph A. Henderson	St. George's Island, Md.	
William T. Husemann	St. Patrick's Creek, Md.	Abandoned 6-3-1897.
George P. Good	St. Patrick's Creek, Md.	
L. E. Raulenberg	Blackistone Island, Md.	
Frederick J. McWilliams	Colton's Point, Md.	
Samuel Trader	St. George's Island, Md.	
-		
John Joe Gibson	Canoe Neck Creek, Md.	Built by I. Willin.
-	Tappahannock, Va.	
John Goldsmith	St. Patrick's Creek, Md.	Used by C.S.A. in the Civil War.
-	-	
William Lucas	Georgetown, D. C.	
Charles Huselman	-	
-	Washington, D. C.	
Thomas L. Crowder	St. George's Island, Md.	Probably built by Thomas L. Crowder or Kenelm Cheseldine. Vessel sunk and abandoned twice between 1890-1893 but was raised and repaired. Abandoned on 6-30-1897.
Joseph Poe	St. George's Island, Md.	
Kenelm Cheseldine	White's Neck Creek, Md.	
George Ball	St. George's Island, Md.	
James C. Bailey	River Springs, Md.	Built by T. H. Kirby. Square rigged. Second round stern bugeye. Rig changed to gasoline screw on 8-15-1928. Burned at Bar Gut Landing, N. J. on 2-21-1936.
"Boss" (J. M.) Bailey	White's Neck Creek, Md.	
Kenelm Cheseldine	White's Neck Creek, Md.	Built by Kenelm Cheseldine. Abandoned 3-14-1916.
-	Alexandria, Va.	
-	Washington, D. C.	
Ephraim Chesser	St. George's Island, Md.	
George Ball	St. George's Island, Md.	
Tyler Chesser	St. George's Island, Md.	
Bud Thrift	Mundy Point, Va.	(Sold in Caribbean in 1941. —(Capsized at sea and lost-1942.
-	Alexandria, Va.	
Ephraim Chesser	St. George's Island, Md.	
Bun Rice	St. George's Island, Md.	
H. Webster Foxwell	Bretton Bay, Md.	Three-masted schooner - later named the "Edna Bright Haugh." Abandoned at Norfolk, Va., in 1938.
Tyler Chesser	St. George's Island, Md.	Log bugeye.
-	Crisfield, Md.	
-	Norfolk, Va.	
Howard Chesser	St. George's Island, Md.	
Wes Chesser	St. George's Island, Md,	

160

APPENDIX "A"

Name of Vessel	Ship #	Ton-nage	Type	Length	Year Built	Where Built
Water Lily	-	-	Sloop	-	-	-
Welcome Return	-	-	Schooner	48	1804	Leonardtown, Md.
Westmoreland	81307	9	Schooner	43	1890	Currioman Bay, Va.
Wide Awake	80415	8	Bugeye	43	1873	Bay Hundred, Md.
William Dickson	80533	7	Schooner	36.6	1875	Washington, D. C.
William D. Clarke	80514	43	Schooner	80	1873	Occoquan, Va.
William Austin	81395	6	Sloop	46.7	1892	Crisfield, Md.
William F. King	81848	7	Sloop	41.6	1902	Hunting Creek, Va.
William & Hopewell	-	-	Ship	-	1767	St. Mary's River, Md.
William & Thomas	-	-	Schooner	-	c.1838	-
Willie Ann	26556	10	Sloop	36.5	1861	Potomac, Va.
Willie Clarence	81464	10	Bugeye	57.5	1892	Oriole, Md.
Wilson & Hunting	80976	419	Schooner	152	1883	Alexandria, Va.
Wm. F. Vilas	81158	21	Bugeye	58	1887	Pocomoke City, Md.
Wm. H. English	-	-	Bugeye	-	-	-
Wm. H. Whiting	81055	26	Pungy	59	1884	Pocomoke City, Md.
Wm. H. H. Bixler	80543	20	Schooner	52.5	1875	Somerset Co., Md.
Wm. M. Austin	-	-	Skipjack	47	-	-
Wm. M. Powell	80992	59	Schooner	78.5	1883	Finney, Va.
Winnie H. Windsor	81060	26	Bugeye	63.1	1884	Solomons Island, Md.
Zephr	28073	30	Pungy	52	1871	Calvert Co., Md.

ADDENDA

Name of Vessel	Ship #	Ton-nage	Type	Length	Year Built	Where Built
Elizabeth Ann	135452	68	Schooner	802	1880	Barren Cr. Springs, Md.
Gladys L	-	-	Bugeye	-	-	-
James A. Whiting	75326	35	Pungy	61	1871	Somerset Co., Md.
Lucy May	-	-	Schooner	-	-	-
Matilda	91951	37	Schooner	60.6	1887	Marion, Md.
Minnie and Emma	91550	77	Schooner	93	1883	Pocomoke City, Md.

NOTE: Mr. Robert H. Burgess who furnished the above information also advised
that Capt. B. S. (Bud) Thrift of Kinsale, Va., skippered the "J. W.
Knowles." The "Thomas B. Schall" had Capt. Bailey and Capt. Dungan as
master at different times and the "Columbia F. C." had Capt. Burton, Capt.
Fisher, and also Capt. Dungan. The master of the "Josephine Wimsatt" was
Capt. Brinsfield and Capt. Garnet Belfield of Coles Point, Va. skippered
the "Mattie F. Dean" and other schooners.

Master**	Home Port or Sailed From	Remarks
James Dingee	St. Patrick's Creek, Md.	
George Tarleton	Bretton Bay, Md.	Built by James Thompson.
John King	Bretton Bay, Md.	
-	Alexandria, Va.	
Bun Rice	St. George's Island, Md.	
-	Annapolis, Md.	
-	Alexandria, Va.	
Grude Clark	St. George's Island, Md.	Sharp sail.
-	Crisfield, Md.	
Vernon Hebb	St. Mary's River, Md.	Ocean-going ship.
John Cumberland	Georgetown, D. C.	
- Lucas	Georgetown, D. C.	
-	Newport News, Va.	
James Dickerson	St. Patrick's Creek, Md.	
-	Perth Amboy, N. J.	
John Twilley, Sr.	St. George's Island, Md.	Owned by John Twilley.
Will Twilley	St. George's Island, Md.	
James Thompson	St. George's Island, Md.	
John Henderson	St. George's Island, Md.	Owned by - Lewis, Coan River,
Edward Henderson	St. George's Island, Md.	Va.
John Joe Gibson	Canoe Neck Creek, Md.	Abandoned 9-11-1911.
Charles A. & George	River Springs, Md.	
W. Ellis	River Springs, Md.	
George W. Ellis	River Springs, Md.	
R. G. Clark	St. George's Island, Md.	
George H. Cullison	St. George's Island, Md.	
J. H. Russell &	Canoe Neck Creek, Md.	Square sail. On 6-30-1924
Jeremiah Gibson	Canoe Neck Creek, Md.	rig changed to gasoline screw.
Wes Chesser, Jr.	St. George's Island, Md.	On 8-20-1929 rig changed back
Jeremiah Gibson	Canoe Neck Creek, Md.	to sail and on 12-18-1931 rig again changed to gasoline screw. Abandoned 9-30-1934.
Bern Thompson	St. George's Island, Md.	
John Beitzell	Fleet's Bay, Va.	Owned by Bern Thompson
W. H. Douglas	Kinsale, Va.	
-	-	Owned by Andrew J. Lewis, Walnut Point, Va.
-	-	Owned by Andrew J. Lewis, Walnut Point, Va.
Hunter Belfield Lodge, Va.		
-	-	Owned by Andrew J. Lewis, Walnut Point, Va.
Hunter Belfield Lodge, Va.		

*Sloop -- Scow sloop or sloop barge.
*Schooner -- Scow schooner or schooner barge.
**Also owner unless otherwise noted.

NOTE: The names of all owners and masters of these vessels are not shown on this list. Further information may be found at the U. S. National Archives, Washington, D. C.

APPENDIX "B"

WORKBOAT RACE ENTRIES

June 21, 1930

SCHOONERS

No.	Boat	Captain	Home Port	Length
1.	William H. Michael	Capt. Davis Price, Sr.	Cambridge, Md.	65 ft.
2.	S. J. Delan	Capt. W. H. Valliant (Owner)	Bellevue, Md.	50 ft.
3.	Stephen H. Douglas	Capt. W. H. Valliant (Owner)	Bellevue, Md.	50 ft.
4.	Thomas A. Jones	Capt. W. H. Valliant (Owner)	Bellevue, Md.	86 ft.
5.	Amanda F. Lewis	Capt. G. T. Rice	Coan, Va.	67 ft.
6.	Emma V. Wills	Capt. Peter C. Smith	Tylerton, Md.	64 ft.
7.	J. S. Smith	Capt. Howard J. Chesser	St. George's Is., Md.	60 ft.
8.	C. W. Willey	Capt. Lafayette Donoho	Oxford, Md.	74 ft.

BUGEYES

No.	Boat	Captain	Home Port	Length
16.	Agnes Leonard	John Meredith	Cambridge, Md.	60 ft.
17.	Florence	Capt. David Mesick, Jr.	Cambridge, Md.	75 ft.
18.	Fanny Lowery	Capt. F. McNamara	Crisfield, Md.	65 ft.
19.	Emma A. Faulkner	Capt. C. S. Leonard	Cambridge, Md.	78 ft.
20.	M. M. Davis	Capt. Johnson S. Evans	Ewell, Md.	55 ft.
21.	Moonlight	Capt. Wells Todd	Crisfield, Md.	56 ft.
22.	Col. R. J. Colton	Capt. Robert M. Pyne	Oxford, Md.	60 ft.
23.	Florence Northam	Capt. Charles O. Chesser	St. George's Is., Md.	65 ft.
24.	Ethel Vail	Capt. G. Walter Chesser	St. George's Is., Md.	54 ft.
25.	Eva Belle	Capt. George W. Smith	Tylerton, Md.	60 ft.
26.	Nettie B. Greenwell	Capt. W. McLaughlin	Wingate, Md.	72 ft.
27.	R. D. E. Hughette	Capt. O. Pope	Oxford, Md.	67 ft.
28.	Little Jennie	Capt. Joseph H. Mills	Oxford, Md.	
29.	Susie E. Parris	Capt. Charles W. Pope	Oxford, Md.	60 ft.

DECKED SKIPJACKS

No.	Boat	Captain	Home Port	Length
36.	America	Capt. Leon Daniel	Wenona, Md.	42 ft.
37.	Geneva May	Capt. William Hawthorn	Wenona, Md.	50 ft.
38.	Robert L. Tawes	Capt. John S. Wheatley	Tangier, Va.	45 ft.
39.	Maud Talmadge	Capt. Willard Crockett	Tangier, Va.	39 ft.
40.	(No Name)	Capt. William Parks	Tangier, Va.	39 ft.
41.	Lena Rose	Capt. William Mister	Wenona, Md.	50 ft.
42.	Myrtle	Capt. Brinkley Taylor	Wenona, Md.	38 ft.
43.	Zingara	Capt. W. H. Valliant	Bellevue, Md.	48 ft.
44.	Ruth	Capt. Ernest H. Jenkins	Fairbank, Md.	44 ft.
45.	William Florence	Capt. Curtis Smith	Tylerton, Md.	45 ft.
46.	Robert J. Webster	Capt. Hobson Burton	Deals Island, Md.	60 ft.
47.	Florence Louise	Capt. Dewey Anderson	Deals Island, Md.	60 ft.
48.	Rew Brothers	Capt. Julius Webster	Wenona, Md.	42 ft.
49.	S. H. Tolley	Capt. Robert J. Parks	Wingate, Md.	55 ft.
50.	Mary E.	Capt. Burke Wingate	Wingate, Md.	50 ft.
51.	Gay Elva	Capt. L. Whitelock	Chance, Md.	40 ft.
52.	W. M. Austin	Capt. R. G. Clark	St. George's Is., Md.	45 ft.
53.	Stanley Norman	Capt. Alfred Reynold	Wingate, Md.	47 ft.
54.	Southern	Capt. Joseph A. Henderson	St. George's Is., Md.	30 ft.
55.	Della Griffith	Capt. Walter Duncan	Oxford, Md.	38 ft.
56.	Ida May	Capt. Orville	Wingate, Md.	47 ft.
57.	Lena Rose	Capt. William Bloodsworth	Cambridge, Md.	42 ft.

APPENDIX "B"

DECKED SKIPJACKS

(Cont'd)

No.	Boat	Captain	Home Port	Length
58.	Wilma & Florence	Capt. Curtis J. Smith	Tylerton, Md.	47 ft.
59.	Mary Elizabeth	Capt. Gordon S. Pope	Oxford, Md.	62 ft.
60.	Omar J. Croswell	Capt. James D. Webster	Solomons, Md.	40 ft.
61.	Lizzie B.	Capt. Bruce Bozman	Champ, Md.	28 ft.
62.	Minnie B.	Capt. Scott Bozman	Champ, Md.	42 ft.
63.	Appolla	Capt. J. Frank Dobson	Olivet, Md.	55 ft.
64.	Reliance	Capt. Lloyd V. Kitwan	Crapo, Md.	44 ft.
65.	Sonny Boy	Capt. Stanford White	Wenona, Md.	30 ft.

OPEN SKIPJACKS

No.	Boat	Captain	Home Port	Length
66.	Theresa Webster	Capt. Alton Walter	Deals Island, Md.	28 ft.
67.	Rosalie Webster	Capt. Winford Scott	Deals Island, Md.	28 ft.
68.	Esther Webster	Capt. William Turner	Deals Island, Md.	28 ft.
69.	Nellie K.	Capt. Frank Danials	Wenona, Md.	30 ft.
70.	Jack Dempsey	Capt. Preston Webster	Deals Island, Md.	28 ft.
71.	Gene Tunney	Capt. Valliant Webster	Deals Island, Md.	28 ft.
72.	Ralph W.	Capt. Ralph Willing	Chance, Md.	31 ft.
73.	Rosa Lee	Capt. Lawson Tyler	Ewell, Md.	28 ft.
74.	Lena Rose	Capt. Herman Marsh	Rhodes Point, Md.	24 ft.

SMITHS ISLAND CRABBING SKIFFS

No.	Boat	Captain	Home Port	Length
79.	Miss Chesterfield	Daniel Dize	Ewell, Md.	19½ ft.
80.	Polly Evans	Capt. Ogdon Evans	Ewell, Md.	19½ ft.
81.	Speedy	Capt. Severn Evans	Ewell, Md.	19 ft.
82.	Cora Katheryn	Capt. James Corbin	Ewell, Md.	19½ ft.
83.	Patsy Lee	Capt. William Raymond	Ewell, Md.	19½ ft.
84.	Rachel Jane	Capt. Harry Evans	Ewell, Md.	19½ ft.
85.	Yankee Doodle	Capt. Gordon Adams	Crisfield, Md.	20 ft.
86.	Marsh Brothers	Capt. Calvin Marsh	Tylerton, Md.	22 ft.
87.	Empress Josephine	Capt. Earnest Evans	Ewell, Md.	19 ft.
88.	Lucky Strike	Capt. Donald Middleton	Ewell, Md.	18.6 ft.
89.	Bernice M.	Capt. Stremghn Marshall	Tylerton, Md.	19½ ft.
90.	Morttra Frances	Capt. Chorlton Marshall	Tylerton, Md.	19 ft.
91.	Margaret C. B.	Capt. B. S. Brom	Tylerton, Md.	18 ft.
92.	The Doris M.	Capt. John Bradshaw	Tylerton, Md.	19 ft.
93.	Margaret T.	Capt. Robby Bradshaw	Tylerton, Md.	19 ft.
94.	Chris Chraf	Capt. Edison Marshall	Tylerton, Md.	18 ft.
95.	Sea Angel	Capt. Glenon Marsh	Tylerton, Md.	19 ft.
96.	Pop Eye	Capt. William Clayton	Tylerton, Md.	18½ ft.
97.	Esther Ralston	Capt. Herman Marsh	Rhodes Point, Md.	19½ ft.

APPENDIX "C"

FEDERAL CENSUS RECORDS

POTOMAC RIVERMEN

St. Mary's County, Maryland - 1860

	Age	
C. C. Spalding	38	Captain - oyster boat
Charles I. Norris	29	Captain - coasting vessel
Somerset Norris	29	Sailor
William H. Brown	-	Surveyor of Customs
Benjamin Foxwell	25	Captain - freight vessel
George H. Colison	38	Captain - coasting vessel
William Dunn	33	Captain - bay vessel
James E. Joy	25	Sailor
William C. Briscoe	55	Fisherman and farmer
George Griggs	65	Pilot
Henry Stanhice	53	Sailor
Thomas Bennett	24	Captain - bay vessel
Joseph T. Abell	31	Sailor
Abel Abell	36	Fisherman
Leonard R. Howard	27	Captain
Walter Chesser	55	Captain - oyster vessel
William Carroll	17	Sailor
John E. Bagby	25	Sailor
Henry Gibson	60	Sailor
Ephraim Chesser	28	Sailor
Thomas Crowder	45	Sailor
George Messeck	45	Sailor
Gabriel Thomas	45	Sailor
Solomon Thomas	23	Sailor
Samuel Trader	26	Sailor
Robert H. Gardiner	40	Captain - bay vessel
William S. Shorter	35	Captain - bay vessel
John A. B. Shermantine	17	Sailor
Marshall Boothe	35	Captain - bay vessel
Charles I. Paul	43	Captain - bay vessel
Charles W. Armsworthy	36	Sailor
Van Buren Foxwell	21	Captain - bay vessel
George Moore	40	Pilot
James Moore	55	Pilot & oyster vessel
Merret Cole	55	Pilot & oyster vessel
George Poe	45	Sailor
William L. Wheatley	49	Captain - bay vessel
H. I. Stone	35	Sailor
John Greenwell	50	Fisherman
John Boothe	24	Sailor
William Medley	30	Captain - bay vessel
William Mowbray	21	Sailor
Joseph Mattingly	35	Fisherman
Ignatius Heard	28	Captain - bay vessel
Richard Langley	38	Fisherman
John Wheeler	45	Captain - wooden vessel
James Mowbray	52	Ship's carpenter
Stephen Foxwell	54	Captain - freight vessel
Solomon Foxwell	23	Sailing Master
Benjamin Foxwell	24	Captain - bay vessel
George E. Paul	35	Sailor
Ignatius W. Norris	37	Captain - freight vessel
James Barron	30	Sailor
John Bullock	68	Fisherman
Francis Thompson	31	Sailor

APPENDIX "C"

St. Mary's County, Maryland - 1860 (Cont'd)

	Age	
Leonard Neale	60	Captain - freight vessel
Kenelm Cheseldine	55	Fisherman
Thomas L. Harden	25	Captain - coasting vessel
Jackson Cheseldine	24	Captain - coasting vessel
Daniel Thompson	24	Sailor
Richard Ellis	29	Sailor
John W. Ellis	30	Sailor
Joseph Mattingly	25	Sailor
John W. Harden	30	Sailor
Robert H. Harden	29	Captain - vessel
Thomas Lloyd	45	Captain - freight vessel
James Brookbank	60	Captain - freight vessel
Thomas Gatton	55	Fisherman
Benjamin F. Graves	38	Captain - bay vessel
Rhewlen Graves	28	Captain - bay vessel
H. H. Goldsmith	-	Captain

St. Mary's County, Maryland - 1870

William C. Bane	58	Sailor
Thomas F. Joy	41	Oysterman
William Watts	35	Sailor
Joseph Hobbs	35	Sailor
Walter Chesser	69	Sailor
Ephraim Chesser	36	Oysterman
Jerome Moor(e)	26	Pilot
George Moor(e)	50	Pilot
George Poe	55	Sailor
Richard Cortney	45	Oysterman
Thomas Crowder	52	Oysterman
Samuel Potter	37	Sailor
James Bullock	28	Fisherman
Julius Devaney	27	Oysterman
Charles Norris	40	Sailor
Benjamin Foxwell	35	Sailor
Solomon Foxwell	33	Sailor
John M. Wheeler	55	Sailor
John F. Russell	30	Sailor
Andrew Cheseldine	36	Sailor
Kelley Cheseldine	28	Sailor
John G. Thompson	22	Sailor
Hiram Jones	50	Oysterman
Charles G. F. Husemann	46	Sailor
John T. Jones	40	Oysterman
William W. Gatton	35	Oysterman

Charles County, Maryland - 1860

Henry Pherson	48	Master Sailor
James Lancaster	34	Master Sailor
Francis Penn	28	Master Sailor
Samuel G. Herbert	35	Master Sailor
James C. Simms	25	Master Sailor
Joseph S. Herbert	38	Master Sailor
Richard H. Herbert	34	Master Sailor
James F. Sutton	44	Keeper of Light Boat
William G. Middleton	35	Master Carpenter
George B. Shannon	32	Master Carpenter
George H. Carpenter	27	Collector

APPENDIX "C"

Charles County, Maryland - 1860 (Cont'd)

	Age	
James T. Middleton	26	Collector
Thomas St. Clair	39	Fisherman
Charles H. Lacy	22	Master Sailor
John F. Zell	22	Sailor
Henry Hannon	52	Captain
Thomas Hannon	21	Captain
Sherrod Hannon	19	Captain

Charles County, Maryland - 1870

C. H. Lacey	42	Sailor
J. Welch	25	Fisherman
L. C. Allen	54	Sailor
Thornton Bell	54	Sailor
A. Franklin	30	Sailor
G. W. Wheeler	40	Sailor
F. Bradley	34	Sea Captain
Z. W. Posey	47	Sailor
L. F. Burroughs	28	Sailor
Henry Pearson	53	Sailor
Henry Woodey	47	Fisherman
G. W. Swann	26	Fisherman
Warren Swann	53	Fisherman
H. M. Hannon	62	Sea Captain
William E. Elkins	32	Sailor

Northumberland County, Virginia - 1860

Henry G. Headley	42	Sailor
William Rice	21	Sailor
Josephus O. Lewis	25	Sailor
Theophilus Sayres	35	Sailor
Thomas A. Richardson	41	Sailor
Lindsey J. N. Jones	30	Sailor
Holland H. Hughes	27	Sailor
William G. Smith	30	Sailor
L. R. Ayres	30	Sailor
J. B. Williams	29	Sailor
Griffin B. Edwards	26	Sailor
Archy Hall	30	Sailor
Anson A. Lewis	17	Sailor
James H. Stephens	44	Sailor
Cyrus Edwards	31	Sailor
Austin J. Dodson	37	Sailor
Eppa S. Headley	38	Sailor
Joseph Bridgman	25	Sailor
William Headley	28	Sailor
James Stephens	29	Sailor
Eth. Jones	28	Sailor
Michell Evans	41	Sailor
Lewis Evans	38	Sailor
Thomas H. Gaskins	29	Sailor
John H. Evans	35	Sailor
Jesse Crowther	51	Sailor
Zach Johnson	40	Oysterman

Northumberland County, Virginia - 1870

Joseph Seha	36	Sailor

APPENDIX "C"

Northumberland County, Virginia - 1870 (Cont'd)

	Age	
Samuel Brown	45	Sailor
Gustavus Haynie	25	Sailor
Ethelbert Jones	34	Sailor
Cyrus L. Haynie	21	Sailor
Lewis Evans	48	Sailor
Alfred Evans	25	Sailor
Lambert Howarth	52	Sailor
William Headley	38	Sailor
Thomas B. Neale	61	Sailor
Theo. Sayres	45	Sailor
William Swann	30	Sailor
Henry Barnes	58	Ship Carpenter

Westmoreland County, Virginia - 1860

G. A. Reed	32	Waterman
J. R. Marchant	47	Waterman
M. A. Hinson	20	Waterman
R. Hinson	23	Waterman
D. Foxwell	75	Ship Carpenter
William Foxwell	45	Ship Carpenter
I. Foxwell	30	Ship Carpenter
James Bryant	55	Ship Carpenter
L. A. Weever	24	Waterman
William Weever	52	Waterman
William H. Bartlet	30	Waterman
M. Kilman	56	Waterman
J. C. Courtney	56	Waterman
W. Mothershead	51	Waterman
H. Winkfield	34	Waterman

Westmoreland County, Virginia - 1870

John Hammonds	30	Sailor
George Reed	44	Sailor
Henry Armstrong	45	Sailor
William Lucas	33	Sailor
John Hinson	45	Sailor
James Hinson	37	Sailor

King George County, Virginia - 1860

William W. Henderson	23	Mariner
Lawrence Brannican	52	Fisherman
John A. Redman	29	Mariner
William L. Pratt	40	Fisherman

King George County, Virginia - 1870

James B. Price	30	Sailor
John Marmaduke	55	Sailor
Benjamin Shelley	29	Sailor

Stafford County, Virginia - 1860

John Knoxville	63	Fisherman

APPENDIX "C"

<u>Stafford County, Virginia - 1860</u> (Cont'd)

	Age	
John Dickerson	40	Fisherman
John Dent	27	Waterman
Nathaniel Finall	45	Fisherman
John A. Evans	·28	Boatman
Barney Agar	26	Boatman
Travers Agar	22	Boatman
Alex Dent	27	Boatman
Sam Dent	25	Boatman
James H. Dent	21	Boatman
Traverse Moncure	31	Captain of steamer
Traverse Segar	38	Boatman

169

APPENDIX "D"

SOME POTOMAC RIVERMEN IN THE FEDERAL CENSUS OF 1880

St. Mary's County, Maryland

John E. Bagley, Pilot
James H. Cunningham, Pilot
Benjamin Cunningham, Pilot
Samuel F. Potter, Pilot
Walter F. Crowder, Pilot
Thomas L. Crowder, Pilot
William P. Courtney, Pilot
David E. Lowe, Pilot
Charles F. Husemann, Blacksmith
  (Tong Maker and Boat Builder)
William West, Sailor
S. Edgar Cullison, Sailor
John Armstrong, Sailor
Walter Chesser, Sailor
Samuel Trader, Sailor
William Simpkins, Sailor
Cadmus Simpkins, Sailor
Tyler Chesser, Sailor
John W. Henderson, Sailor
Alonzo Gibson, Sailor
Richard T. Ball, Sailor
George A. Ball, Sailor
David Evans, Sailor
George Poe, Sailor
John Poe, Sailor
Charles Poe, Sailor
Joshua Hewitt, Sailor
Thomas W. Bennett, Sailor
William Barron, Sailor
James Barron, Sailor
Thomas Goldsborough, Sailor
Solomon Foxwell, Sailor
Charles Norris, Sailor
J. W. Foxwell, Sailor
Nelson Cheseldine, Sailor
John Kenelm Cheseldine, Sailor
John F. Russell, Sailor
Andrew Jackson Cheseldine, Sailor
Jeremiah Gibson, Sailor
George W. Cheseldine, Sailor
Thomas J. Lawrence, Oysterman
John Joseph Gibson, Oysterman
George Columbus Bailey, Oysterman
James Dingee, Oysterman
George Moore, Fisherman
James Moore, Fisherman
Richard Moore, Fisherman
John Trader, Fisherman
George Poe, Fisherman
John Chapman, Fisherman
Francis E. Johnson, Fisherman
John Fenwick, Fisherman
Rodolphus Wilkinson, Fisherman
James Bullock, Fisherman
Benjamin Moore, Fisherman

Charles County, Maryland

James T. Bateman, Sailor
Benton Barnes, Sailor

Charles County, Maryland (Cont'd)

John W. Maddox, Sailor
Louis C. Maddox, Sailor
Massy Posey, Sailor
Alphonsus Haislip, Sailor
John E. Carpenter, Sailor
John P. Ashton, Sailor
John Smart, Sailor
Massena Kendrick, Sailor
Joseph Kendrick, Sailor
Robert A. Clay, Sailor
James Maddox, Sailor
William Kendrick, Sailor
Magruder Dunnington, Sailor
Stanislaus Dunnington, Sailor
John W. Shorter, Sailor
James T. Bailey, Sailor
Thomas Penn, Sailor
Robert Fleury, Sailor
John Stewart, Sailor
Charles H. Lacey, Fisherman
Watson Wheeler, Fisherman
Thomas M. Wheeler, Fisherman
Martin Raynor, Fisherman
Immanuel Scott, Fisherman
James Fletcher, Fisherman
Joseph Dyer, Fisherman
Thomas Johnson, Fisherman
Samuel Johnson, Fisherman
Sandy Maunders, Fisherman

Northumberland County, Virginia

Isaac McArthur, Ship Carpenter
Charles Vanlandingham, Ship Carpenter
James B. Abbott, Ship Carpenter
Samuel J. Lewis, Ship Carpenter
Nelson J. Woodhull, Ship Carpenter
Samuel Nelson, Ship Carpenter
Thomas Parks, Ship Carpenter
Henry McFarland, Ship Carpenter
Luke Griffin, Sailor
William Johnson, Sailor
Cornelius P. Evans, Sailor
Leboles R. Coles, Sailor
Lucuis D. Haynie, Sailor
Willard H. Owens, Sailor
James Marsh, Sailor
Richard Toulson, Sailor
Cyrus L. Haynie, Sailor
Charles B. Kent, Sailor
Cornelius Haynie, Sailor
John Dodson, Sailor
Bertrand Dodson, Sailor
Nathan W. Moore, Sailor
George H. White, Sailor
Thomas W. Crowther, Sailor
Gustavus Rice, Sailor
Charles Kent, Sailor
Joshua Swann, Sailor
William Swann, Sailor

170

APPENDIX "D"

Northumberland County, Virginia (Cont'd)

Gustavus Swift, Sailor
Benjamin Franklin Irwin, Sailor
William H. Gaskins, Sailor
William Lewis, Sailor
Thomas Bundick, Sailor
Thomas E. Richardson, Sailor
James Richardson, Sailor
Octavius Hudson, Sailor
John Hudson, Sailor
John A. Sears, Sailor
David Lindsay, Sailor
Gustavus M. Forbush, Fisherman
Albert M. Haynie, Fisherman
Benedict L. Haynie, Fisherman
John T. Gough, Fisherman
Noah Williams, Fisherman
Bertrand B. Haynie, Fisherman
Benjamin Willis, Fisherman
Wallis Overton, Fisherman
Elias Edwards, Fisherman
Elias W. Edwards, Fisherman
Thomas Humphries, Fisherman
William Humphries, Fisherman
William George, Fisherman
Franklin George, Fisherman
Willard Haynie, Fisherman
Mortimer L. Dodson, Fisherman
Charles J. Dodson, Fisherman
Alpheus Headley, Fisherman
Arthur F. Booth, Fisherman
Joseph S. Booth, Fisherman
John L. Flynt, Fisherman
Lawrence K. Flynt, Fisherman
James A. Headley, Fisherman
John Turner, Fisherman
Archie Turner, Fisherman
Plato Turner, Fisherman
Len Headley, Fisherman
Thomas M. Dodson, Fisherman
Eugene O. Dodson, Fisherman
Monroe Gill, Fisherman
Raleigh Carter, Fisherman
Philip Swift, Fisherman

Westmoreland County, Virginia

Daniel G. Balderson, Boat Builder
Joseph M. Smith, Boat Builder
William Parks, Ship Carpenter
Washington Parks, Ship Carpenter
Edward Tyler, Sailor
Mosley Tate, Sailor
Edgar Owens, Sailor
Lewellin Reed, Sailor
George A. Reed, Sailor
Jackson Bell, Fisherman
Thomas Boyce, Fisherman

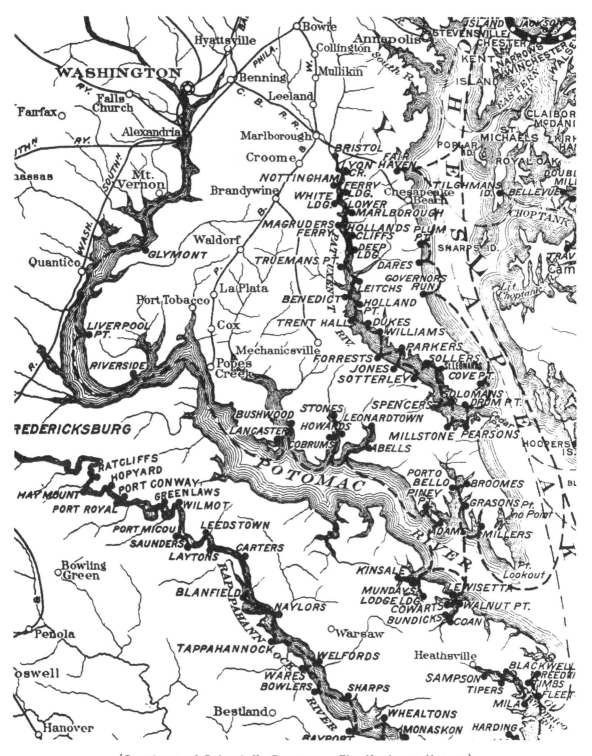

(Courtesy of Robert H. Burgess - The Mariners Museum)

APPENDIX "E"

VIEW OF
POTOMAC RIVER LANDINGS

View from off Quantico (looking u

View of Freestone Point from off Deep

View from off Freestone Point (loo

As seen from the channel by the Steamboat Captains
and Sailing Vessel Masters during the past century.

Off Giesboro' Point

s off Bog Island

Nose bearing N.by E.⁴ E, distant 2⁴ Miles.

Head bearing NE.⅔ E, distant 2⅔ Miles.

an Head bearing NE.⅔ E, distant 2⅔ Miles.

174

APPENDIX "E"

Quantico Station

View of Quanti

Freestone Creek

View looking up the River, Mar

Acquia   Brent's Pt.
Creek

View from off Potomac Creek (looking up), Smith's Pt. bea

Lt. Ho. Persimmon Pt.   Lower Cedar Pt.   Nanjemoy Creek

View, looking up from off Swan Pt., Lower Cedar Pt. Lt. Ho. bearing N. N W. ¼ W., distant 5¼ Miles, Swan Pt. N. NE ¼ E., dist.1¼ Miles.

Mathias Pt.   Mathias Pt. Lt. Ho.   Beacon

View from off Pope's Creek Landing (lo

ation, distant ⅞ of a Mile.

(Point bearing W. ½ N, distant 1½ Miles.

½ W, distant 2 Miles, and Brent's Pt. NW. by W. ½ W, distant 2½ Miles.

Bluff and King George's Points from off White Pt., Bluff Pt. bearing W. NW. ¼ W., distant 2 Miles.

; Mathias' Pt. bearing NW. by W. ½ W, distant 2½ Miles.

176

View of Smith's Pt.,the Lt.Ho.bearing W. ½ S, distant 2 Miles.

View of Point Lookout, the

View off St.Mary's River, Pine

View off Chancellor's Point

View of Priest's Point, S

Piney Pt. Lt. Ho.

Piney Pt. from the Southward, the Lt. Ho. bearing NW. by W, distant 1½ Miles.

. bearing W. SW, distant 3½ Miles.

Mary's River   Priest's Point   Kitt's Pt.

Lt. Ho. bearing NW. ½ W, distant 5 Miles.

St. Mary's

king up the St. Mary's River.

Seminary   Priest's House

le's Creek, St. Mary's River.

178

APPENDIX "E"

View of Breton and St.Clement's Bays, from off King's

Nomini Cliffs fro

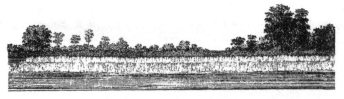

View off Baywood fi

APPENDIX "E"

vr.,Blakistone's Island Lt.bearing N W. by W. ‡ W, distant 3 Miles.

ff Blakistone's Island.

abreast of Bridge Creek.

APPENDIX "F"

Canoe Neck Creek, Maryland
February 29, 1968

Captn Ed:

   Am sending you a lot of Potomac River information which I have collected
during my cruising the river since 1930. I started cruising just after graduating
from Catholic University in June of '30 -- there being no jobs for architects, and
my mother and father found it cheaper to have me on the river than at home.
   Expenses were about 25¢ a day, as fish and fresh vegetables were gifts from
the tidewater farmers or watermen.....there were no other expenses as God furnished
the winds free and plenty of fringe benefits if you predicted the right winds at
the right times.
   I cruised every year with the Sea Scouts of the Corinthian/Capital Yacht Clubs
(except during World War II), and naturally studied the charts inquisitively --
wondering how the points of land and creeks received their names -- then I started
to imagine the historical happenings that occurred along the river's shores.
   And so -- I send this to you for whatever value it may be.....hope some day to
have time (about two years) to really make a detailed study on the derivations of
all the place names -- and make lots of money selling the book.

                    Sincerely,

                    FREDERICK TILP

          * * * * * * * * * * * * * * *

   The list of Potomac River names is in four parts in accord with the U. S.
Coast and Geodetic Survey charts:

        Part "A" - C&G Chart #557 - Chesapeake Bay to Piney Point.

        Part "B" - C&G Chart #558 - Piney Point to lower Cedar Point.

        Part "C" - C&G Chart #559 - Lower Cedar Point to Mattawomen Creek.

        Part "D" - C&G Chart #560 - Mattawomen Creek to Georgetown, D. C.

   Names are listed as one would sail or "tack up" the river, going first from
the Virginia shore, starting at Smith Point; crisscrossing through all the Potomac's
"reaches" to Bladensburg, Maryland, and Georgetown, D. C.
   As the collector of all this information was not present at the time these
places were named, the maps were drawn, and/or when the battles were fought -- he
is, therefore, unable to exactly verify everything noted in this list.

APPENDIX "F"

DERIVATION OF POTOMAC RIVER PLACE NAMES
By Frederick Tilp

```
┌─────────────────────────────────────────────────┐
│                                                   │
│                   PART "A"                        │
│                                                   │
│             COAST & GEODETIC SURVEY               │
│                  CHART #557                       │
│                                                   │
│           CHESAPEAKE BAY TO PINEY POINT           │
│                                                   │
└─────────────────────────────────────────────────┘
```

A-1 SMITH POINT, VIRGINIA, named as "Saint Gregories Poynt" by Father Andrew White who accompanied the Maryland colonists in the sailing ships, Ark and Dove, in 1634. First shown as "Smiths Point" on charts of 1780, named for Captain John Smith of Jamestown, Virginia. Charts of 1721 indicate a large island at the mouth of the Little Wicomico, allowing two entrances to the creek.

A-2 LITTLE WICOMICO CREEK, VIRGINIA, named for an Indian village, "Wieocomoco," (Indian translation - "where houses are building").

Cod Creek, named for local landowner, Colonel Saint Leger Codd, a Protestant Cavalier of 1670.

A-3 HACK CREEK, VIRGINIA, named for Peter Hack, Northumberland County, Virginia, sheriff of 1716.

Cubitt Creek, first shown as "Cupids Creek" because of its romantic setting as noted in will of Richard Hull in 1713.

A-4 HULL CREEK, VIRGINIA, named for local landowner, John Hull, 1774.

A-5 PRESLEY CREEK, VIRGINIA, named for William Presley (member of the House of Burgesses - 1647), who patented 1,150 acres of land here. Nearby was erected Northumberland County's first Court House.

A-6 COD CREEK, VIRGINIA, (see Little Wicomico Creek).

A-7 COAN RIVER, VIRGINIA, named for an Indian village, "Sekacawone," (Indian tr. - "stone people"). English settlers erected a shire named "Chickacoan" in 1651.

Walnut Point, records indicate "no walnuts anywhere around," but many tall poplar trees in the area which boasted a summer resort hotel in the 1890's. From 1910 thru 1940, there was a large, active fish and vegetable packing factory here. Headquarters of the Potomac River Transportation Company steamboats servicing the Potomac to the Wicomico River; the Piankatank, and the Great Wicomico River to Baltimore.

Lake Landing, named for Lake Cowart, local landowner and operator of packing factory. Former steamboat landing.

Bundicks Landing, named for Richard Bundick, local warehouse treasurer in 1870. Former steamboat landing.

Coan Wharf, the "seaport town of entry" site selected by the House of Burgesses in 1680 to serve Northumberland County, named "Chicacony." Formerly a steamboat landing and large packing plant/factory. A cable ferry ran from Coan to Bundicks until 1934 carrying one auto per trip. The home port of the river's last commercial sailing pungy boat, "Amanda F. Lewis."

APPENDIX "F"

A-7 COAN RIVER, VIRGINIA (Continued)

Rowes Landing, the river landing for an architectural mansion, "Springfield" (Built 1828); formerly named "Black Point," home of John Heath, a student at William and Mary College, who founded the Phi Beta Kappa Society at Raleigh Tavern in Williamsburg, Virginia, in 1776.

Lewisetta, named for "Etta Lewis," daughter of local landowner in 1753. Former steamboat landing and factory.

Honest Point, first shown on charts of 1850.

The Glebe, named for "Glebe lands" owned by the local Episcopal Church. Charts of 1841 show this as "Kill Neck Creek."

Cowarts Wharf, named for local family of Cowart who operated the seafood packing plant in 1900 till 1929. Nearby is the home site of Mary Ball, George Washingtons's mother, named "Cherry Hill." Former steamboat landing.

Travis Point, named for local landowner, John Travers, in 1837. Charts of 1841 show nearby "Judith Sound" as "Judas Creek."

A-8 YEOCOMICO RIVER, VIRGINIA, named for an Indian village, "Aiagomoago" (Tr. - "he, that is floating on water, tossed to and fro").

Barns Point, named for original landowners of 1670 -- the Barones family.

Cornish Cove, named for local Irish landowner, William Cornish - 1785. On charts of 1826 was noted as "Cornishes Cove."

Lodge Landing, the site of the first Freemasonry lodge in Virginia. Former steamboat landing.

Harry Hogan Point, named for the last Indian family who lived here, "Harrihokan." Chesapeake Bay skipjacks are still being built here at the Krentz shipyard.

Great House Point, site of an old residence titled "Great House," home of the Bayly family who still care for the grave site and tomb of U.S.N. Midshipman James B. Sigourney who died in a Naval battle with the British off the Yeocomico River in July, 1813.

Kinsale, named for Kinsale by Irish settlers in 1705; town established by the House of Burgesses. Former steamboat landing. Headquarters of Confederate smuggling flotilla of blockade runners to Smith Creek, and to the Patuxent River in Maryland.

Lynch Point, named "Levy Point" in 1667 where the Protestant Virginia Legislature authorized a fort erected for protection from the Catholics who in Saint Mary's City had previously erected a fort.

Lodge Creek, noted on charts of 1826 as "Balls Swamp."

White Point Creek, charts of 1825 to 1868 show as "Tapscotts Creek."
                    1868 as "Saw Mill Branch."
                    1868 to 1940 as "Mill Branch."
                    1940 as "Pretty Point Creek."
                    1940 to 1968 as "White Point Creek."

Mundy Point, first shown on charts of 1825 as "Monday Point." Home port of Virginia's last commercial sailing schooner, "Colombia F. C." Former steamboat landing. Home of the river's largest seafood processing factory (1968).

Hampton Hall Branch, noted on charts of 1841 as "Lees Mill Creek."

APPENDIX "F"

A-9 SANDY POINT, VIRGINIA, noted on the Herrman Map of 1673 as "Sandy Point," probably so named due to the beautiful sandy beaches. Site of the girlhood home of Mary Ball, mother of George Washington.

A-10 BONUMS CREEK, VIRGINIA, named for local landowner, Samuel Bonum, who patented the estate in 1650. Charts of 1825 note this as "Benan Creek."

A-11 POINT LOOKOUT, MARYLAND, named as "Saint Michaells Poynt" by Father Andrew White in 1634. Charts of 1636 note this as "Wiffins Point." First noted as "Point Lookout" on charts of 1660. Site of the southern terminal of a proposed railroad from Washington, D. C., which started work in 1868, but stopped on its southward progress at Mechanicsville, Maryland. Also, the site of the Hammond General Hospital; started in 1862, which resulted in a Confederate Prisoner Camp to hold over 20,000 men.

A-12 CORNFIELD HARBOR, MARYLAND, Fort Lincoln, a heavy gun battery was erected here to aid in protection of the Point Lookout Prison Camp and the National Capital City. A popular and much used anchorage for Chesapeake Bay commercial and freighting sail vessels until their complete death about 1942.

A-13 POTTER CREEK, MARYLAND, named for local landowner's family of Potter in the early 1800's.

A-14 HARRY JAMES CREEK, MARYLAND, named for local landowner family of James about 1785.

A-15 ROWLEY BAY, MARYLAND, named for the local family of "Rawleigh" who migrated here from the Eastern shore of Maryland. One of the members became a Judge in Saint Mary's County Court in the 1800's.

A-16 CALVERT BAY, MARYLAND, named for William Calvert, son of Governor Leonard Calvert, who built his home nearby in 1661. Originally named "Trinity Bay" by Father Andrew White in 1637.

A-17 SMITH CREEK, MARYLAND, named for the Virginia Captain John Smith in 1608. Renamed "Trinity Creek" by Father Andrew White in 1634. Renamed "Smith Creek" during the Protestant Rebellion of 1689.

Wynnes Wharf, named for the Father Wynne, a Jesuit active here in the 1870's. Later named "Benville Wharf" in 1880 for local landowner, Mrs. Anastasia Benville.

Miller Wharf, former steamboat landing, now called "Claytons Point" for the Clayton family who now (1968) reside there.

Kitts Point, named as "Kitts Point" on charts of 1836; then on charts from 1902 to 1923 as "Kitty Point." A ferry was established here to sail across the Saint Mary's River to Saint George's Island in 1639.

Jutland Creek, named for "Jutland," the early home of the Honorable William Bladen, a prominent politician of the pre-Revolutionary War period.

A-18 SAINT MARY'S RIVER, MARYLAND, named for Henrietta Maria, wife of the Royal Grantor, Charles I, in 1634, by Leonard Calvert. In 1572, Spanish explorer Pedro Menendez de Marques entered the Chesapeake Bay to investigate French trespassers, and named the Chesapeake Bay as "Bahia de Santa Maria" -- this has nothing to do with this Saint Mary's River, however. The river was first named "Yowaccomoco" for

APPENDIX "F"

A-18 SAINT MARY'S RIVER, MARYLAND (Continued)
the Indian village there. Charts of 1673 show this as "Saint Georges River."
Southern shore of this creek was the site of the most important coaling station of
the Navy's Potomac Flotilla during the Civil War.

Saint Mary's City, the original capital of the Maryland Province from 1634 until
1695. Maryland's first public ferry was established here in 1638 running from the
city to West Saint Mary's -- the fee per person, horse, or ox was one pound of tobacco.

Pagan Point, named for the Indian name "Pukan" or "Pakana" (Tr. - "pecan nut");
has nothing to do with "pagans" as such.

Carthagena Creek, named by William Hebb in the 1700's who fought in a Naval
engagement along with Lawrence Washington at Carthagena in the West Indies.

Chancellor Point, named for Philip Calvert, the colony's Governor and first
Chancellor, in 1657 who built a beautiful home here.

Portobello Point, named by Edwin Coade (a friend of Lawrence Washington) who
fought a Naval engagement at Portobello in the West Indies. Some authorities say
it was named by William Hebb, who owned the land at this time.

Saint Inigoes Creek, named by Father Andrew White as "Saint Ignatius Creek," but
came to be called "Saint Inigoes." Southern shore of this creek was the site of the
most important coaling station of the Navy's Potomac Flotilla during the Civil War.

Grasons Wharf, named for Governor William Grason (1838) but shown on charts of
1892 as "Jones Wharf" for the Jones family of Cross Manor. It was a famed steamboat
landing.

Tippity-Wichity Island, noted on charts of 1824 as "Lynch Island" for the Lynch
family whose home was located on the adjacent western shore of the river. Local
informants indicate that an Indian family named "Tippity-Wichity" lived there until
the Civil War.

A-19 SAINT GEORGE'S RIVER/ISLAND, MARYLAND, named by the Jesuits who first came into
possession in 1638; keeping the island until 1850 when it was sold to settlers from
Tangier Island. During steamboating days, there were two active wharves on the
Creek -- Hobbs Wharf and Adams Wharf, both having hotels on shore for summer visitors
until about 1930. Home port of the river's last commercial sailing bugeye, "Florence
Northam."

A-20 PINEY POINT, MARYLAND, named for the beautiful loblolly and long leaf yellow
pines ashore; first shown on charts of 1744. This area was the summer social center
of Washington's dignitaries between 1820 and 1910. President James Monroe stayed
here first in the hotel and later in a cottage that became the "summer White House"
of John C. Calhoun, Henry Clay, Daniel Webster, President Franklin Pierce and Teddy
Roosevelt also visited here, to enjoy the ever-present southeast breeze and fine
tasting artesian well water. Site of the last "Work Boat Races" sponsored by the
Baltimore Sun newspapers in the 1930's for the Chesapeake Bay pungy boats, bugeyes,
schooners, and skipjacks.

A-21 HERRING CREEK, MARYLAND, obviously named for the great numbers of herring "running" here in the spring season. First shown on charts of 1744. A favorite spot
for smugglers during the Civil War and Prohibition times, due to the continually
changing channel location and shoaling at the entrance.

A-22 McKAY BEACH, MARYLAND, named for local landowner family of McKay in 1930.

A-23 BLAKE CREEK, MARYLAND, named for the "Black" family living here in 1872.

APPENDIX "F"

A-24 VALLEY LEE, MARYLAND, named for the "Lee" family who lived here, naming their
home "Mount Olive."

A-25 TALL TIMBERS, MARYLAND, obviously named for the tall pine trees growing here.
Started as a summer resort about 1890.

****

PUNGY, "AMANDA F. LEWIS,"
ENTERING COAN RIVER, VIRGINIA, OFF WALNUT POINT
NEAR SUNSET, AUGUST 23, 1930

Photo: H. W. Piper

APPENDIX "F"

DERIVATION OF POTOMAC RIVER PLACE NAMES
By Frederick Tilp

```
+------------------------------------------------+
|                    PART "B"                    |
|                                                |
|             COAST & GEODETIC SURVEY            |
|                  CHART #558                    |
|                                                |
|         PINEY POINT TO LOWER CEDAR POINT       |
+------------------------------------------------+
```

B-1 JACKSON CREEK, VIRGINIA, named for Richard Jackson who lived here in 1737.
First charts, however, in 1744 show this as "Cherives Creek," so named in the time
of Thomas Gerard who established a home ("Wilton") here in 1660.

B-2 GARNER CREEK, VIRGINIA, named for John Garner who patented land here in 1660.
Charts of 1825 show this as "Gardners Creek."

B-3 RAGGED POINT, VIRGINIA, first shown on charts of 1775 as "Ragged Point."

B-4 BLACKBEARDS POND, VIRGINIA, locally known as Long Pond or Rice's Pond. First
shown on charts of 1907 as "Blackbeard's Pond," but no one seems to know who "Blackbeard" was.

B-5 COLES POINT, VIRGINIA, named for a pioneer, Richard Cole, a jovial spirit of
early colonial days, who patented lands here in 1661. Dick Cole's walnut coffin
was inscribed, "Here lies Dick Cole, a grievous sinner - who died a little before
dinner - yet hopes in Heaven to find a place - to satiate his soul with Grace."

B-6 BARNES POINT, VIRGINIA, named for the Barnes family who patented land here in
1780. Charts of 1906 show this as "Grapevine Point."

B-7 LOWER MACHODOC CREEK, VIRGINIA, named for an Indian village "Matchoatoke" (Tr. -
"at the big bad tidal river").

    Narrow Beach, home site of the Allerton family who came to America on the
Pilgrims' ship, "Mayflower."

    Glebe Creek, site of the rector's home of Cople Parish, established in 1650.
"Glebe Lands" in colonial days were the homestead and farm lands set aside by each
parish for support of the clergy. (Maybe we should do this today.)

    Cabin Point, named for "Indian cabins" by the energetic John Mottrom in 1650,
one of George Washington's ancestors.

    Tidewells, named for local landowner family, the "Tidewells."

B-8 KINGCOPSICO POINT, VIRGINIA, named for a local Indian chieftain, the "King
Copsico," though first shown on charts of 1864. Here lived Anna Washington, the
only sister of George Washington's grandfather.

*B-9 NOMINI BAY, VIRGINIA, named for an Indian village, "Onawanient," then corrupted
to "Nawmani," and then to "Nominy."

    Buckner Creek, nearby is a site of ground selected by the House of Burgesses
in 1680 to have a "seaport town of entry" established. The home of John Augustine

APPENDIX "F"

B-9 NOMINI BAY, VIRGINIA

Buckner Creek (Continued)
Washington (brother of George) -- "Bushfield" on the original site has been restored on the southeastern shore.

Snake Island, near Ice House Point was the site where the Indian Princess Pocahontas (while on a visit to the Potomac Indian village in 1611) was betrayed into the hands of Sir Samuel Argall for a "copper kettle." Crazy Snake (her lover), whom King Powhattan had appointed to guard her while on this visit drowned himself when he learned of the betrayal. The island has since borne his name.

Mount Holly, named for nearby eminence covered with holly trees. On the upper reaches of this river are ruins of the famous "double mills" which Councilor Carter built in 1770 -- the mill had two races with two water wheels.

Elbow Point, George Washington's diary of August 27, 1768, notes that he "hauled seine here for sheep heads" (local fish).

Nomini Wharf, at the site of the present bridge was located a ferry in 1862. During the Civil War, this was an active terminal for smugglers of Virginia from Southern Maryland who hauled mainly in salt, arms, medicine, and food.

Currioman Bay, named "Curryoman" by Charles Chilton in 1660, landowner. The home of Colonel Walter Broadhurst, who in 1650 patented land here and built the first Court House for Westmoreland County, Virginia. In 1880 Currioman Bay had four steamboats (3 from Washington and 1 from Baltimore) each week to trade with farmers at Currioman wharf. The water traffic was so heavy with sailing craft that the landowners requested state aid to dredge a channel across the northern neck of Hollis Marsh to the Potomac. However, a terrific northeast storm in the early 1900's washed the entrance open - thus separating "Hollis Marsh" (charts of 1744) from the mainland.

McGuires Wharf, the Virginia terminal of a ferry boat system running daily to Leonardtown until 1934.

B-10 POPLAR HILL CREEK, MARYLAND, named for Poplar Hill Church, the second Protestant Church in Maryland -- the original church being built in 1642.

B-11 HUGGINS POINT, MARYLAND, first shown as "Huggins Point" on charts of 1836, then changed to "Higgins Point" in 1845; then back to "Huggins" in 1907. There have never been any "Higgins" or "Huggins" owned land ashore here.

B-12 BRETTON BAY, MARYLAND, named for William Bretton, clerk of the Provincial Council, who was granted 850 acres here by Lord Baltimore in 1637, which was named "Little Bretton" (Newtown Neck). In 1668 William Bretton sold the plantation to the Jesuits for 40,000 pounds of tobacco.

Leonardtown, named for Benedict Leonard Calvert, the Fourth Lord Baltimore in 1728. Originally named "Seymourtown" in 1708. The Maryland terminal of a ferry from Leonardtown to McGuires Wharf, Virginia, running during Prohibition days. One of the items carried was U. S. Mail. Charts of 1872 indicate the Leonardtown wharf as being named "Blackstones Wharf."

Protestant Point, named for several landowners here with strong Protestant feelings in 1642 in contrast to the many Catholic names on the Bay.

Lovers Point, named "Gough's Point" on charts of 1873; "Abells Wharf" on charts of 1907; and those of 1920 named it "Lovers Point." Families of Gough, Abell, and Love owned property nearby. Former steamboat landing.

Saint Lawrence's Creek, (small creek to the East of Leonardtown). There was a wharf located here and a ferry to Leonardtown until 1890.

APPENDIX "F"

B-12 BRETTON BAY, MARYLAND (Continued)

Paw Paw Point, named on charts of 1898 for the many paw-paw shrubs growing ashore here. "Paw-paw" is a Caribbean Indian word.

Buzzard Point, named for the many buzzards here. (This "buzzard point" idea close to small towns appears on many charts -- probably a place where farmers brought their dead animals.) Note: Washington, D. C. has one, too.

Combs Creek, named for local landowners, the "Combs" family in 1880. A popular boat yard and repair place during the 1800's for large sailing craft.

Beaver Dam Bay, the upper part of Bretton Bay was first known as the beaver dam area, probably due to fresh water beavers there.

B-13 SAINT CLEMENT'S BAY, MARYLAND, named for "Saint Clements Day" of November 23, 1633. It seems that a plot by seamen on the Ark and Dove to prevent the sailing of the ships which were to bring Maryland's first colonists to America was discovered on "Saint Clements Day" while they were still at anchor in Yarmouth, England. There was so much smuggling to Virginia during the Civil War that the Potomac Flotilla of the Federal Navy stationed two patrol boats here for 16 months.

Saint Patrick's Creek, first named by the Jesuits. Shown as "Saint Pauls Creek" on charts of 1774 due to a cartographer's error.

Canoe Neck Creek, first shown on charts of 1667 as "Cannoow Necke" Creek. Though this name may have risen when there were Indians living here, the source of its Indian part ("Canoe") is West Indian name found by Columbus.

Deep Creek, named for the extra "deepness" of this creek, which permitted large sailing vessels to enter and load tobacco and wheat.

Shipping Point, a shipping point from colonial days. A "rolling road" for tobacco once led to the point.

Tomakokin Creek, named for an Indian village, "Tomacookin" (Tr. - "beaver lands").

Miley's Creek, named for an Indian family living here until the 1860's.

Steamboat Landings. Popular landings on this Bay were at Cobrums Wharf (misspelled "Coburn"); Stones Wharf now called Bayside Wharf; Howards Wharf now called Guest Point; and at St. Clement's Shores.

Captain John Lawrence of Canoe Neck Creek, owner and captain of a sailing sloop, "Jane Wright," had the first casualty of the Civil War. On August 15, 1861, he was ordered by the Federal Navy to "heave to" (while sailing from Washington off Smith Point, Maryland). His boat was then sunk by guns from the USS Yankee as the first victim of their scorched earth policy which so stated, "ALL boats on the Potomac operated by Southern Marylanders shall be destroyed."

B-14 COLTON POINT, MARYLAND, named for Richard Colton who reputedly won the land in a card game from a member of the Blackistone family about 1866. Originally shown on charts as "Longworth Point."

B-15 SAINT CLEMENT'S ISLAND, MARYLAND, named for "Saint Clements Day" (see St. Clement's Bay), in 1634 by Father Andrew White. This is the site of the original landing of the Maryland colonists on March 25, 1634. Originally containing 400 acres, and given to Thomas Gerard who gave it to his daughter, Elizabeth Gerard Blackiston, as part of her dowry. The island was then owned by members of the Blackiston family for over 200 years. Renamed "Saint Clement's Island" in 1962 by the Federal Government.

APPENDIX "F"

B-16 HERON ISLAND, MARYLAND, a long sand bar that almost blocks the entrance to St. Clement's Bay; named by Father Andrew White in 1634 as "Herne Island, so called for the infinite swarms of hernes thereon."

B-17 DUKEHARTS CHANNEL, MARYLAND, nearby in St. Katherine's Sound is "River Springs," named for the many underground fresh cold water springs located at the shore line.

B-18 SAINT KATHERINE'S ISLAND and SAINT MARGARET'S ISLAND, MARYLAND, named by Father Andrew White in 1634. Ashore on the mainland is Bluff Point, site of the original home of John Coode who led the Protestant Rebellion of 1689. Home port of the river's last commercial sailing schooner, "Mattie F. Dean."

B-19 BULLOCKS ISLAND, MARYLAND, named for the Bullock family who lived here until the late 1800's.

White Neck Creek. Father Andrew White established the first Indian mission here in 1634 and erected a "rude" chapel. Charts of 1866 show this as "White Snake Creek."

B-20 WICOMICO RIVER, MARYLAND, named for an Indian village, "Wighococomoco" (Tr. - "pleasant village of dwelling sites") by Virginia's Captain John Smith in 1608. The Wicomico Indians lived and prospered along the eastern shores of this river, as there are many shell-heaps ranging from small mounds to several acres in size. The last full-blooded Wicomico Indian died at Port Tobacco in 1885, at the age of 109. Popular steamboat landings in the early 1900's were at Bushwood and Lancaster.

Chaptico Bay, named for an Indian village, "Copticon" (Tr. - "big broad river"). Chaptico town was legislated to be an official "seaport town of entry" in 1683 and was so noted in large letters on charts up to 1774 as an important port.

Manahowic Creek, named for an Indian village (Tr. - "they are merry people"); first shown on John Smith's map of 1608.

Bushwood Wharf, named for "Bushwood Lodge," the homestead of the first member of the Key family, Philip Key -- the great-grandfather of Francis Scott Key. Members of the Blakiston family have resided in this area from colonial times. Bushwood Manor was the dower of Susannah, daughter of Thomas Gerard, who married (1) Robert Slye, and (2) John Coode.

Dolly Boarmans Creek, named of a local resident; first shown on charts of 1902.

Stoddert Point, named for James Stoddert who emigrated here from Scotland in 1650 and settled nearby.

Mills Point, named for a Colonel Mills who built a mansion here in the 1700's.

Allens Fresh, first known as "Allens Mill" in the late 1600's.

Budds Creek, named for the "great number of birds found here" by John Smith in 1608 and so noted as "Birds Creek"; and then some cartographer misspelled it "Budds" in 1774.

Rock Point, probably named for the thriving "rock fish" catches made here, as there are no mineral rocks ashore. A popular fishing place for the past three centuries.

Charleston Creek, named for "Charleston," the family homestead of Daniel Jenifer who lived here in the early 19th century.

B-21 COBB ISLAND, MARYLAND, first shown on charts of 1737 as "Cob Island." No references found to date mention a Mr. "Cob."

APPENDIX "F"

B-21 COBB ISLAND, MARYLAND (Continued)

Neale Sound, named for Captain James Neale, who was granted land here in 1642.

B-22 SWAN POINT, MARYLAND, named for the "numerous swans here" by Captain John Smith in 1608. Incidently, there are also numerous families of "Swann"s living ashore in this area.

B-23 CUCKOLDS CREEK, MARYLAND, an English merchant stopping here for several days in 1739 wrote his firm that "the deers here were as numerous as the 'cuckolds' in Liverpool." Evidently a cartographer heard this and the name became fixed as "Cuckolds Creek."

B-24 PICCOWAXEN CREEK, MARYLAND, named for an Indian village, "Pukewaxen" (Tr. - "ragged, pierced or broken shoes"). First shown on charts of 1649. Two miles of the adjacent shore line contains the largest Indian shell-field on the river.

B-25 MORGANTOWN, MARYLAND, named for Morgan A. Harris, who built a home nearby named "Waverly" in 1782. George Washington's diary relates that his schooner, during February, 1766, ran aground on the dangerous shoals nearby. Ferry boats ran from Morgantown to Wilkersons Wharf on Rosiers Creek, Virginia, for tourists to Colonial Beach beginning in the early 1900's until 1934.

B-26 LOWER CEDAR POINT, MARYLAND, first shown on charts of 1635. Known as the "Coney Island of the Potomac," due to the sandy beach and cool southeasterly winds of the summer. Steamers from Washington ran here weekly during the early 1900's.

B-27 NOMINI CLIFFS, VIRGINIA, most charts from 1775 until 1868 show all these Virginia cliffs as "Hollis Cliffs." Unable to find any reason for naming of the "Horsehead Cliffs."

B-28 STRATFORD CLIFFS, VIRGINIA, named for the nearby restored colonial mansion, "Stratford Hall"; birthplace of three Virginia governors, of two signers of the Declaration of Independence and the Confederate General Robert E. Lee.

B-29 POPES CREEK, VIRGINIA, named for Nathaniel Pope, who patented the nearby estate in 1647. A water mill, located at the headwaters of this creek, once owned by Augustine Washington was in continuous operation for over 230 years.

Bridges Creek, named for Hercules Bridges who patented land here in 1647.

B-30 CHURCH POINT, VIRGINIA, named for the Appomattox "Church," place of George Washington's baptism, which was established here in 1661. Among the first vestry were John Washington and Andrew Monroe.

B-31 MATTOX CREEK, VIRGINIA, named for the Indian village, "Appomattix." Here in 1648, Colonel Nathaniel Pope established the first wharf and warehouse in Westmoreland County, Virginia.

Paynes Point, named for Daniel Payne, a Baltimore shipping merchant who settled here in 1750.

Wirts Wharf, named for the Honorable William Wirt of Maryland, once the Attorney General of the United States. His home, "Wirtland," was built in 1852. Former steamboat landing and tobacco warehouse.

APPENDIX "F"

B-32 MONROE CREEK, VIRGINIA, named for Andrew Monroe, who patented land here in 1650-52. Two miles from Colonial Beach is the birthplace of the President, James Monroe. At the end of oyster dredging by sailing craft in 1930, this creek became the graveyard of over 30 large river sailing craft -- the shores were littered for years with their wooden hulls and masts.

Doctors Point, site of the tombs of the Monroe ancestors.

Colonial Beach, named by real estate developers who created this as a summer resort titled "Classic Shores" in the early 1900's. Charts of 1873 show this as "Millville."

Robbins Grove Point, named for the great numbers of robins which roosted here in the 1920's.

Winkedoodle Point, named for the Indian title, meaning "pleasant or fair."

B-33 WHITE POINT, VIRGINIA, named for the beautiful white sand here by real estate operators in 1895.

B-34 ROSIER CREEK, VIRGINIA, named for John Rozier who patented land here in 1651. Charts of 1775 show this as "Attopan Creek."

Wilkerson Wharf, at Potomac Beach was the Virginia terminal of the Adams ferry boats running from Lower Cedar Point, with bus shuttle to Colonial Beach, ending about 1934.

B-35 UPPER MACHODOC CREEK, VIRGINIA, named for an Indian village, "Machodick" (Tr. - "at the big tidal river").

Dahlgren, named for Admiral John A. Dahlgren, Commandant of the Washington Navy Yard during the Civil War.

Barber Point, named for Colonel Thomas B. B. Baber, who purchased the property from the Washington family in 1828. Charts of 1841 show this as Washington Point.

Gambo Creek, named for the landowner in 1691, Alexander Gamble, a Scottish merchant from Dumfries. On charts of 1841 it was shown as "Gamble Creek"; then probably some cartographer misnamed it as "Gambo Creek." Originally named "Dodson Creek" for landowner, Gervais Dodson, in 1658. The last Virginia landing place of John Wilkes Booth. (See "Popes Creek, Maryland.)

Yates Point, the northern Potomac point of Gambo Creek was named for the local family of "Yates" which was the Virginia terminal of the Hooes ferry (Laidlow ferry) established by Colonel Rice Hooe in 1680. George Washington records usage of this ferry many times during the Revolutionary War. "Barnsfield," the nearby ancestorial home of the Hooe family, was the headquarters of Confederate blockade runners and smugglers -- burned by Union troops.

B-36 PERSIMMON POINT, VIRGINIA, probably named for a grove of outstanding persimmon trees growing here; or possibly from the original name given by the Indians, "Puchaminson." Charts of 1841 show this as "Rosiman Point."

*B-9 NOMINI BAY, VIRGINIA

Hollis Marsh and Cliffs, named for John Hallows who patented land here in 1647. The three cliffs (Nomini, Horsehead, and Stratford) were originally named "Hollis Cliffs."

APPENDIX "F"

DERIVATION OF POTOMAC RIVER PLACE NAMES
By Frederick Tilp

> PART "C"
>
> COAST & GEODETIC SURVEY
> CHART #559
>
> LOWER CEDAR POINT TO MATTAWOMEN CREEK

C-1 POPES CREEK, MARYLAND, named for Francis Pope who originally patented land here. Just south of the creek was located the Maryland terminal of the Laidlow ferry (called the Hooe ferry in Virginia) which ran continuously for over one hundred years. This was the main route for Confederate mail entering to the North, as the cliffs gave the rebels an unobstructed view both up and down the river. An oyster shell mound covering 30 acres and extending a depth of 20 feet is located at the nearby hill top.

Huckleberry, the home site of Thomas A. Jones, a signal agent for the Confederacy. Between April 15 and 22, 1865, Jones helped to conceal John Wilkes Booth and David Herold here. Then Jones sold his small rowing boat to Booth who with Herold started their escape across the river on April 22, 1865.

Railroad Wharf, built at the time of the railroad from Bowie, Maryland, in 1872, with hopes of it crossing the river, joining main lines in Virginia.

C-2 MATHIAS POINT, VIRGINIA, named for Matthias Hooe. Potomac's first scheduled ferry was established by Colonel William Hooe in 1713; one of his sons was named "Matthias" whose name first was shown on charts of 1736.

Commander James H. Ward, USN, the first U. S. Naval officer to die in the Civil War led an attack ashore here on Confederate gun emplacements and cavalry on June 27, 1861, and was killed.

C-3 PORT TOBACCO CREEK, MARYLAND, named for an Indian village, "Potopaco" (Tr. - "the jutting of water inland"). First shown on Captain John Smith's map of 1608. Charts of 1636 show this as "Portobacks," and probably some cartographer corrupted it into "Port Tobacco" without actually checking the exact derivations.

Chapel Point, named for "Saint Thomas Manor Chapel" and manor house erected here on a Jesuit missionary acreage of 4,000 acres granted in 1649. The river's most beautiful view is from the adjacent cemetery (an absolute "MUST" for anyone interested in Potomac's history).

Brents Landing, named for the local landowner family of "Brents" in 1700. Shown on charts of 1873 as "Pear Tree Point." An active steamboat landing until 1932.

Fourth Point, Jesuit records show this in 1662 as being "Fort Point."

Windmill Point, originally named "Thomas Point" on charts of 1794; changed to "Windmill Point" later.

Port Tobacco town, first Charles County seat established in 1727 and called Charleston until 1820; then changed to Port Tobacco. Charts of 1775 show a ferry running from here to a wharf 1/2 mile west of Mathias Point, Virginia.

C-4 UPPER CEDAR POINT, MARYLAND, first shown on charts of 1737. The Potomac's first floating light-ship was established here in 1820.

C-5 NANJEMOY CREEK, MARYLAND, named for an Indian village, "Nushemouck" (Tr. - "one goes on downward"). First shown on John Smith's map of 1608 as "Nussamek."

APPENDIX "F"

C-5 NANJEMOY CREEK, MARYLAND (Continued)

Hilltop Creek, named for the "Tophill" as shown on a survey of land here in 1864.

Burgess Creek, named for nearby landowner. Originally shown as "Avon River" on charts of 1835; then changed to "Mills Creek."

Balls Point, site of the home of Colonel John A. Hughes who, on April 21, 1865, gave "ham sandwiches, whiskey and newspapers" to John Wilkes Booth and his accomplice, Herold, on their flight from Maryland to Virginia.

C-6 RIVERSIDE, MARYLAND, charts of 1813 show this as "William Hamilton's Place" who ran a ferry to Metompkin Point, Virginia. Charts of 1873 note this as "Nanjemoy Landing." A popular steamboat wharf and store here until 1934.

C-7 CHOTANK CREEK, VIRGINIA, named from an Indian village, "Acowehtank" (Tr. - "it flows in the opposite direction." Charts of 1736 show this as "Jotank."

C-8 STUART POINT, VIRGINIA, named for "Mount Stuart," a dwelling of distinction and dignity, originally built by the Stuart family in 1780.

C-9 METOMPKIN POINT, VIRGINIA, named for an Indian village, "Matomkin" (Tr. - "people who dig the earth." Charts of 1713 show this as "Ticks Hole"; while charts of 1861 indicated it as "Tomkin Point."

C-10 SOMERSET BEACH, VIRGINIA, from here eastward to Mathias Point are located the antibellum mansions of the prominent tidewater families such as Fitzhughs, Fowkes, Alexanders, Washington, Dades, and Stuarts.

C-11 FAIRVIEW BEACH, VIRGINIA, originally named "Boyd's Hole." Site of the Virginia terminal of a popular ferry from Maryland Point as shown on charts of 1775.

C-12 MARYLAND POINT, MARYLAND, site of the largest Doeg Indian nation village on the Potomac, who also inhabited the Virginia shores. Charts of 1666 indicate this as "Maryland Indian Point"; and probably a cartographer corrupted this to "Maryland Point."

Railroad Bridge. An Army map of 1866 shows a proposed railroad extending from Bladensburg, Maryland, to Charleston (Port Tobacco); to Trappe, Maryland; to Maryland Point; thence over the river by a bridge or by use of the ferry to "Boyd's Hole, Virginia."

George Washington used the ferry running from Maryland Point many times, noting it as "Widow Martin's Landing."

C-13 PASSAPATANZY CREEK, VIRGINIA, named from an Indian village, "Paspetansy-town" (Tr. - "stream that scoops out banks"). A favorite place for whiskey stills during Prohibition.

C-14 BULL BLUFF, VIRGINIA, site of a Naval magazine established here during the Revolutionary War.

C-15 POTOMAC CREEK, VIRGINIA, named for an Indian village, "Patowmeck-town" (Tr. - "landing place for goods" or "Emporium"). A canal was proposed in 1827 to run from Wipsewisa Creek (south shore of this creek) across the peninsula to Muddy Creek of the Rappahannock River (south of Fredericksburg, Virginia).

APPENDIX "F"

C-15 POTOMAC CREEK, VIRGINIA (Continued)

Marlboro Point, site of a proposed seaport town of entry - "Marlborough-Town"; by the House of Burgesses in 1680.

Belle Plain, site of the wharf where the bodies of Booth and Herold (Abraham Lincoln's assasins) were placed on a steamer for transportation to Washington.

C-16 AQUIA CREEK, VIRGINIA, named for an Indian village, "Quiyough" (Tr. - "tall or high lands") which actually does describe the adjacent shores rising high from the river's shore line.

Brents Point, named for Mistress Margaret Brent of Saint Mary's City, Maryland, who was granted land here in 1652.

Aquia Creek stone quarries furnished all the tidewater of the Chesapeake Bay mills with their "millstones" for grinding of grains. The quarry originally opened in 1750 for use of tombstone work; worked continuously for building purposes until 1931.

Civil War. The south shore was the site of the terminus of the Aquia Creek and Fredericksburg Railroad; was fortified by Confederates and used as headquarters in menacing Federal navigation on the river for about a year.

Coal Landing, named for the wharf here in 1860. Used for coal delivery from.the Georgetown/Cumberland canal, thence to the railroad at Fredericksburg.

C-17 THOMAS POINT, MARYLAND, first noted as "Thom Point" on charts of 1750, changed to Lower Thomas Point; then to Thomas Point. Assumably from a "Thomas" family.

C-18 CLIFTON BEACH, MARYLAND, named from local family of "Clifton" here in 1651, and so shown on charts as "Clifton Point." Popular summer resort in the late 1890's; serviced daily by steamboats from Washington.

C-19 SMITHS POINT, MARYLAND, assumably named from the versatile Captain John Smith. First shown on charts as "Smith Point" of 1737.

C-20 WADES BAY, MARYLAND, named for the original landowner, Zachariah Wade, who lived here in 1665. Adjoining water front farm of 600 acres was purchased by George Washington in 1775.

C-21 DOUGLAS POINT, MARYLAND, named for James Douglass, a Scottish merchant of Dumfries, Virginia, who owned land here in 1761.

C-22 BLUE BANKS, MARYLAND, named for the bluish marl beds that form the banks. First shown on charts of 1894.

C-23 BRENT MARSH, VIRGINIA, named for "Giles Brent," who built a mill here on the headwaters in 1668. Originally shown as "Brents Mill Run"; then charts of 1862 show it as "Meadow Brook." Anchored off here were several hundred wooden ocean-going vessels built during World War I which became such a hazard that they were moved across the river to Mallows Bay, Maryland.

C-24 CLIFTON POINT (Widewater), VIRGINIA, Cook's Ferry ran from here to Sandy Point, Maryland during the Civil War. Off Widewater was President Cleveland's favorite fishing area. Widewater came to make airplane history when Professor Langley's model of a "heavier-than-air plane" flew three thousand feet in 90 seconds in 1903.

APPENDIX "F"

C-25 LIVERPOOL POINT, MARYLAND, named for the Liverpool (England) tobacco merchants who first established their wharf and warehouse here in 1741. First shown on charts of 1813.

C-26 MALLOWS BAY, MARYLAND, originally named as "Marlows Creek" on charts of 1841 for the local landowner family, "Marlow." However, in 1930 there was an abundant growth of water plants named "marsh-mallows" which thrived here for many years. The site of one of the last colonies of snowy white egrets before Federal protection in 1936. Buried in the waters of Mallows Bay are the hulks of vessels towed here from Brent Marsh, Virginia, area.

C-27 SANDY POINT, MARYLAND. Maryland terminal of Cook's ferry from Widewater, Virginia. Charts of 1862 also show a ferry running from here to Colchester in Occoquan Bay, Virginia. A former steamboat landing up until 1944.

C-28 CHOPAWAMSIC ISLAND, VIRGINIA, named for an Indian village, "Chippawamsic" (Tr. - "separation of the inlet"); the delta of this creek actually is "separated" at the inlet. The creek and swamp here was one of the most beautiful wildlife areas on the East Coast until ruined by a Navy/Marine airfield in the 1920's.

   Missouri Mills, a grist mill which served the countryside for a century and a half was located at the headwaters of this creek.

C-29 QUANTICO, VIRGINIA, named for an Indian village, "Quanticott" (Tr. - "at the long tidal stream"). A tobacco warehouse was established here in 1713. During the Civil War it was known as "Evansport" and had the heaviest Confederate battery of guns planted, extending northward along the shore to Freestone Point. In 1872, a "Potomac Town" was planned as the site of a large town development. U. S. Marine Base established here in 1917. On the shores of Quantico Creek during World War I were built two large three-masted sailing schooners for the U. S. Shipping Board.

C-30 SHIPPING POINT, VIRGINIA, the Virginia terminal of "Budds Ferry" running from Goose Bay, Maryland, causing much apprehension during the Civil War to the Federal Navy. First ferry started here in 1757, running to "Roger Chamberlaynes place" on Goose Bay, Maryland.

C-31 POSSUM POINT, VIRGINIA, an English word derived from an Indian name sounding similarly to "possum." Off Possum Point was anchored part of the British fleet in 1814 after the Capital was burned; the sailors destroyed many farms and plantations ashore here. A terrific gale caused many of the sailing vessels to drag anchor.

C-32 COCKPIT POINT, VIRGINIA. Heavy artillery Confederate batteries occupied these heights in 1861-62 making life miserable for Federal small boats going to and from Washington.

C-33 GOOSE BAY, MARYLAND. Maryland terminal of the "Budds Ferry" which was constantly watched by the Federal Navy, during the Civil War. Mrs. Budd of Charles County ran a thriving business ferry to Shipping Point, Virginia, even though the U. S. Army placed large cannons on shore near her ferry to offset the Confederate cannon on the Virginia shore in 1861-62.

C-34 CHICOMUXEN CREEK, MARYLAND, named for an Indian village here - "Chingomuxon" (Tr. - "high land nearby"). First noted on charts of 1850.

   Lintons Wharf and Poseys Wharf were steamboat landings until the 1930's.

196

APPENDIX "F"

C-35 STUMP NECK, MARYLAND, first shown on 1773 charts as "Dogues'Neck" for the Doeg Indians' village. Then an English chart of 1774 shows it as "Stump Neck," assumably someone cut all the trees down leaving a lot of stumps.

Kudds Point, first shown on charts of 1865 where was located "Winthrops Wharf."

C-36 MATTAWOMEN CREEK, MARYLAND, named for an Indian village, "Mataughquamend" (Tr. - "where one goes pleasantly"). Charts of 1666 show this as "Zachia Swamp." Charts of 1673 show this as "Saint Thomas Creek." In 1910 there were six steamboat wharves in active operation on this creek. It is now (in part) a sewer for the adjoining area.

Winthrops Wharf, named for Beckwith Winthrop, Assistant Secretary of the U. S. Navy. Site of the D. C. Marine Corps officers' rifle range, established in 1909.

Grinders Wharf, named for local landowner; operating during the Civil War.

Procters Wharf, a coaling wharf for the discharge of coal from the Cumberland/ Georgetown canal boats for the Naval Powder Factory use.

Mattingly, Nelson, and Dent were named for families owning steamboat wharves up in this creek in the early 1900's.

C-37 POWELLS CREEK, VIRGINIA, named for Nathaniel Powell (the recorder of John Smith's trip up the Potomac in 1608). However, charts of 1657 show this as "Yosocomico" and charts of 1677 as "Yosockeccocoe"; and at long last on charts of 1692 it is shown as "Powells Creek."

C-38 CHERRY HILL, VIRGINIA, first shown on charts of 1841 as "Morgans Point." Site of the former District of Columbia's garbage disposal plant.

C-39 FREESTONE POINT, VIRGINIA, named for the deposits of sandstone (which were easily cut without splitting). Bluffs used by Confederates sniping at Federal shipping during the Civil War.

APPENDIX "F"

DERIVATION OF POTOMAC RIVER PLACE NAMES
By Frederick Tilp

```
PART "D"

COAST & GEODETIC SURVEY
CHARTS #560

MATTAWOMEN CREEK TO GEORGETOWN
```

D-1 OCCOQUAN, VIRGINIA, named for an Indian village, "Aquoconde" (Tr. - "at the end of water"). Charts of 1654 show this as "Ohoquin." At the foot of the Occoquan falls there was a proposed seaport town of entry-town marked by the General Assembly of Virginia and a public warehouse was built in 1734. Some historians indicate that the Spaniards established a mission here in 1570 called "Axacan" - later destroyed by the Indians.

Neabsco Creek, named for the Indian village, "Niobsco" (Tr. - "at the point of rock"). Ocean-going vessels used this creek until about 1840 for trade in ship building, grain, lumber railroad ties, and barrels.

Belmont Bay, named for the large plantation here, "Belmont Mansion," in 1734.

Marumsco Creek, named for an Indian village, "Marumsco" (Tr. - "at the island"). Charts of 1663 and land patents show a "Horne Island" at the mouth of this creek.

Colchester, laid out as a town in 1753; a very popular and prosperous place for travelers due to the fine foods served here in local "ordinaries," during and after the Revolutionary War.

Woodbridge, named obviously for a wooden bridge. Here a ferry was established by direction of the General Assembly in 1681. George Mason received a ferry contract in 1774 and in 1795 he mentions a new toll bridge here and so named the village on the southern shore as "Woodbridge."

Occoquan town. During the 1800's, this town had one of the largest cotton spinning mills and shad/herring fisheries on the East Coast.

D-2 SYCAMORE POINT, VIRGINIA, first noted on charts of 1907. A popular steamboat landing for picnickers from Washington until the early twenties.

D-3 HALLOWING POINT, VIRGINIA, first named on county maps as "Holland Point" in 1660. Charts of 1878 show this as "Hollings Point." The Chapman family of Maryland owned land here for its ferry boat service to "Chapman's Landing" in Maryland established during the colonial era.

Craney Island, named for the numerous cranes here as charts of 1773 show this as "Crane Island" and about three times its present (1968) size.

D-4 INDIAN HEAD, MARYLAND, charts of 1710 show this as "Pamunkey Indian Lands."
                          1776..............."Indian Point"
                          1835..............."Indian Head Lands"
                          1865..............."Indian Head Point"
                          1866..............."Indian Head"

D-5 GLYMONT, MARYLAND, named for a nearby plantation, "Glymont," meaning "happy hill." A popular summer resort for Washingtonians starting in the 1870's. There were two Glymont Landings about 1/4 mile apart -- the upper named "Pyes Landing" (chart of 1862) and the lower landing as "Marburys Landing."

APPENDIX "F"

D-6 CHAPMANS LANDING, MARYLAND, named from the first landowners, the "Chapman" family. The original home on a high bluff overlooking the river was built in 1670 and is still occupied in 1968.

D-7 POMONKEY CREEK, MARYLAND, named for an Indian village, "Pamunkey" (Tr. - "twisting in the lands"). The present town of Fenwick was formerly named "McGhiesport" both for local landowners. The fresh water springs which emptied into the creek were so pure that many sailing vessels anchored off-shore and filled their water casks with the "Pomonkey Spring Water" -- this practice ended in 1926.

D-8 GREENWAY FLATS. These flats are extensive shoals south of Marshall Hall and east of Fort Belvoir. So named for a mansion, "Greenway"; the Shenandoah home of Lord Fairfax who owned Belvoir before the Revolutionary War. It was a favorite place for deep drafted sailing ships to run aground trying to "cut corners here."

D-9 GUNSTON COVE, VIRGINIA, named for the hamlet of Gunston in Staffordshire, England, by the original landowner, George Mason, who built "Gunston Hall" in 1755/58 -- a rare and fine example of American Georgian architecture. The "Cove" was the headquarters of the Potomac Flotilla of three vessels organized and in part sponsored by George Mason for protection of the Potomac in the Revolutionary War.

    Charts of 1653 show the Cove as "Doeg Island Creek"
            1774...................."Pohick Creek"
            1794...................."Baxters Creek"

    Accotink Creek, named for an Indian village, "Accotink" (Tr. - "at the end of the hill") and shown on charts of 1657. Heavy river traffic in this creek was evident, as in 1880 local landowners indicated to Congress that 8,000 acres of farm land was dependent on keeping the creek dredged for passage of the steamers and sailing craft. It is now (in part) a sewer of the adjoining housing developments.

    Pohick Creek, named for an Indian village, "Pohick" (Tr. - "at the water place"). John Smith's map of 1608 shows this as "Pawcohiccora."

    The peninsula between Pohick and Accotink was shown on charts of 1841 as "Wheat Patch Point."

D-10 WHITESTONE POINT, VIRGINIA, the site of "Belvoir Mansion" built by Colonel William Fairfax in 1741, which was burned by the British in 1814.

    Charts of 1669 show this as "Poynt of Pohick"
            1741.............."Rankins Point"
            1814.............."White House"

    Fort Belvoir, originally named "Fort Humphries" from 1927 to 1934.

D-11 DOGUE CREEK, VIRGINIA, named for an Indian village, "Doeg" (Tr. - "little creek").

    Grist Mill, owned by George Washington, located at the headwaters of this creek. It was asserted by Washington that "grains from this mill were equal in quality to any made in this country"; used at Mt. Vernon for baking and distilling purposes and shipped aboard the "Washington schooners."

    Charts of 1657 show this as "Hopkins Creek"
            1797.............."Dogneny Creek"
            1813.............."Epsewassen Stream"

D-12 FERRY POINT, VIRGINIA, named for the ferry boat terminal here "by the Virginia General Assembly in 1745 an act establishing a public ferry from Clifton Neck (Ferry Pt.) to the Maryland shores (between Marshall Hall and Bull Town Cove)." The Clifton

APPENDIX "F"

D-12 FERRY POINT, VIRGINIA (Continued)
Ferry operated continuously until 1808. This area was a favorite for Virginia duellists -- the last being fought here in 1805. The Ferry House and popular artesian well fell into ruins about 1850.

D-13 MOUNT VERNON, VIRGINIA, named for the British Admiral Vernon by Lawrence Washington (Brother of George) in honor of his former Naval Commander and personal friend. John Washington, the great-grandfather of George, applied for a patent to this land in 1669. The original grant included over 5,000 acres, stretching along the Potomac from Dogue Creek to Great Hunting Creek (south of Alexandria). Pollution has killed much of the fish life once enjoyed by George Washington.

D-14 LITTLE HUNTING CREEK, VIRGINIA, first named by Giles Brent of Saint Mary's City in his accounts of 1658 as "Little Hunting Creek." George Washington's schooners docked here to load freight and allow the fresh water to kill worms and barnacles.

D-15 MARSHALL HALL, MARYLAND, named for William Marshall, original grantee of this land in 1651. Public swimming beach was closed here at the local amusement park in 1932 due to river pollution.

D-16 BULL TOWN COVE, MARYLAND. Derivation of name unfound to date. Located on the boundary of Prince George's and Charles Counties; this was the last stronghold of the river "arks" -- floating houses or stores for Potomac rivermen. A favorite stopping place for sailing craft on the way to Washington.

D-17 BRYAN POINT, MARYLAND, named for William Bryan who built "Bryan Hall" about 1800. Site of the U. S. Fish Commission's hatchery where millions of shad and perch were propagated yearly until about 1930 -- pollution stopped this.

D-18 PISCATAWAY CREEK, MARYLAND, named for an Indian village, "Pascattawaye" (Tr. - "high passable bank around a bend in the river"). On the south shore, Captain John Smith, in 1608, noted an Indian village, "Moyaone." This was a harbor for ocean-going vessels in the early colonial days. Shoaling and pollution has shoaled this creek, preventing use only by dredging temporary channels.

Piscataway town, at the headwaters boasted in 1690 several warehouses, and in 1752 the first theatrical performance on the Potomac was given, perhaps to such distinguished Maryland families as the Hansons, Addisons, and the Digges; and Virginia families of note -- the Masons of "Gunston Cove" and Washington of "Mount Vernon."

Civil War encouraged so much smuggling to the Virginia shore that a Federal Naval vessel was assigned here in October, 1861.

Accokeek Creek, named for a small Indian village here, "Aquakick" (Tr. - "where the edge of the hill is"). First shown on charts of 1653.

Farmington Landing had a thriving store and wharf for small river steamers to Alexandria, Virginia, from Civil War days until about 1914.

D-19 FORT WASHINGTON, MARYLAND, named as defense for the federal city by Major Charles l'Enfant who planned the city of Washington. Originally named "Fort Warburton" for the estate on which it was first built, "Warburton Manor," patented in 1661, was the home of the Digges family, prominent in colonial and Revolutionary affairs in Maryland and Virginia.

D-20 SHERIDAN POINT, VIRGINIA, originally shown on charts of 1658 as "Piscatawu Neck." Probably named "Sheridan Point" for the Civil War General Sheridan due to an Army establishment here named "Fort Hunt."

APPENDIX "F"

D-21 SWAN CREEK, MARYLAND, named for the "numerous swans" here-on charts of 1666.

Hatton Point, named for original landowners, the "Hatton" family.

D-22 RIVERVIEW, MARYLAND, a popular "river steamboat landing and resort" from the 1890's until 1936. Pollution stopped public swimming here at the sandy beach.

D-22 BROAD CREEK, MARYLAND, named for its "broad expanse" by English Episcopal settlers in 1650-60. Saint John's Episcopal Church parish was founded at the head-waters in 1692.

Indian Queen Bluffs, named for the "queenly wife" of the Indian Emporer "Chito-machen" who lived here in 1640 who was baptised and married by the Jesuits, later renamed "Mary."

D-23 WELLINGTON, VIRGINIA, named for the "Wellington House" located on the river bank, built in 1760 and occupied by Colonel Tobias Lear, the private and military secretary to General George Washington and afterwards private tutor to his adopted children. Charts of 1862 show this as "Red House." Just north of "Red House" is "Hog Island," noted on many charts as "Hell Hole" (especially those of the Civil War period) as it was an impassable swamp for travelers of that time.

D-24 ROZIER'S BLUFF, MARYLAND, named for Charles Rozier who owned land here in 1776.

Fort Foote, named for Admiral Andrew Hull Foote, a Commandant of the Washington Navy Yard and Commander of the South Atlantic Blockading Squadron during the Civil War. Invasion of Washington by the Confederates during the Civil War was of such concern that U. S. Army Engineer, B. S. Alexander, submitted a design to "block the invading fleet," consisting of iron chains stretched across the river supported by many large wooden floats.

D-25 NEW ALEXANDRIA, VIRGINIA, on the south shore of Great Hunting Creek, so named by a firm of real estate developers in the late 1890's as part of a promotional plan to establish a town along the Washington, Alexandria, and Mount Vernon Electric Railway which ran from Washington city (terminal at 13½ and D Streets, N.W.) to Mount Vernon, Virginia.

Scottish merchants from Dumfries built a warehouse on the south shore of this creek naming it Belhaven in 1732, in honor of the traditional hero of the merchants at that time -- John Hamilton (1656-1708), second Baron Belhaven whose famous speeches in the British Parliament were "the only specimen of Scottish parliamentary oratory which has found its way into English collections of rhetorical masterpieces."

D-26 HUNTING CREEK, VIRGINIA, originally named "Indian Cabin Creek"; then charts of 1669 show it as "Great Mussle Creek." However, Mistress Margaret Brent of Saint Mary's City patented land here in 1654 and so noted it as "Great Hunting Creek," probably to contrast it to "Little Hunting Creek" (near Mt. Vernon). Shipyards prospered on the northern shore until the early 1900's, when pollution killed Alexandria's most beautiful wildlife swamp and changed it into a cesspool of filth (1968).

D-27 ALEXANDRIA, VIRGINIA, named for John Alexander, who purchased 6,000 acres in this area about 1675 for 6,000 pounds of tobacco. The city was looted by the British in 1814 after the capture of Washington. A prosperous seaport in 1880 as the Court House registered 182 sailing vessels here. The last commercial sailing vessel carried oyster shells to the local fertilizer factory in 1944. Maritime influence was so powerful in this city that in 1779 the town acquired a "City Seal" picturing a full sailing ship with a balance equally poised above the ship.

APPENDIX "F"

D-27 ALEXANDRIA, VIRGINIA (Continued)

Jones Point, named for Cadwalder Jones, a British trader with the tidewater Potomac Indians, who established a trading post here in 1682 and left fairly accurate maps of the river in 1699. Also, the site of old Fort Columbia, a fortification of wood and earthworks built for Revolutionary War defense.

D-28 FOX FERRY, MARYLAND, named for George Fox who established a ferry here in the 1800's. During the Civil War smuggling was so prosperous that there were two wharves here named "the upper and the lower." Then, during Prohibition times the ferry was re-activated into a second prosperous operation for the use of corn and rye whiskey importation from Southern Maryland to the thirsty Virginians. Pollution and silt stopped this about 1932.

D-29 OXON CREEK, MARYLAND, named for Oxford College in England by John Addison, who having been to Oxford College and therefore being an "Oxonian," named his first patent of land and estate, "Oxon Hill." Pollution and D. C. dumps have ruined a once beautiful creek and wildlife refuge swamp.

Disneyland. A scheme proposed in 1968 will develop the south shore of Oxon Creek as an "East Coast Disneyland."

Marbury Point, on the north shore, named for Francis Marbury, who was granted land here in 1693. At Shepherds Landing; there was a railroad ferry operating to the Alexandria terminal of the Georgetown/Alexandria canal docks during the late 1800's. An auto ferry operated here for about ten months in 1934. A railroad bridge was erected here during World War I; dismantled 1947.

D-30 BELLEVUE, D. C., named by the U. S. Government in 1873 for the establishment of a naval magazine here; the farm originally located here was named the "Bellville Farm."

D-31 FOUR MILE RUN, VIRGINIA, charts of 1693 show this as "Four Mill Run." A written account of 1706 with chart indicates "Four Mile Creek," as it is four miles above Great Hunting Creek (which is incorrect).
    Charts of 1862 indicate this as "Roaches Mill Run" named for the Roach family who purchased and operated George Washington's former mill located at the headwaters of this creek.
    Brochures printed and distributed by a Georgetown steam packet line before the Civil War indicate the derivation of the name as due to it being a "Four Mile Run" from Georgetown, D. C. to here. (But, the name was "Four Mile Run" even before steamboats were running on the river, so this is incorrect also.)
    Sailing vessels were built along these shores until after the Civil War, and then Virginia's pollution deposits ended all clean activity.

D-32 GIESBORO POINT, D. C., named for an estate located on the nearby hill named "Giesborough" in 1663. Estates of colonial historical distinction in this area were Oxon Hill, Giesborough, Saint Elizabeth's, and Blue Plains.

D-33 ROACHES RUN, D. C., named for the local landowners, the Roach family (see Four Mile Run).

D-34 HAINS POINT, D. C., named for Peter C. Hains, Major of the U. S. Engineers, in charge of the land fill and dredging work of the present East Potomac Park (formerly called the "speedway"). Previously, this entire area was a wildlife and game refuge teeming with birds and game -- then came pollution and man's desire for more land and stone seawalls.

APPENDIX "F"

D-35 GREENLEAF POINT, D. C., named for John Greenleaf who owned this land and sold it for an Army fort in 1803; named then changed to "Arsenal Point." The bodies of John Wilkes Booth and the three other alleged conspirators were buried here for several years.

D-36 ANACOSTIA, D. C., named for an Indian village, "Natoctchtanck" (Tr. - "a town of traders"). An Indian community devoted to agriculture and fishing along this southern shore from Giesboro Point to Bladensburg was mentioned several times in early traveler's accounts.

Anacostia River, first shown on charts as "Saint Isidore's Creek"; then changed to "Saint Thomas Bay"; then to the "Eastern Branch"; and charts of 1927 changed it to the "Anacostia River."

D-37 BUZZARDS POINT, D. C., named on the Hermann map of 1673 as "Turkey Buzzard Point," probably due to the dead bodies of wild animals which may have drifted there due to the currents of the Anacostia River -- and attracted buzzards. During the land ownership by a "Young" family in the 1700's, the point was shown on chart as "Young's Point." A popular fishing "haul-seine point" by the Indians, and early settlers -- they probably deposited excess fish here, and this would have attracted buzzards. Today it is the partial outlet for sewer lines which do not attract buzzards.

D-38 JAMES CREEK, D. C., (which ran along the east wall of Fort McNair to Canal Street). This creek was dredged in 1875 permitting canal boats and sailing craft to deliver building materials to the foot of Jenkin's Hill (site of the U. S. Capitol building).

James Creek Canal ran from a spot west of Buzzards Point, northward to Canal Street, thence northward on South Capitol Street; making several turns westward of Capitol Hill; thence directly west on Constitution Avenue to a spot where the Lincoln Memorial now stands. As pollution increased, the Canal was completely filled in by 1934, mostly with coal ashes, trash, and granite paving blocks.

D-39 TIDAL BASIN, D. C., formerly called "Tiber Bay" which was the mouth of Tiber Creek. Named "Tiber Bay" in 1803 by local real estate operators who had hoped to have the new federal city exceed in grandeur that of ancient Rome (which was built on the "Tiber River"). Sailing ships delivering stone for the Washington Monument moored their craft in Tiber Bay. Named "Tidal Basin" by U. S. Engineers in a designed effort to have tidal currents flush the Washington Channel of pollution and debris from the commercial markets there. (Note: It did not work satisfactorily.)

D-40 ROCHAMBEAU MEMORIAL BRIDGE, D. C., originally called "Long Bridge." Since the first one was built in 1809 of one mile in length, several replacements have been built on the same spot -- running from the intersection of 14th and "D" Streets, S.W. to Columbia Island, Virginia (originally called "Alexander's Island"). Most of the bridges were washed away or burned as in the case of the British invasion of 1814.

D-41 THEODORE ROOSEVELT ISLAND, D. C., originally called "My Lord's Island"; then changed to "Mason's Island," named by George Mason's son who resided here in a home titled "Barbados"; then changed to "Analostan Island," for an Indian village here of the same name; then changed by Congress in 1931 to "Theodore Roosevelt Island." Formerly a beautiful and secluded wildlife reserve, but people and pollution will soon change all this.

D-42 ROCK CREEK, D. C., named for the numerous rocks along its shore by a Scotsman named Ninian Beall who patented 765 acres of land here in 1703 and named his residence "Rock of Cymbarton." At this time there was a river landing on the west side of Rock Creek called "Saw Pit Landing."

APPENDIX "F"

D-43 GEORGETOWN, D. C., named by local landowners George Mason, George Gordon, and George Beall. In 1658, the site was part of Charles County, Maryland; in 1659 was part of Prince George's County; in 1748 - part of Frederick County; in 1776 - part of Montgomery County; and in 1871 finally became part of the District of Columbia. In 1876 seventy-nine commercial sailing vessels and thirty steamboats registered "Georgetown" as their "home port."

B-44 AQUEDUCT BRIDGE, D. C. (located to the north of the present Key Bridge); named for the aqueduct which contained the Georgetown to Alexandria canal; started in 1830 and opened for traffic in 1833. This bridge was superseded by ferry boats consecutively named "Magee's Ferry," "Awbrey's Ferry," and "Mason's Ferry."

D-45 THREE SISTERS ISLAND, D. C., named for three Indian maidens, sisters of an Analostan chief, who, according to tradition, were drowned one night in a whirlpool and on the following morning there appeared three rocky islands.

D-46 WASHINGTON NAVY YARD. Prior to 1799, U. S. Naval construction was performed entirely at private shipyards. Encouraged by the strong interest of General George Washington, Congress approved the establishment of this yard resulting in the construction of 19 wooden sailing, fighting vessels and 3 engine powered vessels; the largest being the "Minnesota" -- a wooden hulled screw frigate of 3,200 tons launched in 1855.

D-47 BLADENSBURG, MARYLAND, named for Thomas Bladen, the colonial Governor of the Province from 1742/1746-47. Originally named "Garrison Landing"; chartered in 1742 to serve the area for transporting tobacco to England -- the last schooner leaving Bladensburg with hogsheads of that leaf in 1842. One hundred years of profitable use was made of this seaport until pollution and silt ruined the importance of the town and the Eastern Branch as a seaport.

D-48 POTOMAC RIVER, named for the "Patowmeck" Indians and so noted on John Smith's map of 1608 (Tr. - "landing place for goods" or even "Emporium") as most Indians living on the river were great "traders" in minerals, bison skins, colored earths, etc."

The source of the Potomac: From a spring located near Kempton, Maryland (the western dividing lines between Maryland and West Virginia) the Potomac River starts from a modest trickle on its journey to the Chesapeake Bay. Near this spring stands the Fairfax Stone with a plaque which explains, "This monument, at the head spring of the Potomac River, marks one of the historical spots of America. Its name is derived from Thomas Lord Fairfax, who owned all the land lying between the Potomac and the Rappahannock Rivers. The first Fairfax Stone, marked "FX" was set in 1746 by Thomas Lewis, a surveyor employed by Lord Fairfax. This is the base point for a western dividing line between Maryland and West Virginia."

The Potomac River has been shown on charts since 1608 as Red River, Maryland River, Elizabeth River, Cohongoronta River, Patowmeck, Wappa-comma River.

APPENDIX "G"

BIBLIOGRAPHY

The Potomac by Frederick Gutheim, Rinehart and Co., Inc., New York - 1949

Narratives of Early Maryland 1633-1684, Edited by Clayton Colman Hall, Charles Scribner's Sons, New York

The Spanish Jesuit Mission in Virginia 1570-1572 by Clifford M. Lewis, S.J., and Albert J. Loomie, S.J., published for The Virginia Historical Society by the University of North Carolina Press

The Calvert Papers No. 1, Fund Publication No. 28, published by the Maryland Historical Society, Baltimore, Maryland - 1889

The Gerard-Cheseldine Family Genealogy by Edwin W. Beitzell - 1947 (Privately printed)

The Archives of Maryland published by the Maryland Historical Society, Baltimore, Maryland

The Beitzell Family Genealogy by Edwin W. Beitzell - 1948 (Privately printed)

Follow the Water by Varley Lang, published by John F. Blair, Winston-Salem, N. C. - 1961

The Lord's Oysters by Gilbert Byron, published by Little, Brown and Company - 1957

Stephen R. Mallory by Joseph T. Durkin, S.J., published by the University of North Carolina Press - 1954

The Chronicles of St. Mary's, Vols. 1-15, published by the St. Mary's County Historical Society, Leonardtown, Maryland

The Bulletin of the Northumberland County (Virginia) Historical Society (Vols. 1-4)

The British Invasion of Maryland 1812-1815 by Wm. M. Marine

Eleanor Calvert and Her Circle by Alice Coyle Torbet, published by the William-Frederick Press, New York - 1950

Daily National Intelligencer

Niles Weekly Register

The Maryland Journal

The Maryland Gazette

A History of the National Capital (2 Vols.) by Wilhelmas Bogart Bryan, published by The Macmillan Co., New York - 1914

U. S. Census Records of Prince George's, St. Mary's, and Charles Counties, Maryland; Northumberland, Westmoreland, King George, and Stafford Counties, Virginia

The National Geographic Magazine

The St. Mary's Beacon (Leonardtown, Maryland)

The Civil War At Sea by Virgil Carrington Jones, published by Holt, Rinehart, Winston - New York, 1960-1961

Chesapeake Bay Log Canoes by M. V. Brewington

Mariners Museum Publication No. 3 - 1937, Newport News, Virginia

APPENDIX "G"

Chesapeake Bay - A Pictorial Maritime History by M. V. Brewington, Cornell Maritime Press, Cambridge, Maryland - 1953

Chesapeake Bay Bugeyes by M. V. Brewington, published by The Mariners Museum, Newport News, Virginia; printed by Dietz Press - 1941

Chesapeake Circle by Robert H. Burgess

This Was Chesapeake Bay by Robert H. Burgess

A History of Maryland by James McSherry, Baltimore - 1852

Lists of Merchant Vessels of the U. S.

A Cruising Guide to the Chesapeake by Fessenden S. Blanchard, published by Dodd Mead & Co., New York - 1950

Official Records of the Union and Confederate Navies in the War of the Rebellion, Series I, Volumes 4 and 5 - Government Printing Office 1896-1897

War of the Rebellion Official Records of the Union and Confederate Armies, Series II, Volume 6

Potomac Landings by Paul Wilstach

Causes of the Maryland Revolution of 1689 by F. E. Sparks

Correspondence, diaries, and manuscripts - The Woodstock College, Woodstock, Maryland

Records of the Columbia Historical Society

History of Travel in America by Seymour Dunbar, Tudor Publishing Co., New York - 1937

The Evening and Sunday Star, Washington, D. C.

The Washington Post, Washington, D. C.

The Chesapeake Skipper (Magazine)

William and Mary Quarterly, Vol. 15

The Chesapeake Bay Pilots by M. V. Brewington (booklet); also in Maryland Historical Magazine, XLVIII, 2, June 1953

History of Charles County, Maryland by James Brown and Margaret Brown Klaptor - 1958

United States National Archives, Department of Commerce Records, Bureau of Lighthouses; also Social and Economics Branch, Ships Records

The Maryland Dents by Harry Wright Newman, Dietz Press, Inc., Richmond, Virginia - 1963

Early Days of Washington by Sally Somervel Mackall (Privately printed - 1899)

Greenleaf and Law in the Federal Capital by Allen C. Clark, Press of W. F. Roberts, Washington, D. C. - 1901

Washington Village and Capital, 1800-1878, by Constance McLaughlin Green, Princeton University Press, Princeton, New Jersey - 1962 (2 Vols.)

Washington City and Capital, Federal Writer's Project, W.P.A., American Guide Series, U. S. Government Printing Office, Washington, D. C. - 1937

INDEX

212

Deagle, Mr., 59
Daily National Intelli-
  gencer, 28, 112
"Daisie," schooner, 54,
  140
"Daisy," sloop, 140
Dalton, John, 19
Dalton, Tristam, 26
Dameron, Luke, 32
Dameron Marshes, Va., 45
"Dana," U.S.S., 39
"Dandy," horse, 53
"Dandy," steamboat, 111
Danials, Capt. Frank, 163
Daniel, Capt. Leon, 162
"Daniel J. Ballard,"
  pungy, 140
"Daniel," schooner, 140
Dare, Virginia, 2
"Dash," sloop, 140
"Dashaway," schooner, 140
Davenport, Col., 44
Davidson's Wharf, 26
Davis, Capt. David, 9
Davis, Jno., 6
Davis, Mitchell, 125
Davis, M. M. (Cell), 58,
  63, 67, 70, 145, 157
Davis, Mr., 42
Davis, President Jeffer-
  son, 46
Dawson, Christopher, 32
Dawson, William, 44
Deale, Md., 59, 71
Deal's Island, 24, 81,
  162, 163
Dean, Augustus, 65, 143
Dean, Mattie F., 63
Dean, William H., 71
Deblois, Lewis, 26
Decatur, Commodore Stephen,
  38
Decourcey, William, 20
Deep Creek, 3, 119, 188
"Defence," ship, 19, 20,
  140
"Defender," dory, 60, 93,
  94, 128, 130
"Defy," pungy, 140
Delahay, Kenneth, 58
Delahay, Mrs. J. R., 58
Delahay, Ronald, 58
Delaware Bay, 60, 88
Delaware Breakwater, 47
Delaware River, 111
Delehay, Francis, 41
"Delight," sloop, 140
de Marques, Pedro Menendez,
  183
Dent, Alex, 168
Dent, Capt. George, 16,
  21, 41
Dent, Dr. Walter B., 119
Dent Family, 12
Dent, General John, 17,
  18
Dent, Helen, 119
Dent, James H., 168
Dent, J. F., 36

Dent, John, 41, 151, 168
Dent, Majr. Wm., 7
Dent, Sam, 168
Dent's Landing, 12
Dent, Stoney, 95, 97, 98
Dent's Wharf, 196
Dent, Thomas, 10, 12
Dent, William, 12
Denwood, Liven, 8
Devaney, Julius, 165
"Devastation," H.M.S., 33
Deveran, Marny, 6
Dickens, Capt. George,
  141, 147
Dickens, Capt. Henry, 141,
  155
Dickerson, Capt. James,
  67, 161
Dickerson, John, 168
Dickson, Capt. William
  (Bill), 75, 99
Dickson, Wm., 10
Dickyson, Wm., 9
Digges Family, 199
Diggs, Madam, 7
Dills, Mr., 41
Dingee, Capt. James, 67,
  161, 169
Diocese of Richmond, 51
Dipple Fishery, 90
"Dirigo," schooner, 140
Disharvon, Calvin, 151
Disneyland, 201
"District of Columbia,"
  steamboat, 116, 117, 123
Dividing Creek, 10, 45,
  150
Dixon, Thomas, 8
Dize, Capt. Daniel, 163
Dobbins, Capt., 44
Dobson, Capt. J. Frank,
  163
Doctors Point, 191
Dodson, Austin J., 166
Dodson, Bertrand, 169
Dodson, Charles J., 170
Dodson Creek, 191
Dodson, Eugene O., 170
Dodson, Gervais, 191
Dodson, John, 169
Dodson, Mortimer L., 170
Dodson, Thomas M., 170
Doeg Indian Nation, 193,
  196, 198
Doeg Island Creek, 198
Dogneny Creek, 198
Dogue Creek, 3, 34, 198,
  199
Dogue's Neck, 196
Dolly Boarman's Creek, 3,
  189
"Dolphin," pungy, 52, 66,
  140
"Dolphin," ship, 16
Doncaster, Md., 63
Donoho, Capt. Lafayette,
  162
Dorchester County, Md.,
  8, 60, 61, 69, 140, 146,
  150, 152, 154, 156

"Dorchester," steamboat,
  116, 117, 118
Dories, 52, 53, 55, 57,
  58, 59, 60, 66, 68,
  70, 71, 76, 77, 79,
  85, 86, 93, 96, 130
"Doris C," dory, 57
Dorsey, Edwd., 7
Dorsey, Jno., 7
Dorsey, Joshua, 7
Dorsey, Samll., 7
Dorsey, Stephen, 8
Dorsey, Walter B., 84
Douglas, Dr. J. H., 42
Douglas, James E., 113
Douglas, John, 113, 114
Douglas Point, 194
Douglass, James, 194
"Dove," pungy, 58, 64,
  68, 69, 142
"Dove," sloop, 140
Downey, Capt. Lum, 149
Downs, James, 55
Downs, Mrs. Helen (Bailey),
  68
"Dragon," U.S.S., 45
Draper, Col. Alonzo G.,
  43, 44, 45
"Dreamland," steamboat,
  53
Dredging Crabs, 105, 107
Dredging, Oyster, 57, 65,
  70, 71, 72, 74, 76, 77,
  78, 79, 80, 81, 82, 85,
  86, 104, 125, 191
Drury, T. T., 39
Ducks, 1, 125, 126, 127,
  133, 134
"Duck," sloop, 142
Dukeharts Bar, 78
Dukeharts Channel, 189
Dulles International Air-
  port, 136
Dumfries, Va., 194, 200
Duncan, Capt. George, 77,
  141, 155
Duncan, Capt. Walter, 162
Duncanson, Robert, 28
"Dun Luce," ship, 16
Dunmore, Lord, 16, 17, 19,
  21, 24
"Dunmore, ship, 16
Dunn, Capt. William, 164
Dunnington, Magruder, 169
Dunnington, Stanislaus,
  169
Dunnock, John A., 71
Dunnock, Levin T., 71
Dyer, Joseph, 169
Dynam, James, 10
Dyson, Chloe, 113
Eagles, 1, 98
"Eagle," ship, 142
Eagles Nest Fishery, 90
"Earl Biscoe," schooner,
  142
Early, General Jubal A.,
  46, 47, 116
Eastern Bay, 73

Eastern Branch, 3, 12, 26,
27, 47, 89, 100, 202,
203
Eastern Shore, 6, 23, 64,
65, 68, 74, 79, 81, 85,
108
"Eastern Shore," steamboat,
120
East India Trade, 26
Easton, Md., 74, 101, 106,
109
Eastport, Md., 71
East Potomac Park, 201
Eaton, Thomas C., Jr., 52
Eden, Governor Robert,
16, 26
"Edith M.," bugeye, 142
"Edith Marcy," bugeye, 67,
142
"Edith Muir," bugeye, 77,
142
"Edna & Nellie," bugeye,
142
"Edna Bright Haugh,"
schooner, 159
"Edna J. Cox," skipjack,
142
"Edward Dean," schooner,
52, 54, 64, 65, 69, 142
Edward, King of England,
66
Edwards, Cyrus, 166
Edwards, Elias, 170
Edwards, Elias W., 170
Edward's Ferry, 36
Edwards, Griffin B., 166
"Edwin H. Stuart," schoon-
er, 142
"Edwin J. Palmer," schoon-
er, 66, 142
Eels, 97, 98, 109
Egerton, Mrs., 22
Egrets, 195
Elbow Point, 187
"Elenora Russell," bugeye,
63, 77, 142
"Elexena," schooner, 142
"Eliza Ann," schooner, 142
Elizabeth City, N. C., 144
"Elizabeth Clarke," schoon-
er, 142
Elizabeth River, 46, 203
Elkins, William E., 166
Elk River, 20
"Ella B," dory, 60
"Ella Covington," bugeye,
58, 142
"Ella F. Cripps," schoon-
er, 63, 85, 142
"Ella G. Pride," bugeye,
142
"Ella Hill," skipjack, 142
"Ella May," dory, 60
Ellenborough, house, 40
Ellicott, James F., 39
Elliott, T., 58
Ellis, Capt. Bernard, 67,
145, 147
Ellis, Capt. Charles A.
(Sandy), 65, 149, 161

Ellis, Capt. Cyrus, 70,
147
Ellis, Capt. George W.,
70, 145, 147, 157, 161
Ellis, Capt. Gilbert,
128, 134
Ellis, Capt. Paul, 70, 147
Ellis, Capt. William
(Billy), 147
Ellis, Delmas (Bee), 128
Ellis, George Cyrus, 70
Ellis, James Edwin, 70
Ellis, John W., 165
Ellis, Mrs. Bessie (Gibson),
70
Ellis, Richard, 165
Ellis, Susan, 55
Ellitt, John, 9
Ellsworth, Col. Ephraim
Elmer, 37, 113
Elm Hollow, 93
Elsey, Petr., 8
"Emma Berry," pungy, 142
"Emma Grant," sloop, 142
"Emma R. Faunce," schoon-
er, 67, 144
"Emma," sloop, 142
"Emma V. Wills," schooner,
58, 65, 144
"Emmett Arthur," sloop,
68, 144
"Endeavor," steamboat,
118
Enfield, house, 39, 46,
49
England, 2, 3, 9, 11, 13,
15, 22, 24, 25, 27, 72,
88, 125, 126, 188, 203
Ennalls, Major, 8
Ennis, Capt. Thomas, 7
"Enola," sloop, 64, 65,
94, 144
"Enquire," sloop, 144
"Enterprise," dory, 134
Entwisle, Capt. Charlie, 116
"E. P. Evans," schooner,
63, 142
Epsewassen Stream, 198
"Erebus," H.M.S., 33
Esperanza, 121
"Essex," U.S.S., 34
"Estelle Randall," steam-
boat, 117
"Ethel," sloop, 64, 144
"Ethel Vail," bugeye, 77,
144
"Etta," schooner, 144
"Eula K," schooner, 144
"Eunice S," skipjack, 144
"Euryalus," H.M.S., 33
"Eva Clarence," bugeye,
67, 144
"Eva Lee," sloop, 144
Evans, Alfred, 167
Evans, Capt. Ernest, 163
Evans, Capt. Harry, 163
Evans, Capt. Johnson A.,
162
Evans, Capt. Ogdon, 163
Evans, Capt. Severn, 163

Evans, Capt. William
Wallace, 108
Evans, Cornelius P., 169
Evans, David, 169
Evans, John A., 168
Evans, John H., 166
Evans, Lewis, 166, 167
Evans, Michell, 166
Evans, O. N., 39
Evansport, Va., 195
"Eva," pungy, 80
Evening Star Newspaper,
49, 59, 111
Everenden, Thos., 8
Ewell, Capt. Harrison,
58, 65, 139, 151
Ewell, Dr. James, 116
Ewell, Md., 162, 163
"Excelsior," steamboat,
115
"Express," steamboat,
113, 114, 115
"Factor," ship, 9
Fagan, Jesse, 71
Fairbank, Md., 162
Fairfax, Col., 24
Fairfax, Col. William,
198
Fairfax County, Va., 12,
19
Fairfax, Lord Thomas,
198, 203
Fairfax Stone, 203
Fair Landing, 90
"Fair Maid," pilot boat,
21, 144
Fairmount, Md., 138, 142,
146, 152
"Fairplay," sloop, 144
Fairview Beach, 193
"Fairview," schooner, 52,
144
"Fairy," H.M.S., 33
Fallers Landing, 90
Fallon, Capt. William,
40, 141
Fall River, Mass., 61,
151
"Fannie Kemp," boat, 67,
144
"Fannie," schooner, 144
"Fanny Shepherd," sloop,
62, 70, 144
"Fanny," ship, 16
Farmington Landing, 199
"Father & Sons," schooner,
144
Faunce, Capt. Con, 63, 68,
93, 94, 96, 157
Faunce, Capt. Evans, 99
Faunce, Capt. Frank, 96,
97, 99
Faunce, Capt. Jacob (Jake)
R., 66, 67, 94, 96, 145,
147, 149
Faunce, Capt. Joe, 96
Faunce, David Mc, 66
Faunce Family, 90
Faunce, John B., 66
Fearson, Mr., 35

214

"Federal Hill," schooner, 144
Felix, Ensign, 45
Fendall, Governor Josias, 14, 15
Fendall's Rebellion, 5, 14
Fenwick, Bishop Benedict, 20
Fenwick, Bishop Edward Dominic, 11
Fenwick, Capt. Edward, 11
Fenwick, Capt. Ignatius, 11, 20, 24, 153
Fenwick, Charles E., 120
Fenwick, Col. Ignatius, 20, 24, 34
Fenwick, Cuthbert, 4, 5, 13
Fenwick, James, 11, 24
Fenwick, John, 169
Fenwick, Joseph, 24
Fenwick, Mary Hill Carroll, 20
Fenwick, Md., 198
Fenwick, Mr., 41
Fenwick, Richard, 20
Fenwick, William, 21, 145
Ferguson, George, 10
Ferry House, 199
Ferry, John, 7
Ferry Point, 198
Ferrys, 15, 16, 36, 38, 111, 113, 117, 121, 180, 182, 183, 186, 189, 191, 192, 193, 194, 195, 198, 201, 202
Fiddler Crab, 107
Fields, W. C., 128
Fields, Wm., 7
Finall, Nathaniel, 168
"Pincastle," sloop, 16, 17
Finn, Capt. William, 143
Finney, Va., 160
"Firefighter," boat, 125
Fish, 1, 2, 3, 11, 16, 50, 55, 59, 60, 68, 70, 72, 77, 82, 88-102, 110, 131, 134, 136
Fishbourne, Ralph, 10
Fish Brokers, 90, 94
Fisher, Alexr., 9
Fishermen, 78, 90-99
Fishing Creek, Md., 148
Fishing Industry, 89, 90, 94, 100, 101, 180, 196
Fishing Island, Md., 150
Fishing Shores, 89
Fish "Kills," 100, 101
Fitch, John, 111
Fitzhugh Family, 193
"Five Brothers," schooner, 144
"Five Sisters," schooner, 144
"Five Sisters," skipjack, 68, 144
"Five Sons," sloop, 144
Flattie, 65, 76 - See also Skipjack

Fleet, Captain Henry, 1, 2, 4, 23, 88
Fleet's Bay, 50, 51, 52, 64, 91, 147, 151, 161
Fletcher, James, 169
Fleury, Robert, 169
Flood's Creek, 3
"Flora," pungy, 144
"Florence Northam," bug-eye, 63, 144, 183
Florida, 2, 47, 62, 70, 139
"Florida," steamboat, 115
Flynt, John L., 170
Flynt, Lawrence K., 170
Foote, Admiral Andrew Hull, 200
Forbush, Capt. Gus, 77, 170
Ford, Capt. Joseph, 21, 29, 58
Ford, N., 41
Forrest, Captain, 18
Forrest, Capt. James, 28
Forrest, Dr. J. W., 36
Forrest, Joseph, 36
Forrest, J. Piett, 39
Forrest, J. W., 39
Forrest, R. K., 145
Forrest, Stoddert and Murdock, 24
Forrest, Uriah, 24
Fort Belvoir, 198
Fort Carroll, 120
Fort Columbia, 201
Fort Foote, 116, 200
Fort Humphries, 198
Fort Hunt, 199
Fort Lincoln, 183
Fort McHenry, 120
Fort McNair, 202
Fort Monroe, Va., 106, 114, 115
Fort Point, 121, 192
Fort St. Inigoes, 121
Fort Stevens, D. C., 46
Fort Warburton, 199
Fort Washington Lighthouse, 113, 124
Fort Washington, Md., 34, 116, 199
Foster's Point, 66
Four Mile Creek, 201
Four Mile Run, 3, 116, 201
Four Mill Run, 201
"Four Sisters," sloop, 144
Fourth Point, 192
"Fowey," ship, 16, 17, 18, 19
Fowke Family, 193
Fowke's Landing, 90
Foxall, Henry, 26
Fox Ferry, 16, 201
Fox, George, 201
"Fox," pungy, 144
Foxwell, A. J., 39
Foxwell, Capt. Benjamin, 60, 76, 139, 145, 164, 165

Foxwell, Capt. H. Webster, 60, 76, 147, 151, 157, 159
Foxwell, Capt. John J., 157
Foxwell, Capt. Solomon, 60, 71, 153, 164, 165, 169
Foxwell, Capt. Stephen, 60, 164
Foxwell, Capt. Van Buren, 60, 164
Foxwell, Capt. William J., 157
Foxwell, D., 167
Foxwell Family, 60
Foxwell, I., 167
Foxwell, J. W., 169
Foxwell, William, 167
France, 24
"Frances Miller," schooner, 146
"Francis J. Ruth," pungy, 59, 60, 146
Francis, Steph., 6
Francis, Thomas, 6, 7
Frand, Nicho., 9
Franklin, A., 166
Frederick County, Md., 203
Frederick, Md., 46
"Fredericksburg," steamboat, 112
Fredericksburg, Va., 37, 111, 194
Frederickstown, Md., 113
Freestone Fishery, 90
Freestone Point, 195, 196
French Fleet, 21, 24
French Revolution, 24
"French Smoot," schooner, 146
Friend, Daniel, 20
Friendly Hall, house, 66
Frigates, 16, 33, 35
Frisby, Esqr., 9
Fulton, Robert, 111, 112, 117
Furbush, John W., 153
Fur Trade, 4, 11
Fyke Nets, 90, 91
"G. A. Kirwin," pungy, 146
"Galena," U.S.S., 47
Galesville, Md., 68
Gamble, Alexander, 191
Gamble Creek, 191
Gambo Creek, 191
Gandy, Capt. John, 141
Gardiner, Capt. Robert H., 164
Gardiner Creek, 3, 186
Gardiner, David, 35
"Garland," ship, 16
Garner, Capt. George. 155
Garner Creek, 186
Garner, John, 186
Garrett, Richard H., 47
Garrison's Landing, 12, 203
Gaskins, Thomas H., 166
Gaskins, William H., 170

Gass, Capt. "Monk," 99
Gatton, Thomas, 165
Gatton, William W., 165
Geese, 1, 126, 127
General Assembly of Virginia, 197, 198
"General Hancock," sloop, 146
"General Monk," ship, 20
"General Washington," ship, 20
Geoghegan, Capt. William C., 116, 118
"George B. Faunce," bugeye, 52, 66, 67, 68, 70, 77, 146
"George," brigantine, 6
George, Franklin, 170
"George H. Bunker," bugeye, 146
"George Leary," steamboat, 115, 116, 117, 118
"George," schooner, 146
"George T. Ash," schooner, 146
Georgetown-Alexandria Canal, 194, 196, 201, 203
Georgetown, D. C., 1, 12, 16, 20, 24, 25, 26, 35, 49, 57, 70, 89, 90, 112, 113, 116, 123, 126, 136, 141, 143, 144, 147, 149, 151, 155, 159, 180, 197, 201, 203
Georgetown Steam Packet Line, 201
Georgetown University, 20, 25, 28
"George Washington," steamboat, 116
George, William, 170
Gerard, Ann, 5
Gerard, Elizabeth, 188
Gerard, Frances, 5
Gerard, John, 5
Gerard, Rose Tucker, 5
Gerard's Cove, 133
Gerard's Creek, 3
Gerard's Reserve, 5
Gerard, Susannah Snow, 5, 189
Gerard, Thomas, 3, 5, 11, 13, 14, 15, 74, 186, 188, 189
German Society of Maryland, 80
Germany, 95
Gettysburgh, Pa., 36, 42
Gibbons, Cardinal James, 51
Gibson, Alonzo, 169
Gibson, Bernard (Jack), 127, 128
Gibson, Bessie, 70
Gibson, Capt. Alfred, 57, 96

Gibson, Capt. Edwin, 55, 57, 59, 60, 61, 62, 64, 65, 68, 77, 94, 96, 101, 102, 125, 151, 155
Gibson, Capt. Garner, 58, 59, 69
Gibson, Capt. George, 69, 143
Gibson, Capt. Henry, 55, 57, 86, 96, 118
Gibson, Capt. Jerry, 55, 61, 62, 67, 77, 139, 161, 169
Gibson, Capt. John, 59, 69, 99
Gibson, Capt. John Joe, 62, 69, 70, 141, 145, 149, 159, 161, 169
Gibson, Capt. Richard (Dick), 65, 102, 127, 128, 134
Gibson, Henry, 164
Gibson, Joe, 127, 128
Gibson, Mary (Beitzell), 55
Gibson, Perry, 59, 69
Gibson's Flats, 76
Gibson, William Thomas (Buddy), 58, 59, 69
Gideon, Commander John Lewis, 20
Giesboro Point, 10, 201
Giesborough Estate, 201
Gill-boats, 49, 51, 57
Gill, Monroe, 170
Gill Nets, 49, 81, 90, 96, 99, 101
"Gilman Dove," schooner, 146
Gilmer, Thomas W., 35
Gird, Capt., 112
Gladstanes, John, 8
Glannitt, John, 9
Glear, Saml., 9
Glebe Creek, 3, 186
Glebe, The (Creek), 3, 182
"Gloucester," ship, 54
Glymont Lighthouse, 113
Glymont, Md., 116, 197
Glymont Plantation, 197
Gobb's Bar, Va., 45
"Golden Lion," ship, 13, 14
Goldsborough, Thomas, 169
Goldsmith, Capt. H. H., 165
Goldsmith, Capt. John M., 39, 46, 159
Goldsmith Farm, 50
Goldstein, Joseph, 123
Good, Capt. George P., 159
Goode, Douglas, 145
Goodman, Benny, 118
Goodrick, Commander Briger, 16
Goodwin, Capt. Tho., 6
Goose Bay, 3, 90, 195

Goose Creek, 3, 27
"Goose," (Punt) Guns, 35, 123, 126, 127
Gordon, Capt. James Alexander, 33, 34, 35
Gordon, George, 12
Gordon, George, 203
Gordon, Mr., 42
Gough Family, 187
Gough, George, 23
Gough, John, 23
Gough, John T., 170
Gough's Point, 187
Gough, Thomas, 23
Gough, T. W., 41
"Governor McLane," Police Boat, 78, 79, 80
Grace Episcopal Church, 54
"Grace," ship, 16
"Gracie Lee," sloop, 146
Graham, Capt. Burton, 139, 143, 147
Graham Family, 59
Graison, Robt., 9
Granger, R., 42
Grant, General U. S., 46, 47
Grant, William, 113, 114
"Grape Shot," sloop, 146
Grapevine Point, 186
Grason, Governor William, 184
Grason's Wharf, 121, 184
"Gratitude," schooner, 45
Graves, Capt. Benjamin F., 165
Graves, Capt. Rhewlen, 165
Great Choptank, 9
"Great Eastern," steamboat, 113
Great Falls, 1, 2, 4, 12, 88, 98
Great House Point, 182
Great Hunting Creek, 3, 199, 200, 201
Great Mills, Md., 11, 30, 36
Great Mussle Creek, 200
Great Wicomico River, Va., 181
Greenback, Va., 150
Green, Capt. Taylor, 67, 141, 149
Green, George, 113, 114
Greenleaf, James, 26
Greenleaf, John, 202
Greenleaf Point, D. C., 47, 116, 202
Greenleaf Wharf, 26
Greenway Flats, 198
Greenway, house, 198
Greenwell, John, 164
Greenwell, Philip, 95, 157
Greenwell's Wharf, 94
Griffin, Luke, 169
Griggs, Capt. George, 164
Griggs, James, 23
Grindal, Francis, 9

222

Sheridan, General Phillip, 46, 199
Sheridan Point, 199
Sherly, Richd., 8
Shermantine, John A. B., 164
Sherwood, Daniel, 10
"Shining Light," pungy, 158
Shipbuilding, 5-11
Shipping Point, Md., 37, 93, 188
Shipping Point, Va., 195
Ships, 5-11, 16, 17
"Shirley," steamboat, 113, 115
Shore, Capt., 37
Shores, Capt. Edgie, 71
Shores, L., 67, 145
Shorter, Capt. William S., 164
Shorter, John W., 169
Shovebottom, Rd., 8
Shreive, Capt. John, 112
Sigourney, Lt. James B., 28, 139, 182
"Silver Spray," bugeye, 158
"Silver Star," schooner, 158
Silviant, Owen, 10
Simmons, Capt. Thomas, 22
Simms, Capt. James C., 165
Simms, Capt. Thomas P., 145
Simms, George, 41
Simons, Mr., 42
Simpkins, Cadmus, 169
Simpkins, Capt. Shill, 63, 145, 147, 153
Simpkins, Capt. Thomas, 64
Simpkins, Capt. William, 63, 145, 155, 169
Simpkins Family, 59
Simpson, Jereh., 10
Simpson, Jeremiah, 10
Sinclair, Capt. Billy, 145
Sinnickson, Va., 154
Sisson, Capt. Richard, 98
Sisters of Charity, 42
Skillinton, Tho., 10
Skinner, Hammond, 62
Skipjacks, 76, 77, 182, 184 - See also Appendices "A" & "B"
"Skysjack," schooner, 158
Slaves, 3, 18, 22, 29, 31, 35, 39, 41, 43, 44, 45, 65, 77, 89
Sloops, 5-11, 13, 16, 17, 27, 35, 39, 44, 57, 58, 59, 61, 64, 67, 68, 70, 71, 77, 81, 85, 86, 93, 94, 96 - See also Appendices "A" & "B"
Slye, Capt. Chap, 116
Slye, Capt. Harry E., 116, 117, 122
Slye, Capt. Robert, 11

Slye, Commander Walter C., 116
Slye, Gerard, 15
Slye, Robert, 14, 15, 189
Small, David, 7
Smallwood Vigilantes, 36
Smart, John, 169
Smith, Anthony, 23, 24
Smith, Biscoe, 23
Smith, Capt. Curtis, 162, 163
Smith, Capt. George W., 162
Smith, Capt. James, 9, 10
Smith, Capt. Joe, 116
Smith, Captain John, 1, 2, 88, 120, 181, 183, 189, 190, 192, 194, 196, 198, 199, 203
Smith, Capt. Peter C., 162
Smith, Capt. Thomas, 20
Smith, Capt. William, 28
Smith, Capt. William H., 42
Smith Creek, 3, 18, 21, 22, 35, 120, 124, 182, 183
Smith, Edmund R., 25
Smith, Esqr., 9
Smith Island, 40, 149
Smith, John, 23
Smith, Joseph M., 170
Smith, Nathan, 7
Smith Point, 38, 52, 180, 181, 188, 194
Smith Point Lighthouse, 113, 124
Smith, President, 9
Smith, Robt., 9
Smith, Walter, 7
Smith, Wm., 8
Smith, William G., 166
Smith, William R., 39
Smithsonian Institution, 57, 62
Smoot, Capt. William Barton, 20
Smoot, Elizabeth, 28
Smoot, Goodman, 15
Smoot, McKay, 23
Smoot, William, 28
Snake Island, 187
Snow, Abel, 14
Snowden, Richd., 6
Snow Hill, 14
Snows, 17
Snow, Susannah, 5
"Sodonia Curley," schooner, 158
Solomon, Isaac, 58
Solomons Island, 58, 61, 63, 65, 67, 70, 75, 120, 138, 140, 142, 144, 146, 148, 150, 154, 156, 160, 163
Somerset Beach, 193
Somerset County, Md., 8, 62, 67, 80, 138, 140, 144, 146, 148, 150, 152, 154, 156, 158, 160

Somerset, Mass., 140
"Somerset," schooner, 158
Somerset Seafood Co., 71
Somers, I. S., 153
Sommers, Capt. James, 63, 143
Sothoron, John H., 36
Southern Maryland, 19, 20, 23, 36, 38, 43, 122, 187, 188, 201
"Southern," skipjack, 158
Southern Steamboat Line, 112
"Southland," steamboat, 117
South River, 16
South Yeoacomaco River, 3
Spalding Bennett, 23
Spalding, Capt. C. C., 41, 164
Spanish Settlement, 2
Sparks, F. E., 14
Spelman, Henry, 1, 88
Spencer, Thomas O., 36
"Splendid," pungy, 66, 158
Spondines, Hugh, 10
"Springfield," house, 182
Spurne, Nicho., 6
Squires, Commander, 16
Stafford County, Va., 19, 58, 78, 90, 138
Staffordshire, England, 198
Stanford, Capt. William J., 62, 63, 143, 145
Stanhice, Henry, 164
Stanton, Edwim, 45
Star-Democrat Newspaper, 73
"Star," sloop, 158
Steamboat Landings, 52, 64, 69, 80, 94, 112, 113, 118, 119, 120, 121, 122, 127, 181, 182, 183, 184, 187, 188, 189, 190, 192, 194, 195, 196, 197, 198, 199, 200
Steamboats, 35, 36, 37, 38, 39, 40, 44, 45, 47, 51, 52, 53, 64, 90, 94, 96, 97, 109, 111-123, 128, 135, 201, 203
Stephens, James, 166
Stephens, James H., 166
Stephens, Wm., 8, 10
Sterling, Capt. John, 108
Stevens, Capt. Henry, 141
Stevens, Tho., 9
Stewart, Capt., 31
Stewart, Capt. Henry, 67, 145
Stewart, General Philip, 32, 33
Stewart, John, 169
Stockton, Commodore, 35
Stoddert, Benjamin, 24
Stoddert, James, 189
Stoddert Point, 189
Stone, F. J., 36, 113, 114

228

Stone, Governor William,
13, 14
Stone, H. I., 164
Stone, John, 7
Stone's Wharf, 69, 94, 95,
188
Stone, T., 21
Stony Point, 90
Stratford Cliffs, 98, 127,
155, 190, 191
Stratford Hall, 5, 11, 190
Street, Mr., 40
Stuart, Dr., 127
Stuart, Dr. Richard, 47
Stuart Family, 193
Stuart Point, 193
Stuart, R. H., 157
Stump Landing, 90
Stump Neck, 90, 196
"Sue," steamboat, 115, 118
Sumers, Solon., 9, 10
Summrs, Saml., 10
"Sunny South," bugeye, 62,
158
Surratt, Mrs. Mary, 47
"Susan E. Parker," schoon-
er, 158
"Susannah," brigantine, 6
Sutton, Capt., 9
Sutton, James F., 165
Sutton, Joseph, 23
Swalm, W. F., 42
Swan, 1, 75, 123, 125,
126, 127
"Swan," boat, 39, 46
Swan Creek, 3, 199
Swann Family, 190
Swann, G. W., 166
Swann, Joshua, 169
Swann, J. Thomas, 155
Swann, Thomas, 23
Swann, Warren, 166
Swann, William, 167, 169
Swan Point, 21, 41, 66,
72, 78, 83, 116, 190
"Swan," sloop, 158
"Swash," 78, 81
Swift, Gustavus, 170
Swift, Philip, 170
"S. Wimsatt," schooner,
156
Sycamore Point, 197
"Sydney," steamboat, 112
Sykes, Representative, 35
"Sylph," dory, 69, 96
Talbot County, Md., 6, 9,
146, 148
"Talbot," steamboat, 117,
118, 120
Tall Timbers, 185
Tangier Island, 59, 78,
162, 184
Tangier Sound, 115
"Tangier," steamboat, 115
Tappahannock, Va., 139, 141,
143, 151, 153, 157, 159
Tapscott's Creek, 182
Tarleton, Capt. George, 161
Tarleton, J. P., 113

Tarleton, Mrs. Mary A., 113
Tarleton, William, 113
"Tartar," sloop, 158
Tate, Mosley, 170
Taveau Creek, 3
Tawes, Gov. J. Millard, 84
Taylor, Capt. Brinkley, 162
Taylor, Capt. John Tawes,
108
Taylor, Capt. Matthew M.,
155
Taylor, Capt. Toby, 125
Taylor, Capt. Will, 145
Taylor, Gen., 29
Taylor, Jenifer, 28
Taylor, Richard, 23
Taylor's Island, Md., 71
"Teaser," sloop, 158
Teel, Mr., 42
Templeman, Augustine, 23
Tench, Thomas, 6
"Tennessee," sloop, 158
Tennesson, Capt. A. C.,
145, 153
Tent Landing Fishery, 90
Texas, 103
Thames River, 1
Thane, Elswyth, 89
"Thelma M," barge, 70
Theodore Roosevelt Island,
202
"Theodore Weems," steam-
boat, 115
Thimble Shoals, 52
"Thomas B. Schall," schoon-
er, 158
Thomas, Capt., 36
Thomas, Capt. Foster, 153
Thomas, Capt. George, 153
Thomas, Capt. George E.,
143
Thomas, Capt. George
Gabriel, 77, 159
Thomas, Capt. George M.,
143
Thomas, Capt. George W.,
143, 145, 151
Thomas, Capt. J. Foster,
143
Thomas, Capt. Randolph,
139, 151, 153
Thomas Family, 59, 194
"Thomas Franklin," schoon-
er, 158
"Thomas Freeborn," steam-
boat, 36, 39
Thomas, Gabriel, 164
Thomas, H., 36
"Thomas H. Kirby," bugeye,
68, 125, 158
Thomas, Jno., 7
Thomas, Lottie L., 61
Thomas, Major John Allen,
18, 20
Thomas, Mrs., 113
Thomas Point, 192, 194
Thomas, Richard (Zarvona),
38
"Thomas," ship, 17
Thomas, Solomon, 164

Thomas, Tyler, 28
"Thomas Warren," sloop,
158
Thomas, William R., 61
Thom Point, 194
Thompson, Capt. Bernard,
139, 143, 161
Thompson, Capt. Golden,
99, 106, 108, 139
Thompson, Capt. Golden,
Jr., 99
Thompson, Capt. Gussie,
99
Thompson, Capt. James, 23,
161
Thompson, Capt. Paul, 99
Thompson, Capt. Roy, 99
Thompson, Daniel, 165
Thompson Family, 59
Thompson, Francis, 164
Thompson, John, 9
Thompson, John G., 165
Thompson, Mr., 16
Thompson, Mrs., 29
Thompson, Richard L., 59,
143
Thompson, "Rome," 57, 59,
141
Thompson, William, 57,
59, 60, 61, 81, 139,
141, 145, 149
Thorton, Col. Presley,
22
"Three Brothers," schoon-
er, 58, 158
"Three Brothers," sloop,
158
"Three Rivers," steamboat,
116, 117, 118, 119
Three Sisters Island, 203
"Three Sisters," schooner,
158
Thrift, Capt. Bud, 159
Tibbs, Noble, 54
Tiber Creek, 27, 112, 202
Ticks Hole, 193
Tidal Basin, D. C., 202
Tide Mills, 127
Tidewater Fisheries, 77,
83, 84
Tidewell Family, 186
Tidewell's, 186
Tilp, Capt. Fred, 62, 180,
181, 186, 192, 197
"Tiny Lou," Police Boat,
83
Tippity-Wichity Island,
184
"Tivoli," steamboat, 118
Tobacco, 4, 11, 12, 14,
23, 24, 26, 28, 29, 32,
93, 188, 190, 195, 203
Todd, Capt. Wells, 162
Toleration Act of 1649,
14, 15
Tomakoken Creek, 3, 188
Tomkin Point, 193
"Tompkins," Shoal, 131
"Tom Young," schooner, 158

"William M. Powell,"
  schooner, 77
"Wm. M. Powell,"
  schooner, 160
Williams, B., 28
Williams, Benjamin, 28
Williamsburg, Va., 2, 16,
  54, 89, 123, 182
Williams, Capt., 80
Williams, Elisha, 32
Williams, J. B., 166
"William," ship, 16
Williams, Noah, 170
Williamsport, Md., 36
Williams Shoal, 66
"Willie Ann," sloop, 160
"Willie Clarence," bugeye,
  67, 160
Willing, Capt. Ralph, 163
Willin, I., 159
Willis, Benjamin, 170
Wilmington, Del., 138, 141
Wilmington, N. C., 46, 47
Wilmington Steamboat Line,
  115
"Wilson & Hunting,"
  schooner, 57, 160
Wilson Line, 116, 123
Wilson, Mrs. Elizabeth,
  22
Wilton, house, 5, 186
Winder, St. Col., 8
Windmill Point, 90, 192
Wingate, Capt. Burke, 162
Wingate, Md., 162
Winkedoodle Point, 191
Winkfield, H., 167
"Winnie H. Windsor," bug-
  eye, 61, 67, 160

"Wm. F. Vilas," bugeye,
  160
Winthrop, Beckwith, 196
Winthrop's Wharf, 196
Wirtland, house, 190
Wirt's Wharf, 190
Wirt, William, 190
Wise, Jackson, 68
Wittman, Md., 158
Woodbridge, Va., 197
Wood, Capt. John Taylor,
  46
Woodey, Henry, 166
Woodhall, Capt. George,
  128, 134
Woodhall, Joe, 128, 134
Woodhall, Valentine, 134
Woodhull, Nelson J., 169
Woodland, Joe, 95
Woods, Joseph, 9
Woolford, Rogr., 9
Worcester County, Md., 158
Work Boat Races, 63, 70
World War I, 54, 55, 57,
  63, 68, 69, 81, 85, 86,
  94, 96, 98, 194, 195,
  201
World War II, 19, 25, 59
  82, 85, 86, 98, 118,
  122, 180
Wright, Caleb S., 37
Wright, Capt. Richard A.,
  145
Wright, Judge, 58
Wright, Robert, 33
"W. W.Corcoran," steam-
  boat, 115
Wyatt, David, 113, 114
Wye River, 106

Wyman, Lt., 37, 39
Wynne Wharf, 120, 183
Xyle, Alexr., 8
"Yankee," U.S.S., 39,
  188
Yates, Charles A., 41
Yates Creek, 39
Yates Family, 191
Yates, Norman, 95
Yates Point, 191
Yates, Richard, 20
Yates, Vachel, 20
Yeoacomico River, 3, 28,
  29, 30, 31, 44, 62, 78,
  94, 121, 124, 141, 182
Yeo, Capt. John, 9
Yeocomico (Yoacomaco),
  1, 183
York, Pa., 49
York River, 1, 2, 52,
  54, 118
York River Line, 115
Yorktown, Va., 54, 123
"Yosockeccocoe," 196
"Yosocomico," 196
Young, Arthur, 89
Young Family, 202
Younghusband, Commander
  Wm., 16
Young, Notley, 26
Young's Point, 202
Zachariah, William, 23
Zachariah, Zachariah, 23
Zachia Swamp, 196
Zarvona, Richard Thomas,
  38
Zell, John F., 166
"Zephr," pungy, 52, 160

SUPPLEMENT TO

LIFE ON THE POTOMAC RIVER

By Edwin W. Beitzell
of St. Mary's County, Maryland

INTRODUCTION

Since the first printing of Life On The Potomac River in 1968 many interested people have forwarded additional data concerning activities on the River. This data is included in the second printing in this supplement. It was realized at the time of the original publication that the book was deficient in covering the activities of the Rivermen on the Virginia side of the Potomac and through the kind efforts of Virginia friends it is believed that this deficiency has been remedied to a considerable degree in this printing.

For some five years prior to the publication of this book in 1968 a diligent search had been made to find a photograph of a "black nancy" boat with no success. Six months after publication a picture was found - A picture of a "nancy" boat is important in a story of the Potomac River because this boat was the forerunner of the Potomac River "dory". "Nancies" continued in use up until about World War I, but in latter years were known as the "poor man's" boat, since many of them were built by the owners, often with little skill and few tools (see story p.57 and drawing p. 105).

THE BLACK NANCY, BROOKLYN

On February 2, 1969, Mrs. Nellie Gass Gibson of Bushwood, Maryland loaned the author a snapshot, taken in 1911 or 1912 of a black nancy boat (and a dory boat) lying in St. Patrick's Creek. On the same day Capt. Garnett Arnold, aged 74, of St. Patrick's Creek was interviewed who indentified the nancy boat as the Brooklyn. He said she was built about 1890 and originally owned by Capt. John Harden of Canoe Neck Creek as she was an old boat when Harden sold her to him in 1911, when he was 16 years old. He paid $25.00 for the boat. At the time of the sale Harden built himself a "dory" boat, the Star, later sold to Garrett Gass, (pictured with the Brooklyn). Capt. Arnold said the Brooklyn was 27 feet in length and about 10 feet in width, and as a result of her width could carry a lot of sail. (Most nancies were rather narrow boats). She could carry 44 bushels of oysters (22½ inch tubs) when fully loaded. She was ribbed, planked lengthwise and had the "new" dory type stern. He sold the Brooklyn to Jim Hogge of Upper Machodoc Creek, Va. in January 1915, after using her as an oyster and fishing boat.

Capt. Arnold also stated with considerable emphasis that Grason Thompson (not "Rome" Thompson as stated in "Life on the Potomac River" p.57) and Charles G. Husemann, both of St. Patrick's Creek were the originators of the Potomac River "dory". This occurred in 1875, when Mr. Thompson's son, Willie, was about 2 years old (born Feb. 18, 1873) and still in diapers. Capt. Arnold said he worked with Willie Thompson and other local area men in the shipyards of Alexandria and Quantico during World War I and Willie told him the story at that time and the group often discussed the matter while working there. He also discussed the matter on many occasions with the older heads on St. Patrick's Creek, such as Charles A. (Sandy) Ellis, Joe Lawrence, John Bryant and James Dingee. So far as known, the Brooklyn was the last black nancy in this area.

The above was also discussed with Capt. Garner Gibson of White's Neck Creek who stated he had always understood that what Capt. Arnold had said was essentially correct.

EDWIN W. BEITZELL

February 13, 1969

Black Nancy, Brooklyn   C. 1911   "Dory" Star

Garry Gass in the Star, After Conversion to Motor

POTOMAC RIVER "DORY" SAILS AGAIN

After a lapse of some 40 years a Potomac River "dory" boat is again under sail, thanks to the interest of Capt. Sam Bailey, Sr., of the 7th District, of St. Mary's County. Capt. Sam, along with many contemporaries such as Captains Frank Ellis, Edward Brown, Willie Owens, Clem Beitzell, Golden Thompson, Henry Gibson, Alton and Walter Cheseldine, and many others in the St. Clement's Island area sailed these "dories" to dredge hundreds of thousands of bushels of oysters. From about 1875, when the dory was developed by the boat builders of St. Partick's and White's Neck Creeks (an improved design of the old "black nancy"), until some years after World War I the deep water oyster bars of the Potomac were white with sail of these boats. At times the Nomini Cliffs on the Virginia shore were obscured completely by the sails of "dories" dredging on Sheep's Head Bar west of St. Clement's Island.

Capt. Sam Bailey's dory, the Shamrock in Canoe Neck Creek.
Skipper Capt. Fred Cheseldine with Don Moore
and members of Capt. Fred Tilp's sailing class --
An activity of the 7th District Optimist Club
August 23, 1970

Capt. Sam's "dory", the Shamrock, was built by John Cheseldine of White's Neck Creek in 1917 for Capt. Freeman Cheseldine. During her first eight years her successive owners were Capt. Matt Bailey and Capt. Walter Goode. Capt. Goode sold her in 1925 to Capt. Edward Brown of St. Patrick's Creek who used her for both dredging and tonging oysters until he had Walter Cheseldine build him a much larger "dory" in 1928. She was then rented to Tom Tolson for some 4 or 5 years and later used by Capt. Brown's sons. She is 30 feet in length and 8 feet 8½ inches in width. After dredging was prohibited in the Potomac in 1931, her sails, masts and centerwell were removed and she was equipped with a 7 h.p. Palmer motor (still used as an auxiliary). She was restored to her original condition by Capt. Garner Gibson, master boat-builder of White's Neck Creek in 1970. Capt. Willie Owens of Canoe Neck Creek took the measurement for the sails and Capt. Garner made the board, centerwell, masts and booms to put her in first class sailing condition. It was necessary for Capt. Sam to go to a sailmaker on the Eastern Shore for the sails.

It was the pleasure of the author with Capt. Fred Cheseldine and Robert Pogue to try out the Shamrock after she was restored. We had a "fresh", Southwest wind and sailed out of St. Patrick's Creek up the Potomac to St. Katherine's Sound, then returned as far as Huggins Point and back to St. Patrick's. It was a "stiff" breeze and we put her washboard under with no danger of capsizing. She was fast, easy to maneuver and responded sharply. It is no wonder that the Rivermen loved these boats and raced each other at every opportunity.

In 1972 Capt. Sam was persuaded to sell the Shamrock to the Harry Lundeberg School of Seamenship at Piney Point, Maryland, where she is being preserved in their Museum of Living Ships, one of the finest on the East Coast of the U.S.A. There are less than a dozen of these fine craft still afloat. It is hoped that more of them will be saved. At least, thanks to the Lundeberg School, they will not completely disappear as has happened with the "black nancy".

Shamrock

Centerwell

Motor

Stern

THE BIRTH OF THE AIRCRAFT CARRIER
(Off Mattawoman Creek, Maryland)
by Frederick Tilp

On November 11, 1861, Confederate lookouts on the Potomac first sighted the Civil War's most incredible armada heading southwards and rounding the river's bend at the Indian Head bluffs. The powerful screw sloop WACHUSETT, the double-ended gunboats TIOGA and PORT ROYAL, and the armed steamer DELAWARE escorted a smaller steamer towing an "unusual craft." Actually it was this "odd craft" that startled the Confederates who were at work constructing batteries on the rocky slopes of Freestone Point, Virginia (about three miles north of Quantico Creek).

Moored to its unusually large and flat deck was a huge balloon with the name INTREPID standing out clearly on its sides -- being carried by America's first aircraft carrier -- the GEORGE WASHINGTON PARKE CUSTIS.

This particular stretch of Potomac River had become the scene of extensive military and naval activity. Troops of both sides were concentrated in the vicinity -- and Union ships (naval, merchant, and fishing) were being forced to run a deadly gauntlet of rebel fire. Serious damage to, and the loss of several vessels bound downriver from Washington due to these shore based Confederate batteries caused the Secretary of War Stanton to order a Federal tug available to tow (under a cover of darkness) all sailing vessels becalmed to a safer spot below Mallows Bay, Maryland.

At the beginning of the war the extent of the battlefronts along the river made reconnaissance a serious problem. A number of balloon observation stations were established on shore from the heights of Indian Head southward to

Thomas Point. The rapidly changing troop movements on the Virginia shore made fast movement of balloons essential.

When balloons were first used in the Civil War, they were inflated from city gas mains and then towed slowly and tortuously (while inflated) to the scene of action. Movement was slow and difficult at best -- and even a small storm off the river's shore could make the operation disastrous.

The Union Army's first "Chief Aeronaut" (as he was called), Professor Thaddeus S. C. Lowe, increased balloon mobility by developing portable gas generating equipment that could be carried in the field. However, Southern Maryland's poor roads near the Potomac made the movement of a wagon train with balloon, gas generators, and supplies far too slow to meet practical battle-field requirements.

To improve balloon mobility, Lowe then proposed the use of a boat especial-ly equipped to launch balloons and carry supplies for their operation. The Navy Department had purchased in August of 1861 a coal barge for the Washington Navy Yard named the GEORGE WASHINGTON PARKE CUSTIS. She was 122 feet long, 14' 6" beam, and a hold depth of 5' 6". This nondescript craft (with an impressive name) was modified for balloon work by covering the hull with a wide, flat, overhanging deck all around and adding a small house on the stern. Gas generators, repair parts, and other necessary facilities for balloon operation were provided, and manned by a crew of Army balloon handlers under Lowe's direction.

The operation of the "balloon boat" as she was called, was entirely an Army affair, except for the lack of motive power and armament which required the Navy for towing and escort services.

By early November 1861, the strange craft and her escorts were ready for service, and the first balloon expedition by carrier left the Washington Navy Yard on the tenth of November. The following day, an operational ascension from the balloon boat was made off Mattawoman Creek where Lowe, accompanied by General Daniel E. Sickles observed the Confederates at work on their fortifica-tions and gun emplacements between Occoquan Bay and Chopawamsic Creek, Virginia.

The results apparently convinced Lowe of the value of his new aircraft carrier, as a few days later he wrote the Commandant of the Washington Navy Yard that: "It is my intention to use permanently the boat lately fitted up for balloon purposes." By January 1862, Lowe's balloon corps had expanded its work to Island #10 in the Mississippi River.

On an Army landing at White House Point (near Fort Belvoir, Virginia) Lowe and his balloon advanced to the forefront of the Army's troops and the Navy's landing craft. An increasing role in waterborn operations at that time is further shown by the order of Commodore Charles Wilkes, USN to "tow a balloon along all sections of the Potomac River, holding it at an elevation of 1,000 feet while examining the surrounding countryside."

After many ascensions of the balloon, the task force worked its way continuously back and forth on the Potomac River until the GEORGE WASHINGTON PARKE CUSTIS was returned to the Washington Navy Yard for repairs in the spring of 1863, and then fell into obscurity.

Even so, the great aircraft carrier task forces of today and even the launching areas of the astronauts to the moon may trace their heritage back to the little GEORGE WASHINGTON PARKE CUSTIS and the balloon pioneers of the Civil War who first operated on the Potomac River.

A model of the balloon boat GEORGE WASHINGTON PARKE CUSTIS.

Author's Note: Actually the first waterborn platform used for balloon operations in the Civil War was in August 1861 (3 months before the CUSTIS was activated), when the little armed steamer FANNY served as a temporary "balloon base" off Fortress Monroe in Hampton Roads, Virginia. After several days of ascensions and examinations of the "secessionists positions" the records showed nothing of continued operations here.

Acknowledgments:
      Photos -- (First) U. S. Naval Institute Proceedings, Annapolis, Maryland.
               (Second) Mariners Museum, Newport News, Virginia.
      Dates and Data -- U. S. Naval Institute Proceedings.

THE SHIP FEDERALIST

A Footnote to the Baltimore Constitutional Procession
by Robert L. Raley

In the Winterthur Newsletter of February 24, 1958, Charles F. Montgomery quoted from the Independent Chronicle and Universal Advertiser (Boston, May 26, 1788) descriptions of various floats in Baltimore's "Grand Procession" to celebrate the ratification of the Federal Constitution by the State of Maryland. This news item was a reprint of a notice first published in the Maryland Journal and Baltimore Advertiser (May 6, 1788). It not only described the displays presented by the House-Carpenters, Painters, and Cabinet-makers, but also listed the names of those who preceded each trade float. The account fills nearly two columns.

After months of dissension, the citizens of Baltimore had been stirred to a pitch of great expectancy by their state's forthcoming ratification of the Constitution. Now assured of its passage, tradesmen and merchants busily prepared for the great ceremony to honor not only the Constitution, but also the idol of the people, George Washington. Merchants postponed sales of their merchandise to enable them to work on their displays. Finally, on May second the papers (M.J.B.A., 1788) announced the arrival of "Captain Barney and the Ship Federalist." Barney's remarkable career was as well known to the citizens of Baltimore as the role the miniature ship was to play in their festivities. Of Maryland ancestry, Barney had first assumed command of a ship at the age of fifteen and later had been brilliantly successful against the English navy during the Revolutionary War. The exact meaning of the paper's reference to Barney's being from "the Cape of Good-Hope" is not precisely clear; however, everyone knew what was meant by the reference that he was "last from Fell's Point, to be employed in the Service of the United States."

The day arrived. Before jubilant crowds the Ship Federalist passed bravely through the streets of Baltimore, "completely office red and manned, rigged and sailed: borne on a carriage drawn by Horses. She displayed the Flag of the United States, and was fully dressed. Being the Seventh Ship in the Line, and having weathered the most dangerous Cape in the Voyage, she lay to under Seven Sails, during the Repast, on Federal Hill, throwing out Signals, and expecting the Arrival of the other Six" (MJBS., May 6, 1788).

Fortunately, this was not the end for this proud little ship. Mathew Cary informs us that "the merchants of Baltimore, to express their veneration for his excellency general Washington, (had) presented him with the little ship Federalist, the same used in the late procession. Captain Barney . . . sailed in her to Mount Vernon" (American Museum, III, No. 4 (1788), 592).

So impressed was Washington by this gift that he not only invited Barney to be his guest for a week at Mount Vernon, but also wrote (June 8, 1788) to William Smith and other gentlemen proprietors of the Ship Federalist:

Gentlemen:

Captain Barney has just arrived here in the miniature ship, called the Federalist; and has done me the honour to offer that beautiful curiosity as a present to me, on your part: I pray you, gentlemen, to accept the warmest expressions of my sensibility for this specimen of American ingenuity; in which the exactitude of the proportions, the neatness of the workmanship, and the elegance of the decorations (which make your present fit to be preserved in a cabinet of curiosities) at the same time they exhibit the skill and taste of the artist, demonstrate that Americans are not inferior to any people whatever in the use of mechanical instruments and the art of shipbuilding.

The unanimity of the agricultural state of Maryland in general, as well
as of the commercial town of Baltimore in particular, expressed in their
decision on the subject of a general government, will not (i persuade myself)
be without its due efficacy on the minds of their neighbours, who, in many
instances, are intimately connected not only by the nature of their produce,
but by the ties of blood and the habits of life. Under these circumstances,
I cannot entertain an idea that the voice of the convention of this state,
which is now in session, will be dissonant from that of her nearly-allied
sister, who is only separated by the Potowmack (sic).

You will permit me, gentlemen, to indulge my feelings in reiterating the
heart-felt wish, that the happiness of this country may equal the desires of
its sincerest friends; and that the patriotic town, of which you are inhabitants
(in the prosperity of which I have always found myself strongly interested)
may not only continue to increase in the same wonderful manner it has formerly
done, but that its trade, manufactures, and other resources of wealth, may be
placed, permanently, in a more flourishing situation than they have hitherto
been.

I am, with sentiments of respect,
Gentlemen,
Your most obedient and most humble servant,
GEORGE WASHINGTON

In less than two months after Washington received this gift, Mount Vernon
was struck by an exceedingly violent storm. On July 23 the prevailing east-
northeast wind changed suddenly to the southeast, bringing with it the
"highest tide that was ever known in this river (Potomac)" (Pennsylvania
Packet, August 6, 1788). The storm, with its high winds, continued through
the 24th. The same newspaper carried word of the many ships lost at sea and
of the considerable damage to shipping and property in Norfolk and Portsmouth.
Even as far north as Alexandria, flood conditions required the rescue by boat
of waterfront residents. At Mount Vernon not only were trees on the estate
extensively damaged, but also the small Ship Federalist foundered and sank a
few feet from the pier where Washington had received from Captain Barney this
token of love and admiration of the people of Baltimore.

NOTE: Similar ships--the Union and the Hamilton--were prominently featured in
the Constitutional Processions of Philadelphia and New York. The Union was
described as 33 feet in length, "a master-piece of elegant workmanship, decor-
ated with emblematical carving; and, what is truly astonishing, was begun and
completed in less than four days" (American Museum, July, 1788). The Ship
Hamilton had a 27-foot keel and a 10-foot beam and was commanded by Captain
Nicholson (Pennsylvania Packet, August 7, 1788). The Union was manned by a
crew including officers of twenty-five men, under John Green, Esq. There is
no evidence to indicate that these ships were any more than parade floats,
unlike their sister ship, the Federalist, a seaworthy vessel.

(Reprinted from the Winterthur Newsletter, February 26, 1962)

OYSTER KNIVES
By Vice Admiral Felix Johnson, U.S.N. Ret.

ADMIRAL JOHNSON
and his collection

The collection of oyster knives pictured was begun in 1954 and now numbers almost 100. The collection includes knives from Australia, Canada, Denmark, England, France, Germany, Japan, Norway, Scotland, Sweden and from most areas of the United States bordering on the sea. There is a great deal of diversity in their origins. For example, there is a curious similarity between the heavy oyster knives used in the Maritime Provinces of Canada and in the Gulf States. In both of these areas, the oyster shuckers open the shells at the hinge, rather than at the lip, as we do on the Chesapeake Bay and its tributaries. The former method requires a much heavier knife than the latter. There is evidence that this style of shucking and oyster knife was first used in Canada and was carried from there to our Gulf Coast by the French Acadians whose forcible expulsion from Nova Scotia to Louisiana in 1755 was memorialized in Longfellow's poem "Evangeline."

The solid steel knives are used mostly on our southeast coast and are called "crackers." The professional shuckers in this area are almost incredibly dexterous in using these knives. First the heavy steel haft is used to knock off a bit of the shell's lip, then the shucker quickly reverses the knife and slips the blade point into the notch to open the oyster.

The Admiral holding (L to R) a Champion Stabber, a knife from France, a "Cracker" knife from Yorktown, Virginia, a "Cul tac" from England and a short blade knife with guard from Japan.

A third type of knife, which is the smallest in the collection, came from Mersea, England. Oysters from the Kentish Coast are tiny compared to ours, although they are justly famous for their delicate flavor. These oysters are also probably the most expensive in the world as their going price is three shillings or about 42 cents each.

The largest knife in the collection also comes from Mersea and is called a "Cul tac." It is actually a culling tool since the oyster shells in that area are too thin to permit use of a culling hammer such as is used here.

My favorite shucking knife is the "Champion Stabber," used on the Eastern Shore, with the Danish knife a close second.

RECOLLECTIONS OF OLD SOUTHWEST WASHINGTON WATERFRONT
By Caroline Wimsatt (Mrs. James F.) Reilly

My Grandfather, William Abell Wimsatt, was the owner of the schooner "Josephine Wimsatt" named after my Grandmother, Josephine Cleary Wimsatt. (See pictures p. 137) Grandfather had a fleet of three of these schooners used to bring lumber up the Potomac River to his wholesale lumber company, Johnson and Wimsatt, at the foot of 12th and Water Streets, S. W. One of the other two vessels was named the "Kinkora" after the County in Ireland, from which my Grandmother Wimsatt's family, the Clearys, had emigrated. The name of the other vessel was the "Rosie Beatrice".

As a child and young girl (until the age of 21) I lived in the Southwest and on my way home from school during childhood I often stopped by the lumber yard and if one of the boats was at the dock, we grandchildren would climb all over her and play. My memories of old Water Street, the docks, the fish wharves, the wholesale produce houses, the barrell makers, Forsberg's Iron Foundary, the Morgue, etc., are very vivid and dearly cherished. I really shudder at the "new" Southwest. My father, William Kurtz Wimsatt, was born in 1878 at the foot of 12th and G Streets on a hill overlooking the Potomac. He lived there for many years before moving to B Street just behind the Smithsonian Museum where I was born. Father told us many fascinating stories of early days on the waterfront when the seiners and duck hunters plied their trade there; of the hard winters and thick ice when the river traffic was stopped; of the busy docks before the channel of the Potomac was filled with silt. He and his friends often swam, and skated too, to Alexandria and back.

Grandmother Wimsatt wrote in her "Recollections" that when she was a girl, Seventh Street was called the Long Pavement and it ran from the Market House to B Street South. She recorded that there was a canal (Tiber Creek) then where B Street North later was about the time of the Civil War. This canal separated the southern part of the city from the Northern part, connecting with the Potomac River at one end, and with the Eastern Branch at the other, making an island of South Washington. Even after the canal had been done away with, for many years this southern part of the city was known as the "Island". Her home was on 7th Street S. W. between C Street and Virginia Avenue and in later years was torn down to make a sub-station for the Southern Railroad. At the foot of 7th Street was the wharf, the landing place for the river boats and many carriages and omnibuses passed before her house every day carrying passengers to the steamboats, one of which ran to Mount Vernon.

Grandmother's family, the Clearys, favored the Confederacy and her Father lost his good government position when it became known that his sympathies were with the Southern Cause. All of her brothers, except one who was studying for the priesthood, entered the Confederate service. Her mother made her son Reuben, who was a Doctor, a Confederate flag. Reuben raised a company of volunteers in Washington, was chosen Captain of it and when he left for the South he carried the flag wrapped around his body under his clothing. As the war went on, feeling became so bitter that the family had to flee Washington and take refuge in Virginia until the end of the War.

Grandfather Wimsatt, who was President and Founder of the Johnson and Wimsatt Lumber Company, first had the yard at 12th and Water Streest, but after the yard was destroyed by fire in 1928 he moved to the block between 9th and 10th on Water Street. He had owned this property for some time, but leased it to the American Ice Company. After the fiasco of Southwest, my father, William Kurtz Wimsatt, who then managed the Company, moved the whole operation to Springfield, Virginia. After all no lumber had come by water for many years!

In a letter dated February 15, 1973, Mrs. Reilly wrote:

> The enclosed etchings are the work of Ruel Pardee Tolman. The view of the National Museum was done from the archway of the entrance to the "Castle" building of the Smithsonian Complex. We children always called it "The White Museum", the other two "The Castle" and "The Red Museum". The rounded pathway went up to the entrance of "The Red Museum".

National Museum

The Pathway

Mr. James McSherry Wimsatt, the brother of Mrs. Reilly, sent some additional Tolman etchings and a picture of the "Kinkora". One of the schooners of Johnson and Wimsatt is partly pictured unloading at 12th and Water Streets S. W. by Tolman. The second etching pictures the "Matanza" an unidentified vessel tied up at the wharf half-way between 9th and 10th Streets on Water Street. Mr. Wimsatt wrote on February 19, 1973, "The building in the center background is the old American Ice Company stable. The tower in the right hand upper corner is the tower on the Forsburg Foundry and Machine Shop building. I think Mr. Tolman took some liberty putting the tower and American flag so close to the American Ice Co. stable. It was, in fact, a block and a half away at the foot of 8th Street S. W.".

Unloading

The Mantanza

Smithsonian Institution

Mr. Wimsatt wrote further, "The 'Kinkora' was a ram and I was often aboard this vessel and some others. My first job with Johnson and Wimsatt was tallying lumber off the 'Rosie Beatrice'. She was a 25 ton schooner that had been converted to power and was driven by a two cylinder Lothrop engine. A man by the name of Edward Hall and I were supposed to take her down river to a shipyard for overhaul, but the trip was never completed. Between half-drunk Eddie and the bed bugs I abandoned ship".

Ram, Kinkora, Off Old Point Comfort, Va.

Rippon Lodge
by Richard Blackburn Black,
Rear Admiral U.S.N.R. (Ret.)

Rippon Lodge

Rippon Lodge was named after the cathedral town of Rippon (now "Ripon") by my 5th Great Grandfather, Richard Blackburn in 1725.

One can imagine Blackburn, the young colonist, arriving in the new land with his household goods and possibly some servants and livestock; quickly riding out to the beautiful site overlooking the mouth of Neabsco Creek, the Potomac, and the distant Maryland shore and exulting in the knowledge that this land, made available to him by the payment of "quit-rents" to Lord Fairfax, was to be his to work and develop into the great plantation it would some day be. Possibly, with the vision and ambition of the young, he could see the stream of barges and shallops plying from his wharf in the Creek out to the ships in the river with great hogsheads of the prime tobacco he was to grow on nearly twenty-one thousand acres he would one day control.

He started the construction of his new home in 1725 as is attested by a roughly scribed date in one of the oaken framing timbers. The house is of frame construction with much of its beaded pine clapboard still intact and most of its hewn oak framing timbers still as sturdy as on the day they were cut from the surrounding forest.

Benjamin Latrobe, the famous architect, who visited Rippon Lodge and its then owner, Colonel Thomas Blackburn in 1796, made color sketches of the house that I was allowed to photograph by Mrs. Ferdinand Latrobe of Baltimore many years ago. Another famous visitor to Rippon Lodge was General George Washington who recorded in his journal that he and Mrs. Washington lodged at Col. Blackburn's in October 1773 and and June 1788. Two of the Blackburn girls married into the Washington Family.

View From Rippon Lodge

247

Latrobe Sketches

Admiral Black wrote on February 15, 1973:

"I like very much the humorous sketch of Col. Thomas Blackburn. We have a photo of a portrait of him and, since he was anything but a good-looking man, I often say that his face was left out on purpose".

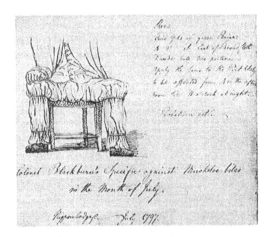

Near the end of the eighteenth century Thomas Blackburn enlarged the house which originally was a simple story-and-a-half Georgian farmhouse. Judge and Mrs. Wade Hampton Ellis purchased and restored Rippon Lodge in 1924 and added a wide columned verandah and a wing at each end. My wife, Aviza Johnson Black, and I acquired the place in 1952 and we have gone on, within our means, with the restoration.

Mrs. Black is honored at Rippon Lodge by having a 17th-18th century shallop named for her. This shallop designed by William Baker, and built in 1960 by James E. Richardson of Cambridge, Maryland is 30 feet long with a two-masted sailing rig and a 30 horsepower marine engine carefully concealed inside a sea-chest.

AUTHOR'S NOTE

A more comprehensive story of "Rippon Lodge" by Admiral Black will be found in the publication of the Historical Society of Fairfax County, Vol. 9, p. 23, 1964-1965.

"Rippon Lodge" prior to restoration and additions by Judge Wade Hampton Ellis starting in 1924

"Rippon Lodge" from the North

"Rippon Lodge" from Southeast

Shallop Aviza Sailing On Chesapeake Bay
Presented to the Chesapeake Bay Maritime Museum
at St. Michaels, Md.
by Admiral Richard B. Black

250

Admiral Black also furnished a copy of a license for the schooner, Speedwell, twelve tons, of Dumfries, Virginia, dated January 14, 1799, to engage in the coastal trade. He wrote, "Note that the Master, John Oliver, could not write and even his 'x' is not well executed. The original was given to me a number of years ago by Mrs. Jack Ratcliffe of Manassas. Her husband is historian of Prince William County".

Hallowing Point

Mr. John W. Hazard of Larks Landing at Hallowing Point has given some interesting history of this area. The following is quoted from several of his letters:

We live on the shore of the Potomac at Hallowing Point right opposite Glymount and have been members of Pohick Church for some years. We have always thought that Pohick Creek (my father used to refer to the church as Pohick on the crick) was named for the old fashioned name for the hickory tree which was pohickory. This, it is said, was derived from the Algonquian word for a mash made of the kernel of the hickory nut, pawcohiccora. There is also an old story hereabouts that the name Hallowing Point derived from the legend that there once was a ferry here. The ferryman supposedly resided on the Maryland shore around Chapman's Point, and when anyone on the Virginia shore wanted a ride, he would 'hallow' for the ferryman.

Craney Island is opposite our house and one of the elders has claimed that when she was a girl, the island was a great deal larger and that there was a farm on it.... two other old timers here remember when there was a cornfield on Craney Island, and the owner rowed out to cultivate it. The old Smoot Sand and Gravel Co. saved it from complete inundation by dumping a couple of barge loads of large rip rap around it. On the old maps it is sometimes shown as Crane Island. The reason for preserving the island was for use for duck blinds. It was for years leased by the Craney Island Club that owned the area between Hallowing Point and the Big Marsh, now happily preserved as a wildlife area. The Island is now a narrow pile of rocks only about 40 to 50 feet wide, on which grow some scrubby trees".

"Some of my ancestors, the Warders, used to sail cordwood from Neabsco Creek up to Washington before the Civil War, and another ancestor, Captain Thomas Bibb, had a business in Fredericksburg and used to ship produce from there to Washington in his boat".

"The print of the vessel carrying cordwood up the river....really looks like a canal boat rather than a schooner. I recall seeing a ram anchored off Solomon's before World War II and it was a real schooner, although the masts were of the same height. The vessel we see here has practically no rigging and what appear to be two leeboards on the port side. However, I have no doubt that rams did carry wood (and other products) up to Washington. The demand caused by the population growth during the Civil War must have been tremendous. This engraving comes from a book Picturesque America which was published after the Civil War".

FORT WASHINGTON
Kiplinger Washington Collection

AUTHOR'S NOTE

Mr. Hazard is Executive Editor of Changing Times and Curator of the Kiplinger Washington Collection. The boat pictured in the engraving may be a scow-schooner or schooner-barge as described in the List of Merchant Sailing Vessels of the U.S..

252

Point Lookout   ?
John W. Hazard Collection

Old Bay Line Between Norfolk & Washington
Steamboats Near Mt. Vernon

U. S. Navy Yard 1861
Kiplingler Washington Collection

Steamboat Era Remembered
by Rod Coggin

It isn't on the menu but you can have a steamboat special with your cheeseburger at Hyatt Headley's.

Headley will serve you stories about steamboats, any day of the week. Its the best thing going.

Headley operates a drug and sundry in Callao, and he has stocked his shelves with steamboat memorabilia. He will point to the carefully lit pictures of old steamboats, and the shelf lined with brass grillwork from actual boats. Especially, he points to the picture of the old "Northumberland".

Headley's eyes twinkle when he recalls the days when the "Northumberland" docked at Cowarts; how she would slish up the river towards Cowarts wharf at 4 in the afternoon, and the first line would be pitched from the floating hotel to the open arms of a kid named Headley down on the wharf.

He will tell you about Captain Bob Hart, and show you the picture of the man who told the Headley kid that if he ever grew tall enough to look through the spokes of the helm he would be signed on as a mate on the "Northumberland". Headley will tell you that it took two people to hold that steering wheel, and that he would watch her steered from Cowarts to Baltimore, via Kinsale, Mundy Point, Lodge, Coan Wharf, Bundicks, Lake, Walnut Point, Cowarts, Lewisetta, and St. Mary's City. Price: $2.50: Dinner, 75 cents: children, 50 cents.

Young Headley would marvel at the red carpet which led up to the passenger salon aboard the Northumberland, and the huge mirrors which hid the smokestacks from bourbon drinkers in "a REAL saloon". He would stay up all night, afraid of missing something, sometimes watching the hissing water ("the boats were so quiet," he says) or exploring the cargo bay filled with livestock, watermelons, and green tomatoes. Arriving the next morning, Headley would step off into another world, Baltimore, a place where Headley recalls a fellow Northern Necker saying, "that man 'Co.' owns everything!"

The steamboats are gone now, all of them, and Headley can tell you how, when and where. He and his wife, the former Virginia Hayden of Callao, rode the last bay steamers from Old Point Comfort until the retirement of the last boat in the early 1960's.

Headley dreams aloud these days of the boats returning, and of the times when, as a kid, he used to ride the few minutes on the "Northumberland" from Cowarts to Lewisetta and walk the miles back home, "just to blow the whistle".

His father was Ross Headley, a Coan River waterman, whose home was at Cowart, Virginia.

Capt. Ross Headley was one of seven sons and he would quote his mother saying, "My Ma used to say, when a steamboat docks here, one of my boys is on her". This was true as the seven Headley sons were all on seven different steamboats at one time in her life. After his steamboat career, Capt. Headley dredged oysters in a skipjack in the fall and winter, fished pound nets in the spring and crabbed in the summer.

Hyatt Headley will tell you that they had a steamboat captain from the little town of Cowart, Captain Emerson O. Harding.

PROUD REMINDER - of the steamboat days, this wooden eagle once perched atop a floating palace. Headley says the eagles were replaced on later boats by powerful searchlights. This one now is mounted in the rear of Headley's Callao store.

(Reprinted from the Northern Neck News by special permission)

254

Steamboats Northumberland and Three Rivers
At Lodge Landing, Va.

The Mariners Museum Collection

Steamboat Westmoreland
With Unidentified Bugeye in the Background

The Mariners Museum Collection

255

List of Captains Sailing Out of the Coan and Yeocomico Rivers
And the Various Vessels They Commanded
by Robert H. Burgess

Mr. Burgess wrote on January 30, 1973, "My father, William Kirk Burgess sailed on dredging craft on the Potomac..... He was born in 1874 near Farnham, Virginia, and as a young man took to the water. Later he went to Baltimore and on into steamboats, the Charlotte, Gaston and Manhattan and on into steamers of the Merchants and Miners, first on deck, quartermaster, engine room and was with that firm coastwise for 18 years. He worked up to Chief Engineer and went deep sea in freighters. He died in Baltimore in May 1941. His career in sailing craft was furnished me in 1953 by his twin brother, George Burgess..... who also dredged on some of the same craft as my father". The list of vessels follows:

Captain	Vessel	Type
Martin O'Malley	Clara M. Leonard	Schooner
Eg. Swift	Thomas J. Parks	Schooner
George Dungan	Pocahontas (Lodge, Va.)	Schooner
Luther Headley	Dorchester	Schooner
Bill Swann	Chief	Pungy
Taylor Swann	Ocean Queen	Pungy
Ben Fisher	Volunteer	Bugeye
Bill Dungan	J. A. Holland	Three Sail Bateau
Ed Rice	George T. Garrison	Schooner
Abb Robinson	*(Thomas Henry Bailey Brown	Pungy
	(Riverdale	Bugeye
John Newsome	John and Jane	Bugeye
" "	** Anna M. Estell	Schooner
" "	Wm. B. Coleman	Pungy
Edgar Headley	Patterson and Bash	Pungy

* – Later named Mildred Addison
** – Sailed to West Indies for pineapples

AUTHOR'S NOTE

Details concerning these sailing vessels and others included in subsequent pages of this Supplement can be found in the "Annual List of Merchant Vessels of the United States", going back to 1868. Data in the lists include the Official Number, Signal Letters, if any, Rig (Type), Name of Vessel, Gross and Net Tonnage, Length, Breadth, Depth, Crew (No. of), When Built, Where Built and Home Port. These annual publications are on file at the U. S. Archives in Washington, D. C. Also at the Archives will be found the record of ownership, masters and other papers relating to each vessel.

Schooner-rigged Bugeye "J. W. Lewis"
Photos by Vernon D. Tate

257

Steamboat Calvert at Washington, D. C.

Photo by Herman Hollerith, Jr.

Mariners Museum Collection

258

Steamboat Potomac

List of Captains Sailing Out of the Yeocomico River
And the Various Vessels They Commanded   1900 to 1960
by W. Norris Parks

Captain	Home Address	Vessel	Type
J. Harvey Bailey	Kinsale, Va.	John E. Bright	Schooner
John P. (Puss) Bailey	Kinsale, Va.	(James A. Garfield	Schooner
		(Minnie May Kirwan	Schooner
		(Levi B. Phillips	Schooner
		(Thomas B. Schall	Schooner
Garnett Belfield	Kinsale, Va.	(E. S. Wilson	Schooner
		(Mattie F. Dean	Schooner
Hunter T. Belfield	Kinsale, Va.	(Etta	Schooner
		(John Kelso	Schooner
		(Nellie	Schooner
		(Edwin C.	Schooner
		(Minnie and Emma	Schooner
Charles Courtney	Kinsale, Va.	Columbia F. C.	Schooner
William H. Douglas	Kinsale, Va.	(Charles P. Finney	Schooner
		(Elizabeth Ann	Schooner
		(Edwin C.	Schooner
		(John Branford	Bugeye
George Dungan	Lodge, Va.	(Columbia F. C.	Schooner
		(Levi B. Phillips	Schooner
John Johnson	Tucker Hill, Va.	Grape Shot	Schooner
Benjamin Nash	Kinsale, Va.	Lillian Ruth	Power Boat
Arthur W. Parks	Kinsale, Va.	(Columbia F. C.	Schooner
		(Lillian Ruth	Power Boat
James K. Parks	Kinsale, Va.	(Ella F. Cripps	Schooner
		(Minnie May Kirwan	Schooner
		(Levi B. Phillips	Schooner
		(Mollie V. Leonard	Bugeye
		(Yeocomico	Power Boat
B. S. Thrift	Kinsale, Va.	(Augusta	Schooner
		(Minnie and Emma	Schooner
		(J. W. Knowles	Schooner
E. Porter (Bud) Thrift	Kinsale, Va.	(Thomas B. Schall	Schooner
		(Minnie and Emma	Schooner
Elwood Thrift	Kinsale, Va.	Widgeon	Schooner
Lloyd Thrift	Kinsale, Va.	Widgeon	Schooner
Warren Reamy	Mundy Point, Va.	Thomas B. Schall	Schooner
Jennings Burton	Kinsale, Va.	Margaret A. Travers	Power Boat[1]
Owner W. J. Courtney	Mundy Point, Va.	Winnie Estelle	Power Boat

(1) Originally a round stern bugeye

Mr. Parks is a native of Kinsale, Va., where his family was involved in stores, canneries and shipping. As a youth he recalls many of these vessels and their captains.

Schooner, Minnie and Emma
At Pier 6, Pratt Street, Baltimore After
Discharging a Cargo of Lumber, Sept. 6, 1933
Photo by Robert H. Burgess

Trailboard on Abandoned Hulk of Bugeye,
A. J. Lawson at Crisfield Md. July 1951,
Now in the Collection of Robert H. Burgess
Photo by Robert H. Burgess

Hulk of Pungy, James A. Whiting Abandoned
At Walnut Point, Coan River, Va. July 1947
Home of Andrew J. Lewis, Owner of Vessel in Right Background
Photo by Robert H. Burgess

Bugeye, Nettie B. Greenwell,
Loaded with Watermelons Approaching Long Dock, Baltimore
Sept. 2, 1933
Photo by Robert H. Burgess

List of Captains, Owners, and Their Vessels
Sailing Out of Colonial Beach, Nomini,
Lower Machodoc, Yeocomico and the Coan River
by Captain Harding Daiger

In several letters written in January and February 1973 Captain Daiger wrote as follows:

I was born on Lower Machodoc Creek on December 19, 1904. I could lay in my bed at night and watch the Washington and Norfolk steamboats go by. The first job I had when I was 18 was as an Oiler on the steamboat, Ocean View of the Whiting Line of Washington, D. C. with Capt. Austin Kelly and later with Capt. James Beach of Alexandria, Va. In 1927, I sailed with Mr. G. W. Fosberg of Washington on his yacht, the Aldot. She was about 80 feet in length. Mr. Fosberg had both a Captain's and an Engineer's license. I then went sailing with Capt. W. L. Smith on the schooner, Josephine Smith. When he came ashore and went into the Store business, I then went Captain of the Josephine Smith until we traded her for the power boat, Bessie L. I went Captain of her and ran oysters to Washington and to the L. R. Carson Packing Co. in Crisfield, Md. I also ran seed oysters from the James River and water melons from the Piankatank River to Baltimore and from Mardella Spring, Md. to Washington, D. C. until she was sold to Henry Clayton in Crisfield.

I can recall my first trip on the Potomac, but not the exact year. I was still a boy and I went on a little schooner, John Willie, with my father. I remember him taking me up the street in Washington to the train tunnel to see the trains go by and they were the first I had seen. He also took me to a silent movie, my first, and he brought back a lot of oranges and bananas to the family which were enjoyed.

When I was running oysters and other freight on the Potomac the gill nets were a problem, particularly at night. Most of them had lights, but they were hard to miss on a dark, rainy night. I ran fish in the Bessie L from the gill fisherman for Capt. Andrew Johnson for awhile when he was broken down. I also did some haul seine fishing and also some menhaden fishing on the boat, Tender Heart, later named the North Beach, of the Standard Products Company of Fairport, Virginia. I have run herring from Capt. Sam Hall's nets above Nomini to Garner Brothers in Lewisetta, Virginia, as many as 90 thousand a trip.

I can recall some deep water trap net fishermen back in the early 1900's who came up from Yeocomico and rented a row of shanties from my Grandfather, Charles E. Daiger near Edgewater Wharf and fished out of the Lower Machodoc. They were Capt. Robert Balderson and his sons, Leonard, Roy and Willie; Capt. Joe Booth; Capt. James Wilkerson; Capt. L. Warthen and Capt. James Jewel. The ones I knew that fished out of Yeocomico were Capt. Buckie Turner and his brother, Capt. George Turner; Capt. Daniel Jewel; Capt. Clarence Jewell and Capt. Warren Reamey. Mr. W. J. Courtney ran a cutting house at Mundy Point. About this same time (1910-1920) Mr. Wiseman from Washington, D. C. and Capt. Harry Miller were running a cutting house at Colonial Beach. They would pick out the best of the roe herring and take them to Washington and put them through a smoking process which made for good-eating. Some sturgeon were still being caught in the Potomac then. My Mother would bake them and they were just about the best fish I can recall eating.

Times were not always good on the River. Sometimes there would be a great strike of oysters or a big glut of fish and the price would drop very low and it would be hard to find a market, but with all the ups and downs it was a good life and I was sorry to see it go. I didn't think this could really happen in my time. One of the main things to do away with the freight boats was the Great Depression in the 30's. We ran oysters to Washington for as low as 5¢ on the bushel and over runage; 15¢ to Crisfield on a charter; 8¢ a bushel for seed oysters from the James River; $100.00 a ton for lime and fertilizer; 8¢ a bushel for wheat to Baltimore; 5¢ a case for large No. 3 tomatoes and $75.00 a trip for water melons.

The worst storm or blow I can recall was in March about 1932. I was in the Josephine Smith as Captain and we had put out our oysters at the 11th Street Wharf in Washington and came on down the Potomac and anchored in Nanjemoy Creek about nightfall. The next morning it was blowing so hard N. W. we went forward and let go the other anchor and all of the chain. The wind increased so that she picked up both anchors and all the chain and went out of there. We had to get those anchors and

264

Captain Harding Daiger
1934

Schooner, Josephine Smith
At Tidwells Canning Factory

Steamboat, Wakefield

come on down the river. It blowed so hard that it blowed the water up in the air at
times so we couldn't see land on either side. She was running her bow split level
with the water, <u>light</u> under bare poles. We eventually wound up in the Lower Machodoc
under a bit of sail.

I can recall, when the schooner, Moffet, sank off St. Katherine's Island in the
Potomac in a March gale. She was loaded with oyster shells from the Rappahannock
River. Her Captain and crew of 2 or 3 men were lost.

AUTHOR'S NOTE
* * * * *

The author well remembers this event and in the summer following when he was
visiting his Uncle, Charles Beitzell, on St. Katherine's Island he went out in a skiff
and saw the top of the Moffet's masts a few feet out of the water. As she was a
menace to river traffic the Coast Guard destroyed her with dynamite. This occurred
about 1918. Fred Cheseldine who was then living on St. Margaret's Island said he
was watching the Moffet during the gale and she was hit by a waterspout.
* * * * *
I have crossed the Chesapeake Bay from Point Lookout to Kedges Straights in
the Bessie L. when I would be afraid to put a man on deck for fear he would be washed
overboard. I have crossed there in the Josephine Smith with single reefed mainsail,
reefed jib and foresail stowed away when her jib would be wet 6 feet up from the water
blowing off the top of the waves.

One experience with ice in the Potomac was when I was with Capt. W. L. Smith
on the Josephine Smith loaded with oysters bound for Washington. We started to run
into ice at Maryland Point Light and we made it as far as Quantico, with the ice
getting heavier all the time. The U. S. Navy tug, Triton, was on her way to Washington so she took a line to the Bugeye, Edith Marcy, Capt. Richard Chesser of St.
Inigoes, Md., and to us. The Captain of the tug would not take any money so Capt.
Smith gave them a 1/2 case of eggs. We had on board a few cases of eggs to sell in
D. C.

In the freeze of 1934, I was in the Lower Machodoc in the Bessie L. loaded with
oysters for Crisfield. The Coast Guard sent a large steel boat with twin diesel
motors to cut a track and it took her all day. It was night when she cut to where
I was anchored. They will not tow a boat out of a harbor. By that time it was dark
and snowing and it was almost two weeks before I got out using this same track.
When I got to the turn by the Black Beacon, the Beacon was down. I got out on the ice
and ran my foot down with hip boots on and I could just feel the bottom with my toe.
The ice was still that thick from being blown in and piling up. It was clear from
there to Crisfield, but I went down around Tangier instead of North to Kedges Straights.

My Grandfather, Charles E. Daiger, owned the schooner Joseph T. Brenan and
later sold it to Robert Bailey. My father, W. A. Daiger, bought a dory boat from
Capt. Boss Bailey and she is in the picture with the Josephine Smith. My father also
ran a Blacksmith shop and built and repaired dredges used on the sailing vessels.
My uncle, Walter Daiger, was mate on the steamboats, Endeavor and Ocean View. He
died on February 11, 1973 in his 90's and probably was the last of the river steamboat officers. I was just an oiler and that didn't make me much of a steamboat man.

The first gasoline engines to come on the River were the Bridge Port, Ordmore,
Faro, Lathrop and then the Mianus, Herbert, Victor, Regal and the Palmer.

One of the largest schooners sailing on the Potomac in my time was the Levi B.
Phillips. The largest sloop was the Flora Elsie; the largest bugeye, the Gladys L.
and the largest bateau (skipjack), the Norma K. The last schooner to leave the
Potomac was the Columbia F. C., Capt. George Dungan, Master.

The steamboats running into Lower Machodoc Creek from Washington to Edgewater
Wharf, owned by my Grandfather, Charles E. Daiger and to Olverson's Wharf, owned by
Ben Olverson were:

Wakefield	Capt. Bailey Reed
	Capt. Chap Slye
Majestic	Capt. Bailey Reed
W. L. Davis	Capt. Austin Kelly

Endeavor   Capt. Austin Kelly
Ocean View   Capt. James Beach
(Capt. Phil Barbour and Capt. Eppie Dodson also were steamboat captains who ran into
the Lower Machodoc)

The last sail boats to dredge oysters in the Potomac out of Machodoc were the
bugeye, Catherine E. Shores, the schooners Kimble and Grapeshot and the sloop, Ethel.
I have seen as many as a dozen flying jib schooners and other boats anchored in the
Machodoc at one time.

The list of sailing vessels is as follows:

Vessel Name	Captain	Home	Owner	Type
Austin	Asbury Evans	Machodoc	Same	Sloop
Birdie May	George Trader	Machodoc	Same	Bugeye
Cape Charles	George Trader	Machodoc	Same	Bugeye
Catherine E. Shores	Edward Barnes	Machodoc	Same	Bugeye
Crockett	Walter Daiger	Machodoc	Same	Schooner
Clara M. Leonard	Jessie Fagan	Nomini	Same	Schooner
Columbia F. C.	(Arthur Parks	Kinsale	W. J. Courtney	Schooner
	(George Dungan	Yeocomico		
C. R. Pryor	Ernest Herbert	Machodoc	Same	Schooner
E. R. S. Daugherty	George Trader	Machodoc	Same	*Pungy
#Elizabeth Clark	Joe Skates	Nomini	Clark Lumber Co.	Schooner
Ella Worden	(William Stanford	Colonial Beach	William Stanford	Schooner
	(George Stanford	Colonial Beach	William Stanford	Schooner
E. P. Evans	William Stanford	Colonial Beach	—	Schooner
Ethel	—	Machodoc	—	Sloop
Eva B.	Charles Boyce	Machodoc	Same	Sloop
Flora Elsie	Walter Wessels	Washington, D.C.	Same	Sloop
Gladys L.	Marshall Pritchard	Coan	Andrew Lewis	Bugeye
Grapeshot	—	Machodoc	—	Schooner
Harriet P. Ely	Ed. Waters	—	—	Schooner
James O. Wright	Harry Miller	Colonial Beach	Same	Bugeye
Joseph T. Brenan	Fletcher Smith	Machodoc	Chas. E. Daiger	Schooner
Josephine Smith	(W. L. Smith	Machodoc	W. A. Daiger	Schooner
	(Willie S. Evans			
	(George W. Kilman			
	(Raymond Chatham			
	(Harding Daiger	Machodoc		
Kimble	Webster Smith	Machodoc	—	Schooner
Levi B. Phillips	— Bailey	Kinsale	—	Schooner
Majestic	Richard Miller	Colonial Beach	Same	Bugeye
Norma K.	—	—	—	Bateau
S. E. Coulbourn	(James Herbert	Machodoc	Same	Pungy
	(William Herbert			
Thomas J. Parks	Walter Daiger	Machodoc	Same	Pungy

Power Boats

Bessie L.	Harding Daiger	Machodoc	(W. A. Daiger	Barge
			(Harding Daiger	
Dora Estelle	Charles Henderson	Machodoc	Same	Barge
Irana	Howard Herbert	Machodoc	Chas. E. Daiger	Barge
##Jane C.	Andrew Johnson	Machodoc	Chas. E. Daiger	Barge
J. C. Drewer	(William Hundley	Machodoc	Same	Barge
	(Walter Hundley	Machodoc	Same	Barge
John Branford	Ernest Harding	Machodoc	—	**Barge
Yeocomico	James Parks	Kinsale	Same	Barge
Yeomac	Garnett Belfield	Coles Point	Same	Barge

*   One of only 3 centerboard pungys built on Chesapeake Bay
** Originally a bugeye, changed from sail to power
\#   Had bullet holes in Main Mast from the battle of the Rappahannock River.
     Capt. Bosman was killed.
\#\# Later named Edith R.

Bugeye, Majestic 1936

Schooner, Federal Hill 1936

Photos by Vernon D. Tate

Baltimore Harbor in the 1930's

Unidentified

Skipjack

Ketch Bugeye

Photos by Vernon D. Tate

Schooner, Sarah W. Wingate
In Baltimore Harbor in 1930's

Photos by Vernon D. Tate

Ram, Edwin & Maud
In Baltimore Harbor in 1930's

Photos by Vernon D. Tate

Memories of a Lifetime on the Potomac River
by Capt. Graham Trader

There were very few boats on either the Maryland or the Virginia side of the Potomac in the early days and this was because the Yankees had taken or destroyed all they could find during the War Between the States. And the war ruined the people and they were slow to get back into the water business.

Some boats were built in the Virginia inlets but they were of the smaller size. Several were built on the Yeocomico before 1900 by William Parks, Wash Parks and Henry Seldon. Seldon was a colored man who built or helped build several pungys. The Potomac Rivermen due to the war had only small boats from which they tonged until about 1875 and the demand for Potomac oysters wasn't as good as for Bay oysters. The Bay Watermen called the oysters from the tributaries "fresh water" oysters and that hurt the trade. But when the dredge had thinned the oysters out in the Bay, plenty of oysters were found in the Potomac and the dredge was brought in there.

About 1870 a blacksmith from Delaware Bay came to Crisfield, Md. There had been for sometime a thriving oyster industry in Delaware Bay and they had devised a dredge for taking oysters. This blacksmith brought with him the design and knowledge of manufacture. Before long he made one or more and persuaded some men to try them out.

One of these men was my great uncle, Samuel Trader, and he claimed to be the first man to drag a dredge in the Potomac River for oysters. This then is the real beginning of the oyster industry in Potomac. Although crude, he saw a possiblity in the operation of the dredge and it soon expanded into a large operation. This began in the early 70's and before the mid 80's several hundred boats were in operation and the oyster industry was booming. In the early days of dredging anything that would sail was put in service but most of the larger boats of that time were unsuited for dredging. A large number were keel pungys which drew too much water for the shoal rocks as did most of the schooners. There were a number of sloops, most of which were brought here from the Delaware Bay region. But they were soon replaced by the bugeyes and flatties which were developed on the Chesapeake and scores of both Bugeyes and Flatties were built almost exclusively on the bay.

In the Potomac the most popular rocks for dredging were Upper Banks and Lower Banks; Hog Island and Lynch's Point on the Virginia side with Jones Shore, Island Bar, Piney Point with Herring Run and Heron Island on Maryland shore. These rocks began to have their boom in early 80's and then began a trek up the river which ended with the discovery of oysters in deep waters at Popes Creek and Upper Cedar Point in 1888. Then came the freshet in the Spring of 1889 which killed 90% or more of the oysters above Blackistone (St. Clement's) Island in Potomac and in the Bay to Sharps Island. Thus ended an era.

This has covered one phase of the growth of the oyster industry but there were numerous obstacles to overcome in the production and marketing of the catch. At first the dredge was dragged by a line and when filled was pulled aboard by hand. The propulsion was always by sails legally and gasoline engines did not come into general use until about 1910. This goes back to getting the dredge filled with oysters and shells aboard. At first it was pulled by hand then someone thought up a spool attached to the mast with handles. This led to a "stump" or upright in mid ship with a spool and handles that were detachable. This was a big improvement but dangerous as several men were killed or injured by the dredge striking a hang and the handle would fly back and clear the deck. There was an iron crank adapted with the same action and it was about 1885 before a patent winder with a ratchet was adopted and wound by hand until about 1910. When gasoline winders or winches came into general use on the larger boat this also brought a larger class of boats into the industry as they would handle a larger dredge. Although there were a large number of boats in the 1500 to 1800 bu. class before 1890 most of the larger boats dropped out between 1890 and 1905.

The boom in oysters in the 80's also created a demand for boats and more than a hundred were built in the 400 to 1200 bu. class in the 80's with many many more in the smaller sizes in the early 90's. I was raised on the Potomac in Lower Machodoc Creek and my earliest recollection of the dredging season I was able to count more than 150 boats in sight of my home on a clear day in a stretch of about 15 miles.

This was about 1897 or 98. The oysters had made a comeback from a low in 1890 but while there was a large number of boats working nobody was catching many oysters or making any money. All oysters were handled in the shells with practically the entire catch going to Baltimore where they were steamed and canned before being put on the market with a small percentage shucked and handled raw, as without refrigeration it was not possible to keep them long or ship long distances. Therefore the larger part of the catch was consumed near the East Coast. None shipped as far as the mid-west except as steamed until about the turn of the century.

Here might be place for the part the Traders took in the development of the oyster industry in the Potomac. While the records show the first of our family arrived in Accomack Co. as a head grant in 1635, there is no notable mention made of them in history so presumably they were just ordinary working people. While they resided in Accomack through the years some of them became sailors and coasters engaged in trading up and down the coast from one port to another buying in the north and selling in the south and vice versa. At least one of them was engaged in this trade. (Maybe this accounts for the name change from Armitreading to the present day Trader). One did some dealing in slaves, not in dealing in the trade in the Indies but buying a few for sale locally in the ports of call up and down the coast. Maybe on orders or for speculation though little is known of this. However the base or home port seems to have remained Accomack County.

Then in the 1850's my great uncle, Samuel Trader, migrated to St. George's Island. The Island was sold by the Jesuits to some men from the Eastern Shore in 1852 or 54. Maybe he was one of them, anyhow, he came to the Island about this time and remained there throughout his lifetime. He was listed as a sailor in the census of St. Mary's County and was engaged in sailing on the Bay and as a sometime pilot, which took up most of his time until the War in 1861-65. He engaged in blockade running during the war but lost all of his boats except a small log canoe which he kept hid or sunk and continued to run throughout the war.

Near the end of the war he acquired a small pungy named the "Defy". I don't know how he acquired her, but she was found abandoned near the Virginia Capes just after the Civil War, loaded with salt. She was a pretty little thing of only about three hundred bushels in size but she was a complete ship with deck and hatches, with a brick chimney and fireplace for cooking in the cabin. She was a full pungy with two masts and a lug foresail without any boom. The sheet was fastened to an eyebolt in the log on each side. In sailing or tacking into the wind you undid sisterhooks in the eyebolt and carried it to the other side and hooked in the eyebolt on the log.

Uncle Sam engaged in carpentering and later made tong shafts for sale to the oystermen and became quite well known as a tong maker on both sides of the river and continued in this until his death in 1916. He always claimed to be the first man to use a dredge with sail power in the Potomac.

My Grandfather remained in Accomack County and acquired a small schooner named the Flying Cloud and engaged in freighting produce from Hunting Creek to Baltimore and Washington, D. C. He hauled mainly sweet potatoes in barrels and Irish potatoes, then in the fall and winter months would buy oysters in Tangier and Pocomoke Sound for sale in Washington, D. C. also Baltimore, Md. About 1875 he was struck by a bolt of lightning while taking in sail in a thunder squall. The lightning struck the top-mast, ran down the mast, struck my grandfather splitting his clothing and one shoe. It followed the main boom out and killed a negro cook standing near the stern of the boat. While he was not killed he was paralized in one side and always walked with a limp and dragged one foot but never spoke another word though he lived until 1910. He was active though handicapped until shortly before his death. Thus my father, George T. Trader, soon became the breadwinner for the family at an early age. He acquired a small sloop, the Phoebe Clark at the age of 19 years and became master of his own boat in 1880. He began tonging oysters in Pocomoke and Tangier Sounds as both places had struck full. They had plenty of market for them to planters from Delaware Bay and Long Island Sound for seed to be used to rehabilitate the depleted rocks in these areas. The price was 12½ cents per basket of about 3 pecks each. Then he was in the Potomac tonging and dredging until 1885 when he purchased a small pungy the E.R.S. Daugherty of about 600 bushels capacity. This was the beginning of the boom in dredging in the Potomac. The Daugherty was one of only three Centerboard Pungys ever built. John Beitzell was master of her for one season about 1896. My father

kept her until 1905 when he had her rebuilt from the keel up, but she was burned
lying at anchor in front of the home place before he had a chance to use her. One
day while he was working in the Phoebe Clark after a Northwester on a low tide,he
with two boys he had working with him picked up and loaded aboard one hundred and
three bushels of oysters at King Copsico Point, which gives one an idea of the amount
of oysters in the river at this time. (In the early 80's). After working the Daugherty three years and making money he purchased the square sail bugeye Cape Charles in
1888. Then with two boats at work he made two excellent seasons. Then came the
freshet of 1889 and set the whole industry back and it never recovered to where it
had been. He sold the Cape Charles in North Carolina in 1898 and quit dredging and
bought and ran oysters to Washington, D. C. where he built up a good trade but after
losing the Daugherty he came ashore, but was not suited for farming. So in 1912 we
bought the square sail bugeye Birdie May with her dredging rig complete. She was
beached to die in 1932. I first came into the picture in 1910. Oysters made a partial
comeback in 1910, but with power winders and larger boats this was shortlived and we
quit dredging in 1916 and began buying oysters and running to Washington, D. C. which
we continued until my father's death in 1936. I kept in the water business until 1968.

Oysters had begun to come back in the upper Potomac by 1905 and thousands of
bushels were used for planting in Rappahannock and other areas of both states. About
this time the area above Lower Cedar Point was closed to dredging, and for some years
tonging for plants and for steam stock was the main livelihood for a large number of
people from both states. The oysters above this line on the rocks were too small for
shucking and still are, but the law will not allow oysters smaller than three inches
to be marketed now, though there are thousands of bushels 2½ inches to 3 inches which
when fat could be shucked and the yield of meats would be good and help relieve the
shortage.

The river was closed to dredging above Lower Cedar Point about 1900 and reserved for tonging and as a seed area for planting purposes. A large amount were
used for steaming in Baltimore and Cambridge, but with the rebirth of the oysters in
the James River the demand dwindled in the Potomac. Then about 1908 another law
closed this area to January 1st. and ran until April 25th for tonging for anything
you could sell. About 1915 the area was closed for everything under three inches.
But Patent Tongs were allowed which enabled the oysters in deep water to be caught
and there were enormous amounts of large oysters which were caught, but Patent Tongs
were outlawed in 1950. This leaves a large area in this part of the river that cannot be worked, which used to supply many oysters and I think it still would if Patent
Tongs were allowed. The oysters on the shoal rocks above the Bridge will not grow
to be more than three inches in length. I had worked this area several seasons prior
to 1925 and could average 40 bushels a day with Patent Tongs in from 5 to 10 fathoms
of water and I have reason to believe there are oysters on these rocks today. They
grow to a large size. I have caught oysters in 15 fathoms at Upper Cedar Point.

I began working in the Potomac with shaft tongs in 1910 in the upper river for
plants and steam stock in March and April. I have worked in the river every year
since except from 1925 to 1932 when there were almost no oysters to catch. Almost
all men who worked these years worked in James River catching seed stock for planting
purposes. I did not go to James River until 1945 but did work part of each season
from 1945 to 1960 in the James. I have worked on every rock in the Potomac from
Point Lookout to and including Maryland Point where I caught 40 bushels one day in
1924. I worked 28 foot shafts for several years and could always find oysters in
deep water, but no more. Now 22 foot shafts are plenty long.

Incidently, while working above the Bridge in 1924 I saw three dredge boats go
up to a 9 fathom lump just above the Metompkin Beacon and come down the river that
afternoon with a total of 600 bushels for the day for which they received $1.25 per
bushel. This was Thanksgiving Day 1924 and dredging was not legal there, but the
Police boats were taking the day off for a holiday and they got away without being
caught. While I have tonged all over the river, I never did any illegal dredging as
four years of legal dredging was enough for me.

While I have spent a lifetime on the river and the work was hard and at times
unrewarding, I have loved it and enjoyed most of it. I would not recommend it to anyone unless he had a love for that kind of life. Unless he had some other trade he
would never get rich and though it is good at times, it can be frustrating. I had
three sons of my own, but did not encourage them to follow in my footsteps and all

three have found other occupations and I think they have all done very well at
their work.

After dredging became so prosperous, naturally every man capable of handling a
boat tried to get into it and a motley crew they were and with the hundreds of boats
engaged, the problem of crews to man them became enormous, with each boat requiring
from four to as many as twelve head on some of the larger schooners. Of course, the
local labor supply was inadequate. They naturally turned to Baltimore and Norfolk
to the shipping offices so-called which were supposed to be employment agencies,
but they were really "flop houses" where tramps and bums collected and where they
were allowed to stop overnight for a small fee and were promised a job. These so-
called shipping offices were nothing more than some rooms in a derelict building
where two or more men had a front for an office to catch the drifters who they would
pick up anywhere they could find them. These were the type of men who were hired to
go down the Bay dredging. Sometimes if there were not enough of these the jails would
be raided and then you really got in trouble. The bums wouldn't work and some of the
jailbirds were ready to cut the Captain's throat or probably had already killed one
or more men. But one bright spot at this time were lots of immigrants coming into
the country. Many Irish and Eastern Europeans, mostly German young men who had left
Germany to avoid the army as all young men of 18 were forced to join the army. The
language barrier was a problem with them and as they did not know how to man the boats
nor to cull oysters and could not understand English, you had a frustrating job on
your hands, for they had to know what to do, and do it now. If you got a crew of all
immigrants they were usually eager to learn and willing to work, so with a little
patience you soon had a good working crew. But if you got one or two bums or outlaws
in the bunch you usually had lots of trouble. You tried to teach them not to throw
oysters back overboard in the daytime, and to watch the outlaws to keep from being
murdered at night. Then if you did fall asleep the whole crew would try to get ashore
and next morning you had no crew to work with. After staying one night in a shipping
office they were infested with lice and in a few days the whole boat was lousy. You
went to the shipping office for a crew which they furnished for about two or three
dollars per man plus about a dollar a day for the time each man had been in the office.
Sometime this would amount to 10 or 12 dollars per man which came out of his wages.
Now wages were $4 to $8 per month. A good cook was about eight dollars a month.
Usually there was an advance of ten or twelve dollars per man plus boots and oilskins
at about eight dollars per man, so he had to work about four or five months to have
a dollar for himself. This left little incentive for them to work and while the
majority of captains provided adequate rations some of them did not and sometimes the
crews were subjected to almost inhuman treatment. Many were beaten and abused beyond
description besides being ill fed, and in cold weather often there was insufficient
clothing. Many captains would not provide them with oilskins or boots. Besides this,
many times the shipping office employed thugs to go around to the lesser barrooms and
drug a number of unsuspecting drinkers and ferry them aboard in the night. You paid
their fee and they delivered. After delivery you would get under way, and by morning
you were well out on the Bay and could look your crew over. And what a crew you had.
Sometimes you would find you had more than you bargained for, but then you had to try
to make a crew of what you had and all kinds were at times shanghied. Sometimes
there were intellectuals of all kinds, even some prominent people, as well as bums
and panhandlers. So you see, the captains had a rather difficult proposition to overcome.

It has been told that some captains would line the crew up in mid deck and fix
the sails to sweep them overboard, to keep from paying them off. While this could
happen and probably did, I never knew of a case actually to happen, though there were
cases reported of men actually being swept overboard accidently and these were probably instances where it was not an accident and was not reported. There were some
captains capable of anything and before about 1890 there was no effective law to protect the crews. While wages were small, provisions were cheap and with everyone making money there was no necessity for not providing proper rations for the crews.
Heck fish were less than 5 cents a lb., navy beans at 2 cents, lard for 5 cents a lb.,
fat back 5 cents and smoked side at 7 cents a lb., potatoes at 50 cents a bushel,
cabbage at $1.50 for 100 lbs. You could feed a man a good healthy ration for less
than $1.50 a week with variety. Corned beef was about 6 cents a lb. with split peas
at $1.50 a bushel. These prices were for good quality products and in most stores
at this time. By buying in quantity you could buy for less than these prices. Still
many crews were ill fed and often the captain awoke in the morning without a crew for
they had managed to get away in the night. Quite often one or more were drowned trying

to get away and their bodies would not be found for days or even weeks. If they got ashore they were sometimes picked up next day, but if they eluded capture they were usually fed by the farmers on shore and would finally get back to town only to be picked up and shipped out again later. I was too late to go through this for when I started dredging the laws had been changed to protect the crews and you had to treat the crews as men, but my father went through the whole era. Though he had some poor crews he only had one or two unruly ones and he put them ashore as soon as he found them out. But he did have some good crews and some of them turned out to be unusually bright. He shipped one young German who got ashore one night but was caught next day and brought back. After being talked to, he agreed to stay for the season, then stayed on the farm the following summer and learned the English language. The following season he came back and dredged that winter. When he left in the spring with about $50 he went to New York, got a job and took up electric engineering at night school and in a short time was employed by an Electric Co. and helped to install electricity in the Hudson Tunnel as an electrical engineer. He had a nice home in Jersey City and raised a family.

With the advent of the dredge the first oysters were found and worked in the lower Potomac and there not having been too much traffic on the river there were few places where provisions could be had except a few staples at some small stores in some harbors on the river. But with a demand for them there soon began a build up of stores and Blacksmith shops to supply the boats. Coan River at this time was the most popular harbor and as most of the boats were owned by Eastern Shore men it was natural for business men of that area to follow. At this time Charles Lewis and his brother, Andrew, purchased land near the mouth of Coan River and started a business, naming the place Lewisetta. L. W. Courtney owned Mundy Point and this soon became a popular harbor for dredge boats also. Capt. E. P. Barnes started a grocery and ship chandlery store at Coles Point on the Lower Machodoc in 1880 which soon became the most popular harbor on Potomac for several years. There soon followed others namely Bretton Bay and Rock Point in Md. and Colonial Beach and Upper Machodoc in Va.

Virginia outlawed dredging in most of her waters about 1890. This included all of the state waters except the western section of the Bay from Smith Point to Windmill Point with Tangier Sound and lower part of Pocomoke Sound. This created quite a problem caused by illegal dredging wherever there were oysters which resulted in a number of battles between the dredgeboats and enforcement officers. One of these took place in the Rappahannock between the shore population and a fleet of sloops supposedly from Md. and New Jersey with at least one cannon fired from the shore. This culminated in the capture of nine boats with the crews and captains, a total of about 65 men, back of Gwynns Island who were carried to Crickett Hill and tried at Mathews Court House. Another pitched battle was fought in the Pocomoke with rifles between a fleet of dredge boats and a police boat in which several boats were captured. No one was injured though several hundred shots were fired by both sides. Maryland also had some areas in which dredging was prohibited and they also had numerous skirmishes and at least two pitched battles on Eastern Shore.

With the advent of the dredge and discovery of oysters in Potomac, there arose the problem of disposal and here began an era. While Baltimore was handling an enormous amount of oysters, there was many thousand bushels of oysters too small for market and with no cull law they were in demand for planting in northern states and some were carried as far as Long Island with most going to Delaware Bay and tributaries. Some of these oysters were not small at all but were on shoal bars and rocks where the larger boats would not float and this was a thriving business as early as 1880 and 82. But transportation being what it was and the development of the James River beds where oysters had been known and utilized since early 1600's this phase of the industry came to an end helped by the freshet of 89. All the potentials of oysters production for the Potomac are based on the amount produced in 1888 but I have no record nor can I find any of a freshet or catastrophe to have killed out the oysters in the upper river before.

Now we know nature changes very slowly if at all and there have been freshets at intervals through the ages and until some way is found to control the amount of run off of fresh water down the river from heavy rainfall in the watershed, there is no way to tell what the actual potential really is or can become. So we know any estimate is truly wishful thinking.

276

* * * * *

Hurricane Agnes with the tremendous flow of fresh water in 1972 wiped out the soft clam (maninose) industry in the Potomac and severely damaged the oyster and crab population in its tributaries.

* * * * *

With the return of the oysters in the 90's there began to spring up a number of shucking houses along the river but these never proved very lucrative in these years. There was no refrigeration, slow transportation and the price of shucked oysters left very little profit. The usual wholesale price for standard size oysters was seldom above 80 cents a gallon, usually from 65 to 80 cents per gallon. Sometimes with a scarcity from bad weather or a freeze $1.00 would be received but this was unusual.

With the advent of better handling methods and better and faster transportation, Baltimore began to loose out to other locations on the Bay. Cambridge was for sometime a big factor and at one time had two steam houses in operation. But these closed about 1916 or soon after and another era came to an end.

Crisfield was also a large user of oysters and from 1910 to the mid twenties was the largest market for oysters on the Bay. One house there, The John Handy Co. could handle more than 5000 bushels per day with several houses almost as large and numerous smaller ones. With oysters, fish and crabs Crisfield was the largest port of entry for number of boats in and out in the United States for some years. But with the freshet in the spring of 1925, the Potomac and most of the Bay production of oysters fell way down and Crisfield was hard hit. Oysters began to come back in 1933 which put some life in Crisfield. Then another freshet in 1936 just about put Crisfield out of the picture as far as oysters were concerned. Unless and until production improves greatly, Crisfield will probably never be what it was in the 1920's.

Through the years many man-made changes have taken place in the oyster picture but none of them seem to make any permanent improvement in the production of oysters. First change was the outlawing of dredging in some areas then a cull law was passed calling for oysters less than 2½ inches to be thrown back overboard, passed about 1892, then it was changed to three inches in 1924 with all dredging abolished in 1930 in the Potomac. Then from some unknown cause there was in 1949 and 1950 almost a total kill of oysters in deep water in the lower Potomac, the lower Bay and also the Rappahannock and again in 1954 though not so bad in the Potomac as the Rappahannock. The biologists came up with a name for it, MSX, which literally translated means "Microbe of the Sea unknown". But most anyone could come up with a name with just as much meaning for $8,000 to $10,000 a year. So with no known cause and no method of prevention we will just have to wait and see if oysters will make a comeback in spite of these obstacles or others now unknown.

I was not born until 1893 so I missed all the earliest days in the oyster trade, but through my father who you might say grew up with it, I learned much of the early days and have tried to set down some of the highlights. First off there were literally piles of oysters in the Potomac prior to 1888 and they were handled in the thousands of bushels. At one time a firm in Baltimore was using barges to transport, having one in the Lower Machodoc and one in the Wicomico buying oysters and a tug to tow them to Baltimore. They would bring them down light, drop a light one and pick up a loaded one. These were of about 6000 bushels capacity and there were dozens of schooners of 1500 to 3000 bushels capacity buying and running to Baltimore. I have known as late as 1898 there were as many as 65 boats buying oysters in the Lower Machodoc with up to 250 boats catching them and at the same time as many boats in the other harbors on the river both market boats and dredge boats. As late as 1924 I have seen 35 market boats in the Upper Machodoc in the tonging season before the dredging season opened November 1st. One of these boats of about 1000 bushels capacity after dredging season opened landed seven loads of oysters from Swann Point to Crisfield in 8 days.

While working with my father in 1913 we caught and landed in one day 585 bushels which we sold at 25 cents a bushel and got paid off at 17 cents. This was the largest amount we caught in one day, although we caught between 800 and 1000 bushels a week, several weeks usually at 40 to 50 cents a bushel and have known others that caught as many and more than that but this was not the usual catch for often 100 bushels was a good weeks catch after the first 15 days of any season. One time Capt. Ned Hayden in

277

Capt. Graham
Trader

Capt. Trader in One of Several Work Boats He Built

Schooner, Clemmie Travers
Photo by Vernon D. Tate

Barge, Dewey and Unidentified Bugeye

Photo by Vernon D. Tate

the schooner, Rosa Beitzell, went to Norfolk to ship a crew as all men working on boats in Virginia had to come from Virginia. Coming back up the Bay he ran over a spar buoy in back of Gwynns Island just after dark which awakened him. He went on deck and knowing where he was called his crew and went to work and when daylight came he steered for Crisfield where he landed 1000 bushels at $1.25 a bushel. This was on prohibited bottom and just one day after the capture of nine boats for illegal dredging as I mentioned before. Naturally, he did not attempt this again. Soon after this some men fitted the B. A. Wagner, a large keel pungy boat with patent tongs and caught as high as 200 bushels a day with four pair of tongs but this did not last long. This was in the Bay back of Gwynns Island.

There was a great deal of commerce on the bay and rivers and quite a number of the larger vessels were used in the trade to the West Indies out of Baltimore Md. The trade was handled almost exclusively by schooners as the pungy was unsuited for this type of sailing. The pungy was developed from the Baltimore or Yankee Clipper with a deep keel and while they were good sailors and quite able they did not handle kindly in a following sea which soon put them out of the running for the West Indies run. They tried building larger ones until they got the Francis J. Ruth of about two thousand bushels capacity, the largest ever built but they were still too wet for the West Indies trade and too deep draft for most of the tributaries, so they soon became a thing of the past. The Bugeye replaced them and in the 80's and 90's the Bugeye both sharp sail and schooner rigged largely replaced the schooner. In turn they were replaced almost entirely by the flattie or skipjack in the early 1900's in fact there were very few skipjacks built after 1920, and only one to three a year built since that time. And now in 1968 there are only a few kept up for dredging in Maryland as there is no dredging except in the Maryland part of the Bay allowed with sail gear as Virginia has almost nowhere that dredging is allowed.

About the time I started to work Capt. E. P. Barnes of Coles Point had two vessels of about 600 - 700 bushels, but they were soon wrecked. Also Lewis Courtney, a merchant at Mundy Point, acquired the 2500 bushel schooner, Columbia F. C. which had been built there for the Columbia Fishing Club. The Club soon dissolved and they sold her to Courtney. She was used as a buy boat and ran oysters and other freight to Baltimore. There was a good deal of freighting in grain, cord-wood, railroad ties and lumber. Courtney and his son W. J. Courtney also acquired the schooners, Etta, the E. P Evans and Bessie Reed which were used in dredging oysters by three men who bought a share in them until about 1915 or 1920 when the dredging was over for the larger boats. The Courtneys also bought the Thomas B. Schall, a schooner of about 2000 bushels and dredged her one or two seasons and then put her to running oysters and other freight to Baltimore. In addition to the store at Mundy Point, the W. J. Courtney Co. owned about 9 tomato canneries in the area. This was in the period 1910-1925. Lewis Brothers on Coan River owned at least two large boats and some smaller boats, but they were used mostly for freighting and did little or no dredging. He went out of business about 1905. From about 1905 until 1930 there were most always four to eight schooners berthed in Kinsale harbor. Most of the boats were owned in Baltimore with local Watermen as Captain. At this time Tom Webster and Capt. Bob Moore of Baltimore owned about 150 schooners, most of which were left over from the fruit trade to the West Indies when steam took over from sail. These men, having so many boats, were glad to put them out to work and most any Riverman with any sailing experience could get one at $40.00 on the hundred of the freight. Capt. Bob Moore who owned a hundred of these schooners used to say "No matter which way the wind blew, some of his boats were running a fair wind". One schooner, loaded with grain, owned in part or wholly by Capt. Puss Bailey of Kinsale was rundown and sunk by a freight ship off Cove Point in the Chesapeake Bay.

I knew a good number of boats and Captains on the Lower Machodoc. Capt. Harding Daiger has a list of them. There was one railway on Coan River owned and operated by Capt. Lew Headley from the 1880's until 1940. Some smaller ones are now operating.

Having lost practically all the boats on the Potomac during the War of 1812 and again in the Civil War, there was a strong demand for boats and many boats large and small were built on the Potomac, with boat yards in almost every tributary on the river.

These were used to carry freight of all kinds to Baltimore, Philadelphia, Washington, Alexandria and Norfolk. There was grain and produce, tobacco, cattle, hogs and anything that would produce money. Also included was wood, lumber and ties and quite a lot of barrel stock as there was a large quantity of large oak timber for making staves.

The wood business, both cordwood for fires and pulp for paper, was for many years the largest commodity handled on the river until the early 1920's when trucks took over from the boats.

Following the Civil War, there was a wood landing and sometime two or three on every tributary on the river with a large number along the river front all the way to Washington, D. C. Most wood was loaded on scows and transferred to other boats. A few large scows were used in the upper river under sail, but they did not handle well under sail. There was one fitted out with gasoline engines from Nanjemoy Creek about 1918, but this was near the end of the era and was soon abandoned.

The last of the wood runners was the "Bertha May" owned by Capt. Parker Gray of Maryland Point, Maryland. He met a tragic death in 1921 or 1922 when he went aboard to get under way to move her from her anchorage near Maryland Point to Upper Nanjemoy Creek. He had a gasoline winder or hoister for raising the anchor and hoisting the sails, also for pumping ship. He started the engine and was wearing a long overcoat at the time the tail of which caught in the gears someway and was beaten to death before he was found by his son.

AUTHOR'S NOTE

Mr. Andrew J. Cummings also related this story in a letter dated March 6, 1969, but gave the name of the schooner as the "Anna B. Bateman".

* * * * *

The era of wood running was not affected too much by the advent of the steamboats on the Potomac, but the steamboats did get practically all of the farm produce plus fish and most all fruit and vegetables. Still most of the grain and tobacco was carried by sail boats until about 1920, which was the beginning of the end for sail boats and by 1940 practically all sail boats on the Potomac were gone.

Also ended about 1905 was a large flotilla of three and four mast schooners running ice from Maine to Washington, D. C. also Baltimore, Maryland. Prior to this time all ice consumed in the cities was gathered in winter and stored for use in warm weather. I well remember, though I was a small boy at the time, of seeing as many as six three and four mast schooners gathered in the river in sight of our home at Lower Machodoc Creek in the morning waiting for a tow to Washington, and others light, bound for Maine or to load freight back to some other port. This to me was one of the most interesting sights of my youth, together with the myriad of dredge boats in season at work in the river. I have counted more than two hundred sail boats in sight early in the morning in the oyster season, and up to 65 market boats waiting to load oysters. Most of them carried from 1000 to 4000 bushels of oysters and they all loaded in a few days.

Three Mast Schooner, "Jennie Thomas"   Sloop, "Flying Scud"
Photos by Vernon D. Tate

At Left, 3 Masted Schooner, "Albert T. Stearns"
Astern are Schooners "Charles E. Balch", "Monhegan" and "Annie F. Conlon"
Discharging Ice at Independent Ice Company, Ninth Street Wharf, Washington, D.C.
July 23, 1892

Mariners Museum Collection

The Indians had been fishing in a crude manner before the English came into the Potomac and made extensive use of them for food and had learned to use the herring and menhaden as fertilizer for their corn and maybe other crops. History tells us that the water was almost alive with fish at times and I can visualize this as in my boyhood as late as 1900, I have seen literally millions of them in the water. The Indians used crude nets and weirs which were a sort of barricade of poles and brush woven together with an opening in the center in which they inserted a hoop or dip net and caught the fish that came through the hole. The white man improved on this method in many ways and began to use nets made of twine. They were knit into a drag or haulsein but the net was knit by hand and was a slow and tedious process. Whole families would spend the long winter nights knitting netting to be used in the nets. They were operated at different points along the river front called fishing shores. Many of these were operated for years at the same place and this was the main source of fresh fish for market in the early days. Some seiners had Ice Houses, filled in winter, to ice the fish for shipment in hot weather. Not all the fishing was done by haulseine as quite a lot of fishing was done with gill nets, especially after they began using linen for twine.

The Faunce family came to the Potomac from Pennsylvania and settled in Washington, D. C. They bought 60 acres of land at Ragged Point about 1888 and operated about 30 pound nets in the area which were the first such nets used in the Potomac. There were four boys in this family, John D., George B., Jake R., and Dave M. George B. took to sailing and was drowned in the capsize of his boat while still a young man. After about 3 years at Ragged Point, John D. went to Virginia Beach and established a fishery there which proved disastrous for the Faunces. They had to launch and land boats from the ocean beach which required the services of an experienced surf man. Capt. John D. fired the surf man he had and took over the boats himself. While trying to beach his boat one day the boat broached side on and capsized, loaded with net and the Capt. was caught under the net and drowned. His death coupled with the heavy expense they had incurred in trying to establish the fishery and the expenses of Dave M. who was living in high style in Norfolk (he was a young man and had rather expensive tastes for a fisherman) contributed to their undoing. They had made big money and were still making money at Ragged Point, but there wasn't enough to pay for the expense of the Virginia Beach fiasco, plus the spending of Dave, so the end came soon after. About 1897 the Ragged Point fishing was closed and sold out in bankruptcy. The nets were sold and men from Maryland and Virginia acquired them and began to fish them. From this time on pound net fishing was on the increase and soon processing plants appeared along the river. The increase lasted until the mid 1920's, when practically all the small independent fisherman was forced out of business when catches became small and there was little market for herring. Some fishermen made some money and saved it but many were no better off than when they started. About the only ones who stayed in were the large corporations with the processing plants and some of these were still fishing in 1968.

AUTHOR'S NOTE

It is believed there were at least 5 sons in the Faunce Family as Capt. J. Melvin Faunce, a grandson of Capt. Jake, speaks of his great-uncle, Capt. Con Faunce, who is mentioned on pp. 63, 68, 93, 94, 96 and 157. Capt. Jake R. Faunce apparently upon leaving Ragged Point, removed to St. Patrick's Creek where he lived for the rest of his life (see p. 66, 67, 94, 96, 145, 147 and 149). There seems to be some doubt that the Faunces were the first to fish pound nets in the Potomac. If so, it had to be earlier than 1888 since Capt. Josiah Beitzell, Sr. after moving to Maryland from Virginia in 1882 and before his death in 1884 hired a net rigger from Washington to come down and teach his sons the art (see p. 53).

* * * * *

Some cotton was used for gill nets but cotton twine had a tendency to fuzz up and looked much larger when wet. It wasn't until after the Civil War that linen came into general use for gill nets and practically all fishing was with haulseine and trot line until about 1880 when the trap or pound nets were introduced. They were quite different from the present trap net but used the same principle of poles and net with bays or false pound but without the funnel as used now. They had what was termed an open mouth and did not retain the fish as well as the later models.

Some haulseins were operated in Colonial days and by 1750 there were quite a few. By 1730 they were in general use all along the river front. One was operated by George Washington at Ferry Landing, at that time a part of Mount Vernon. There was a seine operated near what is now Colonial Beach, one near the Maryland end of Potomac River Bridge, one on the Maryland side at Nanjemoy Creek, one at Passapa- tanzy Creek, Virginia, one at Potomac Creek, one at Aquia Creek, one near Widewater, one at Quantico, one on each side of Occoquan Creek, and one at Hallowing Point. In addition seines were operated near Sandy Point, at Chapmans Point above Glymount, at Bryant's Point above Marshall Hall and maybe others I don't know of. Most of these I have named were operated until about 1905 and some until 1915. Most of these nets were operated for spring fishing during the months of April and May. Until about 1905 all herring were processed in Washington, D. C. for there were no process- ing plants on the Potomac prior to this time. People would drive for miles and even days to the fishing shores to buy herring to salt for home use through the year. They would cut and salt them before returning home and they were much prized as food. Some used them as a staple food and others as a special for breakfast with hot spoon bread and lots of country butter. I have seen as many as fifty 2 and 4 horse teams and wagons in Washington, D. C. in the morning to buy fish for salting, and this was a common sight all along the river front at the seining shores. Around 1900 there were millions of herring processed and salted at the old fishing wharf in Washington, D. C. There was no canning of fish or herring at that time.

About 1880 haulseins were the only means of catching herring and shad commer- cially and they had increased in size until they were enormous. The largest sein was carried to St. Louis in 1896 to the World's Fair. It measured 7 miles of net and lines. These nets had gotten so large that they were stationary or operated at one place and used steam power to haul them ashore. The largest at Freestone Point required a crew of almost a hundred men and was owned by the Neitzey Family, who were also the largest wholesale fish dealers in Washington, D. C. and operated until about 1905. The William Neitzey Co. was still a large wholesale firm until about 1936, then the wholesale fish business died out until about 1950. It was almost non-existent. There are still some wholesale fish dealers in Washington, D. C., but the old fish markets are all gone.

These fishing shores I have named were principally engaged in spring fishing for herring and shad, but there were three seins, one at Passapatanzy, one at Poto- mac Creek and one at Aquia Creek known as winter seines that began fishing after Jan- uary 1st, if the river was open or as soon after as the ice cleared enough to make a haul. These seins caught mostly winter fish such as catfish and perch with some rock fish, but usually it was well into February before many rock fish showed up. Then until mid April or early May they would catch tons of rock fish at times, not every day but several times during the season. I have known of as many as fifteen to twenty tons of rock caught at one haul. These fish sold well and often sold for as much as 40 cents a lb. though sometimes there were too many for the market to handle and the price would drop.

Along with the large seines there were a large number of small seines handled by man power. These seines were manned by six to nine men and were fished usually in the summer time as the men had to stand in the water to handle them, although in cold weather some used body boots or waders that came up under the arms. Some of these men fished through the winter with trot lines catching any fish that would bite, catfish, rock fish, perch and eels. They usually used a seine to catch bait fish in the creeks and inlets and sometimes they would make a haul of good fish for market.

From about 1850 until 1936 shad fishing with gill nets was much used especially before 1900 but shad began to thin out and from 1905 to 1915 gilling for shad dropped off to a trickle. However there was a project started at Bryant's Point Maryland to hatch shad eggs. This project did a grand job for several years and the supply of shad multiplied many many times and from 1915 through the early twenties the Potomac had an abundance of shad. This was one of the leading market fish of this period on the Potomac, but in 1924 or 1925 the hatchery was moved to some place near the head of Chesapeake Bay. It remained there for seven or eight years, then moved back to Bryant's Point and converted to hatching principally Bass and other fresh water fish through the 30's and may still be in operation. Some shad eggs were hatched but they were having trouble getting eggs in sufficient quantity since there were so few nets still in operation and these did not produce enough eggs to justify them.

At one time, about 1885, shad fishing with drift nets became so profitable that quite a number of fishermen from the Delaware Bay came in the river and fished out of Charles County. Then a law was passed that prohibited any non-resident of Charles County from fishing in the Potomac between the spar buoy off Popes Creek and the Buoy on Greenway Flats which took in practically all the river for drift netting for shad. However, out-of-state fishermen did fish in the Potomac for some years by making their nets and boats over to a resident, who then procured licenses for them. Some of these fished as late as 1920.

I spent 14 Springs drifting for shad between 1916 and 1936 and during this time became familiar with many of the old fishermen, some retired and some who were still fishing. This was a period of plenty shad and fair prices compared to the economy at that time. Many were the stories told of experiences they had, some good, some not so good. The best price I received for shad was in 1918. One time I shipped 144 shad, about half were roes for which I received $158.10 net. The roe shad sold for $2.25 each. We paid 25% for commission and freight for shipping. We had boats to pick up each evening and the fish were sold in Washington, D. C. next morning. I don't remember roe shad selling for less than 50 cents each except one time while I was fishing. Buck shad generally sold at half the price for roes.

The largest single drift I made was something over 300 shad and the largest day's catch on two tides was 512. The largest drift was usually made on a runaway tide which sometimes lasted 24 hours or more. We usually laid the nets out two to three hours before slack tide was due, but sometimes a change in the weather could keep you in the river for hours. I caught one drift that lasted from 3:00 a.m. to 5:00 p.m. Three boats of Delaware men caught a gale north west and drifted from Riverside, Maryland to Hollis Marsh in Virginia about 30 miles and they had a hard time all the way. The largest drift I knew about was made by Pete Posey who caught a runaway tide and drifted from Maryland Point to Popes Creek. Flood tide caught him and to save his net from the oyster bar at Port Tobacco, he pulled in fish, net, and all. He landed 558 shad and more than 100 rock fish which just about loaded his gill skiff. Large catches were made at times, but usually they were the result of a miscalculation or a change in the weather when you could not get the net in on account of the wind. I saw several bad storms while I was fishing, but was lucky enough that I was never caught in a real bad one myself.

The scientists claim it requires three years for a shad to mature to spawning age. But from my observations this is the life cycle of the shad for otherwise there would be more large or oversize shad. Usually a roe shad will average 3½ to 4 lbs. at spawning size and it stands to reason if they returned even in a year they would be much larger. I caught one shad that weighed 10½ lbs. and one Spring I caught several that weighed over seven lbs. The largest I ever heard of weighed 18 lbs, a buck caught at Glymount.

The stake net (so called) is a gill net put out and fastened to a stake at each end to catch fish gilled in them. These nets were not used in the Potomac until 1918. Capt. Tom Hayden, a ship carpenter, and fisherman went to North Carolina during World War I to work in a shipyard and became familiar with these nets as they were used extensively in North Carolina. After the war he came home to Alexandria, Virginia, and in partnership with George Grimes of Comorn in King George County, rigged and put out two sets of nets opposite Maryland Point on the Virginia side of the Potomac. They started out in a rather large scale operation with a five man crew and two boats. They fished each net on every tide and caught live fish which sold for top prices in Washington, up to $1,600.00 for one days fishing. Soon these nets were put out all up and down the river. Sometimes they were not fished for two or three days with the result that quite a large number of the fish drowned which soon ruined the demand and affected the price of fresh fish. I have always been opposed to fishing these nets, but the Commission is more after the license fee than anything else. We in the Potomac had always fished floating gill nets but prior to 1928, the fishermen in the Upper Chesapeake perfected a so-called sunken drift net which they had used successfully for shad and later for Winter fishing for rock fish.

In the Winter of 1928, a fisherman from Rock Hall, Maryland with his two sons came to the Potomac with some of these nets and made a killing on Rock fish. The following years several men from the Bay area and some in the Potomac used these nets. The shad was prized for its flavor and for many years was the most popular fish of the Chesapeake. However with dwindling supplies and preparation of convenience (frozen) foods, not to mention its myriad of small bones, the once popular shad is now one of the least popular fish on the fresh market, and except for the roe which is still popular, the shad has become one of the lesser food fishes.

While talking with some of the older fishermen on the Potomac I heard some wild tales and you had to use a good bit of credibility to enjoy some of them. One of the best I can recall occurred one afternoon while I was fishing at Riverside, Maryland. I fished here in the early part of the season from March 15 to about April 15, then moved up the river to Quantico or the White House and Mount Vernon. I had rented a shanty from Mr. Frank Burgess who owned a farm at Riverside and while walking along the shore one afternoon I saw quite a number of clean, almost new looking bricks at or below low water mark. I asked Mr. Burgess if there had been a building along the riverfront at some time past. He was a good bit older than I was and he replied with very straight face "not in my time", and went on to say that the bricks appeared on the beach after a tow of scows loaded with bricks passed Riverside in a heavy South-wester and he surmised that they washed off those scows, about a ¼ mile off shore. His son spoke up and said more than 5000 bricks washed off one scow in that blow.

Capt. Morgan Monroe, who lived at Sandy Point, Maryland, fished gill nets for several years. One year in February a man who fished one of his nets came to his landing and told him there were shad in the river. Capt. Monroe told him he was off his rocker for shad didn't show in the river that early and besides there had been a freeze and the river was full of ice. But nothing would do but he had to try it to satisfy him. Capt. Monroe got out a boat and some net (though they never started fishing here before the middle of March) and made a good catch of shad. He continued to catch shad for two weeks, when they dropped off until April, and they began catching fish again. This is the only instance I know of shad being caught in quantity this early.

There was an article in the Northumberland Echo of November 6, 1969 concerning the "Conway boats" and three of them were mentioned. There was also a fourth, the Ruth Conway. These boats were built originally for the West Indies trade in summer and for freighting on the Chesapeake the rest of the year. About 1905 or 1910, Capt. Harvey Conway of Cambridge, Maryland acquired one of these boats and rebuilt and restored her. Soon after he acquired three others and restored them, one for each of his three sons.

He did a wonderful job of restoring these boats and they were a beautiful sight to see under full sail. I did know the original names of these schooners, but after fifty years the original names have faded out of my mind. I do remember when each of them came out in their new rigs and they went through another era on the Bay transporting oysters in season and freighting produce and fertilizer in the summer. About 1925 or so they were dismantled and turned into barges with engines and have continued to ply the Bay, in good condition to this time in 1969.

One of the schooners was the original named Laurena Clayton. This was one of the best looking schooners on the Bay. She was rigged with a foretopmast and under sail was a beautiful sight.

AUTHOR'S NOTE

In the article to which Capt. Trader refers it was stated that altogether there are some 16 or 17 of these schooners still in service as barges, half of Maryland registration. Of the Conway boats, one is the 102 year old Eugenia, the former Betty Conway, now operated (1969) by Capt. Arthur R. Eubank of Lewisetta. The Carol Ann, once the Ida B. Conway, built in 1873, is operated from Lewisetta by Capt. Tom Letson. The Sarah Conway is owned by Calvin Evans and while laid up in 1969 is still "in the best of shape". These boats haul from grain terminals at Kinsale and Bundick Landing.

From the Northern Neck News,
Friday, October 10, 1947

Sailing Ships Stir Old Memories

The Article in the Northern Neck News on the sailing vessel "James A. Whiting" is a most timely tribute to these ships that played such an important role in transportation, before gasoline engines supplanted them and took from the Bay and its tributaries much of the scenic beauty their white sails and graceful dippling of the white bone at their bow, as they slipped along thru the blue spray of the crested waters, had afforded lovers of the sea. The ships have disappeared and have left nothing to take their place. Most of us have stood on the banks of rivers, when sail boats were dredging, hundreds of them, their white sails fluttering in the breeze against the blue waters, flashing in the sunlight, as they fill and draw away.

Capt. George Trader, owned a pungy that must have been built about the time the "Whiting", She was the "E.R.S. Daugherty".

The "Daugherty" was painted in "pungy style" with pink sides, green bends and a white rail and Capt. Trader must have bought her about 1880. Later he bought the "Cape Charles" a schooner rigged bugeye, which he sold to a man from North Carolina. I suppose her bones are bleaching on the shore of Albemarle Sound.

The Cape Charles was one of the most graceful vessels I ever saw. She had a "flip to her tail" I never saw in another vessel.

Capt. Trader had the "Daugherty" rebuilt in 1908 from stem to stern at a railway in Coan River. He brought her home and bought a new suit of sail. There was a big day on Colonial Beach and he took his family up there in the "Daugherty" with a fresh breeze Southwest and all five sails set mainsail, foresail, top sail, jib and staysail.

There came out of Nomini Creek a gasoline boat, that was something new, being one of the first of the variety and Capt. Trader gave it a chase. The "Daugherty" sailed in well ahead. That was the only trip he ever took in her. He intended to run oysters to Washington as he had been doing for years and had put some oysters on her deck, intending to buy next day.

Somebody set her afire that night and the only thing saved was the jib as they let her anchor go and let her drift up on Granny's Bar, where her hull still lies.

Later Capt. Trader bought the "Birdie May". I have a picture of her that was published in the Washington Star. She was a sister ship to the "Cape Charles" built at the same railway. The years were going on and boats, as well as men, wear out.

The "Birdie May" lies along side the "Daugherty" on Granny's Bar in Machodoc Creek.

There are other hulls in the creek, the '---Coulburn', also the 'Grape Shot' and 'Nellie' in Yeocomico.

I was only a sailor's wife, so my language may not be properly nautical.

MRS. GEORGE TRADER
Coles Point, Virginia

(Reprinted by Special Permission)

NOTE

The author of this article was Mrs. Vivian Steteria Olinda Dobyns Trader, wife of Capt. George T. Trader. Mrs. Trader was born during the Civil War, raised a large family, taught in the neighborhood school when no teacher was available, and was greatly loved throughout the area. She died shortly after this article was written.

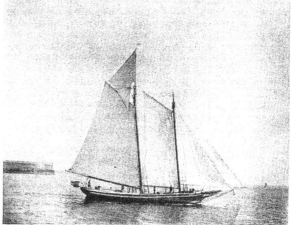

Schooner, John Nelson   Unidentified Schooner

Baltimore Harbor Scenes

Photos by Vernon D. Tate

Miscellaneous Notes

In a letter dated January 19, 1969, Mr. Daniel B. Lloyd of Washington, D. C. mentioned that the Port Tobacco Times of May 1860, carried an advertisement concerning the packet, "Enterprise", over the signature of Capt. Thomas Lloyd, an ancestor. The "Enterprise" plied between Allen's Fresh and the Wicomico Depot and made connections with the "Columbia" and the "St. Nicholas" in the freight trade. The ad also gave the schedule and ports of call of these vessels and referred to Capt. Jere Herbert's warehouse at Tulip Hill.

* * * * *

Mr. James E. Nicholson of Baltimore in a letter dated December 1, 1970, recalled that his father, also named James E. Nicholson, had a power launch, 35 feet in length and equipped with a closed cabin built in White's Neck Creek by Capt. Billy Ellis almost a half century ago. Their trips to St. Mary's County each summer were made in her. Mr. Nicholson, Senior, was a sailmaker in Washington and made sails for many of the Bugeyes and Schooners in the Potomac River trade. He was half owner of the schooner, "Mary Gandy" with Capt. Jimmie Cheseldine, which was used as a "buy boat" and they sold most of their oysters to Weser's Oyster House in Washington. Mr. Nicholson, Jr., also recalled sailing Capt. Warren Yates' nancy boat many times in St. Katherine's Sound as a youngster. He said he remembered so well that she was painted black and the name "Nancy" was painted on her stern in yellow and she had a yellow stripe all around under the gunwales.

* * * * *

Mr. Francis A. Lamb of Colonial Beach wrote on June 21, 1971 concerning the Sloop, "Flora Elsie" (included in Capt. Harding Daiger's list). He said he had always heard that she was one of the fastest boats in the area and remembered that she was a big black Sloop, carrying mainsail, topsail, and three jibs. She was beached and died below Alexandria about 1930.

* * * * *

The writer's eldest brother, Joe Beitzell, who has lived in California for many years, wrote after reading "Life on the Potomac River", several years ago as follows:

"I noted the name of Capt. Willard Haynie in the book and it brought back to mind one of the most memorable experiences of my boyhood. Capt. Willard was a good friend of Papa's dating back to the days when our folks were still living in the Northern Neck (1882). When he would come up from his home in Fairport, Virginia to dredge in the Potomac he would stop in to visit us occasionally. He had the misfortune to lose his first wife and son and he seemed to take a fancy to me because he said I looked so much like the son he had lost. He had married again and had a son, Grover, about my age. On one of his visits, Papa and Mama agreed, much to my delight, to let Capt. Willard take me home with him for a week-end visit. I was only about 8 - 10 years old at the time (somewhere around 1900). We sailed out of Canoe Neck Creek on his pungy, Hattie Whittington, early on a Friday morning, dredged awhile on Heron Island Bar, made a good catch and then sailed down the Potomac to Coan River. There Capt. Willard hired a two-horse rig and drove about 20 - 25 miles further south to Fairport which is located on the Great Wicomico. His wife and son, Grover, were very hospitable and all of us had a great time. Capt. Willard's first wife and son were buried in the back yard of his home and I remember that there were large head stones at the graves".

"When I was about 14 or 15, Papa, Uncle Ernest and I made another trip down there. We sailed down in Papa's old dory, the Defender, and made it down to Indian Creek near the mouth of the Rappahannock in one day, after stopping off to see Capt. Willard on the way. We stayed with Capt. Willard Lankford, Aunt Laura's brother, and visited a lot of friends of the family whose names I can't now remember. But I do remember that all of the people I met in Virginia on the trip were so friendly and entertaining. We had a rough trip home in a heavy wind, but though the old Defender was ugly, she was also sturdy and Papa and Uncle Ern knew how to handle her. I still remember those waves - they seemed to be 10 feet high."

It was the writer's good fortune that he was able to contact Mr. Grover Haynie, Jr., the grandson of Capt. Willard, after this lapse of some 68 years. The family is still living in the same area and Mrs. Grover G. Haynie, Sr., daughter-in-law, of Capt. Willard very kindly sent the following sketch:

"Willard A. Haynie 1860-1929"

"Willard A. Haynie was a native of Northumberland County, Virginia, and he was a waterman all of his life. Among the boats he owned were: "United", a small schooner; "Hattie Whittington", a pungy; "Irene", a bugeye - dredge boat; "Dewey", a large model purse boat; "Aleta", a batteau - dredge rig; and 3 power boats: "Grover G.", named for his son; "Mary E. Haynie", named for his granddaughter, both of the above were built to run oysters to market; and "Sea Gull". As far as I know, Willard Haynie used the "Hattie Whittington", and the "Irene" for dredging in the Potomac before the grounds were closed for dredging". The power boat "Mary E. Haynie" was used to transport the cable, wire and phone equipment to Tangier Island when the telephone system was installed on the Island."

"While dredging in the Potomac River, he used a shipped crew from Baltimore and at times, he had problem keeping the crew. Some of them ran away, as the work was hard, and the shipped crews were not used to such hard work. They were men sent down by a shipping office in Baltimore, and many times it turned out that they were kidnapped and sent down to work on the dredge boats. When the men ran away, Capt. Willard would get a couple of his friends on another boat and someone from St. Mary's County and search for them, as he had already outfitted them in oilskins and boots and they were supposed to work out the cost before they drew any wages".

"One story he often told was about the time that he and another captain had foreign crews and they were talking in their native tongue. He suspected that they were planning to run away and told the other captain, who laughed and said he didn't think so and went to bed. Captain Willard sat up and sure enough, he heard the men tip-toeing on deck. He threw open the hatch and they ran back to the forepeake where they slept. Captain Willard fastened the hatch so they couldn't get out and then went to bed. Sure enough, the other captain's crew ran away that night and he never found them".

"Sometimes Captain Willard would get some of the men from his locality to dredge with him and on one or two occasions, he took his cousin along. The cousin was taken sick with tonsilitis and Captain Willard used an old time remedy (a wool sock with hot wood ashes inside of it around the sick man's throat). After a day or so, the man got better and came on deck to get a drink of water. He hadn't shaved and needed a haircut, and made quite a figure. Just as he stepped on deck, the police boat drew along side to inspect the size of the oysters. The police captain took one look at the sick man and ordered his men to shove the police boat away".

"Captain Willard told many stories of his experiences on the Potomac River, visited with his many friends living there, and also went to the store located there".

"Captain Willard trapped for fish on Gough's Bar in the Chesapeake Bay. He used a small bateau type boat named the "Plunder". After he started to use deeper nets, he bought the "Sea Gull" which he was using at the time of his death. His son, Grover G. Haynie, Sr., carried on the business of trapping until ill-health forced him to sell the boat and rigs in the early 1940's. A dredge, a hand stakepump and other items were given to the Mariners Museum in Newport News where they are on display."

* * * * *

One fine day in February 1973, the writer with his friend, Robert E. T. Pogue, drove down into the Northern Neck of Virginia (one of many such trips) to see Capt. Garnett Belfield and Capt. Melvin Faunce. We had such an enjoyable visit, swapping yarns and memories (Pogue did some oyster tonging during the "Depression" years and also was with the Marine Police for awhile) that it was difficult to do much note-taking.

* * * * *

Capt. Belfield said his first vessel was the Sloop, "Harriet E. Smith" and that he made some kind of a record on his first trip when he sank the vessel twice by running on some piling. He wasn't discouraged though and went on to put in 54 years sailing the Potomac and the Chesapeake. He has done everything from pile driving to running seed oysters out of the James River and lumber and railroad ties up to Philadelphia in the days when the canal still had locks. He recalled being frozen in at Christmas time in Crisfield in 1936, and 1937 was no better, being frozen in at Pocomoke City. The Norfolk boats were only running during the day because of the ice. During the period the people of Tangier Island ran short of supplies, and food and medicine were flown in. A character named "Poor John" Crockett stole the liquor that was included in the supplies and was found the next day lying drunk in the marsh. "Poor John" was over 6 feet tall and in his small boat "stuck out like a sore thumb". One day he and his son were doing some illegal hand-scraping (dredging) and a police boat was seen approaching and the son called out "flatten out Pa, for God's sake, flatten out".

Capt. Belfield also told the story of Capt. John Thompson, a Black man who had the sharp sail Bugeye, "L. F. Petty". In addition to sails the Petty was equipped with a 24 h.p. Lathrop engine which was hard to start. Capt. John had a regular routine he went through each time he started the motor - a turn of the flywheel and he said "Golly day", another turn, "My heavens", turn "Holy Moses", turn "Goodness gracious", turn "God dammit, you can't do me this way".

Capt. Belfield said that during the 1930's Capt. William Stanford made five trips to Baltimore from the Potomac, freighting wheat and other grain, completely alone, no crew whatsoever. He had an engine for getting up the sails.

In addition to the Harriet E. Smith, Capt. Belfield sailed the Schooners:

> Bessie Reed
> E. S. Wilson
> Mattie F. Dean
> Minnie and Emma

Capt. Hunter Belfield owned and sailed:

> Bessie Reed
> Ella F. Cripps
> Etta
> Minnie and Emma
> Lucy May
> Edwin C.
> Nellie

Capt. George Dungan sailed:

> Thomas B. Schall
> Columbia F. C.
> Levi B. Phillips

All of these vessels operated out of the Yeocomico River.

Capt. Belfield also had the W. J. Matthews, formerly the Dorchester, after she had been converted to power. The John Branford, a 67 foot Bugeye built at Fairmount, Maryland in 1900, is still afloat as a power boat, She was owned until recently by Capt. Belfield's son-in-law, Ernest Harding, who runs a shuck house near the Belfield home at Coles Point. Capt. and Mrs. Belfield have a fine restaurant nearby.

Other vessels recalled by Capt. Belfield included:

> Elizabeth Ann - Schooner, died in Wicomico
> John E. Bright - 700 bushel schooner
> Charles F. Rollie - large schooner
> B. W. Bramble - Schooner
> Harp - died at Lodge Landing in the Yeo-
>   comico
> J. W. Knowles - died in Carter's Creek
> Federal Hill - died at Colonial Beach
> Gladys L. - formerly the Miriam, a Bugeye
> Addie Mills - sunk, loaded with watermelons
>   It was said that the seeds
>   swelled and burst her open
> Ruth Conway - formerly the Grason A. sunk
>   loaded with corn

Andrew J. Lewis of Walnut Point in the Coan River owned several vessels. Among them were:

James A. Whiting - Pungy
Matilda - Schooner
George H. Bunker - square sail Bugeye

Capt. Frank Bramble was Master of several of the Lewis vessels and Capt. Elmer Bradshaw was Master of the Matilda for some years. Capt. Peyton Fiddler had the W. J. Matthews, formerly the Schooner, Dorchester for 10 years.

Capt. Gus Rice of Coan River was the Master of the Pungies Joe Smith and Martha Avery in addition to the Amanda F. Lewis.

Capt. Belfield said that one time when he was in Crisfield at the big oyster packing plant of John Handy, a State chemist opened an oyster and said "There's enough germs in this oyster to kill a thousand people". Mr. Handy grabbed the oyster, swallowed it and said, "Well, I've saved 999 lives".

* * * * *

In talking with Capt. Melvin Faunce it was learned that he started working in the Potomac before he was 14 years of age, helping his Uncle, Frank Faunce of St. Patrick's Creek, trapnetting and seining. In a few years he came over to the Virginia side of the River with Capt. Marshall Pritchard running railroad ties from Walnut Point in the Coan. He located in Nomini in 1933, ran fish, oysters and crabs to Washington, did some seine hauling with his brother-in-law, Ridgely Jones, in 1941-1942.

He and Capt. Jones fished 5 trap nets in 30-35 feet of water from 1942 to 1950. In the latter year Capt. Faunce opened a wholesale seafood place on the Washington waterfront. Capt. Jones is still fishing trap nets. Capt. Faunce said many of the fishermen on the Virginia side of the river have gone out of business, the latest were Capt. Roy and Capt. Willie Balderson last year.

After the Southwest fiasco wiped out the seafood dealers on the Washington waterfront, Capt. Faunce had a seafood place at Bladensburg for six years where business was very good and he sold as many as 500 bushels of crabs a week, in season. He returned to Nomini in 1966 and established his present seafood business where he is assisted by his son-in-law, William Howeth. It is a fine, clean, seafood place and if you want the best in crabs and oysters, both in the shell and out, you need go no further.

Capt. Melvin Faunce continues to carry on the century old tradition of his family and it is certain that he would have it no other way.

On the return trip home, Pogue and I had a long conversation concerning the future of the seafood industry on the Potomac. On these trips we usually talk about the old days on the River or the old places of historic interest we know or famous characters of the past and such and thoroughly enjoy each others company. Anway, on this trip we agreed that the Tidewater Fisheries aren't "on the ball" when it comes to oysters in the Potomac River. No oysters have been taken in deep water (too deep for tonging) since dredging and patent tongs were prohibited years ago. We agreed that Capt. Graham Trader had a point when he raised the question as to why this waste of our best oysters. The police force is adequate now to supervise the use of these deep water rocks by the rivermen using patent tongs or even dredges. And on Capt. Trader's second point of the under-size oysters in the Upper Potomac which do not grow to be the legal size we agreed also. Why not utilize these oysters to replenish public oyster grounds or let owners of private ground buy them for planting? In both cases it would give employment to the Rivermen in the off-season. It is realized, of course, that most of the oysters in the upper part of the River were killed as a result of the fresh water from Hurricane Agnes in 1972, but this had happened many times before and the oyster bars recovered in 2 - 3 years due to the shells left on the bottom. It also seems time to use divers to survey the River bottom to learn just what is growing where and to find new productive grounds. In this day of skin-diving it doesn't appear to be an impossible task. We had to agree also with Capt. Harding Daiger that we never expected to see the River die in our time. But it will, if the pollution isn't stopped and some new means developed to promote better utilization of our God-given heritage.

292

Index to Supplement
to
Life on the Potomac River

EDWIN W. BEITZELL

About the Author

Born in St. Mary's County, Maryland, on St. Clement's Bay in 1905, he was educated in the public schools of the County, Leonard Hall High School in Leonardtown and is a graduate of Georgetown University. He is the author of "The Jesuit Missions of St. Mary's County," published in 1960, and has written many oral history articles for the Maryland Historical Magazine, the Chronicles of St. Mary's and other publications. Although employed in Washington, D.C., by The Chesapeake and Potomac Telephone Company for 41 years he kept his roots in St. Mary's County and returned to his boyhood home upon retirement in 1967. The early history of Maryland and Virginia has been his avocation for the past 30 years.

Made in the USA
Middletown, DE
16 July 2024

57362509R00203